SCIENTIFIC KNOWLEDGE

SCIENTIFIC KNOWLEDGE
BASIC ISSUES IN THE PHILOSOPHY OF SCIENCE

Janet A. Kourany
University of Notre Dame

Wadsworth Publishing Company
Belmont, California
A Division of Wadsworth, Inc.

Philosophy Editor: Kenneth King
Editorial Assistant: Debbie Fox
Production: Stacey C. Sawyer, Montara, Calif.
Designer: MaryEllen Podgorski
Compositor: TC Systems
Cover: Stephen Rapley
Print Buyer: Ruth Cole

Printed in the United States of America

5 6 7 8 9 10

ISBN 0-534-06444-2

Library of Congress Cataloging-in-Publication Data

Scientific knowledge.

Bibliography: p.
1. Science–Philosophy. I. Kourany, Janet A.
Q175.3.S327 1986   501   86-23334
ISBN 0-534-06444-2

To my Mother and Father
For all their love and support

CONTENTS

PART 1 PHILOSOPHY OF SCIENCE: AN OVERVIEW   *1*

Ernan McMullin, *Alternative Approaches to the Philosophy of Science*   3

PART 2 EXPLANATION: A MAJOR GOAL OF SCIENTIFIC KNOWLEDGE   **20**

Carl Hempel and Paul Oppenheim, *Studies in the Logic of Explanation*   30

Carl Hempel, *Statistical Explanation*   44

Wesley Salmon, *Why Ask, "Why?"? An Inquiry Concerning Scientific Explanation*   51

Bas van Fraassen, *The Pragmatics of Explanation*   65

Dudley Shapere, *Scientific Theories and Their Domains*   77

Robert Cummins, *Programs in the Explanation of Behavior*   95

Stephen Toulmin, *Ideals of Natural Order*   105

PART 3 THE VALIDATION OF SCIENTIFIC KNOWLEDGE   *112*

Rudolf Carnap, *The Confirmation of Laws and Theories*   122

Karl Popper, *Science: Conjectures and Refutations*   139

Pierre Duhem, *Physical Theory and Experiment*   158

Imre Lakatos, *Falsification and the Methodology of Scientific Research Programmes*   170

Thomas Kuhn, *Objectivity, Value Judgment, and Theory Choice*   197

Ronald Giere, *Testing Theoretical Hypotheses*   208

PART 4   THE HISTORICAL DEVELOPMENT OF SCIENTIFIC KNOWLEDGE   *228*

Karl Popper, *The Rationality of Scientific Revolutions*   235

Thomas Kuhn, *The Function of Dogma in Scientific Research*   253

Thomas Kuhn, *The Nature and Necessity of Scientific Revolutions*   266

Larry Laudan, *Dissecting the Holist Picture of Scientific Change*   276

Paul Oppenheim and Hilary Putnam, *Unity of Science as a Working Hypothesis*   296

Patrick Suppes, *The Plurality of Science*   317

Dudley Shapere, *Unity and Method in Contemporary Science*   326

PART 5   REALISM VERSUS ANTI-REALISM: THE ONTOLOGICAL IMPORT OF SCIENTIFIC KNOWLEDGE   *336*

Bas van Fraassen, *Arguments Concerning Scientific Realism*   343

Arthur Fine, *And Not Anti-Realism Either*   359

Michael Gardner, *Realism and Instrumentalism in Pre-Newtonian Astronomy*   369

Ian Hacking, *Experimentation and Scientific Realism*   388

PREFACE

Logical Positivism was a philosophical movement that began in Vienna in the 1920s and guided philosophy of science for at least thirty years. Since its demise in the 1960s, philosophers of science have not succeeded in developing a unified program of research to take its place. Indeed, philosophers of science continue to disagree not only about the nature of science but also about the aims and methods of philosophy of science itself.

The result of this unsettled state of the field is that very few textbooks in the philosophy of science have been available in recent years. The present anthology is an attempt to remedy this situation. Its aim is to introduce readers to the most basic issues in the philosophy of science without trying to minimize the prevailing controversy. Thus, Part 1 of the book is devoted to an overview of issues and alternative approaches to them that are current in philosophy of science today, whereas Parts 2 through 5 explore the most basic of these issues through essays representing a variety of positions and approaches. All the essays in this book, products of some of the most distinguished scholars in the field, have been chosen for their clarity and philosophical significance: They presuppose no special scientific or philosophical (for example, formal logic) background on the part of the reader. Introductions to each section provide a framework and the necessary background information for the essays.

Many people offered helpful suggestions and advice at various stages of the project. In particular, I would like to thank Robert Audi, Michael Bradie, Myles Brand, Nancy Cartwright, Maurice Finocchiaro, Ronald Giere, Mary Hesse, Noretta Koertge, Isaac Levi, Andrew Lugg, David Malament, Thomas Nickles, Michael Ruse, Husain Sarkar, Abner Shimony, Paul Teller, and Mary Williams. At least as helpful were my colleagues at Notre Dame James Cushing, Michael Detlefsen, Edward Manier, Vaughn McKim, Philip Quinn, Kenneth Sayre, Larry Simon, and especially Ernan McMullin; reviewers Michael Boylan, Georgetown University, Frank F. Fair, Sam Houston State University, Jarrett Leplin, University of North Carolina, Greensboro, Ronald Munson, University of Missouri, St. Louis, and especially Robert Causey, University of Texas; and Wadsworth special projects reviewer Jonas Weisel. Wadsworth philosophy editor Kenneth King, meanwhile, showed remarkable patience and good cheer through all the major and minor crises that arose during the project. My husband and fellow philosopher James Sterba, however, deserves the most thanks—for all the time, energy, and support he contributed in so many ways to the project. Our daughter, Sonya, also contributed to the project in her own special ways.

PHILOSOPHY OF SCIENCE: AN OVERVIEW

1

Are the sciences moving toward a unified account of the world, or are the pictures of reality they provide becoming ever more disparate? Do scientists have any reason to believe that current scientific theories are true when all the scientific theories of the past have turned out to be false? Is there anything that especially distinguishes current theories from past ones? How can scientists test a scientific theory that is about entities and processes no one can observe? These are some questions that philosophers have raised about science—questions, in fact, that we shall deal with in this book.

Why are philosophers so interested in science? On the simplest level, such interest reflects the traditional concern of philosophy with the nature of reality and the foundations and limits of human knowledge. But the answer goes deeper than this, and it affects more than just philosophy. The knowledge science provides is immensely impressive, and this knowledge has had a profound impact on our lives. Indeed, the noted historian of science Herbert Butterfield has said, of the Scientific Revolution that was instrumental in bringing this knowledge into existence:

> It outshines everything since the rise of Christianity and reduces the Renaissance and Reformation to the rank of mere episodes. . . . It changed the character of men's habitual mental operations even in the conduct of the nonmaterial sciences, while transforming the whole diagram of the physical universe and the very texture of human life itself.

Small wonder that science has inspired a deep interest among philosophers.

But science has inspired an equally deep interest among the representatives of other disciplines as well. Philosophers have wanted to explore the general characteristics of science that most directly relate to its function as a knowledge-producing activity—the nature and kinds of its explanations, the nature of its validation procedures, its patterns of development, the truth-status of its theories, and the like. Historians have wanted to know exactly how the concepts, methods, and goals of science have reached their present state of development, what particular factors brought about crucial changes in these at various times and places, and what particular social and economic forces promoted or inhibited these changes. Psychologists have wanted to analyze what types of individuals have engaged in this enterprise, what relationship their personality characteristics and motivation have had to the styles of their research, and, in general, what psychological processes have characterized their research. And sociologists have wanted to understand how far and in what ways such individuals have been influenced by the social and cultural contexts in which they work, to what extent a society's presuppositions have molded the findings of scientific research.

These various approaches to science—the philosophical, the historical, the psychological, and the sociological—are not independent of one another. Thus, for example, alternative philosophical views regarding the nature of theory-testing have shaped alternative sociological views regarding the influence of social factors on scientists' acceptance or rejection of theories. And, in turn, completed sociological research in this area will test and ultimately refine those philosophical views. Similarly, historical data have suggested philosophical views regarding general patterns of scientific development, which might, in turn, help in the construction of more adequate historical narratives. Historical data might also be used to test psychological or sociological hypotheses regarding science: for example, the detailed diaries of experimental investigations, hypotheses, speculations, plans, and incidental observations left by the nineteenth-century English physicist Michael Faraday have been used to test psychological hypotheses regarding scientific inference. Successful psychological or sociological hypotheses might, in turn, disclose the relevance of factors not previously noted when gathering historical data or constructing historical narratives, thereby yielding more successful historical research.

Doubtless a completely adequate picture of science will only emerge with the integration of all these different approaches to science. Unfortunately, such a picture is still a long way off. Indeed, we now lack even the separate approaches themselves in an adequate state of development. What's more, deep controversies exist in the philosophy of science, the history of science, the sociology of science, and the psychology of science—and none more so than in the philosophy of science. The controversies relate not only to particular views on particular questions but also to the methods that should be used in answering those questions and even, on occasion, to the relative importance of the questions themselves. In "Alternative Approaches to the Philosophy of Science," Ernan McMullin surveys the controversy that exists in the philosophy of science, outlining the different approaches currently being pursued in several major areas. His discussion provides a helpful backdrop to the readings that follow in two ways. Read now, before the topics in the rest of the book are covered, it will form an introduction to these topics and their interrelations. Reread later, after the topics are covered and you are well on your way to formulating your own positions on these topics. McMullin's discussion will make explicit some of the subtle but important differences of approach in the different readings. It will then also help to make explicit the approach you, yourself, have adopted in the philosophy of science and the reasons you might formulate for that approach. By then you will be invincible indeed! May you have great success in your venture.

Alternative Approaches to the Philosophy of Science

Ernan McMullin

TWO SENSES OF "SCIENCE"

When one speaks of the philosophy or the history of "science," what is meant by the term "science"? There are two principal senses, very different in their implications for philosopher and historian alike. Science may be regarded as a collection of propositions, ranging from reports of observations to the most abstract theories accounting for these observations. Let us call this S_1. S_1 is the end product of research, the careful statement in approved technical terms of something that has been empirically determined to be so, and perhaps also of a tentative explanation of *why* it is so. S_1 ordinarily contains only those definitions, theories of the measuring instruments involved, and the like, that are needed to allow another scientist, within the bounds of a research paper or book, to grasp the "data," to test their reliability if need be, and to evaluate claims made to generalize or explain them. The *Principia* of Newton would be an example of S_1, as would the average paper or letter in the *Physical Review* today. It will be noted that S_1 does not contain an account of how discoveries were made, of the various false starts, of the ways in which concepts were gradually modified to fit the new problem, of the various extrascientific factors that influenced the author to adopt the theory he is proposing.

S_2 includes all of these. It is "science" considered as the ensemble of activities of the scientist in the pursuit of his goal of scientific observation and understanding. It includes the various influences that affect him significantly, perhaps unknown to himself, in this pursuit. It contains all the propositional formulations, both provisional and "fin-ished," with the reasonings *actually* followed (not just those ultimately reported). In short, S_2 is everything the scientist actually *does* that affects the scientific outcome in any way. S_2 contains S_1; it is, however, far broader and vaguer than S_1. It is not just propositional, for it includes the building of apparatus, the making of measurements, the half-conscious speculation, the rough sketch—all brought into some sort of unity by the aim of accurately describing or explaining some feature of our experience.

It would be impossible ever to convey S_2 fully, even in the case of a relatively simple piece of scientific research. And no one tries to do so because it is S_1 in which everyone (including the scientist himself) is interested. S_1 is the measure of his achievement; it is that part of S_2 which is intersubjective, communicable, in some hopeful sense permanent. Because of its vagueness and singularity, S_2 will be difficult to comprehend; the effort to grasp it may well seem unrewarding or even futile. In the permanent record of the textbook, it is S_1 that figures, and usually in an artificial form that gives practically no clue to the real sequence of events and considerations. S_2 is, for the most part, soon forgotten; indeed, even to begin with, much of it may never have been made explicit. The interest of S_2 is only this, that in a very definite sense it serves to explain how S_1 came to be formulated in the first place.

HISTORY OF SCIENCE

And this, of course, is of special concern to the historian. Thus, he will have to take at least *some*

From Ernan McMullin, "The History and Philosophy of Science: A Taxonomy," *Historical and Philosophical Perspectives of Science*, Roger Stuewer, Ed. *Minnesota Studies in the Philosophy of Science*, Vol. V. Minneapolis: University of Minnesota, 1970, pp. 15-17, 23-30, 42-62. Reprinted by permission.

account of S_2. But there are very different ways of going about writing history of science. As historiography,[1] its first responsibility is to establish what the facts were: who said what, and what he meant by it, and what reasons he adduced. But after that, a considerable difference of emphasis is possible. At one extreme is chronicle, an establishing of the "facts" with a minimum of interpretive addition; at the other is "overview" or "applied history" where history is used to make a philosophical, theological, or political point, and the goal is discovery of an overall pattern rather than determination of contingent singulars. These divergent aims manifest themselves among historians of science as among other historians. But because what they are giving is a record not of battles or of treaties but of *ideas,* intelligibly linked with one another, they are forced to *some* extent, at least, to be interpretive. The historian of science is by definition a historian of ideas.

This suggests yet another sort of emphasis, the "history of ideas" approach now canonized by the establishment of departments and doctorates under that title in many universities in the United States. The historian of ideas has a methodologically very complex task. He has to trace a concept like *matter* or *force* or *democracy* through the writings of one or more people, subordinating the contingent historical particularities to the main aim of grasping what the concept meant and how this meaning was progressively modified. The danger of this approach (as "professional" historians are quick to emphasize) is that it may entirely subordinate history to a quite different sort of enterprise in which the connectives between, or developments of, ideas are created by the writer himself, rather than laboriously recovered from the intractable past. Ideas have a permanence and a transparency that persons and historical events lack. Thus it is tempting when tracing, let us say,

the development of Newton's concept of force to pay more attention to the logical implications or plausible modifications of the concept as *we* see them than to the actual sequence as it occurred in Newton's own thought. The history of ideas can easily become a logical and analogical development whose dynamism lies in the ideas themselves and in the creativity of the person constructing it, rather than in the partial records of the free decisions and semi-opaque mental constructions of men long dead. The connectives of history are *not* always those of logic or analogy. . . .

THREE APPROACHES TO PHILOSOPHY OF SCIENCE

In attempting to define what is meant by a "philosophy" of science, the first problem one encounters is the notorious vagueness of the term "philosophy."[2] Unlike historiography, which is relatively well defined in its method and in the types of evidence on which it draws, "philosophy" can in practice be anything from a cloudy speculative fancy to a piece of formal logic. The term has become almost hopelessly equivocal in modern usage; even in academic contexts, despite the unity implied by a label like "Department of Philosophy," there can be the widest divergence concerning what the aims and methods of the "philosopher" should be. Five strands might be roughly separated. Something may be called "philosophy" because of (1) its concern with the "ultimate causes" of things; or (2) the immediate availability of the prescientific or "ordinary-language" or "core-of-experience" evidence on which it rests; or (3) the generality of the claims it makes; or (4) its speculative character, allied with difficulties in confirmation, particularly empirical confirmation of any kind; or (5) its "second-level" character, the fact that it is concerned with other first-level

---

[1] There is an unfortunate ambiguity in the English word *history.* It signifies both the sequence of events and what is written about the events. Thus, "history" of science (in one sense of the term) is about the "history" of science (in the other). The technical term *historiography* is sometimes used for the former, but is rather cumbrous. We shall rely on context for clarification. *HS* below will, however, always mean the written account, the product of the historian.

[2] I have argued elsewhere that a failure on the part of those writing what they call "philosophy of science" to say what the term "philosophy" means for them leads to this label (at present an honorific one) being used to cover ever broader areas of thought. See "Philosophies of Nature," *New Scholasticism,* 43 (1968), 29–74.

disciplines rather than with the world directly. In practice, some ill-defined combination of these criteria will usually be operative. It is the last (and most recent) of these senses that seems most relevant to the notion of a "philosophy" of science. It is "philosophy" just because it *is* a second-order critical and reflective enterprise. The label "philosophy of science" is of course of very recent origin, even more recent than the separation of the domains of "science" and "philosophy" from which it takes its origin.

There are, it would seem, two quite different ways in which one could set about constructing a reflective philosophy of science (*PS*). One could look outside science itself to some broader context, and in this way derive a theory of what scientific inquiry should look like and how it should proceed. We shall call this an "external" philosophy of science (*PSE*), because its warrant is not drawn from an inspection of the procedures actually followed by scientists. *PSE* will often appear as normative, because it can serve to pass judgment on the adequacy of the methods followed in a particular piece of scientific work, or even in scientific work generally. Since it does not rest upon any analysis of the strategies actually followed by those who would regard themselves as "scientists," it need not be governed by current orthodoxies in this regard. Thus, *PSE* need not take account of the history of science, except as it furnishes illustrations. *PSE* in no way rests upon *HS*, though it must obviously give some sort of plausible reconstruction of *HS* if it is to be taken seriously. If a *PSE* diverges radically in its implied norms from what scientists actually appear to be doing, it is likely to be challenged, and its starting point may be called into question. Yet a surprisingly large divergence can be tolerated; it will be said simply that the "science" under discussion falls short of what "science" ought to be. One thinks, for example, of the account of the nature of science given by Aristotle in his *Posterior Analytics*, so obviously and widely at variance with what might have been inferred from his own extensive contributions to the science of biology.

There are two main types of "external" warrant for an account of the nature of science:

1. *PSM:* If one views science as the ideal of human knowing, or as one specific type of human knowing, it is plausible to suppose that its nature can best be understood by beginning from a general theory of knowing and being. This was essentially the starting point from which both Plato and Aristotle commenced in their discussion of the nature of science; to a large extent it was still the framework within which Descartes constructed his *Discourse on Method*. Such a *PS* can begin from an epistemological or from a phenomenological starting point; it will derive from a more general "metaphysical" theory, therefore; hence the label *PSM*. Since it is a *PSE*, the "metaphysics" here should not be a science-based one (otherwise the warrant would not be extrinsic). When we speak of a *PSM*, therefore, it will be assumed not only that its warrant is basically a "metaphysical" one (another admittedly vague label), but also that it is prior to any analysis of the actual procedures followed in science.

2. *PSL:* To the extent that science is thought of as a logical structure of demonstration or of validation, *PS* becomes akin to a formal logic, whether a deductive logic of demonstration (like the Aristotelian theory of syllogism) or an inductive logic of confirmation (such as that constructed by Carnap). Such a *PS* can be judged as one would any other purely formal system, in terms of consistency, simplicity, and so forth. Only the most general specifications of what would constitute "demonstration" or "inductive evidence" may be needed to get the system construction under way. There may be very little reference to present or past scientific practice; it is not suggested that this logic is the one actually followed by scientists in their work of discovery or of validation. Rather, it is a reconstruction, an idealized formal version of what, for example, proof *really* amounts to in science, whether the scientist knows it or not. It may be interpreted normatively as suggesting how, for instance, scientists *should* proceed when faced with two

competing theories. Or it may be intended *only* as rational reconstruction of a general logic that is intrinsic to scientific inquiry, though not capable of being made operationally specific enough to serve as a methodological manual for the scientist wondering how best to do his work.

The best known recent instance of a *PSL* of this latter type is Carnap's inductive logic. This is a formidably complex and logically fascinating formal system relating various types of confirmation in a mathematically expressible way. But no one has been able to suggest how the basic "measure" utilized by Carnap (that of degree of support of a hypothesis, *H*, on the basis of evidence, *e*) could be related to any actual hypothesis/evidence situation in empirical science. Thus, though Carnap's logic has been (and continues to be) of great interest to logicians, it is not clear that it has led to an understanding of what goes on in scientific inquiry. Yet it qualifies as a *PSL* in intention, at least; the reason for undertaking it, and the general conceptual framework of *hypothesis, evidence, plausibility,* in terms of which it was developed, derived from empirical science. But the justification for it as an intellectual construction lies in its logical interest, rather than in any insight it provides into the actual procedures of the scientist.

Discussions of the nature of science up to the seventeenth century were nearly always "external" in character, though one occasionally finds in the later medieval and Renaissance periods some analysis, for instance, of the actual methods of "composition" and "resolution" followed by scientists. The theory of science was based on a prior metaphysics or on an autonomous logic.[3] And even though

the pioneers of the scientific "revolution" purported to be drawing upon new sources for their methodology, they were still much closer to the *PSM* and *PSL* of the Greek tradition than they were willing to admit. Though Bacon, Boyle, Huygens, and many others depended on their knowledge of the practice of science in their analyses of methodological and epistemological issues, it was only in the nineteenth century that writers like Whewell and Mill took this new source of *PS* with complete seriousness.[4] It is easy to see why the astounding successes of the new mechanics, and the beginnings of a new era in biology, geology, and chemistry, should make it for the first time plausible that if one wished to understand the nature of science, one should look at what scientists actually *do*. No longer did "science," a stable knowledge of the world, seem a remote ideal; in terms of practical success, it had clearly been achieved already.

3. *PSI:* In contrast, therefore, with *PSE* is a philosophy of science which relies for its warrant upon a careful "internal" description of how scientists actually proceed, or have in the past proceeded. The function of different methodological elements (law, hypothesis, predictive validation, etc.) is studied not in the abstract, but in the practice of the scientists themselves.[5] This approach presupposes that one can already identify competent scientists and successful pieces of research. *PSI* is based on what scientists *do* rather than upon what they *say* they are doing; when contemporary scientists set out to give an account of the nature of scientific method, they can sometimes be as remote from scientific practice as were Aristotle or Descartes. They may have some sort of idealized *PS* in mind, an oversimplified isolation of one procedure, perhaps, or even a *PSM* in disguise.[6] A *PS* constructed by a scientist is

---

[3] These were combined in the dominant Aristotelian account of science of this period. See, for example, A. C. Crombie, *Robert Grosseteste and the Origins of Experimental Science, 1100–1700* (Oxford: Clarendon Press, 1953), chapters 4, 11; and E. McMullin, "The Nature of Scientific Knowledge: What Makes It Science?" *Philosophy in a Technological Culture,* ed. G. McLean (Washington, D.C.: Catholic University of America Press, 1964), pp. 28–54. See also the first half of my "Philosophies of Nature."

[4] See my "Empiricism and the Scientific Revolution."

[5] A good example would be Leonard Nash's recent work, *The Nature of the Natural Sciences* (Boston: Little, Brown, 1963).

[6] Examples are not hard to find. One recalls the "pointer-reading" account of scientific method on which Eddington built his

not necessarily *PSI,* and if it is *PSI,* it is not necessarily accurate *PSI.* The evidence on which *PSI* is based is a descriptive account of the procedures by which empirical science is built; though the testimony of scientists is of primary importance in achieving such a description, such testimony cannot be taken without question, especially if there is reason to suppose that the scientist allows a *PSE* or an overly simplified *PSI* to color what he has to say of his own procedures.

By comparison with *PSE, PSI* is a relatively empirical undertaking, not very different in this respect from an empirical science itself. If one wishes to give a *PSI* analysis of the role of models in science, one begins from a carefully documented review of how scientists have made use of models. *PSI* thus differs in several important respects from *PSE* (whether of the traditional *PSM* or *PSL* varieties). It is expressly second-level, in that it takes another intellectual discipline as its object of study. It presupposes an already-functioning methodology, whose pragmatic success is a sufficient warrant of its adequacy as a heuristic. There is no need to ask what science *ought* to look like, in some abstract sense. The very success of modern natural science in prediction and control gives a sufficient reason for taking it as an object of analytic epistemological study in its own right. Furthermore, the claims made in *PSI* are relatively easily confirmed, as a rule; they can usually be settled by an analysis of the interrelations of some elements of descriptive methodology. There is not much affinity, in consequence, between the practitioner of *PSI* and the metaphysician or moralist. (There

is just as little affinity, but for different reasons, between the exponents of *PSM* and *PSL.*) This may help to explain the not infrequent tensions between philosophers of science and other philosophers; the closer to *PSI* the former are, the more likely they are, for example, to plan their conventions in conjunction with those of scientists or historians of science rather than those of philosophers.

Why are *PSI* and *PSL* with their heavily empirical or formal emphases called "philosophy" at all, then? It might seem that *PS* in either of these two genres could just as readily be called "science of science" or "logic of science," or be given an entirely new label. The main reason for retaining the name of "philosophy" is that the logical analysis of method and the drawing out of conceptual implications characteristic of both *PSI* and *PSL* present obvious analogies with the techniques traditional to the philosopher. Granted that the type of evidence called on and the mode of confirmation employed are rather different, there is still a sufficient family resemblance based on the procedures followed. And there is also a sufficient cross-relevance between *PS* of the *PSI* and *PSL* variety and other parts of "philosophy" to make it desirable that they should be studied in conjunction with one another. Besides which, we have already noted the modern tendency to describe all second-order critical discussions, whether they are of art, of history, of literature, of law, as "philosophy of . . . ."

In any discussion of the relevance of history of science to philosophy of science, it makes a very great difference which type of *PS* one has in mind. Clearly, history of science may be of little concern to a practitioner of *PSE* (whether *PSM* or *PSL*), though he cannot be wholly unconcerned about serious divergences between his own account of the nature of science and the course science has actually followed. And he may want to draw upon *HS* for illustrations and indirect support. But the philosopher whose interest is *PSI* has to take history of science very seriously. It furnishes not merely examples but the basic evidence from which his inquiry has to begin. More exactly, *PSI*

---

elaborate "Fundamental Theory"; Bridgman's operationalism also comes readily to mind as an illustration. A recent delightful example is an article by the biochemist J. R. Platt: "The New Baconians," *Science,* 146 (1964), 347–353. He reduces scientific inquiry to what he calls a "Baconian" method of "strong inference," which he compares to climbing a tree, each fork corresponding to a choice between alternative hypotheses; the decision on which way to go at each fork is made on the basis of crucial experiments ("clean results"). He attributes the recent rapid advance of biochemistry to its fidelity to this simple method, and suggests that other parts of science could enjoy equal success if only they could see the methodological light.

can begin either from a historical review or from an account of contemporary practice (or both). But even if a *PSI* practitioner prefers to focus on the details of contemporary practice, leaving the historical dimension of this practice out of account, he cannot draw any sharp distinction between past and present, and thus will have to admit the potential relevance of *HS* to what he is doing, whether he chooses to make use of it or not.

It might be argued that all there is of methodological import in the history of scientific development is likely to find a place somewhere in contemporary scientific practice, so that explicit recourse to the past history of science is unnecessary to the philosopher of science. If he bases his analysis on what scientists are currently doing, he is taking advantage of the learning process that has gone on in science itself over the centuries, as scientists have gradually become more expert in how to go about their experimental and theoretical researches. A pragmatic type of validation procedure has, after all, been at work in science itself; the methodology of today's physicist is by no means the same as that of Galileo.

While this is true up to a point, it will be argued below that *PSI* has to take into account the *developmental* aspect of science, the characteristic ways in which a theory, for instance, is modified in the face of successive anomalies. To do this properly, it will not be enough to examine the science of a particular moment; one will have to follow it over a period, even a considerable period. Besides, it may be important to note the ways in which the procedures of the scientist have changed since Galileo's time and to ask why these changes have occurred. Furthermore, historical distance allows one to isolate and understand much better the influences at work in a piece of scientific research (as in any other human activity). The philosopher may learn more about the nature of explanation in dynamics from a careful analysis of, say, the writings of Newton and his contemporaries than from a review of contemporary relativistic dynamics, not only because the simpler seventeenth-century context may reveal features of method that are more difficult to un-

cover today, but also because the variety of influences at work on Newton, as well as the different nuances his thought took on in successive drafts of his work, permit a more detailed analysis than would ordinarily be possible in the case of some contemporary piece of research. In summary, then, the history of science is relevant to *PSI* for two different sorts of reason: (1) because it provides complete case studies, of a kind one could not recover from contemporary science; (2) more fundamentally, because it allows one to study science in its all-important temporal dimension.

HS AND SOME PHILOSOPHERS

The distinction drawn above between *PSM, PSL,* and *PSI* ought not be taken to imply that any given piece of *PS* conforms to one and only one of these patterns. In practice, one finds philosophers of science calling upon all three sorts of criteria, sometimes even in the same piece of writing, and intermingling them in very complex (and not necessarily consistent) ways. Nevertheless, it is often possible (and when possible, helpful) to characterize a piece of writing in *PS* under one or other of the categories above, depending on which of the three types of warrant seems to dominate in it. There is no reason why an author could not combine logical, metaphysical, and descriptive-empirical elements in constructing a philosophy of science. But it is of paramount importance that he not be misled (or that he not mislead the reader) about what the balance between them in his argument really is.

In particular, it is easy for an author to suppose that what he is presenting is *PSI* when it is in fact *PSE*. This is all the more likely to happen today; because of the sheer weight of evidence available on what the procedures of the scientist are, it is hazardous to put forward any philosophy of science nowadays without some attempt, at least, to make it look like *PSI*, that is, to make it appear to derive from a familiarity with current scientific practice or from an intimate knowledge of the history of science. Yet if, in fact, the genre of writing is really that of *PSM* or *PSL*, there is an obvious danger that the wrong criteria of evaluation will be applied.

Philosophers of science of even the most "external" sort have always made *some* reference, at least, to what they believe the scientific practice of their day to be. But they have not usually turned their attention to *HS*; in the logical-empirical tradition which has dominated much of the work in *PS* of our century, virtually no attention has been paid to *HS* until recently, on the grounds presumably that the logical structures which were the philosopher's concern exhibited themselves readily in any random slice of contemporary scientific inquiry. It did not seem necessary or even desirable, therefore, to undertake first the difficult work of the historian of science as a means of carrying out the task of the philosopher of science.

This has changed in the last decades, and now one is beginning to find case histories dotted here and there throughout the journals of *PS*. But the change has brought with it some methodological headaches. How exactly *should HS* be incorporated in the philosopher's work? What weight should be given it? To what extent ought it be regarded as normative? . . .

Can the philosopher allow himself to be *entirely* governed by what happens (or has in the past happened) in scientific practice? Is there an analogy here between the philosopher formulating a theory to account for the procedures of science and a physicist formulating a theory to account for the behavior of gases? To press such an analogy, to suppose that everything a scientist does contributes positively to a theory of science is clearly wrong. Scientists (unlike gases) can make mistakes; there can be bad pieces of research. And scientists can gradually learn to do things better, so that later science could conceivably be more significant than earlier science. But is there any norm for what should count as a "good" or "bad" piece of research work? any norm, that is, prior to the construction of a *PSI*? If not, how is the practitioner of *PSI* to proceed? Can he leave aside those events in *HS* which don't fit in with his views, on the grounds that they were "bad" science, or at least untypical of the "best" science? Would there

not be a danger of *petitio principii* in such a procedure? Would such a *PS* be genuinely internal?

This is a real difficulty for anyone who purports to be giving a *PSI*. Can a *PSI* be normative? Does not this implicitly convert it into a *PSE*? A *PSI* has no source of autonomous prescientific evidence which would allow it to judge the adequacy of a particular piece of scientific work. Nevertheless, a *PSI* can legitimately point out when such a piece of work departs from the "normal," from the strategies that have proved in the past most "successful." Since it purports to be giving an account of what actually goes on in science, this is as far as it can go. It could not, for example, mount a critique of "normal" procedure itself without becoming a methodologically different sort of undertaking, one intended to define the ideal rather than explore the actual. One last reminder is in order, that in most cases a *PS* will not fall neatly into either category: It will draw from above as well as below. It will be governed by unstated metaphysical presuppositions, logical considerations of consistency, esthetic values, as well as by some knowledge of what has been going on in science these three centuries past. Our purpose in separating these considerations, and in classifying the types of *PS* built on only one of them to the relative exclusion of the others, was to focus attention on an important but often overlooked ambiguity: what counts as evidence in *PS,* and in particular what role *HS* plays in it.

PHILOSOPHY OF SCIENCE: THREE AREAS OF INQUIRY

In the preceding sections, we have been speaking of *PS* as though it were a single well-defined enterprise. This is far from being the case. *PS* comprises all those philosophic inquiries that take science as their starting point or as their object of concern. When discussing the distinction between *PSE* and *PSI* above, we assumed that the problems of *PS* are *epistemological* in nature, so that one could turn either to a more general theory of knowledge or to an inspection of the procedures actually followed in science in order to solve them. But two other sorts of problem have also got to be taken into account; they belong to the domains traditionally called ontology and philosophy of nature respectively. The abbreviations *ES* (epistemology of science), *OS* (ontology of science), and *PN* (philosophy of nature) will be convenient here. *ES* would at one time have been regarded as part of logic. *OS* constitutes a relatively new problematic, although there are some hints of this problematic in Plato's thought and in later medieval discussions of astronomy and optics. *PN* would originally not have been distinguished from "physics" (natural philosophy) itself. The development of Newtonian science profoundly affected all three of these. *ES* was greatly enlarged and strengthened as science itself became more and more sophisticated and self-conscious in its methods. *OS* became a crucial issue only where there was a sufficient body of scientific theory to make a question about its ontological import unavoidable. *PN* became a separate domain only when "philosophy" and "science" themselves began to separate in the post-Newtonian period. Metaphysics and physics had always been distinguished. But a distinction between the "philosophic" and "scientific" approaches to' an issue is of very recent origin. *ES, OS,* and *PN* have come to be grouped together in recent decades under the broad title of "philosophy of science," a title which would have made no sense in Newton's day.[7]

ES is concerned with science as a way of knowing (explaining, proving, discovering, measuring, conceptualizing, etc.). It is a general meth-

odology of empirical science; it is not concerned with particular scientific theories or even with particular domains (biology, chemistry, etc.) except insofar as the difference of domain brings with it a difference of methodology.[8] Most of the published work in what is called "philosophy of science" today would fall into this category. Topics like the nature of explanation in science, the logic of confirmation or discovery, account for more than half of all the essays in current anthologies of *PS* in the United States (in the Pittsburgh, Minnesota, Delaware, and Boston series, for example).[9] Although in principle *ES* is a general theory of scientific method, it is ordinarily elaborated in the context of the most developed sciences, notably mechanics, from which in the past the ideal of scientific method has most often been elaborated. Of late, however, philosophers have begun to realize the negative effects of this concentration of *ES* upon what is in fact a quite untypical part of science. "Explanation" in mechanics means something quite different from explanation in a structural science like biology or chemistry or geology. With the change in *PS* already noted from external (*PSE*) to internal (*PSI*) modes of warrant, *ES* has broadened very much in scope and has grown in sophistication. Because science represents in some sense an ideal of human knowing, *ES* (whether of the *PSE* or *PSI* variety) is highly relevant to the more general issues of epistemology and metaphysics. In some recent instances, indeed, the position adopted in *ES* has determined the entire shape of philosophy, as with logical positivism.

A second area of *PS*, closely related to the first, is the ontology of science (*OS*), the exploration of the ontological relevance of the claims made by empirical science. *OS* reduces, in essence, to a single question: To what extent do the postulational structures of science reveal a "real" structure, whether of the world or of the human mind? Various philosophers have argued that although science makes our experience intelligible by for-

---

[7] In some countries (U.S.S.R., Germany), and in some philosophic traditions (especially those of Aristotle, Aquinas, Kant, and Hegel), this grouping is less common. A strong distinction would be drawn between "theory of science" ("critique of the sciences," etc.) on the one hand, comprising *ES* and *OS*, and *Naturphilosophie* (*PN*) on the other. In the International Congresses of Philosophy, these constitute two different sections, though the assignment of papers to one or the other becomes ever more arbitrary. In the Vienna Congress of 1968, whether one submitted a paper to the "Theory of Science" division or to the "Philosophy of Nature" division seemed to depend largely on one's country of origin or on one's own philosophical standpoint. See my Introduction to the *Naturphilosophie* section of the *Congress Proceedings* (vol. 4, pp. 295–305): "Is There a Philosophy of Nature?" The main reason this distinction is not emphasized by English and American philosophers is that they are skeptical of the possibility of an autonomous philosophy of nature.

[8] Quantum theory has, for instance, suggested to some philosophers that a special multivalued logic is required where noncommuting operators stand for physical parameters.

[9] See E. McMullin, "Recent Work in the Philosophy of Science," *New Scholasticism*, 40 (1966), 478–518.

mulating correlations that enable predictions to be made, we cannot infer from this that scientific theories have any ontological import. They may be no more than arbitrary fictions, convenient instruments of prediction. *OS* is concerned, therefore, not with the general structures of scientific knowing, nor with the specific physical structures that occur in nature, but with the question of how these are related to one another. What, in brief, does science tell us about the world? This question has been a crucial one for philosophers ever since the time of Hume, who was the first to defend a phenomenalist ontology which would deny an intelligible structure to nature, and therefore by implication refuse any sort of realist view of science. There has been a significant difference between the *OS* of scientists and that of philosophers: The former did not have to contend with Hume. For the most part, they have maintained a realist *OS* (with the exception of some physicists working in the area of mechanics, an atypical part of science, as we have already noted). The resolution of this ontological issue is quite crucial for contemporary metaphysics, especially for a metaphysics (like that of process philosophy) which derives part of its warrant from the results of scientific theory.

Empiricist philosophers have paid relatively little attention to *OS,* as a glance at standard United States handbooks of *PS* will show.[10] For an empiricist of Humean sympathies, *OS* is not even a meaningful issue. But apart from this, *ES* and *PN* are much more congenial from the point of view of "research," since there is an abundance of material to work on; new problems arise as new scientific theories are formulated. The philosopher of science who busies himself with *PSI* (whether *ES* or *PN*) can easily leave *OS* out of account altogether; by comparison with other parts of *PS,* the problem it poses tends to seem an intractable one.

Yet it is *OS* that poses the most specifically "philosophical" issue of any part of *PS;* until one has faced this issue, all other findings in *PS* are suspended in the air.

The third area of *PS* depends quite sensitively for its characterization upon the position one adopts in *OS.* Many scientific theories appear to have far-reaching implications for traditional philosophic problems concerning the nature of mind, the relations of space and time, the nature of causality, and so forth. If one defends a realistic or quasi-realistic theory of science, then the implications of relativity theory, of the theory of evolution, of cybernetics, and the like, have to be taken seriously by any philosopher who wishes to understand the most general traits of the physical world. One can describe these implications as a "philosophy of nature," meaning that the scientific theories themselves allow us to formulate a properly "philosophic" cosmology. On the other hand, if a nonrealist *OS* be defended, what passes as *PN* in the other view is likely to be regarded as no more than a speculative extension of science, a series of conceptual clarifications, "philosophical" only in a very loose sense . . . .

PN is obviously very close in methodology to science itself. They seem, in fact, to form a continuum. The conventional modern distinction between philosophy and science, which has come to seem so basic, is not readily applicable here. How is one to specify a demarcation criterion that would mark "philosophy" off from "science" in such works of *PN* as Adolf Grünbaum's *Philosophic Problems of Space and Time?* Much will depend on whether one believes an autonomous *PN* to be possible. Is it possible to construct a *PN* prior to the deliverances of science, based on the "common core of experience" or on the structures of ordinary language, or on an analysis of the general structures of possibility of any knowledge of a physical world? A wide variety of philosophers (neo-Aristotelians, Marxist-Leninists, phenomenologists, Kantians, Hegelians, etc.) maintain that such a *PN* can be developed.

They disagree, however, on how to interpret its relationship with science. Is it altogether autonomous, and thus unaffected by the growth of scientific knowledge? If so, can it perhaps even serve

---

[10] One notable exception is E. Nagel's *The Structure of Science* (New York: Harcourt, Brace and World, 1961). For detailed work in *OS,* see, for example, J.J.C. Smart, *Philosophy and Scientific Realism* (London: Routledge and Kegan Paul, 1963); W. Sellars, "The Language of Theory," in his *Science, Perception and Reality* (New York: Humanities, 1963); G. Maxwell, "The Ontological Status of Theoretical Entities," *Minnesota Studies in the Philosophy of Science,* vol. III (Minneapolis: University of Minnesota Press, 1962), pp. 3–27.

as a norm to judge the adequacy of the categories and methods of the scientist? This strong claim for *PN* can be found in some writers of the Hegelian, Marxist, and Husserlian traditions. A weaker claim would give the prescientific *PN* a limited autonomy only, allowing for the possibility that it might have to be modified in the light of advances in science. In other words, part of the warrant for an adequate *PN* would be the sciences of nature. A philosophy of nature would thus have to balance evidence of two rather different sorts, evidence from some prescientific source (e.g., common experience or the categorial "cuts" of ordinary language) as well as from science. Each of these would in effect be taken seriously as a partial warrant for philosophic assertions about nature; the testimony of one could, however, modify that of the other. The alternative to these two views of *PN* is one which would make it wholly derivative from science, i.e., would deny any source of evidence for a *PN* other than contemporary scientific theory and practice.

The status given a *PN* thus serves as an indicator of the distinction between "philosophy" and "science" a particular philosopher maintains, i.e., of the ways in which he chooses to define these two very vague and dangerously honorific terms. (1) He may deny the existence of a *PN* entirely, in which case all knowledge of nature, however speculative, is by definition "scientific," and "philosophy" is entirely confined to second-order questions about language or method. (2) He may allow a *PN*, but insist that it be entirely derivative from science. In this case, the distinction between "philosophy" and "science" is in terms of speculative character or generality or the like. (3) He may allow a partial warrant for *PN* prior to the constructive activity of science. This gives a very complex notion of "philosophy," since quite different types of evidence can be relevant to it, and it can make first-order assertions about the world, of higher generality than those of science but presumably in a continuum with these. (4) Finally, he may hold out for a completely autonomous *PN* prior to science, in which case he can draw a very sharp distinction between "philosophy" and "science" on the basis of the type of evidence on

which each rests. Since he does not in this case admit science as a source of properly "philosophical" knowledge of nature, he will not have a *PS* concerned with nature; *PS* for him will cover at most only *ES* and *OS*. This rather summary and abstract taxonomy may suffice to bring out the wide variety of approaches that may be covered by our label "philosophy of nature."[11] It would take us much too far afield to evaluate these approaches, and in particular to investigate whether or not there *is* a genuinely autonomous "philosophical" mode of approach to nature different from that followed by the scientist. But perhaps enough has been said to suggest that this part of *PS* is more complex and controversial in character, methodologically speaking, than are *ES* and *OS*. The existence of a *PN* (if it be admitted) suggests that philosophy and science have somehow got to complement one another—or else compete with one another—in the construction of a total world picture.

The distinction just drawn between three different approaches to *PN* can also be expressed in terms of the "external-internal" division above, even though it was originally elaborated in the context of *ES* rather than *PN*. If the warrant for *PN* is independent of science, we have a *PNE*; if it rests upon the theories of science, it is a *PNI*. If there is some external source of evidence for a *PN* but the procedures and theories of science are also taken into account, we have a *PN* of mixed warrant (*PNM*).[12] *OS* can likewise be governed either

---

[11] I have developed this schema in more concrete detail against the background of the major exponents of *PN*, past as well as present, in "Philosophies of Nature." I have argued that this question of the type of warrant on which a *PN* is supposed to rest makes an illuminating basis of distinction between contemporary approaches to nature. The tension between the different possible approaches to knowledge of nature a philosopher may take up has been of very great importance in the Kantian and more recently the Marxist-Leninist schools. For the latter, see my review-article on David Joravsky's book *Soviet Marxism and Natural Science, 1917–1932* (London: Routledge and Kegan Paul, 1961), in *Natural Law Forum*, 8 (1963), 149–159.

[12] These are the *PN1, PN2,* and *PNM,* of my article "Philosophies of Nature." *PNM* seems to me the most defensible sort of *PN;* I have argued elsewhere that it plays an implicit but important role in the heuristics of science (section 9 of the Epilogue to *The Concept of Matter in Modern Thought*).

by external or by internal considerations (or by a combination of the two). One could, for instance, develop a positivist *OSE* on the basis of a Humean phenomenalism. A "pure" *OSI* is less likely; one would not normally wish to base an ontology on an analysis of science exclusively. Metaphysical and epistemological considerations of a more general sort would presumably have to be taken into account in deciding what the ontological implications of scientific theory are . . . .

PHILOSOPHY AND PSYCHOLOGY

What is the relationship between the "philosophic" mode of investigating science and other systematic modes of understanding human activity such as psychology (including variants like psychoanalysis) and sociology?[13] The distinctions we have already drawn may help us to bring some clarity to this question, one which is quite crucial to the currently disputed question of a "logic of discovery" in science.[14] The science we have in mind here is, of course, *S2*. Psychology is not relevant to the understanding of *S1*, but it may well tell us something of the conditions under which *S2* is

furthered. Only *ES* is involved in this correlation with the work of the social sciences; psychology is clearly irrelevant to *OS* and *PN*. *ES₂* is, it would appear, the possible point of contact between *PS* and other modes of "understanding science," understanding it, that is, specifically as a human activity. Understanding is usually thought to involve two "moments": the discovery of regular patterns and the explanation of why these regularities recur in the way they do. Our question, then, reduces to this: What are the principal ways of understanding the patterns that occur in the complex of activities we call scientific research?

The answer we shall hazard is that only two need be considered: the philosophical and the psychological. We can trace regular conceptual or propositional connections, whether these be strictly logical (governed by a specifiable formal rule) or analogical. We can examine the scientist's activity with a view to describing and interrelating propositions implicit in it, the beliefs that guide him, the data he has obtained, the hypotheses he advances, and so forth. We can trace the gradual modification of a concept (like the concept of ether in Newton's thought), where it is possible to give plausible conceptual grounds ("reasons") for the modification's having occurred the way it did. The "pattern" here is a relation between ideas or can somehow be associated with such a relation. The techniques are those of conceptual analysis. The *ideal* here would be that of a complete logical reduction, the discovery of a fully formal system which would simulate the theory or procedure under investigation. But this is rarely possible, since scientists do not follow a strict (i.e., fully specifiable formal-deductive) logic of this sort in the more significant parts of their work. Indeed, to the extent that they do follow fully formal rules, their reasoning is unlikely to be significant, since it is only unfolding something already conceptually and propositionally given.[15]

A *psychological* pattern is, broadly speaking,

---

[13] Other social sciences, like economics and politics, are much less relevant because their "laws" and explanatory hypotheses concern facets of human behavior or of social structure that are remote from the doing of science. Though economic or political situations and motives can obviously influence scientific research, this influence would be best understood as a rule in psychological or sociological terms. If, for example, one were to ask why certain lines of research moved more rapidly than others in the United States over the last two decades, one would have to take into account the availability of federal grants for some types of research and not for others. Note that this is a *psychological* explanation (the efficacy of the economic motive) rather than an economic one. Scientific activity does not lend itself to what we would ordinarily regard as economic or political patterning. To understand the economic situation that made one type of research more desirable to the federal government than another may require quite a bit of economic or political analysis. But this analysis is likely to be of only marginal interest to someone who is trying to discover invariants in scientific activity as such.

[14] R. Blackwell in Chapter 3 of his recent *Discovery in the Physical Sciences* (Notre Dame, Ind.: University of Notre Dame Press, 1969) distinguishes between four possible ways of patterning scientific discovery: logical, psychological, historical, and epistemological. In general, though, distinctions of this sort have not been analyzed by philosophers of science in any detail.

---

[15] This important point I have tried to make in some detail in "Freedom and Creativity in Science," in *Freedom and Man*, ed. J. C. Murray (New York: Kenedy, 1965), pp. 105–130.

some regularity in human behavior, thought to be attributable to the specific personality structure (intellectual abilities, emotional makeup, character, etc.) of the individuals exhibiting it.[16] Since this includes propositional "behavior" (thinking, writing, proving), logical patterns are not going to be easily distinguished from psychological ones.[17] Since people generally obey the *modus ponens* rule in their reasoning, is it not a psychological law as well as a logical one? This is a matter of definition, of course, but logical rules of inference are usually *not* regarded as properly "psychological" laws, even though they are clearly patterns of a quite basic sort in the operation of the human psyche. The reason for not including them in the scope of psychology is that the "dynamism" of these regularities, their ultimate ground, is thought to lie in the propositions rather than in the psychological structures of the thinker . . .. Even if these latter structures were quite different, the assumption is that logical laws would still govern the thinking of the individual, as an ideal to be striven after, even if perhaps not always followed.

To the extent that the scientist's procedures are *not* completely bound by logical rule, however, it would seem that psychological considerations may have to be taken into account. The formula-

tion of a hypothesis, for instance, is not a deductive process. It may be guided by analogies but by definition it goes "beyond the evidence," i.e., beyond what could be arrived at on the basis of formal logic alone. It is relevant, therefore, to inquire whether the pattern of *discovery*, say in science, can be at least partially accounted for in terms of psychological laws and theories.[18] To "account for" it here means to situate it as one human ability among others, to show if possible "how it works," an ambitious mechanistic metaphor but implying nothing much more than that the characteristic stages in discovery should be categorized in some general way. A good example of this sort of effort is Koestler's massive work, *The Act of Creation,*[19] which explores creativity in art, humor, and science, and suggests as an "explanation" of what occurs an ability on man's part to juxtapose hitherto unrelated matrices of thought. Whether this is an "explanation" or only an insightful *description* of what happens can be debated, but it is enough for us to note that insofar as it would "explain," it would do so by pointing to a general human ability (possessed by some to a higher degree than others); it would then go on to break down this complex and puzzling ability into simpler and better understood sub-abilities. Contrast this with a logical explanation of the steps of a mental process, where rules would have to be given to justify each step of the process, or at least to estimate its inductive weight. To "explain" a process psychologically does not of itself justify the term of the process; at best, it only describes how we got there . . ..

A complete epistemology of science (ES_2) cannot, therefore, leave psychological considerations out of account. Admittedly, such considerations are not relevant if we are merely interested in the validity of the scientific claims made, the extent to which they "explain" the data (ES_1). And this is the

[16] It is not necessary to distinguish explicitly between sociology and psychology in this context. Sociology seeks information about the behavior of persons as members of specific groups, and about the interactions of groups considered as units. But insofar as one wishes to *explain* this behavior or these interactions, one must ultimately return to psychology. As a type of *information*, sociology is distinct from psychology. But as modes of *explanation*, they tend to become one. E.g., much has been written about the influence of religion on the growth of science in the seventeenth century. Correlations have been sought between creativity in science and Unitarianism (or Anglicanism or free thought or Christianity). But if such are found, one will still have to ask why a Unitarian should have been a better scientist, and the answer will have to be either *conceptual* (lying in Unitarian belief) or *psychological* (the type of personality structure commonly found among Unitarians). The former approach is the commoner among those philosophers and historians who have discussed this problem (see, for example, R. S. Westfall, *Science and Religion in Seventeenth Century England*, New Haven, Conn.: Yale University Press, 1958) . . ..

[17] The whole question of how logic and psychology are to be situated relative to one another is so dismayingly vast, so amorphous in its ramifications, that these remarks have to be considered as no more than loose generalities.

[18] One of the difficulties about answering this question is that there are so many different sorts of "psychology," ranging from depth psychology to behaviorist studies of animal behavior. Obviously, the implications of each of these for *ES* are likely to differ.

[19] New York: Macmillan, 1964.

perspective in which the problem is most often discussed. But the wider perspective is a valid one, and the question of the methodology appropriate to it is deserving of more attention than it has so far received. Whether at this stage psychology can in fact offer much help on issues such as the nature of creative discovery is another matter. Such questions do not readily lend themselves to investigation in the prevailing behaviorist terms, and it is noteworthy that extensive empirical attempts in recent decades to correlate creativity with other more easily identifiable traits have been unsuccessful.[20] The "explanation" offered by psychology is, besides, of a very modest sort. It is obviously never going to reduce the creative act to specifiable rule; it can only search for some appropriate general categories in which to analyze it. Men have the ability to "see" a particular hypothesis as the best way of explaining the "facts." The distinction—one might almost say the tension—between the psychological and the philosophical modes of approach to this ability soon becomes evident. Are we to rest content with describing it simply as an ability? Or ought we in each case where it operates attempt to specify the logical reasons why the hypothesis *is* the best one, or why it is confirmed by this piece of evidence?

These are the two principal ways of understanding recurrent patterns in the activities of the scientist. But how are these patterns to be *discovered?* This is where the historian comes in, because all these patterns are of themselves "historical," in the sense that they recur in time and can be documented by the ordinary methods of the historian. Does this not suggest that history ought to be added to logic and psychology as a third mode of recovering pattern in science, of "understanding science"? It is important to see why this is not the case. *HS* is not of itself a mode of understanding science, in the ordinary sense of discovering and explaining regularities in the practice of

science. Its goal is to establish the singular, not the universal (as does epistemology or psychology). Insofar as it provides "understanding," it is an understanding of the past singular in its complexity and contingency, a different sense, therefore, of "understanding." To achieve it, the historian may make use of a variety of sciences: psychology, linguistics, sociology, as well as philosophy. But this does not mean that his own effort falls into the same methodological category as theirs. There is ultimately a quite fundamental division here. The historian is concerned with what happened just because it *did* happen. He may call upon universals of all sorts in his effort to establish what happened or why it happened. But his goal is not the assertion of a universal, a pattern, or the interlinking of such patterns. This is the task of the philosopher, the sociologist, the economist, whose use of the materials of history does not commit them to the reconstruction of any specific set of historical events.

History is closely interwoven with these other fields. They are built up inductively from things that happen. But they are not concerned with the particularities of occurrences, only with their exemplification of a certain set of universals. The philosopher of science will discuss the nature of measurement, for instance, without adverting to any specific historic instance of it. The sociologist will assert a correlation between drug addiction and broken homes without giving historical details of the broken homes he investigated in making his generalization. Yet the philosopher and the sociologist have to begin from the activities of real people; they may not invent their material, they have to find it. This can easily be overlooked in the case of philosophy, because it is for the most part at such a high level of generality that specific reference to concrete instances, instances requiring the skill of the historian to establish or unravel them, is rarely found. When a philosopher speaks of the nature of discovery (say) in science, he will often suppose that what he is saying is so intuitively evident to anyone who has even a rudimentary acquaintanceship with science that reliance on specific instances, calling such instances in evidence so to speak, is simply unnecessary.

---

[20] As a glance at such standard collections as *Scientific Creativity: Its Recognition and Development,* ed. C. W. Taylor and F. Barron (New York: Wiley, 1963), will quickly show.

LOGIC AND HISTORY

We have already seen that a philosopher who wishes to find an "external" warrant for a *PS* is likely to look either to a metaphysics (*PSM*) or to the properties of formal systems (*PSL*), whereas someone who relies on "internal" evidence (*PSI*) is likely to look for his evidence either to contemporary science or to episodes in *HS*. Of these approaches, the two that most strongly contrast with one another are the logical and the historical. It may be worth exploring these contrasts in more detail. It defines the ends of a spectrum of possible ways of relating *HS* to *PS*.

The logician and the historian approach the problem of relating two elements in a piece of scientific research in quite different ways. The logician seeks to discover a purely logical structure relating them, a structure of transparent intelligibility in its own right. This structure can be disentangled and its properties studied; it can be used to justify the move from one element to the other. What the historian seeks to establish is the fact that the elements occurred in a certain sequence, whether or not any formal structure can be discerned in their relationship. He may be able to "explain" the historical sequence by showing how it exemplifies some logical or psychological pattern. But his first concern is not with explanation but with a reconstruction of the past, no matter how opaque it seems.

In *PSL* in its most "external" form, science becomes the occasion for the logician to investigate certain formal structures that might not otherwise have come to his attention. His aim is to construct a theory of inference, a theory of confirmation, a semantics of scientific terms, or the like, in such a way that these can stand in their own right as formal systems. The important point is that *PSL*, so construed, does not rest upon an appeal to what is actually going on in science or to *HS*. When an exponent of *PSL* puts forward an inductive logic, he need not be claiming that this is what actually governs scientists in their evaluation of hypotheses. He may even be entirely indifferent to any reference from case studies in *HS*. It need not weaken his case to say that Newton did not follow

the logical plan suggested. What the logician is saying is that in an abstractly described piece of scientific research, the logical relationships between the elements are of the following kind— whether or not the relationships he specifies describe any historical sequence or were grasped by the scientists involved in the research. In this external form, *PSL* is not an empirical study; it is basically of the same character as mathematics or any other formal discipline. It is only in a broad sense that it qualifies as "philosophy." It could be argued that it ought *not* be so described, any more than formal logic would nowadays be described as "philosophy." Nevertheless, this would be a mistake since *PSL* does illuminate the structures of empirical science, and does take its origin in them.[21]

There is an obvious analogy here with the "rational mechanics" of Newton's successors. Newton developed a complex physical theory, which he himself on occasion liked to regard as a quasi-formal mathematical system, thus leaving aside all questions about the operational meaning of the concepts employed and of the empirical adequacy of the system as a means of understanding specific concrete problems, leaving aside in other words what would be regarded as the properly "physical" issues. This "rational mechanics," as it was

---

[21] Two recent instances of *PSL* would be R. Carnap's *Philosophical Foundations of Physics* (New York: Basic Books, 1966), and Kyburg's *Philosophy of Science: A Formal Approach*. Carnap's book deals with probability theory, the logic of measurement, the logic of causal modalities, analyticity, correspondence rules. Kyburg organizes his book "around the concept of a formal system," and explicitly limits himself to *ES*. He leaves aside *OS* ("what does the fact that science exists at all tell us about the world?"), not because he thinks these unimportant, but because a formalist *ES* is, in his view, an indispensable starting point for any adequate discussion of them. His first chapters are characteristically headed "The Concept of a Formal System," "Quantities," "Scientific Terms," "Axioms," "Probability and Error," "Induction and Experiment." He makes extensive use of the predicate calculus and of the logic of relations, and indeed notes in his preface that "the philosophy of science can be understood without knowing physics (though perhaps not without really understanding some science), but it cannot be understood without knowing some logic, an essential ingredient of every science." In the entire text (on the testimony of the careful index at the end), not a single scientist is mentioned, nor are there more than a few references to specific scientific works. Thus the weight of the book in no way rests on a reporting of scientific practice; an item from *HS* would not be relevant to any of the major points that Kyburg is making.

called, was developed at the hands of Euler, La-grange, Laplace, Hamilton, and many others. Its evolution was quite independent of any new empirical information, or any modifications in the empirical bearing of the concepts used. It was guided by purely mathematical principles; its criteria were those of pure mathematics, although its original impetus came from physics. What its proponents sought was a more elegant formal exposition, employing more economical and better defined concepts; this in turn would allow the hidden inconsistencies and vaguenesses of the earlier system to be eliminated. The construction of the well-known "Lagrangian" and "Hamiltonian" functions to help in formulating the state description of a Newtonian mechanical system was an instance of such a development. It was prompted not by any empirical inadequacy of the system but by a desire for conceptual improvement. In technique, the exponents of rational mechanics were mathematicians; its history has been similar to that of a branch of mathematics, even though its starting point was different. It is not, however, applied mathematics, a point that Clifford Truesdell has emphasized.[22] It does not simply apply a given mathematics to the formulation of a physical theory or to the solution of physical problems. Rather, new mathematical concepts have to be developed or old ones modified in response to the needs of the physicist, or as a further elaboration of a formal system first created by the physicist. Thus rational mechanics is not quite reducible either to physics or to mathematics. The analogy with *PSL*, with logic substituted for mathematics, is a fairly exact one; *PSL* likewise is not quite reducible either to philosophy or to logic.

If the logician, instead of considering general epistemological issues inherent in any part of science, turns to specific scientific theories with a view to formalizing them, he will have to take *HS* somewhat more seriously. If he aims to formalize Newtonian mechanics, he can scarcely do this without some reference to the documents. Yet this reference may serve only as a starting point; he may settle for some convenient textbook account of Newtonian mechanics and focus on the logical issues involved in it, without pausing to ask whether the system he is analyzing is really that of Newton. If an objection is raised on this score, the logician is likely to be unmoved; his creative energies are concentrated on formal problems of structure, not on problems of historical interpretation. Thus his analysis of "Newtonian" mechanics is likely to identify this mechanics with a broad class of systems, independent of any particular historical text. Yet he may after all rightly claim that his analysis illuminates (at least to some degree) Newton's own work, its conceptual implications and its weaknesses. And he may well exhibit considerable historical sophistication in deciding how to formalize messy physical concepts like *mass* or *force*.

The value of such an approach to *PS* is that it uncovers logical structures, a thorough grasp of which is indispensable to the full understanding of science or of a particular scientific theory. Its limitations as *PS* have already been alluded to more than once, chief among them a remoteness from the actual workings of science and a danger of escapism (from the point of view of *PS* not that of logic, of course) because of the allure of the free construct. The logical-empiricist school has naturally tended to *PSL* because the characteristically Humean epistemology of the empiricist made it difficult for him to take *HS* seriously as an independent source of philosophical insight. The variety of challenges to empiricism among philosophers of science in the past decade has brought with it a corresponding skepticism about the adequacy of logical reconstructionism as a program for *PS*. It has also opened the way for a much more thorough utilization of *HS* on the part of philosophers . . ..

CAN ONE DO HISTORY AND PHILOSOPHY OF SCIENCE TOGETHER?

This essay has made extensive use of dichotomies as a tool of methodological analysis. But it has

---

[22] *Essays in the History of Mechanics* (Heidelberg: Springer, 1968).

also stressed that works of scholarship rarely fall into a single neat methodological category. One distinction, however, that might seem a reasonably sharp one is that between *HS* and *PS*. Ordinarily, it is easy to tell which of these genres a particular piece of research belongs to. Can they be validly blended in a single work? The answer would seem to be that they can. *PSI,* as we have seen, often involves a careful reading of the history of science as a *warrant* for the philosophical claims made. Such work accomplishes both a historical and a philosophical goal. The writer tries to illuminate the historical instance with all the relevant philosophical analysis he can produce so that, despite its singularity, he may understand it as best he can. He also uses the documented historical instance to make a further philosophical point; it serves not merely as illustration but as evidence for this point. This genre of "history and philosophy of science" (*HPS*) is a complex, even a risky, one . . .. There are obvious dangers involved in combining two methodologies so diverse (not to mention the dangers of infuriating two professional groups whose reflexes are so different!). A good piece of *HPS* will not blur the distinction between the historical and the philosophical points it is making; by making them at the same time, or at least in the same piece, there is no intention of claiming them to be ultimately identical. We have already seen that philosophy and historiography are at bottom irreducible to one another, no matter how closely they may be interlocked in practice. It is important to grasp in as precise a way as possible what the relation is between the historical and the philosophical motifs in such writing. The historical motif is prior and in a sense basic, for on the establishing of the analysis as *history* depends its *warrant* as philosophy. It is ultimately because something happened in a certain way that a point in *PS* can be made to rest partially upon it.

If someone . . . asserts for instance that Galileo's colleagues obtained telescopic results that differed from Galileo's, it is essential that he be correct in the historical claim if it is to serve as warrant and not merely as illustration. An illustration could be replaced by some other apposite

instance if it proved historically inaccurate. But if the philosophical claim in any way *rests* upon the case histories cited, it is weakened if any of these are shown to be unreliable. The *HPS* writer may, of course, choose simply to cite his history from someone else and not attempt to bring any fresh support for the claim that it happened the way it is supposed to have. But even so, by making use of it for philosophical purposes, he will almost certainly have illuminated it, situated it, helped the reader to understand it better. And this, as we have already seen, is one of the two main functions of the historian. By making a series of points of general philosophical relevance in the context of Newton's dynamics, Dudley Shapere (to quote one recent example) has also illuminated Newton's own historical achievement.[23]

There is one particular category of philosophical problem where the *HPS* approach is seen at its best, and where the *PSL* methods of the logician prove inadequate. This is the investigation of the *developmental* aspects of science (S_2). If discovery in science were guided by logical laws, one could write a history of science as it *had* to occur. But, of course, science is not like this; central to it is human creativity, and there are the innumerable contingencies of influence and noninfluence. One can extract the partial logical structures of validation which are implicit in scientific research. But to see how change actually occurs in science, what factors are most often responsible for it, one has to have recourse to the historical record.

This is the approach taken by Mary Hesse, for example, in her *Forces and Fields*.[24] She traces some basic conceptual structures that have re-

---

[23] "Philosophical Significance of Newton's Science," *Texas Quarterly,* 10 (Fall 1967), 201–215. Adolf Grünbaum argues this point cogently, and illustrates it from the historiography of relativity theory, in "The Bearing of Philosophy on History of Science," *Science,* 143 (1964), 1406–12.

[24] London: Nelson, 1961. One of the earliest and still one of the finest achievements of this genre was Pierre Duhem's ten-volume work, *Le Système du Monde* (Paris: Hermann, 1913–59). This is a history of mechanics, with special reference to celestial mechanics, but it also makes use of historical analyses to argue (in contrast to Mary Hesse) a generally positivist view of the nature of scientific theory. The prototype of *HPS* was the pioneering work of William Whewell, *The Philosophy of the Inductive Sciences, Founded upon Their History* (London, 1840).

curred in the analysis of continuous and discontinuous motion in mechanics. In particular, she emphasizes the complex philosophical problems that underlay many of the modifications of concept that occurred as mechanics attained a greater and greater precision. The resultant is good history of science; it also serves as the ground for a variety of epistemological and ontological assertions, notably the assertion of a generally realistic view of scientific constructs.

Thomas Kuhn's influential work, *The Structure of Scientific Revolutions*,[25] puts *HS* to even more striking philosophical use. He distinguishes between fundamental changes of "paradigm" in science ("revolutions" in his terminology), and theoretical developments that leave the basic "paradigm" unchanged. His main thesis is that

changes of paradigm cannot be justified on empirical or even rational grounds, though *post factum* an effort will always be made to provide such rationalization. This is a bold claim; it denies the possibility of any sort of *PSL* applicable to significant advances in science. Indeed, it has seemed to many to call into question the entire set of formalist assumptions on which the logical analysis of science is based. Kuhn's *HPS* is thus the antithesis of *PSL*, which may help to explain the warmth it has generated. For us, the important thing about it is that *only* the history of science can serve as evidence in its support. It is a philosophical statement about the nature of S_2 and about the transformational characteristics of S_1. It could not be derived from a general theory of knowledge, nor could it rest upon a formal logic. Only a sensitive analysis of selected periods in *HS,* an analysis which leaves aside the preconceptions of later methodology, will suffice to tell whether it is correct or not . . . .

---

[25] Chicago: University of Chicago Press, 1962.

EXPLANATION: A MAJOR GOAL OF SCIENTIFIC KNOWLEDGE

2

One of the foremost objectives of science is explanation. But what exactly is a scientific explanation? Are there important characteristics that all and only scientific explanations share, that distinguish them from nonscientific explanations, from pseudoscientific explanations, and from common-sense explanations? Are there, in addition, important contrasts among scientific explanations that divide them into different kinds, appropriate for different kinds of scientific question? Or are the characteristics of scientific explanations so intimately tied to the diverse and changing content, methods, and goals of science that attempted generalizations such as these become fruitless? We shall first consider some general conceptions of scientific explanation most influential in contemporary discussion in the philosophy of science; then we shall turn to some distinctions among scientific explanations that philosophers of science have found significant. Later we shall consider some historically based qualms held by other contemporary philosophers of science to this kind of undertaking.

THE NATURE OF SCIENTIFIC EXPLANATION

In February and March of 1865, after eight years of planting, fertilizing, reaping, and replanting edible pea plants, Gregor Mendel presented the results of his experiments to the Natural Science Society of Brünn. He had crossed, he reported, pure-breeding varieties of peas with contrasted characters like round versus wrinkled seed form, gray-brown versus white seed-coat color, and tall versus dwarf stature. He had then allowed the hybrid offspring (the F_1 generation) to self-fertilize to produce a second (F_2) generation. And he had always observed the same results: The F_1 generation consisted of plants with one of the two contrasted characters, which character Mendel called *dominant;* the F_2 generation consisted of plants of which three-fourths had the dominant character and one-fourth the other, *recessive* character. What could explain these results? Mendel suggested that each different character of his pea plants (such as round seed form, wrinkled seed form, gray-brown seed-coat color, and so on) was associated with a different internal "factor," that fertilization combined factors segregated into different pollen and egg cells, and that such combination was completely random. Thus, for example, when the F_1 (Td) hybrids that resulted from crossing pure-breeding tall (TT) with pure-breeding dwarf (dd) pea plants were self-fertilized, equal numbers of T-factors and d-factors, segregated into different pollen and egg cells, entered randomly into all possible combinations (TT Td dT dd) in equal numbers, thereby yielding the observed 3:1 ratio of dominant to recessive characters in the F_2 generation.

Although Mendel's experiments in plant hybridization and his explanation of their results attracted little attention when they were announced in 1865, they ultimately became the foundation of modern genetics. What characteristics of Mendel's explanation gave it, if not this special status, at least the status of a good scientific explanation? Three influential conceptions of scientific explanation can be applied to this question: the inferential conception, the causal conception, and the erotetic conception. In what follows I shall sketch each of these in turn. Readings representing each will then follow.

The Inferential Conception of Scientific Explanation

What characteristics of Mendel's explanation gave it the status of a good scientific explanation? According to the inferential conception of scientific explanation, Mendel's explanation could be formulated as one or more sound arguments containing: (a) testable statements of fact in the premises, such as the fact that the F_1 generation resulted from crossing pure-breeding tall with pure-breeding dwarf pea plants; (b) testable statements of law in the premises, such as the law that each different character of pea plants is associated with a different internal factor, or that the factor combinations TT Td dT dd are equiprobable; and (c) a statement of what is to be explained in the conclusion, such as that the ratio of dominant to recessive characters in the F_2 generation was $3:1$.

Let me explain: In logic an argument is a set of statements, one or more of which—the premises—are given in justification of the remaining statement, the conclusion. The aim of an argument, of course, is to provide strong grounds for believing the conclusion. This aim is generally fulfilled under two conditions: (1) There is a special logical relation, called *validity*, between the premises and conclusion of the argument, such that if the premises are true, the conclusion either has to be true or is very probably true; and (2) The premises of the argument *are* true. Arguments fulfilling these two conditions are called *sound* arguments.

Consider, for example, the following two arguments:

1. All the coins in Bank A are shiny pennies.
   Sonya has shaken a coin out of Bank A.
   _____
   The coin Sonya has shaken out of Bank A is a shiny penny.

2. 90% of the coins in Bank B are shiny pennies.
   Sonya has shaken a coin out of Bank B.
   _____
   The coin Sonya has shaken out of Bank B is a shiny penny.

In the first argument the logical relation of validity holding between the premises and the conclusion is such that, if the premises are true, then the conclusion *has* to be true. Arguments of this kind, in which the premises, if true, logically guarantee the truth of the conclusion, or at least purport to do so, are called *deductive* arguments. Given the logical relation of validity holding between the premises and conclusion of the first argument, and assuming that the premises *are* true, we have the strongest possible grounds for believing the conclusion. In the second argument, the logical relation of validity holding between the premises and the conclusion is such that, if the premises are true, then the conclusion is *very probably* true. Arguments of this kind, in which the premises, if true, show that the conclusion is very probably true, or at least purport to do so, are called *inductive* arguments. Given the logical relation of validity holding between the premises and conclusion of the second argument, and assuming that the premises *are* true, we have strong, but not conclusive, grounds for believing the conclusion.

According to the inferential conception of scientific explanation, scientific explanations are deductive or inductive arguments—logical *inferences*. These arguments are composed of (1) a conclusion, called the *explanandum*, describing the phenomenon (event, fact, law) to be explained, and (2) a set of premises, called the *explanans*, describing the facts and laws provided to account for the explanandum. As with other arguments, the aim of scientific explanations is to provide strong grounds for believing the explanandum—more precisely, to provide strong grounds for believing that the phenomenon described in the explanandum was to be expected. And as with other arguments, this aim is generally fulfilled under two conditions: (1) There is a logical relation of validity holding between the explanans and explanandum of the explanation, such that if the explanans is true, the explanandum either has to be true or is very probably true; and (2) The explanans *is* true.

But what distinguishes scientific explanations from other arguments? According to the inferential conception, it is the nature of their premises: The explanans statements of scientific explanations are testable by experiment or observation, and they include scientific laws, which may be universal laws or statistical laws (or both). Roughly speaking, universal laws attribute a certain characteristic to all members of a class, whereas statistical laws attribute a certain characteristic only to a specified proportion of the members of a class. Mendel's explanation, for example, included at least one of each: the universal law that each different character of pea plants is associated with a different internal factor, and the statistical law that the factor combinations TT Td dT dd are equiprobable—that is, that the actual factor combinations that occur will be roughly 25% TT, 25% Td, 25% dT, and 25% dd. Scientific explanations have thus been divided into three classes:

1. Deductive-nomological (*D-N*) explanations; that is, deductive explanations that include only universal laws in their explanans (where *nomological* derives from the Greek word *nomos* or *law*)

2. Deductive-statistical (*D-S*) explanations; that is, deductive explanations that include at least one statistical law in their explanans

3. Inductive statistical (*I-S*) explanations; that is, inductive explanations that include at least one statistical law in their explanans

The inferential conception of scientific explanation is presented in two readings that follow. In the first paper, the classic "Studies in the Logic of Explanation," Carl Hempel and Paul Oppenheim discuss deductive-nomological explanations. In the second, "Statistical Explanation," Carl Hempel discusses both deductive-statistical and inductive-statistical explanations, comparing them to deductive-nomological explanations.

The Causal Conception of Scientific Explanation

According to the inferential conception of scientific explanation, as we have seen, a scientific explanation is a deductive or inductive argument. According to the causal conception, on the other hand, although a scientific explanation may sometimes suggest the elements out of which a deductive or inductive argument can be constructed, and although an argument may sometimes exhibit explanatory relations, a scientific explanation is *not* an argument. Indeed, the aim of a scientific explanation, according to the causal conception, is not to show that the phenomenon-to-be-explained was to be expected, but to show how the phenomenon-to-be-explained was brought about, how it fits under universal or statistical regularities that can be causally explained. Explaining the world and what goes on in it means, accordingly, laying bare its inner workings, its underlying causal mechanisms.

The case of Gregor Mendel illustrates this conception. As we have seen, Mendel explained the results of his breeding experiments with pea plants by showing how these results were brought about. Indeed, he first showed that his results fit into a pattern or regularity: Crossing pure breeding varieties of peas with contrasted characters yields all dominant characters in the F_1 generation, and a $3:1$ ratio of dominant to recessive characters in the F_2 generation. Then he causally explained this regularity by referring to the underlying processes of segregation, combination, and transmission of factors that bring it about.

In "Why Ask, 'Why?'?" Wesley Salmon defends a causal conception of scientific explanation.

The Erotetic Conception of Scientific Explanation

Although not all why-questions are requests for scientific explanations—and not all requests for scientific explanations are made by posing why-questions—it seems possible to rephrase any request for a scientific explanation as a why-question. Hence the development of a conception of scientific explanation different from those we have considered: Any request for a scientific explanation can be analyzed as a why-question, and any scientific explanation can be analyzed as an answer to a why-question.

Since the logic of questions is known as erotetic logic, this approach can be called the erotetic conception of scientific explanation. In "The Pragmatics of Explanation," Bas van Fraassen argues for an erotetic conception according to which a why-question is specified by three factors: the topic, the contrast class, and the explanatory relevance relation. Consider, for example, the following why-question posed by Gregor Mendel: Why is it the case that the F_2 generation of pea plants consists of plants of which three-fourths have the dominant character and one-fourth the recessive character? The proposition "The F_2 generation of pea plants consists of plants of which three-fourths have the dominant character and one-fourth the recessive character" is the *topic* of the question. The *contrast class* is a set of propositions containing the topic and alternatives to the topic. In Mendel's question the alternatives to the topic might be: "The F_2 generation of pea plants consists of plants of which all have the dominant character;" "The F_2 generation of pea plants consists of plants of which half have the dominant character and half, the recessive character." In this case Mendel would be asking why the F_2 generation has the proportion of dominant characters it does, rather than the proportion had by the F_1 generation or the proportion had by the parent generation. But Mendel might have wanted to ask, instead, why the F_2 generation has the three-fourths to one-fourth proportion, rather than the F_1 generation, which would involve a different contrast class for his question. Finally, the explanatory *relevance relation* is the respect-in-which a reason is requested, that which determines what shall count as a possible answer (explanation). In Mendel's case, his request was for "events leading up to" the F_2 generation ratio. But, in different circumstances, his request might have been for the function the $3:1$ ratio in the F_2 generation fulfills in the evolution of pea plants—a different explanatory relevance relation.

Finally, concerning Mendel's answer to his question (his scientific explanation), it is of the form "P because A," where P is the topic of his question, and A is the relevant set of Mendel's statements. What criteria can be used to show it was a good answer? Van Fraassen suggests three criteria for evaluating answers relative to the knowledge contexts in which their questions have arisen:

1. Is A acceptable or likely to be true?

2. To what extent does A favor the topic P as against other members of the contrast class; that is, to what extent does A make the topic stand out as more probable than other members of the contrast class?

3. Compared with other possible answers to the question at issue (a) Is A more probable?; (b) Does A favor the topic P to a greater extent?; and (c) Is A made wholly or partially irrelevant by other answers?

In the portion of "The Pragmatics of Explanation" reprinted in this section, van Fraassen discusses some of the considerations that led him to his erotetic conception of scientific explanation.

Summary

We have now considered three conceptions of scientific explanation—the inferential conception, the causal conception, and the erotetic conception. According to the inferential conception, a scientific explanation is a deductive or inductive argument, showing that the phenomenon-to-be-explained was to be expected. According to the causal conception, a scientific explanation exhibits the underlying causal processes by which the phenomenon-to-be-explained was brought about. And according to the erotetic conception, a scientific explanation is simply an answer to a why-question, having no particular form and containing no particular sort of information. How can you choose among these alternative conceptions of scientific explanation? Obviously a careful reading of each selection that follows will be necessary, paying particular attention to the reasons given by each author for his position, the examples offered in support or illustration, and the criticisms the authors at times direct to each other's views. But equally necessary will be a comparison of each conception with actual examples of scientific explanations to see how well the conception illuminates the examples. Obviously, some understanding of the various kinds of scientific explanation available would be helpful for this comparison.

KINDS OF SCIENTIFIC EXPLANATION

In considering different conceptions of scientific explanation, we were trying to capture the traits that all scientific explanations have in common, the traits that distinguish scientific explanations from other kinds of explanation. But the elucidation of important *differences* among scientific explanations would also help us to a clearer understanding of scientific explanation. Although no generally accepted taxonomy of kinds of scientific explanation exists in philosophy of science today, a number of kinds of scientific explanation are generally recognized as important: (1) compositional explanation; (2) evolutionary explanation; (3) functional explanation; and (4) transitional explanation. We shall briefly sketch the distinctive features of each kind; readings illustrating them will then follow.

Compositional Explanation

In a compositional explanation the properties of objects are explained in terms of the properties of their parts—their *composition*. Examples include Mendel's explanation of the breeding patterns of pea plants in terms of internal factors and their behavior, and the explanation of the properties of the chemical elements in terms of their atomic structure. In "Scientific Theories and Their Domains," Dudley Shapere discusses this kind of explanation and the conditions under which it seems appropriate. According to Shapere, such an explanation is given of a *domain*—that is, an associated set of items of information that raise questions of importance for science. More particularly, it is given of an *ordered* domain, a domain in which types of items are first classified, and then those classes themselves are arranged in some pattern, for example a series, according to some ordering principle. Thus, for example, a compositional explanation was given of the periodic table of chemical elements in the last quarter of the nineteenth century, the table which showed that the chemical elements display a periodicity of properties when arranged in a series of increasing atomic weights, the weights increasing by discrete jumps rather than by continuous gradations. The compositional explanation in this case postulated that the atoms of these elements are composed of discrete massive particles whose increase in numbers accounts for the discrete increases of atomic weights, and whose repeating organizational structures account for the periodicity of properties of the chemical elements.

Shapere adds that a compositional explanation is reasonably given for any domain ordered in the way the chemical elements were in the periodic table—that is, for any domain ordered in a periodic way based on a property that jumps in value from one item to the next, the items having values which are integral multiples of a fundamental value. This reasonability of compositional explanation holds especially when other conditions are also fulfilled, such as when compositional explanations have been successful or promising in other domains and the domain under consideration appears to be related to those other domains so as to form part of a larger domain.

Evolutionary Explanation

In an evolutionary explanation the properties of objects are explained in terms of the temporal development of those objects—their *evolution*. Examples include the Darwinian explanation of the biological species in terms of the processes of variation and natural selection, and the explanation of the chemical composition of stars in terms of their age. In "Scientific Theories and Their Domains," Dudley Shapere also discusses evolutionary explanation. According to Shapere, evolutionary explanations, like compositional explanations, are appropriate for domains ordered in certain ways. Consider, for example, the domain of stellar spectroscopy in the late nineteenth century. It contained the classifications of stars based on color and on spectral characteristics (which were thought to identify their chemical composition), where these two systems of classification correlated well. Background information concerning color changes of cooling bodies (from blue or white to red hot) suggested a temporal order for the color classes of stars that correlated with an order for the spectral classes in terms of increasing numbers and intensities of heavy element lines, coupled with decreasing intensities of hydrogen lines. This pattern suggested an evolutionary explanation of the domain, namely, that as stars age they cool, changing in color from blue or white to red; and as they age, higher elements are built up out of hydrogen, so that older stars are composed of a larger proportion of heavier elements.

Shapere also tells us that an evolutionary explanation is reasonably given for any domain ordered in a comparable way—that is, such that the order can be viewed as the increase or decrease of the factors on the basis of which the order is made, and such that the order can be viewed as a temporal one, having a temporal direction. As with compositional explanations, the reasonability of evolutionary explanation holds especially when other conditions are also fulfilled, such as when evolutionary explanations have been successful or promising in other domains and the domain under consideration seems to be related to those domains so as to form part of a larger domain.

Functional Explanation

In a functional explanation, relatively sophisticated capacities of objects are explained in terms of the sophisticated organization of relatively simple capacities of those objects or their components. Thus, for example, in biology the characteristic capacities of the circulatory system, the digestive system, the nervous system, and so on are explained in terms of the interrelated capacities of component organs and structures. Such an explanation exhibits the role or *function* of each of the simpler capacities in the exercise of the more sophisticated capacity.

In "Programs in the Explanation of Behavior," Robert Cummins discusses functional explanations within the area of information processing psychology, suggesting in what sense such explanations do and in what sense they do not explain behavior. According to Cummins, functional explanations explain psychological capacities like the capacity to solve logic problems, speak English, recognize patterns, and the like, in terms of simple capacities like the capacity to store ones and zeros, simple capacities that are organized in a sophisticated way—that is, according to a sophisticated program. Such programs explain capacities, Cummins points out, in the same sense in which we explain how little Johnny is able to build sophisticated audio equipment when we point out that he is able to follow the simple instructions in the kit in the order in which the instructions are given. But such programs do not explain capacities in another sense: They do not direct behavior, in addition to analyzing and describing its direction, in the way that the ordered set of instructions also directs Johnny's behavior. For that kind of an explanation—that is, for an explanation of why capacities are exercised (programs are followed) under appropriate conditions—we need an explanation in terms of the purely physical conditions, the relatively permanent physical changes in the organism, that underlie the acquisition of the capacity.

Transitional Explanation

In a transitional explanation a change of state in an object—a *transition* from one state to another—is explained in terms of a disturbance in the object and the state of the object at the time of the disturbance. The original and clearest model of this kind of explanation occurs in the science of dynamics. Here the change of state of the object is defined in terms of its motion, and the disturbance which causes this change is defined as one or more forces acting on the object.

However, not every motion is explained in this way, by reference to forces acting on an object. Indeed, some motions are held to be natural and self-explanatory, and dynamics distinguishes between these and other motions, and provides a way of explaining only the others. Different systems of dynamics, however, have made this natural-unnatural distinction in different ways, and have provided different concepts of force to explain the unnatural motions. Thus, for example, suppose the ropes by which a horse is pulling a cart happen to break, so that the cart comes to rest. According to Aristotelian dynamics, this would be entirely natural. If left to itself, the cart would remain at rest, and now a force—the horse's pulling—is no longer exerted on the cart, and so it stops. According to Galilean and Newtonian dynamics however, the cart's coming to rest in this way would not be natural. If left to itself, with nothing to stop it, the cart would keep moving forever, at uniform speed—along a track circling the center of the earth for Galileo, and in a straight line right out into space for Newton. The cart's coming to rest must thus be explained—for example, as the result of forces of friction, gravity, and air-resistance. In "Ideals of Natural Order," Stephen Toulmin discusses such differences in dynamical systems, focusing on the seventeenth century and the changes through which Newtonian dynamics finally displaced Aristotelian dynamics.

Summary

We have now surveyed four important kinds of scientific explanation— compositional explanation, evolutionary explanation, functional explanation, and transitional explanation—noting the distinctive features of each. As we have seen, in a compositional explanation, the properties of objects are explained in terms of the properties of their parts. In an evolutionary explanation, the properties of objects are explained in terms of the temporal development of those objects. In a functional explanation, relatively sophisticated capacities of objects are explained in terms of the sophisticated organization of relatively simple capacities of those objects or their components. And in a transitional explanation, a change of state in an object is explained in terms of a disturbance in the object and the state of the object at the time of the disturbance.

Can these four kinds of scientific explanation be characterized in terms of the general conceptions of scientific explanation treated earlier? For example, can functional explanations be formulated as deductive or inductive arguments showing that the phenomenon-to-be-explained was to be expected (the inferential conception)? Can they be formulated as answers to why-questions (the erotetic conception)? Do they exhibit the underlying causal processes by which the phenomenon-to-be-explained was brought about (the causal conception)? If so, do such characterizations help or hinder the understanding of functional explanations? If not, does this show an inadequacy in the general conceptions of scientific explanation? Or does it show an inadequacy in functional explanations—that they do not really explain after all? Are there other kinds of scientific explanation at least as important as the four we have discussed? If so, can they be characterized in a helpful way in terms of the general conceptions of scientific explanation? And finally, which general conception of scientific explanation seems to best capture important characteristics common not only to the four kinds of scientific explanation we have discussed but also to any others you can think of? These are some of the questions you should keep uppermost in your mind as you read through the selections that follow.

Studies in the Logic of Explanation[1]

Carl Hempel
Paul Oppenheim

INTRODUCTION

To explain the phenomena in the world of our experience, to answer the question "why?" rather than only the question "what?" is one of the foremost objectives of empirical science. While there is rather general agreement on this point there exists considerable difference of opinion as to the function and the essential characteristics of scientific explanation. The present essay is an attempt to shed some light on these issues by means of an elementary survey of the basic pattern of scientific explanation and a subsequent more rigorous analysis of the concept of law and the logical structure of explanatory arguments. . . .

ELEMENTARY SURVEY OF SCIENTIFIC EXPLANATION

Some Illustrations

A mercury thermometer is rapidly immersed in hot water; there occurs a temporary drop of the mercury column, which is then followed by a swift rise. How is this phenomenon to be explained? The increase in temperature affects at first only the glass tube of the thermometer; it expands and thus provides a larger space for the mercury inside, whose surface therefore drops. As soon as by heat

conduction the rise in temperature reaches the mercury, however, the latter expands, and as its coefficient of expansion is considerably larger than that of glass, a rise of the mercury level results. This account consists of statements of two kinds. Those of the first kind indicate certain conditions which are realized prior to, or at the same time as, the phenomenon to be explained; we shall refer to them briefly as antecedent conditions. In our illustration, the antecedent conditions include, among others, the fact that the thermometer consists of a glass tube which is partly filled with mercury, and that it is immersed into hot water. The statements of the second kind express certain general laws; in our case, these include the laws of the thermic expansion of mercury and of glass, and a statement about the small thermic conductivity of glass. The two sets of statements, if adequately and completely formulated, explain the phenomenon under consideration: they entail the consequence that the mercury will first drop, then rise. Thus, the event under discussion is explained by subsuming it under general laws, i.e., by showing that it occurred in accordance with those laws, in virtue of the realization of certain specified antecedent conditions.

Consider another illustration: *To an observer in a rowboat, that part of an oar which is under water appears to be bent upwards. The phenomenon is explained by means of general laws—mainly the law of refraction and the law that water is an optically denser medium than air—and by reference to certain antecedent conditions—especially the facts that part of the oar is in the water, part in the air, and that the oar is practically a straight piece of wood. Thus, here again, the question "Why* does the phenomenon occur?" is con-

[1] This essay grew out of discussions with Dr. Paul Oppenheim; it was published in co-authorship with him and is here reprinted with his permission. Our individual contributions cannot be separated in detail; the present author is responsible, however, for the . . . final formulation of the entire text. . . .

Paul Oppenheim and I are much indebted to Professors Rudolf Carnap, Herbert Feigl, Nelson Goodman, and W. V. Quine for stimulating discussions and constructive criticism.

From the Introduction and Parts I and III of Carl Hempel and Paul Oppenheim, "Studies in the Logic of Explanation," *Philosophy of Science*, Vol. 15, pp. 135–175. Copyright © 1948, The Williams and Wilkins Co. Reprinted, with some changes, by permission of the publisher.

strued as meaning "According to what general laws, and by virtue of what antecedent conditions does the phenomenon occur?"

So far, we have considered only the explanation of particular events occurring at a certain time and place. But the question "Why?" may be raised also in regard to general laws. Thus, in our last illustration, the question might be asked: Why does the propagation of light conform to the law of refraction? Classical physics answers in terms of the undulatory theory of light, i.e., by stating that the propagation of light is a wave phenomenon of a certain general type, and that all wave phenomena of that type satisfy the law of refraction. Thus, the explanation of a general regularity consists in subsuming it under another, more comprehensive regularity, under a more general law. Similarly, the validity of Galileo's law for the free fall of bodies near the earth's surface can be explained by deducing it from a more comprehensive set of laws, namely Newton's laws of motion and his law of gravitation, together with some statements about particular facts, namely, about the mass and the radius of the earth.

The Basic Pattern of Scientific Explanation

From the preceding sample cases let us now abstract some general characteristics of scientific explanation. We divide an explanation into two major constituents, the *explanandum* and the *explanans*[2]. By the explanandum, we understand the sentence describing the phenomenon to be explained (not that phenomenon itself); by the explanans, the class of those sentences which are adduced to account for the phenomenon. As was noted before, the explanans falls into two subclasses; one of these contains certain sentences $C_1, C_2, \ldots, C_k$ which state specific antecedent conditions; the other is a set of sentences $L_1, L_2, \ldots, L_r$ which represent general laws.

If a proposed explanation is to be sound, its constituents have to satisfy certain conditions of adequacy, which may be divided into logical and empirical conditions. For the following discussion, it will be sufficient to formulate these requirements in a slightly vague manner. . . .

I. *Logical conditions of adequacy*

(R1) The explanandum must be a logical consequence of the explanans; in other words, the explanandum must be logically deducible from the information contained in the explanans; for otherwise, the explanans would not constitute adequate grounds for the explanandum.

(R2) The explanans must contain general laws, and these must actually be required for the derivation of the explanandum. We shall not make it a necessary condition for a sound explanation, however, that the explanans must contain at least one statement which is not a law; for, to mention just one reason, we would surely want to consider as an explanation the derivation of the general regularities governing the motion of double stars from the laws of celestial mechanics, even though all the statements in the explanans are general laws.

(R3) The explanans must have empirical content; i.e., it must be capable, at least in principle, of test by experiment or observation. This condition is implicit in (R1); for since the explanandum is assumed to describe some empirical phenomenon, it follows from (R1) that the explanans entails at least one consequence of empirical character, and this fact confers upon it testability and empirical content. But the point deserves special mention because . . . certain arguments which have been offered as explanations in the natural and in the social sciences violate this requirement.

II. *Empirical condition of adequacy*

(R4) The sentences constituting the explanans must be true. That in a sound explanation, the statements constituting the explanans have to satisfy some condition of factual correctness is obvious. But it

---

[2] These two expressions, derived from the Latin *explanare,* were adopted in preference to the perhaps more customary terms "explicandum" and "explicans" in order to reserve the latter for use in the context of explication of meaning, or analysis. On explication in this sense, cf. Carnap (1945a), p. 513.

might seem more appropriate to stipulate that the explanans has to be highly confirmed by all the relevant evidence available rather than that it should be true. This stipulation, however, leads to awkward consequences. Suppose that a certain phenomenon was explained at an earlier stage of science by means of an explanans which was well supported by the evidence then at hand, but has been highly disconfirmed by more recent empirical findings. In such a case, we would have to say that originally the explanatory account was a correct explanation, but that it ceased to be one later, when unfavorable evidence was discovered. This does not appear to accord with sound common usage, which directs us to say that on the basis of the limited initial evidence, the truth of the explanans, and thus the soundness of the explanation, had been quite probable, but that the ampler evidence now available makes it highly probable that the explanans is not true, and hence that the account in question is not—and never has been—a correct explanation.[3] (A similar point will be made and illustrated, with respect to the requirement of truth for laws. . . .)

Some of the characteristics of an explanation which have been indicated so far may be summarized in the following schema:

Let us note here that the same formal analysis, including the four necessary conditions, applies to scientific prediction as well as to explanation. The difference between the two is of a pragmatic character. If E is given, i.e., if we know that the phenomenon described by E has occurred, and a suitable set of statements $C_1, C_2, \ldots, C_k, L_1, L_2, \ldots, L_r$ is provided afterwards, we speak of an explanation of the phenomenon in question. If the latter statements are given and E is derived prior to the occurrence of the phenomenon it describes, we speak of a prediction. It may be said, therefore, that an explanation of a particular event is not fully adequate unless its explanans, if taken account of in time, could have served as a basis for predicting the event in question. Consequently, whatever will be said in this article concerning the logical characteristics of explanation or prediction will be applicable to either, even if only one of them should be mentioned.[4]

Many explanations which are customarily offered, especially in prescientific discourse, lack this potential predictive force, however. Thus, we may be told that a car turned over on the road "because" one of its tires blew out while the car was traveling at high speed. Clearly, on the basis of just this information, the accident could not have been predicted, for the explanans provides no explicit general laws by means of which the prediction might be effected, nor does it state adequately the antecedent conditions which would be needed for the prediction. The same point may

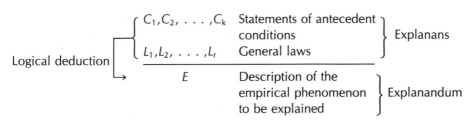

Logical deduction $\left[\begin{array}{l} \left\{ \begin{array}{l} C_1, C_2, \ldots, C_k \quad \text{Statements of antecedent conditions} \\ L_1, L_2, \ldots, L_r \quad \text{General laws} \end{array} \right\} \text{Explanans} \\ \underline{\hspace{5cm}} \\ \rightarrow \quad E \qquad\qquad \text{Description of the empirical phenomenon to be explained} \left.\begin{array}{l}\\\\\end{array}\right\} \text{Explanandum} \end{array} \right.$

[3] (Added in 1964.) Requirement (R4) characterizes what might be called a correct or *true explanation*. In an analysis of the logical structure of explanatory arguments, therefore, that requirement may be disregarded. This is, in fact, what is done in section 7 [a later section, not reprinted here], where the concept of *potential explanation* is introduced. On these and related distinctions, see also section 2.1 of the essay "Aspects of Scientific Explanation" [in Carl G. Hempel, *Aspects of Scientific Explanation and Other Essays in the Philosophy of Science.* New York: Macmillan, 1965]. . . .

be illustrated by reference to W. S. Jevons's view that every explanation consists in pointing out a resemblance between facts, and that in some

[4] (Added in 1964.) This claim is examined in much fuller detail, and reasserted with certain qualifications, in sections 2.4 and 3.5 of the essay "Aspects of Scientific Explanation". . . .

cases this process may require no reference to laws at all and "may involve nothing more than a single identity, as when we explain the appearance of shooting stars by showing that they are identical with portions of a comet."[5] But clearly, this identity does not provide an explanation of the phenomenon of shooting stars unless we presuppose the laws governing the development of heat and light as the effect of friction. The observation of similarities has explanatory value only if it involves at least tacit reference to general laws.

In some cases, incomplete explanatory arguments of the kind here illustrated suppress parts of the explanans simply as "obvious"; in other cases, they seem to involve the assumption that while the missing parts are not obvious, the incomplete explanans could at least, with appropriate effort, be so supplemented as to make a strict derivation of the explanandum possible. This assumption may be justifiable in some cases, as when we say that a lump of sugar disappeared "because" it was put into hot tea, but it surely is not satisfied in many other cases. Thus, when certain peculiarities in the work of an artist are explained as outgrowths of a specific type of neurosis, this observation may contain significant clues, but in general it does not afford a sufficient basis for a potential prediction of those peculiarities. In cases of this kind, an incomplete explanation may at best be considered as indicating some positive correlation between the antecedent conditions adduced and the type of phenomenon to be explained, and as pointing out a direction in which further research might be carried on in order to complete the explanatory account.

The type of explanation which has been considered here so far is often referred to as causal explanation.[6] If E describes a particular event, then the antecedent circumstances described in the sentences C_1, C_2, . . . , C_k may be said jointly to "cause" that event, in the sense that

there are certain empirical regularities, expressed by the laws L_1, L_2, . . . , L_r, which imply that whenever conditions of the kind indicated by C_1, C_2, . . . , C_k occur, an event of the kind described in E will take place. Statements such as L_1, L_2, . . . , L_r, which assert general and unexceptional connections between specified characteristics of events, are customarily called causal, or deterministic, laws. They must be distinguished from the so-called statistical laws which assert that, in the long run, an explicitly stated percentage of all cases satisfying a given set of conditions are accompanied by an event of a certain specified kind. Certain cases of scientific explanation involve "subsumption" of the explanandum under a set of laws of which at least some are statistical in character. Analysis of the peculiar logical structure of that type of subsumption involves difficult special problems. The present essay will be restricted to an examination of the deductive type of explanation, which has retained its significance in large segments of contemporary science, and even in some areas where a more adequate account calls for reference to statistical laws.[7]

---

[6] (Added in 1964.) Or rather, causal explanation is one variety of the deductive type of explanation here under discussion; see section 2.2 of "Aspects of Scientific Explanation."

---

[7] The account given above of the general characteristics of explanation and prediction in science is by no means novel; it merely summarizes and states explicitly some fundamental points which have been recognized by many scientists and methodologists.

Thus, e.g., Mill says: "An individual fact is said to be explained, by pointing out its cause, that is, by stating the law or laws of causation, of which its production is an instance," and "a law or uniformity in nature is said to be explained, when another law or laws are pointed out, of which that law itself is but a case, and from which it could be deduced" (1858, Book III, Chapter XII, section 1). Similarly, Jevons, whose general characterization of explanation was critically discussed above, stresses that "the most important process of explanation consists in showing that an observed fact is one case of a general law or tendency" (1924, p. 533). Ducasse states the same point as follows: "Explanation essentially consists in the offering of a hypothesis of fact, standing to the fact to be explained as case of antecedent to case of consequent of some already known law of connection" (1925, pp. 150–51). A lucid analysis of the fundamental structure of explanation and prediction was given by Popper in (1935), section 12, and, in an improved version, in his work (1945), especially in Chapter 25 and in note 7 for that chapter.

For a recent characterization of explanation as subsumption under general theories, cf., for example, Hull's concise discussion in (1943a), chapter I. A clear elementary examination of certain aspects of explanation is given in Hospers (1946), and a concise survey of many of the essentials of scientific explanation which are considered in the first two parts of the present study may be found in Feigl (1945), pp. 284 ff.

Explanation in the Nonphysical Sciences: Motivational and Teleological Approaches

Our characterization of scientific explanation is so far based on a study of cases taken from the physical sciences. But the general principles thus obtained apply also outside this area.[8] Thus, various types of behavior in laboratory animals and in human subjects are explained in psychology by subsumption under laws or even general theories of learning or conditioning; and while frequently the regularities invoked cannot be stated with the same generality and precision as in physics or chemistry, it is clear at least that the general character of those explanations conforms to our earlier characterization.

Let us now consider an illustration involving sociological and economic factors. In the fall of 1946, there occurred at the cotton exchanges of the United States a price drop which was so severe that the exchanges in New York, New Orleans, and Chicago had to suspend their activities temporarily. In an attempt to explain this occurrence, newspapers traced it back to a large-scale speculator in New Orleans who had feared his holdings were too large and had therefore begun to liquidate his stocks; smaller speculators had then followed his example in a panic and had thus touched off the critical decline. Without attempting to assess the merits of the argument, let us note that the explanation here suggested again involves statements about antecedent conditions and the assumption of general regularities. The former include the facts that the first speculator had large stocks of cotton, that there were smaller speculators with considerable holdings, that there existed the institution of the cotton exchanges with their specific mode of operation, etc. The general regularities referred to are—as often in semi-popular explanations—not explicitly mentioned; but there is obviously implied some form of the law of supply and demand to account for the drop in cotton prices in terms of the greatly increased supply under conditions of practically unchanged demand; besides, reliance is necessary on certain regularities in the behavior of individuals who are trying to preserve or improve their economic position. Such laws cannot be formulated at present with satisfactory precision and generality, and therefore, the suggested explanation is surely incomplete, but its intention is unmistakably to account for the phenomenon by integrating it into a general pattern of economic and socio-psychological regularities.

We turn to an explanatory argument taken from the field of linguistics.[9] In Northern France, there are in use a large variety of words synonymous with the English "bee," whereas in Southern France, essentially only one such word is in existence. For this discrepancy, the explanation has been suggested that in the Latin epoch, the South of France used the word "apicula," the North the word "apis." The latter, because of a process of phonologic decay in Northern France, became the monosyllabic word "é"; and monosyllables tend to be eliminated, especially if they contain few consonantic elements, for they are apt to give rise to misunderstandings. Thus, to avoid confusion, other words were selected. But "apicula", which was reduced to "abelho," remained clear enough and was retained, and finally it even entered into the standard language in the form "abeille." While the explanation here described is incomplete in the sense characterized in the previous section, it clearly exhibits reference to specific antecedent conditions as well as to general laws.[10]

---

[8] On the subject of explanation in the social sciences, especially in history, cf. also the following publications, which may serve to supplement and amplify the brief discussion to be presented here: Hempel (1942); Popper (1945); White (1943); and the articles Cause and Understanding in Beard and Hook (1946).

[9] The illustration is taken from Bonfante (1946), section 3.

[10] While in each of the last two illustrations, certain regularities are unquestionably relied upon in the explanatory argument, it is not possible to argue convincingly that the intended laws, which at present cannot all be stated explicitly, are of a causal rather than a statistical character. It is quite possible that most or all of the regularities which will be discovered as sociology develops will be of a statistical type. Cf., on this point, the suggestive observations in Zilsel (1941), section 8, and (1941a). This issue does not affect, however, the main point we wish to make here, namely that in the social no less than in the physical sciences, subsumption under general regularities is indispensable for the explanation and the theoretical understanding of any phenomenon.

While illustrations of this kind tend to support the view that explanation in biology, psychology, and the social sciences has the same structure as in the physical sciences, the opinion is rather widely held that in many instances, the causal type of explanation is essentially inadequate in fields other than physics and chemistry, and especially in the study of purposive behavior. Let us examine briefly some of the reasons which have been adduced in support of this view.

One of the most familiar among them is the idea that events involving the activities of humans singly or in groups have a peculiar uniqueness and irrepeatability which makes them inaccessible to causal explanation because the latter, with its reliance upon uniformities, presupposes repeatability of the phenomena under consideration. This argument, which, incidentally, has also been used in support of the contention that the experimental method is inapplicable in psychology and the social sciences, involves a misunderstanding of the logical character of causal explanation. Every individual event, in the physical sciences no less than in psychology or the social sciences, is unique in the sense that it, with all its peculiar characteristics, does not repeat itself. Nevertheless, individual events may conform to, and thus be explainable by means of, general laws of the causal type. For all that a causal law asserts is that any event of a specified kind, i.e., any event having certain specified characteristics, is accompanied by another event, which in turn has certain specified characteristics; for example, that in any event involving friction, heat is developed. And all that is needed for the testability and applicability of such laws is the recurrence of events with the antecedent characteristics, i.e., the repetition of those characteristics, but not of their individual instances. Thus, the argument is inconclusive. It gives occasion, however, to emphasize an important point concerning our earlier analysis: When we spoke of the explanation of a single event, the term "event" referred to the occurrence of some more or less complex characteristic in a specific spatio-temporal location or in a certain individual object, and not to *all* the characteristics of that object, or to all that goes on in that space-time region.

A second argument that should be mentioned here[11] contends that the establishment of scientific generalizations—and thus of explanatory principles—for human behavior is impossible because the reactions of an individual in a given situation depend not only upon that situation, but also upon the previous history of the individual. But surely, there is no *a priori* reason why generalizations should not be attainable which take into account this dependence of behavior on the past history of the agent. That indeed the given argument "proves" too much, and is therefore a *non sequitur,* is made evident by the existence of certain physical phenomena, such as magnetic hysteresis and elastic fatigue, in which the magnitude of a specific physical effect depends upon the past history of the system involved, and for which nevertheless certain general regularities have been established.

A third argument insists that the explanation of any phenomenon involving purposive behavior calls for reference to motivations and thus for teleological rather than causal analysis. For example, a fuller statement of the suggested explanation for the break in the cotton prices would have to indicate the large-scale speculator's motivations as one of the factors determining the event in question. Thus, we have to refer to goals sought; and this, so the argument runs, introduces a type of explanation alien to the physical sciences. Unquestionably, many of the—frequently incomplete—explanations which are offered for human actions involve reference to goals and motives; but does this make them essentially different from the causal explanations of physics and chemistry? One difference which suggests itself lies in the circumstance that in motivated behavior the future appears to affect the present in a manner which is not found in the causal explanations of the physical sciences. But clearly, when the action of a person is motivated, say, by the desire to reach a certain objective, then it is not the as yet unrealized future event of attaining that goal which can be said to determine his present behavior, for in-

───────────

[11] Cf., for example, F. H. Knight's presentation of this argument in (1924), pp. 251–52.

deed the goal may never be actually reached; rather—to put it in crude terms—it is (a) his desire, present before the action, to attain that particular objective, and (b) his belief, likewise present before the action, that such and such a course of action is most likely to have the desired effect. The determining motives and beliefs, therefore, have to be classified among the antecedent conditions of a motivational explanation, and there is no formal difference on this account between motivational and causal explanation.

Neither does the fact that motives are not accessible to direct observation by an outside observer constitute an essential difference between the two kinds of explanation; for the determining factors adduced in physical explanations also are very frequently inaccessible to direct observation. This is the case, for instance, when opposite electric charges are adduced in explanation of the mutual attraction of two metal spheres. The presence of those charges, while eluding direct observation, can be ascertained by various kinds of indirect test, and that is sufficient to guarantee the empirical character of the explanatory statement. Similarly, the presence of certain motivations may be ascertainable only by indirect methods, which may include reference to linguistic utterances of the subject in question, slips of pen or tongue, etc.; but as long as these methods are "operationally determined" with reasonable clarity and precision, there is no essential difference in this respect between motivational explanation and causal explanation in physics.

A potential danger of explanation by motives lies in the fact that the method lends itself to the facile construction of *ex post facto* accounts without predictive force. An action is often explained by attributing it to motives conjectured only after the action has taken place. While this procedure is not in itself objectionable, its soundness requires (1) that the motivational assumptions in question be capable of test, and (2) that suitable general laws be available to lend explanatory power to the assumed motives. Disregard of these requirements frequently deprives alleged motivational explanations of their cognitive significance.

The explanation of an action in terms of the agent's motives is sometimes considered as a special kind of teleological explanation. As was pointed out above, motivational explanation, if adequately formulated, conforms to the conditions for causal explanation, so that the term "teleological" is a misnomer if it is meant to imply either a noncausal character of the explanation or a peculiar determination of the present by the future. If this is borne in mind, however, the term "teleological" may be viewed, in this context, as referring to causal explanations in which some of the antecedent conditions are motives of the agent whose actions are to be explained.[12]

Teleological explanations of this kind have to be distinguished from a much more sweeping type, which has been claimed by certain schools of thought to be indispensable, especially in biology. It consists in explaining characteristics of an organism by reference to certain ends or purposes which the characteristics are said to serve. In contradistinction to the cases examined before, the ends are not assumed here to be consciously or subconsciously pursued by the organism in question. Thus, for the phenomenon of mimicry, the explanation is sometimes offered that it serves the purpose of protecting the animals endowed with it from detection by its pursuers and thus tends to preserve the species. Before teleological hypotheses of this kind can be appraised as to their potential explanatory power, their meaning has to be clarified. If they are intended somehow to express the idea that the purposes they refer to are inherent in the design of the universe, then clearly they are not capable of empirical test and thus violate the requirement (R3). . . . In certain cases, however, assertions about the purposes of biological characteristics may be translatable into statements in non-teleological terminology, which assert that those characteristics function in a specific manner which is essential to keeping the organism alive or

---

[12] For a detailed logical analysis of the concept of motivation in psychological theory, see Koch (1941). A stimulating discussion of teleological behavior from the standpoint of contemporary physics and biology is contained in the article (1943) by Rosenblueth, Wiener, and Bigelow. The logic of explanation by motivating reasons is examined more fully in section 10 of the essay "Aspects of Scientific Explanation". . . .

to preserving the species.[13] An attempt to state precisely what is meant by this latter assertion—or by the similar one that without those characteristics, and other things being equal, the organism or the species would not survive—encounters considerable difficulties. But these need not be discussed here. For even if we assume that biological statements in teleological form can be adequately translated into descriptive statements about the life-preserving function of certain biological characteristics, it is clear that (1) the use of the concept of purpose is not essential in these contexts, since the term "purpose" can be completely eliminated from the statements in question, and (2) teleological assumptions, while now endowed with empirical content, cannot serve as explanatory principles in the customary contexts. Thus, e.g., the fact that a given species of butterfly displays a particular kind of coloring cannot be inferred from—and therefore cannot be explained by means of—the statement that this type of coloring has the effect of protecting the butterflies from detection by pursuing birds, nor can the presence of red corpuscles in the human blood be inferred from the statement that those corpuscles have a specific function in assimilating oxygen and that this function is essential for the maintenance of life.

One of the reasons for the perseverance of teleological considerations in biology probably lies in the fruitfulness of the teleological approach as a heuristic device: Biological research which was psychologically motivated by a teleological orientation, by an interest in purposes in nature, has frequently led to important results which can be stated in nonteleological terminology and which increase our knowledge of the causal connections between biological phenomena.

Another aspect that lends appeal to teleological considerations is their anthropomorphic character. A teleological explanation tends to make us feel that we really "understand" the phenomenon in question, because it is accounted for in terms of purposes, with which we are familiar from our own experience of purposive behavior. But it is important to distinguish here understanding in the psychological sense of a feeling of empathic familiarity from understanding in the theoretical, or cognitive, sense of exhibiting the phenomenon to be explained as a special case of some general regularity. The frequent insistence that explanation means the reduction of something unfamiliar to ideas or experiences already familiar to us is indeed misleading. For while some scientific explanations do have this psychological effect, it is by no means universal: The free fall of a physical body may well be said to be a more familiar phenomenon than the law of gravitation, by means of which it can be explained; and surely the basic ideas of the theory of relativity will appear to many to be far less familiar than the phenomena for which the theory accounts.

"Familiarity" of the explanans is not only not necessary for a sound explanation, as has just been noted; it is not sufficient either. This is shown by the many cases in which a proposed explanans sounds suggestively familiar, but upon closer inspection proves to be a mere metaphor, or to lack testability, or to include no general laws and therefore to lack explanatory power. A case in point is the neovitalistic attempt to explain biological phenomena by reference to an entelechy or vital force. The crucial point here is not—as is sometimes said—that entelechies cannot be seen or otherwise directly observed; for that is true also of gravitational fields, and yet, reference to such fields is essential in the explanation of various physical phenomena. The decisive difference between the two cases is that the physical explanation provides (1) methods of testing, albeit indirectly, assertions about gravitational fields, and (2) general laws concerning the strength of gravitational fields and the behavior of objects moving in them. Explanations by entelechies satisfy the analogue of neither of these two conditions. Failure to satisfy the first condition represents a violation of (R3); it renders all statements about entelechies inaccessible to empirical test and thus devoid of empirical meaning. Failure to comply with the

---

[13] An analysis of teleological statements in biology along these lines may be found in Woodger (1929), especially pp. 432 ff; essentially the same interpretation is advocated by Kaufmann in (1944), Chapter 8.

second condition involves a violation of (R2). It deprives the concept of entelechy of all explanatory import; for explanatory power never resides in a concept, but always in the general laws in which it functions. Therefore, notwithstanding the feeling of familiarity it may evoke, the neovitalistic account cannot provide theoretical understanding.

The preceding observations about familiarity and understanding can be applied, in a similar manner, to the view held by some scholars that the explanation, or the understanding, of human actions requires an empathic understanding of the personalities of the agents.[14] This understanding of another person in terms of one's own psychological functioning may prove a useful heuristic device in the search for general psychological principles which might provide a theoretical explanation; but the existence of empathy on the part of the scientist is neither a necessary nor a sufficient condition for the explanation, or the scientific understanding, of any human action. It is not necessary, for the behavior of psychotics or of people belonging to a culture very different from that of the scientist may sometimes be explainable and predictable in terms of general principles even though the scientist who establishes or applies those principles may not be able to understand his subjects empathically. And empathy is not sufficient to guarantee a sound explanation, for a strong feeling of empathy may exist even in cases where we completely misjudge a given personality. Moreover, as Zilsel has pointed out, empathy leads with ease to incompatible results; thus, when the population of a town has long been subjected to heavy bombing attacks, we can understand, in the empathic sense, that its morale should have broken down completely, but we can understand with the same ease also that it should have developed a defiant spirit of resistance. Arguments of this kind often appear quite convincing; but they are of an *ex post facto* character and lack cognitive significance unless they are supple-

mented by testable explanatory principles in the form of laws or theories.

Familiarity of the explanans, therefore, no matter whether it is achieved through the use of teleological terminology, through neovitalistic metaphors, or through other means, is no indication of the cognitive import and the predictive force of a proposed explanation. Besides, the extent to which an idea will be considered as familiar varies from person to person and from time to time, and a psychological factor of this kind certainly cannot serve as a standard in assessing the worth of a proposed explanation. The decisive requirement for every sound explanation remains that it subsume the explanandum under general laws. . . .

LOGICAL ANALYSIS OF LAW AND EXPLANATION

Problems of the Concept of General Law

From our general survey of the characteristics of scientific explanation, we now turn to a closer examination of its logical structure. The explanation of a phenomenon, we noted, consists in its subsumption under laws or under a theory. But what is a law, what is a theory? While the meaning of these concepts seems intuitively clear, an attempt to construct adequate explicit definitions for them encounters considerable difficulties. In the present section, some basic problems of the concept of law will be described and analyzed. . . .

The concept of law will be construed here so as to apply to true statements only. The apparently plausible alternative procedure of requiring high confirmation rather than truth of a law seems to be inadequate: It would lead to a relativized concept of law, which would be expressed by the phrase "sentence S is a law relative to the evidence E." This does not accord with the meaning customarily assigned to the concept of law in science and in methodological inquiry. Thus, for example, we would not say that Bode's general formula for the distance of the planets from the sun was a law relative to the astronomical evidence available in the 1770s, when Bode propounded it, and that it

---

[14] For a more detailed discussion of this view on the basis of the general principles outlined above, cf. Zilsel (1941), sections 7 and 8, and Hempel (1942), section 6.

ceased to be a law after the discovery of Neptune and the determination of its distance from the sun; rather, we would say that the limited original evidence had given a high probability to the assumption that the formula was a law, whereas more recent additional information reduced that probability so much as to make it practically certain that Bode's formula is not generally true, and hence not a law.[15]

Apart from being true, a law will have to satisfy a number of additional conditions. These can be studied independently of the factual requirement of truth, for they refer, as it were, to all logically possible laws, no matter whether factually true or false. Adopting a term proposed by Goodman,[16] we will say that a sentence is *lawlike* if it has all the characteristics of a general law, with the possible exception of truth. Hence, every law is a lawlike sentence, but not conversely.

Our problem of analyzing the notion of law thus reduces to that of explicating the concept of lawlike sentence. We shall construe the class of lawlike sentences as including analytic general statements, such as "A rose is a rose," as well as the lawlike sentences of empirical science, which have empirical content.[17] It will not be necessary to require that each lawlike sentence permissible in explanatory contexts be of the second kind; rather, our definition of explanation will be so constructed as to guarantee the factual character of the totality of the laws—though not of every single one of them—which function in an explanation of an empirical fact.

What are the characteristics of lawlike sentences? First of all, lawlike sentences are statements of universal form, such as "All robins' eggs are greenish-blue," 'All metals are conductors of electricity,' "At constant pressure, any gas expands with increasing temperature." As these examples illustrate, a lawlike sentence usually is not only of universal, but also of conditional form; it makes an assertion to the effect that universally, if a certain set of conditions, C, is realized, then another specified set of conditions, E, is realized as well. The standard form for the symbolic expression of a lawlike sentence is therefore the universal conditional. However, since any conditional statement can be transformed into a nonconditional one, conditional form will not be considered as essential for a lawlike sentence, while universal character will be held indispensable.

But the requirement of universal form is not sufficient to characterize lawlike sentences. Suppose, for example, that a given basket, b, contains at a certain time t a number of red apples and nothing else.[18] Then the statement

(S_1)   Every apple in basket b at time t is red

is both true and of universal form. Yet the sentence does not qualify as a law; we would refuse, for example, to explain by subsumption under it the fact that a particular apple chosen at random from the basket is red. What distinguishes S_1 from a lawlike sentence? Two points suggest themselves, which will be considered in turn, namely, finite scope, and reference to a specified object.

First, the sentence S_1 makes in effect an assertion about a finite number of objects only, and this seems irreconcilable with the claim to universality which is commonly associated with the notion of

---

[15] The requirement of truth for laws has the consequence that a given empirical statement S can never be definitely known to be a law; for the sentence affirming the truth of S is tantamount to S and is therefore capable only of acquiring a more or less high probability, or degree of confirmation, relative to the experimental evidence available at any given time. On this point, cf. Carnap (1946). For an excellent nontechnical exposition of the semantical concept of truth, which is here invoked, the reader is referred to Tarski (1944).

[16] (1947), p. 125.

[17] This procedure was suggested by Goodman's approach in (1947). Reichenbach, in a detailed examination of the concept of law, similarly construes his concept of nomological statement as including both analytic and synthetic sentences; cf. (1947). Chapter VIII.

[18] The difficulty illustrated by this example was stated concisely by Langford (1941), who referred to it as the problem of distinguishing between universals of fact and causal universals. For further discussion and illustration of this point, see also Chisholm (1946), especially pp. 301f. A systematic analysis of the problem was given by Goodman in (1947), especially part III. While not concerned with the specific point under discussion, the detailed examination of counterfactual conditionals and their relation to laws of nature, in Chapter VIII of Lewis (1946), contains important observations on several of the issues raised in the present section.

law.[19] But are not Kepler's laws considered as law-like although they refer to a finite set of planets only? And might we not even be willing to consider as lawlike a sentence such as the following?

(S_2) All the sixteen ice cubes in the freezing tray of this refrigerator have a temperature of less than 10 degrees centigrade.

This point might well be granted; but there is an essential difference between S_1, on the one hand, and Kepler's laws, as well as S_2, on the other: The latter, while finite in scope, are known to be consequences of more comprehensive laws whose scope is not limited, while for S_1 this is not the case.

Adopting a procedure recently suggested by Reichenbach[20], we will therefore distinguish between fundamental and derivative laws. A statement will be called a derivative law if it is of universal character and follows from some fundamental laws. The concept of fundamental law requires further clarification; so far, we may say that fundamental laws, and similarly fundamental lawlike sentences, should satisfy a certain condition of nonlimitation of scope.

It would be excessive, however, to deny the status of fundamental lawlike sentence to all statements which, in effect, make an assertion about a finite class of objects only, for that would rule out also a sentence such as "All robins' eggs are greenish-blue," since presumably the class of all robins' eggs—past, present, and future—is finite. But again, there is an essential difference between this sentence and, say, S_1. It requires empirical knowledge to establish the finiteness of the class of robins' eggs, whereas, when the sentence S_1 is construed in a manner which renders it intuitively unlawlike, the terms "basket b" and "apple" are understood so as to imply finiteness of the class of

apples in the basket at time t. Thus, so to speak, the meaning of its constitutive terms alone—without additional factual information—entails that S_1 has a finite scope. Fundamental laws, then, will have to be construed so as to satisfy a condition of nonlimited scope; our formulation of that condition, however, which refers to what is entailed by "the meaning" of certain expressions, is too vague and will have to be revised later. Let us note in passing that the stipulation here envisaged would bar from the class of fundamental lawlike sentences also such undesirable candidates as "All uranic objects are spherical," where "uranic" means the property of being the planet Uranus; indeed, while this sentence has universal form, it fails to satisfy the condition of nonlimited scope.

In our search for a general characterization of lawlike sentences, we now turn to a second clue which is provided by the sentence S_1. In addition to violating the condition of nonlimited scope, that sentence has the peculiarity of making reference to a particular object, the basket b; and this, too, seems to violate the universal character of a law.[21] The restriction which seems indicated here should again be applied to fundamental lawlike sentences only; for a true general statement about the free fall of physical bodies on the moon, while referring to a particular object, would still constitute a law, albeit a derivative one.

It seems reasonable to stipulate, therefore, that a fundamental lawlike sentence must be of universal form and must contain no essential—i.e., uneliminable—occurrences of designations for particular objects. But this is not sufficient; indeed, just at this point, a particularly serious difficulty presents itself. Consider the sentence

(S_3) Everything that is either an apple in basket b at time t or a sample of ferric oxide is red.

If we use a special expression, say "x is ferple," as synonymous with "x is either an apple in b at t or a

---

[19] The view that laws should be construed as not being limited to a finite domain has been expressed, among others, by Popper (1935), section 13 and by Reichenbach (1947), p. 369.

[20] (1947), p. 361. Our terminology as well as the definitions to be proposed later for the two types of law do not coincide with Reichenbach's, however.

[21] In physics, the idea that a law should not refer to any particular object has found its expression in the maxim that the general laws of physics should contain no reference to specific space-time points, and that spatio-temporal coordinates should occur in them only in the form of differences or differentials.

sample of ferric oxide," then the content of S_3 can be expressed in the form

(S_4)   Everything that is ferple is red.

The statement thus obtained is of universal form and contains no designations of particular objects, and it also satisfies the condition of nonlimited scope; yet clearly, S_4 can qualify as a fundamental lawlike sentence no more than can S_3.

As long as "ferple" is a defined term of our language, the difficulty can readily be met by stipulating that after elimination of defined terms, a fundamental lawlike sentence must not contain essential occurrences of designations for particular objects. But this way out is of no avail when "ferple," or another term of its kind, is a primitive predicate of the language under consideration. This reflection indicates that certain restrictions have to be imposed upon those predicates—i.e., terms for properties or relations—which may occur in fundamental lawlike sentences.[22]

More specifically, the idea suggests itself of permitting a predicate in a fundamental lawlike sentence only if it is purely universal, or, as we shall say, purely qualitative, in character; in other words, if a statement of its meaning does not require reference to any one particular object or spatio-temporal location. Thus, the terms "soft," "green," "warmer than," "as long as," "liquid," "electrically charged," "female," "father of," are purely qualitative predicates, while "taller than the Eiffel Tower," "medieval," "lunar," "arctic," "Ming" are not.[23]

Exclusion from fundamental lawlike sentences of predicates which are not purely qualitative would at the same time ensure satisfaction of the condition of nonlimited scope; for the meaning of a purely qualitative predicate does not require a finite extension; and indeed, all the sentences considered above which violate the condition of nonlimited scope make explicit or implicit reference to specific objects.

The stipulation just proposed suffers, however, from the vagueness of the concept of purely qualitative predicate. The question whether indication of the meaning of a given predicate in English does or does not require reference to some specific object does not always permit of an unequivocal answer since English as a natural language does not provide explicit definitions or other clear explications of meaning for its terms. It seems therefore reasonable to attempt definition of the concept of law not with respect to English or any other natural language, but rather with respect to a formalized language—let us call it a model language L—which is governed by a well-determined system of logical rules, and in which every term either is characterized as primitive or is introduced by an explicit definition in terms of the primitives.

This reference to a well-determined system is customary in logical research and is indeed quite natural in the context of any attempt to develop precise criteria for certain logical distinctions. But it does not by itself suffice to overcome the specific difficulty under discussion. For while it is now readily possible to characterize as not purely qualitative all those among the defined predicates in L whose definiens contains an essential occur-

---

[22] The point illustrated by the sentences S_3 and S_4 above was made by Goodman, who has also emphasized the need to impose certain restrictions upon the predicates whose occurrence is to be permissible in lawlike sentences. These predicates are essentially the same as those which Goodman calls projectible. Goodman has suggested that the problems of establishing precise criteria for projectibility, of interpreting counterfactual conditionals, and of defining the concept of law are so intimately related as to be virtually aspects of a single problem. Cf. his articles (1946) and (1947). One suggestion for an analysis of projectibility has been made by Carnap in (1947). Goodman's note (1947a) contains critical observations on Carnap's proposals.

[23] That laws, in addition to being of universal form, must contain only purely universal predicates was argued by Popper (1935, sections 14, 15). Our alternative expression *purely qualitative predicate* was chosen in analogy to Carnap's term *purely*

qualitative property cf. (1947). The above characterization of purely universal predicates seems preferable to a simpler and perhaps more customary one, to the effect that a statement of the meaning of the predicate must require no reference to particular objects. That formulation might be too restrictive since it could be argued that stating the meaning of such purely qualitative terms as *blue* or *hot* requires illustrative reference to some particular object which has the quality in question. The essential point is that no one specific object has to be chosen; any one in the logically unlimited set of blue or of hot objects will do. In explicating the meaning of *taller than the Eiffel Tower, being an apple in basket* b *at time* t, *medieval*, etc., however, reference has to be made to one specific object or to some one in a limited set of objects.

rence of some individual name, our problem remains open for the primitives of the language, whose meanings are not determined by definitions within the language, but rather by semantical rules of interpretation. For we want to permit the interpretation of the primitives of *L* by means of such attributes as blue, hard, solid, warmer, but not by the properties of being a descendant of Napoleon, or an arctic animal, or a Greek statue; and the difficulty is precisely that of stating rigorous criteria for the distinction between the permissible and the nonpermissible interpretations. Thus the problem of finding an adequate definition for purely qualitative attributes now arises again; namely for the concepts of the meta-language in which the semantical interpretation of the primitives is formulated. We may postpone an encounter with the difficulty by presupposing formalization of the semantical meta-language, the meta-meta-language, and so forth, but somewhere, we will have to stop at a nonformalized meta-language; and for it, a characterization of purely qualitative predicates will be needed and will present much the same problems as nonformalized English, with which we began. The characterization of a purely qualitative predicate as one whose meaning can be made explicit without reference to any one particular object points to the intended meaning but does not explicate it precisely, and the problem of an adequate definition of purely qualitative predicates remains open.

There can be little doubt, however, that there exists a large number of predicates which would be rather generally recognized as purely qualitative in the sense here pointed out, and as permissible in the formulation of fundamental lawlike sentences; some examples have been given above, and the list could be readily enlarged. When we speak of purely qualitative predicates, we shall henceforth have in mind predicates of this kind. . . .

REFERENCES

Beard, Charles A., and Sidney Hook, "Problems of Terminology in Historical Writing." Chapter IV of *Theory and Practice in Historical Study: A Report of the Com-* mittee on *Historiography*. New York, Social Science Research Council, 1946.

Bergmann, Gustav, "Holism, Historicism, and Emergence," *Philosophy of Science*, 11 (1944), 209–21.

Bonfante, G., "Semantics, Language." An Article in P. L. Harriman, ed., *The Encyclopedia of Psychology*. New York, 1946.

Broad, C. D., *The Mind and its Place in Nature*. New York, 1925.

Carnap, Rudolf, *Introduction to Semantics*. Cambridge, Mass., 1942.

Carnap, Rudolf, "On Inductive Logic," *Philosophy of Science*, 12 (1945), 72–97.

Carnap, Rudolf, "The Two Concepts of Probability," *Philosophy and Phenomenological Research*, 5 (1945), 513–32.

Carnap, Rudolf, "Remarks on Induction and Truth," *Philosophy and Phenomenological Research*, 6 (1946), 590–602.

Carnap, Rudolf, "On the Application of Inductive Logic," *Philosophy and Phenomenological Research*, 8 (1947), 133–47.

Chisholm, Roderick M., "The Contrary-to-Fact Conditional," *Mind*, 55 (1946), 289–307.

Church, Alonzo, "Logic, formal," in Dagobert D. Runes, ed. *The Dictionary of Philosophy*. New York, 1942.

Ducasse, C. J., "Explanation, Mechanism, and Teleology," *The Journal of Philosophy*, 22 (1925), 150–55.

Feigl, Herbert, "Operationism and Scientific Method," *Psychological Review*, 52 (1945), 250–59 and 284–88.

Goodman, Nelson, "A Query on Confirmation," *The Journal of Philosophy*, 43 (1946), 383–85.

Goodman, Nelson, "The Problem of Counterfactual Conditionals," *The Journal of Philosophy*, 44 (1947), 113–28.

Goodman, Nelson, "On Infirmities of Confirmation Theory," *Philosophy and Phenomenological Research*, 8 (1947), 149–51.

Grelling, Kurt and Paul Oppenheim, "Der Gestaltbegriff im Lichte der neuen Logik," *Erkenntnis*, 7 (1937–38), 211–25 and 357–59.

Grelling, Kurt and Paul Oppenheim, "Logical Analysis of Gestalt as 'Functional Whole'." Preprinted for distribution at Fifth Internat. Congress for the Unity of Science, Cambridge, Mass., 1939.

Helmer, Olaf and Paul Oppenheim, "A Syntactical Definition of Probability and of Degree of Confirmation," *The Journal of Symbolic Logic*, 10 (1945), 25–60.

Hempel, Carl G., "The Function of General Laws in History." *The Journal of Philosophy*, 39 (1942), 35–48.

Hempel, Carl G., "Studies in the Logic of Confirmation," *Mind*, 54 (1945); Part I: pp. 1–26, Part II: pp. 97–121.

Hempel, Carl G. and Paul Oppenheim, "A Definition of Degree of Confirmation," *Philosophy of Science,* 12 (1945), 98–115.

Henle, Paul, "The Status of Emergence," *The Journal of Philosophy,* 39 (1942), 486–93.

Hospers, John, "On Explanation," *The Journal of Philosophy,* 43 (1946), 337–56.

Hull, Clark L., "The Problem of Intervening Variables in Molar Behavior Theory," *Psychological Review,* 50 (1943), 273–91.

Hull, Clark L., *Principles of Behavior.* New York, 1943.

Jevons, W. Stanley, *The Principles of Science.* London, 1924 (1st ed. 1874).

Kaufmann, Felix, *Methodology of the Social Sciences.* New York, 1944.

Knight, Frank H, "The Limitations of Scientific Method in Economics," in R. Tugwell, ed., *The Trend of Economics.* New York, 1924.

Koch, Sigmund, "The Logical Character of the Motivation Concept," *Psychological Review,* 48 (1941); Part I: pp. 15–38, Part II: pp. 127–154.

Langford, C. H., Review in *The Journal of Symbolic Logic,* 6 (1941), pp. 67–68.

Lewis, C. I., *An Analysis of Knowledge and Valuation.* La Salle, Ill., 1946.

McKinsey, J.C.C., Review of Helmer and Oppenheim (1945). *Mathematical Reviews,* 7 (1946), 45.

Mill, John Stuart, *A System of Logic,* New York, 1858.

Morgan, C. Lloyd, *Emergent Evolution.* New York, 1923.

Morgan, C. Lloyd, *The Emergence of Novelty.* New York, 1933.

Popper, Karl, *Logik der Forschung.* Wien, 1935.

Popper, Karl, *The Open Society and its Enemies.* London, 1945.

Reichenbach, Hans, *Elements of Symbolic Logic.* New York, 1947.

Rosenblueth, A., N. Wiener and J. Bigelow, "Behavior, Purpose, and Teleology," *Philosophy of Science,* 10 (1943), 18–24.

Stace, W. T., "Novelty, Indeterminism and Emergence," *Philosophical Review,* 48 (1939), 296–310.

Tarski, Alfred, "The Semantical Conception of Truth, and the Foundations of Semantics," *Philosophy and Phenomenological Research,* 4 (1944), 341–76.

Tolman, Edward Chase, *Purposive Behavior in Animals and Men.* New York, 1932.

White, Morton G., "Historical Explanation." *Mind,* 52 (1943), 212–29.

Woodger, J. H., *Biological Principles.* New York, 1929.

Zilsel, Edgar, *Problems of Empiricism.* Chicago, 1941.

Zilsel, Edgar, "Physics and the Problem of Historico-Sociological Laws," *Philosophy of Science,* 8 (1941), 567–79.

Statistical Explanation

Carl G. Hempel

LAWS OF STATISTICAL FORM

We now turn our attention to explanations based on nomological statements of a kind we have not so far considered, which have come to play an increasingly important role in empirical science. I will refer to them as *laws or theoretical principles of statistic-probabilistic form,* or as *statistical laws,* for short.

Most of our discussion will be concerned with the explanatory use of statistical laws of a very simple kind; we will call them *laws of basic statistical form.* These are statements to the effect that the statistical probability for an event of kind F to be also of kind G is r, or that

$$p(G,F) = r$$

for short. Broadly speaking, this statement asserts that in the long run the proportion of those instances of F which are also instances of G is approximately r. . . .

For example, the statement that the rolling of a given slightly irregular die (event of kind F) yields an ace (event of kind G) with a probability of .15, i.e., in about 15 percent of all cases in the long run, has this basic statistical form. And so does the law that the half-life of radon is 3.82 days, i.e., that the statistical probability for a radon atom to disintegrate during any given period of 3.82 days is 1/2, which means, roughly, that of a sample of radon containing a large number of atoms, very close to one half of the atoms decay within 3.82 days.

Laws of basic statistical form may be regarded as less stringent counterparts of laws that have the universal conditional form

$$(x) \ (Fx \supset Gx)$$

asserting that any instance of F is an instance of G, as for example: "Any gas expands when heated under constant pressure." Indeed, the two kinds of law share an important feature, which is symptomatic of their nomological character: both make general claims concerning a class of cases that might be said to be potentially infinite. . . . [A] statement which is logically equivalent to a finite conjunction of singular sentences, and which in this sense makes a claim concerning only a finite class of cases, does not qualify as a law and lacks the explanatory force of a nomological statement. Lawlike sentences, whether true or false, are not just conveniently telescoped summaries of finite sets of data concerning particular instances.

For example, the law that gases expand when heated under constant pressure is not tantamount to the statement that in all instances that have so far been observed, or perhaps in all instances that have so far occurred, an increase in the temperature of a gas under constant pressure has been accompanied by an increase in volume. Rather it asserts that a growth in volume is associated with the heating of a gas under constant pressure in *any* case, whether past, present, or future, and whether actually observed or not. It even implies counterfactual and subjunctive conditionals to the effect that if a given body of gas had been heated or were to be heated under constant pressure, its volume would have increased, or would increase, as well.

Similarly, the probabilistic laws of genetics or of radioactive decay are not tantamount to descriptive reports of the frequencies with which some kind of phenomenon has been found to occur in a finite class of observed cases: they assert certain peculiar, namely probabilistic, modes of

From Section 3, "Aspects of Scientific Explanation," in Carl Hempel, *Aspects of Scientific Explanation and Other Essays in the Philosophy of Science.* New York: Free Press, 1965, pp. 376–386. Reprinted by permission.

connection between potentially infinite classes of occurrences. In a statistical law of basic form, as contradistinguished from a statistical description specifying relative frequencies in some finite set, the "reference class" F is not assumed to be finite. Indeed, we might say that a law of the form "$p(G,F) = r$" refers not only to all actual instances of F, but, so to speak, to the class of all its potential instances. Suppose, for example, that we are given a homogeneous regular tetrahedron whose faces are marked "I," "II," "III," "IV." We might then assert that the probability of obtaining a III, i.e., of the tetrahedron's coming to rest on that face upon being tossed out of a dice box, is 1/4. But, while this assertion says something about the frequency with which a III is obtained as a result of rolling the tetrahedron, it cannot be construed as simply specifying that frequency for the class of all tosses which are, in fact, ever performed with the tetrahedron. For we might well maintain our hypothesis even if we were informed that the tetrahedron would actually be tossed only a few times throughout its existence, and in this case, our probability statement would surely not be meant to assert that exactly, or even nearly, one-fourth of those tosses would yield the result III. Moreover, our statement would be perfectly meaningful and might, indeed, be well supported (e.g., by results obtained with similar tetrahedra or with other homogeneous bodies in the form of regular solids) even if the given tetrahedron happened to be destroyed without ever having been tossed at all. What the probability statement attributes to the tetrahedron is, therefore, not the frequency with which the result III is obtained in actual past or future rollings, but a certain *disposition,* namely, the disposition to yield the result III in about one out of four cases, in the long run. This disposition might be characterized by means of a subjunctive conditional phrase: If the tetrahedron were to be tossed a large number of times, it would yield the result III in about one-fourth of the cases.[1] Implica-

tions in the form of counterfactual and subjective conditionals are thus hallmarks of lawlike statements both of strictly universal and of statistical form.

As for the distinction between lawlike sentences of strictly universal form and those of probabilistic or statistical form, it is sometimes thought that statements asserting strictly universal connections, such as Galileo's law or Newton's law of gravitation, rest, after all, only on a finite and thus inevitably incomplete body of evidence; that, therefore, they may well have as yet undetected exceptions; and that accordingly they, too, should be qualified as only probabilistic. But this argument confounds the claim made by a given statement with the evidence available in support of it. On the latter score, all empirical statements are only more or less well supported by the relevant evidence at our disposal; or, in the parlance of some theorists, they have a more or less high logical or inductive probability conferred upon them by that evidence. But the distinction between lawlike statements of strictly universal form and those of probabilistic form pertains, not to the evidential support of the statements in question, but to the claims made by them: roughly speaking, the former attribute (truly or falsely) a certain characteristic to all members of a certain class; the latter, to a specified proportion of its members.

Even if all the supposedly universal laws of empirical science should eventually come to be regarded as reflections of underlying statistical uniformities—an interpretation that the kinetic theory of matter gives to the classical laws of thermodynamics, for example—even then the distinc-

---

[1] Carnap (1951–54, pp. 190–92) has argued in a similar vein that the statistical probability of rolling an ace with a given die is a physical characteristic, which he also calls "the probability state" of the die, and that the relative frequency with which

rollings of the die yield an ace is a symptom of that state, much as the expansion of the mercury column in a thermometer is a symptom of its temperature state.

The dispositional construal I have outlined for the concept of statistical probability appears to be in close accord also with the "propensity interpretation" advocated by Popper. The latter "differs from the purely statistical or frequency interpretation only in this—that it considers the probability as a characteristic property of the experimental arrangement rather than as a property of a sequence"; the property in question is explicitly construed as *dispositional* (Popper 1957, pp. 67–68). See also the discussion of this paper in Körner (1957), pp. 78–89, *passim.* However, the currently available statements of the propensity interpretation are all rather brief; a fuller presentation is to be given in a forthcoming book by Popper.

tion between the two types of law and the corresponding explanations is not wiped out: in fact, it is presupposed in the very formulation of the conjecture.

Nor is a statement of the universal conditional form

$$(x) (Fx \supset Gx)$$

logically equivalent to the corresponding statement of the basic statistical form

$$p(G,F) = 1$$

for . . . the latter asserts only that it is practically certain that in a large number of instances of F, almost all are instances of G; hence the probability statement may be true even if the corresponding statement of strictly universal form is false.

So far, we have dealt only with statistical laws of basic form. Let us now say more generally that *a statement has the form of a statistical law,* or is of probabilistic-statistical character, if it is formulated in terms of statistical probabilities, i.e., if it contains (nonvacuously) the term "statistical probability" or some notational equivalent, or a term—such as "half-life"—which is defined by means of statistical probabilities.

Take, for example, the statement that when two coins are flipped simultaneously, the face shown by one is independent of that shown by the other. This amounts to saying that the probability for the second coin to show heads when the first shows heads is the same as when the first shows tails; and vice versa. Generally, assertions of statistical independence have the form of statistical laws, though they are not of basic statistical form. Similarly, a statement asserting a statistical dependence or "aftereffect" has the form of a statistical law; for example, the statement that in any given area the probability for a day to be cloudy when it follows a cloudy day is greater than when it follows a noncloudy day. Still other laws of statistical form are formulated in terms of mean values of certain variables, such as the mean kinetic energy and the mean free path of the molecules in a gas; the notion of mean value here invoked is defined by reference to statistical probabilities.

By a *statistical explanation,* let us now under-

stand any explanation that makes essential use of at least one law or theoretical principle of statistical form. In the following subsections, we will examine the logical structure of such explanations. We will find that there are two logically different types of statistical explanation. One of them amounts, basically, to the deductive subsumption of a narrower statistical uniformity under more comprehensive ones: I will call it *deductive-statistical explanation.* The other involves the subsumption, in a peculiar nondeductive sense, of a particular occurrence under statistical laws; for reasons to be given later, it will be called *inductive-statistical explanation.*

DEDUCTIVE-STATISTICAL EXPLANATION

It is an instance of the so-called gambler's fallacy to assume that when several successive tossings of a fair coin have yielded heads, the next toss will more probably yield tails than heads. Why this is not the case can be explained by means of two hypotheses that have the form of statistical laws. The first is that the random experiment of flipping a fair coin yields heads with a statistical probability of 1/2. The second hypothesis is that the outcomes of different tossings of the coin are statistically independent, so that the probability of any specified sequence of outcomes—such as heads twice, then tails, then heads, then tails three times—equals the product of the probabilities of the constituent single outcomes. These two hypotheses in terms of statistical probabilities imply *deductively* that the probability for heads to come up after a long sequence of heads is still 1/2.

Certain statistical explanations offered in science are of the same deductive character, though often quite complex mathematically. Consider, for example, the hypothesis that for the atoms of every radioactive substance there is a characteristic probability of disintegrating during a given unit time interval, and that probability is independent of the age of the atom and of all external circumstances. This complex statistical hypothesis explains, by deductive implication, various other statistical aspects of radioactive decay, among them, the following: Suppose that the decay of individual atoms of some radioactive substance is recorded by means of the scintillations produced upon a sensitive screen by the alpha particles emitted by the disintegrating atoms. Then the time intervals separating successive scintillations will vary considerably in length, but intervals of different lengths will occur with different statistical probabilities. Specifically, if the mean time interval between successive scintillations is s seconds, then the probability for two successive scintillations to be separated by more than $n \cdot s$ seconds is $(1/e)^n$, where e is the base of the natural logarithms.[2]

Explanations of the kind here illustrated will be called *deductive-statistical explanations,* or *D-S explanations*. They involve the deduction of a statement in the form of a statistical law from an explanans that contains indispensably at least one law or theoretical principle of statistical form. The deduction is effected by means of the mathematical theory of statistical probability, which makes it possible to calculate certain derivative probabilities (those referred to in the explanandum) on the basis of other probabilities (specified in the explanans), which have been empirically ascertained or hypothetically assumed. What a D-S explanation accounts for is thus always a general uniformity expressed by a presumptive law of statistical form.

Ultimately, however, statistical laws are meant to be applied to particular occurrences and to establish explanatory and predictive connections among them. In the next subsection, we will examine the statistical explanation of particular events. Our discussion will be limited to the case where the explanatory statistical laws are of basic form: this will suffice to exhibit the basic logical differences between the statistical and the deductive-nomological explanation of individual occurrences.

---

[2] Cf. Mises (1939), pp. 272–78, where both the empirical findings and the explanatory argument are presented. This book also contains many other illustrations of what is here called deductive-statistical explanation.

INDUCTIVE-STATISTICAL EXPLANATION

As an explanation of why patient John Jones recovered from a streptococcus infection, we might be told that Jones had been given penicillin. But if we try to amplify this explanatory claim by indicating a general connection between penicillin treatment and the subsiding of a streptococcus infection we cannot justifiably invoke a general law to the effect that in all cases of such infection, administration of penicillin will lead to recovery. What can be asserted, and what surely is taken for granted here, is only that penicillin will effect a cure in a high percentage of cases, or with a high statistical probability. This statement has the general character of a law of statistical form, and while the probability value is not specified, the statement indicates that it is high. But in contrast to the cases of deductive-nomological and deductive-statistical explanation, the explanans consisting of this statistical law together with the statement that the patient did receive penicillin obviously does not imply the explanandum statement, "The patient recovered," with deductive certainty, but only, as we might say, with high likelihood, or near certainty. Briefly, then, the explanation amounts to this argument:

(a) The particular case of illness of John Jones—let us call it j—was an instance of severe streptococcal infection (Sj) which was treated with large doses of penicillin (Pj); and the statistical probability $p (R, S \cdot P)$ of recovery in cases where S and P are present is close to 1; hence, the case was practically certain to end in recovery (Rj).

This argument might invite the following schematization:

(b)
$$p (R, S \cdot P) \text{ is close to } 1$$
$$\underline{Sj \cdot Pj \hspace{3cm}}$$

(Therefore:) It is practically certain (very likely) that Rj

In the literature on inductive inference, arguments thus based on statistical hypotheses have often been construed as having this form or a similar one. On this construal, the conclusion characteristically contains a modal qualifier such as "almost certainly", "with high probability," "very likely," etc. But the conception of arguments having this character is untenable. For phrases of the form "It is practically certain that p" or "It is very likely that p," where the place of p is taken by some statement, are not complete self-contained sentences that can be qualified as either true or false. The statement that takes the place of p—for example, Rj—is either true or false, quite independently of whatever relevant evidence may be available, but it can be qualified as more or less likely, probable, certain, or the like only *relative to some body of evidence*. One and the same statement, such as Rj, will be certain, very likely, not very likely, highly unlikely, and so forth, depending upon what evidence is considered. The phrase "It is almost certain that Rj" taken by itself is therefore neither true nor false; and it cannot be inferred from the premises specified in (b), nor from any other statements.

The confusion underlying the schematization (b) might be further illuminated by considering its analogue for the case of deductive arguments. The force of a deductive inference, such as that from "all F are G" and "a is F" to "a is G," is sometimes indicated by saying that if the premises are true, then the conclusion is necessarily true or is certain to be true—a phrasing that might suggest the schematization

All F are G
a is F

(Therefore:) It is necessary (certain) that a is G.

But clearly the given premises—which might be, for example, "All men are mortal" and "Socrates is a man"—do not establish the sentence "a is G" ("Socrates is mortal") as a necessary or certain truth. The certainty referred to in the informal paraphrase of the argument is relational: the statement "a is G" is certain, or necessary, *relative to the specified premises;* i.e., their truth will guarantee its truth—which means nothing more than that "a is G" is a logical consequence of those premises.

Analogously, to present our statistical explanation in the manner of schema (b) is to misconstrue the function of the words *almost certain* or *very*

likely as they occur in the formal wording of the explanation. Those words clearly must be taken to indicate that on the evidence provided by the explanans, or relative to that evidence, the explanandum is practically certain or very likely, i.e., that

(c) Rj is practically certain (very likely) relative to the explanans containing the sentences "$p(R, S \cdot P)$ is close to 1" and "$Sj \cdot Pj$."[3]

The explanatory argument misrepresented by (b) might therefore suitably be schematized as follows:

(d)
$$\frac{\begin{array}{l} p\,(R,\ S \cdot P) \text{ is close to 1} \\ Sj \cdot Pj \end{array}}{Rj} \quad \text{[makes practically certain (very likely)]}$$

In this schema, the double line separating the "premises" from the "conclusion" is to signify that the relation of the former to the latter is not that of deductive implication but that of inductive support, the strength of which is indicated in square brackets.[4,5]

---

[3] Phrases such as "It is almost certain (very likely) that j recovers," even when given the relational construal here suggested, are ostensibly concerned with relations between propositions, such as those forming the conclusion and the premises of an argument. For the purpose of the present discussion, however, involvement with propositions can be avoided by construing the phrases in question as expressing logical relations between corresponding *sentences,* e.g., the conclusion sentence and the premise sentence of an argument. This construal, which underlies the formulation of (c), will be adopted in this essay, though for the sake of convenience we may occasionally use a paraphrase.

[4] In the familiar schematization of deductive arguments, with a single line separating the premises from the conclusion, no explicit distinction is made between a weaker and a stronger claim, either of which might be intended; namely (i) that the premises logically imply the conclusion and (ii) that, in addition, the premises are true. In the case of our probabilistic argument, (c) expresses a weaker claim, analogous to (i), whereas (d) may be taken to express a "proffered explanation" (the term is borrowed from Scheffler, (1957), section 1) in which, in addition, the explanatory premises are—however tentatively—asserted as true.

[5] The considerations here outlined concerning the use of terms like *probably* and *certainly* as modal qualifiers of individual statements seem to me to militate also against the notion of categorical probability statement that C. I. Lewis sets forth in the following passage (italics the author's):

Our schematization thus reflects explictly the understanding that *almost certain, very likely, practically impossible* and similar expressions often used in the phrasing of probabilistic arguments, including explanations, do not stand for properties possessed by certain propositions or the corresponding sentences, but for relations that some sentences bear to others. According to this understanding, the notion of the explanans of (d) making the explanandum almost certain or very likely is but a special case of the idea of a given statement or set of statements—let us call it the

---

Just as "If *D* then (certainly) *P*, and *D* is the fact "leads to the categorical consequence, "Therefore (certainly) *P*"; so too, "If *D* then probably *P*, and *D* is the fact" leads to a categorical consequence expressed by "It is probable that *P*." And this conclusion is not merely the statement over again of the probability relation between *P* and *D* anymore than "Therefore (certainly) *P*" is the statement over again of "If *D* then (certainly) *P*." "If the barometer is high, tomorrow will probably be fair; and the barometer *is* high" categorically assures something expressed by "Tomorrow will probably be fair." This probability is still relative to the grounds of judgment; but if these grounds are actual, and contain all the available evidence which is pertinent, then it is not only categorical but may fairly be called *the* probability of the event in question. (1946, p. 319).

This position seems to me to be open to just those objections suggested in the main text. If *P* is a statement, then the expressions "certainly *P*" and "probably *P*" as envisaged in the quoted passage are not statements. If we ask how one would go about trying to ascertain whether they were true, we realize that we are entirely at a loss unless and until a reference set of statements or assumptions has been specified relative to which *P* may then be found to be certain, or to be highly probable, or neither. The expressions in question, then, are essentially incomplete; they are elliptic formulations of relational statements; neither of them can be the conclusion of an inference. However plausible Lewis's suggestion may seem, there is no analogue in inductive logic to *modus ponens*, or the "rule of detachment," of deductive logic, which, given the information that *D*, and also "if *D* then *P*," are true statements, authorizes us to detach the consequent *P* in the conditional premise and to assert it as a self-contained statement which must then be true as well.

At the end of the quoted passage, Lewis suggests the important idea that "probably *P*" might be taken to mean that the total relevant evidence available at the time confers high probability upon *P*. But even this statement is relational in that it tacitly refers to some unspecified time, and, besides, his general notion of a categorical probability statement as a conclusion of an argument is not made dependent on the assumption that the premises of the argument include all the relevant evidence available.

It must be stressed, however, that elsewhere in his discussion, Lewis emphasizes the relativity of (logical) probability, and, thus, the very characteristic that rules out the conception of categorical probability statements.

Similar objections apply, I think, to Toulmin's construal of probabilistic arguments; *cf.* Toulmin (1958) and the discussion in Hempel (1960), sections 1–3.

---

grounds or the evidence *e*—conferring more or less strong inductive support or confirmation or credibility upon some statement *h*. To clarify and systematically to elaborate the idea here sketchily characterized is, of course, the objective of various theories of inductive reasoning. It is still a matter of debate to what extent clear criteria and a precise theory for the concept at issue can be developed. Several attempts have been made to formulate rigorous logical theories for a concept of inductive support that admits of numerical or nonnumerical gradations in strength: two outstanding examples of such efforts are Keynes's theory of probability and, especially, Carnap's impressive system of inductive logic.[6] In the latter, the degree to which a sentence, or hypothesis, *h* is confirmed by an evidence sentence *e* is represented by a function $c(h,e)$, whose values lie in the interval from 0 to 1 inclusive, and which satisfies all the basic principles of abstract probability theory; $c(h,e)$ is therefore also referred to as the *logical or inductive* probability of *h* on *e*. This concept of inductive probability as a quantitative logical relation between statements must be sharply distinguished from the concept of statistical probability as a quantitative empirical relation between kinds or classes of events. The two concepts have a common formal structure, however, in virtue of which both of them qualify as probabilities: both are defined, in their respective formal theories, in terms of nonnegative additive set functions whose values range from 0 to 1. Carnap's theory provides an explicit definition of $c(h,e)$ for the case where the sentences *h* and *e* belong to one or another of certain relatively simple kinds of formalized language; the extension of his approach to languages whose logical apparatus would be adequate for the formulation of advanced scientific theories is as yet an open problem.

But, independently of the extent to which the relation of the explanandum to the explanans can be analyzed in terms of Carnap's quantitative con-

---

[6] See Keynes (1921); of Carnap's numerous writings on the subject, *cf.* especially (1945), (1950), (1952), (1962).

cept of inductive probability, probabilistic explanations must be viewed as inductive in the broad sense here adumbrated. To refer to the general notion of inductive support as capable of gradations, without commitment to any one particular theory of inductive support or confirmation, we will use the phrase (*degree of*) *inductive support of h relative to e.*[7]

Explanations of particular facts or events by means of statistic-probabilistic laws thus present themselves as arguments that are *inductive* or *probabilistic* in the sense that the explanans confers upon the explanandum a more or less high degree of inductive support or of logical (inductive) probability; they will therefore be called *inductive-statistical explanations,* or *I-S explanations*. Explanations, such as (d), in which the statistical laws invoked are of basic form, will also be called *I-S explanations of basic form.*

REFERENCES

Carnap, R. "On Inductive Logic." *Philosophy of Science* 12:72–97 (1945).

Carnap, R. *Logical Foundations of Probability*. Chicago: University of Chicago Press 1950; second, revised, edition 1962. Cited in this essay as Carnap (1950).

Carnap, R. "Inductive Logic and Science." *Proceedings of the American Academy of Arts and Sciences,* volume 80:187–97 (1951–54).

Carnap, R. *The Continuum of Inductive Methods*. Chicago: University of Chicago Press, 1952.

Carnap, R. "The Aim of Inductive Logic." In Nagel, Suppes, and Tarski (1962), pp. 303–18.

Helmer, O. and P. Oppenheim. "A Syntactical Definition of Probability and of Degree of Confirmation." *The Journal of Symbolic Logic* 10:25–60 (1945).

Hempel, C. G. "Inductive Inconsistencies." *Synthese* 12:439–69 (1960).

Hempel, C. G. and P. Oppenheim. "A Definition of 'Degree of Confirmation'." *Philosophy of Science* 12:98–115 (1945).

Kemeny, J. G. and P. Oppenheim. "Degree of Factual Support." *Philosophy of Science* 19:307–24 (1952).

Keynes, J. M. *A Treatise on Probability*. London: Macmillan, 1921.

Körner, S. (ed). *Observation and Interpretation: Proceedings of the Ninth Symposium of the Colston Research Society*. New York: Academic Press, and London: Butterworths Scientific Publications, 1957.

Lewis, C. I. *An Analysis of Knowledge and Valuation*. La Salle, Ill.: Open Court Publishing Co., 1946.

Mises, R. von. *Probability, Statistics and Truth*. London: William Hodge & Co., 1939.

Nagel, E., P. Suppes, and A. Tarski (eds.). *Logic, Methodology, and Philosophy of Science. Proceedings of the 1960 International Congress*. Stanford: Stanford University Press, 1962.

Popper, K. R. "The Propensity Interpretation of the Calculus of Probability, and the Quantum Theory." In Körner (1957), pp. 65–70.

Rescher, N. "A Theory of Evidence." *Philosophy of Science* 25:83–94 (1958).

Scheffler, I. "Explanation, Prediction, and Abstraction." *The British Journal for the Philosophy of Science* 7:293–309 (1957).

Toulmin, S. *The Uses of Argument*. Cambridge, England: Cambridge University Press, 1958.

---

[7] Some recent attempts to give precise explications of this general notion have led to concepts that do not have all the formal characteristics of a probability function. One such construal is presented in Helmer and Oppenheim (1945) and, less technically, in Hempel and Oppenheim (1945). Another is the concept of degree of factual support propounded and theoretically developed in Kemeny and Oppenheim (1952). For a suggestive distinction and comparison of different concepts of evidence, see Rescher (1958).

Why Ask, "Why?"?
An Inquiry Concerning Scientific Explanation

Wesley C. Salmon[1]

Concerning the first order question "Why?" I have raised the second order question "Why ask, 'Why?'?" to which you might naturally respond with the third order question "Why ask, 'Why ask, "Why?'?"?" But this way lies madness, to say nothing of an infinite regress. While an infinite sequence of nested intervals may converge upon a point, the series of nested questions just initiated has no point to it, and so we had better cut it off without delay. The answer to the very natural third order question is this: the question "Why ask, 'Why?'?" expresses a deep philosophical perplexity which I believe to be both significant in its own right and highly relevant to certain current philosophical discussions. I want to share it with you.

The problems I shall be discussing pertain mainly to scientific explanation, but before turning to them, I should remark that I am fully aware that many—perhaps most—why-questions are requests for some sort of *justification* (Why did one employee receive a larger raise than another? Because she had been paid less than a male colleague for doing the same kind of job) or *consolation* (Why, asked Job, was I singled out for such extraordinary misfortune and suffering?). Since I have neither the time nor the talent to deal with questions of this sort, I shall not pursue them further, except to remark that the seeds of endless

philosophical confusion can be sown by failing carefully to distinguish them from requests for scientific explanation.

Let me put the question I do want to discuss to you this way. Suppose you had achieved the epistemic status of Laplace's demon—the hypothetical superintelligence who knows all of nature's regularities, and the precise state of the universe in full detail at some particular moment (say now, according to some suitable simultaneity slice of the universe). Possessing the requisite logical and mathematical skill, you would be able to predict any future occurrence, and you would be able to retrodict any past event. Given this sort of apparent omniscience, would your scientific knowledge be complete, or would it still leave something to be desired? Laplace asked no more of his demon; should we place further demands upon ourselves? And if so, what should be the nature of the additional demands?

If we look at most contemporary philosophy of science texts, we find an immediate *affirmative* answer to this question. Science, the majority say, has at least two principal aims—prediction (construed broadly enough to include inference from the observed to the unobserved, regardless of temporal relations) and explanation. The first of these provides knowledge of *what* happens; the second is supposed to furnish knowledge of *why* things happen as they do. This is not a new idea. In the *Posterior Analytics*, Aristotle distinguishes syllogisms which provide scientific understanding from those which do not.[2] In the Port Royal Logic, Ar-

Presidential Address delivered before the Fifty-second Annual Pacific Meeting of the American Philosophical Association in San Francisco, California, March 24, 1978.

[1] The author wishes to express his gratitude to the National Science Foundation for support of research on scientific explanation.

[2] Book I.2, 71b, 17–24.

From *Proceedings and Addresses of the American Philosophical Association*, Vol. 51, No. 6 (Aug., 1978), pp. 683–705. Copyright © 1978 by Wesley C. Salmon. Reprinted by permission.

nauld distinguishes demonstrations which merely convince the mind from those which also enlighten the mind.[3]

This view has not been universally adopted. It was not long ago that we often heard statements to the effect that the business of science is to predict, not to explain. Scientific knowledge is descriptive—it tells us *what* and *how.* If we seek explanations—if we want to know why—we must go outside of science, perhaps to metaphysics or theology. In his Preface to the Third Edition (1911) of *The Grammar of Science,* Karl Pearson wrote, "Nobody believes now that science *explains* anything; we all look upon it as a shorthand description, as an economy of thought."[4] This doctrine is not very popular nowadays. It is now fashionable to say that science aims not merely at describing the world—it also provides *understanding, comprehension,* and *enlightenment.* Science presumably accomplishes such high-sounding goals by supplying scientific explanations.

The current attitude leaves us with a deep and perplexing question, namely, if explanation does involve something over and above mere description, just what sort of thing is it? The use of such honorific near-synonyms as "understanding," "comprehension," and "enlightenment" makes it sound important and desirable, but does not help at all in the philosophical analysis of explanation—scientific or other. What, over and above its complete descriptive knowledge of the world, would Laplace's demon require in order to achieve understanding? I hope you can see that

this is a real problem, especially for those who hold what I shall call "the inferential view" of scientific explanation, for Laplace's demon can infer every fact about the universe, past, present, and future. If the problem does not seem acute, I would quote a remark made by Russell about Zeno's paradox of the flying arrow—"The more the difficulty is meditated, the more real it becomes."[5]

It is not my intention this evening to discuss the details of the various formal models of scientific explanation which have been advanced in the last three decades.[6] Instead, I want to consider the general conceptions which lie beneath the most influential theories of scientific explanation. Two powerful intuitions seem to have guided much of the discussion. Although they have given rise to disparate basic conceptions and considerable controversy, both are, in my opinion, quite sound. Moreover, it seems to me, both can be incorporated into a single overall theory of scientific explanation.

1. The first of these intuitions is the notion that the explanation of a phenomenon essentially involves *locating and identifying its cause or causes.* This intuition seems to arise rather directly from common sense, and from various contexts in which scientific knowledge is applied to concrete situations. It is strongly supported by a number of paradigms, the most convincing of which are explanations of particular occurrences. To explain a given airplane crash, for example, we seek "the cause"—a mechanical failure, perhaps, or pilot error. To explain a person's death again we seek the cause—strangulation or drowning, for instance. I shall call the general view of scientific explanation which comes more or less directly from this fundamental intuition

[3] Antoine Arnauld, *The Art of Thinking* (Indianapolis: Bobbs-Merrill, 1964), p. 330. "Such demonstrations may convince the mind, but they do not enlighten it; and enlightenment ought to be the principal fruit of true knowledge. Our minds are unsatisfied unless they know not only *that* a thing is but *why* it is."

[4] Karl Pearson, *The Grammar of Science,* 3rd ed. (New York: Meridian Books, 1957), p. xi. The first edition appeared in 1892, the second in 1899, and the third was first published in 1911. In the Preface to the Third Edition, Pearson remarked, just before the statement quoted in the text, "Reading the book again after many years, it was surprising to find how the heterodoxy of the eighties had become the commonplace and accepted doctrine of today." Since the "commonplace and accepted doctrine" of 1911 has again become heterodox, one wonders to what extent such changes in philosophic doctrine are mere matters of changing fashion.

[5] Bertrand Russell, *Our Knowledge of the External World* (London: George Allen & Unwin Ltd, 1922), p. 179.

[6] The classic paper by Carl G. Hempel and Paul Oppenheim, "Studies in the Logic of Explanation," which has served as the point of departure for almost all subsequent discussion was first published just thirty years ago in 1948 in *Philosophy of Science,* Vol. 15, pp. 135–175.

the causal conception; Michael Scriven has been one of its chief advocates.[7]

2. The second of these basic intuitions is the notion that all scientific explanation involves *subsumption under laws*. This intuition seems to arise from consideration of developments in theoretical science. It has led to the general "covering law" conception of explanation, as well as to several formal "models" of explanation. According to this view, a fact is subsumed under one or more general laws if the assertion of its occurrence follows, either deductively or inductively, from statements of the laws (in conjunction, in some cases, with other premises). Since this view takes explanations to be arguments, I shall call it *the inferential conception;* Carl G. Hempel has been one of its ablest champions.[8]

Although the proponents of this inferential conception have often chosen to illustrate it with explanations of particular occurrences—e.g., why did the bunsen flame turn yellow on this particular occasion?—the paradigms which give it strongest support are explanations of general regularities. When we look to the history of science for the most outstanding cases of scientific explanations, such examples as Newton's explanation of Kepler's laws of planetary motion or Maxwell's electromagnetic explanation of optical phenomena come immediately to mind.

It is easy to guess how Laplace might have reacted to my question about his demon, and to the two basic intuitions I have just mentioned. The super-intelligence would have everything needed to provide scientific explanations. When, to mention one of Laplace's favorite examples, a seemingly haphazard phenomenon, such as the appearance of a comet, occurs, it can be explained by showing that it actually conforms to natural laws.[9] On Laplace's assumption of determinism, the demon possesses explanations of all happenings in the entire history of the world—past, present, and future. Explanation, for Laplace, seemed to consist in showing how events conform to the laws of nature, and these very laws provide the causal connections among the various states of the world. The Laplacian version of explanation thus seems to conform both to the causal conception and to the inferential conception.

Why, you might well ask, is not the Laplacian view of scientific explanation basically sound? Why do twentieth century philosophers find it necessary to engage in lengthy disputes over this matter? There are, I think, three fundamental reasons: (1) the causal conception faces the difficulty that no adequate treatment of causation has yet been offered; (2) the inferential conception suffers from the fact that it seriously misconstrues the nature of subsumption under laws; and (3) both conceptions have overlooked a central explanatory principle.

The inferential view, as elaborated in detail by Hempel and others, has been the dominant theory of scientific explanation in recent years—indeed, it has become virtually "the received view." From that standpoint, anyone who had attained the epistemic status of Laplace's demon could use the known laws and initial conditions to predict a future event, and when the event comes to pass, the argument which enabled us to predict it would ipso facto constitute an explanation of it. If, as Laplace believed, determinism is true, then every *future* event would thus be amenable to deductive-nomological explanation.

When, however, we consider the explanation of past events—events which occurred earlier than our initial conditions—we find a strange disparity. Although, by applying known laws, we can reliably *retrodict* any past occurrence on the basis of facts subsequent to the event, our intuitions rebel at the idea that we can *explain* events in

---

[7] See, for example, his recent paper, "Causation as Explanation," *Nous*, Vol. 9 (1975), pp. 3–16.

[8] Hempel's conceptions have been most thoroughly elaborated in his monographic essay, "Aspects of Scientific Explanation," in *Aspects of Scientific Explanation and Other Essays in the Philosophy of Science* (New York: Free Press, 1965), pp. 331–496.

[9] P. S. Laplace, *A Philosophical Essay on Probabilities* (New York: Dover Publications, 1951), pp. 3–6.

terms of subsequent conditions. Thus, although our inferences to future events qualify as explanations according to the inferential conception, our inferences to the past do not. Laplace's demon can, of course, construct explanations of past events by inferring the existence of still earlier conditions and, with the aid of the known laws, deducing the occurrence of the events to be explained from these conditions which held in the more remote past. But if, as the inferential conception maintains, explanations are essentially inferences, such an approach to explanation of past events seems strangely roundabout. Explanations demand an asymmetry not present in inferences.

When we drop the fiction of Laplace's demon, and relinquish the assumption of determinism, the asymmetry becomes even more striking. The demon can predict the future and retrodict the past with complete precision and reliability. We cannot. When we consider the comparative difficulty of prediction vs. retrodiction, it turns out that retrodiction enjoys a tremendous advantage. We have records of the past—tree rings, diaries, fossils—but none of the future. As a result, we can have extensive and detailed knowledge of the past which has no counterpart in knowledge about the future. From a newspaper account of an accident, we can retrodict all sorts of details which could not have been predicted an hour before the collision. But the newspaper story—even though it may *report* the explanation of the accident—surely does not *constitute* the explanation. We see that *inference* has a preferred temporal direction, and that *explanation* also has a preferred temporal direction. The fact that these two are opposite to each other is one thing which makes me seriously doubt that explanations are essentially arguments.[10] As we shall see, however, denying that explanations are arguments does not mean that we must give up the *covering law* conception. Subsumption under laws can take a different form.

Although the Laplacian conception bears strong similarities to the received view, there is a fundamental difference which must be noted. Laplace evidently believed that the explanations provided by his demon would be *causal explanations,* and the laws invoked would be *causal laws.* Hempel's deductive-nomological explanations are often casually called "causal explanations," but this is not accurate.[11] Hempel explicitly notes that some laws, such as the ideal gas law

$$PV = nRT$$

are non-causal. This law states a mathematical functional relationship among several quantities—pressure P, volume V, temperature T, number of moles of gas n, universal gas constant R—but gives no hint as to how a change in one of the values would lead causally to changes in others. As far as I know, Laplace did not make any distinction between causal and non-causal laws; Hempel has recognized the difference, but he allows noncausal as well as causal laws to function as covering laws in scientific explanations.

This attitude toward noncausal laws is surely too tolerant. If someone inflates an air mattress of a given size to a certain pressure under conditions which determine the temperature, we can deduce the value of n—the amount of air blown into it. The *subsequent* values of pressure, temperature, and volume are thus taken to explain the quantity of air *previously* introduced. Failure to require covering laws to be causal laws leads to a violation of the temporal requirement on explanations. This is not surprising. The asymmetry of explanation is inherited from the asymmetry of causation—namely, that causes precede their effects. At this point, it seems to me, we experience vividly the force of the intuitions underlying the causal conception of scientific explanation.

There is another reason for maintaining that non-causal laws cannot bear the burden of covering laws in scientific explanations. Non-causal regularities, instead of having explanatory force which enables them to provide understanding of

---

[10] In "A Third Dogma of Empiricism" in Robert Butts and Jaakko Hintikka, eds., *Basic Problems in Methodology and Linguistics* (Dordrecht: D. Reidel Publishing Co., 1977), pp. 149–166, I have given an extended systematic critique of the thesis (dogma?) that scientific explanations are arguments.

[11] Hempel, "Aspects of Scientific Explanation," pp. 352–354.

events in the world, cry out to be explained. Mariners, long before Newton, were fully aware of the correlation between the behavior of the tides and the position and phase of the moon. But inasmuch as they were totally ignorant of the causal relations involved, they rightly believed that they did not understand why the tides ebb and flow. When Newton provided the gravitational links, understanding was achieved. Similarly, I should say, the ideal gas law had little or no explanatory power until its causal underpinnings were furnished by the molecular-kinetic theory of gases. Keeping this consideration in mind, we realize that we must give at least as much attention to the explanations of regularities as we do to explanations of particular facts. I will argue, moreover, that these regularities demand causal explanation. Again, we must give the causal conception its due.

Having considered a number of preliminaries, I should now like to turn my attention to an attempt to outline a general theory of causal explanation. I shall not be trying to articulate a formal model; I shall be focusing upon general conceptions and fundamental principles rather than technical details. I am not suggesting, of course, that the technical details are dispensable—merely that this is not the time or place to try to go into them. Let me say at the outset that I shall be relying very heavily upon works by Russell (especially *The Analysis of Matter* and *Human Knowledge, Its Scope and Limits*) and Reichenbach (especially *The Direction of Time*). Although, to the best of my knowledge, neither of these authors ever published an article, or a book, or a chapter of a book devoted explicitly to scientific explanation, nevertheless it seems to me that a rather appealing theory of causal explanation can be constructed by putting together the insights expressed in the aforementioned works.

Developments in twentieth-century science should prepare us for the eventuality that some of our scientific explanations will have to be statistical—not merely because our knowledge is incomplete (as Laplace would have maintained), but rather, because nature itself is inherently statistical. Some of the laws used in explaining particular events will be statistical, and some of the regulari-

ties we wish to explain will also be statistical. I have been urging that causal considerations play a crucial role in explanation; indeed, I have just said that regularities—and this certainly includes statistical regularities—require causal explanation. I do not believe there is any conflict here. It seems to me that, by employing a statistical conception of causation along the lines developed by Patrick Suppes and Hans Reichenbach,[12] it is possible to fit together harmoniously the causal and statistical factors in explanatory contexts. Let me attempt to illustrate this point by discussing a concrete example.

A good deal of attention has recently been given in the press to cases of leukemia in military personnel who witnessed an atomic bomb test (code name "Smokey") at close range in 1957.[13] Statistical studies of the survivors of the bombings of Hiroshima and Nagasaki have established the fact that exposure to high levels of radiation, such as occur in an atomic blast, is statistically relevant to the occurrence of leukemia—indeed, that the probability of leukemia is closely correlated with the distance from the explosion.[14] A clear pattern of statistical relevance relations is exhibited here. If a particular person contracts leukemia, this fact may be explained by citing the fact that he was, say, 2 kilometers from the hypocenter at the time of the explosion. This relationship is further explained by the fact that individuals located at specific distances from atomic blasts of specified magnitude receive certain high doses of radiation.

This tragic example has several features to which I should like to call special attention:

1. The location of the individual at the time of the blast is statistically relevant to the occurrence of leukemia; the probability of leukemia for a person located 2 kilometers from the hypocen-

[12] Patrick Suppes, *A Probabilistic Theory of Causation* (Amsterdam: North-Holland Publishing Co., 1970); Hans Reichenbach, *The Direction of Time* (Berkeley & Los Angeles: University of California Press, 1956), Chap. IV.

[13] See *Nature*, Vol. 271 (2 Feb. 1978), p. 399.

[14] Irving Copi, *Introduction to Logic*, 4th ed. (New York: Macmillan Publishing Co., 1972), pp. 396–397, cites this example from *No More War* by Linus Pauling.

ter of an atomic blast is radically different from the probability of the disease in the population at large. Notice that the probability of such an individual contracting leukemia is not high; it is much smaller than one-half—indeed, in the case of Smokey it is much less than 1/100. But it is markedly higher than for a random member of the entire human population. It is the *statistical relevance* of exposure to an atomic blast, not a high probability, which has explanatory force.[15] Such examples defy explanation according to an inferential view, which requires high inductive probability for statistical explanation.[16] The case of leukemia is subsumed under a statistical regularity, but it does not "follow inductively" from the explanatory facts.

2. There is a *causal process* which connects the occurrence of the bomb blast with the physiological harm done to people at some distance from the explosion. High energy radiation, released in the nuclear reactions, traverses the space between the blast and the individual. Although some of the details may not yet be known, it is a well-established fact that such radiation does interact with cells in a way which makes them susceptible to leukemia at some later time.

3. At each end of the causal process—i.e., the transmission of radiation from the bomb to the person—there is a *causal interaction*. The radiation is emitted as a result of a nuclear interaction when the bomb explodes, and it is absorbed by cells in the body of the victim. Each of these interactions may well be irreducibly statistical and indeterministic, but that is no reason to deny that they are causal.

4. The causal processes begin at a central place, and they travel outward at a finite velocity. A rather complex set of statistical relevance relations is explained by the propagation of a process, or set of processes, from a common central event.

In undertaking a general characterization of causal explanation, we must begin by carefully distinguishing between causal processes and causal interactions. The transmission of light from one place to another, and the motion of a material particle, are obvious examples of causal processes. The collision of two billiard balls, and the emission or absorption of a photon, are standard examples of causal interactions. Interactions are the sorts of things we are inclined to identify as events. Relative to a particular context, an event is comparatively small in its spatial and temporal dimensions; processes typically have much larger durations, and they may be more extended in space as well. A light ray, traveling to earth from a distant star, is a process which covers a large distance and lasts for a long time. What I am calling a "causal process" is similar to what Russell called a "causal line."[17]

When we attempt to identify causal processes, it is of crucial importance to distinguish them from such pseudo-processes as a shadow moving across the landscape. This can best be done, I believe, by invoking Reichenbach's *mark criterion*.[18] Causal processes are capable of propagating marks or modifications imposed upon them; pseudo-processes are not. An automobile traveling along a road is an example of a causal process. If a fender is scraped as a result of a collision with a stone wall, the mark of that collision will be carried on by the car long after the interaction with the wall occurred. The shadow of a car moving

---

[15] According to the article in *Nature* (note 13), "the eight reported cases of leukemia among 2235 [soldiers] was 'out of the normal range'." Dr. Karl Z. Morgan "had 'no doubt whatever' that [the] radiation had caused the leukemia now found in those who had taken part in the maneuvers."

[16] Hempel's inductive-statistical model, as formulated in "Aspects of Scientific Explanation" (1965), embodied such a high probability requirement, but in "Nachwort 1976"—inserted into a German translation of this article (*Aspekte wissenschaftlicher Erklärung*, Walter de Gruyter, 1977)—this requirement is retracted.

[17] Bertrand Russell, *Human Knowledge, Its Scope and Limits* (New York: Simon and Schuster, 1948), p. 459.

[18] Hans Reichenbach, *The Philosophy of Space and Time* (New York: Dover Publications, 1958), Sec. 21.

along the shoulder is a pseudo-process. If it is deformed as it encounters a stone wall, it will immediately resume its former shape as soon as it passes by the wall. It will not transmit a mark or modification. For this reason, we say that a causal process can transmit information or causal influence; a pseudo-process cannot.[19]

When I say that a causal process has the capability of transmitting a causal influence, it might be supposed that I am introducing precisely the sort of mysterious power Hume warned us against. It seems to me that this danger can be circumvented by employing an adaptation of the "at-at" theory of motion, which Russell used so effectively in dealing with Zeno's paradoz of the flying arrow.[20] The flying arrow—which is, by the way, a causal process—gets from one place to another by being *at* the appropriate intermediate points of space *at* the appropriate instants of time. Nothing more is involved in getting *from* one point *to* another. A mark, analogously, can be said to be propagated from the point of interaction at which it is imposed to later stages in the process if it appears *at* the appropriate intermediate stages in the process *at* the appropriate times without additional interactions which regenerate the mark. The precise formulation of this condition is a bit tricky, but I believe the basic idea is simple, and that the details can be worked out.[21]

If this analysis of causal processes is satisfactory, we have an answer to the question, raised by Hume, concerning the connection between cause and effect. If we think of a cause as one event, and of an effect as a distinct event, then the connection between them is simply a spatio-temporally continuous causal process. This sort of answer did not occur to Hume because he did not distinguish between causal processes and causal interactions. When he tried to analyze the connections between distinct events, he treated them as if they were chains of events with discrete links, rather than processes analogous to continuous filaments. I am inclined to attribute considerable philosophical significance to the fact that each link in a chain has adjacent links, while the points in a continuum do not have next-door neighbors. This consideration played an important role in Russell's discussion of Zeno's paradoxes.[22]

After distinguishing between causal interactions and causal processes, and after introducing a criterion by means of which to discriminate the pseudo-processes from the genuine causal processes, we must consider certain configurations of processes which have special explanatory import. Russell noted that we often find similar structures grouped symmetrically about a center—for example, concentric waves moving across an otherwise smooth surface of a pond, or sound waves moving out from a central region, or perceptions of many people viewing a stage from different seats in a theatre. In such cases, Russell postulates the existence of a central event—a pebble dropped into the pond, a starter's gun going off at a race track, or a play being performed upon the stage—from which the complex array emanates.[23] It is noteworthy that Russell never suggests that the central event is to be explained on the basis of convergence of influences from remote regions upon that locale.

Reichenbach articulated a closely related idea in his *principle of the common cause*. If two or more events of certain types occur at different places, but occur at the same time more frequently than is to be expected if they occurred independently, then this apparent coincidence is to be

---

[19] See my "Theoretical Explanation," Sec. 3, pp. 129–134, in Stephan Körner, ed., *Explanation* (Oxford: Basil Blackwell, 1975), for a more detailed discussion of this distinction. It is an unfortunate lacuna in Russell's discussion of causal lines—though one which can easily be repaired—that he does not notice the distinction between causal processes and pseudo-processes.

[20] See Wesley C. Salmon, ed., *Zeno's Paradoxes* (Indianapolis: Bobbs-Merrill, 1970), p. 23, for a description of this "theory."

[21] I have made an attempt to elaborate this idea in "An 'At-At' Theory of Causal Influence," *Philosophy of Science*, Vol. 44, No. 2 (June 1977), pp. 215–224. Because of a criticism due to Nancy Cartwright, I now realize that the formulation given in this article is not entirely satisfactory, but I think the difficulty can be repaired.

[22] Russell, *Our Knowledge of the External World*, Lecture VI, "The Problem of Infinity Considered Historically." The relevant portions are reprinted in my anthology, *Zeno's Paradoxes*.

[23] Russell, *Human Knowledge*, pp. 460–475.

explained in terms of a common causal anteced-ent.[24] If, for example, all of the electric lights in a particular area go out simultaneously, we do not believe that they just happened by chance to burn out at the same time. We attribute the coincidence to a common cause such as a blown fuse, a downed transmission line, or trouble at the gener-ating station. If all of the students in a dormitory fall ill on the same night, it is attributed to spoiled food in the meal which all of them ate. Russell's similar structures arranged symmetrically about a center obviously qualify as the sorts of coinci-dences which require common causes for their explanations.[25]

In order to formulate his common cause prin-ciple more precisely, Reichenbach defined what he called a *conjunctive fork.* Suppose we have events of two types, *A* and *B,* which happen in conjunction more often than they would if they were statistically independent of one another. For example, let *A* and *B* stand for colorblindness in two brothers. There is a certain probability that a male, selected from the population at random, will have that affliction, but since it is hereditary, occurrences in male siblings are not independent. The probability that both will have it is greater than the product of the two respective probabili-ties. In cases of such statistical dependencies, we invoke a common cause, *C,* which accounts for them; in this case, it is a genetic factor carried by the mother. In order to satisfy the conditions for a conjunctive fork, events of the types *A* and *B* must occur independently in the absence of the com-mon cause *C*—that is, for two unrelated males, the probability of both being colorblind is equal to the product of the two separate probabilities. Fur-thermore, the probabilities of *A* and *B* must each be increased above their overall values if *C* is present. Clearly the probability of colorblindness is greater in sons of mothers carrying the genetic factor than it is among all male children regardless of the genetic make-up of their mothers. Finally,

Reichenbach stipulates, the dependency between *A* and *B* is absorbed into the occurrence of the common cause *C,* in the sense that the probability of *A* and *B* given *C* equals the product of the prob-ability of *A* given *C* and the probability of *B* given *C.* This is true in the colorblindness case. Exclud-ing pairs of identical twins, the question of whether a male child inherits colorblindness from the mother who carries the genetic trait depends only upon the genetic relationship between that child and his mother, not upon whether other sons happened to inherit the trait.[26] Note that screen-ing-off occurs here.[27] While the colorblindness of a brother is statistically relevant to colorblindness in a boy, it becomes irrelevant if the genetic factor is known to be present in the mother.

Reichenbach obviously was not the first phi-losopher to notice that we explain coincidences in terms of common causal antecedents. Leibniz postulated a pre-established harmony for his win-dowless monads which mirror the same world, and the occasionalists postulated God as the coor-dinator of mind and body. Reichenbach was, to the best of my knowledge, the first to give a pre-cise characterization of the conjunctive fork, and to formulate the general principle that conjunctive forks are open only to the future, not to the past.[28] The result is that we cannot explain coincidences on the basis of future effects, but only on the basis of antecedent causes. A widespread blackout is explained by a power failure, not by the looting which occurs as a consequence. (A common ef-fect, *E,* may form a conjunctive fork with *A* and *B,* but only if there is also a common cause, *C.*) The

---

[24] Reichenbach, *The Direction of Time,* Sec. 19.

[25] In "Theoretical Explanation" I discuss the explanatory import of the common cause principle in greater detail.

---

[26] Reichenbach offers the following formal definition of a con-junctive fork *ACB*

$$P(A\&B/C) = P(A/C) \times P(B/C)$$
$$P(A\&B/\overline{C}) = P(A/\overline{C}) \times P(B/\overline{C})$$
$$P(A/C) > P(A/\overline{C})$$
$$P(B/C) > P(B/\overline{C})$$

in *The Direction of Time,* p. 159. I have changed these formulas from Reichenbach's notation into a more standard one.

[27] *C* screens-off *A* from *B* if

$$P(A/C\&B) = P(A/C) \neq P(A/B)$$

[28] *The Direction of Time,* pp. 162–163.

principle that conjunctive forks are not open to the past accounts for Russell's principle that symmetrical patterns emanate from a central source—they do not converge from afar upon the central point. It is also closely related to the operation of the second law of thermodynamics and the increase of entropy in the physical world.

The common cause principle has, I believe, deep explanatory significance. Bas van Fraassen has recently subjected it to careful scrutiny, and he has convinced me that Reichenbach's formulation in terms of the conjunctive fork, as he defined it, is faulty.[29] (We do not, however, agree about the nature of the flaw.) There are, it seems, certain sorts of causal *interactions* in which the resulting effects are more strongly correlated with one another than is allowed in Reichenbach's conjunctive forks. If, for example, an energetic photon collides with an electron in a Compton scattering experiment, there is a certain probability that a photon with a given smaller energy will emerge, and there is a certain probability that the electron will be kicked out with a given kinetic energy (see Figure 1). However, because of the law of conservation of energy, there is a strong correspondence between the two energies—their sum must be close to the energy of the incident photon. Thus, the probability of getting a photon with energy E_1 and an electron with energy E_2, where $E_1 + E_2$ is approximately equal to E (the energy of the incident photon), is much greater than the product of the probabilities of each energy occurring separately. Assume, for example, that there is a probability of 0.1 that a photon of energy E_1 will emerge if a photon of energy E impinges on a given target, and assume that there is a probability of 0.1 that an electron with kinetic energy E_2 will emerge under the same circumstances (where E, E_1, and E_2 are related as the law of conservation of energy demands). In this case the probability of the joint result is not 0.01, the product of the separate

COMPTON SCATTERING

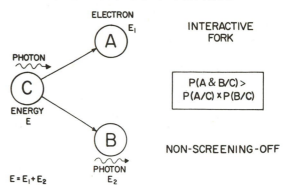

Figure 1

probabilities, but 0.1, for each result will occur if and only if the other does.[30] The same relationships could be illustrated by such macroscopic events as collisions of billiard balls, but I have chosen Compton scattering because there is good reason to believe that events of that type are irreducibly statistical. Given a high energy photon impinging upon the electron in a given atom, there is no way, even in principle, of predicting with certainty the energies of the photon and electron which result from the interaction.

This sort of interaction stands in sharp contrast with the sort of statistical dependency we have in the leukemia example (see Figure 2, which also represents the relationships in the colorblindness case). In the absence of a strong source of radiation, such as the atomic blast, we may assume that the probability of next-door neighbors contracting the disease equals the product of the probabilities for each of them separately. If, however, we consider two next-door neighbors who lived at a distance of 2 kilometers from the hypocenter of the

[29] Bas C. van Fraassen, "The Pragmatics of Explanation," *American Philosophical Quarterly*, Vol. 14, No. 2 (April 1977), pp. 143–150. This paper was presented at the 51st Annual Meeting of the American Philosophical Association, Pacific Division, March 1977.

[30] The relation between $E_1 + E_2$ and E is an approximate rather than a precise equality because the ejected electron has some energy of its own before scattering, but this energy is so small compared with the energy of the incident X ray or γ-ray photon that it can be neglected. When I refer to the probability that the scattered photon and electron will have energies E_1 and E_2, respectively, this should be taken to mean that these energies fall within some specified interval, not that they have exact values.

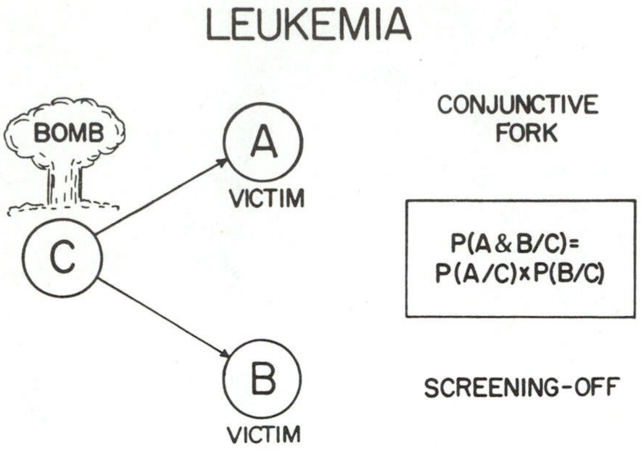

LEUKEMIA

CONJUNCTIVE FORK

$$P(A\&B/C)= P(A/C)\times P(B/C)$$

SCREENING-OFF

Figure 2

atomic explosion, the probability of both of them contracting leukemia is much greater than it would be for any two randomly selected members of the population at large. This apparent dependency between the two leukemia cases is not a direct physical dependency between them; it is merely a statistical result of the fact that the probability for each of them has been enhanced independently of the other by being located in close proximity to the atomic explosion. But the individual photons of radiation which impinge upon the two victims are emitted independently, travel independently, and damage living tissues independently.

It thus appears that there are two kinds of causal forks: (1) Reichenbach's *conjunctive forks*, in which the common cause screens-off the one effect from the other, which are exemplified by the colorblindness and leukemia cases, and (2) *interactive forks*, exemplified by the Compton scattering of a photon and an electron. In forks of the interactive sort, the common cause does not screen-off the one effect from the other. The probability that the electron will be ejected with kinetic energy E_2 given an incident photon of energy E is *not equal to* the probability that the electron will emerge with energy E_2 given an incident photon of energy E and a scattered photon of energy E_1. In the conjunctive fork, the common cause C absorbs the dependency between the effects A and B, for the probability of A and B given C is *equal to* the product of the probability of A given C and the

probability of B given C. In the interactive fork, the common cause C does not absorb the dependency between the effects A and B, for the probability of A and B given C is *greater than* the product of the two separate conditional probabilities.[31]

Recognition and characterization of the interactive fork enables us to fill a serious lacuna in the treatment up to this point. I have discussed causal processes, indicating roughly how they are to be characterized, and I have mentioned causal interactions, but have said nothing about their characterization. Indeed, the criterion by which we distinguished causal processes from pseudo-processes involved the use of marks, and marks are obviously results of causal interactions. Thus, our account stands in serious need of a characterization of causal interactions, and the interactive fork enables us, I believe, to furnish it.

There is a strong temptation to think of events as basic types of entities, and to construe processes—real or pseudo—as collections of events. This viewpoint may be due, at least in part, to the fact that the space-time interval between events is a fundamental invariant of the special theory of relativity, and that events thus enjoy an especially fundamental status. I suggest, nevertheless, that we reverse the approach. Let us begin with processes (which have not yet been sorted out into causal and pseudo) and look at their intersections. We can be reassured about the legitimacy of this new orientation by the fact that the basic space-time structure of both special relativity and general

---

[31] As the boxed formulas in Figures 1 and 2 indicate, the difference between a conjunctive fork and an interactive fork lies in the difference between

$$P(A\&B/C) = P(A/C) \times P(B/C)$$

and

$$P(A\&B/C) > P(A/C) \times P(B/C).$$

The remaining formulas given in Note 26 may be incorporated into the definitions of both kinds of forks. One reason why Reichenbach may have failed to notice the interactive fork is that, in the special case in which

$$P(A/C) = P(B/C) = 1$$

the conjunctive fork shares a fundamental property of the interactive fork, namely, a perfect correlation between A and B given C. Many of his illustrative examples are instances of this special case.

relativity can be built upon processes without direct recourse to events.[32] An electron traveling through space is a process, and so is a photon; if they collide, that is an intersection. A light pulse traveling from a beacon to a screen is a process, and a piece of red glass standing in the path is another; the light passing through the glass is an intersection. Both of these intersections constitute interactions. If two light beams cross one another, we have an intersection without an interaction—except in the extremely unlikely event of a particle-like collision between photons. What we want to say, very roughly, is that when two processes intersect, and both are modified in such ways that the changes in one are correlated with changes in the other—in the manner of an interactive fork (see Figure 3)—we have a causal interaction. There are technical details to be worked out before we can claim to have a satisfactory account, but the general idea seems clear enough.[33]

I should like to commend the principle of the common cause—so construed as to make reference to both conjunctive forks and interactive forks—to your serious consideration.[34] Several of its uses have already been mentioned and illustrated. *First,* it supplies a schema for the straightforward explanations of everyday sorts of otherwise improbable coincidences. *Second,* it is the source of the fundamental temporal asymmetry of causality, and it accounts for the temporal asymmetry we impose upon scientific explanations.

CAUSAL INTERACTION

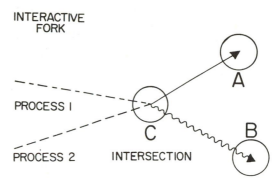

Figure 3

Third, it provides the key to the explication of the concept of causal interaction. These considerations certainly testify to its philosophical importance.

There are, however, two additional applications to which I should like to call attention. *Fourth,* as Russell showed, the principle plays a fundamental role in the causal theory of perception. When various observers (including cameras as well as human beings) arranged around a central region, such as a stage in theatre-in-the-round, have perceptions that correspond systematically with one another in the customary way, we may infer, with reasonable reliability, that they have a common cause—namely, a drama being performed on the stage.[35] This fact has considerable epistemological import.

Fifth, the principle of the common cause can be invoked to support scientific realism.[36] Suppose, going back to a previous example, we have postulated the existence of molecules to provide a causal explanation of the phenomena governed by

[32] For the special theory of relativity, this has been shown by John Winnie in "The Causal Theory of Space-time," in John S. Earman, Clark N. Glymour, and John J. Stachel, eds., *Foundations of Space-Time Theories, Minnesota Studies in the Philosophy of Science,* Vol. VIII (Minneapolis: University of Minnesota Press, 1977), pp. 134–205, which utilizes much earlier results of A. A. Robb. For general relativity, the approach is discussed under the heading "The Geodesic Method" in Adolf Grünbaum, *Philosophical Problems of Space and Time,* 2nd ed. (Dordrecht: D. Reidel Publishing Co., 1973), pp. 735–750.

[33] The whole idea of characterizing causal interactions in terms of forks was suggested by Philip von Bretzel in "Concerning a Probabilistic Theory of Causation Adequate for the Causal Theory of Time," *Synthese,* Vol. 35, No. 2 (June 1977), pp. 173–190, especially Note 13.

[34] It strikes me as an unfortunate fact that this important principle seems to have gone largely unnoticed by philosophers ever since its publication in Reichenbach's *The Direction of Time* in 1956.

[35] Russell, *Human Knowledge,* pp. 491–492.

[36] Scientific realism is a popular doctrine nowadays, and most contemporary philosophers of science probably do not feel any pressing need for additional arguments to support this view. Although I am thoroughly convinced (in my heart) that scientific realism is correct, I am largely dissatisfied with the arguments usually brought in support of it. The argument I am about to outline seems to me more satisfactory than others.

the ideal gas law. We will naturally be curious about their properties—how large they are, how massive they are, how many there are. An appeal to Brownian motion enables us to infer such things. By microscopic examination of smoke particles suspended in a gas, we can ascertain their average kinetic energies, and since the observed system can be assumed to be in a state of thermal equilibrium, we can immediately infer the average kinetic energies of the molecules of the gas in which the particles are suspended. Since average velocities of the molecules are straightforwardly ascertainable by experiment, we can easily find the masses of the individual molecules, and hence, the number of molecules in a given sample of gas. If the sample consists of precisely one mole (gram molecular weight) of the particular gas, the number of molecules in the sample is Avogadro's number—a fundamental physical constant. Thus, the causal explanation of Brownian motion yields detailed quantitative information about the micro-entities of which the gas is composed.

Now, consider another phenomenon which appears to be of an altogether different sort. If an electric current is passed through an electrolytic solution—for example, one containing a silver salt—a certain amount of metallic silver is deposited on the cathode. The amount deposited is proportional to the amount of electric charge which passes through the solution. In constructing a causal explanation of this phenomenon (known as electrolysis), we postulate that charged ions travel through the solution, and that the amount of charge required to deposit a singly charged ion is equal to the charge on the electron. The magnitude of the electron charge was empirically determined through the work of J. J. Thomson and Robert Millikan. The amount of electric charge required to deposit one mole of a monovalent metal is known as the Faraday, and by experimental determination, it is equal to 96,487 coulombs. When this number is divided by the charge on the electron (-1.602×10^{-19} coulombs), the result is Avogadro's number. Indeed, the Faraday is simply Avogadro's number of electron charges.

The fundamental fact to which I wish to call attention is that the value of Avogadro's number ascertained from the analysis of Brownian motion agrees, within the limits of experimental error, with the value obtained by electrolytic measurement. Without a common causal antecedent, such agreement would constitute a remarkable coincidence. The point may be put in this way. From the molecular kinetic theory of gases we can derive the statement form, "The number of molecules in a mole of gas is _____ ." From the electrochemical theory of electrolysis, we can derive the statement form, "The number of electron charges in a Faraday is _____ ." The astonishing fact is that the same number fills both blanks. In my opinion, the instrumentalist cannot, with impunity, ignore what must be an amazing correspondence between what happens when one scientist is watching smoke particles dancing in a container of gas while another scientist in a different laboratory is observing the electroplating of silver. Without an underlying causal mechanism—of the sort involved in the postulation of atoms, molecules, and ions—the coincidence would be as miraculous as if the number of grapes harvested in California in any given year were equal, up to the limits of observational error, to the number of coffee beans produced in Brazil in the same year. Avogadro's number, I must add, can be ascertained in a variety of other ways as well—e.g., X-ray diffraction from crystals—which also appear to be entirely different unless we postulate the existence of atoms, molecules, and ions. The principle of the common cause thus seems to apply directly to the explanation of observable regularities by appeal to unobservable entities. In this instance, to be sure, the common cause is not some sort of event; it is rather a common constant underlying structure which manifests itself in a variety of different situations.

Let me now summarize the picture of scientific explanation I have tried to outline. If we wish to explain a particular event, such as death by leukemia of GI Joe, we begin by assembling the factors statistically relevant to that occurrence—for example, his distance from the atomic explosion, the magnitude of the blast, and the type of shelter he was in. There will be many others, no doubt, but these will do for purposes of illustration. We must also obtain the probability values associated with the relevancy relations. The statistical relevance relations are statistical regularities, and we proceed to explain them. Although this differs substantially from things I have said previously, I no longer believe that the assemblage of relevant factors provides a complete explanation—or much of anything in the way of an explanation.[37] We do, I believe, have a bona fide explanation of an event if we have a complete set of statistically relevant factors, the pertinent probability values, *and* causal explanations of the relevance relations. Subsumption of a particular occurrence under statistical regularities—which, we recall, does not imply anything about the construction of deductive or inductive arguments—is a necessary part of any adequate explanation of its occurrence, but it is not the whole story. The causal explanation of the regularity is also needed. This claim, it should be noted, is in direct conflict with the received view, according to which the mere subsumption—deductive or inductive—of an event under a lawful regularity constitutes a complete explanation. One can, according to the received view, go on to ask for an explanation of any law used to explain a given event, but that is a different explanation. I am suggesting, on the contrary, that if the regularity invoked is not a causal regularity, then a causal explanation of that very regularity must be made part of the explanation of the event.

If we have events of two types, *A* and *B,* whose respective members are not spatio-temporally contiguous, but whose occurrences are correlated with one another, the causal explanation of this regularity may take either of two forms. Either there is a direct causal connection from *A* to *B* or from *B* to *A,* or there is a common cause, *C,* which accounts for the statistical dependency. In either case, those events which stand in the cause-effect relation to one another are joined by a causal process.[38] The distinct events *A, B,* and *C* which are thus related constitute interactions—as defined in terms of an interactive fork—at the appropriate places in the respective causal processes. The interactions *produce* modifications in the causal processes, and the causal processes *transmit* the modifications. Statistical dependency relations arise out of local interactions—there is no action-at-a-distance (as far as macro-phenomena are concerned, at least)—and they are propagated through the world by causal processes. In our leukemia example, a slow neutron, impinging upon a uranium atom, has a certain probability of inducing nuclear fission, and if fission occurs, gamma radiation is emitted. The gamma ray travels through space, and it may interact with a human cell, producing a modification which may leave the cell open to attack by the virus associated with leukemia. The fact that many such interactions of neutrons with fissionable nuclei are occurring in close spatio-temporal proximity, giving rise to processes which radiate in all directions, produces a pattern of statistical dependency relations. After initiation, these processes go on independently of one another, but they do produce relationships which can be described by means of the conjunctive fork.

Causal processes and causal interactions are, of course, governed by various laws—e.g., conservation of energy and momentum. In a causal process, such as the propagation of a light wave or the free motion of a material particle, energy is being transmitted. The distinction between causal processes and pseudo-processes lies in the distinction between the transmission of energy from one space-time locale to another and the mere appearance of energy at various space-time locations. When causal interactions occur—not merely in-

---

[37] Compare Wesley C. Salmon, et al., *Statistical Explanation and Statistical Relevance* (Pittsburgh: University of Pittsburgh Press, 1971), p. 78. There I ask, "What more could one ask of an explanation?" The present paper attempts to present at least part of the answer.

[38] Reichenbach believed that various causal relations, including conjunctive forks, could be explicated entirely in terms of the statistical relations among the events involved. I do not believe this is possible; it seems to me that we must also establish the appropriate connections via causal processes.

tersections of processes—we have energy and/or momentum transfer. Such laws as conservation of energy and momentum are causal laws in the sense that they are regularities exhibited by causal processes and interactions.

Near the beginning, I suggested that deduction of a restricted law from a more general law constitutes a paradigm of a certain type of explanation. No theory of scientific explanation can hope to be successful unless it can handle cases of this sort. Lenz's law, for example, which governs the direction of flow of an electric current generated by a changing magnetic field, can be deduced from the law of conservation of energy. But this deductive relation shows that the more restricted regularity is simply part of a more comprehensive physical pattern expressed by the law of conservation of energy. Similarly, Kepler's laws of planetary motion describe a restricted subclass of the class of all motions governed by Newtonian mechanics. The deductive relations *exhibit* what amounts to a part-whole relationship, but it is, in my opinion, the physical relationship between the more comprehensive physical regularity and the less comprehensive physical regularity which has explanatory significance. I should like to put it this way. An explanation may sometimes provide the materials out of which an argument, deductive or inductive, can be constructed; an argument may sometimes exhibit explanatory relations. It does not follow, however, that explanations are arguments.

Earlier in this discussion, I mentioned three shortcomings in the most widely held theories of scientific explanation. I should now like to indicate the ways in which the theory I have been outlining attempts to cope with these problems. (1) The causal conception, I claimed, has lacked an adequate analysis of causation. The foregoing explications of causal processes and causal interactions were intended to fill that gap. (2) The inferential conception, I claimed, had misconstrued the relation of subsumption under law. When we see how statistical relevance relations can be brought to bear upon facts-to-be-explained, we discover that it is possible to have a *covering law*

conception of scientific explanation without regarding explanations as arguments. The recognition that subsumption of narrower regularities under broader regularities can be viewed as a part-whole relation reinforces that point. At the same time, it suggests a reason for the tremendous appeal of the inferential conception in the first place. (3) Both of the popular conceptions, I claimed, overlooked a fundamental explanatory principle. That principle, obviously, is the principle of the common cause. I have tried to display its enormous explanatory significance. The theory outlined above is designed to overcome all three of these difficulties.

On the basis of the foregoing characterization of scientific explanation, how should we answer the question posed at the outset? What does Laplace's demon lack, if anything, with respect to the explanatory aim of science? Several items may be mentioned. The demon *may* lack an adequate recognition of the distinction between causal laws and non-causal regularities; it *may* lack adequate knowledge of causal processes and of their ability to propagate causal influence; and it *may* lack adequate appreciation of the role of causal interactions in *producing* changes and regularities in the world. None of these capabilities was explicitly demanded by Laplace, for his analysis of causal relations in general was rather superficial.

What does scientific explanation offer, over and above the inferential capacity of prediction and retrodiction, at which the Laplacian demon excelled? It provides knowledge of the mechanisms of *production* and *propagation* of structure in the world. That goes some distance beyond mere recognition of regularities, and of the possibility of subsuming particular phenomena thereunder. It is my view that knowledge of the mechanisms of production and propagation of structure in the world yields scientific understanding, and that this is what we seek when we pose explanation-seeking why questions. The answers are well worth having. That is why we ask not only "What?" but "Why?"

The Pragmatics of Explanation

Bas van Fraassen

A BIASED HISTORY

Current discussion of explanation draws on three decades of debate, which began with Hempel and Oppenheim's "Studies in the Logic of Explanation" (1948).[1] The literature is now voluminous, so that a retrospective must of necessity be biased. I shall bias my account in such a way that it illustrates my diagnoses of the difficulties and points suggestively to the solution I shall offer below.

Hempel: Grounds for Belief

Hempel has probably written more papers about scientific explanation than anyone; but because they are well known I shall focus on the short summary which he gave of his views in 1966.[2] There he lists two criteria for what is an explanation:

explanatory relevance: the explanatory information adduced affords good grounds for believing that the phenomenon did, or does, indeed occur.

testability: the statements constituting a scientific explanation must be capable of empirical test.

In each explanation, the information adduced has two components, one ("the laws"), information supplied by a theory, and the other ("the initial or boundary conditions"), auxiliary factual information. The relationship of providing good grounds is explicated separately for statistical and non-statistical theories. In the latter, the information

implies the fact that is explained; in the former, it *bestows high probability* on that fact.

As Hempel himself points out, the first criterion does not provide either sufficient or necessary conditions for explanation. This was established through a series of examples given by various writers (but especially Michael Scriven and Sylvain Bromberger), which have passed into the philosophical folklore.

First, giving good grounds for belief does not always amount to explanation. This is most strikingly apparent in examples of the asymmetry of explanation. In such cases, two propositions are strictly equivalent (relative to the accepted background theory), and the one can be adduced to explain why the other is the case, but not conversely. Aristotle already gave examples of this sort (*Posterior Analytics,* Book I, Chapter 13). Hempel mentions the phenomenon of the *red shift:* Relative to accepted physics, the galaxies are receding from us if and only if the light received from them exhibits a shift toward the red end of the spectrum. While the receding of the galaxies can be cited as the reason for the red shift, it hardly makes sense to say that the red shift is the reason for their motion. A more simpleminded example is provided by the *barometer,* if we accept the simplified hypothesis that it falls exactly when a storm is coming, yet does not explain (but rather, is explained by) the fact that a storm is coming. In both examples, good grounds of belief are provided by either proposition for the other. The flagpole is perhaps the most famous asymmetry. Suppose that a flagpole, 100 feet high, casts a shadow 75 feet long. We can explain the length of the shadow by noting the angle of elevation of the sun, and appealing to the accepted theory that light travels in straight lines. For given that angle,

---

[1] C. G. Hempel and P. Oppenheim, "Studies in the Logic of Explanation." *Philosophy of Science,* 15 (1948), 135–75.

[2] C. G. Hempel, *Philosophy of Natural Science* (Englewood Cliffs, N.J.: 1966), pp. 48f.; see S. Bromberger, "Why-Questions," (n. 14 below) for some of the counterexamples.

and the height of the pole, trigonometry enables us to deduce the length of the base of the right-angled triangle formed by pole, light ray, and shadow. However, we can similarly deduce the length of the pole from the length of the shadow plus the angle of elevation. Yet if someone asks us why the pole is 100 feet high, we cannot explain that fact by saying "because it has a shadow 75 feet long." The most we could explain that way is how we *came to know,* or how he might himself verify the claim, that the pole is indeed so high.

Second, not every explanation is a case in which good grounds for belief are given. The famous example for this is *paresis:* No one contracts this dreadful illness unless he had latent, untreated syphilis. If someone asked the doctor to explain to him why he came down with this disease, the doctor would surely say, "Because you had latent syphilis which was left untreated." But only a low percentage of such cases are followed by paresis. Hence if one knew of someone that he might have syphilis, it would be reasonable to warn him that, if left untreated, he might contract paresis—but not reasonable to expect him to get it. Certainly we do not have here the high probability demanded by Hempel.

It might be replied that the doctor has only a partial explanation, that there are further factors which medical science will eventually discover. This reply is based on faith that the world is, for macroscopic phenomena at least, deterministic or nearly so. But the same point can be made with examples in which we do not believe that there is further information to be had, even in principle. The half-life of uranium U^{238} is $(4.5) \cdot 10^9$ years. Hence the probability that a given small enough sample of uranium will emit radiation in a specified small interval of time is low. Suppose, however, that it does. We still say that atomic physics explains this, the explanation being that this material was uranium, which has a certain atomic structure, and hence is subject to spontaneous decay. Indeed, atomic physics has many more examples of events of very low probability, which are explained in terms of the structure of the atoms involved. Although there are physicists and philosophers who argue that the theory must there-

fore be incomplete (one of them being Einstein, who said "God does not play with dice") the prevalent view is that it is a contingent matter whether the world is ultimately deterministic or not.

In addition to the above, Wesley Salmon raised the vexing problem of *relevance,* which is mentioned in the title of the first criterion but does not enter into its explication. Two examples that meet the requirements of providing good grounds are:

John Jones was almost certain to recover from his cold because he took vitamin C, and almost all colds clear up within a week of taking vitamin C.

John Jones avoided becoming pregnant during the past year, for he has taken his wife's birth control pills regularly, and every man who takes birth control pills avoids pregnancy.[3]

Salmon assumed here that almost all colds spontaneously clear up within a week. There is then something seriously wrong with these "explanations," since the information adduced is wholly or partly irrelevant. So the criterion would have to be amended at least to read, "provides good and *relevant* grounds." This raises the problem of explicating relevance, also not an easy matter.

The second criterion, of testability, is met by all scientific theories, and by all the auxiliary information adduced in the above examples, so it cannot help to ameliorate these difficulties. . . .

The Difficulties: Asymmetries and Rejections

There are two main difficulties, illustrated by the old paresis and barometer examples, which none of the examined positions can handle. The first is that there are cases, clearly in a theory's domain, where the request for explanation is nevertheless rejected. We can explain why John, rather than his brothers, contracted paresis, for he had syphilis; but not why he, among all those syphilitics, got paresis. Medical science is incomplete, and hopes to find the answer some day. But the exam-

---

[3] W. C. Salmon, *Statistical Explanation and Statistical Relevance* (Pittsburgh: University of Pittsburgh Press, 1971), pp. 33f.

ple of the uranium atom disintegrating just then rather than later is formally similar and we believe the theory to be complete. We also reject such questions as the Aristotelians asked the Galileans: Why does a body free of impressed forces retain its velocity? The importance of this sort of case, and its pervasive character, has been repeatedly discussed by Adolf Grünbaum. It was also noted, in a different context, by Thomas Kuhn.[4] Examples he gives of explanation requests that were considered legitimate in some periods and rejected in others cover a wide range of topics. They include the qualities of compounds in chemical theory (explained before Lavoisier's reform, and not considered something to be explained in the nineteenth century, but now again the subject of chemical explanation). Clerk Maxwell accepted as legitimate the request to explain electromagnetic phenomena within mechanics. As his theory became more successful and more widely accepted, scientists ceased to see the lack of this as a shortcoming. The same had happened with Newton's theory of gravitation, which did not (in the opinion of Newton or his contemporaries) contain an explanation of gravitational phenomena, but only a description. In both cases there came a stage at which such problems were classed as intrinsically illegitimate, and regarded exactly as the request for an explanation of why a body retains its velocity in the absence of impressed forces. While all of this may be interpreted in various ways (such as through Kuhn's theory of paradigms) the important fact for the theory of explanation is that not everything in a theory's domain is a legitimate topic for why-questions; and that what is, is not determinable *a priori*.

The second difficulty is the asymmetry revealed by the barometer, the red shift, and the flagpole examples: Even if the theory implies that one condition obtains when and only when another does, it may be that it explains the one in terms of the other and not vice versa. An example that combines both the first and second difficulty is this: According to atomic physics, each chemi-

cal element has a characteristic atomic structure and a characteristic spectrum (of light emitted upon excitation). Yet the spectrum is explained by the atomic structure, and the question why a substance has that structure does not arise at all (except in the trivial sense that the questioner may need to have the terms explained to him).

To be successful, a theory of explanation must accommodate, and account for, both rejections and asymmetries. I shall now examine some attempts to come to terms with these, and gather from them the clues to the correct account.

Causality: The *Conditio Sine Qua Non*

Why are there no longer any Tasmanian natives? Why are the Plains Indians now living on reservations? Of course it is possible to cite relevant statistics: In many areas of the world, during many periods of history, upon the invasion by a technologically advanced people, the natives were displaced and weakened culturally, physically, and economically. But such a response will not satisfy: What we want is the story behind the event.

In Tasmania, attempts to round up and contain the natives were unsuccessful, so the white settlers simply started shooting them, man, woman, and child, until eventually there were none left. On the American Plains, the whites systematically destroyed the great buffalo herds on which the Indians relied for food and clothing, thus dooming them to starvation or surrender. There you see the story, it moves by its own internal necessity, and it explains why. . . .

Causality: Salmon's Theory

. . . An account of causal explanation which focuses on extended processes has recently been given by Wesley Salmon.[5]

In his earlier theory, to the effect that an expla-

---

[4] T. Kuhn, *The Structure of Scientific Revolutions* (Chicago: University of Chicago Press, 1970), pp. 107f.

[5] W. C. Salmon, "Why ask 'Why'?", presidential address to the Pacific Division of the American Philosophical Association, San Francisco, March 1978. The paper is published in *Proceedings and Addresses of the American Philosophical Association*, 51 (1978), 683–705. [This paper is reprinted above, pp. 51–64. Page references are to this version.]

nation consists in listing statistically relevant factors, Salmon had asked "What more could one ask of an explanation?" He now answers this question:

What does explanation offer, over and above the inferential capacity of prediction and retrodiction . . . ? It provides knowledge of the mechanisms of *production* and *propagation* of structure in the world. That goes some distance beyond mere recognition of regularities, and of the possibility of subsuming particular phenomena thereunder.[6]

The question "What is the causal relation?" is now replaced by "What is a causal process?" and "What is a causal interaction?" In his answer to these questions, Salmon relies to a large extent on Reichenbach's theory of the common cause . . . . But Salmon modifies this theory considerably.

A process is a spatio-temporally continuous series of events. The continuity is important, and Salmon blames some of Hume's difficulties on his picture of processes as chains of events with discrete links.[7] Some processes are causal, or genuine processes, and some are pseudo-processes. For example, if a car moves along a road, its shadow moves along that road too. The series of events in which the car occupies successive points on that road is a genuine causal process. But the movement of the shadow is merely a pseudo-process, because, intuitively speaking, the position of the shadow at later times is not caused by its position at earlier times. Rather, there is shadow *here* now because there is a car here now, and not because there was shadow *there* then.

Reichenbach tried to give a criterion for this distinction by means of probabilistic relations.[8] The series of events A_r is a causal process provided

(1) the probability of A_{r+s} given A_r is greater than or equal to the probability of A_{r+s} given A_{r-t}, which is in turn greater than the probability of A_{r+s} *simpliciter.*

This condition does not yet rule out pseudo-processes, so we add that each event in the series *screens off* the earlier ones from the later ones:

(2) the probability of A_{r+s} given both A_r and A_{r-t} is just that of A_{r+s} given A_r

and, *in addition,* there is no other series of events B_r which screens off A_{r+s} from A_r for all r. The idea in the example is that if A_{r+s} is the position of the shadow at time $r+s$, then B_r is the position of the car at time $r+s$.

This is not satisfactory for two reasons. The first is that (1) reminds one of a well-known property of stochastic processes, called the Markov property, and seems to be too strong to go into the definition of causal processes. Why should not the whole history of the process up to time r give more information about what happens later than the state at time r does by itself? The second problem is that in the addition to (2) we should surely add that B_r must itself be a genuine causal process. For otherwise the movement of the car is not a causal process either, since the movement of the shadow will screen off successive positions of the car from each other. But if we say that B_r must be a genuine process in this stipulation, we have landed in a regress.

Reichenbach suggested a second criterion, called the *mark method,* and (presumably because it stops the threatened regress) Salmon prefers that.

If a fender is scraped as a result of a collision with a stone wall, the mark of that collision will be carried on by the car long after the interaction with the wall occurred. The shadow of a car moving along the shoulder is a pseudo-process. If it is deformed as it encounters a stone wall, it will immediately resume its former shape as soon as it passes by the wall. It will not transmit a mark or modification.[9]

So if the process is genuine then interference with an earlier event will have effects on later events in that process. However, thus phrased, this statement is blatantly a causal claim. How shall we explicate "interference" and "effects"? Salmon will shortly give an account of causal interactions

[6] Op. cit., p. 64.

[7] Ibid., p. 57.

[8] Hans Reichenbach, *The Direction of Time* (Berkeley: University of California Press, 1956), Sects. 19 and 22.

[9] Salmon, op. cit., pp. 56–57.

(see below) but begins by appealing to his "at-at" theory of motion. The movement of the car consists simply in being *at* all these positions *at* those various times. Similarly, the propagation of the mark consists simply in the mark being there, in those later events. There is not, over and above this, a special propagation relation.

However, there is more serious cause for worry. We cannot define a genuine process as one that *does* propagate a mark in this sense. There are features which the shadow carries along in that "at-at" sense, such as that its shape is related, at all times, in a certain topologically definable way to the shape of the car, and that it is black. Other special marks are not always carried—imagine part of a rocket's journey during which it encounters nothing else. So what we need to say is that the process is genuine if, *were* there to be a given sort of interaction at an early stage, there *would be* certain marks in the later stages. . . .

We can, at this point, relativize the notions used to the theory accepted. About some processes, our theory *implies* that certain interactions at an early stage will be followed by certain marks at later stages. Hence we can say that, *relative to the theory* certain processes are classifiable as genuine and others as pseudo-processes. What this does not warrant is regarding the distinction as an objective one. However, if the distinction is introduced to play a role in the theory of explanation, and if explanation is a relation of theory to fact, this conclusion does not seem to me a variation on Salmon's theory that would defeat its purpose.[10]

Turning now to causal interactions, Salmon describes two sorts. These interactions are the "nodes" in the causal net, the "knots" that combine all those causal processes into a causal structure. Instead of "node" or "knot" Reichenbach and Salmon also use "fork" (as in "the road forks"). Reichenbach described one sort, the *conjunctive fork* which occurs when an event C, be-

longing to two processes, is the *common cause* of events A and B, in those separate processes, occurring after C. Here common cause is meant in Reichenbach's original sense:

(3) $P(A \& B/C) = P(A/C) \cdot P(B/C)$
(4) $P(A \& B/\overline{C}) = P(A/\overline{C}) \cdot P(B/\overline{C})$
(5) $P(A/C) > P(A/\overline{C})$
(6) $P(B/C) > P(B/\overline{C})$

which . . . entails that there is a positive correlation between A and B.

In order to accommodate the recalcitrant examples . . . Salmon introduced in addition the *interactive fork,* which is like the preceding one except that (3) is changed to

(3*) $P(A \& B/C) > P(A/C) \cdot P(B/C)$

These forks then combine the genuine causal processes, once identified, into the causal net that constitutes the natural order.

Explanation, on Salmon's new account, consists therefore in exhibiting the relevant part of the causal net that leads up to the events that are to be explained. In some cases we need only point to a single causal process that leads up to the event in question. In other cases we are asked to explain the confluence of events, or a positive correlation, and we do so by tracing them back to forks, that is, common origins of the processes that led up to them.

Various standard problems are handled. The sequence *barometer falling—storm coming* is not a causal process since the relevance of the first to the second is screened off by the common cause of atmospheric conditions. When paresis is explained by mentioning latent untreated syphilis, one is clearly pointing to the causal process, whatever it is, that leads from one to the other—or to their common cause, whatever that is. It must of course be a crucial feature of this theory that ordinary explanations are "pointers to" causal processes and interactions which would, if known or described in detail, give the full explanation.

If that is correct, then each explanation must have, as cash-value, some tracing back (which is possible in principle) of separate causal processes

---

[10] But it might defeat the use of Salmon's theory in metaphysical arguments, for example, his argument for realism at the end of this paper.

to the forks that connect them. There are various difficulties with this view. The first is that to be a causal process, the sequence of events must correspond to a continuous spatio-temporal trajectory. In quantum mechanics, this requirement is not met. It was exactly the crucial innovation in the transition from the Bohr atom of 1913 to the new quantum theory of 1924, that the exactly defined orbits of the electrons were discarded. Salmon mentions explicitly the limitation of this account to macroscopic phenomena (though he does discuss Compton scattering). This limitation is serious, for we have no independent reason to think that explanation in quantum mechanics is essentially different from elsewhere.

Secondly, many scientific explanations certainly do not look as if they are causal explanations in Salmon's sense. A causal law is presumably one that governs the temporal development of some process or interaction. There are also "laws of coexistence," which give limits to possible states or simultaneous configurations. A simple example is Boyle's law for gases (temperature is proportional to volume times pressure, at any given time); another, Newton's law of gravitation; another, Pauli's exclusion principle. In some of these cases we can say that they (or their improved counterparts) were later deduced from theories that replaced "action at a distance" (which is not action at all, but a constraint on simultaneous states) with "action by contact." But suppose they were not so replaceable—would that mean that they could not be used in genuine explanations?

Salmon himself gives an example of explanation "by common cause" which actually does not seem to fit his account. By observations on Brownian motion, scientists determined Avogadro's number, that is, the number of molecules in one mole of gas. By quite different observations, on the process of electrolysis, they determined the number of electron charges equal to one Faraday, that is, to the amount of electric charge needed to deposit one mole of a monovalent metal. These two numbers are equal. On the face of it, this equality is astonishing; but physics can explain this equality by deducing it from the basic theories

governing both sorts of phenomena. The common cause Salmon identifies here is the basic mechanism—atomic and molecular structure—postulated to account for these phenomena. But surely it is clear that, however much the adduced explanation may deserve the name "common cause," it does not point to a relationship between events (in Brownian motion on specific occasions and in electrolysis on specific occasions) which is traced back via causal processes to forks connecting these processes. The explanation is rather that the number found in experiment A at time t is the same as that found in totally independent experiment B at *any* other time t', because of the *similarity* in the physically independent causal processes observed on those two different occasions.

Many highly theoretical explanations at least look as if they escape Salmon's account. Examples here are explanations based on principles of least action, based on symmetry considerations, or, in relativistic theories, on information that relates to space–time as a whole, such as specification of the metric or gravitational field.

The conclusion suggested by all this is that the type of explanation characterized by Salmon, though apparently of central importance, is still at most a subspecies of explanations in general.

The Clues of Causality

Let us agree that science gives us a picture of the world as a net of interconnected events, related to each other in a complex but orderly way. The difficulties we found in the preceding two sections throw some doubt on the adequacy of the terminology of cause and causality to describe that picture; but let us not press this doubt further. The account of explanation suggested by the theories examined can now be restated in general terms as follows:

1. Events are enmeshed in a net of causal relations.

2. What science describes is that causal net.

3. Explanation of why an event happens consists (typically) in an exhibition of salient factors in

the part of the causal net formed by lines "leading up to" that event.

4. Those salient factors mentioned in an explanation constitute (what are ordinarily called) the *cause(s)* of that event.

There are two clear reasons why, when the topic of explanation comes up, attention is switched from the causal net as a whole (or even the part that converges on the event in question) to "salient factors." The first reason is that any account of explanation must make sense of common examples of explanation—especially cases typically cited as scientific explanations. In such actual cases, the reasons cited are particular prior events or initial conditions or combinations thereof. The second reason is that no account of explanation should imply that we can never give an explanation—and to describe the whole causal net in any connected region, however small, is in almost every case impossible. So the least concession one would have to make is to say that the explanation need say no more than that *there is* a structure of causal relations of *a certain sort,* which could *in principle* be described in detail: The salient features are what picks out the "certain sort."

Interest in causation as such focuses attention on (1) and (2), but interest in explanation requires us to concentrate on (3) and (4). Indeed, from the latter point of view, it is sufficient to guarantee the truth of (1) and (2) by *defining*

the causal net = whatever structure of relations science describes

and leaving to those interested in causation as such the problem of describing that structure in abstract but illuminating ways, if they wish.

Could it be that the explanation of a fact or event nevertheless resides solely in that causal net, and that *any* way of drawing attention to it explains? The answer is *no;* in the case of causal explanation, the *explanation* consists in drawing attention to certain ("special," "important") features of the causal net. Suppose for example that I wish to explain the extinction of the Irish elk. There is a very large class of factors that preceded

this extinction and was statistically relevant to it—even very small increases in speed, contact area of the hoof, height, distribution of weight in the body, distribution of food supply, migration habits, surrounding fauna and flora—we know from selection theory that under proper conditions any variation in these can be decisive in the survival of the species. But although, if some of these had been different, the Irish elk would have survived, they are not said to provide the explanation of why it is now extinct. The explanation given is that the process of sexual selection favored males with large antlers, and that these antlers were, in the environment where they lived, encumbering and the very opposite of survival-adaptive. The other factors I mentioned are not spurious causes, or screened off by the development of these huge and cumbersome antlers, because the extinction was the total effect of many contributing factors; but those other factors are not the salient factors.

We turn then to those salient features that are cited in explanation—those referred to as "the cause(s)" or "the real cause(s)." Various philosophical writers, seeking for an objective account of explanation, have attempted to state criteria that single out those special factors. I shall not discuss their attempts. Let me just cite a small survey of their answers: Lewis White Beck says that the cause is that factor over which we have most control; Nagel argues that it is often exactly that factor which is not under our control; Braithwaite takes the salient factors to be the unknown ones; and David Bohm takes them to be the factors which are the most variable.[11]

Why should different writers have given such different answers? The reason was exhibited, I think, by Norwood Russell Hanson, in his discussion of causation:

[11] This survey is found in Zwart, P. J., *Causaliteit* (Assen: van Gorcum, 1967), p. 135, n. 19; references are to Beck's and Nagel's papers in H. Feigl and M. Brodbeck (eds.), *Readings in the Philosophy of Science* (New York: Appleton-Century-Crofts, 1953), pp. 374 and 698; R. B. Braithwaite, *Scientific Explanation* (Cambridge: Cambridge University Press, 1953), p. 320; D. Bohm, *Causality and Chance in Modern Physics* (London: Routledge & Kegan Paul, 1957), *passim.*

There are as many causes of *x* as there are explanations of *x*. Consider how the cause of death might have been set out by a physician as "multiple hemorrhage," by the barrister as "negligence on the part of the driver," by a carriage-builder as "a defect in the brakeblock construction," by a civic planner as "the presence of tall shrubbery at that turning".[12]

In other words, the salient feature picked out as "the cause" in that complex process is salient to a given person because of his orientation, his interests, and various other peculiarities in the way he approaches or comes to know the problem—contextual factors.

It is important to notice that in a certain sense these different answers cannot be combined. The civic planner "keeps fixed" the mechanical constitution of the car, and gives his answer in the conviction that regardless of the mechanical defects, which made a fast stop impossible, the accident need not have happened. The mechanic "keeps fixed" the physical environment; despite the shrubbery obscuring vision, the accident need not have happened if the brakes had been better. What the one varies, the other keeps fixed, and you cannot do both at once. In other words, the selection of the salient causal factor is not simply a matter of pointing to the most interesting one, not like the selection of a tourist attraction; it is a matter of *competing* counterfactuals.

We must accordingly agree with the Dutch philosopher P. J. Zwart who concludes, after examining the above philosophical theories,

It is therefore not the case that the meaning of the sentence "*A* is the cause of *B*" depends on the nature of the phenomena *A* and *B*, but that this meaning depends on the context in which this sentence is uttered. The nature of *A* and *B* will in most cases also play a role, indirectly, but it is in the first place the orientation or the chosen point of view of the speaker that determines what the word *cause* is used to signify.[13]

In conclusion, then, this look at accounts of causation seems to establish that explanatory factors are to be chosen from a range of factors which are (or which the scientific theory lists as) objectively relevant in certain special ways—but that the choice is then determined by other factors that vary with the context of the explanation request. To sum up: No factor is explanatorily relevant unless it is scientifically relevant; and among the scientifically relevant factors, context determines explanatorily relevant ones.

Why-questions

Another approach to explanation was initiated by Sylvain Bromberger in his study of why-questions.[14] After all, a why-question is a request for explanation. Consider the question:

1. Why did the conductor become warped during the short circuit?

This has the general form

2. Why (is it the case that) *P*?

where *P* is a statement. So we can think of "Why" as a function that turns statements into questions.

Question 1 *arises,* or *is in order,* only if the conductor did indeed become warped then. If that is not so, we do not try to answer the question, but say something like: "You are under a false impression, the conductor became warped much earlier," or whatever. Hence Bromberger calls the statement *P* the *presupposition* of the question *Why P?* One form of the rejection of explanation requests is clearly the denial of the presupposition of the corresponding why question.

I will not discuss Bromberger's theory further here, but turn instead to a criticism of it. The following point about why-questions has been made in recent literature by Alan Garfinkel and Jon Dorling, but I think it was first made, and discussed in detail, in unpublished work by Bengt Hannson circulated in 1974.[15] Consider the question

---

[12] N. R. Hanson, *Patterns of Discovery* (Cambridge: Cambridge University Press, 1958), p. 54.

[13] Zwart, op. cit., p. 136; my translation.

[14] S. Bromberger, 'Why-Questions', pp. 86–108, in R. G. Colodny (ed.), *Mind and Cosmos* (Pittsburgh: University of Pittsburgh Press, 1966).

[15] 'Explanation-of-What?', mimeographed and circulated, Stanford University, 1974. The idea was independently developed, by Jon Dorling in a paper circulated in 1976, and reportedly by

3. Why did Adam eat the apple?

This same question can be construed in various ways, as is shown by the variants:

3a. Why was it Adam who ate the apple?
3b. Why was it the apple Adam ate?
3c. Why did Adam *eat* the apple?

In each case, the canonical form prescribed by Bromberger (as in 2 above) would be the same, namely

4. Why (is it the case that) (Adam ate the apple)?

yet there are three different explanation requests here.

The difference between these various requests is that they point to different contrasting alternatives. For example, 3b may ask why Adam ate *the apple* rather than some other fruit in the garden, while 3c asks perhaps why Adam *ate* the apple rather than give it back to Eve untouched. So to 3b, "because he was hungry" is not a good answer, whereas to 3c it is. The correct general, underlying structure of a why-question is therefore

5. Why (is it the case that) *P in contrast to* (other members of) *X*?

where *X*, the *contrast-class*, is a set of alternatives. *P* may belong to *X* or not; further examples are:

Why did the sample burn green (rather than some other color)? Why did the water and copper reach equilibrium temperature 22.5°C (rather than some other temperature)?

In these cases the contrast-classes (colors, temperatures) are "obvious." In general, the contrast-class is not explicitly described because, *in context*, it is clear to all discussants what the intended alternatives are.

This observation explains the tension we feel in the paresis example. If a mother asks why her eldest son, a pillar of the community, mayor of his town, and best beloved of all her sons, has this

dread disease, we answer: because he had latent untreated syphilis. But if that question is asked about this same person, immediately after a discussion of the fact that everyone in his country club has a history of untreated syphilis, *there is no answer*. The reason for the difference is that in the first case the contrast-class is the mother's sons, and in the second, the members of the country club, contracting paresis. Clearly, an answer to a question of form 5 must adduce information that *favors P in contrast to* other members of *X*. Sometimes the availability of such information depends strongly on the choice of *X*. . . .

The Clues Elaborated

The discussions of causality and of why-questions seem to me to provide essential clues to the correct account of explanation. In the former we found that an explanation often consists in listing salient factors, which point to a complete story of how the event happened. The effect of this is to eliminate various alternative hypotheses about how this event did come about, and/or eliminate puzzlement concerning how the event could have come about. But salience is context-dependent, and the selection of the correct "important" factor depends on the range of alternatives contemplated in that context. In N. R. Hanson's example, the barrister wants this sort of weeding out of hypotheses about the death relevant to the question of legal accountability; the carriage-builder, a weeding out of hypotheses about structural defects or structural limitations under various sorts of strain. *The context,* in other words, *determines relevance* in a way that goes well beyond the statistical relevance about which our scientific theories give information. . . .

In the discussion of why-questions, we have discovered a further contextually determined factor. The range of hypotheses about the event which the explanation must "weed out" or "cut down" is not determined solely by the interests of the discussants (legal, mechanical, medical) but also by a range of contrasting alternatives to the event. This *contrast-class* is also determined by context.

Alan Garfinkel in *Explanation and Individuals* (Yale University Press, forthcoming). I wish to express my debt to Bengt Hansson for discussion and correspondence in the autumn of 1975 which clarified these issues considerably for me.

It might be thought that when we request a *scientific* explanation, the relevance of possible hypotheses, and also the contrast-class are automatically determined. But this is not so, for both the physician and the motor mechanic are asked for a scientific explanation. The physician explains the fatality *qua* death of a human organism, and the mechanic explains it *qua* automobile crash fatality. To ask that their explanations be scientific is only to demand that they rely on scientific theories and experimentation, not on old wives' tales. Since any explanation of an individual event must be an explanation of that event *qua* instance of a certain kind of event, nothing more can be asked.

The two clues must be put together. The description of some account as an explanation of a given fact or event, is incomplete. It can only be an explanation with respect to a certain *relevance relation* and a certain *contrast-class*. These are contextual factors, in that they are determined neither by the totality of accepted scientific theories, nor by the event or fact for which an explanation is requested. It is sometimes said that an Omniscient Being would have a complete explanation, whereas these contextual factors only bespeak our limitations due to which we can only grasp one part or aspect of the complete explanation at any given time. But this is a mistake. If the Omniscient Being has no specific interests (legal, medical, economic; or just an interest in optics or thermodynamics rather than chemistry) and does not abstract (so that he never thinks of Caesar's death *qua* multiple stabbing, or *qua* assassination), then no why-questions ever arise for him in any way at all—and he does not have any explanation in the sense that we have explanations. If he does have interests, and does abstract from individual peculiarities in his thinking about the world, then his why-questions are as essentially context-dependent as ours. In either case, his advantage is that he always has all the information needed to answer any specific explanation request. But that information is, in and by itself, not an explanation; just as a person cannot be said to be older, or a neighbor, except in relation to others.

ASYMMETRIES OF EXPLANATION: A SHORT STORY

Asymmetry and Context: the Aristotelian Sieve

That vexing problem about paresis, where we seem both to have and not to have an explanation, was solved by reflection on the contextually supplied contrast-class. The equally vexing, and much older, problem of the asymmetries of explanation, is illuminated by reflection on the other main contextual factor: contextual relevance.

If that is correct, if the asymmetries of explanation result from a contextually determined relation of relevance, then it must be the case that these asymmetries can at least sometimes be reversed by a change in context. In addition, it should then also be possible to account for specific asymmetries in terms of the interests of questioner and audience that determine this relevance. These considerations provide a crucial test for the account of explanation which I propose.

Fortunately, there is a precedent for this sort of account of the asymmetries, namely in Aristotle's theory of science. It is traditional to understand this part of his theory in relation to his metaphysics; but I maintain that the central aspects of his solution to the problem of asymmetry of explanations are independently usable.[16]

Aristotle gave examples of this problem in the *Posterior Analytics* I, 13, and he developed a typology of explanatory factors ("the four causes"). The solution is then simply this. Suppose there are a definite (e.g., four) number of types of explanatory factors (i.e., of relevance relations for why-questions). Suppose also that relative to our background information and accepted theories, the propositions *A* and *B* are equivalent. It may then still be that these two propositions describe factors of different types. Suppose that in a certain con-

---

[16] For a fuller account of Aristotle's solution of the asymmetries, see my "A Reexamination of Aristotle's Philosophy of Science." *Dialogue*, 1980. The story was written in reply to searching questions and comments by Professor J.J.C. Smart, and circulated in November 1976.

text, our interest is in the mode of production of an event, and "Because *B*" is an acceptable answer to "Why *A*?" Then it may well be that *A* does not describe any mode of production of anything, so that, *in this same context,* "Because *A*" would not be an acceptable answer to "Why *B*?"

Aristotle's lantern example (*Posterior Analytics* II, 11) shows that he recognized that in different contexts, verbally the same why-question may be a request for different types of explanatory factors. In modern dress the example would run as follows. Suppose a father asks his teenage son, "Why is the porch light on?" and the son replies "The porch switch is closed and the electricity is reaching the bulb through that switch." At this point you are most likely to feel that the son is being impudent. This is because you are most likely to think that the sort of answer the father needed was something like: "Because we are expecting company." But it is easy to imagine a less likely question context: The father and son are rewiring the house and the father, unexpectedly seeing the porch light on, fears that he has caused a short circuit that bypasses the porch light switch. In the second case, he is *not* interested in the human expectations or desires that led to the depressing of the switch.

Aristotle's fourfold typology of causes is probably an oversimplification of the variety of interests that can determine the selection of a range of relevant factors for a why-question. But in my opinion, appeal to some such typology will successfully illuminate the asymmetries (and also the rejections, since no factor of a *particular* type may lead to a telling answer to the why-question). If that is so then, as I said before, asymmetries must be at least sometimes reversible through a change in context. The story which follows is meant to illustrate this. As in the lantern (or porch light) example, the relevance changes from one sort of efficient cause to another, the second being a person's desires. As in all explanations, the correct answer consists in the exhibition of a single factor in the causal net, which is made salient in that context by factors not overtly appearing in the words of the question.

"The Tower and the Shadow"

During my travels along the Saône and Rhône last year, I spent a day and night at the ancestral home of the Chevalier de St. X . . . , an old friend of my father's. The Chevalier had in fact been the French liaison officer attached to my father's brigade in the first war, which had—if their reminiscences are to be trusted—played a not insignificant part in the battles of the Somme and Marne.

The old gentleman always had *thé à l'Anglaise* on the terrace at five o'clock in the evening, he told me. It was at this meal that a strange incident occurred; though its ramifications were of course not yet perceptible when I heard the Chevalier give his simple explanation of the length of the shadow which encroached upon us there on the terrace. I had just eaten my fifth piece of bread and butter and had begun my third cup of tea when I chanced to look up. In the dying light of that late afternoon, his profile was sharply etched against the granite background of the wall behind him, the great aquiline nose thrust forward and his eyes fixed on some point behind my left shoulder. Not understanding the situation at first, I must admit that to begin with, I was merely fascinated by the sight of that great hooked nose, recalling my father's claim that this had once served as an effective weapon in close combat with a German grenadier. But I was roused from this brown study by the Chevalier's voice.

"The shadow of the tower will soon reach us, and the terrace will turn chilly. I suggest we finish our tea and go inside."

I looked around, and the shadow of the rather curious tower I had earlier noticed in the grounds, had indeed approached to within a yard from my chair. The news rather displeased me, for it was a fine evening; I wished to remonstrate but did not well know how, without overstepping the bounds of hospitality. I exclaimed,

"Why must that tower have such a long shadow? This terrace is so pleasant!"

His eyes turned to rest on me. My question had been rhetorical, but he did not take it so.

"As you may already know, one of my ancestors mounted the scaffold with Louis XVI and Marie Antoinette. I had that tower erected in 1930 to mark the exact spot where it is said that he greeted the Queen when she first visited this house, and presented her with a peacock made of soap, then a rare substance. Since the Queen would have been one hundred and seventy-five years old in 1930, had she lived, I had the tower made exactly that many feet high.''

It took me a moment to see the relevance of all this. Never quick at sums, I was at first merely puzzled as to why the measurement should have been in feet; but of course I already knew him for an Anglophile. He added drily,

''The sun not being alterable in its course, light traveling in straight lines, and the laws of trigonometry being immutable, you will perceive that the length of the shadow is determined by the height of the tower.''

We rose and went inside.

I was still reading at eleven that evening when there was a knock at my door. Opening it I found the housemaid, dressed in a somewhat old-fashioned black dress and white cap, whom I had perceived hovering in the background on several occasions that day. Courtseying prettily, she asked,

''Would the gentleman like to have his bed turned down for the night?''

I stepped aside, not wishing to refuse, but remarked that it was very late—was she kept on duty to such hours? No, indeed, she answered, as she deftly turned my bed covers, but it had occurred to her that some duties might be pleasures as well. In such and similar philosophical reflec-

tions we spent a few pleasant hours together, until eventually I mentioned casually how silly it seemed to me that the tower's shadow ruined the terrace for a prolonged, leisurely tea.

At this, her brow clouded. She sat up sharply.

''What exactly did he tell you about this?'' I replied lightly, repeating the story about Marie Antoinette, which now sounded a bit far-fetched even to my credulous ears.

''The *servants* have a different account,'' she said with a sneer that was not at all becoming, it seemed to me, on such a young and pretty face.

''The truth is quite different, and has nothing to do with ancestors. That tower marks the spot where he killed the maid with whom he had been in love to the point of madness. And the height of the tower? He vowed that shadow would cover the terrace, where he first proclaimed his love, with every setting sun—that is why the tower had to be so high.''

I took this in but slowly. It is never easy to assimilate unexpected truths about people we think we know—and I have had occasion to notice this again and again.

''Why did he kill her?'' I asked finally.

''Because, sir, she dallied with an English brigadier, an overnight guest in this house.''

With these words she arose, collected her bodice and cap, and faded through the wall beside the doorway.

I left early the next morning, making my excuses as well as I could.

Scientific Theories and Their Domains

Dudley Shapere

FRAMEWORK OF THE PRESENT ANALYSIS

If we examine some relatively sophisticated area of science at a particular stage of its development, we find that a certain body of information is, at that stage, taken to be an object for investigation. On a general level, one need only think of the subject matters called "electricity," "magnetism," "light," or "chemistry"; but both within and outside such standard fields, there are more specific examples, such as what are taken to be subfields of the preceding subjects. Further, those general subjects themselves are, in many cases, considered to be related in certain ways. I will refer to such bodies of related items as *domains,* though we will find that, in the sense in which this concept will prove helpful in understanding science, and in particular in understanding the concept of a scientific "theory," more is involved than the mere relatedness of certain items.

The preceding examples are familiar ones, and there might appear to be no problem about considering them to be "fields," or, as I have called them, domains. However, this is far from being the case. In order to bring out some of the complexities involved, let us briefly review certain aspects of the history of those examples.

It is by no means obvious that all the phenomena that we today unhesitatingly group together as forming a unified subject matter or domain under the heading of "electricity" really do form such a unity. Earlier investigators had indeed associated the known phenomena: William Gilbert discovered that some twenty substances besides the previously known amber would, when appropriately rubbed, attract light bodies. His investigations led him to conclude that electric phenomena are due to something of a material nature which is liberated by the rubbing of "electricks."[1] Succeeding workers agreed, holding that electricity consists of one (or two) fluids. However, the nineteenth century, with a larger body of apparently related information available, saw reasons to question the unity of the subject: Was the "electricity" associated with physiological phenomena of the same sort (and to be explained in the same way) as that associated with inanimate objects, or was it peculiar to, and perhaps even the distinguishing characteristic of, living things? Was the "electricity" produced on the *surfaces* of certain objects by rubbing them identical with the "electricity" produced in the *interiors* of certain bodies by a voltaic cell? Even by the time of Faraday, according to Whittaker,

the connection of the different branches of electric science with each other was still not altogether clear. Although Wollaston's experiments of 1801 had in effect proved the identity in kind of the currents derived from frictional and voltaic sources, the question was still regarded as open thirty years afterwards, no satisfactory explanation being forthcoming of the fact that frictional electricity appeared to be a surface phenomenon, whereas voltaic electricity was conducted within the interior substance of bodies. To this

---

[1] E. T. Whittaker, *A History of the Theories of Aether and Electricity* (New York: Thomas Nelson, 1951), Vol. I, p. 35.

From Sections 1 and 3 of "Scientific Theories and Their Domains" by Dudley Shapere, in *The Structure of Scientific Theories,* Frederick Suppe, Ed., 2nd edition (1977), pp. 518–525, 533–555. Reprinted by permission of the author and University of Illinois Press. © 1977 by the Board of Trustees of the University of Illinois.

question Faraday now applied himself; and in 1833 he succeeded in showing that every known effect of electricity—physiological, magnetic, luminous, calorific, chemical, and mechanical—may be obtained indifferently either with the electricity that is obtained by friction or with that obtained from a voltaic battery. Henceforth the identity of the two was beyond dispute.[2]

In *De Magnete*,[3] Gilbert had called attention to a number of differences between electricity and magnetism, which Whittaker summarizes succinctly as follows:

Between the magnetic and electric forces Gilbert remarked many distinctions. The lodestone requires no stimulus of friction such as is needed to stir glass and sulphur into activity. The lodestone attracts only magnetizable substances, whereas electrified bodies attract everything. The magnetic attraction between two bodies is not affected by interposing a sheet of paper or a linen cloth, or by immersing the bodies in water; whereas the electric attraction is readily destroyed by screens. Lastly, the magnetic force tends to arrange bodies in definite orientations; while the electric force merely tends to heap them together in shapeless clusters.[4]

Thus there were strong grounds for believing that electricity and magnetism constituted distinct subjects for investigation, for which different explanations were to be given. Nevertheless, in spite of these clear differences, reasons accumulated over the succeeding two or three centuries for *suspecting* that these differences might prove to be superficial, and that there was some deep relationship to be found between electrical and magnetic phenomena. These considerations were very varied in kind; among them were ones like the following:

The suspicion [in the eighteenth century] was based in part on some curious effects produced by lightning, of a kind which may be illustrated by a paper published in the *Philosophical Transactions* in 1735. A tradesman of Wakefield, we are told, "having put up a great number of knives and forks in a large box, and having placed the box in the corner of a large room,

there happen'd in July, 1731, a sudden storm of thunder, lightning, etc., by which the corner of the room was damaged, the Box split, and a good many knives and forks melted, the sheaths being untouched. The owner emptying the box upon a Counter where some Nails lay, the Persons who took up the knives, that lay upon the Nails, observed that the knives took up the Nails."[5]

Subsequent investigations by Franklin, Oersted, Ampère, and Faraday (among others) of the relationships between electricity and magnetism culminated in the synthetic theories of the latter half of the nineteenth century, among which Maxwell's theory was triumphant. It is clear that in some sense Maxwell's theory provided an "explanation" of (a theory explaining) the phenomena of electricity and magnetism; nevertheless, as we shall see (and also for reasons whose character we shall see), that "theory" became part of a larger body of information which called for a further, deeper explanation.

The phenomena of electricity, particularly in the nineteenth century, also came more and more to be connected with chemical phenomena; and, through this association of electricity with chemistry, the suspicion—growing gradually into an expectation or even a demand—arose that a unified theory of electricity and matter should, in some form, be sought. Indeed, as time progressed, this form itself began to be clearer: The unity should be sought in the structure of the atom. Thus the areas which seemed to offer the possibility of precise clues to that structure—particularly the spectra of the chemical elements and the periodic table—became crucial areas of investigation. Lines of potentially fruitful research in the quest for the expected unifying theory began to be generated.

The relations between electricity and light underwent a similar development. Faraday's demonstration of the effect of a magnetic field on the plane of polarization of a light ray provided one sort of consideration leading to the belief that there was a deeper relationship to be sought between magnetism and hence, because of the de-

---

[2] Ibid., p. 175.

[3] W. Gilbert, *De Magnete* (New York: Dover, 1958), Bk. II, Ch. II, esp. pp. 95–97.

[4] Whittaker, *A History of the Theories of Aether and Electricity*, p. 35.

[5] Ibid., pp. 80–81.

velopments summarized above, electricity and light.

Even in such a cursory survey, dealing with such familiar areas of scientific investigation as electricity, magnetism, chemistry, and light, it becomes clear that the grounds for considering the elements of each such domain as constituting a *unified* subject-matter, and as exhibiting relations with other domains which lead to the formation of larger domains, are highly complex. The general situation, in these cases at least, may be summarized as follows. Although in more primitive stages of science (or, perhaps better, of what will become a science), obvious sensory similarities or general presuppositions usually determine whether certain items of experience will be considered as forming a body or domain, this is less and less true as science progresses (or, one might say, as it becomes more unambiguously scientific). As part of the growing sophistication of science, such associations of items are subjected to criticism, and often are revised on the basis of considerations that are far from obvious and naive. Differences which seemed to distinguish items from one another are concluded to be superficial; similarities which were previously unrecognized or, if recognized, considered superficial, become fundamental. Conversely, similarities which formerly served as bases for association of items come to be considered superficial, and the items formerly associated are no longer, and form independent groupings or come to be associated with other groups. The items themselves often, in the process, come to be redescribed, often, for scientific purposes, in very unfamiliar ways. Even where the earlier or more obvious associations are ultimately retained, they are retained only after criticism, and on grounds that go beyond the mere perceptual similarities or primitive uncritical presuppositions which formed the more obvious bases of their original association.

An important part of gaining an understanding of science, and of the nature of scientific theories in particular, must be to examine the character of such grounds for the establishment of domains. But this question immediately leads to another: For in order that the area constituted by the related items be an area *for investigation,* there must be something problematic about it, something inadequate in our understanding of it. A domain, in the sense in which that term will be used here, is not *merely* a body of related information; it is a body of related information about which there is a problem, well defined usually and raised on the basis of specific considerations ("good reasons"). In addition, that problem must be considered important (also on reasonable grounds, not on the basis of some "subjective value judgment"); it must be worth making the effort to resolve. Further, as we shall see, it must—in general, though in certain rather well-circumscribed sorts of cases not necessarily—be capable of being "handled" at the current stage of science.

In earlier stages of the development of a field, curiosity, general puzzlement, or general uncritical presuppositions undoubtedly play a predominant role in generating such problems—in determining whether an area is problematic and worth investigating. With the advance of science, however, and indeed constituting in part the very notion of scientific progress, the considerations leading to certain questions being raised about a domain, and to considering them important, become more specific, precise, and subject to constraints: The generation of problems and priorities becomes more a matter of reasoning. Investigation of the character of this reasoning constitutes another aspect of the attempt to gain an understanding of science. More specifically, and more directly relevant to our present concerns, such analysis will help us to understand the nature and function of scientific theories. For as we shall see, different sorts of questions, reflecting different sorts of inadequacies, can arise, even regarding the same domain; and we shall find that only certain of these sorts of questions are answered in terms of what are commonly and appropriately referred to as "theories."

A further aspect of scientific reasoning which arises at this point concerns the ways in which, at least often when problems arise at sophisticated stages of science, it is possible to formulate promising lines of research to pursue in attempting to answer those problems, and, sometimes, to assign at least rough rankings of degree of promise to such lines of research, thereby establishing research priorities. Further, expectations—sometimes amounting to demands—arise regarding the character of any satisfactory solution to those problems, even in advance of having any such solution (and therefore certain proposed solutions are judged as more or less "attractive"). And in many cases these expectations or demands do succeed in anticipating the actual solution ultimately arrived at; but whether they do or do not, reasons are given supporting the expectations, and the character of those reasons must be analyzed. (In addition, of course, the patterns of reasoning in cases in which the actual solution is *not* in agreement with those expectations or demands must also be analyzed.) Again, in primitive stages of a science, such conclusions are no doubt based primarily on general and uncritical presuppositions.[6] But it is characteristic of sophisticated science that it tends more and more to depend on reasoned arguments for the generation of lines of research, the judgment of them as more or less "promising," and the generation of expectations regarding the character of possible answers to problems. An understanding of such reasoning is essential if we are to understand the nature of science, and in particular of scientific theories.

We may summarize the preceding discussion in terms of five major questions.

1. *What considerations (or, better, types of considerations, if such types can be found) lead scientists to regard a certain body of information as a body of information—that is, as constituting a unified subject matter or domain to be examined or dealt with?*

2. *How is description of the items of the domain achieved and modified at sophisticated stages of scientific development?*

3. *What sorts of inadequacies, leading to the need for further work, are found in such bodies of information, and what are the grounds for*

considering these to be inadequacies or problems requiring further research? (Included here are questions not only regarding the generation of scientific problems about domains, but also of scientific priorities—the questions of importance of the problems and of the "readiness" of science to deal with them.)

4. *What considerations lead to the generation of specific lines of research, and what are the reasons (or types of reasons) for considering some lines of research to be more promising than others in the attempt to resolve problems about the domain?*

5. *What are the reasons for expecting (sometimes to the extent of demanding) that answers of certain sorts, having certain characteristics, be sought for those problems?*

Clearly, a further question, not explicitly emerging from our earlier discussion, also needs to be raised:

6. *What are the reasons (or types of reasons) for accepting a certain solution of a scientific problem regarding a domain as adequate?*

Of these six questions, only the last has been seriously and carefully examined by philosophers of science (in connection, largely, with discussions of "inductive logic"). In the present paper, however, I will focus on aspects of certain of the other five which are relevant to the understanding of the nature and function of scientific theories.

It must not be supposed, however, that complete answers to one of these questions will be wholly independent of answers to the others, so that they can be dealt with in isolation from one another in a piecemeal attack; we will, indeed, discover interdependencies. Nor should it be supposed that there are not other questions which must be dealt with in the attempt to understand the nature of science—though I would argue that the above are very central ones. But in any case, a complete understanding of scientific reasoning would include a treatment of all these questions.[7]

---

[6] The roots and character of some of the most general of such presuppositions have been analyzed in my essay, "The Development of Scientific Categories," forthcoming.

[7] It is necessary to emphasize this point; for many, perhaps most, philosophers of science, even when they have raised such questions as 1 to 5, have denied that they were relevant to the

And a complete and systematic investigation of all of them would serve as a test (and at the same time, as seems to be the case in so many scientific investigations, a clarification) of three general assumptions about science, each successive one of which constitutes a stronger claim than, and presupposes the truth of, its predecessors. Traditionally, these three assumptions have been widely accepted (though not without occasional and recurrent opposition) as true of science; today, however, they are being subjected to powerful attack, in one form or another, from a number of quarters. The assumptions may be stated as follows:

I. *Scientific development and innovation are often appropriately describable as rational.* (Obviously, there is a question here of the appropriate precise sense or senses of *rational;* however, as was indicated above, the proposed investigation itself would provide, in part at least, a specification of such a sense or senses, and thus be simultaneously a test and a clarification of the assumption. Such a procedure seems to be common in scientific inquiry, and itself requires analysis which it has never received, the classical philosophical attitude having been that "meanings" must be specified completely and precisely before any test can be undertaken—a procedure which, even if it is clear itself, is rarely if ever realized in any inquiry whatever.) I will call this the *postulate* (or *hypothesis*) *of scientific rationality.*

II. *The rationality involved in specific cases is often generalizable as principles applicable in many other cases.* (It might be supposed that the truth of II—and also perhaps of III—is a necessary condition for calling a subject or method "rational." However, at least one writer has in effect denied II while apparently maintaining I: "The coherence displayed by the research tradition . . . may not imply even the existence of an underlying body of

rules and assumptions."[8] That is, science, in its "normal" stages, operates according to an underlying rationale, even though any attempt to express that rationale in terms of explicit *rules* is, the author claims, usually [and perhaps always and necessarily] doomed to failure. Because of this possibility, it seems advisable to keep these postulates separated.) I will call this the *postulate* (or *hypothesis*) *of the generalizability of scientific reasoning.*

III. *These principles can in some sense be systematized.* This may be called the *postulate* (or *hypothesis*) *of the systematizability of scientific reasoning principles.*

The present essay can deal only with some aspects of the six questions listed above, and, in fact, will deal only with those aspects that are relevant to the concept of a scientific *theory.* It cannot pretend to deal with all aspects of that concept (or with all uses of the term *theory*). Even within these limitations, it cannot claim completeness: It is no more than a preliminary and, in many cases, only a suggestive rather than thoroughly detailed examination of the issues. . . .

THEORETICAL PROBLEMS, LINES OF RESEARCH, AND SCIENTIFIC THEORIES

We have examined, to the extent that is relevant to present concerns, the concept of a domain. In doing so, we have made a distinction between those problems that are concerned with the clarification of the domain itself, and other problems calling for a "deeper" account of the domain. The former type of problems will henceforth be referred to as *domain problems;* the latter I will call *theoretical problems,* inasmuch as answers to them are called "theories." . . . In the present part, I will consider theoretical problems and the characteristics of answers to them.

It will not, however, be possible to give a complete classification and analysis of types of such

attempt to understand science; for, according to those philosophers, such questions (with the possible exception of certain aspects of 2) have to do only with the "psychology," "sociology," or "history" of science, rather than with its "logic," which alone is relevant to the *understanding* of science.

[8] T. S. Kuhn, *The Structure of Scientific Revolutions* (Chicago: University Chicago Press, 1970), p. 46.

problems, and therefore of theories; I am not sure that such complete classification can or should be given. I will focus on types of theories that are, in some natural sense, paradigmatically *explanatory,* and, yet more specifically, on two types of such theories, which I will call (a) *compositional* and (b) *evolutionary.* The types of problems calling for such answers will be similarly designated. To anticipate briefly, a compositional problem is one which calls for an answer in terms of constituent parts of the individuals making up the domain and the laws governing the behavior of those parts. The parts sought need not be "elementary," though in the cases to be considered here, they are.[9] Evolutionary problems, on the other hand, call for answers in terms of the development of the individuals making up the domain; paradigm examples are the Darwinian theory of biological evolution, theories of stellar evolution, and theories of the evolution of the chemical elements. There are types of theories which do not fit into these two categories, at least not easily: The "theory" constructed on the basis of the fundamental postulates of thermodynamics is an example, as is the special theory of relativity. But the two types to be considered are centrally important, and I believe that an understanding of them is a prerequisite to an understanding of other types represented by these and other examples. At any rate, they will illustrate certain general features of "theoretical problems" and the "theories" which are answers to those problems. I will begin with three case studies, from which such general features, as well as specific features, of these two types of theories will emerge.

The Periodic Table of Chemical Elements

A type of domain whose analysis will prove particularly fruitful are *ordered* domains—that is, domains in which types of items are classified, and those classes themselves arranged in some pattern, for example, a series, according to some rule or ordering principle. The series may (as in the case of the periodic table of chemical elements) or may not (as in the case of spectral classifications of stars, for example, the Morgan-Keenan-Kellman system) be periodic (repeating). Orderings of domains are themselves suggestive of several different sorts of lines of further research. As we would expect from our earlier discussion, some such problems (and associated lines of research) have to do with clarification and extension of the domain—for example, refinements of measurements of the property or properties on the basis of which the ordering is made, with a view to refining the ordering; or the search for other properties which vary concomitantly with those properties.[10] Answers to such problems are not what one would naturally call "theories." (However, one might "hypothesize" that a certain property varies concomitantly with the ordering property, even though the former may not be directly measurable with current techniques, and even though there is no very clear theoretical basis for the hypothesis, though the hypothesis seems needed on other grounds. In such case, we might find the word *theory* being used.) Nor does the fact that the ordering sometimes allows predictions to be made (for example, predictions of new elements and their properties on the basis of the periodic table) turn such ordered domains into "theories."[11] (In

---

[9] Such theories are related to, and indeed are a subclass of, the "existence theories" discussed in "Notes toward a Post-Positivistic Interpretation of Science"—theories, briefly, which make existence claims. Field theories are examples of existence theories which are not readily subsumable under the present heading of "compositional theories."

[10] In the case of ordered domains, one can speak of domain problems having to do with the *incompleteness* of the domain, because of unoccupied places in the ordering; for example, Mendeleev and other pioneers of the periodic table gave reasons for considering there to be "gaps" in their orderings—for considering certain elements to exist which had not yet been discovered. Discovery of such elements, however—though filling in those gaps—while it did increase current knowledge, did not, in any usual sense of the word, increase "understanding" or provide "explanation" of the system of elements.

[11] It is true that, especially in the decade before 1870, several alternative orderings of the chemical elements had been suggested. (See F. P. Venable, *The Development of the Periodic Law* (Easton, Pa.: Chemical Publishing, 1896); J. W. van Spronsen, *The Periodic System of Chemical Elements: A History of the First Hundred Years* (New York: Elsevier, 1969); for a collection of primary sources, see D. M. Knight, ed., *Classical*

particular, the periodic table is not "explanatory," even though predictions can be made on its basis alone.[12])

On the other hand, there are other kinds of problems and lines of research suggested by or-

dered domains which are concerned with attempts to construct "theories." The mere existence of an ordering relation, and still more, of a periodicity in that ordering, raises the question of accounting for that order; and the more extensive, detailed, and precise the ordering, the more strongly the existence of such an account is indi-

---

Scientific Papers: Chemistry, Second Series (New York: American Elsevier, 1970). Could those proposed "orderings" be called "theories"? The question is an empirical one of usage, and what we find is that terms like "classification," "system," "table," or "law" are used; but the term "theory" is used also, but only very occasionally. This is true not only of present usage, but also, as far as I have been able to determine, in regard to the proposals made during the decade 1860 to 1870. The rarity with which the term "theory" is applied to such cases is, I think, significant. However, even to the extent to which one might be tempted to use it in reference to the ordering of the domain of chemical elements, none of the analysis given here would be vitiated. For our purposes, all that is relevant is that *once the character of the ordering had been determined, that ordering itself became part of the domain.* That is, even if the ordering is considered to have been "theoretical" at a certain stage, nevertheless once it had been settled on through the work of Mendeleev and Meyer, it became an integral aspect of the body of information which was to be accounted for—that is, it became part of the domain. (And in any case, an "ordering" would be a very different *kind* of theory from a compositional one.)

As to the use of the term "law" in reference to the periodic table, it is important to remember the historical background of that term in this connection. In his paper of 1871, Mendeleev stated the "periodic law" as follows: "The properties of simple bodies, the constitution of their compounds, as well as the properties of the last, are periodic functions of the atomic weights of the elements." (D. Mendeleev, "The Periodic Law of the Chemical Elements," *The Chemical News*, Vols. XL (1879) and XLI (1880) (translation of the 1871 article); reprinted in Knight, *Classical Scientific Papers*, pp. 273–309; quotation is on p. 267. Interestingly, Freund refers to this article as "The Periodical Regularities of the Chemical Elements": I. Freund, *The Study of Chemical Composition: An Account of Its Method and Historical Development* (New York: Dover, 1968, reprint of the 1904 edition), p. 500. But "the true function, expressing how the properties depend on the atomic weights, is unknown to us." (Mendeleev, in Knight, *Classical Scientific Papers*, p. 288.) That is, Mendeleev, like nearly all other workers in the late nineteenth century, conceived this functional relationship to be a mathematical one *whose precise form remained to be discovered;* and although he was not averse to calling his periodic table a "law," it is clear that he (like others) considered the true expression of this law to be a mathematical one, and that his statement of it was only a vague one which however was clear enough to allow rough results to be achieved. Again in his Faraday lecture of 1889, Mendeleev expressed the same view: "The Periodic Law has shown that our chemical individuals display a harmonic periodicity of properties, dependent on their masses. Now, natural science has long been accustomed to deal with periodicities observed in nature, to seize them with the vise of mathematical analysis, to submit them to the rasp of experiment." (Mendeleev, "The Periodic Law of the Chemical Elements," Faraday Lecture, June 4, 1889; reprinted in Knight, *Classical Scientific Papers*, pp. 322–344; quotation on page 328.) But after discussing the inadequacies of attempted formulations of this function, and listing what he took to be requirements of an adequate expression of it, he found it necessary to conclude that "although greatly enlarging our vision, even now

the periodic law needs further improvements in order that it may become a trustworthy instrument in further discoveries" (ibid., p. 337). This was the universal view: that the true "law" was yet to be found (earlier, Mendeleev had explicitly declared that "I designate by the name of *Periodic Law* the mutual relations between the properties of the elements and their atomic weights, relations which are applicable to all the elements, and which are of the nature of a periodic function"; see Freund, *The Study of Chemical Composition*, p. 469). As late as 1900, this was still the view: "We have not been able to predict *accurately* any one of the properties of one of these [noble] gases from a knowledge of those of the others; an approximate guess is all that can be made. The conundrum of the periodic table has yet to be solved." (Ramsay and Travers, *Argon and Its Companions*, 1900; quoted in Freund, *The Study of Chemical Composition*, p. 500.) The relevance of this disheartened conclusion to the present point is made clear by Ida Freund's comment: "The special feature of the conundrum thus referred to by Professor Ramsey is how to find the formula for the function which would correlate the numerics of the atomic weight with the properties susceptible of quantitative measurement. Another aspect of it is that of the expression of the atomic weights themselves by means of a general algebraic formula. This problem is an attractive one, and several attempts have been made to solve it, in spite of the fact that the only indications of the direction in which success may be expected are of negative nature" (Freund, *The Study of Chemical Composition*, p. 500).

Thus, although the periodic table was widely referred to as a law, the general opinion of the time was that it could be called a "law" only in a rather loose sense, the true law being the precise mathematical expression of the "function" relating the atomic weights and the other properties of the elements and, presumably, their compounds. Views claiming that the table should be called a law because it permits prediction must take into account this feature of the historical situation. (van Spronsen, *The Periodic System of Chemical Elements,* makes a deliberate decision to refer to it as the periodic "system" rather than "law," and so forth.)

[12] In some respects, similar remarks hold for the multitude of conclusions about stars (for example, regarding distances, masses, intrinsic luminosity, ages, chemical composition, internal structure—few of which are "directly observable" in anything like a positivistic sense, if in any natural sense at all) which can be drawn on the basis of the Hertzsprung-Russell diagram, the astrophysical analogue of the periodic table. In this case, however, more of a "theoretical" character has become embedded in the use of the H-R diagram than in the corresponding use of the periodic table for prediction of missing elements. Indeed, a close comparison of these two cases would demonstrate clearly the absurdity of claims that scientific predictions and other conclusions always, and in some sense that is both normal and univocal, involve or presuppose the use of "theories." Such an investigation would also reveal much of importance about the interactions and interpenetrations of "theory" and "classification." The latter is, in many cases, far from being unintellectual drudge work.

cated.[13] But further, the existence of such an ordering tends to make some properties appear more significant than others (for example, atomic weight), and those properties are then looked upon as furnishing "clues" to the discovery of the presumed deeper account. These and other features of ordered and periodic domains are illustrated by the case of the periodic table.

By the early 1870s, it had become finally clear that if the chemical elements were arranged in a table ordered according to atomic weights, and if due allowance were made for undiscovered elements, then certain periodicities in the properties of the elements (as well as certain "horizontal relationships") would be revealed.[14] Many investigators refused to believe that any further problem was raised by these relationships; to them, the "elements" were truly fundamental, not composed of anything more elementary. This was the case particularly among working chemists, to whom the "atom" of the physicists had never been at all useful, and indeed appeared to be mere speculation.[15] However, the relationships between the ele-

ments, reflecting both order and periodicity, indicated to many that there was some more fundamental composition of the elements.[16] So extensive, detailed, and precise were those relationships that even the existence of exceptions, in which the order or the periodicity, one or the other, had to be violated if the other were satisfied, could not shake the conviction of an underlying composition which would, ultimately, remove even those anomalies. (It is perhaps significant that, for a long period, only one such anomaly was known which appeared anywhere near troublesome.[17]) Hence the conviction grew that the

---

[13] This is *one* motivation of the attempt, mentioned in the preceding paragraph, to refine the measurement of the ordering properties: to test the strength of the indication that there is a deeper account to be found.

[14] Relations between isolated groups of elements had been noted much earlier and held to be indications of some common composition at least of the elements so related. As early as the second decade of the century, Döbereiner had constructed "triads" of related elements: For example, he found the (then supposed) atomic weight of strontium (50) to be the mean of those of calcium (27.5) and barium (72.5), and this was taken as grounds for questioning the independent existence of strontium. Later, groups of more than three elements were found to be related, and again compositional theories of various sorts were suggested for those elements. Such views, of course, were based only on what are now called "vertical" rather than on "horizontal" relationships, which were disclosed fully only by the periodic table. In general, nineteenth-century science found many reasons besides the relations embodied in the periodic table for supposing the chemical elements, or at least some of them, to have common constituents; certainly there is no ground for the allegation that the view of the transmutability of the elements had died with the alchemists and was not revived until the work of Rutherford and Soddy; it is one of the liveliest strands in nineteenth-century science. A good survey is W. V. Farrar, "Nineteenth-Century Speculations on the Complexity of the Chemical Elements," *British Journal for the History of Science*, Vol. II (1965), pp. 297–323, though he neglects to include explicit discussion of the important isomeric theories of the elements.

[15] For the opposition of chemists to physical atoms, see D. M. Knight, *Atoms and Elements: A Study of Theories of Matter in*

England in the Nineteenth Century (London: Hutchinson, 1967); W. H. Brock, *The Atomic Debates* (Leicester: Leicester University Press, 1967); and W. McGucken, *Nineteenth-Century Spectroscopy: Development of the Understanding of Spectra 1802–1897* (Baltimore: Johns Hopkins University Press, 1969). In this connection, perhaps Lavoisier's conception of elements as "the substances into which we are capable, by any means, to reduce bodies by decomposition" (A. L. Lavoisier, *Elements of Chemistry* [New York: Dover, 1965], p. xxiv) joined with Dalton's views and a too-rigid empiricism to discourage many chemists from "unscientific," "metaphysical" speculations about the composition of the elements. Mendeleev himself, though on other occasions he was not at all averse to such speculations, remarked in his Faraday lecture that "the periodic law, based as it is on the solid and wholesome ground of experimental research, has been evolved independently of any conception as to the nature of the elements; it does not in the least orginate in the idea of an unique matter; and it has no historical connection with that relic of the torments of classical thought, and therefore it affords no more indication of the unity of matter or of the compound character of our elements, than the law of Avogadro, or the law of specific heats, or even the conclusions of spectrum analysis" (Knight, *Classical Scientific Papers: Chemistry, Second Series*, p. 332). The statement following the word "therefore," of course, is a complete *non sequitur*.

[16] The situation was, however, complicated (a) by the fact that what were and were not elements was not always clear, and (b) by the fact that atomic weights were not well known and were difficult to measure, especially without making certain assumptions. With these and other difficulties to overcome, much "theory" was used in the attempt to construct orderings of the elements before Mendeleev and Meyer. See the references in footnote 11.

[17] The one case which approached being a clear one, because of the large difference in atomic weight involved, was that of tellurium and iodine—though, as we shall see momentarily, even this case was not as clear as van Spronsen makes out. Although the ordering of cobalt and nickel was also anomalous, "The atomic weights of the latter pair of elements differed so slightly that at first the extent of the problem was not appreciated, the more so because their properties differed so little" (van Spronsen, *The Periodic System of Chemical Elements*, p. 236). The third anomaly, with regard to the order of argon and potassium, was not known until 1894, and even then there were difficulties about determining the atomic weight of argon. It was with the discovery of this anomaly, according to van Spronsen, that "the problem became extremely disturbing" (ibid.). Even

periodic table was to be given some deeper explanation; and in particular, since the fundamental ordering factor, the atomic weight, increased by discrete "jumps" (which were, in most cases, rather close to integral values) rather than by continuous gradations, that deeper explanation was expected to be in terms of discrete components. Thus that composition was to be understood in terms of constituent *massive* particles (whose step-by-step increase in numbers was reflected in the increases of atomic weights which furnished the ordering principle of the table), and the structure of which involved repetitions at various intervals (reflected in the periodicity of *other* properties of the domain which were "significant," that is, which were related in the periodicity of the table).

This expectation increased in strength until it reached the status of a *demand*, reinforced by the following considerations: (a) more and more other areas revealed themselves as domains in which an atomistic explanation was expected (for example, the case of chemical spectroscopy, to be discussed below); (b) atomistic explanations became more and more successful (statistical mechanics) or at least more and more promising (Kelvin's vortex atom was applied in a great many areas) in other domains; and (c) reasons accumulated . . . for suspecting the domain under consideration (the chemical elements related through the periodic table) to be itself related, as part of a larger domain, to others, including ones in which atomistic explanations were either expected, demanded, or actually provided. All three of these

sorts of considerations were, of course, open to question: (a') the expectations of atomistic explanations in other areas could be criticized as not being sufficiently well founded, and in any case as only expectations; (b') the atomistic explanations advanced in other areas were perhaps not as completely successful (statistical mechanics still had its difficulties, and the vortex atom was in no case applied in precise mathematical detail[18]) or necessary (perhaps "phenomenological thermodynamics" was all that was needed in the domain of heat) as was claimed; and (c') although some relationships between the domain under consideration and others did exist, there were also differences which might obviate the suspicion that those domains should be looked upon as parts of a higher domain requiring a unitary and, in particular, compositional explanation. But the considerations leading to the expectation of a compositional theory to account for the periodic table were strong enough to constitute reasons in favor of a search for such a theory; that expectation, and the research which it guided, were not shaken substantially by such considerations as (a') to (c'), any more than they were disturbed by the tellurium-iodine anomaly. Nor were they shaken by the failure of successive atomistic theories to account successfully for the features of the periodic table, and still less by the opposition of the energeticists and the positivistically minded philosophers, to whom *any* atomistic explanation was unscientific. Considerations (a) to (c), when added to the indications of the periodic table itself (the domain constituted by the periodic table, that is), were strong enough to constitute reasons in favor of a search for such a theory. That the reasons were not logically conclusive did not make them any the less reasons, and good ones, relative to the state of science at the time, nor did it make action in accordance with them any the less rational.

This discussion is clearly generalizable as a principle of reasonable scientific research:

> *To the extent that a domain D satisfies the following conditions or some subset thereof, it is*

---

the case of tellurium and iodine was not admitted as clear by many authorities, including Mendeleev himself, who in 1889 declared triumphantly that "the periodic law enabled us also to detect errors in the determination of the atomic weight of several elements . . . Berzelius had determined the atomic weight of *tellurium* to be 128, while the periodic law claimed for it an atomic weight below that of iodine, which had been fixed by Stas at 126.5, and which was certainly not higher than 127. Brauner then undertook the investigation, and he has shown that the true atomic weight of tellurium is lower than that of iodine, being near to 125" (Faraday Lecture, in Knight, *Classical Scientific Papers: Chemistry, Second Series*, p. 339; for an amusing if vitriolic response to Brauner's work, see Freund, *The Study of Chemical Composition*, p. 505). As to the fourth anomaly, that of the pair protoactinium-thorium, it never presented a problem, as protoactinium was discovered in 1918, five years after Moseley, Rydberg, and Van den Broek demonstrated that atomic number, rather than atomic weight, provided the fundamental ordering principle.

---

[18] For the vortex atom, see McGucken, *Nineteenth-Century Spectroscopy*, esp. pp. 165–175.

reasonable to expect (or demand) that a compositional theory be sought for D:

(Ci) *D is ordered;*

(Cii) *the order is periodic;*

(Ciii) *the order is discrete* (that is, based on a property which "jumps" in value from one item to the succeeding one), *the items having values which are* (within the limits of experimental error) *integral multiples of a fundamental value;*

(Civ) *the order and periodicity are extensive, detailed, and precise;*[19]

(Cv) *compositional explanatory theories are expected for other domains;*

(Cvi) *compositional theories have been successful or promising in other domains;*

(Cvii) *there is reason to suppose that the domain under consideration is related to such other domains so as to form part of a larger domain.*[20]

Although this principle can and will be generalized still further in a number of respects, I will refer to it (or to the more generalized version of it) as the *principle of compositional reasoning.*

In the light of this principle, one might even speak of the "degree of rationality" involved in pursuing a search for a compositional theory: The pursuit of a certain line of research in the expectation of finding a compositional theory for a given domain is more rational, the more of points (Ci) to (Cvii) are satisfied, and the more each of them is satisfied. And the demand that any acceptable theory accounting for the periodic table be a compositional theory is also the more rational, the more of (Ci) to (Cvii) are satisfied, and the more each of them is satisfied. (Such demands are therefore not "dogmatic" in the sense of being irrational, even though the explanation ultimately accepted might not be in accord with those demands. Of course, the extent to which the demands are justified should always be appreciated.) This notion of "degree of rationality" will be found also applicable to other kinds of scientific research and expectations, theoretical or otherwise.[21]

The *problem* regarding the domain, in the case of the periodic table, then becomes not merely to give an account of the domain, but more specifically, to give a compositional theory for it. Lines of research which it is reasonable to pursue are indicated by the character of the theory expected on the basis of the characteristics of the domain, and are made still more specific by other considerations to be discussed later ("background information").

Spectroscopy

Some of the complexity of reasoning in science, however, begins to reveal itself when we investigate another area of late nineteenth-century science which was widely expected to eventuate in a compositional theory. Almost from its inception, spectroscopy was aimed not only at the identification of chemical elements through their characteristic spectra, but also at the development of an explanatory theory having to do with atoms or molecules. As early as 1836, the British spectroscopist Talbot had written: "The definite rays emitted by certain substances, as, for example, the

---

[19] Thus, because it fails to satisfy this condition to a very high degree, Bode's "law," which gives a simple mathematical ordering relationship approximating the distances of the planets out to Uranus reasonably well, cannot be *clearly* included as part of a domain concerning the planets. Ordering only seven items, it is not very extensive; nor is it very detailed, not holding for Neptune or Pluto at all, and not relating to any other planetary characteristics besides distance; nor is it very precise, since it holds only approximately for the planets to which it does apply. In other words, the failure of a theory of (say) the origin of the solar system to account for Bode's "law" cannot be considered a very great weakness of that theory. For such a theory is only weakly (that is, only to the rather low degree that Bode's "law" is extensive, detailed, and precise) required to account for that "law." It is not clear, in other words, that Bode's ordering really sets a *problem* regarding the planets. To put the point more generally, membership in a domain is also a "matter of degree," and is thus subject to debate. That is, whether a theory is reasonably to be expected to account for a certain item is itself a matter which can be questioned. This kind of move in defense of a theory has often been made in the history of science.

[20] (Cv) to (Cvii) clearly have to do with determinations of the "importance" of the problem.

[21] The whole tenor of the present analysis has been in the direction of making the line between "science" and "nonscience" a matter of degree rather than a sharp distinction in terms of some "line of demarcation."

yellow rays of the salts of soda, possess a fixed and inviolable character, which is analogous in some measures to the fixed proportion in which all bodies combine according to the atomic theory. It may be expected, therefore, that optical researches, carefully conducted, may throw some additional light upon chemistry."[22] And half a century later, Rydberg, one of the leading figures in the field, maintained that spectral data "relate to the motions of the least parts of matter, the atoms themselves, in a way that we can expect . . . to find the most simple functions to express the relations between the form of moving bodies, their dimensions, and the active forces."[23] Hence studies of those data could be expected to lead to "a more exact knowledge of the nature of the constitution of atoms."[24]

Thus, throughout the history of the subject, an intimate connection was presumed to obtain between the characteristic lines of the spectra of chemical elements and the characteristics (usually associated in this case, especially in the nineteenth century, with vibrations)[25] of ultimate constituents of chemical substances. So widespread was this belief that one authority on the history of spectroscopy declares that "I have found no spectroscopist who did not admit an atomic theory. As we have seen, 'understanding spectra' became almost synonymous with 'understanding atoms and molecules,' and to spectroscopists atoms and molecules were as real as spectra themselves. Thus the end of the century's anti-atomistic movement, which had its origin in the application of thermodynamics to chemical phenomena, could only have met with resistance from spectroscopists. It had apparently no influence on spectroscopy."[26]

And yet it was not until 1885 that Balmer discovered the first clear and unambiguous ordering relationship between any spectral lines. Thus, *contrary to the case of the periodic table, the conviction that a compositional theory would be found for the spectral domain was not based on ordering relationships, but preceded their discovery.* On what, then, was the expectation based that spectra would be accounted for in terms of a compositional theory? Undoubtedly it had its roots partly in considerations (Cv) to (Cvii) above (having to do with expectation or achievement of success by compositional theories in related domains), together with analogues of (Ciii) and (Civ). Although there was no *ordering* of lines in the sense of there being a known formula relating them (or even a qualitative expression of reasonable generality and precision, of their arrangements), and measurements of their positions were not related to one another by integral multiples of

---

[22] McGucken, *Nineteenth-Century Spectroscopy*, p. 8. Jammer is thus in error in stating that "Mitscherlich [1864] was the first to point out that spectroscopy should be regarded not only as a method of chemical analysis . . . but also as a clue to the secrets of the inner structure of the atom and the molecule." M. Jammer, *The Conceptual Development of Quantum Mechanics* (New York: McGraw-Hill, 1966), p. 63. Mitscherlich had declared that "[The difference in the spectra of the elements and compounds] appeared to me of great importance, because by the observation of the spectra a new method is found of recognizing the internal structure of the hitherto unknown elements, and of chemical compounds." A. Mitscherlich, "On the Spectra of Compounds and of Simple Substances," *Philosophical Magazine*, 4, 28 (1864), p. 169; quoted in C. L. Maier, "The Role of Spectroscopy in the Acceptance of an Internally Structured Atom, 1860–1920," Ph.D. dissertation, University of Wisconsin (1964), p. 38. Maier's comment on this passage is: "To suggest that Mitscherlich is here implying an internal structure of the elemental atoms would be a distortion in terms of the context of the times. He refers to the internal structure of elements and compounds, not of atoms and molecules. It is far more probable that Mitscherlich had reference to the utility of this new spectral distinction in deciding whether elements and compounds were actually structured into entities such as the atom and molecule than that the atoms themselves were internally structured" (pp. 38–39). Maier could not, of course, have had Jammer's later remark in mind here, but his point certainly holds against the latter. However, perhaps Jammer was thinking only of Daltonian "atoms," in which case his remark would be perfectly in order. In this connection, Maier's own reference to "elemental atoms" is confusing: As he himself notes, it is perfectly correct to interpret Mitscherlich's statement as referring to a possible internal structure of the elements (Daltonian atoms).

[23] McGucken, *Nineteenth-Century Spectroscopy*, p. 155.

[24] Ibid., p. 155. It is certainly necessary to reject Dingle's assertion that "Rydberg's work, fundamentally important though it is, was purely empirical" (H. Dingle, "A Hundred Years of Spectroscopy," *British Journal for the History of Science*, Vol. I (1963), p. 209). Maier argues effectively against Dingle's interpretation (Maier, "The Role of Spectroscopy," pp. 102ff.).

[25] See Maier's discussion of what he calls "the acoustical analogy" and its guidance of the search for mathematical formulas relating the spectral lines (Maier, "The Role of Spectroscopy," Ch. III). McGucken's discussion is also highly illuminating in this connection and complements that of Maier very well (McGucken, *Nineteenth-Century Spectroscopy*).

[26] Ibid., p. 204.

some fundamental value, nevertheless the lines of elements are in general discrete (though not always sharp) and, furthermore, maintain their relative positions, as well as a number of other characteristics (for example, under similar conditions, intensity and degree of sharpness), with great preciseness. Thus Rydberg could adduce as a reason for investigating spectra not only that they related to atomic motions, but also that spectral data were "without comparison the richest and most uniform of all relating to all of the known elements."[27]

But a further consideration, which did not emerge from our study of the case of the periodic table, enters into this case: namely, the existence, in another domain, of a way of approaching problems which, by analogy, could offer promise here. Almost from the outset, it was felt by many that the key to success in this domain lay in constructing a theory of atomistic (or molecular) vibrations on the analogy of sound: The various spectral lines of an element would prove understandable as harmonics of a fundamental vibration and could be revealed by an appropriate Fourier analysis. (Indeed, rather than believing that the discovery of an ordering formula would provide a clue to construction of an atomic or molecular theory, many spectroscopists before Balmer believed that the key to discovery of that ordering formula lay in a consideration of the harmonics of fundamental atomic vibrations.) This case differs from ones in which a theory is *related,* or for which there is good reason to suspect is related, as part of a larger domain to the one under consideration.[28] In

the present case, the domain from which the analogue approach is taken need not be so related, that is, what relations there are between it and the domain under consideration are either very general, very tenuous, or not very "significant." Furthermore, what is borrowed is not necessarily the theory of the original domain, but rather an analogue thereof: At best, it is possible to speak only of *adapting* that theory, not of *applying* it without alteration (as one would attempt to do if expecting to unify two related domains). (Of course, such adaptation often involves *interpreting* the current domain so as to make adaptation or application of the imported approach possible; in the present case, the lines had to be looked at—and there was good ground for such interpretation—as records of wavelengths of vibrations, and the explanatory entities, therefore, as vibrators.) Indeed, the adaptation may not, in its original application, even have been compositional. Nor, in fact, need it have been a "theory"; it may have been merely a mathematical technique or a way of approaching a problem. Needless to say, such analogical adaptations are available in the case of ordered domains also.

Thus the present case allows us to give a more general formulation of conditions (Ciii) and (Civ) for compositional theories, and to add a further condition (Cviii). In the present case, of course, with the qualification to be mentioned below, conditions (Ci) and (Cii), having to do specifically with ordered and periodic domains, are inapplicable[29]:

(Ciii') *the items of the domain have discrete values that are preserved (at least under similar conditions) from situation to situation (or, their relations to one another are preserved from situation to situation), even though no general formula (or qualitative*

---

[27] Ibid., p. 155. In our terms, Rydberg here adduces the high degree of "readiness" in addition to "importance" as an argument for investigating spectra.

[28] In this kind of case, where there is not good reason to suspect that the two domains are related as parts of a larger domain, it is appropriate to speak of the importation of ideas from one domain into another as based on "analogy." Where there are such good reasons, it is more appropriate to speak of such importation as being based on "evidence" (or, more generally, on "reasons"). No doubt there are always *some* grounds, at least very weak ones, for suspecting that two domains may be related as parts of a larger domain; and to this extent, the difference between introducing new ideas on the basis of "analogy" and on the basis of "evidence" is a matter of degree—as is the distinction between principles (Cvii) and (Cviii), which will be discussed below. But this fact does not sanction the obliteration of the distinction by those who maintain that all hypotheses in science are introduced on the basis of "analogy."

[29] It should be recalled that (Ci) and (Cii) did not *have* to be fulfilled in order that a compositional theory could be reasonably expected; their fulfillment, above and beyond the fulfillment of some of the other conditions, only provided increased grounds for expecting such a theory. Condition (Ciii), concerned with discreteness and integral multiplicity, while even it is not a *necessary* condition for expecting a compositional theory, does perhaps by itself provide stronger grounds for such expectation, other things being equal, than condition (Ci) alone would. It should be noted that condition (Ci) is undoubtedly susceptible to considerable generalization.

principle) expressing the relations of those values is known. (The existence of the preserved relations is, of course, a rational incentive to suspect the existence of such a general formula and to search for it. In this sense, (Ciii') may be seen as implying an analogue of (Ci), namely: (Ci') *there is reason* (in this case, in the preservation of relations of lines) *for supposing an ordering formula to exist.* If such a formula is found, as in the case of Balmer's discovery, the domain becomes, to the extent that the formula deals with a proportion of the totality of items (lines) of the domain, ordered. If the formula does not yield values of the items which are integral multiples of a fundamental value, then the rationale for expecting a compositional theory will be more complex, depending in general on (Cviii), below.

(Civ') *a number of features of an extensive range of items of the domain are open, with techniques available, to detailed and precise description or measurement.*

(Cviii) *a theory (or, more generally, a technique or method) which has been successful or promising in another domain (even though, unlike the case of (Cvii), that domain is not related or suspected of being related as part of a larger domain to the domain D under consideration) shows promise of being adaptable, with an appropriate interpretation of the items of D, to D.*

In spite of the fact that this and other forms of reasoning take place in science, there are often alternative lines of reasoning available which lead to different conclusions; and the issue of which line has the strongest arguments in its favor is not always clear-cut. Thus, whether a certain body of information constitutes a domain or not; whether a certain item is or is not a part of a domain (that is, whether or not a theory for that domain is responsible for accounting for that item); the extent to which a certain problem is important; the extent to which the state of science is "ready" to investigate a certain problem; the degree of promise of a certain proposed line of research; whether a cer-

tain specific sort of answer to a problem is reasonably to be expected; whether a certain proposed answer to a problem is adequate—all these can be, and in any given situation in the history of science are apt to be, debated. This is not to say that such issues are *never* unambiguously clear, and still less to say that they do not, in general, become more so as science progresses: For substantive scientific knowledge, as it accumulates, imposes more and more stringent conditions on the character and interrelations of domains, the kinds of questions that can reasonably be asked regarding them, the reasons for considering those problems important and ready for investigation, the moves that it is reasonable to make in trying to answer the problems, the kinds of answers to those problems that can be expected to be found, and the conditions an answer must satisfy if it is to be acceptable. Nevertheless, in all these respects, what is maintained by scientists is of a hypothetical nature, and there is generally room for disagreement, without it being perfectly clear which side has the strongest reasons in its favor.

Thus, for example, although most, if not all, prominent spectroscopists of the nineteenth century believed with Talbot, Mitscherlich, and Rydberg that spectral lines are produced by atoms, there were some who did not believe that a study of those lines would lead, at least easily, to knowledge of the constitution of atoms. There were two distinct lines of argument by which this conclusion was arrived at. On the one hand, Kayser and Runge, two of the leading figures in the history of spectroscopy, held that, although spectral lines are ultimately produced by atoms, their study could provide us only with knowledge of *molecules*, not of atoms. Their reasons for this attitude were complex, having to do partly with experimental results and partly with conceptions of how those results could have been produced.[30] On the other hand, yet another major figure, Arthur Schuster, was pessimistic about the possibility, or at least the ease, of gaining insight through spectra even into the nature and structure of molecules,

---

[30] McGucken, *Nineteenth-Century Spectroscopy,* p. 156; the reasons behind this attitude are surveyed by that author on pp. 73–83.

much less of atoms—not because spectra do not have their origin in the vibrations of atoms or molecules, but because spectra are too complex.

[W]e must not too soon expect the discovery of any grand and very general law [from investigation of spectra], for the constitution of what we call a molecule is no doubt a very complicated one, and the difficulty of the problem is so great that were it not for the primary importance of the result which we may finally hope to obtain, all but the most sanguine might well be discouraged to engage in an enquiry which, even after many years of work, may turn out to have been fruitless. We know a great deal more about the forces which produce the vibrations of sound than about those which produce the vibrations of light. To find out the different tunes sent out by a vibrating system is a problem which may or may not be solvable in certain special cases, but it would baffle the most skillful mathematician to solve the inverse problem and to find out the shape of a bell by means of the sounds which it is capable of sending out. And

this is the problem which ultimately spectroscopy hopes to solve in the case of light.[31]

These examples only illustrate some of the kinds of disagreements to which science, for all its accumulated knowledge and constraints, is subject.[32] Nevertheless, the existence of such disagreements, and the frequent unclarity as to which view is correct, do not mean that no rationale exists in science and its development: the viewpoints *often*, if not always, have reasoned arguments in their favor, even if those arguments are not always telling or accepted. And the situation may, and often does, become more clear-cut with further research. The possibility of rationally based disagreements, in fact, plays an important role in science: The possibility helps to ensure that reasonable alternatives will be explored.

Stellar Spectral Classification and Stellar Evolution

We saw that, in the case of the periodic table, the expectation of a compositional theory arose almost immediately; few workers, however, were interested in questions of the evolution of the elements.[33] On the other hand, it was not long after the first spectral classifications of stars were published that those classifications were associated with expectations (and presentations) of an evolutionary theory explaining the classification. In fact, some of the pioneers of stellar classification

---

[31] Ibid., pp. 125–126. Maier conveys a picture of mass desertions of the field of spectroscopy: "As the complexity of spectra became apparent, more and more workers turned away from it as a method of practical analysis. . . . The field of chemical analysis was left to a few stalwarts. . . ." (Maier, "The Role of Spectroscopy," p. 40). Though this is perhaps something of an exaggeration, considering the widespread employment of spectral analysis by astronomers, it was undoubtedly a very common attitude. Even Kayser, in 1910, had come to the point of declaring that "there is little prospect that in the future qualitative analysis will apply spectroscopic methods to a large extent . . . I come to the conclusion that quantitative spectroscopic analysis has shown itself as impractical" (quoted in ibid., p. 41). It is interesting to note that this attitude was repeated by Niels Bohr, who finally gave a successful explanation of spectra in atomistic terms: "The spectra was a very difficult problem. . . . One thought that this is marvelous, but it is not possible to make progress there. Just as if you have the wing of a butterfly, then certainly it is very regular with the colors and so on, but nobody thought that one could get the basis of biology from the coloring of the wing of a butterfly" (quoted by J. Heilbron and T. Kuhn, "The Genesis of the Bohr Atom," in R. McCormmach, ed., *Historical Studies in the Physical Sciences* [Philadelphia: University of Pennsylvania Press, 1969], Vol. I, p. 257).

[32] A splendid example of several different kinds of disagreement of the sorts discussed here is found in the debates regarding interpretation of the photoelectric effect in the years immediately preceding Einstein's "Concerning a Heuristic Point of View about the Creation and Transformation of Light" (*Annalen der Physik*, 17 (1905), pp. 132–148; translated in H. Boorse and L. Motz, eds., *The World of the Atom* [New York: Basic Books, 1966], Vol. I, pp. 545–557) and in the succeeding years up to Compton's interpretation of his X-ray scattering experiments in 1924. Historical aspects of the case are well presented in M. Klein, "Einstein's First Paper on Quanta," *The Natural Philosopher*, No. 2 (New York: Blaisdell, 1963), pp. 57–86, and R. Stuewer, "Non-Einsteinian Interpretations of the Photoelectric Effect," in R. Stuewer, ed., *Historical and Philosophical Perspectives of Science* (Minneapolis: University of Minnesota Press, 1970), pp. 246–263.

[33] For descriptions of such theories, see Venable, *The Development of the Periodic Law*, and van Spronsen, *The Periodic System of Chemical Elements*. It is highly significant that a large proportion of these evolutionary theories of the chemical elements were proposed by men whose primary work, or a considerable part of whose work, lay in fields outside chemistry. An explanation of this phenomenon will be offered shortly.

[34] A. Clerke, *Problems of Astrophysics* (London: Black, 1903), pp. 179–180. One is reminded here of McGucken's statement, quoted earlier, that in the nineteenth century, " 'understanding spectra' became almost synonymous with 'understanding atoms and molecules' " (McGucken, *Nineteenth-Century Spectroscopy*, p. 204). There were, as usual, dissenters from the prevailing view: The British astronomer Maunder wrote in 1892 that "spectrum type does not primarily or usually denote epoch of stellar life, but rather a fundamental difference of chemical constitution" (O. Struve and V. Zebergs, *Astronomy of the Twentieth Century* [New York: Macmillan, 1962], p. 187). Once again we are reminded of the attitudes of some chemists toward compositional theories of the elements.

were among those who presented such theories. So strong and persistent was this tendency that by the end of the century, the historian of astronomy Agnes Clerke could write that "Modes of classifying the stars have come to be equivalent to theories of their evolution."[34] It will prove illuminating to examine the roots of this difference between the case of the periodic table and that of astronomical spectral classifications.

By 1863, the work of Huggins and others had established, on the basis of spectral analysis, that the stars are composed of the same elements as are found on earth. Classification of stars on the basis of spectral features began at about the same time with the work of Secchi, Vogel, and others. The resulting classifications correlated well with the colors of the stars.

At this point, there was no clear order or sequence among the different classes.[35] However, some astronomers (notably Vogel), on the analogy of changes in cooling materials in terrestrial cases, proposed that the different colors (and therefore the correlated spectral classes) were indications of an *evolutionary sequence*. The hottest (and, on this view, the youngest) stars would be blue or white, while red stars were in their old age.[36]

Further, some writers, noting the presence of strong hydrogen lines in the spectra of the white (and therefore, on the theory under consideration, young) stars, conjoined to that theory a hypothesis about the composition of the elements: Generally, either that of Prout, according to which all ele-

ments are composed of hydrogen (and whose atomic weights would therefore be expected to be integral multiples of that of hydrogen), or else some other view of the fundamental composition of the elements (for example, a modification of Prout's hypothesis, to the effect that the ultimate constituents had an atomic weight of one-half that of hydrogen, thus removing what was to the Prout hypothesis an embarrassing anomaly, namely that of chlorine, with a well-documented atomic weight of 35.5).[37] And on the basis of that combination of a theory of the composition of the elements and a theory of stellar evolution, they proceeded to develop an evolutionary theory of the chemical elements (Prout's own view having been, at least in its usually understood form, purely compositional): As stars age, higher elements are built up out of hydrogen, so that older stars are composed of a larger proportion of heavier elements.[38] This view, though it was not without its immediately obvious difficulties, found some support in the fact that, as a general trend, there are an increasing number of higher element lines as we proceed through the spectral classes, ordered according to color, from white to red.[39] Thus, in summary, the older stars were held to be red and composed of heavier elements—on the assumption, of course, that the *total* composition of a star was accurately reflected in the spectral observations of its surface. (It was not until 1921 that Saha demonstrated that the differences of spectra did not reflect even a difference of *atmospheric* composition, but merely one of temperature. The differences in chemical composition of most stars, though highly significant for interpreta-

---

[35] Even the *Henry Draper Catalogue of Stellar Spectra*, which became the basis of modern classifications, in its first volume of 1890, divided the stars into sixteen classes denoted by the letters *A* through *Q* (with *J* omitted), the alphabetical order not corresponding to any ordering among the classes. It was only early in the twentieth century that some of these groups were omitted, or combined and relettered, and the order changed, ultimately becoming the present O-B-A-F-G-K-M-R-N-S ("Oh, be a fine girl, kiss me right now, sweet"), an arrangement which does provide a sequential ordering.

[36] Other theories, for example, that of Lockyer, held that some red stars are young and heating up—according to Lockyer through meteoritic impacts—to the white stage, while others had cooled from the hotter stage. It is worth noting that an alternative view of the colors of stars had been proposed earlier: Doppler had suggested that blue stars are moving toward us, while red stars are moving away. Such an interpretation, however, would imply corresponding shifts of spectral lines, which are not observed.

[37] Such views of element composition were combined with a variety of theories of stellar evolution other than the one under consideration.

[38] There were also theories according to which greater age saw a greater *breakdown* of heavier elements, *ending* with the ultimate constituents.

[39] The existence of this trend does not itself seem to have been taken as a basis for class orderings in the early stages of astronomical spectroscopy: Criteria of ordering would have had to be complex and quite beyond the knowledge of the times. It was, however, clear enough, once the classes had been ordered according to color, to provide additional support for that proposed ordering.

tion of their energy production, internal structure, and evolution, are small. The assumption made by the early astrophysicists, however, was certainly the reasonable one to make at the time.[40])

The situation seems to have been this: While the spectral classes did admit of at least a rough

ordering[41] in terms of increasing numbers and intensities of heavy element lines (coupled with decreasing intensities of hydrogen lines), such orderings were not in general made by pre-twentieth-century pioneers[42] *except* in conjunction with a theory (or analogy) imported into the domain, namely, the color changes that take place with cooling.[43] Nevertheless, a sequential ordering of spectral classes on the basis of decreasing hydrogen and increasing heavier element lines could have been achieved, at least in rough fashion, even without importation of the "background information" (as I will call it) concerning colors of cooling bodies. And if it had been so achieved, its existence would of itself have served as good ground for suspecting that an evolutionary process might be involved, simply on the basis of the fact that the ordering was based on (depending on which end one cared to look from) increase or decrease of certain factors.

However, importation of the background information concerning color changes of cooling bodies made three further contributions to the interpretation of the sequential ordering as an indicator of a possible evolutionary process. First, it increased the strength of the suggestion that an evolutionary sequence might be involved by showing that the sequential ordering of the domain on the basis of lines could be correlated with a *temporal* order having to do with the cooling process. Second, it suggested a *direction* of the evolution—a direction which could not have been extracted from the ordering on the basis of lines alone, unless one made arbitrary assumptions (for example, that the evolution is from "simple" to "complex"). For, the final death of a star being a cold, burned-out state, the red stars should be the oldest. (Unfortunately, the suggestion was not clear with regard to the beginning of the se-

---

[40] The history of vicissitudes in the presumed relation between spectral classification and evolution of stars is a fascinating one, worth examining for the insight it would provide regarding the rationale of scientific change. By 1928, one of the major theoreticians of astrophysics, James Jeans, could write that, although "[t]he early spectroscopists believed that the spectrum of a star provided a sure indication of the star's age," Saha's ionization and excitation theory had shown that "[t]he linear sequence into which the spectra of stars fall is merely one of varying surface temperature. Clearly this circumstance robs stellar spectra of all direct evolutionary significance" (J. H. Jeans, *Astronomy and Cosmogony* [New York: Dover, 1961], p. 166). "The problem of stellar evolution is now seen to be quite distinct from that of explaining the distribution of stars in the [Hertzsprung-] Russell diagram, and, furthermore, the problem can expect no assistance from the observed distribution of stars in this diagram" (ibid., p. 172). Only a few more years were to pass before the pendulum began to swing back in the direction of a connection between spectral classification and stellar evolution— though that connection came to be seen as far subtler and more complex than anything envisioned by the early pioneers like Vogel and Lockyer. Those later views of a connection between spectral classification and stellar evolution, however, involve a deep penetration of "theory" into the domain (as summarized in the classification and the H-R diagram). (For example, Chalonge's system, by relying heavily on the "Balmer jump" in hydrogen spectra as a basis for spectral classification, ties itself closely to the theory of the hydrogen atom; by this means, it becomes highly useful and precise, even though it is limited in applicability to early-type stars [approximately G0 and earlier] which show hydrogen lines and the Balmer jump with sufficient clarity in their spectra.) Analysis of the modern conceptual situation in this area, though it would be very instructive as to the interrelations of "theory" and "observation," and as to the ways in which a new "theory" accounts for such a domain (consisting of an intimate mixture of older classification and later theory), and therefore as to the nature of theories, is too involved to be discussed here.

[41] As was mentioned above, the attempt to lay out such an ordering would not have been free of difficulties. For example, many spectral lines had not been identified, so that the correlation of "lateness" of spectral type with "heaviness" of composition, rather tenuous at best, could not always be assured. Again, what are now called O- and B-type stars have weaker hydrogen lines than A-type (white) ones, even though they are bluer and hence, on the theory under consideration (as well as according to modern astronomy), hotter.

[42] Recall the case of the *Draper Catalogue*, discussed in footnote 35.

[43] This importation was also supported by the obvious explanation of starlight in terms of the stars being hot and radiating. The resultant loss of energy by radiation would also be clearly suggestive of an evolutionary process. Again, an importation into the stellar domain is at work—in this case, supported by the newly verified view that the stars have the same composition as the earth, so that the same processes and laws can be expected to be at work in both (that is, reasons have been found for supposing the terrestrial and stellar domains to be, in this respect, parts of a larger domain).

[44] Lockyer's reasoning was apparently vindicated later by Miss Maury's discovery that, despite the fact that red stars had the same lines in their spectra, in some such stars the lines were more strongly defined than in others. Hertzsprung, in 1905, established by statistical arguments the validity of Miss Maury's conjecture that this indicated that there were two radically different types of red stars. H. N. Russell, a few years later, used this fact in his construction of a new version of Lockyer's general view of stellar evolution. See Struve and Zebergs, *Astronomy of the Twentieth Century*, pp. 195–200.

quence: Were the white stars like Sirius the youngest, blazing forth suddenly at their birth, and gradually burning themselves down to a red old age? Or as Lockyer maintained, were certain red stars young, gradually heating up by some process, if not Lockyer's meteoritic one, to white maturity, after which they declined to a second red stage just preceding death?[44]) And third, by itself constituting the outline, at least, of a theory, an answer to the evolutionary problem regarding the domain, it suggested directions which research could take—directions in which the theory needed to be laid out in detail.[45]

In spite of the residual ambiguity, in this case regarding the beginning of the temporal process of stellar evolution, we can see clearly at work here two more principles of reasonable scientific research, this time applying to the (or a) way in which a problem arises, with regard to a domain, for which an *evolutionary* answer (explanatory theory) can reasonably be expected and sought:

(Ei) *If a domain is ordered, and if that ordering is one which can be viewed as the increase or decrease of the factor(s) on the basis of which the ordering is made, then it is reasonable to suspect that the ordering may be the result of an evolutionary process, and it is reasonable to undertake research to find such an answer (which we have called an evolutionary theory).*

(Eii) *The reasonableness of such expectation is increased if there is a way (for example, by application or adaptation of some background information such as a theory from another domain, whether unrelated or [preferably] related) of viewing that sequential ordering as a temporal one, and still more if a way is provided of viewing that ordering as having a temporal direction.*

Clearly, there are also analogues for evolutionary theories of conditions (Civ) to (Cviii) which were stated earlier for the case of compositional theories. I will call (Ei) and (Eii) together the *principle of evolutionary reasoning*. It should be added that (Ei) *alone* constitutes only a weak reason for undertaking research in quest of an evolutionary theory; for, without (Eii), little or no specific direction is provided for research.

Condition (Ei) was not applied in science before the second half of the nineteenth century;[46] its acceptance as a new general reasoning principle was due in no small measure to the success of Darwin's evolutionary account of biological species. The principle was, however, only gradually accepted, and this perhaps explains (together with the very real difficulties involved in the attempt) the failure, as it seems to us, of pioneers in stellar spectroscopy to try to order the classes unless they did so with an evolutionary idea already in mind. In any case, this example shows that new reasoning principles, as well as new substantive information, can be introduced into science as part of its maturation. Today the principle seems a natural one to use—so much so, in fact, that we often have difficulty in understanding why it was not applied by earlier thinkers.

Why was it, then, that condition (Ei) was applied by a considerable number of workers in the

---

[45] This third point leads to a suggestion that I am not prepared to develop fully in the present paper. Thus far, I have been speaking of theories as answers to questions. While there is a point to this, it should be remembered that those questions themselves, in the cases considered, involve a general idea of what their answer will be like. In this sense—and it is a sense which seems *prima facie* to fit a great many cases in the history of science—a theory is *gradually developed* by a process of increasingly precise and detailed statement of the initial vague idea; there is then no single point in time at which one can say unambiguously that the theory has been *arrived at*. It would then be misleading to speak, in all cases, as if there were a single event of proposing an answer to the theoretical problem. If this suggestion is borne out, as I strongly suspect it will be, one source of philosophers' difficulties with the notion of "theory" will have been exposed: For when does an idea become precise enough to be called a "theory"? The difference would seem to be more a matter of shading than of sharpness. Theory development would then be more appropriately describable, in some cases at least, as a *process of convergence from generality to (relative) precision* than as a precisely datable event like answering a question.

[46] The few exceptions—most notably, the Kant-Laplace "nebular hypothesis" of the origin of the solar system—are not, however, paradigm examples of evolutionary theories. They have to do with the *origin* of a system and its development only to a certain stage, after which, as far as the theory is concerned, it ceases to develop further. Such theories, while they do have much in common with paradigmatically evolutionary theories, should perhaps be distinguished from them as a separate category of "genetic theories."

domain of astronomical spectral classification, but only rarely in that of the periodic table, where one also had a sequential ordering, and even theories, like Prout's, of the composition of the elements? (Recall that Prout's view that elements are built of hydrogen was seen by most of its adherents only as a compositional theory, not an evolutionary one.) Perhaps chemists were so used to thinking of "elements" as "always having been there" that, despite the view of some of them that the elements were *composed* of something still more elementary, they found it difficult to think of them as having been built up in a historical sense. Astronomers, on the other hand, were more used to thinking in terms of origins and development,[47] and many of them evinced a lively interest in the new biological ideas. But there is also a less speculative and sociological answer to the question: for *astronomical evolutionary theories played the same role vis-à-vis the periodic table that the "background information" regarding cooling of hot bodies played vis-à-vis spectral classification* (the role, namely, summarized in condition (Eii), above). That is, having interpreted spectral sequences as temporal, theories of stellar evolution could now be applied to interpret the increasing sequence of atomic weights in turn as a temporal, and as a temporally directed, one. Without this application of (Eii), the sequence of chemical elements, even seen as composed of increasing numbers of like parts, could *at best* suggest, in accor-

dance with (Ei), that there might be something evolutionary involved. But that alone would have provided only weak incentive and, even more important, guidance in the search for such a theory. Thus the comparative absence, among chemists, of theories of the evolution of the elements is quite understandable in terms of the need of some way of satisfying (Eii) before the search for an evolutionary theory of the elements could seem attractive.[48] And if chemists also had an occupational block against seeing the use of the "Darwinian" principle (Ei), the comparative absence among them of interest in an evolutionary theory of the elements would be still more understandable.

I would not want to claim that (Ei) and (Eii) cover all the kinds of reasoning involved whenever an evolutionary theory is suspected and sought. In particular, the case of biological evolutionary theories is undoubtedly too complex to be dealt with adequately in terms of them. But the present case does illustrate one sort of reasoning pattern involved in the expectation of and search for such theories, and a very fundamental and important one at that. (The same qualifications should be understood in regard to the reasoning principles extracted from the other two cases dealt with above, dealing with compositional theories.) . . .

---

[47] At least in the sense of "genetic theories," if not strictly speaking of evolutionary ones; see preceding footnote. Also, the view of stars as radiating bodies called for an evolutionary theory, as was pointed out in footnote 43.

[48] In the light of this need, it is no wonder that theories of the evolution of the chemical elements tended to be proposed by men who worked in areas other than chemistry—and, in particular, in areas in which evolutionary theories were being developed. It is almost as if a theory of chemical evolution *needed* to come from another (appropriate) area (see footnote 33). Note, too, that the application of theories from those domains to the chemical one was based on good reasons—in particular, on the similarity of composition of earth and stars, as established by spectral analysis.

Programs in the Explanation of Behavior

Robert Cummins

The idea that programs of instructions explain behavior is now a commonplace in psychology. The literature which has grown up in information-processing psychology since the early fifties is large and increasingly influential, so I need not document my claim that many psychologists think behavior is explained by programs. But, although the idea is now familiar, it is controversial; controversial, moreover, in a way which is bound to attract and deserve philosophical attention. For while there are many disagreements concerning *which* programs explain behavior, there is a much more fundamental disagreement concerning what *sort* of explanation is being offered, and even concerning whether what is being offered is or could be an explanation at all. A program, after all, is not a law; it is more like a narrative. And a play-by-play account of behavior, while useful data, can hardly be explanatory.

The purpose of this paper is to set forth a sense in which programs can and do explain behavior, and to distinguish this from a number of senses in which they do not. Once we are tolerably clear concerning the sort of explanatory strategy being employed, two rather interesting facts emerge: (1) though it is true that programs are "internally represented," this fact has no explanatory interest; (2) programs which are couched purely in information-processing terms may have an explanatory interest for a given range of behavior which is independent of physiological explanations of the same range of behavior.

INTRODUCTION

What might be meant, then, by the claim that programs explain behavior, or are theories of behavior?

The first point I want to make is that we are all quite familiar in everyday life with appeals to programs in explaining behavior. Suppose we want to know how little Johnny, a boy innocent of electronics, is able to build sophisticated audio equipment. We all know the answer: He follows the instructions in the manuals that come with the kits. He can do what each instruction specifies—i.e., he already has the capacities required by each instruction—and he can follow the list, in the sense in which this means simply adhering to the specified order. Anyone who does what the instructions specify in the order specified, whether knowingly or by sheer accident, winds up having completed a very sophisticated task.

What the manual does is analyze a certain sophisticated performance into unsophisticated performances in a sophisticated order. This allows Johnny to build an amplifier, but it also allows us to *explain how* Johnny is able to do such a thing given his meager capacities. Any set of instructions—recipes, a teacher's rules for doing long division, the directions on your hot-water heater for relighting the pilot light—can, with a slight change from the usual point of view, be seen as an explanatory analysis of a complex capacity. The source of explanatory power in these cases is obvious: Ability to execute a sophisticated performance is reduced without remainder to abilities which are, relatively speaking, simple and antecedently understood.

So the appeal to programs in explaining behavior is a commonplace. And a little reflection on this commonplace has put us in a position to sharpen the claim we are investigating: Programs explain behavioral *capacities,* and they do this by analyzing the exercise of a complex capacity into the organized exercise of relatively less problem-

Reprinted from "Programs in the Explanation of Behavior," *Philosophy of Science* 44 (1977), pp. 269–284, 286–287, by permission of the author and the Philosophy of Science Association.

atic capacities. The question answered is, "How is the individual able to do such and such?", and in the process we are provided with a more or less detailed analytical description of what the individual does (can do) when he does such and such. The performance is sliced up into independently significant "steps" in a way that is evidently nonarbitrary in at least the minimal sense that not any old way of slicing will work: We may slice our original capacity up into capacities our individual has not got, or into capacities that are more problematic than the original.

With this much under our belts, it is only a short step to the recognition that appealing to a program in explanation of a behavioral capacity is an instance of one of the two standardly available strategies for explaining capacities of any kind. Let us detour briefly into general philosophy of science and give a rough description of these two strategies. An understanding of how they differ and how they are supposed to fit together will prove useful in the subsequent discussion.

THE EXPLANATION OF CAPACITIES[1]

Psychological capacities are a species of disposition. Familiar nonpsychological examples are buoyancy, solubility in water, and flexibility. To attribute a disposition to something is (in part) to say what it would do were certain conditions to hold: It would float or dissolve were it placed in water; it would bend were it stressed. The point of the subjunctive construction is that a thing may have a certain disposition even though it never satisfies the requisite conditions, and hence never *manifests* its disposition. Thus to attribute a disposition to something is to say that its behavior is subject to a certain law, a law special to that kind of thing. The law of a water-soluble thing is: Were it placed in water it would dissolve, *ceteris paribus*. This is not a universal law, and hence the question arises as to why the things that are sub-

ject to it *are* subject to it. There must be (and are) certain features peculiar to water-soluble things which explain why *they are,* and other things *are not,* subject to this law. To explain a disposition, then, is to explain why the associated law holds of the disposed objects and not other things.[2]

There are two distinct strategies one may employ in explaining a capacity. The first of these I call the *Subsumption Strategy*. This strategy should be familiar from chemistry and physics, and a single illustration should make it sufficiently clear what I have in mind. Consider the simple disposition that Brian O'Shaughnessy ([7]) calls elevancy: the tendency of an object to rise in water of its own accord. (Elevancy, of course, is not the same as buoyancy; concrete sailboats are buoyant, but not elevant.) To explain elevancy, we must explain why freeing a submerged elevant object causes it to rise. This we may do as follows. In every case, the ratio of an elevant object's mass to its nonpermeable volume is less than the mass per unit volume of water. Archimedes' Principle tells us that water exerts on a submerged object an upward force equal to the weight of the water displaced. In the case of an elevant object, this force evidently exceeds the weight of the object by some amount f. Freeing the object changes the net force on it from zero to a net force of magnitude f in the direction of the surface, and the object rises accordingly. Here we subsume the connection between freeings and risings under a general law connecting changes in net force with changes in motion, and we do this by citing a feature of elevant objects that allows us (via Archimedes' Principle) to exhibit freeing them under water as an

---

[1] This matter is discussed from a different perspective in [4].

[2] The dispositions I have in mind here are ordinary household dispositions such as flexibility, together with the standard dispositions treated in chemistry and physics texts, e.g., acidity conceived as the capacity to "donate" protons. I wish to rule out such things as the tendency of masses to coalesce in space according to an inverse square law (which may not be a disposition at all (see [2])), and philosopher's inventions such as the "disposition" a certain bit of beach has to be covered by my body on a certain day (given "appropriate conditions," e.g., sunshine on the crucial day and my intention to go to the beach on that day if it is fine). Concentration on cases like these is unlikely to be helpful (unless our question is, "Why, exactly, *aren't* these genuine full-fledged dispositions?"). For more on the explanation of dispositions, see [1].

instance of introducing a net force in the direction of the surface.[3]

The Subsumption Strategy is evidently of little use in explaining psychological capacities. Perhaps certain reflexes can be handled in this way, but little else can be expected to yield to this strategy without further ado.

The further ado in question is what I call the *Analytical Strategy*. Rather than subsume the dispositional regularity under a law not special to the disposed objects, the Analytical Strategy proceeds by analyzing a disposition into a number of other relatively less problematic dispositions such that organized manifestation of these analyzing dispositions amounts to a manifestation of the analyzed disposition. Schematic diagrams in electronics provide a familiar and transparent example of this sort of analysis in a physical science context. Since each symbol represents any physical object whatever having a certain capacity, a schematic diagram of a complex device constitutes an analysis of the electronic capacities of the device as a whole into the capacities of its components. Such an analysis allows us to explain how the device as a whole exercises the analyzed capacity, for it allows us to see exercises of the analyzed capacity as programmed exercises of the analyzing capacities. In this case, the "program" is given by the lines indicating how the components are connected, together with such statements as Ohm's law.

Functional analysis in biology is essentially similar. The biologically significant capacities of an entire organism are explained by analyzing the organism into a number of "systems"—the circulatory system, the nervous system, etc.—each of which has its characteristic capacities. These capacities are in turn analyzed into capacities of component organs and structures. Ideally, this strategy is pressed until pure physiology takes over, i.e., until the analyzing capacities are amenable to the Subsumption Strategy. We can easily imagine biologists expressing their analyses in a form analogous to the schematic diagrams of electrical engineering, with special symbols for pumps, filters, pipes, and so on.[4]

A natural assumption—and a correct one, I think—is that the Analytical Strategy must eventually terminate in dispositions which yield to the Subsumption Strategy. For without this assumption, the apparent explanatory progress afforded by the Analytical Strategy is *mere* appearance. That strategy makes progress only insofar as the analyzing capacities are relatively less problematic as compared to the capacity analyzed. We undermine such progress if we suppose that our analyzing capacities might ultimately prove resistant to the Subsumption Strategy, for to suppose this is to allow that these capacities may be utterly mysterious and inexplicable from the point of view of physical science: We shall be barred from any account of why some things and not others obey the associated law. One needn't endorse any starry-eyed claims about the unity of science to find this prospect unwelcome.[5]

Ultimate applicability of the Subsumption Strategy thus constitutes a constraint on particular applications of the Analytical Strategy. This is of

---

[3] I have called this strategy the Subsumption Strategy because I need a name for it, and *subsumption* captures one central element in the strategy that is absent from, and irrelevant to, the other strategy I want to discuss. But the name is potentially misleading in that it might suggest that mere subsumption under law is all that is involved. That more than mere subsumption is involved is brought out as follows. We can easily imagine a property Φ and a disposition D such that "All and only the things having D have Φ" is both true and lawlike, yet such that the presence of Φ does not explain the regularity associated with D. For instance, "All and only the acids turn litmus red" is true and lawlike, yet we cannot explain the disposition to "donate" protons by appeal to this law. I have treated the contrast between explaining a disposition and merely subsuming it in somewhat more detail, though in a different context, in [3].

[4] For a more detailed discussion of the Analytical Strategy in a somewhat different context, see [4].

[5] The prospect is especially unwelcome in psychology for the following reason. Most capacities of interest to psychologists are or can be acquired (or lost) in ways more or less familiar to learning theorists, and this applies to capacities which are primitive from the point of view of analysis as well as to capacities which are analytically complex. Now it seems clear that the *acquisition* (or loss) of an analytically primitive capacity will be inexplicable unless we can see it in terms of a relatively permanent physical change in the organism: The onset of the capacity must stand to some physical change as, for instance, the onset of elevancy in the football stands to its inflation. (For a brief treatment of this point, see [1].)

some importance, for we shall see shortly that it is difficult to make any clear *sense* of this constraint, let alone satisfy it, when an information-processing program is appealed to in explaining a psychological capacity. I think a more or less vague sense of this problem underlies much of the skepticism such appeals have aroused.

FOLLOWING INSTRUCTIONS: TWO SENSES

So much for our detour into general philosophy of science. We may return now to the specific problem at hand, namely clarifying the claim that programs explain behavior. Let us review the plot. First, we have found that it is a commonplace to explain a behavioral capacity by appeal to a program. Second, we have seen that this is an instance of a familiar and respectable explanatory strategy. And finally, we have achieved some grip on what this strategy is supposed to accomplish and how it is supposed to accomplish it. We are now prepared for more heady matters.

It is useful to recognize that recipes, manuals of instructions, rules for doing long division and the like can and do play an explanatory role in addition to the heuristic roles they are designed to play. It is useful if only because it shows that appealing to a program in explaining a behavioral capacity is not a novel and mysterious strategy invented by computer zealots. On the other hand, such examples can be extremely misleading in that the recipe or manual is an object in the environment: a complex stimulus which directs behavior in addition to merely analyzing behavior and describing its direction. Nothing is more obvious, however, than that an organism does not exercise its psychologically interesting capacities by consciously following an external program of instructions. This obvious fact has led some, presumably to preserve the analogy intact, to suppose that the required program is "there" all right, but "internally represented" in the brain, and "tacitly known and followed." Others, rightly suspicious of this talk of "internalization," have been led to reject the appeal to programs altogether.

From our present vantage point, this dispute should seem odd. We have just seen that appealing to a program to explain a capacity is an instance of an explanatory strategy which makes no use of the notion of being instructed to do something. We could express our analyses of electronic circuits explicitly in program form rather than in schematic diagrams, but it would evidently be pointless to suggest that the circuit does what it does because an "internally respresented" program directs its performance, telling it what to do when. This suggests that theorists who speak thus of internalization may have lost their grip on the point of their own strategy.

We can begin to sort this out if we distinguish two senses in which something or someone might be said to "follow instructions." The more familiar sense, though by no means the better understood sense, is what we might call the *imperative sense:* The individual does what the instructions say to do, and does these things *because he is so instructed.* Thus recipes, manuals, etc. The other sense we might call the *descriptive sense:* The individual or system does what the instructions say to do in the order specified and so on, but not necessarily because he or it is so instructed. It is the possibility of taking programs as descriptive in this way which allows us to speak sensibly of brains and machines executing programs, for this sense does not have the implication that the individual or whatever does what it does because of the program. Unlike the recipe case, the program is an analytical description of what happens only. It is a theorist's tool, not a cause. This point is regrettably obscured—perhaps fudged—by the use of such phrases as "internalizing a program." Such phrases encourage—and often incorporate—a confusion between an analysis of a capacity and a cause of its exercise. The inevitable result is complete mystification as to what sort of explanation is being offered. Conversely, once we are clear about the explanatory strategy being employed, we find we have no need of, and no place for, the idea that the program actually directs performance in addition to describing and analyzing its direction.

In at least one clear sense, then, to claim that a

thing—an organism or brain or whatever—can execute a program is to claim that exercise of a certain relatively sophisticated capacity of that thing can be analyzed into the organized exercise of certain relatively less sophisticated capacities of that thing or its parts. Since the program specifies the organization in question, it evidently provides a kind of narrative description of performance as well. It describes what happens in what order, and identifies these happenings as exercises of certain relatively simple capacities. But it does not explain *why* these capacities are exercised in the order specified, whereas the fact that the cook is looking at a printed recipe does help explain just this sort of fact.

Applications of the Analytical Strategy become more interesting as the gap in sophistication and type between analyzing and analyzed capacities grows large. When the gap is large, we trade sophisticated abilities for sophisticated organization. This is the idea behind the assembly line, and it is the idea behind Watson's treatment of habit as a sequence of conditioned reflexes ([8]). As organization becomes more sophisticated, pressure grows to explain why things happen in the order they do. The pressure isn't very great in Watson's case because each response is supposed to produce the next stimulus in a physiologically unproblematic way. But it is important to see that *some* such supposition is required. As the organization grows in complexity, the question becomes correspondingly more difficult to answer. But it is a perfectly good question, and the need for an answer is only obscured by modes of speech which suggest that an internalized program directs matters. To say a capacity is explained by the fact that a certain program is "internalized" suggests that, having discovered *which* program is executed, we needn't explain *why* it is executed, i.e., why matters follow the particular course specified. This is trying to have the recipe and eat it too. Something causes events to take the course specified by the program, but the program itself is not the responsible party.

Now it might seem that this must be wrong: Surely a computer does some of the things it does because it is programmed to do them, and surely

to program a computer is to bring it about that a certain program is internally represented in the machine. Or again, surely it is sometimes right to say that a cook does some of the things he does because of a certain recipe; the recipe *directs* his behavior—indeed, I said this myself a few pages back. Now when the cook has memorized the recipe, surely it cannot be wholly wrong to say that his *memory* directs his behavior, that he does what he does because of his memory, and isn't his memory of the recipe an internal representation of the recipe?

I think there is a way of interpreting these remarks so as to preserve their truth, but no way of interpreting them which preserves their interest as well. Let us begin by asking what is required for a program to be represented in a device or system. I think this matter is a good deal less complicated than has often been supposed, for it seems that for a program *P* to be represented in a system *S* it is sufficient that *S* executes *P*.[6] To see that it is sufficient, notice that there must be some relatively permanent structural features of *S* which ultimately account, via the Subsumption Strategy, for *S*'s capacity to execute *P*, structural features the acquisition (or loss) of which accounts for the acquisition (or loss) of that capacity. Now it seems that it must always be possible to harness these features as the required representations, each instruction being assigned to whatever structural features of *S* account (via the Subsumption Strategy) for the capacity that instruction specifies.[7] Once this assignment is made, we are free to think of the structural features underlying a given instruction as encoding that instruction, i.e., as an alternate symbolic representation of it.

Now let us imagine a certain system *S* which executes a certain program *P,* and hence represents *P* as well. In the execution of *P* by *S,* events

---

[6] Perhaps I should say explicitly here that, as I use the term, to say *S executes P* is to attribute a capacity to *S; executes* is therefore to be distinguished from *is executing, has executed,* etc.

[7] If *S* is capable of following the program, then it is capable of following each instruction. Hence, each instruction expresses a capacity of *S* (or one of its parts).

take the course they do because *S* is structured in a certain way. Evidently S is not structured in this way *because P is represented in S*. Hence, if we are to insist that events take the course they do because *P* is represented in *S,* we must say that *S*'s being structured in the way it is just *is P*'s being represented in *S*. This seems plausible enough. Of course, it will not always be the case that a system representing a certain program executes that program, a written token of the program itself being an example of a system which represents the program but does not execute it. And even a system which does execute the program may represent that program in virtue of features which are quite irrelevant to execution, e.g., in virtue of the instructions being printed on various parts. But this problem may be avoided in a natural way by restricting attention to a stronger concept of representation which requires that each instruction be represented by those structural features which account for the system's capacity to execute it. We have just seen that systems that *do* execute the program are bound to represent it in virtue of the very facts which explain execution, and hence these systems are bound to strongly represent the program. Taking advantage of this, we can see that to say that *P* is (strongly) represented in *S* could be thought of as a way of attributing to *S* the structure which accounts for execution of *P* by *S*. Construed along these lines it is true that in the execution of *P* by *S,* events take the course they do because *P* is (strongly) represented in *S*.

It is true . . . , but not interesting. To say that *S* strongly represents *P* adds nothing to the fact that *S* executes *P* beyond what is already required by our methodological constraint, viz., that, like all dispositions, execution ultimately be explicable (via the Subsumption Strategy) by appeal to structural features of *S*. No constraint is put on what these features must be beyond what is already imposed by the requirement that *S*'s capacity to follow *P* be explained. Indeed, we cannot say whether a representation *R* of *P* in *S* is a strong representation until we have determined whether, for each instruction, the features of *S* which *R* assigns to that instruction are such as to account for *S*'s capacity to execute that instruction.

If this is correct, then, though there is a sense in which it is true to say that a system *S* is capable of doing what a certain program *P* specifies because *P* is represented in *S,* saying this cannot have any explanatory force whatever. We do explain a complex capacity in a perfectly familiar way when we exhibit performance as execution of a program. But we cannot go on to explain why the program is executed, i.e., why events take the direction specified, by appealing to the fact that the program is represented in the executing system.[8] . . .

Once persuaded of this result we must ask why the stories about programming a computer and memorizing a recipe seemed so compelling.[8] What we were able to salvage from these stories is this: For a computer to be programmed or a recipe memorized is just for the program or recipe to be represented in the computer or cook by the very structural features which account for the capacities in question. This evidently leads nowhere, yet the examples are surely not entirely without point. For one thing, when we program a computer we do something to it—feed in cards or whatever—which *alters* it in a relatively permanent way, i.e., in a way which endures until the machine is programmed again, something wears out or the like. Now it is perfectly in order to say that the computer executes the program because it was altered in a certain way, and this seems to be part of what underlies the misleading remark that the computer does what it does—i.e., follows the program—because it is programmed to do it. And perhaps something analogous partly underlies the equally misleading remark that the cook follows the recipe because he has memorized it.

Another thing that is at work here is an adumbrated but genuine application of the Analytical

---

[8] To these stories we might add the following. "For a program *P* to be represented in *S* is (sometimes) for *S* to have certain *information* available. And certainly it can't be wholly wrong to say that *S* can do certain things because certain information is available to *S*." Of course this is right, provided the "things *S* can do because the information is available" are not the very things specified by *P,* for otherwise to say the information is available will just be a misleading way of saying that *S* is structured in a way which explains its capacity to follow *P*.

Strategy. When we say that the cook stirs the candy while heating it because the recipe he has memorized required this, *part* of what we do is point to a recipe, or the existence of a recipe, which exhibits the role or function of stirring while heating in relation to the larger project the cook is engaged in when he stirs while heating. In the same way, a flow chart for doing long division tells us what bringing down the next digit contributes to getting a quotient. If someone who follows (descriptively) this chart when he finds quotients now "brings down the next digit," we may explain why he does what he does in the sense in which this means explaining what his current doing contributes to his larger undertaking. This sort of fact is not unnaturally expressed by saying that he is bringing down the next digit because the chart requires it at this point. But its naturalness does not prevent it from being dangerous in the hands of philosophers and psychologists.

So there is something—perhaps two things—legitimate in talk of computers doing what they do because they are programmed to do it, or cooks doing what they do because they have memorized a recipe which requires it. But it is not what the words lead us to expect when we take them as the sort of context-free expressions of literal truth beloved of scientists and philosophers. When we get a glimmer of what *is* legitimate in such talk we find that it lends no support whatever to the idea that execution is explained by representation.

INFORMATION PROCESSING PROGRAMS

Skeptical Preliminaries

By now it should seem more or less obvious that organisms—and indeed devices of all kinds—execute programs, and that complex capacities can be explained in a certain familiar and respectable sense by appeal to the fact that certain programs are executed. Indeed, once we see that this claim does not involve trying to have our recipe and eat it too, it seems that we are left with something no one could possibly deny. This is quite right, I

think, provided we neglect the kind of programs everyone finds most interesting, namely information-processing programs (hereafter often abbreviated IP)—programs for manipulating symbols.

Executing a program in the descriptive sense we have staked out seems a simple matter: A device—be it brain or computer—executes the program if it does what each instruction says to do and it does these things in the order specified.[9] So program execution seems to come down to instruction execution, and to execute an instruction in the descriptive sense is just to do what the instruction says to do.

The problem with this thought is that, depending on what sort of instruction is under consideration, it may be far from clear what counts as doing what that instruction says to do. It is perhaps clear enough whether some device is, say, closing the relays labeled *A* through *D,* and hence clear enough whether it is executing the instruction, "CLOSE RELAYS *A* THROUGH *D*." But how about, "CARRY ALL BUT THE LEAST SIGNIFICANT DIGIT"? If our program consists of instructions like this, what sense can we make of the claim that a bunch of relays or flip-flops or neurons does what the program says to do? Perhaps we can explain, via the Subsumption Strategy, the electrochemical capacities of neurons, but this will not help us to satisfy the constraint we placed on analysis if the capacities our analysis appeals to are capacities to manipulate symbols. Come to think of it, do we even know what it would be *like* to explain a capacity of that kind via the Subsumption Strategy? It is evident that there is no set of physical features a thing must have to have a capacity to perform a given symbolic operation: All

---

[9] A more precise formulation would run as follows: Were *d* to execute instructions 1 through *n,* then normally *d* would subsequently execute instruction $n + 1$, for all $0 < n < m$, where there are *m* instructions. Even this is faulty: What counts as the "next instruction" depends on which instructions have already been executed, and on the initial state of the device. The initial state determines the first instruction, and together these determine the second instruction, and so on. In this way, different initial states determine different *paths* through the program. The definition above, then, may be taken to define path execution, execution then being defined thus: *d* executes *P* iff *d* executes each path through *P.*

adding machines add, but they are physically as disparate as wind-up alarm clocks and transistor radios. Indeed, it is hard to see how the physical facts could bear at all on whether or not a device executes a program of information processes, for such programs say nothing whatever about physical make-up. Early researchers were quite clear about this matter. Thus Newell, Shaw, and Simon, reporting on the "Logic Theorist" in [6], stressed that the theory they were proposing was entirely neutral with respect to the physical properties a thing must have for their theory to be true of it. This seems to flout our constraint. The problem raised here has already been hinted at: No matter how elementary a symbolic transaction is, specifying a capacity to perform it is not specifying a physical disposition, and this makes it difficult to see how the Subsumption Strategy could ever get a grip on the atomic capacities such a program deals with.

Salvage

Of course I have been willfully dense in the foregoing in order to bring out a certain problem. I have been exhibiting what one of my graduate students once called a prejudice in favor of thin symbols. If a smear of ink can be a numeral, i.e., represent a number, why not a closed relay or a neural connection?

This is fair enough, and useful up to a point. Evidently, in the right circumstances, an execution of the instruction to close relays A through D could count as execution of the instruction to carry all but the least significant digit. But under what circumstances? Well, very roughly and intuitively, closing relays A through D must stand to other transactions in the device as the instruction to carry all but the least significant digit stands to the other instructions in the program. There must be, in some sense yet to be explained, an "isomorphism of structure" between the information-processing program and some program couched in physical terms. Even this very crude formulation is enough to make it clear that the concept of execution for IP programs is a tricky affair. The problem is that, given any physical transaction you like,

and any symbolic operation you like, there will generally be some set of conditions—some context—in which that physical transaction would count as a performance of that symbolic operation. This follows more or less obviously from the reflection that the "fat symbols"—neurons or whatever—are, from our point of view, in code. In a cypher, any numeral can, taken independently, be assigned any significance whatever. It is only a definite context which places any constraint on the significance to be assigned to an individual numeral, the requirement being that when each numeral is assigned a meaning by a determinate rule, a coherent message should result. We cannot get at program execution one instruction at a time for reasons exactly analogous to those preventing us from getting at cypher significance one numeral at a time.

Actually, cyphers are easier than nervous systems in two respects. First, although there are indefinitely many different ways to make sense of a cypher if there are any ways at all, what we are after is the intended message. Thus there is a unique right answer among the infinity of workable solutions, and we generally can tell, given the context, whether a given solution is the right one by this criterion. But when we are attempting to treat transactions in the nervous system as symbolic operations, there is no "intended interpretation": We are seeking an interpretation which will be theoretically fruitful, and, as is the case with scientific description generally, there is no way to tell in advance whether a given way of describing matters will prove a help or a hindrance. The fact that workable solutions are not unique, and that the first one we hit on may not be the best, is often forgotten simply because it is so difficult to come up with any workable solution at all. But there is no reason to suppose that the criterion of theoretical fruitfulness selects a unique solution as *the correct solution*.

The second respect in which cyphers are easier is more serious: We know how to individuate numerals in standard notation, and we know that numerals are the significant units in a cypher. In short, we know what to assign significance *to*. But we do not know this about organisms. This introduces a truly radical indeterminancy into the problem: Perhaps equally workable solutions can be based on incommensurable ways of individuating the physical parts and transactions to be treated.

This point is worth hammering home. I once purchased a plastic model of a computer circuit consisting, according to the directions, of three flip-flops whose interconnections could be varied in all the standard ways. By ignoring this interpretation in favor of another, it is possible to view the device as consisting of six cells, each capable of assuming eight states, whose interconnections can be varied in a great variety of nonstandard ways. Had the thing grown out of the ground in the outback, there would evidently be no point in asking which interpretation is *right*. The only question would be, which is more useful for the purposes at hand, for instance, explaining the behavior of a large containing system. This is precisely our situation with respect to organisms.

It evidently makes sense, though complicated sense, to treat systems of flip-flops as systems of symbols whose values are determined by their states. And this allows us to make sense of the claim that such systems execute information processing programs, for when we have a rule which tells us which part to treat as which symbol, and which states count as which values, what we have is a way—though not a unique way—of translating an information processing program into one specifying physically described transactions. Given that *this* makes sense, an analogous claim about organic systems *makes sense* as well. The constraint placed on the Analytical Strategy now applies in a straightforward way, for when I have provided the translation, I have specified in physical terms the capacities to which my analysis ultimately appeals.

There is nothing irredeemably mysterious, then, about saying that organic systems execute information processing programs. But given that we *can* say this, we must ask, why anyone should *want* to, especially in the light of the two facts we have just uncovered, viz., (i) that a "translation" into a program dealing in physically specified capacities is ultimately required anyway, and (ii) that

the resulting analyses will be radically *non-unique* in this sense: Two completely incommensurable analyses of the same complex capacity may both be correct; two incommensurable IP programs for performing the same complex task may have adequate but different physical translations both of which are programs the organism may truly be said to execute. Indeed, this much seems demonstrable with my simple plastic computer cell.[10]

I will conclude by suggesting two rather unexciting reasons why someone might want to continue down the information processing trail in psychology in spite of these facts. First, there is a pragmatic motivation. The Analytical Strategy, we said, is most interesting when the difference in type and sophistication between analyzed capacity and analyzing capacities is very large, i.e., when sophisticated abilities are traded in on sophisticated organization of simple capacities. Now the mathematical theory of rule-governed symbol manipulations—the theory of algorithms mainly developed by Turing—provides highly developed techniques for making such trades, provided the capacities are specified as capacities to perform symbolic operations. The prospect of promoting the capacity to store ones and zeros into the capacity to solve logic problems, speak English, recognize patterns and the like has proved irresistible as an explanatory strategy just as it has proved irresistible as an engineering strategy. The computer provides a valuable aid: As the organization gets very sophisticated it becomes difficult to tell whether we have made a successful trade. Running the program on a computer settles the matter with relative ease. So the first point is simply that the Analytical Strategy is facilitated by

---

[10] We might reduce the indeterminacy by requiring that a "correct" information processing program be translatable into some *particular* program dealing only in physically specified capacities, e.g., the one which comes to have preferred explanatory status in physiology. This seems to render the information processing program entirely useless, but actually it does not. What the requirement amounts to is this: the preferred physiological program must have an information processing translation which accounts, via the Analytical Strategy, for the information processing capacities of the organism. I touch on this point again below.

couching the problem in terms amenable to powerful existing analytical techniques.

My second suggestion is slightly more interesting. Some behavior is naturally described from the start in something approaching IP terms. Adding is behavior, but an adding machine is something which adds, not something which prints ink marks of such and such shapes. Some adders don't print at all, and there are various notational systems in use. Once we see this, it is clear that what makes something an adder is the fact that its behavior is subject to a certain systematic interpretation. What makes a device an adder is thus a set of facts akin to the set of facts which makes a page of cyphers an expression of a certain message. If we want to theorize about adders, and "adding behavior," therefore, we will have to abandon the vocabulary of physical capacities. Of course, every adder is some physical object or other, and each case of adding is some physical transaction or other. But there is no set of physically specifiable characteristics a thing *must* have to be an adder, though there are indefinitely many different sets of such characteristics which are sufficient. Thus, if we want to explain capacities like the capacity to add, an IP analysis recommends itself from the start precisely because it abstracts from the physical nitty-gritty. Perhaps we don't so much want to know how the little ink marks are made, but rather how it is that the device always manages to print something interpretable as a *sum*. This, it seems, requires a particular analysis of adding (chosen from the many possible analyses) and a demonstration that certain physical transactions in the device can be systematically treated as performances of the symbolic operations appealed to in that analysis. In short, we need to show that a certain IP program is executed, and to explain at the physical level why it is executed, i.e., why matters take the complex course specified. This suggests that in discussing the requirement that an information processing program be translatable into a program trafficking only in physically specified capacities we have been viewing matters from the wrong direction. Perhaps what we should say is that the (or a) preferred physical analysis of an organism's physically specified capacities must have an information processing translation which accounts, via the Analytical Strategy, for that organism's information processing capacities (i.e., those of its capacities which it can be seen to share with other organisms and devices only when described in information processing terms).

Whether psychologists should ask questions about organisms analogous to the one I raised about adders is a matter I would not presume to pronounce upon. It seems clear enough that some *do* (especially about verbal behavior), and perhaps this is reason enough for a philosopher to subject such questions to critical scrutiny. A methodological principle I follow is that the theories scientists put forward are to be accepted more or less at face value: Serious theorizing is to be presumed innocent of conceptual confusion, though not of falsehood, until proven guilty. It thus has the status of data: It is to be explained if possible and explained away only as a last resort. I have therefore presumed that programs do explain psychological capacities in some sense, the question being *what* sense. If you do not like the sense I found, and cannot find a better, perhaps you will prefer to settle for no sense at all. . . .

REFERENCES

[1] Cummins, R. "Dispositions, States and Causes." *Analysis* 34 (1974): 194–204.

[2] Cummins, R. "States, Causes and the Law of Inertia." *Philosophical Studies* 29 (1976): 21–36.

[3] Cummins, R. "The Philosophical Problem of Truth of." *The Canadian Journal of Philosophy* 5 (1975): 103–122.

[4] Cummins, R. "Functional Analysis." *The Journal of Philosophy* 72 (1975): 741–765.

[5] Fodor, J. "The Appeal to Tacit Knowledge in Psychological Explanation." *The Journal of Philosophy* 65 (1968): 627–640.

[6] Newell, A., H. Simon and J. Shaw, "Elements of a Theory of Human Problem Solving." *Psychological Review* 65 (1958): 151–166.

[7] O'Shaughnessy, B. "The Powerlessness of Dispositions." *Analysis* 31 (1970): 1–15.

[8] Watson, J. *Behaviorism.* New York: Norton, 1930.

Ideals of Natural Order

Stephen Toulmin

. . . [C]onsider the seventeenth-century revolution in dynamics. To bring out clearly the central change this involved, we must begin by looking at the popular caricature of pre-Galilean theories of motion, which can ultimately be traced back to Aristotle. "Men's ideas about dynamics before Galileo," this caricature suggests, "rest upon a simple mistake. Aristotle was a philosopher, or at best a naturalist, rather than a true scientist: He may have been skilled at collecting specimens and miscellaneous information, but he was bad at explaining things; and he put forward certain clearly mistaken views about the ways in which the motion of a body is related to the forces acting on it. The benighted man asserted that the effect of a given force acting continuously upon a given body was to keep it in motion at a constant speed; whereas we have now looked and seen that a constant force produces not a constant speed but a constant acceleration. Aristotle's successors, having an exaggerated idea of his intellectual capacities, trusted to his words rather than to their own eyes, and only the work of that obstinately common-sensical genius Galileo—who refused to allow himself to be befuddled by mere words, and insisted on submitting even the most august and authoritative doctrines to the test of experience—led to this chimera being blown away into the oblivion where it properly belonged."

So stated, this may be less a caricature than the caricature of a caricature; though in less blatant forms, or in part, or by implication, one comes across this view often enough. Still, the picture implicit in this account, both of Aristotelian mechanics and of Galileo's own contribution to our thought, embodies a collection of anachronisms and legends exceptional even for the history of science—a subject in which the George Washingtons have for too long been chopping down their fathers' cherry trees. What one must protest against is not only the intrinsic unlikelihood that a man of Aristotle's capacities could have fallen for so elementary a blunder; but even more, the way in which this caricature degrades a fascinating episode into a prosaic one.

What, then, is wrong? To begin with, this picture gives Aristotle credit for attempting to do something he never seems to have envisaged. It treats him as putting forward a mathematical relationship of the sort familiar from modern dynamical theory. The relationship in question could be written either in words, as

Force varies as Weight times Speed

or alternatively in symbolic shorthand, as

$$F \propto W \times V$$

But this can be read into Aristotle's works only through an anachronism. We scarcely encounter this sort of mathematical equation before the sixteenth century A.D.—not just because the notation employed had yet to be developed, but because the very ideas implicit in the use of such equations were worked out only in the years immediately preceding 1600.

Of course, if we accept this equation as an expression of Aristotle's view, and interpret it in modern terms, we shall find it sadly mistaken. For nowadays it would be natural to take the symbol for speed as meaning "instantaneous velocity," and the symbol for force in its standard Newtonian sense—both of them notions formulated with complete clarity only in 1687. At once objections arise. The term *weight* now appears entirely out of place, and should presumably be replaced by the term *mass*; and even so, the ratio of the force act-

From Chapter 3 of *Foresight and Understanding: An Enquiry into the Aims of Science* by Stephen Toulmin (1961), pp. 47–61. Reprinted by permission of the author and Indiana University Press.

ing on a body to its mass surely determines not its velocity but its acceleration. Yet the question ought to be asked: Are we taking Aristotle in a sense which he ever intended? If we read things into him, it will not be surprising if we end up by finding him seriously at fault.

How else, then, can Aristotle's thesis be taken? In general, his practice in the *Physics* is to put forward, not precise equations, but at most ratios or proportionalities relating (say) the lengths of time different bodies will take to go the same distances when different degrees of effort are exerted upon them. He presents these examples as concerned with *tasks*, posing his questions in the form: "If such-and-such a task takes such-and-such a time, how long will such-and-such another task take?—e.g., if one man can shift a given body 100 yards by himself in 1 hour, how large a body can two men jointly shift through the same distance in the same time? Aristotle concludes that, within limits, the amount a body can be displaced by a given effort will vary in inverse proportion to the size of the body to be moved; and also, that a given body can be displaced in a set time through a distance directly proportional to the effort available.

Of course (he allows) beyond certain limits this sort of ratio does not apply: A body may be so large that it can be shifted only by a team of men and will not respond at all to one man working single-handed—he cites the instance of a team of men moving a ship. And he further remarks, with equal truth, that the effect one can achieve by a given effort depends entirely on the resistances to be overcome. A team of men pulling a ship will take longer to go from one point to another across rough ground than to move it the same distance over smoother ground. As a first approximation, and lacking any better definition of "resistance," Aristotle accordingly puts forward the further proportionality: The distance travelled in a given time will vary inversely as the strength of the resistance offered to motion.

Three things need saying about these ratios of Aristotle before we look at the dynamical innovations of the seventeenth century. The first is this:

Aristotle concentrated his attention on the motion of bodies against appreciable resistance, and on the length of time required for a complete change of position from one place to another. For a variety of reasons, he never really tackled the problem of defining "velocity" in the case when one considers progressively shorter and shorter periods of time—i.e., instantaneous velocity. Nor was he prepared to pay serious attention to the question how bodies would move if all resisting agencies were effectively or completely removed. As things turned out, his hesitations were unfortunate; yet his reasons for hesitating are understandable, and in their way laudable. Though he was a philosopher—and so, in some people's eyes, bound to have had his head in the clouds and his feet off the ground—Aristotle was always unwilling to be drawn into discussing impossible or extreme examples. Leaving aside free fall for the moment as a special case, all the motions we observe going on close around us happen as they do (he saw) through a more or less complete balance between two sets of forces: those tending to maintain the motion and those tending to resist it. In real life, too, a body always takes a definite time to go a definite distance. So the question of instantaneous velocity would have struck him as over-abstract; and he felt the same way about the idea of a completely unresisted motion, which he dismissed as unreal. In point of fact (I suppose) he was right. Even in the interstellar void, where the obstacles to the motion of a body are for practical purposes entirely negligible, there do nevertheless remain some minute, if intermittent, resistances.

In the second place: If we pay attention directly to the kinds of motion Aristotle himself thought typical, we shall find that his rough proportionalities retain a respected place even in twentieth-century physics. Interpreted not as rival laws of nature to Newton's, but as generalizations about familiar experience, many of the things he said are entirely true. One can even represent him as having spoken more wisely than he knew. For, where he argued only for rough, qualitative ratios connecting gross measures of distances and time, contemporary physics actually recognizes an exact mathematical equation corresponding closely to them—though, of course, one that relates instantaneous variables of a kind Aristotle himself never employed.

This equation is known as Stokes' Law. It relates the speed at which a body will move when placed in a resisting medium, such as a liquid, to the force acting on it and the thickness (viscosity) of the medium. According to Stokes, the body's speed under those circumstances will be directly proportional to the force moving it, and inversely proportional to the liquid's viscosity. Suppose we take a billiard ball and drop it through liquids of different viscosities in turn—water and honey and mercury: In each case it will accelerate for a moment, and then move steadily down at a limiting (terminal) speed determined by the viscosity of the liquid in question. If the impressed force is doubled, the speed of fall will be doubled: If one liquid is twice as viscous as another, the billiard ball will travel at only half the speed.

The third point combines these two previous ones. The fact is that Aristotle based his analysis on one particular explanatory conception or *paradigm,* which he formulated by considering examples of a standard type; and he used these examples as objects of comparison when trying to understand and explain *any* kind of motion. If you want to understand the motion of a body (in his view), you should think of it as you would think of a horse and cart; i.e., you should look for two factors—the external agency (the horse) keeping the body (the cart) in motion, and the resistances (the roughness of the road and the friction of the cart) tending to bring the motion to a stop. Explaining the phenomenon means recognizing that the body is moving at the rate appropriate to an object of its weight, when subjected to just that particular balance of force and resistance. Steady motion under a balance of actions and resistances is the natural thing to expect. Anything which can be shown to exemplify this balance will thereby be explained.

In the case of bodies moving against a sufficiently slight resistance, as we all know, Aristotle's analysis ceases to apply. If you drop a billiard ball through air instead of through water or treacle, it will go on accelerating for a long time: Under normal terrestrial conditions, it could never fall far enough to reach the "terminal velocity" at which Stokes' Law would begin to apply. The factor of paramount importance in this case will for once be the initial period of acceleration, and that was something to which Aristotle paid very little attention. If he had thought more about the problem of acceleration, indeed, he might have seen the need for something more sophisticated than his simple proportionalities.

As things turned out, Strato, the very first of Aristotle's followers to take an active interest in mechanics, turned his attention at once to this very phenomenon. Yet, for many reasons—some of them intellectual, some of them historical—neither he nor his ancient successors made any great progress beyond Aristotle's ratios. It was left to the Oxford mathematicians of the early fourteenth century to add an adequate definition of acceleration to Aristotle's previous accounts of speed, and so to pave the way for the work of Stevin and Galileo and Newton.

So much for the background: What, then, did happen in dynamics during the seventeenth century? Certainly the popular caricature is wrong in one respect: Men did not suddenly become aware that Aristotle's views about motion were false, whereas their predecessors had trusted blindly in their truth. Aristotle himself stated his ratios as applying only within certain limits, and John Philoponos (around A.D. 500) made it absolutely clear that projectiles and freely falling bodies could be explained only by bringing in some radically new conception. The problem was *how* to remedy matters.

In retrospect we can see that the paradigm at the heart of Aristotle's analysis had to be abandoned and replaced by another, which placed proper importance on acceleration. Yet this was not easy: Men were accustomed to think of motion as a balance between force and resistance, as much on the basis of everyday experience as through "blind trust in Aristotle's authority." They took the necessary steps hesitantly, a bit at a time, and in the face of their inherited commonsense. The most radical single step was taken by Galileo, yet even he stopped short of the conclusion which is generally credited to him.

There is nothing uniquely natural or rational, Galileo rightly insisted, in a terrestrial body coming to rest when outside forces are removed: Rest and uniform motion alike, he argues, are "natural" for a body on the Earth. Let us only approach gradually toward the extreme case of zero resistance, which Aristotle had denounced as impossible, and we shall recognize this. Think of a ship (say) on a calm sea and imagine the resistances to motion progressively reduced until we could neglect them entirely. If that were to happen, said Galileo, the ship would retain its original motion without change. If it had originally been at rest, it would remain at rest until some outside force started it moving; while, if it were originally moving, it would go on traveling along the same course at the same speed until it met an obstacle. Continuous, steady motion could therefore be just as natural and self-explanatory as rest, and outside resistances alone could bring terrestrial bodies to a halt.

By this step, Galileo went a long way toward the classical Newtonian view, but he did not go the whole way. True, he had exchanged Aristotle's paradigm of natural motion—the horse and cart being pulled along against resistances at a constant speed—for a very different one. For Aristotle, all continuous terrestrial motion was a "phenomenon," or departure from the regular order of things, and he would have asked: "What is to keep Galileo's imaginary ship moving?" Galileo, however, now demanded only that we account for *changes* in the motion of bodies. His ship could move forever without a motive force.

Now this result looks, at first sight, very like our modern "law of inertia." Yet Galileo's paradigm was no more identical with our own than Aristotle's had been. For what he envisaged as his ideal case was a ship moving unflaggingly across the ocean along a Great Circle track, for lack of any external force to speed it up or slow it down. He saw that uniform motion could be quite as natural as rest; but this "uniform motion" took place along a closed horizontal track circling the center of the Earth; and Galileo took such circular

motion as entirely natural and self-explanatory. He does not seem to have regarded the ship as constrained by its own weight from flying off the Earth on a tangent—the image which can clearly be found in Newton.

Indeed, if Galileo's imagined ship *had* taken off from the sea and disappeared off into space along a Euclidean straight line, he would have been no less surprised—in fact, *more* surprised—than we. We should have one possible hypothesis at hand to explain this amazing event—namely, that the action of gravity on the ship had been suspended, so that it was no longer constrained to remain in contact with the Earth's surface and could fly off along its natural path. For Galileo, however, this option was not yet available: In his eyes, some active force alone could have obliged the ship to travel in a perfectly rectilinear path, instead of cruising of its own accord round its natural Great Circle track.

When we turn to Newton we find that the ideal of natural motion has changed yet again. The fundamental example is completely idealized. From now on, a body's motion is treated as self-explanatory only when it is free from all forces, even including its own weight. Galileo could explain his conception of "inertia" by referring to real objects—ships moving on the sea. Newton started his theory by offering us a completely abstract example as the paradigm—namely, a body moving at uniform speed in a Euclidean straight line—and this, as Aristotle would have retorted, is the last thing we should ever encounter in the real world. But, then, Newton does not have to claim that, as a matter of fact, any actual body moves exactly as his first law specifies. He is providing us, rather, with a criterion for telling in what respects a body's motion calls for explanation and what impressed forces we must bring to light if we are to succeed in explaining it. Only if a body ever were left completely to itself would it move steadily along a straight line, and no real body ever actually is placed in this extreme position. This is, for Newton, simply a dynamical ideal, the sole kind of motion which would be self-explanatory, free of all complexity, calling for no further comment—if it ever happened.

It should be clear, by now, why I present Newton's first law of motion or principle of inertia as an "ideal of natural order"—one of those standards of rationality and intelligibility which (as I see it) lie at the heart of scientific theory. At their deepest point, the seventeenth-century changes in dynamics, which had been brewing ever since the early 1300s, involved the replacement of Aristotle's commonsensical paradigm by Newton's new, idealized one. From some angles, this could look like a regression: From now on it was necessary, for theoretical purposes, to relate familiar everyday happenings to idealized, imaginary states-of-affairs that never in practice occur—ideals to which even the motions of the planets can only approximate. Yet the change paid dividends. Once this new theoretical ideal was accepted, the single hypothesis of universal gravitation brought into an intelligible pattern a dozen classes of happenings, many of which had previously been entirely unexplained; and, in the resulting theory, Newton could display a whole new range of relationships and necessities as part of the intelligible order of Nature.

This example has illustrated how the idea of explanation is tied up with our prior patterns of expectation, which in turn reflect our ideas about the order of Nature. To sum up: Any dynamical theory involves some explicit or implicit reference to a standard case or "paradigm." This paradigm specifies the manner in which, in the natural course of events, bodies may be expected to move. By comparing the motion of any actual body with this standard example, we can discover what, if anything, needs to be regarded as a "phenomenon." If the motion under examination turns out to be a phenomenon—i.e., "an event . . . whose cause is in question" as being "highly unexpected"—the theory must indicate how we are to set about accounting for it. (In Newton's theory, this is the prime task of the second law of motion.) By bringing to light causes of the appropriate kind, e.g., Newtonian "forces," we may reconcile the phenomenon to the theory; and if this can be done we shall have achieved our "explanation." Every step of the procedure—from the initial identification of "phenomena" requiring explanation to the

final decision that our explanation is satisfactory—is governed and directed by the fundamental conceptions of the theory.

No wonder that the replacement of one ideal of natural motion by another represents so profound a change in dynamics. Men who accept different ideals and paradigms have really no common theoretical terms in which to discuss their problems fruitfully. They will not even *have* the same problem: Events which are "phenomena" in one man's eyes will be passed over by the other as "perfectly natural." These ideals have something "absolute" about them, like the "basic presuppositions" of science about which R. G. Collingwood wrote.

If that is so, the problem at once arises: How do we know which presuppositions to adopt? Certainly, explanatory paradigms and ideals of natural order are not "true" or "false," in any naive sense. Rather, they "take us farther (or less far)," and are theoretically more or less "fruitful." At a first, everyday level of analysis, Aristotle's paradigm of uniform, resisted motion had genuine merits. But a complete mathematical theory of dynamics required a different ideal. It was no good first taking uniform, resisted motion as one's paradigm, and supposing that one could later explain how bodies would move in the absence of resistances by canceling out the counteracting forces: That way inevitably led to the unhelpful conclusion that a completely unresisted motion was inconceivable—since the attempt to describe it in everyday terms entangles one in contradictions. (Suppose you reduce the resistances finally to zero, then, in Aristotle's ratio of motive force to resistance, the denominator becomes zero; and you are landed in all the difficulties which spring from "dividing by nought.") On the contrary: It was necessary to proceed in the opposite direction. One must first start by taking entirely unresisted motion as one's ideal of perfectly simple and natural motion and only later introduce resistances—showing how, as they are progressively allowed for, the uniform acceleration produced by a single force gives way to the uniform terminal speed of a horse and cart.

Changes in our ideals of natural order may

sometimes be justifiable, but they do have to be justified positively. In due course uniform rectilinear motion became as natural and self-explanatory to Newton's successors as rest had been for Aristotle. Yet neither view of inertia was self-evidently correct: Each must be known by its fruits. So its tenure as the fundamental ideal of dynamics was conditional and provisional. For just as long as we continue to operate with the fundamental notions of the Newtonian theory, his principle of inertia keeps its place in physics. Yet, at the most refined level of analysis, it has already lost its authority. As one consequence of the twentieth-century changeover to relativity physics, the conception of "natural motion" expressed in Newton's first law has again had to be reconsidered. The implications of the resulting amendments in our ideas may have been less drastic than those which flowed from the seventeenth-century revolution, yet—at the theoretical level—the change has been nonetheless profound.

. . . The general point I am making does not apply only to abstract and highly developed sciences, such as dynamics. We use similar patterns of thought in the common affairs of daily life; and, in a sense, the task of science is to extend, improve on, and refine the patterns of expectation we display every day. There is a continual interplay between the two fields.

Suppose, for example, that we look out of the window into the street. One car travels steadily down the road, comes into sight, passes our window, and goes on out of sight again: It may well escape our attention. Another car comes down the road haltingly, perhaps jerking and backfiring, perhaps only stopping dead and starting up again several times: Our attention is immediately arrested, and we begin to ask questions—"Why is it behaving like that?" From this example it is only a step to the case of a practical astronomer, for whom the continued motion round its orbit of the planet Jupiter is no mystery, but for whom questions would immediately arise if the planet were suddenly to fly off along a tangent to its orbit and out into space: "What made it do that?" And from this it is only one further step to the mathematicians' point of view, according to which, if left to

itself, Jupiter ought to travel, not in a closed orbit, but in a straight line—so that even its normal, elliptical path demands explanation.

All the same: Though the form of this thought pattern is preserved, its content changes drastically, and one popular epigram about explanation is falsified in the process. For it is often said that "explanation" consists in relating things with which we are unfamiliar (and which so need explaining) to others which are familiar to us (and so stand in no need of explanation). At a certain level this epigram has a point. If you are explaining something *to somebody*—what might be called an explanation *ad hominem*—it is sensible to start from things he knows about and understands, and to relate the things he finds mysterious back to those which he finds intelligible. This is one of the purposes of "models" in the physical sciences. The beginner in electricity is helped to understand the relations between voltage, current, and resistance by having the flow of electricity in a wire compared with the flow of water down a tube: "Don't you see? Voltage is like the head of water in the system, resistance is like the narrowness of a pipe, and the current of water or electricity depends in each case on both factors."

Scientific discoveries, however, do not consist in arguments which are plausible *ad hominem*, but rather in explanations which will stand on their own feet. In these explanations, the relation between the "familiar" and the "unfamiliar" may be reversed. Revert for a moment to Newtonian dynamics: The ideal of inertial motion which underlies Newtonian explanations can hardly be described as *familiar*. (Aristotle would laugh at that suggestion.) If we were to insist on accounting for the "unfamiliar" in terms of the "familiar," instead of vice versa, we should never be able to shake ourselves loose of Aristotelian dynamics. Aristotle's paradigm is familiar in a way that Newton's never can be; and the Newtonian program of treating the motion of horses and carts as being something highly complex, which can be understood only by starting from planets and projectiles and then allowing for a multiplicity of interfering forces—remains rather paradoxical to the commonsense mind. . . .

THE VALIDATION OF SCIENTIFIC KNOWLEDGE

3

In the last section we saw that scientific theories are regularly proposed to explain observed phenomena. Indeed, that is a major goal of scientific theories. Yet before they can become accepted explanations, part of scientific knowledge, scientific theories must prove their mettle. Until then they are merely hypotheses, and, as the history of science shows, even highly plausible hypotheses all too frequently turn out false. But how do scientific theories prove their mettle? What is the method by which they are tested and found acceptable or unacceptable in science?

It is a commonplace that scientific theories are tested by the results of observation and experiment. Indeed, that is the hallmark of the empirical method, which is held to be a primary source of the success of science. But since scientific theories typically deal with unobservable entities and processes, such as genes and natural selection and electromagnetic fields, they cannot be directly tested by observation. Their mode of observational testing is, instead, indirect. More specifically, what theories postulate about unobservable entities and processes has consequences for observable states of affairs; these consequences, in fact, constitute the empirical content of the theories. Hence scientific theories are tested by deducing from them consequences regarding observable states of affairs and then comparing these consequences with the results of observation and experiment.

Consider, for example, the transition from the phlogiston theory to the oxygen theory in the history of chemistry—the so-called "Chemical Revolution." When the oxygen theory was proposed by Lavoisier in the 1770s, the phlogiston theory was the generally accepted theory of combustion and calcination (slow combustion). According to the latter theory, combustibles and metals contained an "inflammable principle" called *phlogiston*, which they released on combustion and calcination, leaving ashy substances (elementary earths) as residues. The phlogiston theory thus implied that combustibles like wood and charcoal would lose weight on combustion. For if, as the phlogiston theory said, these substances were compounds of elementary earths and phlogiston, and if, as the theory said, combustion was a process in which phlogiston was given off, then it was deducible from the theory that these substances would lose weight whenever they underwent combustion. The phlogiston theory had other true observational consequences as well. For example, it implied that when metallic ores, in smelting, were heated with charcoal, they would turn into metals—the phlogiston would be transferred from the charcoal to the metallic elementary earths to produce metallic compounds, that is, metals.

But the phlogiston theory also had false observational consequences. For example, although it implied that metals and combustibles, such as sulfur and phosphorus, would lose weight on calcination and combustion, the fact was that they *gained* weight. And it was facts like this, anomalous for the phlogiston theory, that the oxygen theory was proposed to explain and *did* explain. Thus, if, as the oxygen theory said, metals and sulfur and phosphorus were elementary earths, and if, as that theory said, calcination and combustion were processes in which oxygen was absorbed from the air, then it was deducible from the theory that these substances would gain weight whenever they underwent calcination or combustion. The oxygen theory had many other true observational consequences. For example, the theory implied that combustion would not occur in a vacuum and that it would soon cease in an enclosed volume of air. The theory even implied that the combined weights of the *two* products (ashy residues and airs given off) of the combustion of substances like wood and charcoal would be greater than the weight of the original substances.

But what followed from these various true and false observational consequences of the phlogiston and oxygen theories? What judgments regarding the two theories could they support, and by what process of reasoning? Regarding such questions there has been—and still is—much disagreement in the philosophy of science. In fact, there are no fewer than six major approaches to such questions of theory testing currently in the forefront of discussion: (1) justificationism; (2) falsificationism; (3) conventionalism;

(4) the methodology of scientific research programmes; (5) Thomas Kuhn's sociological approach; and (6) the testing paradigm of scientific inference. In what follows I shall briefly explain each of these approaches.

JUSTIFICATIONISM

What followed from the various true and false observational consequences of the phlogiston and oxygen theories? Justificationists would say that the oxygen theory was shown to be very probably true by its observational consequences, whereas the phlogiston theory was shown to be definitely false by its observational consequences. Let me explain. According to justificationism, since theories have an infinite number of observational consequences to be compared with the results of observation and experiment, theories can never be "verified"—that is, definitely shown to be true. They can, however, still be partially justified or "confirmed" to different degrees, showing that they are, to a greater or lesser degree, probably true. More specifically, each true consequence of a theory, regardless of whether it was taken into account when developing the theory or only discovered after the theory was already developed, is a positive instance of the theory adding to the degree of confirmation or degree of probability of the theory. And if a great many positive instances of the theory have been observed, while no negative instances have been observed—of course, the instances should be as diversified as possible—then the degree of confirmation or probability of the theory will be high. (Some justificationists hold that such degrees of confirmation will ultimately be capable of expression in quantitative terms and that a sufficiently developed inductive logic will tell scientists how to calculate them.) If, on the other hand, even a single negative instance is observed, then the theory will have been falsified. Hence, justificationists would conclude that, since a great many positive instances of the oxygen theory *were* observed in the years after the enunciation of that theory, while no negative instances were observed, the oxygen theory was shown to be highly probable. At the same time, the phlogiston theory was shown to be definitely false by its ever-accumulating negative instances. Small wonder that scientists abandoned the phlogiston theory in favor of the oxygen theory.

Rudolf Carnap, one of the most important advocates of justificationism, presents and defends that position in "The Confirmation of Laws and Theories."

FALSIFICATIONISM

Falsificationists would agree that the phlogiston theory was shown to be definitely false at the time of the Chemical Revolution, but would claim that the oxygen theory was only shown to be *possibly* true—not, as the justificationists would say, very probably true. What is the difference? Falsificationists would explain that neither the truth nor the probable truth or "degree of confirmation" of a theory can be validly inferred from the truth of those of its observational consequences that scientists have examined. After all, such examined observational consequences, however numerous, represent a vanishingly small proportion of the infinite set of observational consequences of the theory. What's more, the entire examination has taken place in one tiny part of the universe during one tiny period of its duration, even though the theory being tested applies to the entire universe during the entire period of its duration. (Think of someone trying to infer the qualities of the Atlantic Ocean after having observed only a few drops of its water drawn during a one-minute interval from one spot on the beach at Coney Island!) The result is that the examined observational consequences of a theory provide very poor support for any claim about a theory's truth or even probable truth.

But if true observational consequences cannot furnish scientists with valid support for claiming that a theory is true or even probably true, *false* observational consequences *can* furnish scientists with valid support for claiming that a theory is *false*, since a true theory cannot have false consequences. Falsificationists conclude that scientific testing is to be understood as a method of eliminating false theories by observation and experiment rather than a method of discovering true theories. And theories that are *not* eliminated in the testing process—that is to say, theories that are "corroborated"—are tentatively accepted because, unlike falsified theories, they *may* be true.

With regard to the Chemical Revolution, then, the falsificationist would say that the phlogiston theory was shown to be false, whereas the oxygen theory was shown to be possibly true. The falsificationist would hasten to add, however, that the oxygen theory was shown to be possibly true not by the facts that Lavoisier had taken into account when developing his new theory (though the justificationist would say that such facts had confirmatory value), but only by those facts that could have falsified the new theory once it was developed.

Karl Popper, currently the leading exponent of falsificationism, articulates and defends that position in "Science: Conjectures and Refutations."

CONVENTIONALISM

Conventionalists would disagree with both the justificationist and falsificationist accounts of the Chemical Revolution. Indeed, conventionalists would maintain that experimental results showed neither that the phlogiston theory was false nor that the oxygen theory was probably or even possibly true. Both theories could have accommodated all the experimental results. The oxygen theory was accepted and the phlogiston theory rejected because the former system was simpler, more coherent, more economical, and so on, than the latter system. And the same is true of any theory choice. Theories are not chosen on empirical grounds; given sufficient ingenuity, facts can be accommodated by any conceptual framework. Rather, theories are chosen by *convention*, on the basis of considerations like simplicity.

Conventionalists justify their stand by pointing out that theory testing is a more complicated process than justificationists and falsificationists allow. To test a theory, as justificationists and falsificationists have noted, consequences must be derived from it that can be compared with the results of observation and experiment. But, as these individuals have *not* noted, such consequences derive not from the hypothesis to be tested in isolation, but from that hypothesis in conjunction with a whole system of accented theories. Thus, if the derived consequence is false, what deductively follows is not the falsity of the hypothesis under test but rather the falsity of a *conjunction* of theories one of which is the hypothesis at issue.

Consider, for example, one of the false consequences of the phlogiston theory, that metals will lose weight on calcination. According to justificationists and falsificationists, this consequence (as well as others) falsified the phlogiston theory. But the phlogiston theory alone does not entail this consequence. To derive it, a number of additional hypotheses were needed: that phlogiston has weight; that nothing having weight is added to metals as they calcinate; that if something having weight is removed in a process while nothing having weight is added, then the result will weigh less than the original; and so on. Thus, what deductively followed from the observed weight increase of metals after calcination was not the falsity of the phlogiston theory, but the falsity of the *conjunction* of the phlogiston theory with these auxiliary hypotheses.

A number of options were then available. Scientists could have rejected the phlogiston theory, as Lavoisier did. Or scientists could have rejected one or more of the auxiliary hypotheses, as many phlogistonists did. For example, they could have hypothesized that phlogiston had negative weight (as phlogistonists had earlier done); that is, they could have rejected the first auxiliary hypothesis. Or they could have hypothesized that something having weight—for example, Boyle's fire particles or Cavendish's precipitated water—was added to the metals as their phlogiston was released, which would have involved rejecting the second auxiliary hypothesis. Or they could have hypothesized, as de Morveau did in 1772, that if phlogiston is lighter than air, then removing it from a body immersed in air will cause that body to weigh more; that is, they could have rejected the third auxiliary hypothesis. So long as these or other kinds of revision succeeded in satisfying the requirements of experiment, they were all logically acceptable. And only considerations like simplicity could have decided among them. But, conventionalists assure us, the same is true in the case of any theory.

Pierre Duhem, a highly influential physicist, historian, and philosopher of science of the early part of this century, gives a forceful presentation of conventionalism in "Physical Theory and Experiment."

THE METHODOLOGY OF SCIENTIFIC RESEARCH PROGRAMMES

Advocates of the methodology of scientific research programmes—Imre Lakatos and his followers—have amended the conventionalist account of theory testing in a number of ways. They grant conventionalists that a negative experimental result can never falsify a theory, but only a whole system of theories—that is, the conjunction of a theory under test and a set of auxiliary hypotheses. They grant conventionalists, therefore, that any theory can be saved from negative experimental results by suitable revisions of its auxiliary hypotheses. But they suggest that a standard is (and ought to be) imposed by scientists on the revisions by which a theory may be saved, a standard clearer and more rigorous than the conventionalists' simplicity, coherence, economy, or what have you. Indeed, if such a standard were not imposed, they emphasize, theory choice would be left to subjective taste or scientific fashion, leaving too much leeway for dogmatic adherence to a favorite theory.

But what standard do (and should) scientists impose on the revisions by which a theory may be saved? Lakatos and his followers suggest the following: Each revision made in a theory's auxiliary hypotheses to save that theory from a negative experimental result should render that theory and its auxiliary hypotheses capable of predicting all the facts they had previously predicted, together with the previously anomalous fact *and at least one new fact*. Then saving a theory with the help of auxiliary hypotheses that satisfy this standard will represent scientific progress, while saving a theory with the help of auxiliary hypotheses that do not satisfy this standard will represent scientific degeneration; and the degree of progress will be measured by the degree to which a theory and its auxiliary hypotheses lead to the discovery of new facts. But then, any scientific theory will be appraised together with its auxiliary hypotheses (as conventionalists said), and also together with its predecessors (as conventionalists did *not* say), so that we may see by what sort of change it was brought about. That is to say, the unit of appraisal will be a *series* of theory-systems, rather than a single theory-system (as with conventionalists) or a single theory (as with justificationists and falsifications).

In the history of science, according to Lakatos, the series of theory-systems we have been discussing tend to be characterized by a remarkable continuity evolving from the "scientific research programmes" set out at their start. These scientific research programmes each consist of (1) a set of central theoretical assumptions (what we have been calling the "theory" and what Lakatos calls the "hard core" of the programme); (2) a directive that bids scientists to develop auxiliary hypotheses to save the central theoretical assumptions from negative experimental results (Lakatos calls this the "negative heuristic" of the programme); and (3) suggestions for developing such auxiliary hypotheses (Lakatos calls this the "positive heuristic" of the programme). If a research programme's development leads to scientific progress, it is successful, and if its development leads to scientific degeneration, it is unsuccessful—in which case its hard core of theoretical assumptions may have to be abandoned. In his "Falsification and the Methodology of Scientific Research Programmes," Lakatos emphasizes that the main problems of theory assessment cannot be satisfactorily explored except in this framework of scientific research programmes.

Regarding the Chemical Revolution, then, advocates of the methodology of scientific research programmes would grant conventionalists that the phlogiston and oxygen research programmes were both able to accommodate the main facts about combustion and calcination by 1785, though both programmes still faced some outstanding anomalies as well. But advocates of the methodology of scientific research programmes would quickly add that only the oxygen research programme accommodated these facts in a progressive way—that is, anticipated them in a coherent pattern of development. The phlogiston research programme, on the other hand, coped with these facts in a degenerating way—that is, in an incoherent manner *after* their discovery within the oxygen programme. The result was that, from 1785 on, the number of chemists who abandoned the phlogiston programme for the oxygen programme increased steadily, first in France, and then abroad.

THOMAS KUHN'S SOCIOLOGICAL APPROACH

But note that chemists did not abandon the phlogiston programme all at the same time; indeed, the scientific community's gradual shift of allegiance from the phlogiston programme to the oxygen programme, beginning in 1785, took at least seven years. What's more, not all chemists finally did abandon the phlogiston programme. For example, Henry Cavendish and Joseph Priestley, two of the greatest chemists of the period, were never reconciled to the oxygen theory. Facts like these, Thomas Kuhn would point out, dealing as they do with scientists well-versed in questions of scientific appraisal, are inexplicable from the point of view of the methodology of scientific research programmes. And they are inexplicable as well, Kuhn would add, from the points of view of justificationism, falsificationism, and conventionalism. For certainly, from these points of view, scientists should have found the oxygen theory well confirmed or well corroborated or simpler or progressive, and the phlogiston theory falsified or overly complex or degenerating, by some relatively definite time.

The problem, Kuhn would venture, is that the methodology of scientific research programmes, as well as justificationism, falsificationism, and conventionalism, make the question of theory assessment look simpler and more straightforward than it is. Indeed, as Kuhn points out in "Objectivity,

Value Judgment, and Theory Choice," scientists use at least five criteria of theory assessment:

1. *Accuracy:* A theory's consequences should be in qualitative and quantitative agreement with the results of existing experiments and observations.

2. *Consistency:* A theory should be consistent with itself and with other currently accepted theories applicable to related aspects of nature.

3. *Scope:* A theory's consequences should extend far beyond the particular observations, laws, or subtheories it was initially designed to explain.

4. *Simplicity:* A theory should bring order to phenomena that in its absence would be individually isolated and, as a set, confused.

5. *Fruitfulness:* A theory should disclose new phenomena or previously unnoted relationships among phenomena already known.

But these criteria of theory assessment are individually imprecise—scientists may legitimately differ about their application to concrete cases—and, when applied together, the criteria repeatedly conflict with one another. As a consequence, scientists fully committed to the same criteria of theory assessment may nonetheless reach different conclusions when choosing between competing theories. The shared criteria of theory assessment, in short, function as values that influence theory choice rather than as rules that determine it, and they need to be fleshed out by individual idiosyncratic factors to explain the particular theoretical choices that particular scientists make. Finally, such criteria are not fixed once and for all except in a very rough sense: Both their application and, more obviously, the relative weights attached to them have varied markedly with time and field of specialization, many of these variations associated with particular changes of theory.

Kuhn cautions, however, that such imprecision and conflict and incompleteness and variation in scientists' criteria for theory assessment do not justify the view that theory choice is a product of subjective taste or scientific fashion. For, he notes, objectivity is analyzable in terms of criteria like accuracy and consistency. If these criteria do not supply all the guidance that we have customarily expected of them, then it may be the nature rather than the limits of objectivity that is shown.

THE TESTING PARADIGM OF SCIENTIFIC INFERENCE

At least most of the scientists who participated in the Chemical Revolution thought they were determining the true, or at least the truer, system of chemistry when they debated the merits of the phlogiston and oxygen theories vis-à-vis the theories' various true and false observational consequences. However, according to Kuhn's sociological approach—as well as the methodology of scientific research programmes and conventionalism—the truth or falsity of these theories cannot be so determined by observational consequences. Indeed, according to these views, scientists accept or reject a theory on the basis of its accuracy, consistency, scope, simplicity, and fruitfulness (for Kuhn's sociological approach), or its progressiveness (for the research programmes of the methodology of scientific research programmes), or its relative simplicity (for conventionalism). But nothing regarding the truth or falsity of the theory is held to follow from such features of it. Were the scientists of the Chemical Revolution simply confused about what they were doing? Are most scientists equally confused? Or are justificationism or falsificationism—approaches that allow questions regarding a theory's truth or falsity to be settled by reference to its observational consequences—more promising accounts of theory testing after all, despite the problems that have been pointed out in them?

There is yet a further possibility: the so-called testing paradigm of scientific inference, presented by Ronald Giere in "Testing Theoretical Hypotheses." According to Giere, the unit of appraisal in science is a theoretical hypothesis—that is, a construct that identifies elements of a theoretical model or defined type of system with elements of a real system of objects and then goes on to claim that such a real system of objects exhibits the structure of the model. Such units of appraisal are extremely limited in scope—far more so than, for example, the theories of Carnap, Popper, or Kuhn, or the systems of theories of Duhem, or the research programmes of Lakatos. Indeed, the claim that the solar system is a Newtonian particle system (that is, fits a Newtonian model) is an example of a theoretical hypothesis for Giere, as is the claim that heating mercury until a red ash appears on its surface fits a phlogiston model.

An appropriate test of such an hypothesis—and this is the leading idea of the testing paradigm—is a physical process with special properties, namely, a high probability of a positive outcome if the hypothesis is true and a high probability of a negative outcome if the hypothesis is false. The result of such a test is not, as with justificationism, a reevaluation of the degree of probability of the hypothesis relative to the newly augmented total available evidence for it, but a simple acceptance of the hypothesis as true or rejection of it as false. In short, an hypothesis is either accepted because it has passed an appropriate test, or rejected because it has not. It is not accepted because it has a high probability of being true relative to its evidence.

But what is the justification for the general decision rule, central to the testing paradigm, to accept a theoretical hypothesis as true if the outcome of an appropriate test is positive, and to reject a theoretical hypothesis as false if the outcome of an appropriate test is negative? Giere sets for himself the task of determining the acceptable decision principle that leads to this general decision rule. In this way he hopes to elucidate why the general decision rule should be accepted. The decision principle Giere comes up with is the principle that tells decision makers to choose options that have expected values at least as great as some minimum established either by the decision makers or by the decision context. One important consequence of this account is that no theoretical hypothesis is regarded as true for all purposes or in any possible context: The acceptance of a theoretical hypothesis is automatically relativized to a scientific context.

SUMMARY

So, what is the method by which theories are tested and judged acceptable or unacceptable in science? In the foregoing I have sketched six major approaches to this question currently in the forefront of discussion: (1) justificationism; (2) falsificationism; (3) conventionalism; (4) the methodology of scientific research programmes; (5) Thomas Kuhn's sociological approach; and (6) the testing paradigm of scientific inference. As we have seen, these six approaches share certain features in common, though they also differ in crucial respects. Thus, they all allow that a scientific theory is tested by deducing from it consequences regarding observable states of affairs that are then compared with the results of observation and experiment, but they differ regarding what might follow from such a comparison. For justificationism, falsificationism, and the testing paradigm of scientific inference, true observational consequences will warrant a judgment regarding the truth of a theory—either that it is probably true (for justificationism), or that it is possibly true (for falsificationism), or simply that it is true (for the testing paradigm)—whereas false observational consequences will warrant a judgment that the theory is false. For conventionalism, the methodology of scientific research programmes, and Kuhn's sociological approach, on the other hand, neither true nor false observational consequences will warrant any judgment regarding the truth or falsity of the theory. Again, for justificationism, falsificationism, and Kuhn's sociological approach, the units of scientific knowledge and appraisal are theories, whereas for the other approaches these units are different—either systems of theories (for conventionalism), or research programmes (for the methodology of scientific research programmes), or theoretical hypotheses (for the testing paradigm of scientific inference).

The result of these differences, as we have seen, is that the accounts of scientific episodes suggested by the different approaches will be different: in such accounts scientists will be drawing different conclusions for different reasons at different times about different units of scientific knowledge and appraisal. This result, however, suggests a way to decide among the six approaches: As you study the selections that follow, aside from attending to the cogency of the arguments offered for each approach, see to what extent each approach makes sense of the history of science. Does it help us to understand why scientists said and did what they did? Does it help us, at least in some cases, to evaluate what scientists said and did—to distinguish good science from bad science and both from non-science? These are some of the questions you should have uppermost in your mind as you read through the selections that follow.

The Confirmation of Laws and Theories

Rudolf Carnap

The observations we make in everyday life as well as the more systematic observations of science reveal certain repetitions or regularities in the world. Day always follows night; the seasons repeat themselves in the same order; fire always feels hot; objects fall when we drop them; and so on. The laws of science are nothing more than statements expressing these regularities as precisely as possible.

If a certain regularity is observed at all times and all places, without exception, then the regularity is expressed in the form of a "universal law." An example from daily life is "All ice is cold." This statement asserts that any piece of ice—at any place in the universe, at any time, past, present, or future—is (was, or will be) cold. Not all laws of science are universal. Instead of asserting that a regularity occurs in *all* cases, some laws assert that it occurs in only a certain percentage of cases. If the percentage is specified or if in some other way a quantitative statement is made about the relation of one event to another, then the statement is called a "statistical law"—for example, "Ripe apples are usually red" or "Approximately half the children born each year are boys." Both types of law—universal and statistical—are needed in science. The universal laws are logically simpler, and for this reason we shall consider them first. In the early part of this discussion "laws" will usually mean universal laws.

Universal laws are expressed in the logical form of what is called in formal logic a "universal conditional statement." (. . . [W]e shall occasionally make use of symbolic logic, but only in a very elementary way.) For example, let us consider a law of the simplest possible type. It asserts that, whatever x may be, if x is P, then x is also Q. This is written symbolically as follows:

$$(x)\ (Px \supset Qx)$$

The expression "(x)" on the left is called a "universal quantifier." It tells us that the statement refers to *all* cases of x, rather than to just a certain percentage of cases. "Px" says that x is P, and "Qx" says that x is Q. The symbol "$\supset$" is a connective. It links the term on its left to the term on its right. In English, it corresponds roughly to the assertion, "If . . . , then . . . ."

If "x" stands for any material body, then the law states that, for any material body x, if x has the property P, it also has the property Q. For instance, in physics we might say, "For every body x, if that body is heated, that body will expand." This is the law of thermal expansion in its simplest, nonquantitative form. In physics, of course, one tries to obtain quantitative laws and to qualify them so as to exclude exceptions; but, if we forget about such refinements, then this universal conditional statement is the basic logical form of all universal laws. Sometimes we may say that, not only does Qx hold whenever Px holds, but the reverse is also true; whenever Qx holds, Px holds also. Logicians call this a biconditional statement—a statement that is conditional in both directions. But of course this does not contradict the fact that in all universal laws we deal with universal conditionals, because a biconditional may be regarded as the conjunction of two conditionals.

Not all statements made by scientists have this logical form. A scientist may say, "Yesterday in Brazil, Professor Smith discovered a new species of butterfly." This is not the statement of a law. It

From Chapters 1, 2, 3, 23, and 24 of *Philosophical Foundations of Physics* by Rudolf Carnap, pp. 3–6, 19–35, 225–235. Copyright © 1966 by Basic Books, Inc., publishers. Reprinted by permission of the publishers.

speaks about a specified single time and place; it states that something happened at that time and place. Because statements such as this are about single facts, they are called "singular" statements. Of course, all our knowledge has its origin in singular statements—the particular observations of particular individuals. One of the big, perplexing questions in the philosophy of science is how we are able to go from such singular statements to the assertion of universal laws.

When statements by scientists are made in the ordinary word language, rather than in the more precise language of symbolic logic, we must be extremely careful not to confuse singular with universal statements. If a zoologist writes in a textbook, "The elephant is an excellent swimmer," he does not mean that a certain elephant, which he observed a year ago in a zoo, is an excellent swimmer. When he says "the elephant," he is using *the* in the Aristotelian sense; it refers to the entire class of elephants. All European languages have inherited from the Greek (and perhaps also from other languages) this manner of speaking in a singular way when actually a class or type is meant. The Greeks said, "Man is a rational animal." They meant, of course, all men, not a particular man. In a similar way, we say "the elephant" when we mean all elephants or "tuberculosis is characterized by the following symptoms . . ." when we mean not a singular case of tuberculosis, but all instances.

It is unfortunate that our language has this ambiguity, because it is a source of much misunderstanding. Scientists often refer to universal statements—or rather to what is expressed by such statements—as "facts." They forget that the word *fact* was originally applied (and we shall apply it exclusively in this sense) to singular, particular occurrences. If a scientist is asked about the law of thermal expansion, he may say, "Oh, thermal expansion. That is one of the familiar, basic facts of physics." In a similar way, he may speak of the fact that heat is generated by an electric current, the fact that magnetism is produced by electricity, and so on. These are sometimes considered familiar "facts" of physics. To avoid misunderstandings, we prefer not to call such statements "facts."

Facts are particular events. "This morning in the laboratory, I sent an electric current through a wire coil with an iron body inside it, and I found that the iron body became magnetic." That is a fact unless, of course, I deceived myself in some way. However, if I was sober, if it was not too foggy in the room, and if no one has tinkered secretly with the apparatus to play a joke on me, then I may state as a factual observation that this morning that sequence of events occurred.

When we use the word *fact* we will mean it in the singular sense in order to distinguish it clearly from universal statements. Such universal statements will be called "laws" even when they are as elementary as the law of thermal expansion or, still more elementary, the statement "All ravens are black." I do not know whether this statement is true, but, assuming its truth, we will call such a statement a law of zoology. Zoologists may speak informally of such "facts" as "the raven is black" or "the octopus has eight arms," but, in our more precise terminology, statements of this sort will be called "laws."

Later we shall distinguish between two kinds of law—empirical and theoretical. Laws of the simple kind that I have just mentioned are sometimes called "empirical generalizations" or "empirical laws." They are simple because they speak of properties, like the color black or the magnetic properties of a piece of iron, that can be directly observed. The law of thermal expansion, for example, is a generalization based on many direct observations of bodies that expand when heated. In contrast, theoretical, nonobservable concepts, such as elementary particles and electromagnetic fields, must be dealt with by theoretical laws. We will discuss all this later. I mention it here because otherwise you might think that the examples I have given do not cover the kind of laws you have perhaps learned in theoretical physics.

To summarize, science begins with direct observations of single facts. Nothing else is observable. Certainly a regularity is not directly observable. It is only when many observations are compared with one another that regularities are discovered. These regularities are expressed by statements called "laws." . . .

INDUCTION AND STATISTICAL PROBABILITY

. . . Let us now ask how we arrive at such laws. On what basis are we justified in believing that a law holds? We know, of course, that all laws are based on the observation of certain regularities. They constitute indirect knowledge, as opposed to direct knowledge of facts. What justifies us in going from the direct observation of facts to a law that expresses certain regularities of nature? This is what in traditional terminology is called "the problem of induction."

Induction is often contrasted with deduction by saying that deduction goes from the general to the specific or singular, whereas induction goes the other way, from the singular to the general. This is a misleading oversimplification. In deduction, there are kinds of inferences other than those from the general to the specific; in induction there are also many kinds of inference. The traditional distinction is also misleading because it suggests that deduction and induction are simply two branches of a single kind of logic. John Stuart Mill's famous work, *A System of Logic,* contains a lengthy description of what he called "inductive logic" and states various canons of inductive procedure. Today we are more reluctant to use the term "inductive inference." If it is used at all, we must realize that it refers to a kind of inference that differs fundamentally from deduction.

In deductive logic, inference leads from a set of premises to a conclusion just as certain as the premises. If you have reason to believe the premises, you have equally valid reason to believe the conclusion that follows logically from the premises. If the premises are true, the conclusion cannot be false. With respect to induction, the situation is entirely different. The truth of an inductive conclusion is never certain. I do not mean only that the conclusion cannot be certain because it rests on premises that cannot be known with certainty. Even if the premises are assumed to be true and the inference is a valid inductive inference, the conclusion may be false. The most we can say is that, with respect to given premises, the conclu-

sion has a certain degree of probability. Inductive logic tells us how to calculate the value of this probability.

We know that singular statements of fact, obtained by observation, are never absolutely certain because we may make errors in our observations; but, in respect to laws, there is still greater uncertainty. A law about the world states that, in any particular case, at any place and any time, if one thing is true, another thing is true. Clearly, this speaks about an infinity of possible instances. The actual instances may not be infinite, but there is an infinity of possible instances. A physiological law says that, if you stick a dagger into the heart of any human being, he will die. Since no exception to this law has ever been observed, it is accepted as universal. It is true, of course, that the number of instances so far observed of daggers being thrust into human hearts is finite. It is possible that some day humanity may cease to exist; in that case, the number of human beings, both past and future, is finite. But we do not know that humanity will cease to exist. Therefore, we must say that there is an infinity of possible instances, all of which are covered by the law. And, if there is an infinity of instances, no number of finite observations, however large, can make the "universal" law certain.

Of course, we may go on and make more and more observations, making them in as careful and scientific a manner as we can, until eventually we may say, "This law has been tested so many times that we can have complete confidence in its truth. It is a well-established, well-founded law." If we think about it, however, we see that even the best-founded laws of physics must rest on only a finite number of observations. It is always possible that tomorrow a counterinstance may be found. At no time is it possible to arrive at *complete* verification of a law. In fact, we should not speak of "verification" at all—if by the word we mean a definitive establishment of truth—but only of confirmation.

Interestingly enough, although there is no way in which a law can be verified (in the strict sense), there is a simple way it can be falsified. One need find only a single counterinstance. The knowledge of a counterinstance may, in itself, be uncertain.

You may have made an error of observation or have been deceived in some way. But, if we assume that the counterinstance is a fact, then the negation of the law follows immediately. If a law says that every object that is *P* is also *Q* and we find an object that is *P* and not *Q*, the law is refuted. A million positive instances are insufficient to verify the law; one counterinstance is sufficient to falsify it. The situation is strongly asymmetric. It is easy to refute a law; it is exceedingly difficult to find strong confirmation.

How do we find confirmation of a law? If we have observed a great many positive instances and no negative instance, we say that the confirmation is strong. How strong it is and whether the strength can be expressed numerically is still a controversial question in the philosophy of science. We will return to this in a moment. Here we are concerned only with making clear that our first task in seeking confirmation of a law is to test instances to determine whether they are positive or negative. This is done by using our logical schema to make predictions. A law states that (x) $(Px \supset Qx)$; hence, for a given object a, $Pa \supset Qa$. We try to find as many objects as we can (here symbolized by "a") that have the property P. We then observe whether they also fulfill the condition Q. If we find a negative instance, the matter is settled. Otherwise, each positive instance is additional evidence adding to the strength of our confirmation.

There are, of course, various methodological rules for efficient testing. For example, instances should be diversified as much as possible. If you are testing the law of thermal expansion, you should not limit your tests to solid substances. If you are testing the law that all metals are good conductors of electricity, you should not confine your tests to specimens of copper. You should test as many metals as possible under various conditions—hot, cold, and so on. We will not go into the many methodological rules for testing; we will only point out that in all cases the law is tested by making predictions and then seeing whether those predictions hold. In some cases, we find in nature the objects that we wish to test. In other cases, we have to produce them. In testing the law of ther-

mal expansion, for example, we do not look for objects that are hot; we take certain objects and heat them. Producing conditions for testing has the great advantage that we can more easily follow the methodological rule of diversification; but whether we create the situations to be tested or find them ready-made in nature, the underlying schema is the same.

A moment ago I raised the question of whether the degree of confirmation of a law (or a singular statement that we are predicting by means of the law) can be expressed in quantitative form. Instead of saying that one law is "well founded" and that another law "rests on flimsy evidence," we might say that the first law has a .8 degree of confirmation, whereas the degree of confirmation for the second law is only .2. This question has long been debated. My own view is that such a procedure is legitimate and that what I have called "degree of confirmation" is identical with logical probability.

Such a statement does not mean much until we know what is meant by "logical probability." Why do I add the adjective "logical"? It is not customary practice; most books on probability do not make a distinction between various kinds of probability, one of which is called "logical." It is my belief, however, that there are two fundamentally different kinds of probability, and I distinguish between them by calling one "statistical probability" and the other "logical probability." It is unfortunate that the same word, "probability," has been used in two such widely differing senses. Failing to make the distinction is a source of enormous confusion in books on the philosophy of science as well as in the discourse of scientists themselves.

Instead of "logical probability," I sometimes use the term "inductive probability," because in my conception this is the kind of probability that is meant whenever we make an inductive inference. By "inductive inference" I mean not only inference from facts to laws, but also any inference that is "nondemonstrative"; that is, an inference such that the conclusion does not follow with logical necessity when the truth of the premises is granted. Such inferences must be expressed in degrees of what I call "logical probability" or "inductive probability." To see clearly the distinction between this type of probability and statistical probability, it will be useful to glance briefly at the history of probability theory.

The first theory of probability, now usually called the "classical theory," was developed during the eighteenth century. Jacob Bernoulli (1654–1705) was the first to write a systematic treatise about it, and the Reverend Thomas Bayes made an important contribution. Toward the end of the century, the great mathematician and physicist Pierre Simon de Laplace wrote the first large treatise on the subject. It was a comprehensive mathematical elaboration of a theory of probability and may be regarded as the climax of the classical period.

The application of probability throughout the classical period was mostly to such games of chance as dice, cards, and roulette. Actually, the theory had its origin in the fact that some gamblers of the time had asked Pierre Fermat and other mathematicians to calculate for them the exact probabilities involved in certain games of chance. So the theory began with concrete problems, not with a general mathematical theory. The mathematicians found it strange that questions of this sort could be answered even though there was no field of mathematics available for providing such answers. As a consequence, they developed the theory of combinatorics, which could then be applied to problems of chance.

What did these men who developed the classical theory understand by "probability"? They proposed a definition that is still found in elementary books on probability: Probability is the ratio of the number of favorable cases to the number of all possible cases. Let us see how this works in a simple example. Someone says, "I will throw this die. What is the chance that I will throw either an ace or a deuce?" The answer, according to the classical theory, is as follows. There are two "favorable" cases, that is, cases that fulfill the conditions specified in the question. Altogether, there are six possible ways the die can fall. The ratio of favorable to possible cases is therefore 2 : 6 or

1 : 3. We answer the question by saying that there is a probability of 1/3 that the die will show either a deuce or an ace.

All this seems quite clear, even obvious, but there is one important hitch to the theory. The classical authors said that, before one can apply their definition of probability, it must be ensured that all the cases involved are equally probable. Now we seem trapped in a vicious circle. We attempt to define what we mean by probability, and in so doing we use the concept of "equally probable." Actually, proponents of the classical theory did not put it in just those terms. They said that the cases must be "equipossible." This in turn was defined by a famous principle that they called "the principle of insufficient reason." Today it is usually called "the principle of indifference." If you do not know of any reason why one case should occur rather than another, then the cases are equipossible.

Such, in brief, was the way probability was defined in the classical period. A comprehensive mathematical theory has been built on the classical approach, but the only question that concerns us here is whether the foundation of this theory— the classical definition of probability—is adequate for science.

Slowly, during the nineteenth century, a few critical voices were raised against the classical definition. In the twentieth century, about 1920, both Richard von Mises and Hans Reichenbach made strong criticisms of the classical approach.[1] Mises said that "equipossibility" cannot be understood except in the sense of "equiprobability." If this is what it means, however, we are indeed caught in a vicious circle. The classical tradition, Mises asserted, is circular and therefore unusable.

Mises had still another objection. He granted that, in certain simple cases, we can rely on common sense to tell us that certain events are equipossible. We can say that heads and tails are equipossible outcomes when a coin is flipped be-

---

[1] On the views of Mises and Reichenbach, see Richard von Mises, *Probability, Statistics, and Truth* (New York: Macmillan, 1939), and Hans Reichenbach, *The Theory of Probability* (Berkeley, Calif.: University of California Press, 1949).

cause we know of no reason why one should turn up rather than the other. Similarly with roulette; there is no reason why the ball should fall into one compartment rather than another. If playing cards are of the same size and shape, with identical backs, and are well shuffled, then one card is as likely to be dealt to a player as any other. Again, the conditions of equipossibility are fulfilled. But, Mises went on, none of the classical authors pointed out how this definition of probability could be applied to many other situations. Consider mortality tables. Insurance companies have to know the probability that a forty-year-old man in the United States with no serious diseases will live to the same date in the following year. They must be able to calculate probabilities of this sort because they are the basis on which the company determines its rates.

What, Mises asked, are the equipossible cases for a man? Mr. Smith applies for life insurance. The company sends him to a doctor. The doctor reports that Smith has no serious diseases and that his birth certificate shows him to be forty years old. The company looks at its mortality tables; then, on the basis of the man's probable life expectancy, it offers him insurance at a certain rate. Mr. Smith may die before he reaches forty-one, or he may live to be a hundred. The probability of surviving one more year goes down and down as he gets older. Suppose he dies at forty-five. This is bad for the insurance company because he paid only a few premiums, and now they have to pay $20,000 to his beneficiary. Where are the equipossible cases? Mr. Smith may die at the age of forty, of forty-one, of forty-two, and so on. These are the possible cases. But they are not equipossible; that he will die at the age of 120 is extremely improbable.

A similar situation prevails, Mises pointed out, in applying probability to the social sciences, to weather prediction, and even to physics. These situations are not like games of chance, in which the possible outcomes can be classified neatly into *n* mutually exclusive, completely exhaustive cases that fulfill the conditions of equipossibility. A small body of radioactive substance will, in the next second, either emit an alpha particle or it will

not. The probability that it will emit the particle is, say, .0374. Where are the equipossible cases? There are none. We have only two cases: either it will emit the alpha particle in the next second or it will not emit it. This was Mises' chief criticism of the classical theory.

On the constructive side, both Mises and Reichenbach had this to say. What we really mean by probability has nothing to do with counting cases. It is a measurement of "relative frequency." By "absolute frequency," we mean the total number of objects or occurrences; for example, the number of people in Los Angeles who died last year of tuberculosis. By "relative frequency," we mean the ratio of this number to that of a larger class being investigated, say, the total number of inhabitants of Los Angeles.

We can speak of the probability that a certain face of a die will be thrown, Mises said, not only in the case of a fair die, where it is 1/6, but also in cases of all types of loaded dice. Suppose someone asserts that the die he has is loaded and that the probability it will show an ace is not 1/6, but less than 1/6. Someone else says, "I agree with you that the die is loaded, but not in the way you believe. I think that the probability of an ace is greater than 1/6." Mises pointed out that, in order to learn what the two men mean by their divergent assertions, we must look at the way they try to settle their argument. They will, of course, make an empirical test. They will toss the die a number of times, keeping a record of the number of throws and the number of aces.

How many times will they toss the die? Suppose they make 100 throws and find that the ace comes up 15 times. This is slightly less than 1/6 of 100. Will this not prove that the first man is right? "No," the other man might say. "I still think the probability is greater than 1/6. One hundred throws is not sufficient for an adequate test." Perhaps the men continue tossing the die until they have made 6,000 throws. If the ace has turned up fewer than 1,000 times, the second man may decide to give up. "You are right," he says. "It is less than 1/6."

Why do the men stop at 6,000? It may be that they are tired of making throws. Perhaps they made a bet of a dollar about which way the die was loaded, and for a mere dollar they do not want to spend three more days on additional throws. But the decision to stop at 6,000 is purely arbitrary. If, after 6,000 throws, the number of aces is very close to 1,000, they might regard the question as still undecided. A small deviation could be due to chance, rather than to a physical bias in the die itself. In a longer run, the bias might cause a deviation in the opposite direction. To make a more decisive test, the men might decide to go on to 60,000 throws. Clearly, there is no finite number of throws, however large, at which they could stop the test and say with positive assurance that the probability of an ace is 1/6 or less than 1/6 or more.

Since no finite number of tests is sufficient for determining a probability with certainty, how can that probability be defined in terms of frequency? Mises and Reichenbach proposed that it be defined, not as relative frequency in a finite series of instances, but as the *limit* of the relative frequency in an endless series. (It was this definition that distinguished the views of Mises and Reichenbach from those of R. A. Fisher, in England, and other statisticians who had also criticized the classical theory. They introduced the frequency concept of probability, not by definition, but as a primitive term in an axiom system). Of course, Mises and Reichenbach were well aware—although they have often been criticized as though they had not been—that no observer can ever have the complete infinite series of observations available. But I think that their critics were wrong when they said that the new definition of probability has no application. Both Reichenbach and Mises have shown that many theorems can be developed on the basis of their definition, and, with the help of these theorems, we can say something significant. We cannot say with certainty what the value of a probability is, but, if the series is long enough, we can say what the probability *probably* is. In the die example, we might say that the probability that the probability of throwing an ace is greater than 1/6 is very small. Perhaps the value of this probability of a probability can even be calculated. The facts

that the limit concept is used in the definition and that reference is made to an infinite series certainly do cause complications and difficulties, both logical and practical. They do not, however, make the definition meaningless, as some critics have asserted.

Reichenbach and Mises agreed in the view that this concept of probability, based on the limit of a relative frequency in an infinite series, is the only concept of probability acceptable in science. The classical definition, derived from the principle of indifference, had been found inadequate. No new definition other than that of Mises and Reichenbach had been found that was superior to the old. But now the troublesome question of single instances arose once more. The new definition worked very well for statistical phenomena, but how could it be applied to a single case? A meteorologist announces that the probability of rain tomorrow is 2/3. "Tomorrow" refers to one particular day and no other. Like the death of the man applying for life insurance, it is a single, unrepeated event; yet we want to attribute to it a probability. How can this be done on the basis of a frequency definition?

Mises thought that it could not be done; therefore, probability statements for single cases should be excluded. Reichenbach, however, was aware that, in both science and everyday life, we constantly make probability statements about single events. It would be useful, he thought, to find a plausible interpretation for such statements. In weather prediction, it is easy to give such an interpretation. The meteorologist has available a large number of reports of past observations of the weather, as well as data concerning the weather for today. He finds that today's weather belongs to a certain class, and that in the past, when weather of this class occurred the relative frequency with which rain fell on the following day was 2/3. Then, according to Reichenbach, the meteorologist makes a "posit"; that is, he assumes that the observed frequency of 2/3, based on a finite but rather long series of observations, is also the limit of the infinite series. In other words, he estimates the limit to be in the neighborhood of 2/3. He then makes the statement, "The probability of rain tomorrow is 2/3."

The meteorologist's statement, Reichenbach maintained, should be regarded as an elliptical one. If he expanded it to its full meaning, he would say, "According to our past observations, states of weather such as that we have observed today were followed, with a frequency of 2/3, by rain on the following day." The abbreviated statement seems to apply probability to a single case, but that is only a manner of speaking. The statement really refers to relative frequency in a long series. The same would be true of the statement, "On the next throw of the die, the probability of an ace is 1/6." The "next throw" is, like "the weather tomorrow," a single, unique event. When we attribute probability to it, we are really speaking elliptically about relative frequency in a long series of throws.

In this way, Reichenbach found an interpretation for statements that attributed probability to single events. He even tried to find an interpretation for statements attributing probability to general hypotheses in science. We will not enter into that here because it is more complicated and because (in contrast to his interpretation of singular probability predictions) it has not found general acceptance.

The next important development in the history of probability theory was the rise of the *logical* conception. It was proposed after 1920 by John Maynard Keynes, the famous British economist, and has since been elaborated by many writers. Today there is a spirited controversy between proponents of this logical conception and those who favor the frequency interpretation. . . .

INDUCTION AND LOGICAL PROBABILITY

To John Maynard Keynes, probability was a logical relation between two propositions. He did not try to define this relation. He even went so far as to say that no definition could be formulated. Only by intuition, he insisted, can we understand what probability means. His book, *A Treatise on Probability*,[2] gave a few axioms and definitions, expressed in symbolic logic, but they are not very sound from a modern point of view. Some of Keynes's axioms were actually definitions. Some of his definitions were really axioms. But his book is interesting from a philosophical standpoint, especially those chapters in which he discusses the history of probability theory and what can be learned today from earlier points of view. His central contention was that when we make a probability statement, we are not making a statement about the world but only about a logical relation between two other statements. We are saying only that one statement has a logical probability of so-and-so much with respect to another statement.

I use the phrase "so-and-so much." Actually Keynes was more cautious. He doubted that probability in general could be made a quantitative concept, that is, a concept with numerical values. He agreed, of course, that this could be done in special cases, such as the throw of a die, in which the old principle of indifference applied. The die is symmetrical, all its faces are alike, we have no reason to suspect it is loaded, and so on. The same is true of other games of chance, in which conditions are carefully arranged to produce physical symmetry, or, at least, symmetry with respect to our knowledge and ignorance. Roulette wheels are made so that their various sectors are equal. The wheel is carefully balanced to eliminate any bias that might cause the ball to stop at one number rather than another. If someone flips a coin, we have no reason to suppose that heads will show rather than tails.

In restricted situations of this sort, Keynes said, we can legitimately apply something like the classical definition of probability. He agreed with other critics of the principle of indifference that it had been used in the classical period in much too wide a sense and that it had been wrongly applied to many situations, such as the prediction that to-

---

[2] John Maynard Keynes, *Treatise on Probability* (London: Macmillan, 1921).

morrow the sun will rise. It is true, he said, that in games of chance and other simple situations, the principle of indifference is applicable, and numerical values can be given to probability. In most situations, however, we have no way of defining equipossible cases and, therefore, no justification for applying the principle. In such cases, Keynes said, we should not use numerical values. His attitude was cautious and skeptical. He did not want to go too far, to tread on what he regarded as thin ice, so he restricted the quantitative part of his theory. In many situations in which we do not hesitate to make bets, to attribute numerical values to probability predictions, Keynes cautioned against the practice.

The second important figure in the rise of the modern logical approach to probability is Harold Jeffreys, an English geophysicist. His *Theory of Probability,* first published in 1939 by Oxford Press, defends a conception closely related to that of Keynes. When Keynes published his book (it came out in 1921, so he probably wrote it in 1920), the very first publications on probability by Mises and Reichenbach had just appeared. Keynes apparently did not know about them. He criticized the frequency approach, but he did not discuss it in detail. By the time Jeffreys wrote his book, the frequency interpretation had been fully developed, so his book was much more explicit in dealing with it.

Jeffreys said flatly that the frequency theory is entirely wrong. He affirmed Keynes's view that probability refers not to frequency but to a logical relation. He was much more daring than the cautious Keynes. He believed that numerical values *could* be assigned to probability in a large number of situations, especially in all those situations in which mathematical statistics is applied. He wanted to deal with the same problems that interested R. A. Fisher and other statisticians, but he wanted to deal with them on the basis of a different concept of probability. Because he made use of an indifference principle, I believe that some of his results are open to the same objections that were raised against the classical theory. It is difficult, however, to find specific statements in his book to criticize. His axioms, taken one after the

other, are acceptable. Only when he tries to derive theorems from one certain axiom does he, in my opinion, go astray.

The axiom in question is stated by Jeffreys as follows: "We assign the larger number on given data to the more probable proposition (and therefore equal numbers to equally probable propositions)." The part included in the parenthesis obviously says only that, if p and q are equally probable on the basis of evidence r, then equal numbers are to be assigned to p and q as their probability values with respect to evidence r. The statement tells us nothing about the conditions under which we are to regard p and q as equally probable with respect to r. Nowhere else in his book does Jeffreys state those conditions. Later in his book, however, he interprets this axiom in a most surprising way in order to establish theorems about scientific laws. "If there is no reason to believe one hypothesis rather than another," he writes, "the probabilities are equal." In other words, if we have insufficient evidence for deciding whether a given theory is true or false, we must conclude that the theory has a probability of 1/2.

Is this a legitimate use of the principle of indifference? In my view, it is a use that was rightly condemned by critics of the classical theory. If the principle of indifference is to be used at all, there must be some sort of symmetry in the situation, such as the equality of the faces of a die or the sectors of a roulette wheel, that enables us to say that certain cases are equally probable. In the absence of such symmetries in the logical or physical features of a situation, it is unwarranted to assume equal probabilities merely because we know nothing about the relative merits of rival hypotheses.

A simple illustration will make this clear. According to Jeffreys' interpretation of his axiom, we could assume a probability of 1/2 that there are living organisms on Mars because we have neither sufficient reason to believe this hypothesis nor sufficient reason to believe its negation. In the same way, we could reason that the probability is 1/2 that there are animals on Mars and 1/2 that there are human beings there. Each assertion, considered by itself, is an assertion about which we have no sufficient evidence one way or the other. But these assertions are related to each other in such a way that they cannot have the same probability values. The second assertion is stronger than the first because it implies the first, whereas the first does not imply the second. Therefore, the second assertion has less probability than the first; the same relation holds between the third and the second. We must be extremely careful, therefore, in applying even a modified principle of indifference, or we are likely to run into such inconsistencies.

Jeffreys' book has been harshly criticized by mathematical statisticians. I agree with their criticism only with respect to the few places where Jeffreys develops theorems that cannot be derived from his axioms. On the other hand, I would say that both Keynes and Jeffreys were pioneers who worked in the right direction.[3] My own work on probability is in the same direction. I share their view that logical probability is a logical relation. If you make a statement affirming that, for a given hypothesis, the logical probability with respect to given evidence is .7, then the total statement is an analytic one. This means that the statement follows from the definition of logical probability (or from the axioms of a logical system) without reference to anything outside the logical system, that is, without reference to the structure of the actual world.

In my conception, logical probability is a logical relation somewhat similar to logical implication; indeed, I think probability may be regarded as a partial implication. If the evidence is so strong that the hypothesis follows logically from it—is logically implied by it—we have one extreme case in which the probability is 1. (Probability 1 also occurs in other cases, but this is one special case where it occurs.) Similarly, if the negation of a hypothesis is logically implied by the evidence, the logical probability of the hypothesis is 0. In

between, there is a continuum of cases about which deductive logic tells us nothing beyond the negative assertion that neither the hypothesis nor its negation can be deduced from the evidence. On this continuum inductive logic must take over. But inductive logic is like deductive logic in being concerned solely with the statements involved, not with the facts of nature. By a logical analysis of a stated hypothesis *h* and stated evidence *e*, we conclude that *h* is not logically implied but is, so to speak, partially implied by *e* to the degree of so-and-so much.

At this point, we are justified, in my view, in assigning numerical value to the probability. If possible, we should like to construct a system of inductive logic of such a kind that for any pair of sentences, one asserting evidence *e* and the other stating a hypothesis *h*, we can assign a number giving the logical probability of *h* with respect to *e*. (We do not consider the trivial case in which the sentence *e* is contradictory; in such instances, no probability value can be assigned to *h*.) I have succeeded in developing possible definitions of such probabilities for very simple languages containing only one-place predicates, and work is now in progress for extending the theory to more comprehensive languages. Of course, if the whole of inductive logic, which I am trying to construct on this basis, is to be of any real value to science, it should finally be applicable to a quantitative language such as we have in physics, in which there are not only one- or two-place predicates, but also numerical magnitudes such as mass, temperature, and so on. I believe that this is possible and that the basic principles involved are the same as the principles that have guided the work so far in the construction of an inductive logic for the simple language of one-place predicates.

When I say I think it is possible to apply an inductive logic to the language of science, I do not mean that it is possible to formulate a set of rules, fixed once and for all, that will lead automatically, in any field, from facts to theories. It seems doubtful, for example, that rules can be formulated to enable a scientist to survey a hundred thousand sentences giving various observational reports and then find, by a mechanical application of those

[3] A technical evaluation of the work of Keynes and Jeffreys, and others who defended logical probability, will be found in section 62 of my *Logical Foundations of Probability* (Chicago: University of Chicago Press, 1950). Six nontechnical sections of this book were reprinted as a small monograph, *The Nature and Application of Inductive Logic* (Chicago: University of Chicago Press, 1951).

rules, a general theory (system of laws) that would explain the observed phenomena. This is usually not possible, because theories, especially the more abstract ones dealing with such nonobservables as particles and fields, use a conceptual framework that goes far beyond the framework used for the description of observation material. One cannot simply follow a mechanical procedure based on fixed rules to devise a new system of theoretical concepts, and with its help a theory. Creative ingenuity is required. This point is sometimes expressed by saying that there cannot be an inductive machine—a computer into which we can put all the relevant observational sentences and get, as an output, a neat system of laws that will explain the observed phenomena.

I agree that there cannot be an inductive machine if the purpose of the machine is to invent new theories. I believe, however, that there can be an inductive machine with a much more modest aim. Given certain observations e and a hypothesis h (in the form, say, of a prediction or even of a set of laws), then I believe it is in many cases possible to determine, by mechanical procedures, the logical probability, or degree of confirmation, of h on the basis of e. For this concept of probability, I also use the term "inductive probability," because I am convinced that this is the basic concept involved in all inductive reasoning and that the chief task of inductive reasoning is the evaluation of this probability.

When we survey the present situation in probability theory, we find a controversy between advocates of the frequency theory and those who, like Keynes, Jeffreys, and myself, speak in terms of a logical probability. There is, however, one important difference between my position and that of Keynes and Jeffreys. They reject the frequency concept of probability. I do not. I think the frequency concept, also called statistical probability, is a good scientific concept, whether introduced by an explicit definition, as in the systems of Mises and Reichenbach, or introduced by an axiom system and rules of practical application (without explicit definition), as in contemporary mathematical statistics. In both cases, I regard this concept as important for science. In my opinion, the logical

concept of probability is a second concept, of an entirely different nature, though equally important.

Statements giving values of statistical probability are not purely logical; they are factual statements in the language of science. When a medical man says that the probability is "very good" (or perhaps he uses a numerical value and says .7) that a patient will react positively to a certain injection, he is making a statement in medical science. When a physicist says that the probability of a certain radioactive phenomenon is so-and-so much, he is making a statement in physics. Statistical probability is a scientific, empirical concept. Statements about statistical probability are "synthetic" statements, statements that cannot be decided by logic but which rest on empirical investigations. On this point I agree fully with Mises, Reichenbach, and the statisticians. When we say, "With this particular die the statistical probability of throwing an ace is .157," we are stating a scientific hypothesis that can be tested only by a series of observations. It is an empirical statement because only an empirical investigation can confirm it.

As science develops, probability statements of this sort seem to become increasingly important, not only in the social sciences, but in modern physics as well. Statistical probability is involved not only in areas where it is necessary because of ignorance (as in the social sciences or when a physicist is calculating the path of a molecule in a liquid), but also as an essential factor in the basic principles of quantum theory. It is of the utmost importance for science to have a theory of statistical probability. Such theories have been developed by statisticians and, in a different way, by Mises and Reichenbach.

On the other hand, we also need the concept of logical probability. It is especially useful in metascientific statements, that is, statements about science. We say to a scientist, "You tell me that I can rely on this law in making a certain prediction. How well established is the law? How trustworthy is the prediction?" The scientist today may or may not be willing to answer a metascientific question of this kind in quantitative terms. But I believe that, once inductive logic is sufficiently developed, he could reply, "This hypothesis is confirmed to degree .8 on the basis of the available evidence." A scientist who answers in this way is making a statement about a logical relation between the evidence and the hypothesis in question. The sort of probability he has in mind is logical probability, which I also call "degree of confirmation." His statement that the value of this probability is .8 is, in this context, not a synthetic (empirical) statement, but an analytic one. It is analytic because no empirical investigation is demanded. It expresses a logical relation between a sentence that states the evidence and a sentence that states the hypothesis. . . .

THEORIES AND NONOBSERVABLES

One of the most important distinctions between two types of laws in science is the distinction between what may be called (there is no generally accepted terminology for them) empirical laws and theoretical laws. Empirical laws are laws that can be confirmed directly by empirical observations. The term "observable" is often used for any phenomenon that can be directly observed, so it can be said that empirical laws are laws about observables.

Here, a warning must be issued. Philosophers and scientists have quite different ways of using the terms "observable" and "nonobservable." To a philosopher, "observable" has a very narrow meaning. It applies to such properties as "blue," "hard," or "hot." These are properties directly perceived by the senses. To the physicist, the word has a much broader meaning. It includes any quantitative magnitude that can be measured in a relatively simple, direct way. A philosopher would not consider a temperature of, perhaps, 80 degrees centigrade, or a weight of 93 1/2 pounds, an observable because there is no direct sensory perception of such magnitudes. To a physicist, both are observables because they can be measured in an extremely simple way. The object to be weighed is placed on a balance scale. The tem-

perature is measured with a thermometer. The physicist would not say that the mass of a molecule, let alone the mass of an electron, is something observable, because here the procedures of measurement are much more complicated and indirect. But magnitudes that can be established by relatively simple procedures—length with a ruler, time with a clock, or frequency of light waves with a spectrometer—are called observables.

A philosopher might object that the intensity of an electric current is not really observed. Only a pointer position was observed. An ammeter was attached to the circuit and it was noted that the pointer pointed to a mark labeled 5.3. Certainly the current's intensity was not observed. It was *inferred* from what was observed.

The physicist would reply that this was true enough, but the inference was not very complicated. The procedure of measurement is so simple, so well established, that it could not be doubted that the ammeter would give an accurate measurement of current intensity. Therefore, it is included among what are called observables.

There is no question here of who is using the term "observable" in a right or proper way. There is a continuum which starts with direct sensory observations and proceeds to enormously complex, indirect methods of observation. Obviously no sharp line can be drawn across this continuum; it is a matter of degree. A philosopher is sure that the sound of his wife's voice, coming from across the room, is an observable. But suppose he listens to her on the telephone. Is her voice an observable or isn't it? A physicist would certainly say that when he looks at something through an ordinary microscope, he is observing it directly. Is this also the case when he looks into an electron microscope? Does he observe the path of a particle when he sees the track it makes in a bubble chamber? In general, the physicist speaks of observables in a very wide sense compared with the narrow sense of the philosopher, but, in both cases, the line separating observable from nonobservable is highly arbitrary. It is well to keep this in mind whenever these terms are encountered in a book by a philosopher or scientist. Individual authors will draw the line where it is most convenient, depending on their points of view, and there is no reason why they should not have this privilege.

Empirical laws, in my terminology, are laws containing terms either directly observable by the senses or measurable by relatively simple techniques. Sometimes such laws are called empirical generalizations, as a reminder that they have been obtained by generalizing results found by observations and measurements. They include not only simple qualitative laws (such as "All ravens are black") but also quantitative laws that arise from simple measurements. The laws relating pressure, volume, and temperature of gases are of this type. Ohm's law, connecting the electric potential difference, resistance, and intensity of current, is another familiar example. The scientist makes repeated measurements, finds certain regularities, and expresses them in a law. These are the empirical laws. . . . [T]hey are used for explaining observed facts and for predicting future observable events.

There is no commonly accepted term for the second kind of laws, which I call *theoretical laws.* Sometimes they are called abstract or hypothetical laws. "Hypothetical" is perhaps not suitable because it suggests that the distinction between the two types of laws is based on the degree to which the laws are confirmed. But an empirical law, if it is a tentative hypothesis, confirmed only to a low degree, would still be an empirical law although it might be said that it was rather hypothetical. A theoretical law is not to be distinguished from an empirical law by the fact that it is not well established, but by the fact that it contains terms of a different kind. The terms of a theoretical law do not refer to observables even when the physicist's wide meaning for what can be observed is adopted. They are laws about such entities as molecules, atoms, electrons, protons, electromagnetic fields, and others that cannot be measured in simple, direct ways.

If there is a static field of large dimensions, which does not vary from point to point, physicists call it an observable field because it can be measured with a simple apparatus. But if the field changes from point to point in very small dis-

tances, or varies very quickly in time, perhaps changing billions of times each second, then it cannot be directly measured by simple techniques. Physicists would not call such a field an observable. Sometimes a physicist will distinguish between observables and nonobservables in just this way. If the magnitude remains the same within large enough spatial distances, or large enough time intervals, so that an apparatus can be applied for a direct measurement of the magnitude, it is called a *macroevent.* If the magnitude changes within such extremely small intervals of space and time that it cannot be directly measured by simple apparatus, it is a *microevent.* (Earlier authors used the terms "microscopic" and "macroscopic", but today many authors have shortened these terms to "micro" and "macro".)

A microprocess is simply a process involving extremely small intervals of space and time. For example, the oscillation of an electromagnetic wave of visible light is a microprocess. No instrument can directly measure how its intensity varies. The distinction between macro- and microconcepts is sometimes taken to be parallel to observable and nonobservable. It is not exactly the same, but it is roughly so. Theoretical laws concern nonobservables, and very often these are microprocesses. If so, the laws are sometimes called microlaws. I use the term "theoretical laws" in a wider sense than this, to include all those laws that contain nonobservables, regardless of whether they are microconcepts or macroconcepts.

It is true, as shown earlier, that the concepts "observable" and "nonobservable" cannot be sharply defined because they lie on a continuum. In actual practice, however, the difference is usually great enough so there is not likely to be debate. All physicists would agree that the laws relating pressure, volume, and temperature of a gas, for example, are empirical laws. Here the amount of gas is large enough so that the magnitudes to be measured remain constant over a sufficiently large volume of space and period of time to permit direct, simple measurements which can then be generalized into laws. All physicists would agree that laws about the behavior of single molecules are theoretical. Such laws concern a microprocess about which generalizations cannot be based on simple, direct measurements.

Theoretical laws are, of course, more general than empirical laws. It is important to understand, however, that theoretical laws cannot be arrived at simply by taking the empirical laws, then generalizing a few steps further. How does a physicist arrive at an empirical law? He observes certain events in nature. He notices a certain regularity. He describes this regularity by making an inductive generalization. It might be supposed that he could now put together a group of empirical laws, observe some sort of pattern, make a wider inductive generalization, and arrive at a theoretical law. Such is not the case.

To make this clear, suppose it has been observed that a certain iron bar expands when heated. After the experiment has been repeated many times, always with the same result, the regularity is generalized by saying that this bar expands when heated. An empirical law has been stated, even though it has a narrow range and applies only to one particular iron bar. Now further tests are made of other iron objects with the ensuing discovery that every time an iron object is heated it expands. This permits a more general law to be formulated, namely that all bodies of iron expand when heated. In similar fashion, the still more general laws "All metals . . . ," then "All solid bodies . . ." are developed. These are all simple generalizations, each a bit more general than the previous one, but they are all empirical laws. Why? Because in each case the objects dealt with are observable (iron, copper, metal, solid bodies); in each case the increases in temperature and length are measurable by simple, direct techniques.

In contrast, a theoretical law relating to this process would refer to the behavior of molecules in the iron bar. In what way is the behavior of the molecules connected with the expansion of the bar when heated? You see at once that we are now speaking of nonobservables. We must introduce a theory—the atomic theory of matter—and we are quickly plunged into atomic laws involving concepts radically different from those we had before. It is true that these theoretical concepts differ from concepts of length and temperature only in the degree to which they are directly or indirectly observable, but the difference is so great that there is no debate about the radically different nature of the laws that must be formulated.

Theoretical laws are related to empirical laws in a way somewhat analogous to the way empirical laws are related to single facts. An empirical law helps to explain a fact that has been observed and to predict a fact not yet observed. In similar fashion, the theoretical law helps to explain empirical laws already formulated, and to permit the derivation of new empirical laws. Just as the single, separate facts fall into place in an orderly pattern when they are generalized in an empirical law, the single and separate empirical laws fit into the orderly pattern of a theoretical law. This raises one of the main problems in the methodology of science. How can the kind of knowledge that will justify the assertion of a theoretical law be obtained? An empirical law may be justified by making observations of single facts. But to justify a theoretical law, comparable observations cannot be made because the entities referred to in theoretical laws are nonobservables.

Before taking up this problem, some remarks made . . . earlier . . . about the use of the word "fact" should be repeated. It is important in the present context to be extremely careful in the use of this word because some authors, especially scientists, use "fact" or "empirical fact" for some propositions which I would call empirical laws. For example, many physicists will refer to the "fact" that the specific heat of copper is .090. I would call this a law because in its full formulation it is seen to be a universal conditional statement: "For any x, and any time t, if x is a solid body of copper, then the specific heat of x at t is .090." Some physicists may even speak of the law of thermal expansion, Ohm's law, and others, as facts. Of course, they can then say that theoretical laws help explain such facts. This sounds like my statement that empirical laws explain facts, but the word "fact" is being used here in two different ways. I restrict the word to particular, concrete facts that can be spatiotemporally specified, not thermal expansion in general, but *the* expansion of this iron bar observed this morning at ten o'clock when it was heated. It is important to bear in mind the restricted way in which I speak of facts. If the word "fact" is used in an ambiguous manner, the important difference between the ways in which empirical and theoretical laws serve for explanation will be entirely blurred.

How can theoretical laws be discovered? We cannot say, "Let's just collect more and more data, then generalize beyond the empirical laws until we reach theoretical ones." No theoretical law was ever found that way. We observe stones and trees and flowers, noting various regularities and describing them by empirical laws. But no matter how long or how carefully we observe such things, we never reach a point at which we observe a molecule. The term "molecule" never arises as a result of observations. For this reason, no amount of generalization from observations will ever produce a theory of molecular processes. Such a theory must arise in another way. It is stated not as a generalization of facts but as a hypothesis. The hypothesis is then tested in a manner analogous in certain ways to the testing of an empirical law. From the hypothesis, certain empirical laws are derived, and these empirical laws are tested in turn by observation of facts. Perhaps the empirical laws derived from the theory are already known and well confirmed. (Such laws may even have motivated the formulation of the theoretical law.) Regardless of whether the derived empirical laws are known and confirmed, or whether they are new laws confirmed by new observations, the confirmation of such derived laws provides indirect confirmation of the theoretical law.

The point to be made clear is this. A scientist does not start with one empirical law, perhaps Boyle's law for gases, and then seek a theory about molecules from which this law can be derived. The scientist tries to formulate a much more general theory from which a variety of empirical laws can be derived. The more such laws, the greater their variety and apparent lack of connection with one another, the stronger will be the

theory that explains them. Some of these derived laws may have been known before, but the theory may also make it possible to derive new empirical laws which can be confirmed by new tests. If this is the case, it can be said that the theory made it possible to predict new empirical laws. The prediction is understood in a hypothetical way. If the theory holds, certain empirical laws will also hold. The predicted empirical law speaks about relations between observables, so it is now possible to make experiments to see if the empirical law holds. If the empirical law is confirmed, it provides indirect confirmation of the theory. Every confirmation of a law, empirical or theoretical, is, of course, only partial, never complete and absolute. But in the case of empirical laws, it is a more direct confirmation. The confirmation of a theoretical law is indirect, because it takes place only through the confirmation of empirical laws derived from the theory.

The supreme value of a new theory is its power to predict new empirical laws. It is true that it also has value in explaining known empirical laws, but this is a minor value. If a scientist proposes a new theoretical system, from which no new laws can be derived, then it is logically equivalent to the set of all known empirical laws. The theory may have a certain elegance, and it may simplify to some degree the set of all known laws, although it is not likely that there would be an essential simplification. On the other hand, every new theory in physics that has led to a great leap forward has been a theory from which new empirical laws could be derived. If Einstein had done no more than propose his theory of relativity as an elegant new theory that would embrace certain known laws—perhaps also simplify them to a certain degree—then his theory would not have had such a revolutionary effect.

Of course it was quite otherwise. The theory of relativity led to new empirical laws which explained for the first time such phenomena as the movement of the perihelion of Mercury and the bending of light rays in the neighborhood of the sun. These predictions showed that relativity theory was more than just a new way of expressing the old laws. Indeed, it was a theory of great predictive power. The consequences that can be derived from Einstein's theory are far from being exhausted. These are consequences that could not have been derived from earlier theories. Usually a theory of such power does have an elegance, and a unifying effect on known laws. It is simpler than the total collection of known laws. But the great value of the theory lies in its power to suggest new laws that can be confirmed by empirical means.

CORRESPONDENCE RULES

An important qualification must now be added. . . . The statement that empirical laws are derived from theoretical laws is an oversimplification. It is not possible to derive them directly because a theoretical law contains theoretical terms, whereas an empirical law contains only observable terms. This prevents any direct deduction of an empirical law from a theoretical one.

To understand this, imagine that we are back in the nineteenth century, preparing to state for the first time some theoretical laws about molecules in a gas. These laws are to describe the number of molecules per unit volume of the gas, the molecular velocities, and so forth. To simplify matters, we assume that all the molecules have the same velocity. (This was indeed the original assumption; later it was abandoned in favor of a certain probability distribution of velocities.) Further assumptions must be made about what happens when molecules collide. We do not know the exact shape of molecules, so let us suppose that they are tiny spheres. How do spheres collide? There are laws about colliding spheres, but they concern large bodies. Since we cannot directly observe molecules, we assume their collisions are analogous to those of large bodies; perhaps they behave like perfect billiard balls on a frictionless table. These are, of course, only assumptions; guesses suggested by analogies with known macrolaws.

But now we come up against a difficult problem. Our theoretical laws deal exclusively with the behavior of molecules, which cannot be seen. How, therefore, can we deduce from such laws a law about observable properties such as the pressure or temperature of a gas or properties of sound waves that pass through the gas? The theoretical laws contain only theoretical terms. What we seek are empirical laws containing observable terms. Obviously, such laws cannot be derived without having something else given in addition to the theoretical laws.

The something else that must be given is this: a set of rules connecting the theoretical terms with the observable terms. Scientists and philosophers of science have long recognized the need for such a set of rules, and their nature has been often discussed. An example of such a rule is "If there is an electromagnetic oscillation of a specified frequency, then there is a visible greenish-blue color of a certain hue." Here something observable is connected with a nonobservable microprocess.

Another example is "The temperature (measured by a thermometer and, therefore, an observable in the wider sense explained earlier) of a gas is proportional to the mean kinetic energy of its molecules." This rule connects a nonobservable in molecular theory, the kinetic energy of molecules, with an observable, the temperature of the gas. If statements of this kind did not exist, there would be no way of deriving empirical laws about observables from theoretical laws about nonobservables.

Different writers have different names for these rules. I call them "correspondence rules." P. W. Bridgman calls them operational rules. Norman R. Campbell speaks of them as the "Dictionary".[4] Since the rules connect a term in one terminology with a term in another terminology, the use of the rules is analogous to the use of a French-English dictionary. What does the French word "cheval" mean? You look it up in the dictionary and find that it means "horse". It is not really that simple when a set of rules is used for connecting nonobservables with observables; nevertheless, there is

---

[4] See Percy W. Bridgman, *The Logic of Modern Physics* (New York: Macmillan, 1927) and Norman R. Campbell, *Physics: The Elements* (Cambridge: Cambridge University Press, 1920). Rules of correspondence are discussed by Ernest Nagel, *The Structure of Science* (New York: Harcourt, Brace & World, 1961), pp. 97–105.

an analogy here that makes Campbell's "Dictionary" a suggestive name for the set of rules.

There is a temptation at times to think that the set of rules provides a means for defining theoretical terms, whereas just the opposite is really true. A theoretical term can never be explicitly defined on the basis of observable terms, although sometimes an observable can be defined in theoretical terms. For example, "iron" can be defined as a substance consisting of small crystalline parts, each having a certain arrangement of atoms and each atom being a configuration of particles of a certain type. In theoretical terms then, it is possible to express what is meant by the observable term "iron", but the reverse is not true.

There is no answer to the question, "Exactly what is an electron?" . . . [T]his question . . . is the kind that philosophers are always asking scientists. They want the physicist to tell them just what he means by "electricity," "magnetism," "gravity," "a molecule." If the physicist explains them in theoretical terms, the philosopher may be disappointed. "That is not what I meant at all," he will say. "I want you to tell me, in ordinary language, what those terms mean." Sometimes the philosopher writes a book in which he talks about the great mysteries of nature. "No one," he writes, "has been able so far, and perhaps no one ever will be able, to give us a straightforward answer to the question, 'What is electricity?' And so electricity remains forever one of the great, unfathomable mysteries of the universe."

There is no special mystery here. There is only an improperly phrased question. Definitions that cannot, in the nature of the case, be given, should not be demanded. If a child does not know what an elephant is, we can tell him it is a huge animal with big ears and a long trunk. We can show him a picture of an elephant. It serves admirably to define an elephant in observable terms that a child can understand. By analogy, there is a temptation to believe that, when a scientist introduces theoretical terms, he should also be able to define them in familiar terms. But this is not possible. There is no way a physicist can show us a picture of electricity in the way he can show his child a picture of an elephant. Even the cell of an organism, although it cannot be seen with the unaided eye, can be represented by a picture because the cell can be seen when it is viewed through a microscope. But we do not possess a picture of the electron. We cannot say how it looks or how it feels, because it cannot be seen or touched. The best we can do is to say that it is an extremely small body that behaves in a certain manner. This may seem to be analogous to our description of an elephant. We can describe an elephant as a large animal that behaves in a certain manner. Why not do the same with an electron?

The answer is that a physicist can describe the behavior of an electron only by stating theoretical laws, and these laws contain only theoretical terms. They describe the field produced by an electron, the reaction of an electron to a field, and so on. If an electron is in an electrostatic field, its velocity will accelerate in a certain way. Unfortunately, the electron's acceleration is an unobservable. It is not like the acceleration of a billiard ball, which can be studied by direct observation. There is no way that a theoretical concept can be defined in terms of observables. We must, therefore, resign ourselves to the fact that definitions of the kind that can be supplied for observable terms cannot be formulated for theoretical terms. . . .

Science: Conjectures and Refutations

Karl Popper

There could be no fairer destiny for any . . . theory than that it should point the way to a more comprehensive theory in which it lives on, as a limiting case.

Albert Einstein

Mr. Turnbull had predicted evil consequences, . . . and was now doing the best in his power to bring about the verification of his own prophecies.

Anthony Trollope

I

When I received the list of participants in this course and realized that I had been asked to speak to philosophical colleagues I thought, after some hesitation and consultation, that you would probably prefer me to speak about those problems which interest me most, and about those developments with which I am most intimately acquainted. I therefore decided to do what I have never done before: to give you a report on my own work in the philosophy of science since the autumn of 1919 when I first began to grapple with the problem *"When should a theory be ranked as scientific?"* or *"Is there a criterion for the scientific character or status of a theory?"*

The problem which troubled me at the time was neither "When is a theory true?" nor "When is a theory acceptable?" My problem was different. I wished to distinguish between science and pseudo-science, knowing very well that science

often errs, and that pseudo-science may happen to stumble on the truth.

I knew, of course, the most widely accepted answer to my problem: that science is distinguished from pseudo-science—or from "metaphysics"—by its *empirical method,* which is essentially *inductive,* proceeding from observation or experiment. But this did not satisfy me. On the contrary, I often formulated my problem as one of distinguishing between a genuinely empirical method and a non-empirical or even a pseudo-empirical method—that is to say, a method which, although it appeals to observation and experiment, nevertheless does not come up to scientific standards. The latter method may be exemplified by astrology, with its stupendous mass of empirical evidence based on observation—on horoscopes and on biographies.

But as it was not the example of astrology which led me to my problem I should perhaps briefly describe the atmosphere in which my problem arose and the examples by which it was stimulated. After the collapse of the Austrian Empire there had been a revolution in Austria: The air was full of revolutionary slogans and ideas, and new and often wild theories. Among the theories which interested me Einstein's theory of relativity was no doubt by far the most important. Three others were Marx's theory of history, Freud's psychoanalysis, and Alfred Adler's so-called "individual psychology."

There was a lot of popular nonsense talked about these theories, and especially about relativity (as still happens even today), but I was fortunate in those who introduced me to the study of this theory. We all—the small circle of students to which I belonged—were thrilled with the result of

A lecture given at Peterhouse, Cambridge, in Summer 1953, as part of a course on developments and trends in contemporary British philosophy, organized by the British Council; originally published under the title "Philosophy of Science: a Personal Report" in *British Philosophy in Mid-Century* Ed. C. A. Mace, 1957.

Eddington's eclipse observations, which in 1919 brought the first important confirmation of Einstein's theory of gravitation. It was a great experience for us, and one which had a lasting influence on my intellectual development.

The three other theories I have mentioned were also widely discussed among students at that time. I myself happened to come into personal contact with Alfred Adler, and even to cooperate with him in his social work among the children and young people in the working-class districts of Vienna where he had established social guidance clinics.

It was during the summer of 1919 that I began to feel more and more dissatisfied with these three theories—the Marxist theory of history, psychoanalysis, and individual psychology; and I began to feel dubious about their claims to scientific status. My problem perhaps first took the simple form, "What is wrong with Marxism, psychoanalysis, and individual psychology? Why are they so different from physical theories, from Newton's theory, and especially from the theory of relativity?"

To make this contrast clear I should explain that few of us at the time would have said that we believed in the *truth* of Einstein's theory of gravitation. This shows that it was not my doubting the *truth* of those other three theories which bothered me, but something else. Yet neither was it that I merely felt mathematical physics to be more *exact* than the sociological or psychological type of theory. Thus what worried me was neither the problem of truth, at that stage at least, nor the problem of exactness or measurability. It was rather that I felt that these other three theories, though posing as sciences, had in fact more in common with primitive myths than with science; that they resembled astrology rather than astronomy.

I found that those of my friends who were admirers of Marx, Freud, and Adler were impressed by a number of points common to these theories and especially by their apparent *explanatory power*. These theories appeared to be able to explain practically everything that happened within the fields to which they referred. The study of any of them seemed to have the effect of an intellectual conversion or revelation, opening your eyes to a new truth hidden from those not yet initiated. Once your eyes were thus opened you saw confirming instances everywhere: The world was full of *verifications* of the theory. Whatever happened always confirmed it. Thus its truth appeared manifest; and unbelievers were clearly people who did not want to see the manifest truth, who refused to see it, either because it was against their class interest, or because of their repressions which were still "unanalysed" and crying aloud for treatment.

The most characteristic element in this situation seemed to me the incessant stream of confirmations, of observations which "verified" the theories in question; and this point was constantly emphasized by their adherents. A Marxist could not open a newspaper without finding on every page confirming evidence for his interpretation of history, not only in the news, but also in its presentation—which revealed the class bias of the paper—and especially of course in what the paper did *not* say. The Freudian analysts emphasized that their theories were constantly verified by their "clinical observations." As for Adler, I was much impressed by a personal experience. Once, in 1919, I reported to him a case which to me did not seem particularly Adlerian, but which he found no difficulty in analyzing in terms of his theory of inferiority feelings, although he had not even seen the child. Slightly shocked, I asked him how he could be so sure. "Because of my thousandfold experience," he replied; whereupon I could not help saying, "And with this new case, I suppose, your experience has become thousand-and-one-fold."

What I had in mind was that his previous observations may not have been much sounder than this new one; that each in its turn had been interpreted in the light of "previous experience," and at the same time counted as additional confirmation. What, I asked myself, did it confirm? No more than that a case could be interpreted in the light of the theory. But this meant very little, I reflected, since every conceivable case could be interpreted in the light of Adler's theory, or equally of Freud's. I may illustrate this by two very different examples of human behavior: that of a man who pushes a child into the water with the intention of drowning it, and that of a man who sacrifices his life in an attempt to save the child. Each of these two cases can be explained with equal ease in Freudian and in Adlerian terms. According to Freud the first man suffered from repression (say, of some component of his Oedipus complex), while the second man had achieved sublimation. According to Adler the first man suffered from feelings of inferiority (producing perhaps the need to prove to himself that he dared to commit some crime), and so did the second man (whose need was to prove to himself that he dared to rescue the child). I could not think of any human behavior which could not be interpreted in terms of either theory. It was precisely this fact—that they always fitted, that they were always confirmed—which in the eyes of their admirers constituted the strongest argument in favor of these theories. It began to dawn on me that this apparent strength was in fact their weakness.

With Einstein's theory the situation was strikingly different. Take one typical instance—Einstein's prediction, just then confirmed by the findings of Eddington's expedition. Einstein's gravitational theory had led to the result that light must be attracted by heavy bodies (such as the sun), precisely as material bodies were attracted. As a consequence it could be calculated that light from a distant fixed star whose apparent position was close to the sun would reach the earth from such a direction that the star would seem to be slightly shifted away from the sun; or, in other words, that stars close to the sun would look as if they had moved a little away from the sun, and from one another. This is a thing which cannot normally be observed since such stars are rendered invisible in daytime by the sun's overwhelming brightness; but during an eclipse it is possible to take photographs of them. If the same constellation is photographed at night one can measure the distances on the two photographs, and check the predicted effect.

Now the impressive thing about this case is the *risk* involved in a prediction of this kind. If observation shows that the predicted effect is definitely absent, then the theory is simply refuted. The theory is *incompatible with certain possible results of*

observation—in fact with results which everybody before Einstein would have expected.[1] This is quite different from the situation I have previously described, when it turned out that the theories in question were compatible with the most divergent human behavior, so that it was practically impossible to describe any human behavior that might not be claimed to be a verification of these theories.

These considerations led me in the winter of 1919–20 to conclusions which I may now reformulate as follows.

1. It is easy to obtain confirmations, or verifications, for nearly every theory—if we look for confirmations.

2. Confirmations should count only if they are the result of *risky predictions;* that is to say, if, unenlightened by the theory in question, we should have expected an event which was incompatible with the theory—an event which would have refuted the theory.

3. Every 'good' scientific theory is a prohibition: It forbids certain things to happen. The more a theory forbids, the better it is.

4. A theory which is not refutable by any conceivable event is non-scientific. Irrefutability is not a virtue of a theory (as people often think) but a vice.

5. Every genuine *test* of a theory is an attempt to falsify it, or to refute it. Testability is falsifiability; but there are degrees of testability: Some theories are more testable, more exposed to refutation, than others; they take, as it were, greater risks.

6. Confirming evidence should not count *except when it is the result of a genuine test of the theory;* and this means that it can be presented as a serious but unsuccessful attempt to falsify the theory. (I now speak in such cases of "corroborating evidence.")

---

[1] This is a slight oversimplification, for about half of the Einstein effect may be derived from the classical theory, provided we assume a ballistic theory of light.

7. Some genuinely testable theories, when found to be false, are still upheld by their admirers—for example by introducing *ad hoc* some auxiliary assumption, or by reinterpreting the theory *ad hoc* in such a way that it escapes refutation. Such a procedure is always possible, but it rescues the theory from refutation only at the price of destroying, or at least lowering, its scientific status. (I later described such a rescuing operation as a *conventionalist twist* or a *conventionalist stratagem*.)

One can sum up all this by saying that *the criterion of the scientific status of a theory is its falsifiability, or refutability, or testability.*

II

I may perhaps exemplify this with the help of the various theories so far mentioned. Einstein's theory of gravitation clearly satisfied the criterion of falsifiability. Even if our measuring instruments at the time did not allow us to pronounce on the results of the tests with complete assurance, there was clearly a possibility of refuting the theory.

Astrology did not pass the test. Astrologers were greatly impressed, and misled, by what they believed to be confirming evidence—so much so that they were quite unimpressed by any unfavorable evidence. Moreover, by making their interpretations and prophecies sufficiently vague they were able to explain away anything that might have been a refutation of the theory had the theory and the prophecies been more precise. In order to escape falsification they destroyed the testability of their theory. It is a typical soothsayer's trick to predict things so vaguely that the predictions can hardly fail, that they become irrefutable.

The Marxist theory of history, in spite of the serious efforts of some of its founders and followers, ultimately adopted this soothsaying practice. In some of its earlier formulations (for example, in Marx's analysis of the character of the "coming social revolution") their predictions were testable, and in fact falsified.[2] Yet instead of ac-

cepting the refutations the followers of Marx reinterpreted both the theory and the evidence in order to make them agree. In this way they rescued the theory from refutation; but they did so at the price of adopting a device which made it irrefutable. They thus gave a "conventionalist twist" to the theory; and by this stratagem they destroyed its much advertised claim to scientific status.

The two psychoanalytic theories were in a different class. They were simply non-testable, irrefutable. There was no conceivable human behavior which could contradict them. This does not mean that Freud and Adler were not seeing certain things correctly: I personally do not doubt that much of what they say is of considerable importance and may well play its part one day in a psychological science which is testable. But it does mean that those "clinical observations" which analysts naively believe confirm their theory cannot do this any more than the daily confirmations which astrologers find in their practice.[3]

---

[2] See, for example, my *Open Society and Its Enemies*, Ch. 15, Section iii, and notes 13–14.

[3] "Clinical observations," like all other observations, are *interpretations in the light of theories* (see below, Sections iv ff.); and for this reason alone they are apt to seem to support those theories in the light of which they were interpreted. But real support can be obtained only from observations undertaken as tests (by "attempted refutations"); and for this purpose *criteria of refutation* have to be laid down beforehand: It must be agreed which observable situations, if actually observed, mean that the theory is refuted. But what kind of clinical responses would refute to the satisfaction of the analyst not merely a particular analytic diagnosis but psychoanalysis itself? And have such criteria ever been discussed or agreed upon by analysts? Is there not, on the contrary, a whole family of analytic concepts, such as "ambivalence" (I do not suggest that there is no such thing as ambivalence), which would make it difficult, if not impossible, to agree upon such criteria? Moreover, how much headway has been made in investigating the question of the extent to which the (conscious or unconscious) expectations and theories held by the analyst influence the "clinical responses" of the patient? (To say nothing about the conscious attempts to influence the patient by proposing interpretations to him, etc.) Years ago I introduced the term *Oedipus effect* to describe the influence of a theory or expectation or prediction *upon the event which it predicts* or describes: It will be remembered that the causal chain leading to Oedipus' parricide was started by the oracle's prediction of this event. This is a characteristic and recurrent theme of such myths, but one which seems to have failed to attract the interest of the analysts, perhaps not accidentally. (The problem of confirmatory dreams suggested by the analyst is discussed by Freud, for example in *Gesammelte Schriften*, III, 1925, where he says on p. 314: "If anybody asserts that most of the dreams which can be utilized in an analysis . . . owe their origin to [the analyst's] suggestion, then no objection can be made from the point of view of analytic theory. Yet there is nothing in this fact," he surprisingly adds, "which would detract from the reliability of our results.")

And as for Freud's epic of the Ego, the Super-ego, and the Id, no substantially stronger claim to scientific status can be made for it than for Homer's collected stories from Olympus. These theories describe some facts, but in the manner of myths. They contain most interesting psychological suggestions, but not in a testable form.

At the same time I realized that such myths may be developed and become testable, that historically speaking all—or very nearly all—scientific theories originate from myths, and that a myth may contain important anticipations of scientific theories. Examples are Empedocles' theory of evolution by trial and error, or Parmenides' myth of the unchanging block universe in which nothing ever happens and which, if we add another dimension, becomes Einstein's block universe (in which, too nothing ever happens, since everything is, four-dimensionally speaking, determined and laid down from the beginning). I thus felt that if a theory is found to be non-scientific, or "metaphysical" (as we might say), it is not thereby found to be unimportant, or insignificant, or "meaningless," or "nonsensical."[4] But it cannot claim to be backed by empirical evidence in the scientific sense—although it may easily be, in some genetic sense, the "result of observation."

(There were a great many other theories of this pre-scientific or pseudo-scientific character, some of them, unfortunately, as influential as the Marxist interpretation of history; for example, the racialist interpretation of history—another of those impressive and all-explanatory theories which act upon weak minds like revelations.)

Thus the problem which I tried to solve by proposing the criterion of falsifiability was neither a problem of meaningfulness or significance, nor a problem of truth or acceptability. It was the problem of drawing a line (as well as this can be done) between the statements, or systems of statements, of the empirical sciences, and all other statements—whether they are of a religious or of a metaphysical character, or simply pseudo-scientific. Years later—it must have been in 1928 or 1929—I called this first problem of mine the *problem of demarcation*. The criterion of falsifiability is a solution to this problem of demarcation, for it says that statements or systems of statements, in order to be ranked as scientific, must be capable of conflicting with possible, or conceivable, observations.

III

Today I know, of course, that this *criterion of demarcation*—the criterion of testability, or falsifiability, or refutability—is far from obvious; for even now its significance is seldom realized. At that time, in 1920, it seemed to me almost trivial, although it solved for me an intellectual problem which had worried me deeply, and one which also had obvious practical consequences (for example, political ones). But I did not yet realize its full implications, or its philosophical significance. When I explained it to a fellow student of the Mathematics Department (now a distinguished mathematician in Great Britain), he suggested that I should publish it. At the time I thought this absurd; for I was convinced that my problem, since it was so important for me, must have agitated many scientists and philosophers who would surely have reached my rather obvious solution. That this was not the case I learnt from Wittgenstein's work, and from its reception; and so I published my results thirteen years later in the form of a criticism of Wittgenstein's *criterion of meaningfulness*.

Wittgenstein, as you all know, tried to show in the *Tractatus* (see, for example, his propositions 6.53; 6.54; and 5) that all so-called philosophical or metaphysical propositions were actually non-propositions or pseudo-propositions, that they were senseless or meaningless. All genuine (or meaningful) propositions were truth functions of the elementary or atomic propositions which described "atomic facts," i.e., facts which can in

---

[4] The case of astrology, nowadays a typical pseudo-science, may illustrate this point. It was attacked, by Aristotelians and other rationalists, down to Newton's day, for the wrong reason—for its now accepted assertion that the planets had an "influence" upon terrestrial ("sublunar") events. In fact Newton's theory of gravity, and especially the lunar theory of the tides, was historically speaking an offspring of astrological lore. Newton, it seems, was most reluctant to adopt a theory which came from the same stable as for example, the theory that "influenza" epidemics are due to an astral "influence." And Galileo, no doubt for the same reason, actually rejected the lunar theory of the tides; and his misgivings about Kepler may easily be explained by his misgivings about astrology.

principle be ascertained by observation. In other words, meaningful propositions were fully reducible to elementary or atomic propositions which were simple statements describing possible states of affairs, and which could in principle be established or rejected by observation. If we call a statement an "observation statement" not only if it states an actual observation but also if it states anything that *may* be observed, we shall have to say (according to the *Tractatus,* 5 and 4.52) that every genuine proposition must be a truth-function of, and therefore deducible from, observation statements. All other apparent propositions will be meaningless pseudo-propositions; in fact they will be nothing but nonsensical gibberish.

This idea was used by Wittgenstein for a characterization of science, as opposed to philosophy. We read (for example in 4.11, where natural science is taken to stand in opposition to philosophy): "The totality of true propositions is the total natural science (or the totality of the natural sciences)." This means that the propositions which belong to science are those deducible from *true* observation statements; they are those propositions which can be *verified* by true observation statements. Could we know all true observation statements, we should also know all that may be asserted by natural science.

This amounts to a crude verifiability criterion of demarcation. To make it slightly less crude, it could be amended thus: "The statements which may possibly fall within the province of science are those which may possibly be verified by observation statements; and these statements, again, coincide with the class of *all* genuine or meaningful statements." For this approach, then, *verifiability, meaningfulness, and scientific character all coincide.*

I personally was never interested in the so-called problem of meaning; on the contrary, it appeared to me a verbal problem, a typical pseudo-problem. I was interested only in the problem of demarcation, i.e., in finding a criterion of the scientific character of theories. It was just this interest which made me see at once that Wittgenstein's verifiability criterion of meaning was intended to play the part of a criterion of demarca-

tion as well, and which made me see that, as such, it was totally inadequate, even if all misgivings about the dubious concept of meaning were set aside. For Wittgenstein's criterion of demarcation—to use my own terminology in this context—is verifiability, or deducibility from observation statements. But this criterion is too narrow (*and* too wide): It excludes from science practically everything that is, in fact, characteristic of it (while failing in effect to exclude astrology). No scientific theory can ever be deduced from observation statements, or be described as a truth-function of observation statements.

All this I pointed out on various occasions to Wittgensteinians and members of the Vienna Circle. In 1931–2 I summarized my ideas in a largish book (read by several members of the Circle but never published, although part of it was incorporated in my *Logic of Scientific Discovery*); and in 1933 I published a letter to the Editor of *Erkenntnis* in which I tried to compress into two pages my ideas on the problems of demarcation and induction.[5] In this letter and elsewhere I described the problem of meaning as a pseudo-problem, in contrast to the problem of demarcation. But my contribution was classified by members of the Circle as a proposal to replace the verifiability criterion of *meaning* by a falsifiability criterion of *mean-*

---

[5] My *Logic of Scientific Discovery* (1959, 1960, 1961), here usually referred to as *L.Sc.D.,* is the translation of *Logik der Forschung* (1934), with a number of additional notes and appendices, including (on pp. 312–14) the letter to the Editor of *Erkenntnis* mentioned here in the text, which was first published in *Erkenntnis,* 3, 1933, pp. 426 f.

Concerning my never published book mentioned here in the text, see R. Carnap's paper "Ueber Protokollstäze" (On Protocol-Sentences), *Erkenntnis,* 3, 1932, pp. 215–28, where he gives an outline of my theory on pp. 223–8 and accepts it. He calls my theory "procedure B," and says (p. 224, top): "Starting from a point of view different from Neurath's [who developed what Carnap calls on p. 223 "procedure A"], Popper developed procedure B as part of his system." And after describing in detail my theory of tests, Carnap sums up his views as follows (p. 228): "After weighing the various arguments here discussed, it appears to me that the second language form with procedure B—that is, in the form here described—is the most adequate among the forms of scientific language at present advocated . . . in the . . . theory of knowledge." This paper of Carnap's contained the first published report of my theory of critical testing. (See also my critical remarks in *L.Sc.D.,* note 1 to Section 29, p. 104, where the date *1933* should read *1932. . . .*)

ing—which effectively made nonsense of my views.[6] My protests that I was trying to solve, not their pseudo-problem of meaning, but the problem of demarcation, were of no avail.

My attacks upon verification had some effect, however. They soon led to complete confusion in the camp of the verificationist philosophers of sense and nonsense. The original proposal of verifiability as the criterion of meaning was at least clear, simple, and forceful. The modifications and shifts which were now introduced were the very opposite.[7] This, I should say, is now seen even by the participants. But since I am usually quoted as one of them I wish to repeat that although I created this confusion I never participated in it. Neither falsifiability nor testability were proposed by me as criteria for meaning; and although I may plead guilty to having introduced both terms into the discussion, it was not I who introduced them into the theory of meaning.

Criticism of my alleged views was widespread and highly successful. I have yet to meet a criticism of my views.[8] Meanwhile, testability is being widely accepted as a criterion of demarcation.

---

[6] Wittgenstein's example of a nonsensical pseudo-proposition is: "Socrates is identical." Obviously, "Socrates is not identical" must also be nonsense. Thus the negation of any nonsense will be nonsense, and that of a meaningful statement will be meaningful. *But the negation of a testable (or falsifiable) statement need not be testable,* as was pointed out, first in my *L.Sc.D.,* (e.g., pp. 38 f.) and later by my critics. The confusion caused by taking testability as a criterion of *meaning* rather than of *demarcation* can easily be imagined.

[7] The most recent example of the way in which the history of this problem is misunderstood is A. R. White's "Note on Meaning and Verification," *Mind,* 63, 1954, pp. 66 ff. J. L. Evan's article, *Mind,* 62, 1953, pp. 1 ff., which Mr. White criticizes, is excellent, in my opinion, and unusually perceptive. Understandably enough, neither of the authors can quite reconstruct the story. (Some hints may be found in my *Open Society,* notes 46, 51 and 52 to Ch. 11; . . .)

[8] In *L.Sc.D.* I discussed, and replied to, some likely objections which afterwards were indeed raised, without reference to my replies. One of them is the contention that the falsification of a natural law is just as impossible as its verification. The answer is that this objection mixes two entirely different levels of analysis (like the objection that mathematical demonstrations are impossible since checking, no matter how often repeated, can never make it quite certain that we have not overlooked a mistake). On the first level, there is a logical asymmetry: One singular statement—say, about the perihelion of Mercury—can formally falsify Kepler's laws, but these cannot be formally verified by any number of singular statements. The attempt to minimize this asymmetry can only lead to confusion. On another level, we

IV

I have discussed the problem of demarcation in some detail because I believe that its solution is the key to most of the fundamental problems of the philosophy of science. . . . [B]ut only one of them—the *problem of induction*—can be discussed here at any length.

I had become interested in the problem of induction in 1923. Although this problem is very closely connected with the problem of demarcation, I did not fully appreciate the connection for about five years.

I approached the problem of induction through Hume. Hume, I felt, was perfectly right in pointing out that induction cannot be logically justified. He held that there can be no valid logical[9] arguments allowing us to establish "*that those instances, of which we have had no experience, resemble those, of which we have had experience.*" Consequently, "*even after the observation of the frequent or constant conjunction of objects, we have no reason to draw any inference concerning any object beyond those of which we have had experience.*" For "*shou'd it be said that we have experience*"[10]—experience teaching us that objects constantly conjoined with certain other

---

may hesitate to accept any statement, even the simplest observation statement; and we may point out that every statement involves *interpretation in the light of theories,* and that it is therefore uncertain. This does not affect the fundamental asymmetry, but it is important: Most dissectors of the heart before Harvey observed the wrong things—those which they expected to see. There can never be anything like a completely safe observation, free from the dangers of misinterpretation. (This is one of the reasons why the theory of induction does not work.) The "empirical basis" consists largely of a mixture of *theories* of lower degree of universality (of "reproducible effects"). But the fact remains that, relative to whatever basis the investigator may accept (at his peril), he can test his theory only by trying to refute it.

[9] Hume does not say "logical" but "demonstrative," a terminology which, I think, is a little misleading. The following two quotations are from the *Treatise of Human Nature,* Book I, Part III, Sections vi and xii. (The italics are all Hume's.)

[10] This and the next quotation are from *loc. cit.,* Section vi. See also Hume's *Enquiry Concerning Human Understanding,* Section IV, Part II, and his *Abstract,* edited 1938 by J. M. Keynes and P. Sraffa, p. 15, and quoted in *L.Sc.D.,* new appendix *VII, text to note 6.

objects continue to be so conjoined—then, Hume says, "I wou'd renew my question, *why from this experience we form any conclusion beyond those past instances, of which we have had experience.*" In other words, an attempt to justify the practice of induction by an appeal to experience must lead to an *infinite regress.* As a result we can say that theories can never be inferred from observation statements, or rationally justified by them.

I found Hume's refutation of inductive inference clear and conclusive. But I felt completely dissatisfied with his psychological explanation of induction in terms of custom or habit.

It has often been noticed that this explanation of Hume's is philosophically not very satisfactory. It is, however, without doubt intended as a *psychological* rather than a philosophical theory; for it tries to give a causal explanation of a psychological fact—*the fact that we believe in laws,* in statements asserting regularities or constantly conjoined kinds of events—by asserting that this fact is due to (i.e., constantly conjoined with) custom or habit. But even this reformulation of Hume's theory is still unsatisfactory; for what I have just called a "psychological fact" may itself be described as a custom or habit—the custom or habit of believing in laws or regularities; and it is neither very surprising nor very enlightening to hear that such a custom or habit must be explained as due to, or conjoined with, a custom or habit (even though a different one). Only when we remember that the words "custom" and "habit" are used by Hume, as they are in ordinary language, not merely to *describe* regular behavior, but rather to *theorize about its origin* (ascribed to frequent repetition), can we reformulate his psychological theory in a more satisfactory way. We can then say that, like other habits, *our habit of believing in laws is the product of frequent repetition*—of the repeated observation that things of a certain kind are constantly conjoined with things of another kind.

This genetico-psychological theory is, as indicated, incorporated in ordinary language, and it is therefore hardly as revolutionary as Hume thought. It is no doubt an extremely popular psychological theory—part of "common sense," one

might say. But in spite of my love of both common sense and Hume, I felt convinced that this psychological theory was mistaken; and that it was in fact refutable on purely logical grounds.

Hume's psychology, which is the popular psychology, was mistaken, I felt, about at least three different things: (a) the typical result of repetition; (b) the genesis of habits; and especially (c) the character of those experiences or modes of behavior which may be described as "believing in a law" or "expecting a law-like succession of events."

a. The typical result of repetition—say, of repeating a difficult passage on the piano—is that movements which at first needed attention are in the end executed without attention. We might say that the process becomes radically abbreviated, and ceases to be conscious: It becomes "physiological." Such a process, far from creating a conscious expectation of law-like succession, or a belief in a law, may on the contrary begin with a conscious belief and destroy it by making it superfluous. In learning to ride a bicycle we may start with the belief that we can avoid falling if we steer in the direction in which we threaten to fall, and this belief may be useful for guiding our movements. After sufficient practice we may forget the rule; in any case, we do not need it any longer. On the other hand, even if it is true that repetition may create unconscious expectations, these become conscious only if something goes wrong (we may not have heard the clock tick, but we may hear that it has stopped).

b. Habits or customs do not, as a rule, *originate* in repetition. Even the habit of walking, or of speaking, or of feeding at certain hours, *begins* before repetition can play any part whatever. We may say, if we like, that they deserve to be called "habits" or "customs" only after repetition has played its typical part; but we must not say that the practices in question originated as the result of many repetitions.

c. Belief in a law is not quite the same thing as behavior which betrays an expectation of a lawlike succession of events; but these two are sufficiently closely connected to be treated together. They may, perhaps, in exceptional cases, result from a mere repetition of sense impressions (as in the case of the stopping clock). I was prepared to concede this, but I contended that normally, and in most cases of any interest, they cannot be so explained. As Hume admits, even a single striking observation may be sufficient to create a belief or an expectation—a fact which he tries to explain as due to an inductive habit, formed as the result of a vast number of long repetitive sequences which had been experienced at an earlier period of life.[11] But this, I contended, was merely his attempt to explain away unfavorable facts which threatened his theory; an unsuccessful attempt, since these unfavorable facts could be observed in very young animals and babies—as early, indeed, as we like. "A lighted cigarette was held near the noses of the young puppies," reports F. Bäge. "They sniffed at it once, turned tail, and nothing would induce them to come back to the source of the smell and sniff again. A few days later, they reacted to the mere sight of a cigarette or even of a rolled piece of white paper, by bounding away, and sneezing."[12] If we try to explain cases like this by postulating a vast number of long repetitive sequences at a still earlier age we are not only romancing, but forgetting that in the clever puppies' short lives there must be room not only for repetition but also for a great deal of novelty, and consequently of non-repetition.

But it is not only that certain empirical facts do not support Hume; there are decisive arguments of a *purely logical* nature against his psychological theory.

The central idea of Hume's theory is that of *repetition, based upon similarity* (or "resemblance"). This idea is used in a very uncritical way. We are led to think of the water drop that hollows the stone, of sequences of unquestionably like events slowly forcing themselves upon us, as does the tick of the clock. But we ought to realize that in a psychological theory such as Hume's, only repetition-for-us, based upon similarity-for-us, can be allowed to have any effect upon us. We must respond to situations as if they were equivalent; *take* them as similar; *interpret* them as repetitions. The clever puppies, we may assume, showed by their response, their way of acting or of reacting, that they recognized or interpreted the second situation as a repetition of the first—that they expected its main element, the objectionable smell, to be present. The situation was a repetition-for-them because they responded to it by *anticipating* its similarity to the previous one.

This apparently psychological criticism has a purely logical basis which may be summed up in the following simple argument. (It happens to be the one from which I originally started my criticism.) The kind of repetition envisaged by Hume can never be perfect; the cases he has in mind cannot be cases of perfect sameness; they can only be cases of similarity. Thus *they are repetitions only from a certain point of view.* (What has the effect upon me of a repetition may not have this effect upon a spider.) But this means that, for logical reasons, there must always be a point of view—such as a system of expectations, anticipations, assumptions, or interests—*before* there can be any repetition; which point of view, consequently, cannot be merely the result of repetition. (See now also appendix *x, (1), to my *L.Sc.D.*)

We must thus replace, for the purposes of a psychological theory of the origin of our beliefs, the naive idea of events which are similar by the idea of events to which we react by *interpreting* them as being similar. But if this is so (and I can see no escape from it), then Hume's psychological theory of induction leads to an infinite regress, precisely analogous to that other infinite regress which was discovered by Hume himself, and used by him to explode the logical theory of induction. For what do we wish to explain? In the example of the puppies we wish to explain behavior which

---

[11] *Treatise,* Section xiii; Section xv, Rule 4.

[12] F. Bäge, "Zur Entwicklung, etc." *Zeitschrift f. Hundeforschung,* 1933; cp. D. Katz, *Animals and Men,* Ch. VI, footnote.

may be described as *recognizing or interpreting* a situation as a repetition of another. Clearly, we cannot hope to explain this by an appeal to earlier repetitions, once we realize that the earlier repetitions must also have been repetitions-for-them, so that precisely the same problem arises again: that of *recognizing or interpreting* a situation as a repetition of another.

To put it more concisely, similarity-for-us is the product of a response involving interpretations (which may be inadequate) and anticipations or expectations (which may never be fulfilled). It is therefore impossible to explain anticipations, or expectations, as resulting from many repetitions, as suggested by Hume. For even the first repetition-for-us must be based upon similarity-for-us, and therefore expectations—precisely the kind of thing we wished to explain.

This shows that there is an infinite regress involved in Hume's psychological theory.

Hume, I felt, had never accepted the full force of his own logical analysis. Having refuted the logical idea of induction he was faced with the following problem: How do we actually obtain our knowledge, as a matter of psychological fact, if induction is a procedure which is logically invalid and rationally unjustifiable? There are two possible answers: (1) We obtain our knowledge by a non-inductive procedure. This answer would have allowed Hume to retain a form of rationalism. (2) We obtain our knowledge by repetition and induction, and therefore by a logically invalid and rationally unjustifiable procedure, so that all apparent knowledge is merely a kind of belief—belief based on habit. This answer would imply that even scientific knowledge is irrational, so that rationalism is absurd, and must be given up. (I shall not discuss here the age-old attempts, now again fashionable, to get out of the difficulty by asserting that though induction is of course logically invalid if we mean by *logic* the same as *deductive logic*, it is not irrational by its own standards, as may be seen from the fact that every reasonable man applies it *as a matter of fact*: It was Hume's great achievement to break this uncritical identification of the question of fact—*quid*

facti?—and the question of justification or validity—*quid juris?* . . .

It seems that Hume never seriously considered the first alternative. Having cast out the logical theory of induction by repetition he struck a bargain with common sense, meekly allowing the re-entry of induction by repetition, in the guise of a psychological theory. I proposed to turn the tables upon this theory of Hume's. Instead of explaining our propensity to expect regularities as the result of repetition, I proposed to explain repetition-for-us as the result of our propensity to expect regularities and to search for them.

Thus I was led by purely logical considerations to replace the psychological theory of induction by the following view. Without waiting, passively, for repetitions to impress or impose regularities upon us, we actively try to impose regularities upon the world. We try to discover similarities in it, and to interpret it in terms of laws invented by us. Without waiting for premises we jump to conclusions. These may have to be discarded later, should observation show that they are wrong.

This was a theory of trial and error—of *conjectures and refutations*. It made it possible to understand why our attempts to force interpretations upon the world were logically prior to the observation of similarities. Since there were logical reasons behind this procedure, I thought that it would apply in the field of science also; that scientific theories were not the digest of observations, but that they were inventions—conjectures boldly put forward for trial, to be eliminated if they clashed with observations; with observations which were rarely accidental but as a rule undertaken with the definite intention of testing a theory by obtaining, if possible, a decisive refutation.

V

The belief that science proceeds from observation to theory is still so widely and so firmly held that my denial of it is often met with incredulity. I have even been suspected of being insincere—of denying what nobody in his senses can doubt.

But in fact the belief that we can start with pure observations alone, without anything in the nature of a theory, is absurd; as may be illustrated by the story of the man who dedicated his life to natural science, wrote down everything he could observe, and bequeathed his priceless collection of observations to the Royal Society to be used as inductive evidence. This story should show us that though beetles may profitably be collected, observations may not.

Twenty-five years ago I tried to bring home the same point to a group of physics students in Vienna by beginning a lecture with the following instructions: "Take pencil and paper; carefully observe, and write down what you have observed!" They asked, of course, *what* I wanted them to observe. Clearly the instruction "Observe!" is absurd.[13] (It is not even idiomatic, unless the object of the transitive verb can be taken as understood.) Observation is always selective. It needs a chosen object, a definite task, an interest, a point of view, a problem. And its description presupposes a descriptive language, with property words; it presupposes similarity and classifications, which in its turn presupposes interests, points of view, and problems. "A hungry animal," writes Katz,[14] "divides the environment into edible and inedible things. An animal in flight sees roads to escape and hiding places. . . . Generally speaking, objects change . . . according to the needs of the animal." We may add that objects can be classified, and can become similar or dissimilar, *only in this way—by being related to needs and interests*. This rule applies not only to animals but also to scientists. For the animal a point of view is provided by its needs, the task of the moment, and its expectations; for the scientist by his theoretical interests, the special problem under investigation, his conjectures and anticipations, and the theories which he accepts as a kind of background: his frame of reference, his "horizon of expectations."

The problem "Which comes first, the hypothesis (*H*) or the observation (*O*)" is soluble, as is the problem "Which comes first, the hen (*H*) or the egg (*O*). The reply to the latter is "An earlier kind of egg"; to the former, "An earlier kind of hypothesis." It is quite true that any particular hypothesis we choose will have been preceded by observations—the observations, for example, which it is designed to explain. But these observations, in their turn, presupposed the adoption of a frame of reference, a frame of expectations, a frame of theories. If they were significant, if they created a need for explanation and thus gave rise to the invention of a hypothesis, it was because they could not be explained within the old theoretical framework, the old horizon of expectations. There is no danger here of an infinite regress. Going back to more and more primitive theories and myths we shall in the end find unconscious, *inborn* expectations.

The theory of inborn *ideas* is absurd, I think; but every organism has inborn *reactions* or *responses;* and among them, responses adapted to impending events. These responses we may describe as "expectations" without implying that these "expectations" are conscious. The newborn baby "expects," in this sense, to be fed (and, one could even argue, to be protected and loved). In view of the close relation between expectation and knowledge we may even speak in quite a reasonable sense of "inborn knowledge." This "knowledge" is not, however, *valid a priori;* an inborn expectation, no matter how strong and specific, may be mistaken. (The newborn child may be abandoned, and starve.)

Thus we are born with expectations; with "knowledge" which, although not *valid a priori,* is *psychologically or genetically a priori,* i.e., prior to all observational experience. One of the most important of these expectations is the expectation of finding a regularity. It is connected with an inborn propensity to look out for regularities, or with a *need* to *find* regularities, as we may see from the pleasure of the child who satisfies this need.

This "instinctive" expectation of finding regularities, which is psychologically *a priori,* corresponds very closely to the "law of causality"

---

[13] See Section 30 of *L.Sc.D.*

[14] Katz, *loc. cit.*

which Kant believed to be part of our mental outfit and to be *a priori* valid. One might thus be inclined to say that Kant failed to distinguish between psychologically *a priori* ways of thinking or responding and *a priori* valid beliefs. But I do not think that his mistake was quite as crude as that. For the expectation of finding regularities is not only psychologically *a priori,* but also logically *a priori:* It is logically prior to all observational experience, for it is prior to any recognition of similarities, as we have seen; and all observation involves the recognition of similarities (or dissimilarities). But in spite of being logically *a priori* in this sense the expectation is not valid *a priori*. For it may fail: We can easily construct an environment (it would be a lethal one) which, compared with our ordinary environment, is so chaotic that we completely fail to find regularities. (All natural laws could remain valid: Environments of this kind have been used in the animal experiments mentioned in the next section.)

Thus Kant's reply to Hume came near to being right; for the distinction between an *a priori* valid expectation and one which is both genetically *and* logically prior to observation, but not *a priori* valid, is really somewhat subtle. But Kant proved too much. In trying to show how knowledge is possible, he proposed a theory which had the unavoidable consequence that our quest for knowledge must necessarily succeed, which is clearly mistaken. When Kant said, "Our intellect does not draw its laws from nature but imposes its laws upon nature," he was right. But in thinking that these laws are necessarily true, or that we necessarily succeed in imposing them upon nature, he was wrong.[15] Nature very often resists quite successfully, forcing us to discard our laws as refuted; but if we live we may try again.

To sum up this logical criticism of Hume's psy-

chology of induction we may consider the idea of building an induction machine. Placed in a simplified "world" (for example, one of sequences of colored counters), such a machine may through repetition "learn," or even "formulate," laws of succession which hold in its "world." If such a machine can be constructed (and I have no doubt that it can) then, it might be argued, my theory must be wrong; for if a machine is capable of performing inductions on the basis of repetition, there can be no logical reasons preventing us from doing the same.

The argument sounds convincing, but it is mistaken. In constructing an induction machine we, the architects of the machine, must decide *a priori* what constitutes its "world"; what things are to be taken as similar or equal; and what *kind* of "laws" we wish the machine to be able to "discover" in its "world." In other words we must build into the machine a framework determining what is relevant or interesting in its world: The machine will have its "inborn" selection principles. The problems of similarity will have been solved for it by its makers who thus have interpreted the "world" for the machine.

VI

Our propensity to look out for regularities, and to impose laws upon nature, leads to the psychological phenomenon of *dogmatic thinking* or, more generally, dogmatic behavior: We expect regularities everywhere and attempt to find them even where there are none; events which do not yield to these attempts we are inclined to treat as a kind of 'background noise'; and we stick to our expectations even when they are inadequate and we ought to accept defeat. This dogmatism is to some extent necessary. It is demanded by a situation which can only be dealt with by forcing our conjectures upon the world. Moreover, this dogmatism allows us to approach a good theory in stages, by way of approximations: If we accept defeat too easily, we may prevent ourselves from finding that we were very nearly right.

It is clear that this *dogmatic attitude,* which

---

[15] Kant believed that Newton's dynamics was *a priori* valid. (See his *Metaphysical Foundation of Natural Science,* published between the first and the second editions of the *Critique of Pure Reason*.) But if, as he thought, we can explain the validity of Newton's theory by the fact that our intellect imposes its laws upon nature, it follows, I think, that our intellect *must succeed* in this; which makes it hard to understand why *a priori* knowledge such as Newton's should be so hard to come by. . . .

makes us stick to our first impressions, is indicative of a strong belief; while a *critical attitude,* which is ready to modify its tenets, which admits doubt and demands tests, is indicative of a weaker belief. Now according to Hume's theory, and to the popular theory, the strength of a belief should be a product of repetition; thus it should always grow with experience, and always be greater in less primitive persons. But dogmatic thinking, an uncontrolled wish to impose regularities, a manifest pleasure in rites and in repetition as such, are characteristic of primitives and children; and increasing experience and maturity sometimes create an attitude of caution and criticism rather than of dogmatism.

I may perhaps mention here a point of agreement with psychoanalysis. Psychoanalysts assert that neurotics and others interpret the world in accordance with a personal set pattern which is not easily given up, and which can often be traced back to early childhood. A pattern or scheme which was adopted very early in life is maintained throughout, and every new experience is interpreted in terms of it; verifying it, as it were, and contributing to its rigidity. This is a description of what I have called the dogmatic attitude, as distinct from the critical attitude, which shares with the dogmatic attitude the quick adoption of a schema of expectations—a myth, perhaps, or a conjecture of hypothesis—but which is ready to modify it, to correct it, and even to give it up. I am inclined to suggest that most neuroses may be due to a partially arrested development of the critical attitude; to an arrested rather than a natural dogmatism; to resistance to demands for the modification and adjustment of certain schematic interpretations and responses. This resistance in its turn may perhaps be explained, in some cases, as due to an injury or shock, resulting in fear and in an increased need for assurance or certainty, analogous to the way in which an injury to a limb makes us afraid to move it, so that it becomes stiff. (It might even be argued that the case of the limb is not merely analogous to the dogmatic response, but an instance of it.) The explanation of any concrete case will have to take into account the weight of the difficulties involved in making the

necessary adjustments—difficulties which may be considerable, especially in a complex and changing world: We know from experiments on animals that varying degrees of neurotic behavior may be produced at will by correspondingly varying difficulties.

I found many other links between the psychology of knowledge and psychological fields which are often considered remote from it—for example, the psychology of art and music; in fact, my ideas about induction originated in a conjecture about the evolution of Western polyphony. But you will be spared this story.

VII

My logical criticism of Hume's psychological theory, and the considerations connected with it (most of which I elaborated in 1926–7, in a thesis entitled "On Habit and Belief in Laws"[16]), may seem a little removed from the field of the philosophy of science. But the distinction between dogmatic and critical thinking, or the dogmatic and the critical attitude, brings us right back to our central problem. For the dogmatic attitude is clearly related to the tendency to *verify* our laws and schemata by seeking to apply them and to confirm them, even to the point of neglecting refutations, whereas the critical attitude is one of readiness to change them—to test them, to refute them, to *falsify* them, if possible. This suggests that we may identify the critical attitude with the scientific attitude, and the dogmatic attitude with the one which we have described as pseudo-scientific.

It further suggests that genetically speaking the pseudo-scientific attitude is more primitive than, and prior to, the scientific attitude, that it is a pre-scientific attitude. And this primitivity or priority also has its logical aspect. For the critical attitude is not so much opposed to the dogmatic attitude as superimposed upon it: Criticism must be directed

---

[16] A thesis submitted under the title *Gewohnheit und Gesetzerlebnis* to the Institute of Education of the City of Vienna in 1927. (Unpublished.)

against existing and influential beliefs in need of critical revision—in other words, dogmatic beliefs. A critical attitude needs for its raw material, as it were, theories or beliefs which are held more or less dogmatically.

Thus science must begin with myths and with the criticism of myths—neither with the collection of observations, nor with the invention of experiments, but with the critical discussion of myths, and of magical techniques and practices. The scientific tradition is distinguished from the pre-scientific tradition in having two layers. Like the latter, it passes on its theories; but it also passes on a critical attitude toward them. The theories are passed on, not as dogmas, but rather with the challenge to discuss them and improve upon them. This tradition is Hellenic: It may be traced back to Thales, founder of the first *school* (I do not mean "of the first *philosophical* school," but simply "of the first school") which was not mainly concerned with the preservation of a dogma. . .

The critical attitude, the tradition of free discussion of theories with the aim of discovering their weak spots so that they may be improved upon, is the attitude of reasonableness, of rationality. It makes far-reaching use of both verbal argument and observation—of observation in the interest of argument, however. The Greeks' discovery of the critical method gave rise at first to the mistaken hope that it would lead to the solution of all the great old problems; that it would establish certainty; that it would help to *prove* our theories, to *justify* them. But this hope was a residue of the dogmatic way of thinking; in fact nothing can be justified or proved (outside of mathematics and logic). The demand for rational proofs in science indicates a failure to keep distinct the broad realm of rationality and the narrow realm of rational certainty: It is an untenable, an unreasonable demand.

Nevertheless, the role of logical argument, of deductive logical reasoning, remains all-important for the critical approach; not because it allows us to prove our theories, or to infer them from observation statements, but because only by purely deductive reasoning is it possible for us to discover what our theories imply, and thus to criticize them

effectively. Criticism, I said, is an attempt to find the weak spots in a theory, and these, as a rule, can be found only in the more remote logical consequences which can be derived from it. It is here that purely logical reasoning plays an important part in science.

Hume was right in stressing that our theories cannot be validly inferred from what we can know to be true—neither from observations nor from anything else. He concluded from this that our belief in them was irrational. If *belief* means here our inability to doubt our natural laws and the constancy of natural regularities, then Hume is again right: This kind of dogmatic belief has, one might say, a physiological rather than a rational basis. If, however, the term *belief* is taken to cover our critical acceptance of scientific theories—a *tentative* acceptance combined with an eagerness to revise the theory if we succeed in designing a test which it cannot pass—then Hume was wrong. In such an acceptance of theories there is nothing irrational. There is not even anything irrational in relying for practical purposes upon well-tested theories, for no more rational course of action is open to us.

Assume that we have deliberately made it our task to live in this unknown world of ours, to adjust ourselves to it as well as we can, to take advantage of the opportunities we can find in it, and to explain it, *if* possible (we need not assume that it is), and as far as possible, with the help of laws and explanatory theories. *If we have made this our task, then there is no more rational procedure than the method of trial and error—of conjecture and refutation,* of boldly proposing theories, of trying our best to show that these are erroneous, and of accepting them tentatively if our critical efforts are unsuccessful.

From the point of view here developed, all laws, all theories remain essentially tentative, or conjectural, or hypothetical, even when we feel unable to doubt them any longer. Before a theory has been refuted we can never know in what way it may have to be modified. That the sun will always rise and set within twenty-four hours is still proverbial as a law established by induction beyond reasonable doubt. It is odd that this example is still in use, though it may have served well enough in the days of Aristotle and Pytheas of Massalia—the great traveler who for centuries was called a liar because of his tales of Thule, the land of the frozen sea and the *midnight sun*.

The method of trial and error is not, of course, simply identical with the scientific or critical approach—with the method of conjecture and refutation. The method of trial and error is applied not only by Einstein but, in a more dogmatic fashion, by the amoeba also. The difference lies not so much in the trials as in a critical and constructive attitude towards errors; errors which the scientist consciously and cautiously tries to uncover in order to refute his theories with searching arguments, including appeals to the most severe experimental tests which his theories and his ingenuity permit him to design.

The critical attitude may be described as the conscious attempt to make our theories, our conjectures, suffer in our stead in the struggle for the survival of the fittest. It gives us a chance to survive the elimination of an inadequate hypothesis—when a more dogmatic attitude would eliminate it by eliminating us. (There is a touching story of an Indian community which disappeared because of its belief in the holiness of life, including that of tigers.) We thus obtain the fittest theory within our reach by the elimination of those which are less fit. (By "fitness" I do not mean merely "usefulness" but truth. . . .) I do not think that this procedure is irrational or in need of any further rational justification.

VIII

Let us now turn from our logical criticism of the *psychology of experience* to our real problem—the problem of *the logic of science*. Although some of the things I have said may help us here, insofar as they may have eliminated certain psychological prejudices in favor of induction, my treatment of the *logical problem of induction* is completely independent of this criticism, and of all psychological considerations. Provided you do not dogmatically believe in the alleged psycholog-

ical fact that we make inductions, you may now forget my whole story with the exception of two logical points: my logical remarks on testability or falsifiability as the criterion of demarcation; and Hume's logical criticism of induction.

From what I have said it is obvious that there was a close link between the two problems which interested me at that time: demarcation, and induction or scientific method. It was easy to see that the method of science is criticism, i.e., attempted falsifications. Yet it took me a few years to notice that the two problems—of demarcation and of induction—were in a sense one.

Why, I asked, do so many scientists believe in induction? I found they did so because they believed natural science to be characterized by the inductive method—by a method starting from, and relying upon, long sequences of observations and experiments. They believed that the difference between genuine science and metaphysical or pseudo-scientific speculation depended solely upon whether or not the inductive method was employed. They believed (to put it in my own terminology) that only the inductive method could provide a satisfactory *criterion of demarcation*.

I recently came across an interesting formulation of this belief in a remarkable philosophical book by a great physicist—Max Born's *Natural Philosophy of Cause and Chance*.[17] He writes: "Induction allows us to generalize a number of observations into a general rule: that night follows day and day follows night . . . . But while everyday life has no definite criterion for the validity of an induction, . . . science has worked out a code, or rule of craft, for its application." Born nowhere reveals the contents of this inductive code (which, as his wording shows, contains a "definite criterion for the validity of an induction"); but he stresses that "there is no logical argument" for its acceptance: "It is a question of faith," and he is therefore "willing to call induction a metaphysical principle." But why does he believe that such a code of valid inductive rules

---

[17] Max Born, *Natural Philosophy of Cause and Chance*, Oxford, 1949, p. 7.

must exist? This becomes clear when he speaks of the "vast communities of people ignorant of, or rejecting, the rule of science, among them the members of antivaccination societies and believers in astrology. It is useless to argue with them; I cannot compel them to accept the same criteria of valid induction in which I believe: the code of scientific rules." This makes it quite clear that *"valid induction" was here meant to serve as a criterion of demarcation between science and pseudo-science.*

But it is obvious that this rule or craft of "valid induction" is not even metaphysical: It simply does not exist. No rule can ever guarantee that a generalization inferred from true observations, however often repeated, is true. (Born himself does not believe in the truth of Newtonian physics, in spite of its success, although he believes that it is based on induction.) And the success of science is not based upon rules of induction, but depends upon luck, ingenuity, and the purely deductive rules of critical argument.

I may summarize some of my conclusions as follows:

1. Induction, i.e., inference based on many observations, is a myth. It is neither a psychological fact, nor a fact of ordinary life, nor one of scientific procedure.

2. The actual procedure of science is to operate with conjectures: to jump to conclusions—often after one single observation (as noticed, for example, by Hume and Born).

3. Repeated observations and experiments function in science as *tests* of our conjectures or hypotheses, i.e., as attempted refutations.

4. The mistaken belief in induction is fortified by the need for a criterion of demarcation which, it is traditionally but wrongly believed, only the inductive method can provide.

5. The conception of such an inductive method, like the criterion of verifiability, implies a faulty demarcation.

6. None of this is altered in the least if we say that induction makes theories only probable rather than certain. . . .

IX

If, as I have suggested, the problem of induction is only an instance or facet of the problem of demarcation, then the solution to the problem of demarcation must provide us with a solution to the problem of induction. This is indeed the case, I believe, although it is perhaps not immediately obvious.

For a brief formulation of the problem of induction we can turn again to Born, who writes: ". . . no observation or experiment, however extended, can give more than a finite number of repetitions"; therefore, "the statement of a law—B depends on A—always transcends experience. Yet this kind of statement is made everywhere and all the time, and sometimes from scanty material."[18]

In other words, the logical problem of induction arises from (a) Hume's discovery (so well expressed by Born) that it is impossible to justify a law by observation or experiment, since it "transcends experience"; (b) the fact that science proposes and uses laws "everywhere and all the time." (Like Hume, Born is struck by the "scanty material," i.e., the few observed instances upon which the law may be based.) To this we have to add (c) *the principle of empiricism,* which asserts that in science only observation and experiment may decide upon the *acceptance or rejection* of scientific statements, including laws and theories.

These three principles, (a), (b), and (c), appear at first sight to clash; and this apparent clash constitutes the *logical problem of induction.*

Faced with this clash, Born gives up (c), the principle of empiricism (as Kant and many others, including Bertrand Russell, have done before him), in favor of what he calls a "metaphysical principle"; a metaphysical principle which he does not even attempt to formulate; which he vaguely describes as a "code or rule of craft"; and of which I have never seen any formulation which even looked promising and was not clearly untenable.

---

[18] *Natural Philosophy of Cause and Chance,* p. 6.

But in fact the principles (a) to (c) do not clash. We can see this the moment we realize that the acceptance by science of a law or of a theory is *tentative only;* which is to say that all laws and theories are conjectures, or tentative *hypotheses* (a position which I have sometimes called "hypotheticism"); and that we may reject a law or theory on the basis of new evidence, without necessarily discarding the old evidence which originally led us to accept it.[19]

The principle of empiricism (c) can be fully preserved, since the fate of a theory, its acceptance or rejection, is decided by observation and experiment—by the result of tests. So long as a theory stands up to the severest tests we can design, it is accepted; if it does not, it is rejected. But it is never inferred, in any sense, from the empirical evidence. There is neither a psychological nor a logical induction. *Only the falsity of the theory can be inferred from empirical evidence, and this inference is a purely deductive one.*

Hume showed that it is not possible to infer a theory from observation statements; but this does not affect the possibility of refuting a theory by observation statements. The full appreciation of this possibility makes the relation between theories and observations perfectly clear.

This solves the problem of the alleged clash between the principles (a), (b), and (c), and with it Hume's problem of induction.

X

Thus the problem of induction is solved. But nothing seems less wanted than a simple solution to an age-old philosophical problem. Wittgenstein and his school hold that genuine philosophical problems do not exist,[20] from which it clearly follows that they cannot be solved. Others among my contemporaries do believe that there are philosophi-

cal problems, and respect them, but they seem to respect them too much; they seem to believe that they are insoluble, if not taboo, and they are shocked and horrified by the claim that there is a simple, neat, and lucid, solution to any of them. If there is a solution it must be deep, they feel, or at least complicated.

However this may be, I am still waiting for a simple, neat, and lucid criticism of the solution which I published first in 1933 in my letter to the Editor of *Erkenntnis,*[21] and later in *The Logic of Scientific Discovery.*

Of course, one can invent new problems of induction, different from the one I have formulated and solved. (Its formulation was half its solution.) But I have yet to see any reformulation of the problem whose solution cannot be easily obtained from my old solution. I am now going to discuss some of these reformulations.

One question which may be asked is this: How do we really jump from an observation statement to a theory?

Although this question appears to be psychological rather than philosophical, one can say something positive about it without invoking psychology. One can say first that the jump is not from an observation statement, but from a problem-situation, and that the theory must allow us *to explain* the observations which created the problem (that is, *to deduce* them from the theory strengthened by other accepted theories and by other observation statements, the so-called initial conditions). This leaves, of course, an immense number of possible theories, good and bad; and it thus appears that our question has not been answered.

But this makes it fairly clear that when we asked our question we had more in mind than "How do we jump from an observation statement to a theory?" The question we had in mind was, it now appears, "How do we jump from an observation statement to a *good* theory?" But to this the answer is: by jumping first to *any* theory and then testing it, to find whether it is good or not; i.e., by

---

[19] I do not doubt that Born and many others would agree that theories are accepted only tentatively. But the widespread belief in induction shows that the far-reaching implications of this view are rarely seen.

[20] Wittgenstein still held this belief in 1946. . . .

[21] See note 5 above.

repeatedly applying the critical method, eliminating many bad theories, and inventing many new ones. Not everybody is able to do this; but there is no other way.

Other questions have sometimes been asked. The original problem of induction, it was said, is the problem of *justifying* induction, i.e., of justifying inductive inference. If you answer this problem by saying that what is called an "inductive inference" is always invalid and therefore clearly not justifiable, the following new problem must arise: How do you justify your method of trial and error? Reply: the method of trial and error is a *method of eliminating false theories* by observation statements; and the justification for this is the purely logical relationship of deducibility, which allows us to assert the falsity of universal statements if we accept the truth of singular ones.

Another question sometimes asked is this: Why is it reasonable to prefer non-falsified statements to falsified ones? To this question some involved answers have been produced, for example, pragmatic answers. But from a pragmatic point of view the question does not arise, since false theories often serve well enough: Most formulas used in engineering or navigation are known to be false, although they may be excellent approximations and easy to handle; and they are used with confidence by people who know them to be false.

The only correct answer is the straightforward one: because we search for truth (even though we can never be sure we have found it), and because the falsified theories are known or believed to be false, while the non-falsified theories may still be true. Besides, we do not prefer *every* non-falsified theory—only one which, in the light of criticism, appears to be better than its competitors, which solves our problems, which is well tested, and of which we think, or rather conjecture or hope (considering other provisionally accepted theories), that it will stand up to further tests.

It has also been said that the problem of induction is "Why is it *reasonable* to believe that the future will be like the past?" and that a satisfactory answer to this question should make it plain that such a belief is, in fact, reasonable. My reply is that it is reasonable to believe that the future will be very different from the past in many vitally im-

portant respects. Admittedly it is perfectly reasonable to *act* on the assumption that it will, in many respects, be like the past, and that well-tested laws will continue to hold (since we can have no better assumption to act upon); but it is also reasonable to believe that such a course of action will lead us at times into severe trouble, since some of the laws upon which we now heavily rely may easily prove unreliable. (Remember the midnight sun!) One might even say that to judge from past experience, and from our general scientific knowledge, the future will *not* be like the past, in perhaps most of the ways which those have in mind who say that it will. Water will sometimes not quench thirst, and air will choke those who breathe it. An apparent way out is to say that the future will be like the past *in the sense that the laws of nature will not change,* but this is begging the question. We speak of a "law of nature" only if we think that we have before us a regularity which does not change; and if we find that it changes, then we shall not continue to call it a "law of nature." Of course our search for natural laws indicates that we hope to find them, and that we believe that there are natural laws, but our belief in any particular natural law cannot have a safer basis than our unsuccessful critical attempts to refute it.

I think that those who put the problem of induction in terms of the *reasonableness* of our beliefs are perfectly right if they are dissatisfied with a Humean, or post-Humean, skeptical despair of reason. We must indeed reject the view that a belief in science is as irrational as a belief in primitive magical practices—that both are a matter of accepting a "total ideology," a convention or a tradition based on faith. But we must be cautious if we formulate our problem, with Hume, as one of the reasonableness of our *beliefs.* We should split this problem into three—our old problem of demarcation, or of how to *distinguish* between science and primitive magic; the problem of the rationality of the scientific or critical *procedure,* and of the role of observation within it; and lastly the problem of the rationality of our *acceptance* of theories for scientific and for practical purposes. To all these three problems solutions have been offered here.

One should also be careful not to confuse the

problem of the reasonableness of the scientific procedure and the (tentative) acceptance of the results of this procedure—i.e., the scientific theories—with the problem of the rationality or otherwise *of the belief that this procedure will succeed.* In practice, in practical scientific research, this belief is no doubt unavoidable and reasonable, there being no better alternative. But the belief is certainly unjustifiable in a theoretical sense, as I have argued (in Section V). Moreover, if we could show, on general logical grounds, that the scientific quest is likely to succeed, one could not understand why anything like success has been so rare in the long history of human endeavors to know more about our world.

Yet another way of putting the problem of induction is in terms of probability. Let *t* be the theory and *e* the evidence: We can ask for *P(t,e)*, that is to say, the probability of *t*, given *e*. The problem of induction, it is often believed, can then be put thus: Construct a *calculus of probability* which allows us to work out for any theory *t* what its probability is, relative to any given empirical evidence *e*; and show that *P(t,e)* increases with the accumulation of supporting evidence, and reaches high values—at any rate, values greater than 1/2.

In *The Logic of Scientific Discovery* I explained why I think that this approach to the problem is fundamentally mistaken.[22] To make this clear, I introduced there the distinction between *probability* and *degree of corroboration or confirmation.* (The term "confirmation" has lately been so much used and misused that I have decided to surrender it to the verificationists and to use for my own purposes "corroboration" only. The term *"probability"* is best used in some of the many senses which satisfy the well-known calculus of probability, axiomatized, for example, by Keynes, Jeffreys, and myself; but nothing of course depends on the choice of words, as long as we do not *assume,* uncritically, that degree of corroboration must also be a probability—that is to say, that it must satisfy the calculus of probability.)

I explained in my book why we are interested in theories with a *high degree of corroboration.* And I explained why it is a mistake to conclude from this that we are interested in *highly probable* theories. I pointed out that the probability of a statement (or set of statements) is always the greater the less the statement says: It is inverse to the content or the deductive power of the statement, and thus to its explanatory power. Accordingly every interesting and powerful statement must have a low probability; and vice versa: A statement with a high probability will be scientifically uninteresting, because it says little and has no explanatory power. Although we seek theories with a high degree of corroboration, *as scientists we do not seek highly probable theories but explanations; that is to say, powerful and improbable theories.*[23] The opposite view—that science aims at high probability—is a characteristic development of verificationism: If you find that you cannot verify a theory, or make it certain by induction, you may turn to probability as a kind of *Ersatz* for certainty, in the hope that induction may yield at least that much. . . .

---

[22] *L.Sc.D.* (see note 5 above), Ch. x, especially Sections 80 to 83, also Section 34 ff. See also my note "A Set of Independent Axioms for Probability," *Mind,* N.S. 47, 1938, p. 275. (This note has since been reprinted, with corrections, in the new appendix ii of *L.Sc.D.* . . .)

[23] A definition, in terms of probabilities . . . of *C(t,e),* i.e., of the degree of corroboration (of a theory *t* relative to the evidence *e*) satisfying the demands indicated in my *L.Sc.D.,* Sections 82 to 83, is the following:

$$C(t,e) = E(t,e) \, (1 + P(t)P(t,e))$$

where $E(t,e) = (P(e,t) - P(e))/(P(e,t) + P(e))$ is a (non-additive) measure of the explanatory power of *t* with respect to *e*. Note that *C(t,e)* is not a probability: it may have values between −1 (refutation of *t* by *e*) and $C(t,t) \leq +1$. Statements *t* which are lawlike and thus non-verifiable cannot even reach $C(t,e) = C(t,t)$ upon empirical evidence *e*. *C(t,t)* is the *degree of corroborability* of *t*, and is equal to the *degree of testability* of *t*, or to the *content* of *t*. Because of the demands implied in point (6) at the end of Section I above, I do not think, however, that it is possible to give a complete formalization of the idea of corroboration (or, as I previously used to say, of confirmation).

(Added 1955 to the first proofs of this paper:)

See also my note 'Degree of Confirmation', *British Journal for the Philosophy of Science,* 5, 1954, pp. 143 ff. (See also 5, pp. 334.) I have since simplified this definition as follows (B.J.P.S., 1955, 5, p. 359:)

$$C(t,e) = (P(e,t) - P(e))/(P(e,t) - P(et) + P(e))$$

For a further improvement, see *B.J.P.S.* 6, 1955, p. 56.

Physical Theory and Experiment

Pierre Duhem

An Experiment in Physics Is Not Simply the Observation of a Phenomenon; It Is, Besides, the Theoretical Interpretation of This Phenomenon

. . . What exactly is an experiment in physics? This question will undoubtedly astonish more than one reader. Is there any need to raise it, and is not the answer self-evident? What more does "doing an experiment in physics" mean to anybody than producing a physical phenomenon under conditions such that it may be observed exactly and minutely by means of appropriate instruments?

Go into this laboratory; draw near this table crowded with so much apparatus: an electric battery, copper wire wrapped in silk, vessels filled with mercury, coils, a small iron bar carrying a mirror. An observer plunges the metallic stem of a rod, mounted with rubber, into small holes; the iron oscillates and, by means of the mirror tied to it, sends a beam of light over to a celluloid ruler, and the observer follows the movement of the light beam on it. There, no doubt, you have an experiment; by means of the vibration of this spot of light, this physicist minutely observes the oscillations of the piece of iron. Ask him now what he is doing. Is he going to answer, "I am studying the oscillations of the piece of iron carrying this mirror?" No, he will tell you that he is measuring the electrical resistance of a coil. If you are astonished and ask him what meaning these words have, and what relation they have to the phenomena he has perceived and that you have at the same time perceived, he will reply that your question would require some very long explanations, and he will recommend that you take a course in electricity.

It is indeed the case that the experiment you have seen done, like any experiment in physics, involves two parts. In the first place, it consists in the observation of certain facts; in order to make this observation it suffices for you to be attentive and alert enough with your senses. It is not necessary to know physics; the director of the laboratory may be less skillful in this matter of observation than the assistant. In the second place, it consists in the interpretation of the observed facts; in order to make this interpretation it does not suffice to have an alert attention and practiced eye; it is necessary to know the accepted theories and to know how to apply them—in short, to be a physicist. Any man can, if he sees straight, follow the motions of a spot of light on a transparent ruler and see if it goes to the right or to the left or stops at such and such a point; for that he does not have to be a great cleric. But if he does not know electrodynamics, he will not be able to finish the experiment, he will not be able to measure the resistance of the coil.

Let us take another example. Regnault is studying the compressibility of gases; he takes a certain quantity of gas, encloses it in a glass tube, keeps the temperature constant, and measures the pressure the gas supports and the volume it occupies.

There you have, it will be said, the minute and exact observation of certain phenomena and certain facts. Certainly, in the hands and under the eyes of Regnault, in the hands and under the eyes of his assistants, concrete facts were produced; was the recording of these facts that Regnault reported his intended contribution to the advancement of physics? No. In a sighting device Regnault saw the image of a certain surface of mercury become level with a certain line; is that what he recorded in the report of his experiments? No, he recorded that the gas occupied a volume having such and such a value. An assistant raised and lowered the lens of a cathetometer until the image of another height of mercury became level with the hairline of the lens; he then observed the disposition of certain lines on the scale and on the vernier of the cathetometer; is that what we find in Regnault's memoir? No, we read there that the pressure supported by the gas had such and such a value. Another assistant saw the thermometer's liquid oscillate between two line-marks; is that what he reported? No, it was recorded that the temperature of the gas had varied between such and such degrees.

Now, what is the value of the volume occupied by the gas, what is the value of the pressure it supports, what is the degree of temperature to which it is brought? Are they three concrete objects? No, they are three abstract symbols which only physical theory connects to the facts really observed.

In order to form the first of these abstractions, the value of the volume of the enclosed gas, and to make it correspond with the observed fact, namely, the mercury becoming level with a certain line-mark, it was necessary to calibrate the tube, that is to say, to appeal not only to the abstract ideas of arithmetic and geometry and the abstract principles on which they rest, but also to the abstract idea of mass and to the hypotheses of general mechanics as well as of celestial mechanics which justify the use of the balance for the comparison of masses; it was necessary to know the specific weight of mercury at the temperature when the calibration was made, and for that its specific weight at 0° had to be known, which cannot be done without invoking the laws of hydrostatics; to know the law of the expansion of mercury, which is determined by means of an apparatus where a lens is used, certain laws of optics are assumed; so that the knowledge of a good many chapters of physics necessarily precedes the formation of that abstract idea, the volume occupied by a certain gas.

More complex by far and more intimately tied up with the most profound theories of physics is the genesis of that other abstract idea, the value of the pressure supported by the gas. In order to define and measure it, it has been necessary to use ideas of pressure and of force of cohesion that are so delicate and so difficult to acquire; it has been necessary to call for the help of Laplace's formula for the level of a barometer, a formula drawn from the laws of hydrostatics; it has been necessary to bring in the law of the compressibility of mercury whose determination is related to the most delicate and controversial questions of the theory of elasticity.

Thus, when Regnault did an experiment he had facts before his eyes and he observed phenomena, but what he transmitted to us of that experiment is not a recital of observed facts; what he gave us are abstract symbols which accepted theories permitted him to substitute for the concrete evidence he had gathered.

What Regnault did is what every experimental physicist necessarily does; that is why we can state the following principle . . . ..

An experiment in physics is the precise observation of phenomena accompanied by an *interpretation* of these phenomena; this interpretation substitutes for the concrete data really gathered by observation abstract and symbolic representations which correspond to them by virtue of the theories admitted by the observer. . . .

An Experiment in Physics Can Never Condemn an Isolated Hypothesis but Only a Whole Theoretical Group

The physicist who carries out an experiment, or gives a report of one, implicitly recognizes the accuracy of a whole group of theories. Let us accept this principle and see what consequences we may deduce from it when we seek to estimate the role and logical import of a physical experiment.

In order to avoid any confusion we shall distinguish two sorts of experiments: experiments of *application*, which we shall first just mention, and experiments of *testing*, which will be our chief concern.

You are confronted with a problem in physics to be solved practically; in order to produce a certain effect you wish to make use of knowledge acquired by physicists; you wish to light an incandescent bulb; accepted theories indicate to you the means for solving the problem; but to make use of these means you have to secure certain information; you ought, I suppose, to determine the electromotive force of the battery of generators at your disposal; you measure this electromotive force: That is what I call an experiment of application. This experiment does not aim at discovering whether accepted theories are accurate or not; it merely intends to draw on these theories. In order to carry it out, you make use of instruments that these same theories legitimize; there is nothing to shock logic in this procedure.

But experiments of application are not the only ones the physicist has to perform; only with their aid can science aid practice, but it is not through them that science creates and develops itself; besides experiments of application, we have experiments of testing.

A physicist disputes a certain law; he calls into doubt a certain theoretical point. How will he justify these doubts? How will he demonstrate the inaccuracy of the law? From the proposition under indictment he will derive the prediction of an experimental fact; he will bring into existence the conditions under which this fact should be produced; if the predicted fact is not produced, the proposition which served as the basis of the prediction will be irremediably condemned.

F. E. Neumann assumed that in a ray of polarized light the vibration is parallel to the plane of polarization, and many physicists have doubted this proposition. How did O. Wiener undertake to transform this doubt into a certainty in order to condemn Neumann's proposition? He deduced from this proposition the following consequence: If we cause a light beam reflected at 45° from a plate of glass to interfere with the incident beam polarized perpendicularly to the plane of incidence, there ought to appear alternately dark and light interference bands parallel to the reflecting surface; he brought about the conditions under which these bands should have been produced and showed that the predicted phenomenon did not appear, from which he concluded that Neumann's proposition is false, viz., that in a po-

larized ray of light the vibration is not parallel to the plane of polarization.

Such a mode of demonstration seems as convincing and as irrefutable as the proof by reduction to absurdity customary among mathematicians; moreover, this demonstration is copied from the reduction to absurdity, experimental contradiction playing the same role in one as logical contradiction plays in the other.

Indeed, the demonstrative value of experimental method is far from being so rigorous or absolute: The conditions under which it functions are much more complicated than is supposed in what we have just said; the evaluation of results is much more delicate and subject to caution.

A physicist decides to demonstrate the inaccuracy of a proposition; in order to deduce from this proposition the prediction of a phenomenon and institute the experiment which is to show whether this phenomenon is or is not produced, in order to interpret the results of this experiment and establish that the predicted phenomenon is not produced, he does not confine himself to making use of the proposition in question; he makes use also of a whole group of theories accepted by him as beyond dispute. The prediction of the phenomenon, whose nonproduction is to cut off debate, does not derive from the proposition challenged if taken by itself, but from the proposition at issue joined to that whole group of theories; if the predicted phenomenon is not produced, not only is the proposition questioned at fault, but so is the whole theoretical scaffolding used by the physicist. The only thing the experiment teaches us is that among the propositions used to predict the phenomenon and to establish whether it would be produced, there is at least one error; but where this error lies is just what it does not tell us. The physicist may declare that this error is contained in exactly the proposition he wishes to refute, but is he sure it is not in another proposition? If he is, he accepts implicitly the accuracy of all the other propositions he has used, and the validity of his conclusion is as great as the validity of his confidence.

Let us take as an example the experiment imagined by Zenker and carried out by O. Wiener. In order to predict the formation of bands in certain circumstances and to show that these did not appear, Wiener did not make use merely of the famous proposition of F. E. Neumann, the proposition which he wished to refute; he did not merely admit that in a polarized ray vibrations are parallel to the plane of polarization; but he used, besides this, propositions, laws, and hypotheses constituting the optics commonly accepted: He admitted that light consists in simple periodic vibrations, that these vibrations are normal to the light ray, that at each point the mean kinetic energy of the vibratory motion is a measure of the intensity of light, that the more or less complete attack of the gelatine coating on a photographic plate indicates the various degrees of this intensity. By joining these propositions, and many others that would take too long to enumerate, to Neumann's proposition, Wiener was able to formulate a forecast and establish that the experiment belied it. If he attributed this solely to Neumann's proposition, if it alone bears the responsibility for the error this negative result has put in evidence, then Wiener was taking all the other propositions he invoked as beyond doubt. But this assurance is not imposed as a matter of logical necessity; nothing stops us from taking Neumann's proposition as accurate and shifting the weight of the experimental contradiction to some other proposition of the commonly accepted optics; as H. Poincaré has shown, we can very easily rescue Neumann's hypothesis from the grip of Wiener's experiment on the condition that we abandon in exchange the hypothesis which takes the mean kinetic energy as the measure of the light intensity; we may, without being contradicted by the experiment, let the vibration be parallel to the plane of polarization, provided that we measure the light intensity by the mean potential energy of the medium deforming the vibratory motion.

These principles are so important that it will be useful to apply them to another example; again we choose an experiment regarded as one of the most decisive ones in optics.

We know that Newton conceived the emission theory for optical phenomena. The emission theory supposes light to be formed of extremely thin projectiles, thrown out with very great speed by the sun and other sources of light; these projectiles penetrate all transparent bodies; on account of the various parts of the media through which they move, they undergo attractions and repulsions; when the distance separating the acting particles is very small these actions are very powerful, and they vanish when the masses between which they act are appreciably far from each other. These essential hypotheses joined to several others, which we pass over without mention, lead to the formulation of a complete theory of reflection and refraction of light; in particular, they imply the following proposition: The index of refraction of light passing from one medium into another is equal to the velocity of the light projectile within the medium it penetrates, divided by the velocity of the same projectile in the medium it leaves behind.

This is the proposition that Arago chose in order to show that the theory of emission is in contradiction with the facts. From this proposition a second follows: Light travels faster in water than in air. Now Arago had indicated an appropriate procedure for comparing the velocity of light in air with the velocity of light in water; the procedure, it is true, was inapplicable, but Foucault modified the experiment in such a way that it could be carried out; he found that the light was propagated less rapidly in water than in air. We may conclude from this, with Foucault, that the system of emission is incompatible with the facts.

I say the *system* of emission and not the *hypothesis* of emission; in fact, what the experiment declares stained with error is the whole group of propositions accepted by Newton, and after him by Laplace and Biot, that is, the whole theory from which we deduce the relation between the index of refraction and the velocity of light in various media. But in condemning this system as a whole by declaring it stained with error, the experiment does not tell us where the error lies. Is it the fundamental hypothesis that light consists in projectiles thrown out with great speed by luminous bodies? Is it in some other assumption concerning the actions experienced by light corpuscles due to the media through which they move? We know nothing about that. It would be rash to believe, as

Arago seems to have thought, that Foucault's experiment condemns once and for all the very hypothesis of emission, i.e., the assimilation of a ray of light to a swarm of projectiles. If physicists had attached some value to this task, they would undoubtedly have succeeded in founding on this assumption a system of optics that would agree with Foucault's experiment.

In sum, the physicist can never subject an isolated hypothesis to experimental test, but only a whole group of hypotheses; when the experiment is in disagreement with his predictions, what he learns is that at least one of the hypotheses constituting this group is unacceptable and ought to be modified; but the experiment does not designate which one should be changed.

We have gone a long way from the conception of the experimental method arbitrarily held by persons unfamiliar with its actual functioning. People generally think that each one of the hypotheses employed in physics can be taken in isolation, checked by experiment, and then, when many varied tests have established its validity, given a definitive place in the system of physics. In reality, this is not the case. Physics is not a machine which lets itself be taken apart; we cannot try each piece in isolation and, in order to adjust it, wait until its solidity has been carefully checked. Physical science is a system that must be taken as a whole; it is an organism in which one part cannot be made to function except when the parts that are most remote from it are called into play, some more so than others, but all to some degree. If something goes wrong, if some discomfort is felt in the functioning of the organism, the physicist will have to ferret out through its effect on the entire system which organ needs to be remedied or modified without the possibility of isolating this organ and examining it apart. The watchmaker to whom you give a watch that has stopped separates all the wheelworks and examines them one by one until he finds the part that is defective or broken. The doctor to whom a patient appears cannot dissect him in order to establish his diagnosis; he has to guess the seat and cause of the ailment solely by inspecting disorders affecting the whole body. Now, the physicist concerned with remedying a limping theory resembles the doctor and not the watchmaker.

A "Crucial Experiment" Is Impossible in Physics

Let us press this point further, for we are touching on one of the essential features of experimental method, as it is employed in physics.

Reduction to absurdity seems to be merely a means of refutation, but it may become a method of demonstration: In order to demonstrate the truth of a proposition it suffices to corner anyone who would admit the contradictory of the given proposition into admitting an absurd consequence. We know to what extent the Greek geometers drew heavily on this mode of demonstration.

Those who assimilate experimental contradiction to reduction to absurdity imagine that in physics we may use a line of argument similar to the one Euclid employed so frequently in geometry. Do you wish to obtain from a group of phenomena a theoretically certain and indisputable explanation? Enumerate all the hypotheses that can be made to account for this group of phenomena; then, by experimental contradiction eliminate all except one; the latter will no longer be a hypothesis, but will become a certainty.

Suppose, for instance, we are confronted with only two hypotheses. Seek experimental conditions such that one of the hypotheses forecasts the production of one phenomenon and the other the production of quite a different effect; bring these conditions into existence and observe what happens; depending on whether you observe the first or the second of the predicted phenomena, you will condemn the second or the first hypothesis; the hypothesis not condemned will be henceforth indisputable; debate will be cut off, and a new truth will be acquired by science. Such is the experimental test that the author of the *Novum Organum* called the *"fact of the cross,"* borrowing this expression from the crosses that at an intersection indicate the various roads.

We are confronted with two hypotheses concerning the nature of light; for Newton, Laplace, or Biot light consisted of projectiles hurled with extreme speed, but for Huygens, Young, or Fresnel light consisted of vibrations whose waves are propagated within an ether. These are the only two possible hypotheses as far as one can see: Either the motion is carried away by the body it excites and remains attached to it, or else it passes from one body to another. Let us pursue the first hypothesis; it declares that light travels more quickly in water than in air; but if we follow the second, it declares that light travels more quickly in air than in water. Let us set up Foucault's apparatus; we set into motion the turning mirror; we see two luminous spots formed before us, one colorless, the other greenish. If the greenish band is to the left of the colorless one, it means that light travels faster in water than in air, and that the hypothesis of vibrating waves is false. If, on the contrary, the greenish band is to the right of the colorless one, that means that light travels faster in air than in water, and that the hypothesis of emissions is condemned. We look through the magnifying glass used to examine the two luminous spots, and we notice that the greenish spot is to the right of the colorless one; the debate is over; light is not a body, but a vibratory wave motion propagated by the ether; the emission hypothesis has had its day; the wave hypothesis has been put beyond doubt, and the crucial experiment has made it a new article of the scientific credo.

What we have said in the foregoing paragraph shows how mistaken we should be to attribute to Foucault's experiment so simple a meaning and so decisive an importance; for it is not between two hypotheses, the emission and wave hypotheses, that Foucault's experiment judges trenchantly; it decides rather between two sets of theories, each of which has to be taken as a whole, i.e., between two entire systems, Newton's optics and Huygens' optics.

But let us admit for a moment that in each of these systems everything is compelled to be necessary by strict logic, except a single hypothesis; consequently, let us admit that the facts, in condemning one of the two systems, condemn once and for all the single doubtful assumption it contains. Does it follow that we can find in the "crucial experiment" an irrefutable procedure for transforming one of the two hypotheses before us into a demonstrated truth? Between two contradictory theorems of geometry there is no room for a third judgment; if one is false, the other is necessarily true. Do two hypotheses in physics ever constitute such a strict dilemma? Shall we ever dare to assert that no other hypothesis is imaginable? Light may be a swarm of projectiles, or it may be a vibratory motion whose waves are propagated in a medium; is it forbidden to be anything else at all? Arago undoubtedly thought so when he formulated this incisive alternative: Does light move more quickly in water than in air? "Light is a body. If the contrary is the case, then light is a wave." But it would be difficult for us to take such a decisive stand; Maxwell, in fact, showed that we might just as well attribute light to a periodical electrical disturbance that is propagated within a dielectric medium.

Unlike the reduction to absurdity employed by geometers, experimental contradiction does not have the power to transform a physical hypothesis into an indisputable truth; in order to confer this power on it, it would be necessary to enumerate completely the various hypotheses which may cover a determinate group of phenomena; but the physicist is never sure he has exhausted all the imaginable assumptions. The truth of a physical theory is not decided by heads or tails. . . .

Are Certain Postulates of Physical Theory Incapable of Being Refuted by Experiment?

We recognize a correct principle by the facility with which it straightens out the complicated difficulties into which the use of erroneous principles brought us.

If, therefore, the idea we have put forth is correct, namely, that comparison is established necessarily between the *whole* of theory and the *whole* of experimental facts, we ought in the light of this principle to see the disappearance of the obscurities in which we should be lost by thinking that we are subjecting each isolated theoretical hypothesis to the test of facts.

Foremost among the assertions in which we shall aim at eliminating the appearance of paradox, we shall place one that has recently been often formulated and discussed. Stated first by G. Milhaud in connection with the *"pure bodies"* of chemistry,[1] it has been developed at length and forcefully by H. Poincaré with regard to principles of mechanics;[2] Edouard Le Roy has also formulated it with great clarity.[3]

That assertion is as follows: Certain fundamental hypotheses of physical theory cannot be contradicted by any experiment, because they constitute in reality *definitions,* and because certain expressions in the physicist's usage take their meaning only through them.

Let us take one of the examples cited by Le Roy:

When a heavy body falls freely, the acceleration of its fall is constant. Can such a law be contradicted by experiment? No, for it constitutes the very definition of what is meant by "falling freely." If while studying the fall of a heavy body we found that this body does not fall with uniform acceleration, we should conclude not that the stated law is false, but that the body does not fall freely, that some cause obstructs its motion, and that the deviations of the observed facts from the law as stated would serve to discover this cause and to analyze its effects.

Thus, M. Le Roy concludes, "laws are verifiable, taking things strictly . . . , because they constitute the very criterion by which we judge appearances as well as the methods that it would be necessary to utilize in order to submit them to an inquiry whose precision is capable of exceeding any assignable limit."

Let us study again in greater detail, in the light of the principles previously set down, what this comparison is between the law of falling bodies and experiment.

Our daily observations have made us acquainted with a whole category of motions which we have brought together under the name of motions of heavy bodies; among these motions is the falling of a heavy body when it is not hindered by any obstacle. The result of this is that the words *free fall of a heavy body* have a meaning for the man who appeals only to the knowledge of common sense and who has no notion of physical theories.

On the other hand, in order to classify the laws of motion in question the physicist has created a theory, the theory of weight, an important application of rational mechanics. In that theory, intended to furnish a symbolic representation of reality, there is also the question of "free fall of a heavy body," and as a consequence of the hypotheses supporting this whole scheme free fall must necessarily be a uniformly accelerated motion.

The words *free fall of a heavy body* now have two distinct meanings. For the man ignorant of physical theories, they have their *real* meaning, and they mean what common sense means in pronouncing them; for the physicist they have a *symbolic* meaning, and mean "uniformly accelerated motion." Theory would not have realized its aim if the second meaning were not the sign of the first, if a fall regarded as free by common sense were not also regarded as uniformly accelerated, or *nearly* uniformly accelerated, since common-sense observations are essentially devoid of precision, according to what we have already said.

This agreement, without which the theory would have been rejected without further examination, is finally arrived at: A fall declared by common sense to be nearly free is also a fall whose acceleration is nearly constant. But noticing this crudely approximate agreement does not satisfy us; we wish to push on and surpass the degree of precision which common sense can claim. With the aid of the theory that we have imagined, we put together apparatus enabling us to recognize with sensitive accuracy whether the fall of a body is or is not uniformly accelerated;

[1] G. Milhaud, "La Science rationnelle," *Revue de Métaphysique et de Morale,* IV (1896), 280. Reprinted in *Le Rationnel* (Paris, 1898), p. 45.

[2] H. Poincaré, "Sur les Principes de la Mécanique," *Bibliotheque du Congrès International de Philosophie,* III: *Logique et Histoire des Sciences* (Paris, 1901), p. 457; "Sur la valeur objective des théories physiques," *Revue de Métaphysique et de Morale,* X (1902), 263; *La Science et l'Hypothèse,* p. 110.

[3] E. Le Roy, "Un positivesme nouveau," *Revue de Métaphysique et de Morale,* IX (1901), 143–144.

this apparatus shows us that a certain fall regarded by common sense as a free fall has a slightly variable acceleration. The proposition which in our theory gives its symbolic meaning to the words *free fall* does not represent with sufficient accuracy the properties of the real and concrete fall that we have observed.

Two alternatives are then open to us.

In the first place, we can declare that we were right in regarding the fall studied as a free fall and in requiring that the theoretical definition of these words agree with our observations. In this case, since our theoretical definition does not satisfy this requirement, it must be rejected; we must construct another mechanics on new hypotheses, a mechanics in which the words *free fall* no longer signify "uniformly accelerated motion," but "fall whose acceleration varies according to a certain law."

In the second alternative, we may declare that we were wrong in establishing a connection between the concrete fall we have observed and the symbolic free fall defined by our theory, that the latter was too simplified a scheme of the former, that in order to represent suitably the fall as our experiments have reported it the theorist should give up imagining a weight falling freely and think in terms of a weight hindered by certain obstacles like the resistance of the air, that in picturing the action of these obstacles by means of appropriate hypotheses he will compose a more complicated scheme than a free weight but one more apt to reproduce the details of the experiment; in short, . . . we may seek to eliminate by means of suitable "corrections" the "causes of error," such as air resistance, which influenced our experiment.

M. Le Roy asserts that we shall prefer the second to the first alternative, and he is surely right in this. The reasons dictating this choice are easy to perceive. By taking the first alternative we should be obliged to destroy from top to bottom a very vast theoretical system which represents in a most satisfactory manner a very extensive and complex set of experimental laws. The second alternative, on the other hand, does not make us lose anything of the terrain already conquered by physical theory; in addition, it has succeeded in so large a number of cases that we can bank with interest on a new success. But in this confidence accorded the law of fall of weights, we see nothing analogous to the certainty that a mathematical definition draws from its very essence, that is, to the kind of certainty we have when it would be foolish to doubt that the various points on a circumference are all equidistant from the center.

We have here nothing more than a particular application of the principle set down [in the second section]. A disagreement between the concrete facts constituting an experiment and the symbolic representation which theory substitutes for this experiment proves that some part of this symbol is to be rejected. But which part? This the experiment does not tell us; it leaves to our sagacity the burden of guessing. Now among the theoretical elements entering into the composition of this symbol there is always a certain number which the physicists of a certain epoch agree in accepting without test and which they regard as beyond dispute. Hence, the physicist who wishes to modify this symbol will surely bring his modification to bear on elements other than those just mentioned.

But what impels the physicist to act thus is *not* logical necessity. It would be awkward and ill-inspired for him to do otherwise, but it would not be doing something logically absurd; he would not for all that be walking in the footsteps of the mathematician mad enough to contradict his own definitions. More than this, perhaps some day by acting differently, by refusing to invoke causes of error and take recourse to corrections in order to reestablish agreement between the theoretical scheme and the fact, and by resolutely carrying out a reform among the propositions declared untouchable by common consent, he will accomplish the work of a genius who opens a new career for a theory.

Indeed, we must really guard ourselves against believing forever warranted those hypotheses which have become universally adopted conventions, and whose certainty seems to break through experimental contradiction by throwing the latter back on more doubtful assumptions. The history of physics shows us that very often the human mind has been led to overthrow such principles completely, though they have been regarded by common consent for centuries as inviolable axioms, and to rebuild its physical theories on new hypotheses.

Was there, for instance, a clearer or more certain principle for thousands of years than this one: In a homogeneous medium, light is propagated in a straight line? Not only did this hypothesis carry all former optics, catoptrics, and dioptrics, whose elegant geometric deductions represented at will an enormous number of facts, but it had become, so to speak, the physical definition of a straight line. It is to this hypothesis that any man wishing to make a straight line appeals, the carpenter who verifies the straightness of a piece of wood, the surveyor who lines up his sights, the geodetic surveyor who obtains a direction with the help of the pinholes of his alidade, the astronomer who defines the position of stars by the optical axis of his telescope. However, the day came when physicists tired of attributing to some cause of error the diffraction effects observed by Grimaldi, when they resolved to reject the law of the rectilinear propagation of light and to give optics entirely new foundations; and this bold resolution was the signal of remarkable progress for physical theory.

On Hypotheses Whose Statement Has No Experimental Meaning

This example, as well as others we could add from the history of science, should show that it would be very imprudent for us to say concerning a hypothesis commonly accepted today: "We are certain that we shall never be led to abandon it because of a new experiment, no matter how precise it is." Yet M. Poincaré does not hesitate to enunciate it concerning the principles of mechanics.[4]

To the reasons already given to prove that these principles cannot be reached by experimental refutation, M. Poincaré adds one which seems even more convincing: Not only can these principles not be refuted by experiment because they are the universally accepted rules serving to discover in our theories the weak spots indicated by these refutations, but also, they cannot be refuted by experiment because *the operation which would claim to compare them with the facts would have no meaning.*

Let us explain that by an illustration.

The principle of inertia teaches us that a material point removed from the action of any other body moves in a straight line with uniform motion. Now, we can observe only relative motions; we cannot, therefore, give an experimental meaning to this principle unless we assume a certain point chosen or a certain geometric solid taken as a fixed reference point to which the motion of the material point is related. The fixation of this reference frame constitutes an integral part of the statement of the law, for if we omitted it, this statement would be devoid of meaning. There are as many different laws as there are distinct frames of reference. We shall be stating one law of inertia when we say that the motion of an isolated point assumed to be seen from the earth is rectilinear and uniform, and another when we repeat the same sentence in referring the motion to the sun, and still another if the frame of reference chosen is the totality of fixed stars. But then, one thing is indeed certain, namely, that whatever the motion of a material point is, when seen from a first frame of reference, we can always and in infinite ways choose a second frame of reference such that seen from the latter our material point appears to move in a straight line with uniform motion. We cannot, therefore, attempt an experimental verification of the principle of inertia; false when we refer the motions to one frame of reference, it will become true when selection is made of another term of comparison, and we shall always be free to choose the latter. If the law of inertia stated by taking the earth as a frame of reference is contradicted by an observation, we shall substitute for it the law of inertia whose statement refers the motion to the sun; if the latter in its turn is contraverted, we shall replace the sun in the statement of the law by the system of fixed stars, and so forth. It is impossible to stop this loophole.

---

[4] H. Poincaré, "Sur les Principes de la Mécanique," *Bibliothèque du Congrès international de Philosophie,* Sec. III: "Logique et Histoire des Sciences" (Paris, 1901), pp. 475, 491.

The principle of the equality of action and re-action, analyzed at length by M. Poincaré,[5] provides room for analogous remarks. This principle may be stated thus: "The center of gravity of an isolated system can have only a uniform rectilinear motion."

This is the principle that we propose to verify by experiment. "Can we make this verification? For that it would be necessary for isolated systems to exist. Now, these systems do not exist; the only isolated system is the whole universe.

"But we can observe only relative motions; the absolute motion of the center of the universe will therefore be forever unknown. We shall never be able to know if it is rectilinear and uniform or, better still, the question has no meaning. Whatever facts we may observe, we shall hence always be free to assume our principle is true."

Thus many a principle of mechanics has a form such that it is absurd to ask one's self: "Is this principle in agreement with experiment or not?" This strange character is not peculiar to the principles of mechanics; it also marks certain fundamental hypotheses of our physical or chemical theories.[6]

For example, chemical theory rests entirely on the "law of multiple proportions"; here is the exact statement of this law:

Simple bodies A, B, and C may by uniting in various proportions form various compounds M, M¹, ... The masses of the bodies A, B, and C combining to form the compound M are to one another as the three numbers a, b, and c. Then the masses of the elements A, B, and C combining to form the compound M¹ will be to one another as the numbers xa, yb, and zc (x, y, and z being three whole numbers).

Is this law perhaps subject to experimental test? Chemical analysis will make us acquainted with the chemical composition of the body M¹ not exactly but with a certain approximation. The uncertainty of the results obtained can be extremely small; it will never be strictly zero. Now, in what-

ever relations the elements A, B, and C are combined within the compound M¹, we can always represent these relations, with as close an approximation as you please, by the mutual relations of three products xa, yb, and zc, where x, y, and z are whole numbers; in other words, whatever the results given by the chemical analysis of the compound M¹, we are always sure to find three integers x, y, and z thanks to which the law of multiple proportions will be verified with a precision greater than that of the experiment. Therefore, no chemical analysis, no matter how refined, will ever be able to show the law of multiple proportions to be wrong.

In like manner, all crystallography rests entirely on the "law of rational indices" which is formulated in the following way:

A trihedral being formed by three faces of a crystal, a fourth face cuts the three edges of this trihedral at distances from the summit which are proportional to one another as three given numbers, the parameters of the crystal. Any other face whatsoever should cut these same edges at distances from the summit which are to one another as xa, yb, and zc, where x, y, and z are three integers, the indices of the new face of the crystal.

The most perfect protractor determines the direction of a crystal's face only with a certain degree of approximation; the relations among the three segments that such a face makes on the edges of the fundamental trihedral are always able to get by with a certain error; now, however small this error is, we can always choose three numbers x, y, and z such that the mutual relations of these segments are represented with the least amount of error by the mutual relations of the three numbers xa, yb, and zc; the crystallographer who would claim that the law of rational indices is made justifiable by his protractor would surely not have understood the very meaning of the words he is employing.

The law of multiple proportions and the law of rational indices are mathematical statements deprived of all physical meaning. A mathematical statement has physical meaning only if it retains a meaning when we introduce the word "nearly" or "approximately." This is not the case with the

---

[5] Ibid., pp. 472ff.

[6] P. Duhem, *Le Mixte et la Combinaison chimique: Essai sur l'évolution d'une idée* (Paris, 1902), pp. 159–161.

statements we have just alluded to. Their object really is to assert that certain relations are *commensurable* numbers. They would degenerate into mere truisms if they were made to declare that these relations are approximately commensurable, for any incommensurable relation whatever is always approximately commensurable; it is even as near as you please to being commensurable.

Therefore, it would be absurd to wish to subject certain principles of mechanics to *direct* experimental test; it would be absurd to subject the law of multiple proportions or the law of rational indices to this *direct* test.

Does it follow that these hypotheses placed beyond the reach of direct experimental refutation have nothing more to fear from experiment? That they are guaranteed to remain immutable no matter what discoveries observation has in store for us? To pretend so would be a serious error.

Taken in isolation these different hypotheses have no experimental meaning; there can be no question of either confirming or contradicting them by experiment. But these hypotheses enter as essential foundations into the construction of certain theories of rational mechanics, of chemical theory, of crystallography. The object of these theories is to represent experimental laws; they are schematisms intended essentially to be compared with facts.

Now this comparison might some day very well show us that one of our representations is ill adjusted to the realities it should picture, that the corrections which come and complicate our schematism do not produce sufficient concordance between this schematism and the facts, that the theory accepted for a long time without dispute should be rejected, and that an entirely different theory should be constructed on entirely different or new hypotheses. On that day some one of our hypotheses, which taken in isolation defied direct experimental refutation, will crumble with the system it supported under the weight of the contradictions inflicted by reality on the consequences of this system taken as a whole.[7]

In truth, hypotheses which by themselves have no physical meaning undergo experimental testing in exactly the same manner as other hypotheses. Whatever the nature of the hypothesis is, we have seen . . . that it is never in isolation contradicted by experiment; experimental contradiction always bears as a whole on the entire group constituting a theory without any possibility of designating which proposition in this group should be rejected.

There thus disappears what might have seemed paradoxical in the following assertion: Certain physical theories rest on hypotheses which do not by themselves have any physical meaning.

Good Sense Is the Judge of Hypotheses Which Ought to Be Abandoned

When certain consequences of a theory are struck by experimental contradiction, we learn that this theory should be modified but we are not told by the experiment what must be changed. It leaves to the physicist the task of finding out the weak spot that impairs the whole system. No absolute principle directs this inquiry, which different physicists may conduct in very different ways without having right to accuse one another of illogicality. For instance, one may be obliged to safeguard certain fundamental hypotheses while he tries to reestablish harmony between the consequences of the theory and the facts by complicating the schematism in which these hypotheses are applied, by invoking various causes of error, and by multiplying corrections. The next physicist, disdainful of these complicated artificial procedures, may decide to change some one of the essential assumptions supporting the entire system. The first physicist does not have the right to condemn in advance the boldness of the second one, nor does the latter have the right to treat the timidity of the

---

[7] At the International Congress of Philosophy held in Paris in 1900, M. Poincaré developed this conclusion: "Thus is explained how experiment may have been able to edify (or suggest) the principles of mechanics, but will never be able to overthrow them." Against this conclusion, M. Hadamard offered various remarks, among them the following: "Moreover, in conformity with a remark of M. Duhem, it is not *an* isolated hypothesis but the whole group of the hypotheses of mechanics that we can try to verify experimentally." *Revue de Métaphysique et de Morale,* VIII (1900), 559.

first physicist as absurd. The methods they follow are justifiable only by experiment, and if they both succeed in satisfying the requirements of experiment each is logically permitted to declare himself content with the work that he has accomplished.

That does not mean that we cannot very properly prefer the work of one of the two to that of the other. Pure logic is not the only rule for our judgments; certain opinions which do not fall under the hammer of the principle of contradiction are in any case perfectly unreasonable. These motives which do not proceed from logic and yet direct our choices, these "reasons which reason does not know" and which speak to the ample "mind of finesse" but not to the "geometric mind," constitute what is appropriately called good sense.

Now, it may be good sense that permits us to decide between two physicists. It may be that we do not approve of the haste with which the second one upsets the principles of a vast and harmoniously constructed theory whereas a modification of detail, a slight correction, would have sufficed to put these theories in accord with the facts. On the other hand, it may be that we may find it childish and unreasonable for the first physicist to maintain obstinately at any cost, at the price of continual repairs and many tangled-up stays, the worm-eaten columns of a building tottering in every part, when by razing these columns it would be possible to construct a simple, elegant, and solid system.

But these reasons of good sense do not impose themselves with the same implacable rigor that the prescriptions of logic do. There is something vague and uncertain about them; they do not reveal themselves at the same time with the same degree of clarity to all minds. Hence, the possibility of lengthy quarrels between the adherents of an old system and the partisans of a new doctrine, each camp claiming to have good sense on its side, each party finding the reasons of the adversary inadequate. The history of physics would furnish us with innumerable illustrations of these

quarrels at all times and in all domains. Let us confine ourselves to the tenacity and ingenuity with which Biot by a continual bestowal of corrections and accessory hypotheses maintained the emissionist doctrine in optics, while Fresnel opposed this doctrine constantly with new experiments favoring the wave theory.

In any event this state of indecision does not last forever. The day arrives when good sense comes out so clearly in favor of one of the two sides that the other side gives up the struggle even though pure logic would not forbid its continuation. After Foucault's experiment had shown that light traveled faster in air than in water, Biot gave up supporting the emission hypothesis; strictly, pure logic would not have compelled him to give it up, for Foucault's experiment was *not* the crucial experiment that Arago thought he saw in it, but by resisting wave optics for a longer time Biot would have been lacking in good sense.

Since logic does not determine with strict precision the time when an inadequate hypothesis should give way to a more fruitful assumption, and since recognizing this moment belongs to good sense, physicists may hasten this judgment and increase the rapidity of scientific progress by trying consciously to make good sense within themselves more lucid and more vigilant. Now nothing contributes more to entangle good sense and to disturb its insight than passions and interests. Therefore, nothing will delay the decision which should determine a fortunate reform in a physical theory more than the vanity which makes a physicist too indulgent toward his own system and too severe toward the system of another. We are thus led to the conclusion so clearly expressed by Claude Bernard: The sound experimental criticism of a hypothesis is subordinated to certain moral conditions; in order to estimate correctly the agreement of a physical theory with the facts, it is not enough to be a good mathematician and skillful experimenter; one must also be an impartial and faithful judge.

Falsification and the Methodology of Scientific Research Programmes[1]

Imre Lakatos

SCIENCE: REASON OR RELIGION?

For centuries knowledge meant proven knowledge—proven either by the power of the intellect or by the evidence of the senses. Wisdom and intellectual integrity demanded that one must desist from unproven utterances and minimize, even in thought, the gap between speculation and established knowledge. The proving power of the intellect or the senses was questioned by the sceptics more than two thousand years ago; but they were browbeaten into confusion by the glory of Newtonian physics. Einstein's results again turned the tables and now very few philosophers or scientists still think that scientific knowledge is, or can be, proven knowledge. But few realize that with this the whole classical structure of intellectual values falls in ruins and has to be replaced: One cannot simply water down the ideal of proven truth—as some logical empiricists do—to the ideal of "probable truth"[2] or—as some sociologists of knowledge do—to "truth by [changing] consensus."[3] . . .

---

[1] This paper is a considerably improved version of my [1968b] and a crude version of my [1970]. Some parts of the former are here reproduced without change with the permission of the Editor of the *Proceedings of the Aristotelian Society*. In the preparation of the new version I received much help from Tad Beckman, Colin Howson, Clive Kilmister, Larry Laudan, Eliot Leader, Alan Musgrave, Michael Sukale, John Watkins and John Worrall.

[2] The main contemporary protagonist of the ideal of "probable truth" is Rudolf Carnap. For the historical background and a criticism of this position, cf. Lakatos [1968a].

[3] The main contemporary protagonists of the ideal of "truth by consensus" are Polanyi and Kuhn. For the historical background and a criticism of this position, cf. Musgrave [1969a], Musgrave [1969b] and Lakatos [1970].

FALLIBILISM VERSUS FALSIFICATIONISM

Dogmatic (or Naturalistic) Falsificationism. The Empirical Basis

. . . *According to the "justificationists" scientific knowledge consisted of proven propositions.* Having recognized that strictly logical deductions enable us only to infer (transmit truth) but not to prove (establish truth), they disagreed about the nature of those propositions (axioms) whose truth can be proved by extralogical means. *Classical intellectualists* (or "rationalists" in the narrow sense of the term) admitted very varied—and powerful—sorts of extralogical "proofs" by revelation, intellectual intuition, experience. These, with the help of logic, enabled them to prove every sort of scientific proposition. *Classical empiricists* accepted as axioms only a relatively small set of "factual propositions" which expressed the "hard facts." Their truth-value was established by experience and they constituted the *empirical basis* of science. In order to prove scientific *theories* from nothing else but the narrow empirical basis, they needed a logic much more powerful than the deductive logic of the classical intellectualists: *"inductive logic."* All justificationists, whether intellectualists or empiricists, agreed that a singular statement expressing a "hard fact" may *disprove* a universal theory; . . . but few of them thought that a finite conjunction of factual propositions might be sufficient to *prove* "inductively" a universal theory.[4]

---

[4] Indeed, even some of these few shifted, following Mill, the rather obviously insoluble problem of inductive proof (of uni-

---

From Sections 1, 2, and 3 of "Falsification and the Methodology of Scientific Research Programmes" by Imre Lakatos, in *Criticism and the Growth of Knowledge*, Imre Lakatos and Alan Musgrave, Eds. (1970), pp. 91–92, 94–125, 127–138, 189–195. Reprinted by permission of Cambridge University Press.

Justificationism, that is, the identification of knowledge with proven knowledge, was the dominant tradition in rational thought throughout the ages. Scepticism did not deny justificationism: It only claimed that there was (and could be) no proven knowledge and *therefore* no knowledge whatsoever. For the sceptics "knowledge" was nothing but animal belief. Thus justificationist scepticism ridiculed objective thought and opened the door to irrationalism, mysticism, superstition.

This situation explains the enormous effort invested by classical rationalists in trying to save the synthetical *a priori* principles of intellectualism and by classical empiricists in trying to save the certainty of an empirical basis and the validity of inductive inference. For all of them *scientific honesty demanded that one assert nothing that is unproven.* However, both were defeated: Kantians by non-Euclidean geometry and by non-Newtonian physics, and empiricists by the logical impossibility of establishing an empirical basis (as Kantians pointed out, facts cannot prove propositions) and of establishing an inductive logic (no logic can infallibly increase content). It turned out that *all theories are equally unprovable.*

Philosophers were slow to recognize this, for obvious reasons: Classical justificationists feared that once they conceded that theoretical science is unprovable, they would have also to concede that it is sophistry and illusion, a dishonest fraud. The philosophical importance of *probabilism* (or *"neojustificationism"*) lies in the denial that such a concession is necessary.

Probabilism was elaborated by a group of Cambridge philosophers who thought that although scientific theories are equally unprovable, they have different degrees of probability (in the sense of the calculus of probability) relative to the available empirical evidence.[5] *Scientific honesty then requires less than had been thought: It consists in uttering only highly probable theories; or even in merely specifying, for each scientific theory, the evidence, and the probability of the theory in the light of this evidence.*

Of course, replacing proof by probability was a major retreat for justificationist thought. But even this retreat turned out to be insufficient. It was soon shown, mainly by Popper's persistent efforts, that under very general conditions all theories have zero probability, whatever the evidence; *all theories are not only equally unprovable but also equally improbable.*[6]

Many philosophers still argue that the failure to obtain at least a probabilistic solution of the problem of induction means that we "throw over almost everything that is regarded as knowledge by science and common sense."[7] It is against this background that one must appreciate the dramatic change brought about by falsificationism in evaluating theories and, in general, in the standards of intellectual honesty. Falsificationism was, in a sense, a new and considerable retreat for rational thought. But since it was a retreat from utopian standards, it cleared away much hypocrisy and muddled thought, and thus, in fact, it represented an advance.

First I shall discuss a most important brand of falsificationism: dogmatic (or "naturalistic")[8] falsificationism. Dogmatic falsificationism admits the fallibility of *all* scientific theories without qualification, but it retains a sort of infallible empirical basis. It is strictly empiricist without being inductivist: It denies that the certainty of the empirical basis can be transmitted to theories. *Thus dogmatic falsificationism is the weakest brand of justificationism.*

It is extremely important to stress that admitting [fortified] empirical counterevidence as a final arbiter against a theory does not make one a dogmatic falsificationist. Any Kantian or inductivist will agree to such arbitration. But both the Kantian

---

versal from particular propositions) to the slightly less obviously insoluble problem of proving *particular* factual propositions from other *particular* factual propositions.

[5] The founding fathers of probabilism were intellectualists; Carnap's later efforts to build up an empiricist brand of probabilism failed. Cf. my [1968a], p. 367 and also p. 361, footnote 2.

[6] For a detailed discussion, cf. my [1968a], especially pp. 353 ff.

[7] Russell [1943], p. 683. For a discussion of Russell's justificationism, cf. my [1962], especially pp. 167 ff.

[8] For the explanation of this term, cf. *below,* footnote 14.

and the inductivist, while bowing to a negative crucial experiment, will also specify conditions of how to establish, entrench one unrefuted theory more than another. Kantians held that Euclidean geometry and Newtonian mechanics were established with certainty; inductivists held they had probability 1. For the dogmatic falsificationist, however, empirical *counter*evidence is the *one and only* arbiter which may judge a theory.

The hallmark of dogmatic falsificationism is then the recognition that all theories are equally conjectural. Science cannot *prove* any theory. But although science cannot *prove*, it can *disprove*: It "can perform with complete logical certainty [the act of] repudiation of what is false,"[9] that is, there is an absolutely firm empirical basis of facts which can be used to disprove theories. Falsificationists provide new—very modest—standards of scientific honesty: They are willing to regard a proposition as "scientific" not only if it is a proven factual proposition, but even if it is nothing more than a falsifiable one, that is, if there are factual propositions available at the time with which it may clash, or, in other words, if it has potential falsifiers.[10]

Scientific honesty then consists of specifying, in advance, an experiment such that if the result contradicts the theory, the theory has to be given up.[11] The falsificationist demands that once a proposition is disproved, there must be no prevarication: The proposition must be unconditionally rejected. To (non-tautologous) unfalsifiable propositions the dogmatic falsificationist gives short shrift: He brands them "metaphysical" and denies them scientific standing.

Dogmatic falsificationists draw a sharp demarcation between the theoretician and the experimenter: The theoretician proposes, the experimenter—in the name of Nature—disposes. As

Weyl put it: "I wish to record my unbounded admiration for the work of the experimenter in his struggle to wrest interpretable facts from an unyielding Nature who knows so well how to meet our theories with a decisive *No*—or with an unaudible *Yes*."[12] Braithwaite gives a particularly lucid exposition of dogmatic falsificationism. He raises the problem of the objectivity of science: "To what extent, then, should an established scientific deductive system be regarded as a free creation of the human mind, and to what extent should it be regarded as giving an objective account of the facts of nature?" His answer is: "The form of a statement of a scientific hypothesis, and its use to express a general proposition, is a human device; what is due to Nature are the observable facts which refute or fail to refute the scientific hypothesis . . . [In science] we hand over to Nature the task of deciding whether any of the contingent lowest-level conclusions are false. This objective test of falsity it is which makes the deductive system, in whose construction we have very great freedom, a deductive system of scientific hypotheses. Man proposes a system of hypotheses: Nature disposes of its truth or falsity. Man invents a scientific system, and then discovers whether or not it accords with observed fact."[13]

According to the logic of dogmatic falsificationism, science grows by repeated overthrow of theories with the help of hard facts. For instance, according to this view, Descartes's vortex theory of gravity was refuted—and eliminated—by the *fact* that planets moved in ellipses rather than in Cartesian circles; Newton's theory, however, explained successfully the then available facts, both those which had been explained by Descartes's theory and those which refuted it. Therefore Newton's theory replaced Descartes's theory. Analo-

---

[9] Medawar [1967], p. 144.

[10] This discussion already indicates the vital importance of a demarcation between provable factual and unprovable theoretical propositions for the dogmatic falsificationist.

[11] "*Criteria of refutation* have to be laid down beforehand: It must be agreed which observable situations, if actually observed, mean that the theory is refuted" (Popper [1963], p. 38, footnote 3).

[12] Quoted in Popper [1934], Section 85, with Popper's comment: "I fully agree."

[13] Braithwaite [1953], pp. 367–8. For the "incorrigibility" of Braithwaite's observed facts, cf. his [1938]. While in the quoted passage Braithwaite gives a forceful answer to the problem of scientific objectivity, in another passage he points out that "except for the straightforward generalizations of observable facts . . . complete refutation is no more possible than is complete proof" ([1953], p. 19). . . .

gously, as seen by falsificationists, Newton's theory was, in turn, refuted—proved false—by the anomalous perihelion of Mercury, while Einstein's explained that too. Thus science proceeds by bold speculations, which are never proved or even made probable, but some of which are later eliminated by hard, conclusive refutations and then replaced by still bolder, new and, at least at the start, unrefuted speculations.

Dogmatic falsificationism, however, is untenable. It rests on two false assumptions and on a too narrow criterion of demarcation between scientific and non-scientific.

The *first assumption* is that there is a natural, *psychological* borderline between theoretical or speculative propositions on the one hand and factual or observational (or basic) propositions on the other. (I shall call this—following Popper—the *naturalistic doctrine of observation*.)

The *second assumption* is that if a proposition satisfies the psychological criterion of being factual or observational (or basic) then it is true; one may say that it was *proved* from facts. (I shall call this the *doctrine of observational (or experimental) proof*.)[14]

These two assumptions secure for the dogmatic falsificationist's deadly disproofs an empirical basis from which proven falsehood can be carried by deductive logic to the theory under test.

These assumptions are complemented by a *demarcation criterion:* Only those theories are "scientific" which forbid certain observable states of affairs and therefore are factually disprovable. *Or, a theory is "scientific" is it has an empirical basis.*[15]

But both assumptions are false. Psychology testifies against the first, logic against the second, and, finally, methodological judgment testifies against the demarcation criterion. I shall discuss them in turn.

1. A first glance at a few characteristic examples already undermines the *first assumption*. Galileo claimed that he could "observe" mountains on the moon and spots on the sun and that these "observations" refuted the time-honoured theory that celestial bodies are faultless crystal balls. But his "observations" were not "observational" in the sense of being observed by the—unaided—senses: Their reliability depended on the reliability of his telescope—and of the optical theory of the telescope—which was violently questioned by his contemporaries. It was not Galileo's—pure, untheoretical—*observations* that confronted Aristotelian *theory* but rather Galileo's "observations" in the light of his optical theory that confronted the Aristotelians' "observations" in the light of their theory of the heavens. . . . This leaves us with two inconsistent theories, *prima facia* on a par. Some empiricists may concede this point and agree that Galileo's "observations" were not genuine observations; but they still hold that there is a "natural demarcation" between statements impressed on an empty and passive mind directly by the senses—only these constitute genuine "immediate knowledge"—and between statements which are suggested by impure, theory-impregnated sensations. . . . But it transpires from the work of Kant and Popper . . . that . . . there are and can be no sensations unimpregnated by expectations and therefore *there is no natural (i.e., psychological) demarcation between observational and theoretical propositions*. . . .

2. But even if there was such a natural demarcation, logic would still destroy the *second assumption* of dogmatic falsificationism. For the truth-value of the "observational" propositions cannot be indubitably decided: *No factual proposition can ever be proved from an*

---

[14] For these assumptions and their criticism, cf. Popper [1934], Sections 4 and 10. It is because of this assumption that—following Popper—I call this brand of falsificationism "naturalistic." Popper's "basic propositions" should not be confused with the basic propositions discussed in this section; cf. *below*, footnote 35.

It is important to point out that these two assumptions are also shared by many justificationists who are not falsificationists: They may add to experimental proofs "intuitive proofs"—as did Kant—or "inductive proofs"—as did Mill. Our falsificationist accepts experimental proofs *only*.

[15] The empirical basis of a theory is the set of its potential falsifiers: the set of those observational propositions which may disprove it.

experiment. Propositions can only be derived from other propositions, they cannot be derived from facts: One cannot prove statements from experiences—"no more than by thumping the table."[16] This is one of the basic points of elementary logic, but one which is understood by relatively few people even today.[17]

If factual propositions are unprovable, then they are fallible. If they are fallible, then clashes between theories and factual propositions are not "falsifications" but merely inconsistencies. Our imagination may play a greater role in the formulation of "theories" than in the formulation of "factual propositions",[18] but they are both fallible. Thus *we cannot prove theories and we cannot disprove them either.*[19] The demarcation between the soft, unproven "theories" and the hard, proven "empirical basis" is nonexistent: *All* propositions of science are theoretical and, incurably, fallible. . . .

3. Finally, even if there were a natural demarcation between observation statements and theories, and even if the truth-value of observation statements could be indubitably established, dogmatic falsificationism would still be useless for eliminating the most important class of what are commonly regarded as scientific theories. For even if experiments *could* prove experimental reports, their disproving power would still be miserably restricted: *Exactly the most admired scientific theories simply fail to forbid any observable state of affairs.*

To support this last contention, I shall first tell a characteristic story and then propose a general argument.

The story is about an imaginary case of planetary misbehaviour. A physicist of the pre-Einsteinian era takes Newton's mechanics and his law of gravitation (N), the accepted initial conditions, I, and calculates, with their help, the path of a newly discovered small planet, p. But the planet deviates from the calculated path. Does our Newtonian physicist consider that the deviation was forbidden by Newton's theory and therefore that, once established, it refutes the theory N? No. He suggests that there must be a hitherto unknown planet p' which perturbs the path of p. He calculates the mass, orbit, etc., of this hypothetical planet and then asks an experimental astronomer to test his hypothesis. The planet p' is so small that even the biggest available telescopes cannot possibly observe it: The experimental astronomer applies for a research grant to build yet a bigger one.[20] In three years' time the new telescope is ready. Were the unknown planet p' to be discovered, it would be hailed as a new victory of Newtonian science. But it is not. Does our scientist abandon Newton's theory and his idea of the perturbing planet? No. He suggests that a cloud of cosmic dust hides the planet from us. He calculates the location and properties of this cloud and asks for a research grant to send up a satellite to test his calculations. Were the satellite's instruments (possibly new ones, based on a little-tested theory) to record the existence of the conjectural cloud, the result would be hailed as an outstanding victory for Newtonian science. But the cloud is not found. Does our scientist abandon Newton's theory, together with the idea of the perturbing planet and the idea of the cloud which hides it? No. He sug-

---

[16] Cf. Popper [1934], Section 29.

[17] It seems that the first philosopher to emphasize this might have been Fries in 1837 (cf. Popper [1934], Section 29, footnote 3). This is of course a special case of the general thesis that logical relations, like probability or consistency, refer to *propositions*. Thus, for instance, the proposition "nature is consistent" is false (or, if you wish, meaningless), for nature is not a proposition (or a conjunction of propositions).

[18] Incidentally, even this is questionable. Cf. below, pp. 188ff.

[19] As Popper put it, "No conclusive disproof of a theory can ever be produced"; those who wait for an infallible disproof before eliminating a theory will have to wait forever and "will never benefit from experience" ([1934], Section 9).

[20] If the tiny conjectural planet were out of the reach even of the biggest *possible* optical telescopes, he might try some quite novel instrument (like a radiotelescope) in order to enable him to "observe it," that is, to ask Nature about it, even if only indirectly. (The new "observational" theory may itself not be properly articulated, let alone severely tested, but he would care no more than Galileo did.)

gests that there is some magnetic field in that region of the universe which disturbed the instruments of the satellite. A new satellite is sent up. Were the magnetic field to be found, Newtonians would celebrate a sensational victory. But it is not. Is this regarded as a refutation of Newtonian science? No. Either yet another ingenious auxiliary hypothesis is proposed or . . . the whole story is buried in the dusty volumes of periodicals and the story never mentioned again.[21]

This story strongly suggests that even a most respected scientific theory, like Newton's dynamics and theory of gravitation, may fail to forbid any observable state of affairs.[22] Indeed, *some scientific theories forbid an event occurring in some specified finite spatio-temporal region (or briefly, a "singular event") only on the condition that no other factor* (possibly hidden in some distant and unspecified spatio-temporal corner of the universe) *has any influence on it.* But then *such theories never alone contradict a "basic" statement:* They contradict at most a conjunction of a basic statement describing a spatio-temporally singular event and of a universal non-existence statement saying that no other relevant cause is at work anywhere in the universe. And the dogmatic falsificationist cannot possibly claim that such universal non-existence statements belong to the empirical basis—that they can be observed and proved by experience.

Another way of putting this is to say that some scientific theories are normally interpreted as containing a *ceteris paribus* clause[23]: in such cases it is always a specific theory *together* with this clause which may be refuted. But such a refutation is inconsequential for the *specific* theory under test because by replacing the *ceteris paribus* clause by a different one the *specific* theory can always be retained whatever the tests say.

If so, the "inexorable" disproof procedure of dogmatic falsificationism breaks down in these cases *even if* there were a firmly established empirical basis to serve as a launching pad for the arrow of the *modus tollens:* The prime target remains hopelessly elusive.[24] And as it happens, it is exactly the most important, "mature" theories in the history of science which are *prima facie* undisprovable in this way.[25] Moreover, by the standards of dogmatic falsificationism all probabilistic theories also come under this head, for no finite sample can ever *disprove* a universal probabilistic theory[26]; probabilistic theories, like theories with a *ceteris paribus* clause, have no empirical basis. But then the dogmatic falsificationist relegates the most important scientific theories *on his own admission* to metaphysics where rational discussion—consisting, by his standards, of proofs and disproofs—has no place, since a metaphysical theory is neither provable nor disprovable. The demarcation criterion of dogmatic falsificationism is thus still strongly antitheoretical.

(Moreover, *one can easily argue that* ceteris paribus *clauses are not exceptions, but the rule in science.* Science, after all, must be demarcated from a curiosity shop where funny local—or cosmic—oddities are collected and displayed. The assertion that "all Britons died from lung cancer between 1950 and 1960" is logically possible and might even have been true. But if it has been only an occurrence of an event with minute probability, it would have only curiosity value for the crankish fact-collector; it would have a macabre

---

[21] At least not until a new research program supersedes Newton's programme which happens to explain this previously recalcitrant phenomenon. In this case, the phenomenon will be unearthed and enthroned as a "crucial experiment". . . .

[22] Popper asks, "What kind of clinical responses would refute to the satisfaction of the analyst not merely a particular diagnosis but psychoanalysis itself?" ([1963], p. 38, footnote 3.) But what kind of observation would refute to the satisfaction of the Newtonian not merely a particular version but Newtonian theory itself?

[23] This *ceteris paribus* clause must not normally be interpreted as a separate premise. . . .

[24] Incidentally, we might persuade the dogmatic falsificationist that his demarcation criterion was a very naive mistake. If he gives it up but retains his two basic assumptions, he will have to ban theories from science and regard the growth of science as an accumulation of proven basic statements. This indeed is the final stage of classical empiricism after the evaporation of the hope that facts can prove or at least disprove theories.

[25] This is no coincidence. . . .

[26] Cf. Popper [1934], Chapter VIII.

entertainment value, but no scientific value. A proposition might be said to be scientific only if it aims at expressing a causal connection: Such connection between being a Briton and dying of lung cancer may not even be intended. Similarly, "All swans are white," if true, would be a mere curiosity unless it asserted that swanness *causes* whiteness. But then a black swan would not refute this proposition, since it may only indicate *other causes* operating simultaneously. Thus "all swans are white" is either an oddity and easily disprovable or a scientific proposition with a *ceteris paribus* clause and therefore undisprovable. *Tenacity of a theory against empirical evidence would then be an argument for rather than against regarding it as "scientific." "Irrefutability" would become a hallmark of science.)* . . .

To sum up: Classical justificationists only admitted proven theories; neoclassical justificationists probable ones; dogmatic falsificationists realized that in either case no theories are admissible. They decided to admit theories if they are disprovable—disprovable by a finite number of observations. But even if there were such disprovable theories—those which can be contradicted by a finite number of observable facts—they are still logically too near to the empirical basis. For instance, on the terms of the dogmatic falsificationist, a theory like "All planets move in ellipses" may be disproved by five observations; therefore the dogmatic falsificationist will regard it as scientific. A theory like "All planets move in circles" may be disproved by four observations; therefore the dogmatic falsificationist will regard it as still more scientific. The acme of scientificness will be a theory like "All swans are white," which is disprovable by one single observation. On the other hand, he will reject all probabilistic theories together with Newton's, Maxwell's, Einstein's theories, as unscientific, for no finite number of observations can ever disprove them.

If we accept the demarcation criterion of dogmatic falsificationism, *and* also the idea that facts can prove "factual" propositions, we have to declare that the most important, if not all, theories ever proposed in the history of science are metaphysical, that most, if not all, of the accepted pro-

gress is pseudo-progress, that most, if not all, of the work done is irrational. If, however, still accepting the demarcation criterion of dogmatic falsificationism, we deny that facts can prove propositions, then we certainly end up in complete scepticism: Then all science is undoubtedly irrational metaphysics and should be rejected. *Scientific theories are not only equally unprovable, and equally improbable, but they are also equally undisprovable.* But the recognition that not only the theoretical but *all* the propositions in science are fallible means the total collapse of *all* forms of dogmatic falsificationism as theories of scientific rationality.

Methodological Falsificationism. The "Empirical Basis."

The collapse of dogmatic falsificationism because of fallibilistic arguments seems to bring us back to square one. If *all* scientific statements are fallible theories, one can criticize them only for inconsistency. But then, in what sense, if any, is science empirical? If scientific theories are neither provable, nor probabilifiable, nor disprovable, then the sceptics seem to be finally right: Science is no more than vain speculation and there is no such thing as progress in scientific knowledge. Can we still oppose scepticism? *Can we save scientific criticism from fallibilism?* Is it possible to have a fallibilistic theory of scientific progress? In particular, if scientific criticism is fallible, on what ground can we ever eliminate a theory?

A most intriguing answer is provided by *methodological falsificationism.* Methodological falsificationism is a brand of conventionalism; therefore, in order to understand it, we must first discuss conventionalism in general.

There is an important demarcation between *"passivist"* and *"activist" theories of knowledge.* "Passivists" hold that true knowledge is Nature's imprint on a perfectly inert mind: Mental *activity* can only result in bias and distortion. The most influential passivist school is classical empiricism. "Activists" hold that we cannot read the book of Nature without mental activity, without interpreting it in the light of our expectations or theories.[27] Now *conservative "activists"* hold that we are born with our basic expectations; with them we turn the world into "our world" but must then live for ever in the prison of our world. The idea that we live and die in the prison of our "conceptual frameworks" was developed primarily by Kant; pessimistic Kantians thought that the real world is forever unknowable because of this prison, while optimistic Kantians thought that God created our conceptual framework to fit the world. . . . But *revolutionary activists* believe that conceptual frameworks can be developed and also replaced by new, *better* ones; it is *we* who create our "prisons" and we can also, critically, demolish them. . . .

New steps from conservative to revolutionary activism were made by Whewell and then by Poincaré, Milhaud and Le Roy. . . . Poincaré, Milhaud and Le Roy . . . preferred to explain the continuing historical success of Newtonian mechanics by a *methodological decision* taken by scientists: After a considerable period of initial empirical success scientists may *decide* not to allow the theory to be refuted. Once they have taken this decision, they solve (or dissolve) the apparent anomalies by auxiliary hypotheses or other "conventionalist stratagems."[28] This *conservative conventionalism* has, however, the disadvantage of making us unable to get out of our self-imposed prisons, once the first period of trial-and-error is over and the great decision taken. It cannot solve the problem of the elimination of those theories which have been triumphant for a long period. According to conservative conventionalism, experiments may have sufficient power to refute young theories, but not to refute old, established theories: *As science grows, the power of empirical evidence diminishes.*[29]

Poincaré's critics refused to accept his idea, that, although the scientists build their conceptual frameworks, there comes a time when these frameworks turn into prisons which cannot be demolished. This criticism gave rise to two rival schools of *revolutionary conventionalism*: Duhem's simplicism and Popper's methodological falsificationism.[30]

Duhem accepts the conventionalists' position that no physical theory ever crumbles merely under the weight of "refutations," but claims that it still may crumble under the weight of "continual repairs, and many tangled-up stays" when "the worm-eaten columns" cannot support "the tottering building" any longer[31]; then the theory loses its original simplicity and has to be replaced. But falsification is then left to subjective taste or, at best, to scientific fashion, and leaves too much leeway for dogmatic adherence to a favorite theory. . . .

Popper set out to find a criterion which is both more objective and more hard-hitting. He could not accept the emasculation of empiricism, inherent even in Duhem's approach, and proposed a methodology which allows experiments to be powerful even in "mature" science. Popper's

---

[27] This demarcation—and terminology—is due to Popper; cf. especially his [1934], Section 19 and his [1945], Chapter 23 and footnote 3 to Chapter 25.

[28] Cf. especially Poincaré [1891] and [1902]; Milhaud [1896]; Le Roy [1899] and [1901]. It was one of the chief philosophical merits of conventionalists to direct the limelight to the fact that any theory can be saved by "conventionalist stratagems" from refutations. (The term *conventionalist stratagem* is Popper's; cf. the critical discussion of Poincaré's conventionalism in his [1934], especially Sections 19 and 20.)

[29] Poincaré first elaborated his conventionalism only with regard to geometry (cf. his [1891]). Then Milhaud and Le Roy generalized Poincaré's idea to cover all branches of accepted physical theory. Poincaré's [1902] starts with a strong criticism of the Bergsonian Le Roy against whom he defends the empirical (falsifiable or "inductive") character of all physics *except for* geometry and mechanics. Duhem, in turn, criticized Poincaré: In his view there was a possibility of overthrowing even Newtonian mechanics.

[30] The *loci classici* are Duhem's [1905] and Popper's [1934]. Duhem was not a *consistent* revolutionary conventionalist. Very much like Whewell, he thought that conceptual changes are only *preliminaries* to the final—if perhaps distant—"natural classification":"The more a theory is perfected, the more we apprehend that the logical order in which it arranges experimental laws is the reflection of an ontological order." In particular, he refused to see Newton's mechanics *actually* "crumbling" and characterized Einstein's relativity theory as the manifestation of a "frantic and hectic race in pursuit of a novel idea" which "has turned physics into a real chaos where logic loses its way and commonsense runs away frightened" (Preface—of 1914—to the second edition of his [1905]).

[31] Duhem [1905], Chapter VI, Section 10.

methodological falsificationism is both conventionalist and falsificationist, but he "differs from the [conservative] conventionalists in holding that the statements decided by agreement are *not* [spatio-temporally] universal but [spatio-temporally] singular"[32]; and he differs from the dogmatic falsificationist in holding that the truth-value of such statements cannot be proved by facts but, in some cases, may be decided by agreement.[33]

The *conservative conventionalist* (or methodological justificationist, if you wish) makes unfalsifiable by *fiat* some (spatio-temporally) universal theories, which are distinguished by their explanatory power, simplicity, or beauty. Our *revolutionary conventionalist* (or "methodological falsificationist") makes unfalsifiable by *fiat* some (spatio-temporally) singular statements which are distinguishable by the fact that there exists at the time a "relevant technique" such that "anyone who has learned it" will be able to *decide* that the statement is "acceptable."[34] Such a statement may be called an "observational" or "basic" statement, but only in inverted commas.[35] Indeed, the very selection of all such statements is a matter of a decision, which is not based on exclusively psychological considerations. This decision is then followed by a second kind of decision concerning the separation of the set of *accepted* basic statements from the rest.

These *two decisions* correspond to the *two assumptions* of dogmatic falsificationism. But there are important differences. First, the methodological falsificationist is not a justificationist, he has no illusions about "experimental proofs" and is fully aware of the fallibility of his decisions and the risks he is taking.

The methodological falsificationist realizes

that in the "experimental techniques" of the scientist fallible theories are involved,[36] "in the light of which" he interprets the facts. In spite of this he "applies" these theories, he regards them in the given context not as theories under test but as *unproblematic background knowledge,* "which we accept (tentatively) as unproblematic while we are testing the theory."[37] He may call these theories—and the statements whose truth-value he decides in their light—"observational," but this is only a manner of speech which he inherited from naturalistic falsificationism.[38] The methodological falsificationist *uses our most successful theories as extensions of our senses* and widens the range of theories which can be applied in testing far beyond the dogmatic falsificationist's range of strictly observational theories. For instance, let us imagine that a big radio-star is discovered with a system of radio-star satellites orbiting it. We should like to test some gravitational theory on this planetary system—a matter of considerable interest. Now let us imagine that Jodrell Bank succeeds in providing a set of space-time co-ordinates of the planets which is inconsistent with the theory. We shall take these statements as potential falsifiers. Of course, these basic statements are not "observational" in the usual sense but only " 'observational.' " They describe planets that neither the human eye nor optical instruments can reach. Their truth-value is arrived at by an "experimental technique." This "experimental technique" is based on the "application" of a well-corroborated theory of radio-optics. Calling these statements "observational" is no more than a manner of saying that, in the context of his problem, that is, in testing our gravitational theory, the methodological falsificationist uses radio-optics uncritically, as "background knowledge." *The need for decisions to demarcate the theory under test from unproblematic background knowledge is a characteristic*

---

[32] Popper [1934], Section 30.

[33] *In this section I discuss the "naive" variant of Popper's methodological falsificationism. Thus, throughout the section "methodological falsificationism" stands for "naive methodological falsificationism"; for this "naivety," cf. below, pp. 181–182.*

[34] Popper [1934], Section 27.

[35] Op cit. Section 28. For the non-basicness of these methodologically "basic" statements, cf. e.g. Popper [1934] *passim* and Popper [1959], p. 35, footnote *2.

[36] Cf. Popper [1934], end of Section 26 and also his [1968], pp. 291–2.

[37] Cf. Popper [1963], p. 390.

[38] Indeed, Popper carefully puts "observational" in quotes; cf. his [1934], Section 28.

feature of this brand of methodological falsificationism.[39] (This situation does not really differ from Galileo's "observation" of Jupiter's satellites; moreover, as some of Galileo's contemporaries rightly pointed out, he relied on a virtually nonexistent optical theory—which then was less corroborated, and even less articulated, than present-day radio-optics. On the other hand, calling the reports of our human eye "observational" only indicates that we "rely" on some vague physiological theory of human vision.[40])

This consideration shows the conventional element in granting—in a given context—the (methodologically) "observational" status to a theory.[41] Similarly, there is a considerable conventional element in the decision concerning the actual truth-value of a basic statement which we take after we have decided which "observational theory" to apply. One single observation may be the stray result of some trivial error: In order to reduce such risks, methodological falsificationists prescribe some safety control. The simplest such control is to repeat the experiment (it is a matter of convention how many times). . . .

This is how the methodological falsificationist establishes his "empirical basis." (He uses quotation marks in order "to give ironical emphasis" to the term.[42]) This "basis" can be hardly called a "basis" by justificationist standards: There is nothing proven about it—it denotes "piles driven into a swamp."[43] Indeed, if this "empirical basis" clashes with a theory, the theory may be *called* "falsified", but it is not falsified in the sense that it is disproved. Methodological "falsification" is very different from dogmatic falsification. If a theory is falsified, it is proven false; if it is "falsified",

it may still be true. If we follow up this sort of "falsification" by the actual "elimination" of a theory, we may well end up by eliminating a true, and accepting a false, theory (a possibility which is thoroughly abhorrent to the old-fashioned justificationist). . . .

The methodological falsificationist separates rejection and disproof, which the dogmatic falsificationist had conflated. . . . He is a fallibilist but his fallibilism does not weaken his critical stance: He turns fallible propositions into a "basis" for a hard-line policy. On these grounds he proposes a *new demarcation criterion*: Only those theories—that is, non-"observational" propositions—that forbid certain "observable" states of affairs, and therefore may be "falsified"and rejected, are "scientific"; or, briefly, a *theory is "scientific" (or "acceptable") if it has an "empirical basis."* This criterion brings out sharply the difference between dogmatic and methodological falsificationism.[44] . . .

But even these three decisions are not sufficient to enable us to "falsify" a theory which cannot explain anything "observable" without a *ceteris paribus* clause.[45] No finite number of "observations" is enough to "falsify" such a theory. However, if this is the case, how can one reasonably defend a methodology which claims to "interpret natural laws or theories as . . . statements which are partially decidable, i.e., which are, for logical reasons, not verifiable but, in an asymmetrical way, falsifiable . . . ?[46] How can we interpret theories like Newton's theory of dynamics and gravitation as "one-sidedly decidable"?[47] How can we make in such cases genuine "attempts to weed out false theories—to find the weak points of a theory in order to reject it if it is falsified by the test"?[48] How can we draw them

---

[39] This demarcation plays a role both in the *first* and in the *fourth* type of decisions of the methodological falsificationist. (For the *fourth* decision, cf. below, p. 180.)

[40] For a fascinating discussion, cf. Feyerabend [1969].

[41] One wonders whether it would not be better to make a break with the terminology of naturalistic falsificationism and rechristen observational theories *"touchstone theories."*

[42] Popper [1963], p. 387.

[43] Popper [1934], Section 30; also cf. Section 29: "The Relativity of Basic Statements."

[44] The demarcation criterion of the dogmatic falsificationist was: A theory is "scientific" if it has an empirical basis (see *above,* p. 173).

[45] Cf. *above,* pp. 175–176.

[46] Popper [1933].

[47] Popper [1933].

[48] Popper [1957], p. 133.

into the realm of rational discussion? The methodological falsificationist solves the problem by making a further (*fourth type*) *decision:* When he tests a theory together with a *ceteris paribus* clause and finds that this conjunction has been refuted, he must decide whether to take the refutation also as a refutation of the specific theory. For instance, he may accept Mercury's "anomalous" perihelion as a refutation of the treble conjunction N_3 of Newton's theory, the known initial conditions, and the *ceteris paribus* clause. Then he tests the initial conditions "severely"[49] and may decide to relegate them into the "unproblematic background knowledge." This decision implies the refutation of the double conjunction N_2 of Newton's theory and the *ceteris paribus* clause. Now he has to take the crucial decision: whether to relegate also the *ceteris paribus* clause into the pool of "unproblematic background knowledge." He will do so if he finds the *ceteris paribus* clause well corroborated.

How can one test a *ceteris paribus* clause severely? By assuming that there *are* other influencing factors, by specifying such factors, and by testing these specific assumptions. If many of them are refuted, the *ceteris paribus* clause will be regarded as well corroborated. . . .

Thus, with the help of this fourth type of decision,[50] our methodological falsificationist has finally succeeded in interpreting even theories like Newton's theory as "scientific." . . .

To sum up: The methodological falsificationist offers an interesting solution to the problem of combining hard-hitting criticism with fallibilism. Not only does he offer a philosophical basis for falsification after fallibilism had pulled the carpet from under the feet of the dogmatic falsificationist, but he also widens the range of such criticism very considerably. By putting falsification in a new setting, he saves the attractive code of honour of the dogmatic falsificationist: that scientific honesty consists in specifying, in advance, an experiment such that if the result contradicts the theory, the theory has to be given up.[51]

Methodological falsificationism represents a considerable advance beyond both dogmatic falsificationism and conservative conventionalism. It recommends risky decisions. But the risks are daring to the point of recklessness and one wonders whether there is no way of lessening them.

Let us first have a closer look at the risks involved.

Decisions play a crucial role in this methodology—as in any brand of conventionalism. Decisions, however, may lead us disastrously astray. The methodological falsificationist is the first to admit this. But this, he argues, is the price which we have to pay for the possibility of progress.

One has to appreciate the dare-devil attitude of our methodological falsificationist. He feels himself to be a hero who, faced with two catastrophic alternatives, dared to reflect coolly on their relative merits and choose the lesser evil. One of the alternatives was sceptical fallibilism, with its "anything goes" attitude, the despairing abandonment of all intellectual standards, and hence of the idea of scientific progress. Nothing can be established, nothing can be rejected, nothing even communicated: The growth of science is a growth of chaos, a veritable Babel. For two thousand years, scientists and scientifically minded philosophers chose justificationist illusions of some kind to escape this nightmare. . . . Our methodological falsificationist proudly rejects such escapism: he dares to measure up to the full impact of fallibilism and yet escape skepticism by a daring and risky conventionalist policy, with no dogmas. He is fully aware of the risks but insists that *one has to choose between some sort of methodological falsificationism and irrationalism.* He offers a game in which one has little hope of winning, but claims that it is still better to play than to give up. . . .

But is not the firm strategy of the brand of methodological falsificationism hitherto discussed

---

[49] For a discussion of this important concept of Popperian methodology, cf. my [1968a], pp. 397 ff.

[50] This type of decision belongs, in an important sense, to the same category as the first decision: It demarcates, by decision, problematic from unproblematic knowledge. Cf. *above* p. 179, text to footnote 39.

[51] See *above,* p. 172.

too firm? Are not the decisions it advocates bound to be *too arbitrary?* Some may even claim that all that distinguishes methodological from dogmatic falsificationism is that *it pays lip-service to fallibilism!*

To criticize a theory of criticism is usually very difficult. Naturalistic falsificationism was relatively easy to refute, since it rested on an empirical psychology of perception: One could show that it was simply *false.* But how can methodological falsificationism be falsified? No disaster can ever disprove a non-justificationist theory of rationality. Moreover, how can we ever recognize an epistemological disaster? We have no means to judge whether the verisimilitude of our successive theories increases or decreases.[52] At this stage we have not yet developed a general theory of criticism even for scientific theories, let alone for theories of rationality[53]: therefore, if we want to falsify our methodological falsificationism, we have to do it before having a theory of how to do it.

If we look at history of science, if we try to see how some of the most celebrated falsifications happened, we have to come to the conclusion that either some of them are plainly irrational or that they rest on rationality principles radically different from the ones we just discussed. First of all, our falsificationist must deplore the fact that stubborn theoreticians frequently challenge experimental verdicts and have them reversed. In the falsificationist conception of scientific "law and order" we have described there is no place for such successful appeals. Further difficulties arise from the falsification of theories to which a *ceteris paribus* clause is appended.[54] Their falsification as

it occurs in actual history is *prima facie* irrational by the standards of our falsificationist. By his standards, scientists frequently seem to be irrationally slow: For instance, eighty-five years elapsed between the acceptance of the perihelion of Mercury as an anomaly and its acceptance as a falsification of Newton's theory, in spite of the fact that the *ceteris paribus* clause was reasonably well corroborated. On the other hand, scientists frequently seem to be irrationally rash: For instance, Galileo and his disciples accepted Copernican heliocentric celestial mechanics in spite of the abundant evidence against the rotation of the Earth; or Bohr and his disciples accepted a theory of light emission in spite of the fact that it ran counter to Maxwell's well-corroborated theory.

Indeed, it is not difficult to see at least two crucial characteristics common to both dogmatic and our methodological falsificationism which are clearly dissonant with the actual history of science: that (1) *a test is—or must be made—a two-cornered fight between theory and experiment so that in the final confrontation only these two face each other; and* (2) *the only interesting outcome of such conf.ontation is (conclusive) falsification:* "[*the only genuine*] *discoveries are refutations of scientific hypotheses.*"[55] However, history of science suggests that (1') tests are—at least—three-cornered fights between rival theories and experiment and (2') some of the most interesting experiments result, *prima facie,* in confirmation rather than falsification.

But if—as seems to be the case—the history of science does not bear out our theory of scientific rationality, we have two alternatives. One alternative is to abandon efforts to give a rational explanation of the success of science. Scientific method (or "logic of discovery"), conceived as the discipline of rational appraisal of scientific theories—and of criteria of *progress*—vanishes. We, may, of course, still try to explain *changes* in "paradigms" in terms of social psychology. . . . This is

---

[52] I am using here *"verisimilitude"* in Popper's sense: the difference between the truth content and falsity content of a theory. For the risks involved in estimating it, cf. my [1968a], especially pp. 395 ff.

[53] I tried to develop such a general theory of criticism in my [1970].

[54] The falsification of theories depends on the high degree of corroboration of the *ceteris paribus* clause. This, however, is not always the case. This is why the methodological falsificationist may advise us to rely on our "scientific instinct" (Popper [1934], Section 18, footnote 2) or "hunch" (Braithwaite [1953], p. 20).

[55] Agassi [1959]; he calls Popper's idea of science "scientia negativa" (Agassi [1968]).

Polanyi's and Kuhn's way.[56] The other alternative is to try at least to *reduce* the conventional element in falsificationism (we cannot possibly eliminate it) and replace the *naive* versions of methodological falsificationism—characterized by the theses (1) and (2) above—by a *sophisticated* version which would give a new *rationale* of falsification and thereby rescue methodology and the idea of scientific *progress*. This is Popper's way, and the one I intend follow.

Sophisticated versus Naive Methodological Falsificationism. Progressive and Degenerating Problemshifts.

Sophisticated falsificationism differs from naive falsificationism both in its rules of *acceptance* (or "demarcation criterion") and its rules of *falsification* or elimination. For the naive falsificationist any theory which can be interpreted as experimentally falsifiable is "acceptable" or "scientific."[57] For the sophisticated falsificationist a theory is "acceptable" or "scientific" only if it has corroborated excess empirical content over its predecessor (or rival), that is, only if it leads to the discovery of novel facts. This condition can be analysed into two clauses: that the new theory has excess empirical content ("*acceptability*"₁) and that some of this excess content is verified ("*acceptability*"₂). The first clause can be checked instantly . . . by a *priori* logical analysis; the second can be checked only empirically and this may take an indefinite time.

Again, for the naive falsificationist a theory is *falsified* by a ("fortified" . . .) "observational" statement which conflicts with it (or rather, which he decides to interpret as conflicting with it). The sophisticated falsificationist regards a scientific theory *T* as falsified if and only if another theory *T'* has been proposed with the following characteristics: (1) *T'* has excess empirical content over *T;* that is, it predicts *novel* facts, that is, facts improb-

able in the light of, or even forbidden, by *T;*[58] (2) *T'* explains the previous success of *T*, that is, all the unrefuted content of *T* is contained (within the limits of observational error) in the content of *T'*; and (3) some of the excess content of *T'* is corroborated.[59]

In order to be able to appraise these definitions we need to understand their problem background and their consequences. First, we have to remember the conventionalists' methodological discovery that no experimental result can ever kill a theory: any theory can be saved from counterinstances either by some auxiliary hypothesis or by a suitable reinterpretation of its terms. Naive falsificationists solved this problem by relegating—in crucial contexts—the auxiliary hypotheses to the realm of unproblematic background knowledge, eliminating them from the deductive model of the test-situation and thereby *forcing* the chosen theory into logical isolation, in which it becomes a sitting target for the attack of test-experiments. But since this procedure did not offer a suitable guide for a rational reconstruction of the history of science, we may just as well completely rethink our approach. Why aim at falsification at any price? Why not rather impose certain standards on the theoretical adjustments by which one is allowed to save a theory? Indeed, some such standards have been well known for centuries, and we find them expressed in age-old wisecracks against *ad hoc* explanations, empty prevarications, face-saving, linguistic tricks.[60] We have already seen that Duhem adumbrated such stan-

---

[56] Feyerabend, who contributed probably more than anybody else to the spread of Popper's ideas, seems now to have joined the enemy camp. Cf. his intriguing [1970].

[57] Ct. *above*, p. 179.

[58] I use "*prediction*" in a wide sense that includes "*postdiction*."

[59] *For a detailed discussion of these acceptance and rejection rules and for references to Popper's work,* cf. my [1968a], pp. 375–90. For some qualifications (concerning continuity and consistency as regulative principles), cf. *below,* pp. 190–191. . . .

[60] Molière, for instance, ridiculed the doctors of his *Malade Imaginaire*, who offered the *virtus dormitiva* of opium as the answer to the question as to why opium produced sleep. One might even argue that Newton's famous dictum *hypotheses non fingo* was really directed against *ad hoc* explanations—like his own explanation of gravitational forces by an aether-model in order to meet Cartesian objections.

[61] Cf. *above*, p. 177.

dards in terms of "simplicity" and "good sense."[61] But *when* does lack of "simplicity" in the protective belt of theoretical adjustments reach the point at which the theory *must* be abandoned?[62] In what sense was Copernican theory, for instance, "simpler" than Ptolemaic?[63] The vague notion of Duhemian "simplicity" leaves, as the naive falsificationist correctly argued, the decision very much to taste and fashion.[64]

Can one improve on Duhem's approach? Popper did. His solution—a sophisticated version of methodological falsificationism—is more objective and more rigorous. Popper agrees with the conventionalists that theories and factual propositions can always be harmonized with the help of auxiliary hypotheses: He agrees that the problem is how to demarcate between scientific and pseudoscientific *adjustments,* between rational and irrational changes of theory. According to Popper, saving a theory with the help of auxiliary hypotheses which satisfy certain well-defined conditions represents scientific progress; but saving a theory with the help of auxiliary hypotheses which do not, represents degeneration. Popper calls such inadmissible auxiliary hypotheses *ad hoc* hypotheses, mere linguistic devices, "conventionalist stratagems."[65] But then any scientific theory has to be appraised together with its auxiliary hypotheses, initial conditions, etc., and, especially, together with its predecessors so that we may see by what sort of *change* it was brought about. Then, of course, what we appraise is a *series of theories* rather than isolated *theories.*

Now we can easily understand why we formulated the criteria of acceptance and rejection of sophisticated methodological falsificationism as we did.[66] But it may be worth while to reformulate them slightly, couching them explicitly in terms of *series of theories.*

Let us take a series of theories, T_1, T_2, T_3, . . . where each subsequent theory results from adding auxiliary clauses to (or from semantical reinterpretations of) the previous theory in order to accommodate some anomaly, each theory having at least as much content as the unrefuted content of its predecessor. Let us say that such a series of theories is *theoretically progressive (or "constitutes a theoretically progressive problemshift")* if each new theory has some excess empirical content over its predecessor; that is, if it predicts some novel, hitherto unexpected fact. Let us say that a theoretically progressive series of theories is also *empirically progressive (or "constitutes an empirically progressive problemshift")* if some of this excess empirical content is also corroborated, that is, if each new theory leads us to the actual discovery of some *new fact.*[67] Finally, let us call a problemshift *progressive* if it is both theoretically and empirically progressive, and *degenerating* if it is not.[68] We "*accept*" problemshifts as "scientific" only if they are at least theoretically progressive; if they are not, we "*reject*" them as "pseudoscientific." Progress is measured by the degree to which a problemshift is progressive, by the degree to which the series of theories leads us to the discovery of novel facts. We regard a theory in the series

---

[62] Incidentally, Duhem agreed with Bernard that experiments alone—without simplicity considerations—can decide the fate of theories in physiology. But in physics, he argued, they cannot ([1905] Chapter VI, Section I).

[63] Koestler correctly points out that only Galileo created the myth that the Copernican theory was simple (Koestler [1959], p. 476); in fact, "the motion of the earth [had not] done much to simplify the old theories, for though the objectionable equants had disappeared, the system was still bristling with auxiliary circles" (Dreyer [1906], Chapter XIII).

[64] Cf. *above*, p. 177.

[65] Popper [1934], sections 19 and 20. I have discussed in some detail—under the heads "monster-barring," "exception-barring," "monster-adjustment"—such stratagems as they appear in informal, quasi-empirical mathematics; cf. my [1963–4].

[66] Cf. *above,* p. 182.

[67] If I already know P_1: "Swan A is white," P_ω: "All swans are white" represents no progress, because it may only lead to the discovery of such further similar facts as P_2: "Swan B is white." So-called "empirical generalizations" constitute no progress. A *new* fact must be improbable or even impossible in the light of previous knowledge. Cf. *above,* p. 182. . . .

[68] The appropriateness of the term "problemshift" for a series of theories rather than of problems may be questioned. I chose it partly because I have not found a more appropriate alternative—"theoryshift" sounds dreadful—partly because theories are always problematical, they never solve all the problems they have set out to solve. Anyway, in the second half of the paper, the more natural term "research programme" will replace "problemshifts" in the most relevant contexts.

"falsified" when it is superseded by a theory with higher corroborated content. . . .

This demarcation between progressive and degenerating problemshifts sheds new light on the appraisal of *scientific—or rather, progressive—explanations*. If we put forward a theory to resolve a contradiction between a previous theory and a counterexample in such a way that the new theory, instead of offering a content-increasing (scientific) *explanation,* only offers a content-decreasing (linguistic) *reinterpretation,* the contradiction is resolved in a merely semantical, unscientific way. *A given fact is explained scientifically only if a new fact is also explained with it.* . . .

Sophisticated falsificationism thus shifts the problem of how to appraise *theories* to the problem of how to appraise *series of theories*. Not an isolated *theory,* but only a series of theories can be said to be scientific or unscientific: to apply the term "scientific" to one *single* theory is a category mistake.[69]

The time-honoured empirical criterion for a satisfactory theory was agreement with the observed facts. Our empirical criterion for a series of theories is that it should produce new facts. *The idea of growth and the concept of empirical character are soldered into one.*

This revised form of methodological falsificationism has many new features. First, it denies that "in the case of a scientific theory, our decision depends upon the results of experiments. If these confirm the theory, we may accept it until we find a better one. If they contradict the theory, we reject it."[70] It denies that "what ultimately decides the fate of a theory is the result of a test, i.e., an agreement about basic statements."[71] Contrary to naive falsificationism, *no experiment, experimental report, observation statement or well-corroborated low-level falsifying hypothesis alone can lead to falsification. . . . There is no falsification before the emergence of a better theory.*[72] But then the distinctively negative character of naive falsificationism vanishes; criticism becomes more difficult, and also positive, constructive. But, of course, if falsification depends on the emergence of better theories, on the invention of theories which anticipate new facts, then falsification is *not* simply a relation between a theory and the empirical basis, but a multiple relation between competing theories, the original "empirical basis," and the empirical growth resulting from the competition. Falsification can thus be said to have a *"historical character."*[73] Moreover, some of the theories which bring about falsification are frequently proposed *after* the "counterevidence." This may sound paradoxical for people indoctrinated with naive falsificationism. Indeed, this epistemological theory of the relation between theory and experiment differs sharply from the epistemological theory of naive falsificationism. The very term "counterevidence" has to be abandoned in the sense that no experimental result must be interpreted directly as "counterevidence." If we still want to retain this time-honoured term, we have to redefine it like this: "Counterevidence to T_1" is a corroborating instance to T_2, which is either inconsistent with or independent of T_1 (with the *proviso* that T_2 is a theory which satisfactorily explains the empirical success of T_1). This shows that *"cru-*

---

[69] Popper's conflation of "theories" and "series of theories" prevented him from getting the basic ideas of sophisticated falsificationism across more successfully. His ambiguous usage led to such confusing formulations as "Marxism [as the core of a series of theories or of a research programme] is irrefutable" and, at the same time, "Marxism [as a particular conjunction of this core and some specified auxiliary hypotheses, initial conditions and a *ceteris paribus* clause] has been refuted." (Cf. Popper [1963].)

Of course, there is nothing wrong in saying that an isolated, single theory is "scientific" if it represents an advance on its predecessor, as long as one clearly realizes that in this formulation we appraise the theory as the outcome of—and in the context of—a certain historical development.

[70] Popper [1945], Vol. II, p. 233. Popper's more sophisticated attitude surfaces in the remark that "concrete and practical con-

sequences can be *more* directly tested by experiment" (*ibid;* my italics).

[71] Popper [1934], Section 30.

[72] "In most cases we have, before falsifying a hypothesis, another one up our sleeves" (Popper [1959], p. 87, footnote *I). But, as our argument shows, we *must* have one. Or, as Feyerabend put it: "The best criticism is provided by those theories which can replace the rivals they have removed" ([1965], p. 227). He notes that in *some* cases "alternatives will be quite indispensable for the purpose of refutation" (*ibid,* p. 254). But according to our argument *refutation without an alternative shows nothing but the poverty of our imagination in providing a rescue hypothesis.* . . .

[73] Cf. my [1968a], pp. 387 ff.

cial counterevidence"—or "*crucial experiments*"—can be recognized as such among the scores of anomalies only *with hindsight,* in the light of some superseding theory.[74]

Thus the crucial element in falsification is whether the *new theory* offers any novel, excess information compared with its predecessor and whether some of this excess information is corroborated. Justificationists valued "confirming" instances of a theory; naive falsificationists stressed "refuting" instances; for the methodological falsificationists it is the—rather rare—corroborating instances of the *excess* information which are the crucial ones; these receive all the attention. We are no longer interested in the thousands of trivial verifying instances nor in the hundreds of readily available anomalies: The few crucial *excess-verifying instances* are decisive.[75] This consideration rehabilitates—and reinterprets—the old proverb: *Exemplum docet, exempla obscurant.*

"Falsification" in the sense of naive falsificationism (corroborated counterevidence) is not a *sufficient* condition for eliminating a specific theory: In spite of hundreds of known anomalies we do not regard it as falsified (that is, eliminated) until we have a better one.[76] Nor is "falsification" in the naive sense *necessary* for falsification in the sophisticated sense: A progressive problemshift does not have to be interspersed with "refuta-

tions." Science can grow without any "refutations" leading the way. Naive falsificationists suggest a linear growth of science, in the sense that theories are followed by powerful refutations which eliminate them; these refutations in turn are followed by new theories.[77] It is perfectly *possible* that theories be put forward "progressively" in such a rapid succession that the "refutation" of the *n*th appears only as the corroboration of the $n + 1$-th. The problem fever of science is raised by proliferation of rival theories rather than counterexamples or anomalies.

This shows that the slogan of *proliferation of theories* is much more important for sophisticated than for naive falsificationism. For the naive falsificationist science grows through repeated experimental overthrow of theories; new rival theories proposed before such "overthrows" may speed up growth but are not absolutely necessary . . . ; constant proliferation of theories is optional but not mandatory. For the sophisticated falsificationist proliferation of theories cannot wait until the accepted theories are "refuted" (or until their protagonists get into a Kuhnian crisis of confidence).[78] While naive falsificationism stresses "the urgency of replacing a *falsified* hypothesis by a better one,"[79] sophisticated falsificationism stresses the urgency of replacing *any* hypothesis by a better one. Falsification cannot "compel the theorist to search for a better theory,"[80] simply because falsification cannot precede the better theory.

The problem-shift from naive to sophisticated falsificationism involves a semantic difficulty. For the naive falsificationist a "refutation" is an experimental result which, by force of his decisions, is made to conflict with the theory under test. But according to sophisticated falsificationism one must not take such decisions before the alleged "refuting instance" has become the confirming instance of a new, better theory. Therefore when-

---

[74] In the distorting mirror of naive falsificationism, new theories which replace old refuted ones are themselves born unrefuted. Therefore they do not believe that there is a relevant difference between anomalies and crucial counterevidence. For them, anomaly is a dishonest euphemism for counterevidence. But in actual history new theories are born refuted: They inherit many anomalies of the old theory. Moreover, frequently it is *only* the new theory which dramatically predicts that fact which will function as crucial counterevidence against its predecessor, while the "old" anomalies may well stay on as "new" anomalies. . . .

[75] *Sophisticated falsificationism adumbrates a new theory of learning; cf. below,* p. 186.

[76] It is clear that the theory T' may have excess corroborated empirical content over another theory T even if both T and T' are refuted. Empirical content has nothing to do with truth or falsity. Corroborated contents can also be compared irrespective of the refuted content. Thus we may see the rationality of the elimination of Newton's theory in favour of Einstein's, even though Einstein's theory may be said to have been born—like Newton's—"refuted." We have only to remember that "qualitative confirmation" is a euphemism for "quantitative disconfirmation." (Cf. my [1968a], pp. 384–6.)

[77] Cf. Popper [1934], Section 85, p. 279 of the 1959 English translation.

[78] Also cf. Feyerabend [1965], pp. 254–5.

[79] Popper [1959], p. 87, footnote *I.

[80] Popper [1934], Section 30.

ever we see terms like "refutation," "falsification," "counterexample," we have to check in each case whether these terms are being applied in virtue of decisions by the naive or by the sophisticated falsificationist.[81]

Sophisticated methodological falsificationism offers new standards for intellectual honesty. Justificationist honesty demanded the acceptance of only what was proven and the rejection of everything unproven. Neojustificationist honesty demanded the specification of the probability of any hypothesis in the light of the available empirical evidence. The honesty of naive falsificationism demanded the testing of the falsifiable and the rejection of the unfalsifiable and the falsified. Finally, the honesty of sophisticated falsificationism demanded that one should try to look at things from different points of view, to put forward new theories which anticipate novel facts, and to reject theories which have been superseded by more powerful ones.

Sophisticated methodological falsificationism blends several different traditions. From the empiricists it has inherited the determination to learn primarily from experience. From the Kantians it has taken the activist approach to the theory of knowledge. From the conventionalists it has learned the importance of decisions in methodology.

I should like to emphasize here a further distinctive feature of sophisticated methodological empiricism: the crucial role of excess corroboration. For the inductivist, learning about a new theory is learning how much confirming evidence supports it; about refuted theories one *learns* nothing (learning, after all, is to build up proven or probable *knowledge*). For the dogmatic falsificationist, learning about a theory is learning whether it is refuted or not; about confirmed theories one learns nothing (one cannot prove or probabilify

anything) about refuted theories one learns that they are disproved.[82] For the sophisticated falsificationist, learning about a theory is primarily learning which new facts it anticipated; indeed, for the sort of Popperian empiricism I advocate, the only relevant evidence is the evidence anticipated by a theory, and *empiricalness (or scientific character) and theoretical progress are inseparably connected.* . . .

This idea is not entirely new. Leibnitz, for instance, in his famous letter to Conring in 1678, wrote: "It is the greatest commendation of an hypothesis (next to [proven] truth) if by its help predictions can be made even about phenomena or experiments not tried."[83] Leibnitz's view was widely accepted by scientists. But since all appraisal of a scientific theory was before Popper appraisal of its degree of justification, this position was regarded by some logicians as untenable. Mill, for instance, complains in 1843 in horror that "it seems to be thought that an hypothesis . . . is entitled to a more favourable reception, if besides accounting for all the facts previously known, it has led to the anticipation and prediction of others which experience afterwards verified."[84] Mill had a point; this appraisal was in conflict both with justificationism and with probabilism: Why should an event *prove* more, if it was anticipated by the theory than if it was known already before? As long as *proof* was the only criterion of the scientific character of a theory, Leibnitz's criterion could only be regarded as irrelevant.[85] Also, the *probability* of a theory given

---

[81] . . . Possibly it would be better in future to abandon these terms altogether, just as we have abandoned terms like "*inductive* (or experimental) proof." Then we may call (naive) "refutations" anomalies, and (sophisticatedly) "falsified" theories "superseded" ones. Our "ordinary" language is impregnated not only by "inductivist" but also by falsificationist dogmatism. A reform is overdue.

[82] For a defense of this theory of "learning from experience," cf. Agassi [1969].

[83] Cf. Leibnitz [1678]. The expression in brackets shows that Leibnitz regarded this criterion as second best and thought that the best theories are those which are proved. Thus Leibnitz's position—like Whewell's—is a far cry from fully fledged sophisticated falsificationism.

[84] Mill [1843], vol. II, p. 23.

[85] This was J. S. Mill's argument (*ibid*). He directed it against Whewell, who thought that "consilience of inductions" or successful prediction of improbable events *verifies* (that is, *proves*) a theory. (Whewell [1858], pp. 95–6.) No doubt, *the basic contradiction both in Whewell's and in Duhem's philosophy of science is their conflation of heuristic power and proven truth. Popper separated the two.*

evidence cannot possibly be influenced, as Keynes pointed out, by *when* the evidence was produced; the probability of a theory given evidence can depend only on the theory and the evidence,[86] and not upon whether the evidence was produced before or after the theory.

In spite of this convincing justificationist criticism, the criterion survived among some of the best scientists, since it formulated their strong dislike of merely *ad hoc* explanations, which "though [they] truly express the facts [they set out to explain, are] not born out by any other phenomena."[87]

But it was only Popper who recognized that the *prima facie* inconsistency between the few odd, casual remarks against *ad hoc* hypotheses on the one hand and the huge edifice of justificationist philosophy of knowledge must be solved by demolishing justificationism and by introducing new, non-justificationist criteria for appraising scientific theories based on anti-adhocness.

Let us look at a few examples. Einstein's theory is not better than Newton's *because* Newton's theory was "refuted" but Einstein's was not: There are many known "anomalies" to Einsteinian theory. Einstein's theory is better than—that is, represents progress compared with—Newton's theory *anno 1916* (that is, Newton's laws of dynamics, law of gravitation, the known set of initial conditions, "minus" the list of known anomalies such as Mercury's perihelion) *because* it explained everything that Newton's theory had successfully explained, and it explained also *to some extent* some known anomalies and, in addition, forbade events like transmission of light along straight lines near large masses about which Newton's theory had said nothing but which had been permitted by other well-corroborated scientific theories of the day; moreover, *at least some* of the unexpected excess Einsteinian content was in fact *corroborated* (for instance, by the eclipse experiments). . . .

Let us finally consider how much conventionalism remains in sophisticated falsificationism. Certainly *less* than in naive falsificationism. We need *fewer* methodological decisions. The *"fourth-type decision"* which was essential for the naive version[88] has become completely redundant. To show this we only have to realize that if a scientific theory, consisting of some "laws of nature," initial conditions, auxiliary theories (but without a *ceteris paribus* clause) conflicts with some factual propositions we do not have to decide which—explicit or "hidden"—part to replace. We may try to replace *any* part and only when we have hit on an explanation of the anomaly with the help of some content-increasing change (or auxiliary hypothesis), and nature corroborates it, do we move on to eliminate the "refuted" complex. Thus sophisticated falsification is a slower but possibly safer process than naive falsification.

Let us take an example. Let us assume that the course of a planet differs from the one predicted. Some conclude that this refutes the dynamics and gravitational theory applied: The initial conditions and the *ceteris paribus* clause have been ingeniously corroborated. Other conclude that this refutes the initial conditions used in the calculations: Dynamics and gravitational theory have been superbly corroborated in the last two hundred years and all suggestions concerning further factors in play failed. Yet others conclude that this refutes the underlying assumption that there were no other factors in play except for those which were taken into account: These people may possibly be motivated by the metaphysical principle that any explanation is only approximative because of the infinite complexity of the factors involved in determining any single event. Should we praise the first type as *"critical,"* scold the second type as *"hack,"* and condemn the third as *"apologetic"*? No. We do not need to draw any conclusions about such "refutation." We never reject a specific theory simply by *fiat*. If we have an inconsistency like the one mentioned, we do not have

---

[86] Keynes [1921], p. 305. But cf. my [1968a], p. 394.

[87] This is Whewell's critical comment on an *ad hoc* auxiliary hypothesis in Newton's theory of light (Whewell [1858], Vol. II, p. 317.)

[88] Cf. *above*, p. 180.

to decide which ingredients of the theory we regard as problematic and which ones as unproblematic: We regard all ingredients as problematic in the light of the conflicting accepted basic statement and try to replace all of them. If we succeed in replacing some ingredient in a "progressive" way (that is, the replacement has more corroborated empirical content than the original), we call it "falsified." . . .

The first, second, and third type decisions of naive falsificationism[89] however, cannot be avoided, but as we shall show, the conventional element in the second decision—and also in the third—can be slightly reduced. We cannot avoid the decision which sort of propositions should be the "observational" ones and which the "theoretical" ones. We cannot avoid either the decision about the truth-value of some "observational propositions." These decisions are vital for the decision whether a problemshift is empirically progressive or degenerating.[90] But the sophisticated falsificationist may at least mitigate the arbitrariness of this second decision by allowing for an *appeal procedure*.

Naive falsificationists do not lay down any such appeal procedure. They accept a basic statement if it is backed up by a well-corroborated falsifying hypothesis,[91] and let it overrule the theory under test—even though they are well aware of the risk.[92] But there is no reason why we should not regard a falsifying hypothesis—and the basic statement it supports—as being just as problematic as a falsified hypothesis. Now how exactly can we expose the problematicality of a basic statement? On what grounds can the protagonists of the "falsified" theory appeal and win?

Some people may say that we might go on testing the basic statement (or the falsifying hypothesis) "by their deductive consequences" until agreement is finally reached. In this testing we deduce—in the same deductive model—further consequences from the basic statement either with the help of the theory under test or some other theory which we regard as unproblematic. Although this procedure "has no natural end," we always come to a point when there is no further disagreement.[93]

But when the theoretician appeals against the verdict of the experimentalist, the appeal court does not normally cross-question the basic statement directly but rather questions the *interpretative theory* in the light of which its truth-value had been established.

One typical example of a series of successful appeals is the Proutians' fight against unfavourable experimental evidence from 1815 to 1911. For decades Prout's theory *T* ("that all atoms are compounds of hydrogen atoms and thus 'atomic weights' of all chemical elements must be expressible as whole numbers") and falsifying "observational" hypotheses, like Stas's "refutation" *R* ("the atomic weight of chlorine is 35·5") confronted each other. As we know, in the end *T* prevailed over *R*.[94]

The first stage of any serious criticism of a scientific theory is to reconstruct, improve, its logical deductive articulation. Let us do this in the case of Prout's theory *vis à vis* Stas's refutation. First of all, we have to realize that in the formulation we just quoted, *T* and *R* were *not* inconsistent (Physicists rarely articulate their theories sufficiently to be pinned down and caught by the critic.) In order to show them up as inconsistent we have to put them in the following form. *T*: "the atomic weight of all pure (homogeneous) chemical elements are multiples of the atomic weight of hydrogen," and *R*: "chlorine is a pure (homogeneous) chemical element and its atomic weight is 35·5." The last statement is in the form of a falsifying hypothesis

---

[89] Cf. *above,* pp. 178 and 179.

[90] Cf. *above,* p. 183.

[91] Popper [1934], Section 22.

[92] Cf. e.g., Popper [1959], p. 107, footnote *2. Also cf. *above,* pp. 180–181.

[93] This is argued in Popper [1934], Section 29.

[94] Agassi claims that this example shows that we may "stick to the hypothesis in the face of known facts in the hope that the facts will adjust themselves to theory rather than the other way round" [1966], p. 18). But *how* can facts "adjust themselves"? Under which *particular* conditions should the theory win? Agassi gives no answer.

which, if well corroborated, would allow us to use basic statements of the form B: "Chlorine X is a pure (homogeneous) chemical element and its atomic weight is 35·5"—where X is the proper name of a "piece" of chlorine determined, say, by its space-time co-ordinates.

But how well-corroborated is R? The first component of it says that R_1: "Chlorine X is a pure chemical element." This was the verdict of the experimental chemist after a rigorous application of the "experimental techniques" of the day.

Let us have a closer look at the fine-structure of R_1. In fact R_1 stands for a conjunction of two longer statements, T_1 and T_2. The first statement, T_1, could be this: "If seventeen chemical purifying procedures P_1, P_2 . . . P_{17} are applied to a gas, what remains will be pure chlorine." T_2 is then: "X was subjected to the seventeen procedures P_1, P_2 . . . P_{17}." The careful "experimenter" carefully applied all seventeen procedures: T_2 is to be accepted. But the conclusion that therefore what remained *must* be pure chlorine is a "hard fact" only in virtue of T_1. The experimentalist, while *testing T, applied T_1*. He *interpreted* what he saw in the light of T_1: The result was R_1. *Yet in the monotheoretical model of the explanatory theory under test this interpretative theory does not appear at all.*

But what if T_1, the interpretative theory, is false? Why not "apply" T rather than T_1 and claim that atomic weights *must be* whole numbers? Then *this* will be a "hard fact" in the light of T, and T_1 will be overthrown. Perhaps additional new purifying procedures must be invented and applied.

The problem is then *not* when we should stick to a *"theory"* in the face of *"known facts"* and when the other way round. The problem is *not* what to do when "theories" clash with "facts." Such a "clash" is only suggested by the *"monotheoretical deductive model."* Whether a proposition is a *"fact"* or a *"theory"* in the context of a test-situation depends on our methodological decision. "Empirical basis of a theory" is a mono-theoretical notion, it is *relative* to some mono-theoretical deductive structure. We may use it as first approximation; but in case of "appeal" by the theoretician, we must use a *pluralistic model*. In

the pluralistic model the clash is not "between theories and facts" but between two high-level theories: between an *interpretative theory* to provide the facts and an *explanatory theory* to explain them; and the interpretative theory may be on quite as high a level as the explanatory theory. The clash is then not any more between a logically higher-level theory and a lower-level falsifying hypothesis. The problem should not be put in terms of whether a *"refutation"* is real or not. The problem is how to repair an *inconsistency* between the "explanatory theory" under test and the—explicit or hidden—"interpretative" theories; or, if you wish, *the problem is which theory to consider as the interpretative one which provides the "hard" facts and which the explanatory one which "tentatively" explains them*. In a mono-theoretical model we regard the higher-level theory as an *explanatory theory to be judged by the "facts"* delivered from outside (by the authoritative experimentalist): In the case of a clash we reject the explanation.[95] In a pluralistic model we may decide, alternatively, to regard the higher-level theory as an *interpretative theory to judge the "facts"* delivered from outside: In case of a clash we may reject the "facts" as "monsters." In a pluralistic model of testing, several theories—more or less deductively organized—are soldered together.

This argument alone would be enough to show the correctness of the conclusion, which we drew from a different earlier argument, that experiments do not simply overthrow theories, that no theory forbids a state of affairs specifiable in advance.[96] It is not that we propose a theory and Nature may shout NO; rather, we propose a maze of theories, and Nature may shout INCONSISTENT. . . .

The problem is then *shifted* from the old prob-

---

[95] The decision to use some monotheoretical model is clearly vital for the naive falsificationist to enable him to reject a theory on the *sole* ground of experimental evidence. *It is in line with the necessity for him to divide sharply, at least in a test-situation, the body of science into two: the problematic and the unproblematic.* (Cf. above p. 178–179) *It is only the theory he decides to regard as problematic which he articulates in his deductive model of criticism.*

[96] Cf. *above*, p. 174.

lem of replacing a theory refuted by "facts" to the new problem of how to resolve inconsistencies between closely associated theories. Which of the mutually inconsistent theories should be eliminated? The sophisticated falsificationist can answer that question easily: One has to try to replace first one, then the other, then possibly both, and opt for that new set-up which provides the biggest increase in corroborated content, which provides the most progressive problemshift.[97]

Thus we have established an appeal procedure in case the theoretician wishes to question the negative verdict of the experimentalist. The theoretician may demand that the experimentalist specify his "interpretative theory,"[98] and he may then replace it—to the experimentalist's annoyance—by a better one in the light of which his originally "refuted" theory may receive positive appraisal.[99]

But even this appeal procedure cannot do more than *postpone* the conventional decision. For the verdict of the appeal court is not infallible either. When we decide whether it is the replacement of the "interpretative" or of the "explanatory" theory that produces novel facts, we again

must take a decision about the acceptance or rejection of basic statements. But then we have only *postponed*—and possibly *improved*—the decision, not avoided it.[100] The difficulties concerning the empirical basis which confronted "naive" falsificationism cannot be avoided by "sophisticated" falsificationism either. Even if we regard a theory as "factual," that is, if our slow-moving and limited imagination cannot offer an alternative to it (as Feyerabend used to put it), we have to make, at least occasionally and temporarily, decisions about its truth-value. *Even then, experience still remains, in an important sense, the "impartial arbiter"[101] of scientific controversy.* We cannot get rid of the problem of the "empirical basis," if we want to learn from experience[102]: but we can make our learning less dogmatic—but also less fast and less dramatic. By regarding some observational theories as problematic we may make our methodology more flexible: but we cannot articulate and include *all* "background knowledge" (or "background ignorance"?) into our critical deductive model. This process is bound to be piecemeal and some conventional line must be drawn at any given time.

There is one objection even to the sophisticated version of methodological falsificationism which cannot be answered without some concession to Duhemian "simplicism." The objection is the so-called "tacking paradox." According to our definitions, adding to a theory completely disconnected low-level hypotheses may constitute a "progressive shift." It is difficult to eliminate such makeshift shifts without demanding that "the additional assertions must be connected with the contradicting assertion *more intimately* than by mere conjunction."[103] This, of course, is a sort of sim-

---

[97] For instance, in our earlier example (cf. *above*, p. 178 ff.) some may try to replace the gravitational theory with a new one and others may try to replace the radio-optics by a new one: We choose the way which offers the more spectacular growth, the more progressive problemshift.

[98] Criticism does not *assume* a fully articulated deductive structure: It creates it. (Incidentally, this is the main message of my [1963–4].)

[99] A classical example of this pattern is Newton's relation to Flamsteed, the first Astronomer Royal. For instance, Newton visited Flamsteed on 1 September 1694, when working full time on his lunar theory; told him to reinterpret some of his data since they contradicted his own theory; and he explained to him exactly how to do it. Flamsteed obeyed Newton and wrote to him on 7 October: "Since you went home, I examined the observations I employed for determining the greatest equations of the earth's orbit, and considering the moon's places at the times. . . ., I find that (*if, as you intimate, the earth inclines on that side the moon that is*) you may abate abt 20″ from it . . . ." Thus Newton constantly criticized and corrected Flamsteed's observational theories. Newton taught Flamsteed, for instance, a better theory of the refractive power of the atmosphere; Flamsteed accepted this and corrected his original "data." One can understand the constant humiliation and slowly increasing fury of this great observer, having his data criticized and improved by a man who, on his own confession, made no observations himself: It was this feeling—I suspect—which led finally to a vicious personal controversy.

[100] The same applies to the third type of decision. If we reject a stochastic hypothesis only for one which, in our sense, supersedes it, the exact form of the "rejection rules" becomes *less* important.

[101] Popper [1945], Vol. II, Chapter 23, p. 218.

[102] Agassi is then wrong in his thesis that "observation reports may be accepted as false and hence the problem of the empirical basis is thereby disposed of" (Agassi [1966], p. 20).

[103] Feyerabend [1965], p. 226.

plicity requirement which would assure the continuity in the series of theories which can be said to constitute *one* problemshift.

This leads us to further problems. For one of the crucial features of sophisticated falsificationism is that it replaces the concept of *theory* as the basic concept of the logic of discovery by the concept of *series of theories. It is a succession of theories and not one given theory which is appraised as scientific or pseudo-scientific.* But the members of such series of theories are usually connected by a remarkable *continuity* which welds them into *research programmes.* This *continuity*—reminiscent of Kuhnian "normal science"—plays a vital role in the history of science; the main problems of the logic of discovery cannot be satisfactorily discussed except in the framework of a *methodology of research programmes.*

A METHODOLOGY OF SCIENTIFIC RESEARCH PROGRAMMES

I have discussed the problem of objective appraisal of scientific growth in terms of progressive and degenerating problemshifts in series of scientific theories. The most important such series in the growth of science are characterized by a certain *continuity* which connects their members. This continuity evolves from a genuine research programme adumbrated at the start.[104] The programme consists of methodological rules: Some tell us what paths of research to avoid (*negative heuristic*), and others what paths to pursue (*positive heuristic*).

Even science as a whole can be regarded as a huge research programme with Popper's supreme heuristic rule: "Devise conjectures which have more empirical content than their predecessors." Such methodological rules may be formulated, as

Popper pointed out, as metaphysical principles.[105] For instance, the *universal* anticonventionalist rule against exception-barring may be stated as the metaphysical principle: "Nature does not allow exceptions." This is why Watkins called such rules "influential metaphysics."[106]

But what I have primarily in mind is not science as a whole, but rather *particular* research programmes, such as the one known as "Cartesian metaphysics." Cartesian metaphysics, that is, the mechanistic theory of the universe—according to which the universe is a huge clockwork (and system of vortices) with push as the only cause of motion—functioned as a powerful heuristic principle. It discouraged work on scientific theories—like [the "essentialist" version of] Newton's theory of action at a distance—which were inconsistent with it (*negative heuristic*). On the other hand, it encouraged work on auxiliary hypotheses which might have saved it from apparent counterevidence—like Keplerian ellipses (positive heuristic).[107]

Negative Heuristic: The "Hard Core" of the Programme.

All scientific research programmes may be characterized by their *"hard core."* The negative heuristic of the programme forbids us to direct the *modus tollens* at this "hard core." Instead, we must use our ingenuity to articulate or even invent "auxiliary hypotheses," which form a *protective belt* around this core, and we must redirect the *modus tollens* to *these.* It is this protective belt of auxiliary hypotheses which has to bear the brunt of tests and get adjusted and re-adjusted, or even completely replaced, to defend the thus-hardened core. A research programme is successful if all this leads to a progressive problemshift, unsuccessful if it leads to a degenerating problemshift.

---

[104] One may point out that the negative and positive heuristic gives a rough (implicit) definition of the "conceptual framework" (and consequently of the language). The recognition that the history of science is the history of research programmes rather than of theories may therefore be seen as a partial vindication of the view that the history of science is the history of conceptual frameworks or of scientific languages.

[105] Popper [1934], Sections II and 70. I use "metaphysical" as a technical term of naive falsificationism: A contingent proposition is "metaphysical" if it has no "potential falsifiers."

[106] Watkins [1958]. . . .

[107] For this Cartesian research programme, cf. Popper [1958] and Watkins [1958], pp. 350–1.

The classical example of a successful research programme is Newton's gravitational theory, possibly the most successful research programme ever. When it was first produced, it was submerged in an ocean of "anomalies" (or, if you wish, "counterexamples"[108]), and opposed by the observational theories supporting these anomalies. But Newtonians turned, with brilliant tenacity and ingenuity, one counter-instance after another into corroborating instances, primarily by overthrowing the original observational theories in the light of which this "contrary evidence" was established. In the process they themselves produced new counter-examples which they again resolved. They "turned each new difficulty into a new victory of their programme."[109]

In Newton's program the negative heuristic bids us to divert the *modus tollens* from Newton's three laws of dynamics and his law of gravitation. This "core" is "irrefutable" by the methodological decision of its protagonists: Anomalies must lead to changes only in the "protective" belt of auxiliary, "observational" hypotheses and initial conditions.[110]

I have given a contrived micro-example of a progressive Newtonian problemshift.[111] If we analyse it, it turns out that each successive link in this exercise predicts some new fact; each step represents an increase in empirical content: The example constitutes a *consistently progressive theoretical shift*. Also, each prediction is in the end verified; although on three subsequent occasions they may have seemed momentarily to be "refuted."[112] While "theoretical progress" (in the sense here described) may be verified immediately . . . , "empirical progress" cannot, and in a research programme we may be frustrated by a long

series of "refutations" before ingenious and lucky content-increasing auxiliary hypotheses turn a chain of defeats—*with hindsight*—into a resounding success story, either by revising some false "facts" or by adding novel auxiliary hypotheses. We may then say that we must require that each step of a research programme be consistently content-increasing: that each step constitute a *consistently progressive theoretical problemshift*. All we need in addition to this is that at least every now and then the increase in content should be seen to be retrospectively corroborated: The programme as a whole should also display an *intermittently progressive empirical shift*. We do not demand that each step produce *immediately* an *observed* new fact. Our term *intermittently* gives sufficient *rational* scope for dogmatic adherence to a programme in face of *prima facie* "refutations."

The idea of "negative heuristic" of a scientific research programme rationalizes classical conventionalism to a considerable extent. We may rationally decide not to allow "refutations" to transmit falsity to the hard core as long as the corroborated empirical content of the protecting belt of auxiliary hypotheses increases. But our approach differs from Poincaré's justificationist conventionalism in the sense that, unlike Poincaré's, we maintain that if and when the programme ceases to anticipate novel facts, its hard core might have to be abandoned: that is, *our* hard core, unlike Poincaré's, may crumble under certain conditions. In this sense we side with Duhem who thought that such a possibility must be allowed for;[113] but for Duhem the reason for such crumbling is purely *aesthetic*,[114] while for us it is mainly *logical and empirical*.

Positive Heuristic: The Construction of the "Protective Belt" and the Relative Autonomy of Theoretical Science.

Research programmes, besides their negative heuristic, are also characterized by their positive heuristic.

---

[108] For the clarification of the concepts of "counterexample" and "anomaly" cf. *above*, p. 180. . . .

[109] Laplace [1796], Livre IV, Chapter ii.

[110] The actual hard core of a programme does not actually emerge fully armed like Athene from the head of Zeus. It develops slowly, by a long, preliminary process of trial and error. In this paper this process is not discussed.

[111] Cf. *above*, pp. 174–175. For *real* examples, cf. my [1970].

[112] The "refutation" was each time successfully diverted to "hidden lemmas"; that is, to lemmas emerging, as it were, from the *ceteris paribus* clause.

[113] Cf. *above*, p. 177.

[114] Ibid.

Even the most rapidly and consistently progressive research programmes can digest their "counter-evidence" only piecemeal: Anomalies are never completely exhausted. But it should not be thought that yet unexplained anomalies—"puzzles" as Kuhn might call them—are taken in random order, and the protective belt built up in an eclectic fashion, without any preconceived order. The order is usually decided in the theoretician's cabinet, independently of the *known* anomalies. Few theoretical scientists engaged in a research programme pay undue attention to "refutations." They have a long-term research policy which anticipates these refutations. This research policy, or order of research, is set out—in more or less detail—in the *positive heuristic* of the research programme. The negative heuristic specifies the "hard core" of the programme which is "irrefutable" by the methodological decision of its protagonists; the positive heuristic consists of a partially articulated set of suggestions or hints on how to change, develop the "refutable variants" of the research programme, how to modify, sophisticate, the "refutable" protective belt.

The positive heuristic of the programme saves the scientist from becoming confused by the ocean of anomalies. The positive heuristic sets out a programme which lists a chain of ever more complicated *models* simulating reality: The scientist's attention is riveted on building his models following instructions which are laid down in the positive part of his programme. He ignores the *actual* counterexamples, the available "*data*."[115] Newton first worked out his programme for a planetary system with a fixed point-like sun and one single point-like planet. It was in this model that he derived his inverse square law for Kepler's ellipse. But this model was forbidden by Newton's own third law of dynamics; therefore, the model had to be replaced by one in which both sun and planet revolved round their common centre of gravity. This change was not motivated by any observation (the data did not suggest an "anomaly" here) but by a theoretical difficulty in developing the programme. Then he worked out the programme for more planets as if there were only heliocentric but no interplanetary forces. Then he worked out the case where the sun and planets were not mass-points but mass-*balls*. Again, for this change he did not *need* the observation of an anomaly; infinite density was forbidden by an (inarticulated) touchstone theory, therefore planets *had* to be extended. This change involved considerable mathematical difficulties, held up Newton's work—and delayed the publication of the *Principia* by more than a decade. Having solved this "puzzle," he started work on *spinning balls* and their wobbles. Then he admitted interplanetary forces and started work on *perturbations*. At this point he started to look more anxiously at the facts. Many of them were beautifully explained (qualitatively) by this model, many were not. It was then that he started to work on *bulging* planets, rather than round planets, etc.

Newton despised people who, like Hooke, stumbled on a first naive model but did not have the tenacity and ability to develop it into a research programme, and who thought that a first version, a mere aside, constituted a "discovery." He held up publication until his programme had achieved a remarkable progressive shift.[116]

Most, if not all, Newtonian "puzzles," leading to a series of new variants superseding each other, were foreseeable at the time of Newton's first naive model and no doubt Newton and his colleagues *did* foresee them: Newton must have been

---

[115] If a scientist (or mathematician) has a positive heuristic, he refuses to be drawn into observation. He will "lie down on his couch, shut his eyes and forget about the data." (Cf. my [1963–4], especially pp. 300 ff., where there is a detailed case study of such a programme.) Occasionally, of course, he will ask Nature a shrewd question: he will then be encouraged by Nature's *YES*, but not discouraged by its *NO*.

[116] Reichenbach, following Cajori, gives a different explanation of what delayed Newton in the publication of his *Principia*: "To his disappointment he found that the observational results disagreed with his calculations. Rather than set any theory, however beautiful, before the facts, Newton put the manuscript of his theory into his drawer. Some twenty years later, after new measurements of the circumference of the earth had been made by a French expedition, Newton saw that the figures on which he had based his test were false and that the improved figures agreed with his theoretical calculation. It was only after this test that he published his law . . . . The story of Newton is one of the most striking illustrations of the method of modern science" (Reichenbach [1951], pp. 101–2). Feyerabend criticizes Reichenbach's account (Feyerabend [1965], p. 229), but does not give an alternative *rationale*.

fully aware of the blatant falsity of his first variants.[117] Nothing shows the existence of a positive heuristic of a research programme clearer than this fact: This is why one speaks of "models" in research programmes. A "*model*" is a set of initial conditions (possibly together with some of the observational theories) which one knows is *bound* to be replaced during the further development of the programme, and one even knows, more or less, how. This shows once more how irrelevant "refutations" of any specific variant are in a research programme: Their existence is fully expected, the positive heuristic is there as the strategy both for predicting (producing) and digesting them. Indeed, if the positive heuristic is clearly spelt out, the difficulties of the programme are mathematical rather than empirical.[118]

One may formulate the "positive heuristic" of a research programme as a "metaphysical" principle. For instance, one may formulate Newton's programme like this: "The planets are essentially gravitating spinning-tops of roughly spherical shape." This idea was never *rigidly* maintained: The planets are not *just* gravitational, they have also, for example, electromagnetic characteristics which may influence their motion. Positive heuristic is thus in general more flexible than negative heuristic. Moreover, it occasionally happens that when a research programme gets into a degenerating phase, a little revolution or a *creative shift* in its positive heuristic may push it forward again.[119] It is better therefore to separate the "hard core" from the more flexible metaphysical principles expressing the positive heuristic.

Our considerations show that the positive heuristic forges ahead with almost complete disregard of "refutations": It may seem that it is the "*verifications*"[120] rather than the refutations which pro-

vide the contact points with reality. Although one must point out that any "verification" of the $n + 1$-th version of the programme is a refutation of the nth version, we cannot deny that *some* defeats of the subsequent versions are always foreseen: It is the "verifications" which keep the programme going, recalcitrant instances notwithstanding.

We may appraise research programmes, even after their "elimination," for their *heuristic power:* How many new facts did they produce, how great was "their capacity to explain their refutations in the course of their growth"?[121]

(We may also appraise them for the stimulus they gave to mathematics. The real difficulties for the theoretical scientist arise rather from the *mathematical difficulties* of the programme than from anomalies. The greatness of the Newtonian programme comes partly from the development—by Newtonians—of classical infinitesimal analysis which was a crucial precondition of its success.)

Thus the methodology of scientific research programmes accounts for the *relative autonomy of theoretical science:* a historical fact whose rationality cannot be explained by the earlier falsificationists. Which problems scientists working in powerful research programmes rationally choose is determined by the positive heuristic of the programme rather than by psychologically worrying (or technologically urgent) anomalies. The anomalies are listed but shoved aside in the hope that they will turn, in due course, into corroborations of the programme. Only those scientists have to rivet their attention on anomalies who are either engaged in trial-and-error exercises . . . or who work in a degenerating phase of a research programme when the positive heuristic ran out of steam. (All this, of course, must sound repugnant to naive falsificationists who hold that once a theory is "refuted" by experiment (by *their* rule book), it is irrational (and dishonest) to develop it further: One has to replace the old "refuted" theory by a new, unrefuted one.) . . .

---

[117] For a further discussion of Newton's research programme, cf. my [1970].

[118] For this point cf. Truesdell [1960].

[119] Soddy's contribution to Prout's programme or Pauli's to Bohr's (old quantum theory) programme are typical examples of such creative shifts.

[120] A "verification" is a corroboration of excess content in the expanding programme. But, of course, a "verification" does not *verify* a programme: It shows only its heuristic power.

[121] Cf. my [1963–4], pp. 324–30. Unfortunately in 1963–4 I had not yet made a clear terminological distinction between theories and research programmes, and this impaired my exposition of a research programme in informal, quasi-empirical mathematics. There are fewer such shortcomings in my [1971].

REFERENCES

Agassi [1959]: "How are Facts Discovered?" *Impulse,* **3,** No. 10, pp. 2–4.

Agassi [1966]: "Sensationalism," *Mind,* N.S. **75,** pp. 1–24.

Agassi [1968]: "The Novelty of Popper's Philosophy of Science." *International Philosophical Quarterly,* **8,** pp. 442–63.

Agassi [1969]: "Popper on Learning from Experience," in Rescher (*ed.*): *Studies in the Philosophy of Science,* 1969.

Braithwaite [1938]: "The Relevance of Psychology to Logic," *Aristotelian Society Supplementary Volumes,* **17,** pp. 19–41.

Braithwaite [1953]: *Scientific Explanation,* 1953.

Dryer [1906]: *History of the Planetary Systems from Thales to Kepler,* 1906.

Duhem [1905]: *La Théorie Physique, Son Objet et Sa Structure,* 1905. English translation of the second (1914) edition: *The Aim and Structure of Physical Theory,* 1954.

Einstein [1949]: "Autobiographical Notes," in Schilpp (*ed.*): *Albert Einstein, Philosopher-Scientist,* **1,** pp. 2–95.

Feyerabend [1965]: "Reply to Criticism," in Cohen and Wartofsky (*eds.*): *Boston Studies in the Philosophy of Science,* II, pp. 223–61.

Feyerabend [1969]: "Problems of Empiricism II," in Colodny (*ed.*): *The Nature and Function of Scientific Theory,* 1969.

Feyerabend [1970]: "Against Method," *Minnesota Studies for the Philosophy of Science,* **4,** 1970.

Hempel [1952]: "Some Theses on Empirical Certainty," *The Review of Metaphysics,* **5,** pp. 620–1.

Keynes [1921]: *A Treatise on Probability,* 1921.

Koestler [1959]: *The Sleepwalkers,* 1959.

Lakatos [1962]: "Infinite Regress and the Foundations of Mathematics," *Aristotelian Society Supplementary Volume,* **36,** pp. 155–84.

Lakatos [1963–4]: "Proofs and Refutations," *The British Journal for the Philosophy of Science,* **14,** pp. 1–25, 120–39, 221–43, 296–342.

Lakatos [1968a]: "Changes in the Problem of Inductive Logic," in Lakatos (*ed.*): *The Problem of Inductive Logic,* 1968, pp. 315–417.

Lakatos [1968b]: "Criticism and the Methodology of Scientific Research Programmes," in *Proceedings of the Aristotelian Society,* **69,** pp. 149–86.

Lakatos [1970]: *The Changing Logic of Scientific Discovery,* 1970.

Lakatos [1971]: *Proofs and Refutations and Other Essays in the Philosophy of Mathematics,* 1971.

Laplace [1796]: *Exposition du Système du Monde,* 1796.

Leibniz [1678]: Letter to Conring, 19.3.1678.

Le Roy [1899]: "Science et Philosophie," *Revue de Mé-*taphysique et de Morale, **7,** pp. 375–425, 503–62, 706–31.

Le Roy [1901]: "Un Positivisme Nouveau," *Revue de Métaphysique et de Morale,* **9,** pp. 138–53.

Medawar [1967]: *The Art of the Soluble,* 1967.

Milhaud [1896]: "*La Science Rationnelle,*" *Revue de Métaphysique et de Morale,* **4,** pp. 280–302.

Mill [1843]: *A System of Logic, Ratiocinative and Inductive, Being a Connected View of the Principles of Evidence, and the Methods of Scientific Investigation,* 1843.

Musgrave [1969a]: *Impersonal Knowledge,* Ph.D. Thesis, University of London, 1969.

Musgrave [1969b]: Review of Ziman's "Public Knowledge: An Essay Concerning the Social Dimensions of Science," in *The British Journal for the Philosophy of Science,* **20,** pp. 92–4.

Neurath [1935]: "Pseudorationalismus der Falsifikation," *Erkenntnis,* **5,** pp. 353–65.

Poincaré [1891]: "Les géométries non euclidiennes," *Revue des Sciences Pures et Appliquées,* **2,** pp. 769–74.

Poincaré [1902]: *La Science et l'Hypothèse,* 1902.

Popper [1933]: "Ein Kriterium des empirischen Charakters theoretischer Systeme," *Erkenntnis,* **3,** pp. 426–7.

Popper [1934]: *Logik der Forschung,* 1935 (expanded English edition: Popper [1959]).

Popper [1935]: "Induktionslogik und Hypothesenwahrscheinlichkeit," *Erkenntnis,* **5,** pp. 170–2.

Popper [1945]: *The Open Society and its Enemies,* I–II, 1945.

Popper [1957]: "The Aim of Science," *Ratio,* **1,** pp. 24–35.

Popper [1958]: "Philosophy and Physics"; published in *Atti del XII Congresso Internazionale di Filosofia,* Vol. **2,** 1960, pp. 363–74.

Popper [1959]: *The Logic of Scientific Discovery,* 1959.

Popper [1963]: *Conjectures and Refutations,* 1963.

Popper [1968]: "Remarks on the Problems of Demarcation and Rationality," in Lakatos and Musgrave (*eds.*): *Problems in the Philosophy of Science,* 1968, pp. 88–102.

Reichenbach [1951]: *The Rise of Scientific Philosophy,* 1951.

Russell [1943]: "Reply to Critics," in Schilpp (*ed.*): *The Philosophy of Bertrand Russell,* 1943, pp. 681–741.

Truesdell [1960]: "The Program toward Rediscovering the Rational Mechanics in the Age of Reason," *Archive of the History of Exact Sciences,* **1,** pp. 3–36.

Watkins [1957]: "Between Analytic and Empirical," *Philosophy,* **32,** pp. 112–31.

Watkins [1958]: "Influential and Confirmable Metaphysics," *Mind,* N.S. **67,** pp. 344–65.

Watkins [1960]: "When are Statements Empirical?" *British Journal for the Philosophy of Science,* **10,** pp. 287–308.

Whewell [1837]: *History of the Inductive Sciences, from the Earliest to the Present Time*. Three volumes, 1837.

Whewell [1840]: *Philosophy of the Inductive Sciences, Founded upon their History*. Two volumes, 1840.

Whewell [1858]: *Novum Organon Renovatum*. Being the second part of the philosophy of the inductive sciences. Third edition, 1858.

Wisdom [1963]: "The Refutability of 'Irrefutable' Laws," *The British Journal for the Philosophy of Science*, **13,** pp. 303–6.

Objectivity, Value Judgment, and Theory Choice

Thomas Kuhn

In the penultimate chapter of a controversial book first published fifteen years ago, I considered the ways scientists are brought to abandon one time-honored theory or paradigm in favor of another. Such decision problems, I wrote, "cannot be resolved by proof." To discuss their mechanism is, therefore, to talk "about techniques of persuasion, or about argument and counterargument in a situation in which there can be no proof." Under these circumstances, I continued, "lifelong resistance [to a new theory] . . . is not a violation of scientific standards. . . . Though the historian can always find men—Priestley, for instance—who were unreasonable to resist for as long as they did, he will not find a point at which resistance becomes illogical or unscientific."[1] Statements of that sort obviously raise the question of why, in the absence of binding criteria for scientific choice, both the number of solved scientific problems and the precision of individual problem solutions should increase so markedly with the passage of time. Confronting that issue, I sketched in my closing chapter a number of characteristics that scientists share by virtue of the training that licenses their membership in one or another community of specialists. In the absence of criteria able to dictate the choice of each individual, I argued, we do well to trust the collective judgment of scientists trained in this way. "What better criterion could there be," I asked rhetorically, "than the decision of the scientific group?"[2]

A number of philosophers have greeted remarks like these in a way that continues to surprise me. My views, it is said, make of theory choice "a matter for mob psychology."[3] Kuhn believes, I am told, that "the decision of a scientific group to adopt a new paradigm cannot be based on good reasons of any kind, factual or otherwise."[4] The debates surrounding such choices must, my critics claim, be for me "mere persuasive displays without deliberative substance."[5] Reports of this sort manifest total misunderstanding, and I have occasionally said as much in papers directed primarily to other ends. But those passing protestations have had negligible effect, and the misunderstandings continue to be important. I conclude that it is past time for me to describe, at greater length and with greater precision, what has been on my mind when I have uttered statements like the ones with which I just began. If I have been reluctant to do so in the past, that is largely because I have preferred to devote attention to areas in which my views diverge more sharply from those currently received than they do with respect to theory choice.

What, I ask to begin with, are the characteristics of a good scientific theory? Among a number of quite usual answers I select five, not because

[1] *The Structure of Scientific Revolutions*, 2d ed. (Chicago, 1970), pp. 148, 151–52, 159. All the passages from which these fragments are taken appeared in the same form in the first edition, published in 1962.

[2] Ibid., p. 170.

[3] Imre Lakatos, "Falsification and the Methodology of Scientific Research Programs," in I. Lakatos and A. Musgrave. eds., *Criticism and the Growth of Knowledge* (Cambridge, 1970), pp. 91–195. The quoted phrase, which appears on p. 178, is italicized in the original.

[4] Dudley Shapere. "Meaning and Scientific Change," in R. G. Colodny. ed., *Mind and Cosmos: Essays in Contemporary Science and Philosophy*. University of Pittsburgh Series in the Philosophy of Science, vol. 3 (Pittsburgh, 1966), pp. 41–85. The quotation will be found on p. 67.

[5] Israel Scheffler, *Science and Subjectivity* (Indianapolis, 1967), p. 81.

From *The Essential Tension: Selected Studies in Scientific Tradition and Change* by Thomas Kuhn (1977), pp. 320–339. © 1977 by the University of Chicago. Reprinted by permission of the author and University of Chicago Press.

they are exhaustive, but because they are individually important and collectively sufficiently varied to indicate what is at stake. First, a theory should be accurate: Within its domain, that is, consequences deducible from a theory should be in demonstrated agreement with the results of existing experiments and observations. Second, a theory should be consistent, not only internally or with itself, but also with other currently accepted theories applicable to related aspects of nature. Third, it should have broad scope: In particular, a theory's consequences should extend far beyond the particular observations, laws, or subtheories it was initially designed to explain. Fourth, and closely related, it should be simple, bringing order to phenomena that in its absence would be individually isolated and, as a set, confused. Fifth—a somewhat less standard item, but one of special importance to actual scientific decisions—a theory should be fruitful of new research findings: It should, that is, disclose new phenomena or previously unnoted relationships among those already known.[6] These five characteristics—accuracy, consistency, scope, simplicity, and fruitfulness— are all standard criteria for evaluating the adequacy of a theory. If they had not been, I would have devoted far more space to them in my book, for I agree entirely with the traditional view that they play a vital role when scientists must choose between an established theory and an upstart competitor. Together with others of much the same sort, they provide *the* shared basis for theory choice.

Nevertheless, two sorts of difficulties are regularly encountered by the men who must use these criteria in choosing, say, between Ptolemy's astronomical theory and Copernicus's, between the oxygen and phlogiston theories of combustion, or between Newtonian mechanics and the quantum theory. Individually the criteria are imprecise: Individuals may legitimately differ about their application to concrete cases. In addition, when deployed together, they repeatedly prove to conflict with one another; accuracy may, for example, dictate the choice of one theory, scope the choice of its competitor. Since these difficulties, especially the first, are also relatively familiar, I shall devote little time to their elaboration. Though my argument does demand that I illustrate them briefly, my views will begin to depart from those long current only after I have done so.

Begin with accuracy, which for present purposes I take to include not only quantitative agreement but qualitative as well. Ultimately it proves the most nearly decisive of all the criteria, partly because it is less equivocal than the others but especially because predictive and explanatory powers, which depend on it, are characteristics that scientists are particularly unwilling to give up. Unfortunately, however, theories cannot always be discriminated in terms of accuracy. Copernicus's system, for example, was not more accurate than Ptolemy's until drastically revised by Kepler more than sixty years after Copernicus's death. If Kepler or someone else had not found other reasons to choose heliocentric astronomy, those improvements in accuracy would never have been made, and Copernicus's work might have been forgotten. More typically, of course, accuracy does permit discriminations, but not the sort that lead regularly to unequivocal choice. The oxygen theory, for example, was universally acknowledged to account for observed weight relations in chemical reactions, something the phlogiston theory had previously scarcely attempted to do. But the phlogiston theory, unlike its rival, could account for the metals' being much more alike than the ores from which they were formed. One theory thus matched experience better in one area, the other in another. To choose between them on the basis of accuracy, a scientist would need to decide the area in which accuracy was more significant. About that matter chemists could and did differ without violating any of the criteria outlined above, or any others yet to be suggested.

However important it may be, therefore, accuracy by itself is seldom or never a sufficient crite-

---

[6] The last criterion, fruitfulness, deserves more emphasis than it has yet received. A scientist choosing between two theories ordinarily knows that his decision will have a bearing on his subsequent research career. Of course he is especially attracted by a theory that promises the concrete successes for which scientists are ordinarily rewarded.

rion for theory choice. Other criteria must function as well, but they do not eliminate problems. To illustrate I select just two—consistency and simplicity—asking how they functioned in the choice between the heliocentric and geocentric systems. As astronomical theories both Ptolemy's and Copernicus's were internally consistent, but their relation to related theories in other fields was very different. The stationary central earth was an essential ingredient of received physical theory, a tight-knit body of doctrine that explained, among other things, how stones fall, how water pumps function, and why the clouds move slowly across the skies. Heliocentric astronomy, which required the earth's motion, was inconsistent with the existing scientific explanation of these and other terrestrial phenomena. The consistency criterion, by itself, therefore, spoke unequivocally for the geocentric tradition.

Simplicity, however, favored Copernicus, but only when evaluated in a quite special way. If, on the one hand, the two systems were compared in terms of the actual computational labor required to predict the position of a planet at a particular time, then they proved substantially equivalent. Such computations were what astronomers did, and Copernicus's system offered them no labor-saving techniques; in that sense it was not simpler than Ptolemy's. If, on the other hand, one asked about the amount of mathematical apparatus required to explain, not the detailed quantitative motions of the planets, but merely their gross qualitative features—limited elongation, retrograde motion, and the like—then, as every schoolchild knows, Copernicus required only one circle per planet, Ptolemy two. In that sense the Copernican theory was the simpler, a fact vitally important to the choices made by both Kepler and Galileo and thus essential to the ultimate triumph of Copernicanism. But that sense of simplicity was not the only one available, nor even the one most natural to professional astronomers, men whose task was the actual computation of planetary position.

Because time is short and I have multiplied examples elsewhere, I shall here simply assert that these difficulties in applying standard criteria of choice are typical and that they arise no less force-

fully in twentieth-century situations than in the earlier and better-known examples I have just sketched. When scientists must choose between competing theories, two men fully committed to the same list of criteria for choice may nevertheless reach different conclusions. Perhaps they interpret simplicity differently or have different convictions about the range of fields within which the consistency criterion must be met. Or perhaps they agree about these matters but differ about the relative weights to be accorded to these or to other criteria when several are deployed together. With respect to divergences of this sort, no set of choice criteria yet proposed is of any use. One can explain, as the historian characteristically does, why particular men made particular choices at particular times. But for that purpose one must go beyond the list of shared criteria to characteristics of the individuals who make the choice. One must, that is, deal with characteristics that vary from one scientist to another without thereby in the least jeopardizing their adherence to the canons that make science scientific. Though such canons do exist and should be discoverable (doubtless the criteria of choice with which I began are among them), they are not by themselves sufficient to determine the decisions of individual scientists. For that purpose the shared canons must be fleshed out in ways that differ from one individual to another.

Some of the differences I have in mind result from the individual's previous experience as a scientist. In what part of the field was he at work when confronted by the need to choose? How long had he worked there; how successful had he been; and how much of his work depended on concepts and techniques challenged by the new theory? Other factors relevant to choice lie outside the sciences. Kepler's early election of Copernicanism was due in part to his immersion in the Neoplatonic and Hermetic movements of his day; German Romanticism predisposed those it affected toward both recognition and acceptance of energy conservation; nineteenth-century British social thought had a similar influence on the availability and acceptability of Darwin's concept of the struggle for existence. Still other significant differences are functions of personality. Some scientists place more premium than others on originality and are correspondingly more willing to take risks; some scientists prefer comprehensive, unified theories to precise and detailed problem solutions of apparently narrower scope. Differentiating factors like these are described by my critics as subjective and are contrasted with the shared or objective criteria from which I began. Though I shall later question that use of terms, let me for the moment accept it. My point is, then, that every individual choice between competing theories depends on a mixture of objective and subjective factors, or of shared and individual criteria. Since the latter have not ordinarily figured in the philosophy of science, my emphasis upon them has made my belief in the former hard for my critics to see.

What I have said so far is primarily simply descriptive of what goes on in the sciences at times of theory choice. As description, furthermore, it has not been challenged by my critics, who reject instead my claim that these facts of scientific life have philosophic import. Taking up that issue, I shall begin to isolate some, though I think not vast, differences of opinion. Let me begin by asking how philosophers of science can for so long have neglected the subjective elements which, they freely grant, enter regularly into the actual theory choices made by individual scientists? Why have these elements seemed to them an index only of human weakness, not at all of the nature of scientific knowledge?

One answer to that question is, of course, that few philosophers, if any, have claimed to possess either a complete or an entirely well-articulated list of criteria. For some time, therefore, they could reasonably expect that further research would eliminate residual imperfections and produce an algorithm able to dictate rational, unanimous choice. Pending that achievement, scientists would have no alternative but to supply subjectively what the best current list of objective criteria still lacked. That some of them might still do so even with a perfected list at hand would then be an index only of the inevitable imperfection of human nature.

That sort of answer may still prove to be cor-

rect, but I think no philosopher still expects that it will. The search for algorithmic decision procedures has continued for some time and produced both powerful and illuminating results. But those results all presuppose that individual criteria of choice can be unambiguously stated and also that, if more than one proves relevant, an appropriate weight function is at hand for their joint application. Unfortunately, where the choice at issue is between scientific theories, little progress has been made toward the first of these desiderata and none toward the second. Most philosophers of science would, therefore, I think, now regard the sort of algorithm which has traditionally been sought as a not quite attainable ideal. I entirely agree and shall henceforth take that much for granted.

Even an ideal, however, if it is to remain credible, requires some demonstrated relevance to the situations in which it is supposed to apply. Claiming that such demonstration requires no recourse to subjective factors, my critics seem to appeal, implicitly or explicitly, to the well-known distinction between the contexts of discovery and of justification.[7] They concede, that is, that the subjective factors I invoke play a significant role in the discovery or invention of new theories, but they also insist that that inevitably intuitive process lies outside of the bounds of philosophy of science and is irrelevant to the question of scientific objectivity. Objectivity enters science, they continue, through the processes by which theories are tested, justified, or judged. Those processes do not, or at least need not, involve subjective factors at all. They can be governed by a set of (objective) criteria shared by the entire group competent to judge.

I have already argued that that position does not fit observations of scientific life and shall now assume that that much has been conceded. What is now at issue is a different point: whether or not this invocation of the distinction between contexts of discovery and of justification provides even a plausible and useful idealization. I think it does

---

[7] The least equivocal example of this position is probably the one developed in Scheffler, *Science and Subjectivity,* Chap. 4.

not and can best make my point by suggesting first a likely source of its apparent cogency. I suspect that my critics have been misled by science pedagogy or what I have elsewhere called textbook science. In science teaching, theories are presented together with exemplary applications, and those applications may be viewed as evidence. But that is not their primary pedagogic function (science students are distressingly willing to receive the word from professors and texts). Doubtless *some* of them were *part* of the evidence at the time actual decisions were being made, but they represent only a fraction of the considerations relevant to the decision process. The context of pedagogy differs almost as much from the context of justification as it does from that of discovery.

Full documentation of that point would require longer argument than is appropriate here, but two aspects of the way in which philosophers ordinarily demonstrate the relevance of choice criteria are worth noting. Like the science textbooks on which they are often modelled, books and articles on the philosophy of science refer again and again to the famous crucial experiments: Foucault's pendulum, which demonstrates the motion of the earth; Cavendish's demonstration of gravitational attraction; or Fizeau's measurement of the relative speed of sound in water and air. These experiments are paradigms of good reason for scientific choice; they illustrate the most effective of all the sorts of argument which could be available to a scientist uncertain which of two theories to follow; they are vehicles for the transmission of criteria of choice. But they also have another characteristic in common. By the time they were performed no scientist still needed to be convinced of the validity of the theory their outcome is now used to demonstrate. Those decisions had long since been made on the basis of significantly more equivocal evidence. The exemplary crucial experiments to which philosophers again and again refer would have been historically relevant to theory choice only if they had yielded unexpected results. Their use as illustrations provides needed economy to science pedagogy, but they scarcely illuminate the character of the choices that scientists are called upon to make.

Standard philosophical illustrations of scientific choice have another troublesome characteristic. The only arguments discussed are, as I have previously indicated, the ones favorable to the theory that, in fact, ultimately triumphed. Oxygen, we read, could explain weight relations, phlogiston could not; but nothing is said about the phlogiston theory's power or about the oxygen theory's limitations. Comparisons of Ptolemy's theory with Copernicus's proceed in the same way. Perhaps these examples should not be given since they contrast a developed theory with one still in its infancy. But philosophers regularly use them nonetheless. If the only result of their doing so were to simplify the decision situation, one could not object. Even historians do not claim to deal with the full factual complexity of the situations they describe. But these simplifications emasculate by making choice totally unproblematic. They eliminate, that is, one essential element of the decision situations that scientists must resolve if their field is to move ahead. In those situations there are always at least some good reasons for each possible choice. Considerations relevant to the context of discovery are then relevant to justification as well; scientists who share the concerns and sensibilities of the individual who discovers a new theory are ipso facto likely to appear disproportionately frequently among that theory's first supporters. That is why it has been difficult to construct algorithms for theory choice, and also why such difficulties have seemed so thoroughly worth resolving. Choices that present problems are the ones philosophers of science need to understand. Philosophically interesting decision procedures must function where, in their absence, the decision might still be in doubt.

That much I have said before, if only briefly. Recently, however, I have recognized another, subtler source for the apparent plausibility of my critics' position. To present it, I shall briefly describe a hypothetical dialogue with one of them. Both of us agree that each scientist chooses between competing theories by deploying some Bayesian algorithm which permits him to compute a value for $p(T,E)$, i.e., for the probability of a theory T on the evidence E available both to him and to the other members of his professional group at a particular period of time. "Evidence," furthermore, we both interpret broadly to include such considerations as simplicity and fruitfulness. My critic asserts, however, that there is only one such value of p, that corresponding to objective choice, and he believes that all rational members of the group must arrive at it. I assert, on the other hand, for reasons previously given, that the factors he calls objective are insufficient to determine in full any algorithm at all. For the sake of the discussion I have conceded that each individual has an algorithm and that all their algorithms have much in common. Nevertheless, I continue to hold that the algorithms of individuals are all ultimately different by virtue of the subjective considerations with which each must complete the objective criteria before any computations can be done. If my hypothetical critic is liberal, he may now grant that these subjective differences do play a role in determining the hypothetical algorithm on which each individual relies during the early stages of the competition between rival theories. But he is also likely to claim that, as evidence increases with the passage of time, the algorithms of different individuals converge to the algorithm of objective choice with which his presentation began. For him the increasing unanimity of individual choices is evidence for their increasing objectivity and thus for the elimination of subjective elements from the decision process.

So much for the dialogue, which I have, of course, contrived to disclose the non sequitur underlying an apparently plausible position. What converges as the evidence changes over time need only be the values of p that individuals compute from their individual algorithms. Conceivably those algorithms themselves also become more alike with time, but the ultimate unanimity of theory choice provides no evidence whatsoever that they do so. If subjective factors are required to account for the decisions that initially divide the profession, they may still be present later when the profession agrees. Though I shall not here argue the point, consideration of the occasions on which a scientific community divides suggests that they actually do so.

My argument has so far been directed to two points. It first provided evidence that the choices scientists make between competing theories depend not only on shared criteria—those my critics call objective—but also on idiosyncratic factors dependent on individual biography and personality. The latter are, in my critics' vocabulary, subjective, and the second part of my argument has attempted to bar some likely ways of denying their philosophic import. Let me now shift to a more positive approach, returning briefly to the list of shared criteria—accuracy, simplicity, and the like—with which I began. The considerable effectiveness of such criteria does not, I now wish to suggest, depend on their being sufficiently articulated to dictate the choice of each individual who subscribes to them. Indeed, if they were articulated to that extent, a behavior mechanism fundamental to scientific advance would cease to function. What the tradition sees as eliminable imperfections in its rules of choice I take to be in part responses to the essential nature of science.

As so often, I begin with the obvious. Criteria that influence decisions without specifying what those decisions must be are familiar in many aspects of human life. Ordinarily, however, they are called, not criteria or rules, but maxims, norms, or values. Consider maxims first. The individual who invokes them when choice is urgent usually finds them frustratingly vague and often also in conflict one with another. Contrast "He who hesitates is lost" with "Look before you leap," or compare "Many hands make light work" with "Too many cooks spoil the broth." Individually maxims dictate different choices, collectively none at all. Yet no one suggests that supplying children with contradictory tags like these is irrelevant to their education. Opposing maxims alter the nature of the decision to be made, highlight the essential issues it presents, and point to those remaining aspects of the decision for which each individual must take responsibility himself. Once invoked, maxims like these alter the nature of the decision process and can thus change its outcome.

Values and norms provide even clearer examples of effective guidance in the presence of conflict and equivocation. Improving the quality of life is a value, and a car in every garage once followed from it as a norm. But quality of life has other aspects, and the old norm has become problematic. Or again, freedom of speech is a value, but so is preservation of life and property. In application, the two often conflict, so that judicial soul-searching, which still continues, has been required to prohibit such behavior as inciting to riot or shouting fire in a crowded theater. Difficulties like these are an appropriate source for frustration, but they rarely result in charges that values have no function or in calls for their abandonment. That response is barred to most of us by an acute consciousness that there are societies with other values and that these value differences result in other ways of life, other decisions about what may and what may not be done.

I am suggesting, of course, that the criteria of choice with which I began function not as rules, which determine choice, but as values, which influence it. Two men deeply committed to the same values may nevertheless, in particular situations, make different choices as, in fact, they do. But that difference in outcome ought not to suggest that the values scientists share are less than critically important either to their decisions or to the development of the enterprise in which they participate. Values like accuracy, consistency, and scope may prove ambiguous in application, both individually and collectively; they may, that is, be an insufficient basis for a *shared* algorithm of choice. But they do specify a great deal: what each scientist must consider in reaching a decision, what he may or may not consider relevant, and what he can legitimately be required to report as the basis for the choice he has made. Change the list, for example by adding social utility as a criterion, and some particular choices will be different, more like those one expects from an engineer. Subtract accuracy of fit to nature from the list, and the enterprise that results may not resemble science at all, but perhaps philosophy instead. Different creative disciplines are characterized, among other things, by different sets of shared values. If philosophy and engineering lie too close to the sciences, think of literature or the plastic arts. Milton's failure to set *Paradise Lost* in a Coperni-

can universe does not indicate that he agreed with Ptolemy but that he had things other than science to do.

Recognizing that criteria of choice can function as values when incomplete as rules has, I think, a number of striking advantages. First, as I have already argued at length, it accounts in detail for aspects of scientific behavior which the tradition has seen as anomalous or even irrational. More important, it allows the standard criteria to function fully in the earliest stages of theory choice, the period when they are most needed but when, on the traditional view, they function badly or not at all. Copernicus was responding to them during the years required to convert heliocentric astronomy from a global conceptual scheme to mathematical machinery for predicting planetary position. Such predictions were what astronomers valued; in their absence, Copernicus would scarcely have been heard, something which had happened to the idea of a moving earth before. That his own version convinced very few is less important than his acknowledgment of the basis on which judgments would have to be reached if heliocentricism were to survive. Though idiosyncrasy must be invoked to explain why Kepler and Galileo were early converts to Copernicus's system, the gaps filled by their efforts to perfect it were specified by shared values alone.

That point has a corollary which may be more important still. Most newly suggested theories do not survive. Usually the difficulties that evoked them are accounted for by more traditional means. Even when this does not occur, much work, both theoretical and experimental, is ordinarily required before the new theory can display sufficient accuracy and scope to generate widespread conviction. In short, before the group accepts it, a new theory has been tested over time by the research of a number of men, some working within it, others within its traditional rival. Such a mode of development, however, *requires* a decision process which permits rational men to disagree, and such disagreement would be barred by the shared algorithm which philosophers have generally sought. If it were at hand, all conforming scientists would make the same decision at the same time. With standards for acceptance set too low, they would move from one attractive global viewpoint to another, never giving traditional theory an opportunity to supply equivalent attractions. With standards set higher, no one satisfying the criterion of rationality would be inclined to try out the new theory, to articulate it in ways which showed its fruitfulness or displayed its accuracy and scope. I doubt that science would survive the change. What from one viewpoint may seem the looseness and imperfection of choice criteria conceived as rules may, when the same criteria are seen as values, appear an indispensable means of spreading the risk which the introduction or support of novelty always entails.

Even those who have followed me this far will want to know how a value-based enterprise of the sort I have described can develop as a science does, repeatedly producing powerful new techniques for prediction and control. To that question, unfortunately, I have no answer at all, but that is only another way of saying that I make no claim to have solved the problem of induction. If science did progress by virtue of some shared and binding algorithm of choice, I would be equally at a loss to explain its success. The lacuna is one I feel acutely, but its presence does not differentiate my position from the tradition.

It is, after all, no accident that my list of the values guiding scientific choice is, as nearly as makes any difference, identical with the tradition's list of rules dictating choice. Given any concrete situation to which the philosopher's rules could be applied, my values would function like his rules, producing the same choice. Any justification of induction, any explanation of why the rules worked, would apply equally to my values. Now consider a situation in which choice by shared rules proves impossible, not because the rules are wrong but because they are, as rules, intrinsically incomplete. Individuals must then still choose and be guided by the rules (now values) when they do so. For that purpose, however, each must first flesh out the rules, and each will do so in a somewhat different way even though the decision dictated by the variously completed rules may prove unanimous. If I now assume, in addition, that the group is large enough so that individual differences distribute on some normal curve, then any argument that justifies the philosopher's choice by rule should be immediately adaptable to my choice by value. A group too small, or a distribution excessively skewed by external historical pressures, would, of course, prevent the argument's transfer.[8] But those are just the circumstances under which scientific progress is itself problematic. The transfer is not then to be expected.

I shall be glad if these references to a normal distribution of individual differences and to the problem of induction make my position appear very close to more traditional views. With respect to theory choice, I have never thought my departures large and have been correspondingly startled by such charges as "mob psychology," quoted at the start. It is worth noting, however, that the positions are not quite identical, and for that purpose an analogy may be helpful. Many properties of liquids and gases can be accounted for on the kinetic theory by supposing that all molecules travel at the same speed. Among such properties are the regularities known as Boyle's and Charles's law. Other characteristics, most obviously evaporation, cannot be explained in so simple a way. To deal with them one must assume that molecular speeds differ, that they are distributed at random, governed by the laws of chance. What I have been suggesting here is that theory choice, too, can be explained only in part by a theory which attributes the same properties to all the scientists who must

---

[8] If the group is small, it is more likely that random fluctuations will result in its members' sharing an atypical set of values and therefore making choices different from those that would be made by a larger and more representative group. External environment—intellectual, ideological, or economic—must systematically affect the value system of much larger groups, and the consequences can include difficulties in introducing the scientific enterprise to societies with inimical values or perhaps even the end of that enterprise within societies where it had once flourished. In this area, however, great caution is required. Changes in the environment where science is practiced can also have fruitful effects on research. Historians often resort, for example, to differences between national environments to explain why particular innovations were initiated and at first disproportionately pursued in particular countries, e.g., Darwinism in Britain, energy conservation in Germany. At present we know substantially nothing about the minimum requisites of the social milieux within which a sciencelike enterprise might flourish.

do the choosing. Essential aspects of the process generally known as verification will be understood only by recourse to the features with respect to which men may differ while still remaining scientists. The tradition takes it for granted that such features are vital to the process of discovery, which it at once and for that reason rules out of philosophical bounds. That they may have significant functions also in the philosophically central problem of justifying theory choice is what philosophers of science have to date categorically denied.

What remains to be said can be grouped in a somewhat miscellaneous epilogue. For the sake of clarity and to avoid writing a book, I have throughout this paper utilized some traditional concepts and locutions about the viability of which I have elsewhere expressed serious doubts. For those who know the work in which I have done so, I close by indicating three aspects of what I have said which would better represent my views if cast in other terms, simultaneously indicating the main directions in which such recasting should proceed. The areas I have in mind are: value invariance, subjectivity, and partial communication. If my views of scientific development are novel—a matter about which there is legitimate room for doubt—it is in areas such as these, rather than theory choice, that my main departures from tradition should be sought.

Throughout this paper I have implicitly assumed that, whatever their initial source, the criteria or values deployed in theory choice are fixed once and for all, unaffected by their participation in transitions from one theory to another. Roughly speaking, but only very roughly, I take that to be the case. If the list of relevant values is kept short (I have mentioned five, not all independent) and if their specification is left vague, then such values as accuracy, scope, and fruitfulness are permanent attributes of science. But little knowledge of history is required to suggest that both the application of these values and, more obviously, the relative weights attached to them have varied markedly with time and also with the field of application. Furthermore, many of these varia-

tions in value have been associated with particular changes in scientific theory. Though the experience of scientists provides no philosophical justification for the values they deploy (such justification would solve the problem of induction), those values are in part learned from that experience, and they evolve with it.

The whole subject needs more study (historians have usually taken scientific values, though not scientific methods, for granted), but a few remarks will illustrate the sort of variations I have in mind. Accuracy, as a value, has with time increasingly denoted quantitative or numerical agreement, sometimes at the expense of qualitative. Before early modern times, however, accuracy in that sense was a criterion only for astronomy, the science of the celestial region. Elsewhere it was neither expected nor sought. During the seventeenth century, however, the criterion of numerical agreement was extended to mechanics, during the late eighteenth and early nineteenth centuries to chemistry and such other subjects as electricity and heat, and in this century to many parts of biology. Or think of utility, an item of value not on my initial list. It too has figured significantly in scientific development, but far more strongly and steadily for chemists than for, say, mathematicians and physicists. Or consider scope. It is still an important scientific value, but important scientific advances have repeatedly been achieved at its expense, and the weight attributed to it at times of choice has diminished correspondingly.

What may seem particularly troublesome about changes like these is, of course, that they ordinarily occur in the aftermath of a theory change. One of the objections to Lavoisier's new chemistry was the roadblocks with which it confronted the achievement of what had previously been one of chemistry's traditional goals: the explanation of qualities, such as color and texture, as well as of their changes. With the acceptance of Lavoisier's theory such explanations ceased for some time to be a value for chemists; the ability to explain qualitative variation was no longer a criterion relevant to the evaluation of chemical theory. Clearly, if such value changes had occurred as rapidly or been as complete as the theory changes to which they related, then theory choice would be value choice, and neither could provide justification for the other. But, historically, value change is ordinarily a belated and largely unconscious concomitant of theory choice, and the former's magnitude is regularly smaller than the latter's. For the functions I have here ascribed to values, such relative stability provides a sufficient basis. The existence of a feedback loop through which theory change affects the values which led to that change does not make the decision process circular in any damaging sense.

About a second respect in which my resort to tradition may be misleading, I must be far more tentative. It demands the skills of an ordinary language philosopher, which I do not possess. Still, no very acute ear for language is required to generate discomfort with the ways in which the terms "objectivity" and, more especially, "subjectivity" have functioned in this paper. Let me briefly suggest the respects in which I believe language has gone astray. "Subjective" is a term with several established uses: In one of these it is opposed to "objective," in another to "judgmental." When my critics describe the idiosyncratic features to which I appeal as subjective, they resort, erroneously I think, to the second of these senses. When they complain that I deprive science of objectivity, they conflate that second sense of subjective with the first.

A standard application of the term "subjective" is to matters of taste, and my critics appear to suppose that that is what I have made of theory choice. But they are missing a distinction standard since Kant when they do so. Like sensation reports, which are also subjective in the sense now at issue, matters of taste are undiscussable. Suppose that, leaving a movie theater with a friend after seeing a western, I exclaim: "How I liked that terrible potboiler!" My friend, if he disliked the film, may tell me I have low tastes, a matter about which, in these circumstances, I would readily agree. But, short of saying that I lied, he cannot disagree with my report that I liked the film or try to persuade me that what I said about my reaction was wrong. What is discussable in my remark is not my characterization of my internal state, my

exemplification of taste, but rather my *judgment* that the film was a potboiler. Should my friend disagree on that point, we may argue most of the night, each comparing the film with good or great ones we have seen, each revealing, implicitly or explicitly, something about how he *judges* cinematic merit, about his aesthetic. Though one of us may, before retiring, have persuaded the other, he need not have done so to demonstrate that our difference is one of judgment, not taste.

Evaluations or choices of theory have, I think, exactly this character. Not that scientists never say merely, I like such and such a theory, or I do not. After 1926 Einstein said little more than that about his opposition to the quantum theory. But scientists may always be asked to explain their choices, to exhibit the bases for their judgments. Such judgments are eminently discussable, and the man who refuses to discuss his own cannot expect to be taken seriously. Though there are, very occasionally, leaders of scientific taste, their existence tends to prove the rule. Einstein was one of the few, and his increasing isolation from the scientific community in later life shows how very limited a role taste alone can play in theory choice. Bohr, unlike Einstein, did discuss the bases for his judgment, and he carried the day. If my critics introduce the term "subjective" in a sense that opposes it to judgmental—thus suggesting that I make theory choice undiscussable, a matter of taste—they have seriously mistaken my position.

Turn now to the sense in which "subjectivity" is opposed to "objectivity," and note first that it raises issues quite separate from those just discussed. Whether my taste is low or refined, my report that I liked the film is objective unless I have lied. To my judgment that the film was a potboiler, however, the objective–subjective distinction does not apply at all, at least not obviously and directly. When my critics say I deprive theory choice of objectivity, they must, therefore, have recourse to some very different sense of subjective, presumably the one in which bias and personal likes or dislikes function instead of, or in the face of, the actual facts. But that sense of subjective does not fit the process I have been describing any better than the first. Where factors dependent on individual biography or personality must be introduced to make values applicable, no standards of factuality or actuality are being set aside. Conceivably my discussion of theory choice indicates some limitations of objectivity, but not by isolating elements properly called subjective. Nor am I even quite content with the notion that what I have been displaying are limitations. Objectivity ought to be analyzable in terms of criteria like accuracy and consistency. If these criteria do not supply all the guidance that we have customarily expected of them, then it may be the meaning rather than the limits of objectivity that my argument shows.

Turn, in conclusion, to a third respect, or set of respects, in which this paper needs to be recast. I have assumed throughout that the discussions surrounding theory choice are unproblematic, that the facts appealed to in such discussions are independent of theory, and that the discussions' outcome is appropriately called a choice. Elsewhere I have challenged all three of these assumptions, arguing that communication between proponents of different theories is inevitably partial, that what each takes to be facts depends in part on the theory he espouses, and that an individual's transfer of allegiance from theory to theory is often better described as conversion than as choice. Though all these theses are problematic as well as controversial, my commitment to them is undiminished. I shall not now defend them, but must at least attempt to indicate how what I have said here can be adjusted to conform with these more central aspects of my view of scientific development.

For that purpose I resort to an analogy I have developed in other places. Proponents of different theories are, I have claimed, like native speakers of different languages. Communication between them goes on by translation, and it raises all translation's familiar difficulties. That analogy is, of course, incomplete, for the vocabulary of the two theories may be identical, and most words function in the same ways in both. But some words in the basic as well as in the theoretical vocabularies of the two theories—words like "star" and "planet," "mixture" and "compound," or "force" and "matter"—do function differently.

Those differences are unexpected and will be discovered and localized, if at all, only by repeated experience of communication breakdown. Without pursuing the matter further, I simply assert the existence of significant limits to what the proponents of different theories can communicate to one another. The same limits make it difficult or, more likely, impossible for an individual to hold both theories in mind together and compare them point by point with each other and with nature. That sort of comparison is, however, the process on which the appropriateness of any word like "choice" depends.

Nevertheless, despite the incompleteness of their communication, proponents of different theories can exhibit to each other, not always easily, the concrete technical results achievable by those who practice within each theory. Little or no translation is required to apply at least some value criteria to those results. (Accuracy and fruitfulness are most immediately applicable, perhaps followed by scope. Consistency and simplicity are far more problematic.) However incomprehensible the new theory may be to the proponents of tradition, the exhibit of impressive concrete results will persuade at least a few of them that they must discover how such results are achieved. For that purpose they must learn to translate, perhaps by treating already published papers as a Rosetta stone or, often more effective, by visiting the innovator, talking with him, watching him and his students at work. Those exposures may not result in the adoption of the theory; some advocates of the tradition may return home and attempt to adjust the old theory to produce equivalent results. But others, if the new theory is to survive, will find that at some point in the language-learning process they have ceased to translate and begun instead to speak the language like a native. No process quite like choice has occurred, but they are practicing the new theory nonetheless. Furthermore, the factors that have led them to risk the conversion they have undergone are just the ones this paper has underscored in discussing a somewhat different process, one which, following the philosophical tradition, it has labeled theory choice.

Testing Theoretical Hypotheses

Ronald N. Giere

INTRODUCTION

Philosophers of science concerned with theories and the nature of evidence tend currently to fall into several only partially overlapping groups. One group follows its logical empiricist ancestors at least to the extent of believing that there is a "logic" in the relation between theories and evidence. This logic is now most often embedded in the theory of a rational (scientific) agent. Bayesian agents are currently most popular, but there are notable dissenters from The Bayesian Way such as Henry Kyburg and Isaac Levi. Another group derives its inspiration from the historical criticisms of logical empiricism begun a generation ago by such writers as Gerd Buchdahl, Paul Feyerabend, N. R. Hanson, Thomas Kuhn, and Stephen Toulmin. Partly because their roots tend to be in intellectual history, and partly in reaction to logical empiricism, this group emphasizes the evolution of scientific ideas and downplays the role of empirical data in the development of science. For these thinkers, the rationality of science is to be found in the historical process of science rather than in the (idealized) minds of scientists. If there is something that can rightfully be called a middle group, it consists mainly of the followers of the late Imre Lakatos, who skillfully blended Popper's version of empiricism with elements of Kuhn's account of scientific development. Yet Lakatos's "methodology of scientific research programmes" also locates the ultimate rationality of science in a larger historical process rather than in relations between particular hypotheses and particular bits of data.

The author's research has been supported in part by a grant from the National Science Foundation.

I shall be arguing for a theory of science in which the driving rational force of the scientific process is located in the testing of highly specific theoretical models against empirical data. This is not to deny that there are elements of rationality throughout the scientific enterprise. Indeed, it is only as part of an overall theory of science that one can fully comprehend what goes on in tests of individual hypotheses. Yet there is a "logic" in the parts as well as in the whole. Thus I agree with contemporary students of probability, induction, and the foundations of statistics that the individual hypothesis is a useful unit of analysis. On the other hand, I reject completely the idea that one can reduce the rationality of the scientific process to the rationality of individual agents. The rationality of science is to be found not so much in the heads of scientists as in objective features of its methods and institutions.

In this paper I shall not attempt even to outline an overall theory of science. Rather, I shall concentrate on clarifying the nature of tests of individual hypotheses, bringing in further elements of a broader theory of science only when necessary to advance this narrower objective. My account of how individual hypotheses are tested is not entirely new. Indeed, it is a version of the most ancient of scientific methods, the method of hypothesis, or, the hypothetico-deductive (H-D) method. But some elements of the account are new, and some have been borrowed from other contexts.

MODELS, HYPOTHESES, AND THEORIES

Views about the nature of evidence and its role in science depend crucially on views about the na-

From Testing Scientific Theories, John Earman, Ed., *Minnesota Studies in the Philosophy of Science,* Vol. X (1983), pp. 269–298. Reprinted by permission of University of Minnesota Press.

ture of hypotheses and theories. The major divergences of current opinion in the philosophy of science are correlated with strong differences as to just what the highly honorific title "theory" should apply. For the moment I shall avoid the term "theory" and speak of "models" and "hypotheses" instead.

My use of the term "model" (or "theoretical model") is intended to capture current scientific usage—at least insofar as that usage is itself consistent. To this end, I would adopt a form of the "semantic" or definitional view of theories (hereafter, models). On this view, one creates a model by defining a type of system. For most purposes one can simply identify the model with the definition. But to avoid the consequence that rendering the definition in another language would create a different model, it is convenient to invent an abstract entity, the system defined, and call it the model. This move also preserves consistency with the logician's and mathematician's notion of a model as a set of objects that satisfies a given linguistic structure. For present purposes it will make no difference whether we focus on the definition itself or its nonlinguistic counterpart, so long as there is no presumption that in referring to "the model" one is thereby committed to there being any such thing in the empirical world.

Philosophers differ as to the appropriate form of these definitions. I much prefer the state-space approach of van Fraassen or Suppe to the set-theoretical approach of Suppes, Sneed, and Stegmüller, partly because the former seems better to correspond to scientific practice.[1] Here a system is defined by a set of state variables and system laws that specify the physically possible states of the system and perhaps also its possible evolutions. Thus, for example, classical thermodynamics may

be understood as defining an ideal gas in terms of three variables, pressure, volume and temperature, and as specifying that these are related by the law $PV = kT$. Similarly, classical mechanics defines a Newtonian particle system in terms of a 6n-dimensional space (three components each of position and momentum for each particle) and Newton's laws of motion. A wide variety of models in population genetics (with states given by gene frequencies and development governed by Mendel's laws) are also easily expressed in this framework. So also are learning models in psychology and models of inventory and queuing in economics.

Viewed as definitions, theoretical models have by themselves no empirical content—they make no claims about the world. But they may be *used* to make claims about the world. This is done by identifying elements of the model with elements of real systems and then claiming that the real system exhibits the structure of the model. Such a claim I shall call a *theoretical hypothesis*. These are either true or false. From a logical point of view, the definition of a model amounts to the definition of a predicate. A theoretical hypothesis, then, has the logical form of predication: This is an *X*, where the corresponding definition tells what it is to be an *X*.

Our primary concern here is with the testing of theoretical hypotheses and the role of such tests in the overall practice of science. For such purposes, the *logical* differences between statements and definitions are not very important. More important are the implications of this difference for what we take to be the form of the major claims of science.

Since Aristotle it has been assumed that the overall goal of science is the discovery of *true universal generalizations* of the form: All A's are B. Moreover, it has often been supposed that the wider the scope of the antecedent the better. Thus Newton's Law of Universal Gravitation, interpreted as a generalization covering "all bodies," is seen as the epitome of a scientific conclusion. Philosophers, beginning with Hume, have reduced the concept of physical necessity to that of universality, and scientific explanation has been analyzed in terms of derivation from a generalization. Within this framework it is easy to regard a

[1] Bas C. van Fraassen, On the Extension of Beth's Semantics of Physical Theories. *Philosophy of Science* 37 (1970): 325–339; Frederick Suppe, Theories, Their Formulations and the Operational Imperative. *Synthèse* 25* (1973); 129–164; Patrick Suppes, What is a Scientific Theory?, in *Philosophy of Science Today* S. Morgenbesser, ed., (New York: Basic Books, 1967), pp. 55–67; Joseph Sneed, *The Logical Structure of Mathematical Physics* (Dordrecht, Holland: D. Reidel, 1971); Wolfgang Stegmüller, *The Structure and Dynamics of Theories* (New York: Springer, 1976).

theory as simply a conjunction of universal generalizations. This would mean that testing a theory is just testing universal generalizations.

The distinction between models and hypotheses permits a view of the goals of science that is more particularized, or at least more restricted—and therefore, I think, more applicable to the contemporary practice of science. The simplest form of a theoretical hypothesis is the claim that a particular, identifiable real system fits a given model. Though extremely limited in scope, such claims may be very complex in detail and wide-ranging in space and time. The claim that the solar system is a Newtonian particle system (together with a suitable set of initial conditions) contains the whole mechanical history of this system—so long as it has been or will be a system of the designated type. Moreover (although this is more controversial), the same hypothesis contains all the different *possible histories* of this system that could result from different, but physically possible, initial conditions. Thus even a very particular theoretical hypothesis may contain a tremendous amount of empirical content.

Contrary to what some philosophers have claimed, one can have a science that studies but a single real system. Current geological models of the earth are not less than scientific, or scientifically uninteresting, simply because the only hypotheses employing these models refer to a single entity limited in time and space. Nor would models of natural selection be in any way scientifically suspect if there were no life anywhere else in the universe. Geology, however, is atypical. The models of a typical science are intended to apply to one or more *kinds* of systems, of which there are numerous, if only finitely many, instances.

What then is a "theory"? It is tempting to identify a theory with a generalized model; for example, the theory of particle mechanics with a generalized Newtonian model (i.e., one in which the number of particles is left unspecified). But most physicists would immediately reject the suggestion that "Newton's theory" is just a definition. And most scientists would react similarly concerning the theories in their fields. They think that "theories" have empirical content. This is a good

reason to use the term "theory" to refer to a more or less generalized theoretical hypothesis asserting that one or more specified kinds of systems fit a given type of model.[2] This seems broad enough to encompass all the sciences, including geology and physics.

Testing a theory, then, means testing a theoretical hypothesis of more or less restricted scope. This is an important qualification because the scope of a hypothesis is crucial in any judgment of the bearing of given evidence on that hypothesis. Knowing what kind of thing we are testing, we can now turn to an analysis of empirical tests. Here I shall not be challenging, but defending, a time-honored tradition.

THE HYPOTHETICO-DEDUCTIVE TRADITION

To put things in proper perspective, it helps to recall that the hypothetico-deductive method had its origins in Greek science and philosophy. Its most successful employment, of course, was in astronomy. Recast in the above terminology, the goal of astronomy was to construct a model of the heavens that one could use to deduce the motions of the various heavenly bodies as they appear from the earth. "Saving the phenomena" was thus a *necessary* requirement for an acceptable hypothesis. The methodological issue, then as well as now, was whether it is also *sufficient*.

Greek astronomers were well aware that the phenomena could be equally well saved by more than one hypothesis. This methodological fact was exemplified by the construction of both heliocentric and geocentric models. But it was also evident

---

[2] Here I depart from the view I have taken in previous papers and in my elementary text, *Understanding Scientific Reasoning* (New York: Holt, Reinhart and Winston, 1979). I have generally used the term "theory" to refer to a generalized definition or a model—which has no empirical content. But this usage has met sufficient resistance from scientists and science students that I have decided to compromise in the interests of communication. The underlying view of the scientific enterprise, however, is the same. My view here parallels that of Sneed and Stegmüller, although the parallel is difficult to see through the forest of set theory in which they hide their views.

on general logical grounds. Every student of Aristotle's logic knew that it is possible to construct more than one valid syllogism yielding the same true conclusion, and that this could be done as easily with false premises as with true. Truth of the conclusion provides no logical ground for truth of the premises. This obvious logical principle generated a methodological controversy that continues to this day. If two different hypotheses both saved the phenomena, there could be no *logical* reason to prefer one to the other. Some thinkers seemed content to regard any empirically adequate hypothesis acceptable and did not attempt to argue that one was fundamentally better. Others, however, wished to regard one model as representing the *actual* structure of the heavens, and this requires some way of picking out the correct hypothesis from among those that merely save the phenomena.

In the ensuing centuries of debate, the antirealists clearly had logic on their side. The realists, however, did offer several suggestions as to what, in addition to saving the phenomena, justified regarding a hypothesis as uniquely correct. Some appealed to the internal simplicity, or harmony, of the model itself. But this suggestion met the same objections it meets today. There is no objective criterion of simplicity. And there is no way to justify thinking that the simpler of two models, by whatever criterion, is more likely to provide a true picture of reality. Of course one may prefer a model regarded as simpler for *other* reasons having nothing to do with truth, but we shall not be concerned with such reasons here.

Another suggestion, and one I shall explore further in this paper, is that true hypotheses are revealed by their ability to *predict* phenomena before they are known. This suggestion appears explicitly in the late sixteenth century in the writings of Christopher Clavius, although it must certainly have been advanced earlier.[3] In any case, it became a standard part of the methodology of conti-

nental philosophers in the seventeenth century. Thus Descartes, in *Principles of Philosophy* (that is, *natural philosophy*) writes: "We shall know that we have determined these causes correctly only when we see that we can explain in terms of them, not merely the effects we had originally in mind, but also all other phenomena of which we did not previously think."[4]

Leibniz agrees as follows: "Those hypotheses deserve the highest praise (next to truth) . . . by whose aid predictions can be made, even about phenomena or observations which have not been tested before. . . ."[5] The best statement I know, however, occurs in the preface to Huygens's *Treatise on Light* (1690). Having carefully distinguished the deduction of theorems from "certain and incontestable principles" (as in geometry) from the testing of principles by verifying their consequences (the method of science), he continues:

It is possible in this way to attain a degree of probability which very often is scarcely less than complete certainty. This happens when the things which have been demonstrated by means of the assumed principles agree perfectly with the phenomena which experiment brings to light; especially when there are a great number of them, and, furthermore, principally, when one conceives of and foresees new phenomena which must follow from the hypotheses one employs, and which are found to agree with our expectations."[6]

Huygens refers to the three conditions (agreement, number, and anticipation of new phenomena) as "proofs of probability"—meaning that their satisfaction confers probability on the assumed hypotheses. This is noteworthy because Huygens was one of the first students of probability in its modern form. Yet it would be at least a century, and arguably two, before there were any serious

---

[3] R. M. Blake, Theory of Hypothesis among Renaissance Astronomers, in *Theories of Scientific Method*, ed. E. H. Madden (Seattle: University of Washington Press, 1960).

[4] René Descartes, *Principles of Philosophy*, Part III, Sec. 42, in *Descartes: Philosophical Writings*, trans. E. Anscombe and P. Geach (Edinburgh: Nelson, 1954), p. 223.

[5] L. E. Loemker, *Leibniz: Philosophical Papers and Letters*, 2 vols. (Chicago: University of Chicago Press, 1956), Vol. 1, p. 288. See also the paper On the Method of Distinguishing Real from Imaginary Phenomena. In Loemker, Vol. 2, p. 604.

[6] Christiaan Huygens, *Treatise on Light*, trans. S. P. Thompson (London: Macmillan, 1912).

attempts to develop and justify the hypothetical method using ideas from the theory of probability.

In the eighteenth century, the success of Newton's physics sanctified Newton's methodology, including his professed abhorrence of "hypotheses." The method of hypothesis was apparently thought to be almost as discredited as Cartesian physics and Ptolemaic astronomy. Inference to general laws "by induction" from the phenomena was the methodological rule of the day. Interest in the hypothetical method did not revive until the triumphs of wave theories of optics in the nineteenth century—association with scientific success being the apparent standard against which methodological principles are in fact judged. Thus by the third quarter of the nineteenth century we find such eminent methodologists as Whewell and Jevons expounding the virtues of hypotheses with explicit reference to the remarkable predictions that had been based on the wave theory of light. Whewell, for example, writes: "If we can predict new facts which we have not seen, as well as explain those which we have seen, it must be because our explanation is not a mere formula of observed facts, but a truth of a deeper kind.[7] This passage is typical of many of Whewell's writings.

Whewell's homage to the methodological virtues of successful prediction did not go unchallenged. Mill, in particular, denigrated the celebrated predictions of the wave theory as "well calculated to impress the uninformed," but found it "strange that any considerable stress should be laid upon such coincidences by persons of scientific attainments." Moreover, Mill goes on to explain why "coincidences" between "prophecies" and "what comes to pass" should not count for a hypothesis any more than simple agreement with the predicted occurrence. I shall pass over the details of his argument here.[8] Of more interest for this brief survey is that the essentials of the exchange between Whewell and Mill were repeated more than a half-century later in a similar exchange between Peirce and John Maynard Keynes.

In many of his scattered writings, Peirce advocated versions of the following "rule of prediction": "A hypothesis can only be received upon the ground of its having been *verified* by successful *prediction*"[9] Unlike his many predecessors who either lacked the necessary concepts, did not think to apply them, or did not know how, Peirce attempted to justify his rule by explicit appeal to considerations of *probability*. But even this appeal was not decisive. Keynes, whose own view of scientific reasoning incorporated a theory of probability, examined Peirce's arguments for the rule of prediction and concluded that "the peculiar virtue of prediction" was "altogether imaginary." Addressing the details of Keynes's argument would again take us too far afield.[10] I shall only pause to suggest that there must be methodological principles beyond a commitment to concepts of probability that separate the tradition of Huygens, Whewell, and Peirce from that of Bacon, Mill, and Keynes.

Among contemporary methodologists, the main defenders of the hypothetico-deductive method seem to be Popper and his intellectual descendents. Elie Zahar and Alan Musgrave have even advocated a special role for successful "novel predictions" in a Lakatosian research programme.[11] Yet these writers seem to me not to be the legitimate heirs of Huygens, Whewell, or Peirce. For the main stream of the hypothetico-deductive tradition, confirmation of a hypothesis through the verification of its consequences, particularly its *predicted* consequences, provides a reason to believe or accept that the hypothesis is *true*. Popper explicitly denies that there can be any

---

[7] William Whewell, *Philosophy of Discovery* (London: J. W. Parker, 1860), p. 273.

[8] John Stuart Mill, *Logic* (8th ed.) (London, 1881), Book III, Ch. XIV, Sec. 6.

[9] C. S. Peirce, *Collected Papers of Charles Sanders Peirce*, 8 vols. (Cambridge, Mass.: Harvard University Press, 1931–1958), 2.739.

[10] John Maynard Keynes, *A Treatise on Probability* (London: Macmillan, 1921), pp. 304–306.

[11] E. G. Zahar, *Why Did Einstein's Programme Supersede Lorentz's? The British Journal for the Philosophy of Science* 24 (1973): 95–123 and 223–262. Alan E. Musgrave, *Logical Versus Historical Theories of Confirmation. The British Journal for the Philosophy of Science* 25 (1974): 1–23.

such reasons. No matter how "severely tested" and "well-corroborated" a hypothesis might be, it remains a "conjecture" whose truth we have no more reason to believe than we did on the day it was first proposed. Similarly, for Lakatos or Zahar the success of a novel prediction is merely one sign of a "progressive" research programme—not a sign of the truth of any particular theory or hypothesis. Only if one accepts the "problem shift" that replaces "reasons to regard as true" with the very different notions of "corroboration" or "progress" can one place these methodological suggestions firmly within the hypothetico-deductive tradition.

Similar remarks apply to those who take their methodological cues from Quine. Insofar as Quine belongs in the hypothetico-deductive tradition, it is that of the antirealists among the classical astronomers. Saving the phenomena is the main thing. Simplicity in one's hypotheses is desirable, but not because of any supposed link between simplicity and truth. Simplicity is desirable in itself or because it contributes to some pragmatic end such as economy of thought. Similarly with prediction. Hypotheses that are useful in making reliable predictions are desirable, but not because this makes them any more likely to be true. Rather, there is pragmatic value in being able to foresee the future, and we value hypotheses with this virtue without thereby ascribing to them any "truth of a deeper kind."

In championing the hypothetico-deductive method of testing scientific hypotheses, I am adopting only the "realist" tradition of Huygens, Whewell, Peirce, and, in part, Popper. I am not defending the more pragmatic or conventionalist versions represented by Quine.[12] Nevertheless, most of the following account is compatible with the subtle antirealism of van Fraassen's *The Scientific Image*.[13] Just how I would differ from van Fraassen will be explained later.

---

[12] Still less am I defending the logical shadow of the hypothetico-deductive tradition recently criticized by Clark Glymour in *Theory and Evidence* (Princeton: Princeton University Press, 1980), pp. 29–48.

[13] Bas C. van Fraassen, *The Scientific Image* (Oxford: Oxford University Press, 1980).

TESTS OF THEORETICAL HYPOTHESES

The secret to understanding the rationale of the H-D method is to focus not on the meager logical relations between hypothesis and data but on the notion of a *test* of the hypothesis. What kind of a thing is such a test? What is the purpose of testing hypotheses? What are the possible results of a test? How one answers these fundamental questions will to a large extent determine one's view of the legitimacy of the H-D method.

The ancient idea of a test as an *ordeal* is suggestive because it implies that a test is a process, a procedure to which a hypothesis is subjected. Furthermore, the idea that the purpose of the ordeal is to determine a person's guilt or innocence suggests that the purpose of testing a hypothesis is to determine its truth or falsity. Finally, to complete the analogy, those subjected to ordeals are pronounced guilty or innocent depending on whether they pass or fail the test. This suggests that hypotheses may be pronounced true or false depending on whether they pass or fail the test. Analogies, of course, are not arguments. But by developing the analogy we may be led to a better understanding of tests of theoretical hypotheses.

One way in which we scientific philosophers of the twentieth century have advanced beyond our predecessors is that we now accept the idea that no empirical data could possibly determine *with certainty* that any theoretical hypothesis is *true*. Opinions still differ over whether *falsity* may be so determined. I shall take the liberal position that neither truth nor falsity can be determined with certainty. In the language of testing, no test of a theoretical hypothesis can be completely reliable.

Almost all contemporary students of scientific method would agree that the relevant notion of reliability is to be understood and explicated using concepts of *probability*. But just what role probability plays is a matter of deep disagreement. Many philosophers assume that probability is to be introduced as a measure applied to hypotheses themselves. Thus any test would result in the assignment of a probability to the hypothesis in question. That no test is completely reliable means that this probability is always less than one. I am convinced that this is not the way to go. No model of science that places the relations between evidence and hypotheses *within* the probability calculus will prove adequate. Since I cannot argue so general a thesis here, however, I shall proceed with the constructive task of developing an alternative account. This account *uses* probability without attempting to make scientific inference itself a species of probability calculation.[14]

The way probability enters our account is through the characterization of what constitutes an "appropriate" test of a theoretical hypothesis. So far we have concluded only that a test of a hypothesis is a process whose result provides the basis for our "verdict" either that the hypothesis is true or that it is false. This general characterization, however, is satisfied by the procedure of flipping a coin and calling the hypothesis true if heads comes up and false if tails. This procedure has the virtue that our chances of reaching the *correct* conclusion are fifty-fifty regardless of the truth or falsity of the hypothesis. But no one would regard this as a satisfactory way of "testing" hypotheses. It does, however, suggest that an "appropriate" test would be one that has *higher* probabilities for leading us to the correct conclusion. We shall follow this suggestion.

Thinking about tests in this way throws new light on the classical objections to the method of hypothesis. Let us assume for the moment that our powers of deduction and observation are perfect. This will allow us to concentrate on the nature of tests themselves. At least some realists among the classical astronomers may be viewed as advocating a testing procedure that recommended calling a hypothesis true if and only if it saves the phe-

nomena. Following this procedure, the chances of calling a hypothesis false if it is in fact true are (ideally) zero. A true hypothesis cannot have false consequences. The defect of the procedure is that the chances of calling a false hypothesis true are at best simply not known. One might even argue that this probability is high on the ground that there are many, perhaps even infinitely many, false hypotheses that would also save the phenomena. The odds seem overwhelming that the hypothesis in question is one of these. What is needed to improve the procedure, therefore, is some way of increasing the chances that a false hypothesis will be rejected. This must be done in such a way, however, that the probability of rejecting a true hypothesis is not increased. It would be trivially easy to design a procedure guaranteed to reject false hypotheses: simply reject *any* proposed hypothesis, regardless of the evidence. Unfortunately this procedure is also guaranteed to reject any true hypothesis as well.

The above considerations suggest characterizing an *appropriate test* as a procedure that has *both* an appropriately high probability of leading us to accept true hypotheses as true and to reject false hypotheses as false. Alternatively, an appropriate test of a hypothesis is a procedure that is reasonably *unlikely* to lead us either to accept a false hypothesis or to reject a true one. This characterization still requires considerable elaboration and refinement, but it makes clear the kind of account we seek.

One immediate task is to clarify the interpretation of probability assumed in the above characterization of a good test. By a "procedure" I mean an actual process in the real world. If such a procedure is to have probabilities for leading to different results, these must be *physical* probabilities. Our account thus presupposes an acceptable physical interpretation of probability, something many philosophers regard as impossible. Here I would agree with those who reject attempts to reduce physical probability to relative frequency, and opt for some form of "propensity" interpretation. But since this is again too big an issue to be debated here, I shall proceed under the assumption that there is *some* acceptable physical inter-

14 I have elaborated on the deep philosophical differences between these two approaches to scientific inference in Testing vs. Information Models of Statistical Inference. In *Logic, Laws and Life,* ed. R. G. Colodny (Pittsburgh: University of Pittsburgh Press, 1977), pp. 19–70. For further references see this article and the review essay Foundations of Probability and Statistical Inference. In *Current Research in Philosophy of Science,* ed. P. D. Asquith and Henry Kyburg, Jr. (East Lansing: Philosophy of Science Association, 1978).

pretation of probability.[15] Moreover, we must assume that we can at least sometimes have good empirical grounds for judging the relevant physical probabilities to be high.

EXAMPLE: FRESNEL'S MODEL OF DIFFRACTION

An example may help to flesh out the relatively abstract outline presented so far. This example is appropriate in many ways, one being its historical association with the re-emergence of the H-D method of testing in the early eighteen-hundreds after a century in the shadows of Newtonian methodological orthodoxy.

Wave models of optical phenomena had been developed by Hooke and Huygens at the end of the seventeenth century. Particle models were favored by Newton and the later Newtonians. At that time, the evidence for either type of model was genuinely ambiguous. Each type of model explained some phenomena better than the others. The then recently discovered phenomenon of polarization, for example, was an embarrassment to both, though perhaps more so to wave theorists. In general, particle models dominated eighteenth-century theorizing, perhaps partly because of greater empirical success but also, I think, because of the general triumph of Newtonianism. In any case, for most of the eighteenth century there was little serious work on wave models until Thomas Young took up the cause around 1800. The scientific establishment, including the French Academy of Sciences, was then dominated by particle theorists. Laplace, for example, published a particle model of double refraction in 1808. But interest in optics was obviously high, since the

Academy prizes in 1810 and 1818, for example, were for treatments of double refraction and diffraction respectively.

The diffraction prize eventually went to Augustin Fresnel for a wave model. In Fresnel's models, diffraction patterns are produced by the interference of secondary wave fronts originating at the edges of an object placed between a point light source and screen. Fresnel developed special cases of this general model for a single straight edge, a narrow body with parallel edges, and a narrow slit. The calculated patterns agreed well with known experimental results.

Fresnel's memoir was referred to a Commission in which well-known advocates of particle models, Laplace, Poisson, and Biot, held a majority. The commission was apparently not fully convinced by the evidence Fresnel had presented, and Poisson devised a further test. He applied Fresnel's model to the case of a shadow produced by a circular disk and deduced that the resulting diffraction pattern would have a bright spot at the center of the shadow. Even from superficial accounts of this incident it seems clear that no one involved had ever seen such a spot. Moreover, it seems that Poisson and his fellow Commissioners did not expect the spot to appear. It certainly was not a consequence of any current particle models that such a spot should exist. The experiment was performed by François Arago, and apparently also by Fresnel. The spot appeared as predicted, and the Commissioners yielded.[16]

Now let us consider this episode in light of the framework outlined earlier. Assuming sufficient familiarity with the kind of *model* Fresnel proposed, the next question is just what *hypotheses* were at issue. There are a number of possibilities. (i) The specific set-up in Arago's laboratory fits the model. (ii) Any similar set-up with a circular disk, etc., would fit the model. (iii) All types of diffraction phenomena fit this sort of model. (iv) All opti-

[15] I have myself developed a propensity interpretation in several papers beginning with Objective Single-Case Probabilities and the Foundations of Statistics, in P. Suppes, L. Henkin, A. Joja, and Cr. C. Moisil, eds. Logic, Methodology and Philosophy of Science, IV (Amsterdam: North-Holland, 1973), pp. 467–83. For later references see also A Laplacean Formal Semantics for Single Case Propensities, *Journal of Philosophical Logic* 5 (1976):321–353.

[16] The above account is based entirely on secondary sources such as E. T. Whittaker's A *History of the Theories of Aether and Electricity* (London: Thomas Nelson & Sons, 1910; rev. ed. 1951; Torchbook edition, 1960).

cal phenomena fit a similar wave model. Which of these hypotheses were tested by Arago's experiments, and which did the Commission accept in awarding Fresnel the prize?

The episode, I suggest, is best understood taking the hypothesis of most direct concern to be the third of the above four: Fresnel's models capture diffraction phenomena in general. Following the terminology suggested earlier, this hypothesis could be designated "Fresnel's theory of diffraction." Of course everyone was also concerned with whether Arago's set-up fit the model, and this is a consequence of Fresnel's theory. The second hypothesis is also a consequence of Fresnel's theory, but once people were convinced that the model applied to Arago's apparatus, this generalization was not problematic. Enough was known of the general stability of optical phenomena by that time that this simple generalization could legitimately be taken for granted once it was firmly established for a single case. The emphasis placed by empiricist philosophers on such generalizations is quite misleading.

One reason for focusing on Fresnel's theory of diffraction rather than on a broader wave theory of light is that Arago's experiments provide an appropriate test of Fresnel's theory, but not of the broader theory—in spite of the fact that the former is a logical consequence of the latter. This follows from our characterization of an appropriate test of a hypothesis, as we shall now see.

At the time of Arago's experiments, techniques for dealing with optical phenomena were sufficiently well developed that it was very probable that the spot would be observed—given that the Fresnel-Poisson model does fit this situation. So, given that Fresnel's theory is true, it was very unlikely that it should mistakenly have been rejected. This aspect of the test was entirely appropriate to the circumstances. But what if Fresnel's theory had been false? How probable was it that the testing process should have yielded the predicted spot even if Fresnel's models did not really capture diffraction phenomena? To answer this question we must first decide just how much of the episode to include within the "testing process."

According to common interpretations of the discovery/justification distinction, the decisive testing process began when Poisson constructed a Fresnel-style model for the circular disk and deduced that the spot should appear. Nothing that happened earlier is relevant to the confirmation of any of the hypotheses we have considered. I expect that many who reject a discovery/justification distinction would nevertheless agree with this conclusion. And indeed, this view of the matter follows naturally from the doctrine that there is a "direct" evidential relationship, analogous to deduction, between hypothesis and evidence. But this is not our view. On our account, the relationship between hypothesis and evidence is mediated by the testing process, and there is no a priori reason why incidents that occurred before the actual formulation of the hypothesis should not be relevant to the character of this process. In particular, the process by which a hypothesis is selected for consideration might very well influence its content and thus the likelihood of discovering a further consequence to be true.

The Commissioners apparently did not regard Fresnel's success in explaining the diffraction pattern of straight edges as decisive. Why? Was this just prejudice? Or did they have good reasons for not regarding these familiar patterns as being part of a good test of Fresnel's models? I think the latter is the case. From Fresnel's own account it is clear that the straight-edge pattern acted as a constraint on his theorizing. He was unwilling to consider any model that did not yield the right pattern for straight edges. Thus we know that the probability of *any* model he put forward yielding the correct pattern for straight edges was near unity, independently of the general correctness of that model. Since the straight-edge pattern thus had no probability of leading to rejection of any subsequently proposed hypothesis that was in fact false, this pattern could not be part of a good test of any such hypothesis.

We could regard agreement with the straight-edge pattern as a test of a hypothesis if we knew the probability that Fresnel should pick out a satisfactory model using this, together with similar data, as a constraint. At best this probability is simply unknown. And given the frequency with which even experienced scientists come up with unsatisfactory models, there is reason to judge such probabilities to be fairly low. In either case we fail to have a good test of the hypothesis.

The case with the spot is quite different. We know that this result did *not* act as a constraint on Fresnel's choice of models. Suppose, then, that Fresnel had come up with a model that applied satisfactorily to straight edges and the like but was *not* correct for diffraction phenomena in general. The corresponding theory would therefore be false. What is the probability that any model selected in this way should nevertheless yield the correct answer for the disk? In answering this question we must also take into account the fact that the disk experiment was specifically chosen because it seemed to Poisson and others that no such phenomenon existed. So the consequence selected for the test was one that knowledgeable people thought unlikely to be true. Given all these facts, it seems clear that the test was quite likely to lead to a rejection of any false theory that Fresnel might have proposed. And this judgment about the test was one that could easily be made by everyone involved. My view is that they did make this judgment, implicitly if not explicitly, concluded that Poisson's proposed test was quite adequate, and, when the result came in, acted accordingly.

In thinking about this and similar examples it is crucial to remember that the probabilities involved are physical probabilities inherent in the actual scientific process itself. If one slips into thinking in terms of probability relations among hypotheses, or between evidence and hypotheses, one will necessarily misunderstand this account of the nature of empirical testing. In particular, one must not imagine that to estimate the probability of not finding the spot one must be able to calculate the probability of this result as a weighted average of its probabilities relative to all possible alternative theories. No such probabilities are involved. Rather, one needs only to estimate the chances that *any* model generated and tested in this way should fail to cover the general class of diffraction phenomena and nevertheless give the right result for an experiment devised as the disk

experiment was in fact devised. My contention is that the participants' knowledge of the whole situation justified concluding that this chance was low.

There remains the question of why Arago's experiment does not provide an appropriate test of a more general wave theory of all optical phenomena. Let us regard this more general theory as a conjunction of theories restricted to various types of optical phenomena: reflection, refraction, polarization, etc. A Fresnel theory of light would say that Fresnel's models are adequate for this whole range of phenomena. Now since Fresnel's theory of diffraction is one conjunct in this larger theory, and since the test is a diffraction experiment, the probabilities of mistaken acceptance or rejection of a more general theory are identical to those for the more restricted theory. Is the experiment not then an equally good test of the broader theory? A positive answer would be a strong objection to this account of empirical testing since it seems intuitively clear that it would not have been correct to accept the broader theory on the basis of these experiments.

The objection fails, however, because the *appropriateness* of a test need not be solely a function of the absolute *magnitude* of the relevant probabilities. It may depend also on what other tests of the theory might be possible, and in this case there were much better tests available. Since Fresnel's model was selected using mainly diffraction phenomena as constraints, the falsity of a general Fresnel theory of light would be much *more likely* to be demonstrated by experiments on phenomena *other* than diffraction. In particular, one would want a phenomenon to which such wave models had not yet been applied. Many such phenomena were familiar at the time. In fact, no such experiments were necessary because it was almost immediately apparent that there were many phenomena, e.g., polarization, for which Fresnel's model gave no account whatsoever.

Many recent philosophers have objected to the H-D method because it satisfies a "converse consequence condition." That is, if T is confirmed by the truth of some consequence, O, then if T' implies T, T' is equally confirmed. In particular, T and H, for any H, is confirmed. And, granted that a logical consequence of any hypothesis is at least as well confirmed as the hypothesis itself, by confirming T we can equally well confirm any H whatsoever. The above discussion shows that such objections are based on an oversimplified view of the H-D method—indeed, a version to which few if any serious defenders of the H-D method ever subscribed.[17]

THE ROLE OF NOVEL PREDICTIONS

As we have seen, many champions of the H-D method have suggested that successful predictions are sufficient for the confirmation of hypotheses; some, such as Peirce, have taken them to be necessary as well. Critics argued that successful predictions were neither necessary nor sufficient. From our present perspective we can see why the defenders were on the right track even though their critics were technically correct. First let us give the critics their due.

That successful predictions are *not sufficient* is easily seen by imagining other possible sequences of events in the Fresnel example. Suppose that Biot had repeated Fresnel's calculations for a straight edge and persuaded Arago to repeat these measurements. Of course Biot's prediction would have been verified, but no one would have regarded this replication as providing a decisive test of Fresnel's hypothesis regarding this experiment or of the general adequacy of his approach to diffraction phenomena. Why? Because the imagined process would not have been a good test of the hypothesis. The process had a high probability of supporting Fresnel's hypothesis if it were true. But it also had a high probability of supporting the hypothesis even if it were false. The many previous experiments with straight edges had pro-

vided ample evidence for the empirical generalization that this type of experiment yielded the indicated diffraction pattern. So regardless of the truth or falsity of Fresnel's hypothesis, it was highly probable that the hypothesis would be supported. This violates our conditions for a good test of a hypothesis. Both Mill and Keynes used this sort of example in their analyses of the prediction criterion, though each within a quite different framework.

This same counterexample also shows why many H-D theorists have insisted on novel predictions. If a predicted result is not novel, there will be a more or less well-justified low-level empirical hypothesis linking the type of experiment and the type of result. This makes it likely that the test will justify the hypothesis no matter whether it is true or false. Thus it is difficult to have a good test unless the prediction is novel. This point seems to have been missed by empiricist critics of the H-D method such as Mill and Keynes, although perhaps the true value of novelty was also not sufficiently understood by either Whewell or Peirce.

That successful predictions are *not necessary* is also easily demonstrated by an imaginary variation on the same example. It has been claimed that the bright spot in the center of a circular shadow was observed in the early part of the eighteenth century by J. N. Delisle.[18] It seems pretty clear that none of the principles in the case had ever heard of these supposed observations. But suppose they did occur and were published. Imagine, then, that Laplace, but not Fresnel, knew of these results, and upon reading Fresnel's memoir recalled Delisle's unexplained observations. It would not have taken him long to apply Fresnel's method to the case and conclude that Fresnel's model explained Delisle's results. I think the Commission would have been equally convinced that

---

[17] This objection was first advanced by C. G. Hempel in his classic Studies in the Logic of Confirmation, *Mind* 54 (1945):1–26 and 97–121. It forms much of the basis of Glymour's discussion in *Theory and Evidence*.

[18] The reference to Delisle's observations appears in a footnote in Whittaker's *History* (Torchbook edition, p. 108). However, Whittaker gives no references and there are no other entries under "Delisle" in the index. Here is a case where *historical* research might alter one's *methodological* appraisal of a scientific episode.

Fresnel's theory was correct. But whether or not they would have been, they should have been. It was about as improbable that Fresnel, ignorant of Delisle's results, should have developed an inadequate model that nevertheless explained Delisle's results, as it was that an inadequate model should have happened to predict correctly the result of Arago's later experiment. In either case the conditions for a good test are satisfied.

Returning to the champions of the prediction rule, it is clear that they overstated their case. But they were fundamentally correct in thinking that the fact that a result was predicted successfully may be *relevant* to the confirmation of a hypothesis. The conditions that define an appropriate test of a hypothesis are themselves contingent empirical hypotheses about the actual process by which a particular hypothesis is tested. This is due to the fact that the relevant probabilities are *physical* probabilities embodied in the testing process. Judging a process to constitute a good test of a hypothesis thus requires judging that the relevant physical probabilities are high. All sorts of empirical facts about the case may be relevant to these judgments—including facts about when a specified consequence of a hypothesis became known, and to whom.

Let us imagine yet another variant on the Fresnel example. Suppose that someone named Delisle really did observe the spot and that Fresnel, but not other principles in the case, knew of Delisle's results right from the beginning of his work on diffraction. So in addition to explaining the standard diffraction patterns for straight edges, etc., Fresnel was all along seeking a model that would also explain the existence of the spot—and he succeeded. But suppose further that Fresnel suppressed all mention of disks and spots in his memoir, and the rest of the story proceeds as in real life. On our analysis this would be a case of scientific dishonesty, even fraud. The Commission would have had every reason to think that a good test had been performed. But they would have been deceived, for in fact it would have not been a good test. It is not in fact unlikely that a model designed to accommodate a given result should in

fact do so. And this is true no matter whether the corresponding hypothesis is true or false. It is possible, therefore, to be justifiably mistaken about whether a given experiment constitutes a good test or not.

We can go further. One might object that it does not matter whether Fresnel *knew* of Delisle's result, but only whether he *used* this knowledge in selecting a model of diffraction. This is in principle correct. The probability of fit between model and observation is not influenced if the observations play no role in the selection of the model. But it is exceedingly difficult to be confident that no such selection pressure existed when the result was known to the developer of the model. One can always be more confident of the goodness of a test if the result was not previously known. So it is a sound methodological rule to prefer results that were genuinely predicted even though this is not strictly necessary for a good test. The methodological good sense of the champions of prediction was better than their justifications.

Finally, our account of testing theoretical hypotheses reveals the methodological insight in Popper's claims that to test a hypothesis severely, one must attempt sincerely to refute it. Far from introducing irrelevant psychological considerations into a supposed logical relationship between evidence and hypothesis, Popper is highlighting (though in an exaggerated and misleading fashion) one aspect of good tests. Not only is the process by which the *hypothesis* was selected relevant to our judgment of the quality of a test; the process of selecting the *prediction* to be investigated is also relevant. This process can be one that makes it more or less likely that the test will reveal the falsity of the hypothesis—if it is indeed false. In particular, if a knowledgeable scientist such as Poisson investigates a model with the express intent of discovering an inadequacy, and finds a consequence he thinks likely to be false, that is good reason to think that the test has a high probability of discovering a false consequence—if there are any to be discovered. Of course a scientist need not be attempting to refute the hypothesis in question; he may just be trying to devise the best possible test. But the knowledge that a given consequence was selected for investigation in a well-informed attempt to refute the hypothesis is relevant to the judgment as to how good the test might be.

THE LOGIC OF TESTS

A good test of a hypothesis is a physical process with specified stochastic properties, namely, a high probability of one outcome if H is true and another if H is false. That this process has one outcome rather than the other, however, also has *epistemic* consequences. If a good test has a favorable outcome, we are to "conclude" that H is true, "accept" H as being true, or some such thing. One must provide some account of the rationale, or "logic," of this step from the physical outcome to the epistemic conclusion. Here I shall follow those who regard the epistemic step as a kind of *decision*. This opens the way to a decision-theoretic analysis of scientific inference. But since we have renounced probabilities of hypotheses, our decision theory must be "classical," or "non-Bayesian," decision theory.

Casting the problem in decision-theoretic terms, we realize immediately that what really needs to be justified is not so much the decision to accept (or reject) any particular hypothesis, but the general *decision rule* that tells us, for each possible outcome of the experiment, whether to accept or reject the hypothesis. It is so obvious which of the four possible decision rules is correct that most traditional accounts of the H-D method do not even note the epistemic step from physical outcome to accepted conclusion. To understand the logic of the step, however, it is useful to consider the full range of possibilities.

In any test of a theoretical hypothesis there are four possible epistemic results, two correct and two incorrect. The correct ones are accepting H if it is true and rejecting H if it is false. The incorrect ones are rejecting H if it is true and accepting H if it is false. Now to conceptualize the problem in decision-theoretic terms we must assume that it is possible to assign some kind of "value" to these

possible results. For the moment we shall not worry what kind of value this is or whether it has the formal properties of utility. And just for convenience (it makes no difference to the argument), we shall suppose that both correct results have the same value (which we may set arbitrarily at 1) and that both incorrect results also have the same value (which we may set arbitrarily at 0). Finally, let α be the probability that the prediction is false even though H is true and β be the probability that the prediction is true even though H is false. For the moment it will not matter much what these probabilities are so long as they are strictly between zero and one half. With these assumptions we can represent the "decision" to accept or reject H in a two by two matrix (Figure 1). Each of the four possible outcomes is labeled with its respective value and probability (conditional on the hypothesis being true or false).

The meta-decision problem of choosing a decision rule for making the object-level decision is represented as a four-by-two matrix (Figure 2). The obvious decision rule to accept H if and only if the prediction is true is represented as (A, R), and the others are represented accordingly. The outcomes are labeled with the appropriate *expected* values of applying the rule conditional on the truth or falsity of the hypothesis. We are now in a position to consider in a systematic way why the obvious rule is correct.

We have arrived in "meta-meta land." What principle do we use to justify a decision rule to guide our actual decisions? The least controversial principle that might possibly apply—namely,

	Hypothesis true	Hypothesis false
Accept Hypothesis	$Pr = 1 - \alpha$ $V = 1$	$Pr = \beta$ $V = 0$
Reject Hypothesis	$Pr = \alpha$ $V = 0$	$Pr = 1 - \beta$ $V = 1$

Figure 1

	Hypothesis true	Hypothesis false
(A, A)	1	0
(A, R)	$1 - \alpha$	$1 - \beta$
(R, A)	α	β
(R, R)	0	1

Figure 2

dominance—fails to be applicable. Since (A, A) is best if H is true and (R, R) is best if H is false, no one choice of decision rule dominates all others. But the next least controversial principle does apply—namely, *maximin* (it would be "minimax" if we measured our values as losses rather than gains). Maximin recommends the intuitively obvious decision rule (A, R). The justification for this recommendation is that following (A, R) guarantees the greatest "security level," that is, the highest minimum expected gain whether the hypothesis is true or not. In either case, our expected gain can be no lower than the smaller of $(1 - \alpha)$ or $(1 - \beta)$. Since α and β are both less than one-half, no other decision rule can guarantee a greater security level.

The trouble with an appeal to the maximin principle is that it justifies too much. It sanctions the (A, R) rule as long as α and β are less than one-half, which means that any test of a hypothesis is acceptable as long as the probabilities of accepting true hypotheses and rejecting false ones are strictly greater than one-half. This is certainly not in general acceptable for tests of scientific hypotheses. We need a somewhat stronger principle that can force the probabilities of correct acceptance and rejection to be appropriately greater than one-half.

One general decision strategy that has some theoretical backing and seems well suited to the present context is *satisficing*.[19] This strategy may

be understood as a strengthening of maximin. To apply this strategy we must assume that there is some way to set a value that is the minimum regarded as a "satisfactory" outcome of the decision process. This is the *satisfaction level* for the particular decision problem at hand. This level is not a function of the given decision matrix but is imposed "from the outside" either by a decision maker or by the decision context. The decision problem will have a *satisfactory* choice only if the security level is at least as great as the imposed satisfaction level. Otherwise there simply will not be any choice sanctioned by this strategy.

Satisficing has not been much studied by decision theorists and philosophers because it does not conform to the standard conditions for a solution to the fundamental meta-decision problem. That problem is: For any decision matrix, devise a general rule that selects a uniquely rational choice from among all the given possible options. Any rule that does not guarantee some choice of options cannot be a solution to this problem. By invoking satisficing when it does not reduce to maximin, we are rejecting the standard formulation of the fundamental problem of decision theory. And in making satisficing the basis for our acceptance or rejection of hypotheses we would similarly be rejecting a standard, if often implicit, formulation of the basic theoretical problem of scientific inference: For any hypothesis and any evidence, define a uniquely rational function that gives the degree to which the evidence "supports" the hypothesis. On our account, the decision matrix corresponding to an appropriate test must have satisfactory payoffs for the evidence to count either for or against the hypothesis. If the evidence is not part of an appropriate test, the hypothesis is simply neither accepted nor rejected. Neither conclusion is justified.

The demand for a unique solution to any decision problem may have some merit in the context of *practical* decision making. Here one often cannot refuse to make some choice. But science is different. It is not required that scientists be able to say at any moment, given whatever happens to be known at that time, whether some specified hypothesis should be accepted or rejected. One may

---

[19] For an authoritative introduction to satisficing see H. A. Simon, *Models of Man* (New York: Wiley, 1957), pp. 196–206 and also chapters 14 and 15.

simply say that sufficiently good tests are lacking. The other side of the coin is that scientists are not helpless in the face of inadequate tests. They may devise and carry out tests they have explicitly designed to be adequate according to the standards of their field. The scientific enterprise, after all, is not simply a matter of evaluating hypotheses in light of available information, but an active seeking out of information to answer definite (and often theoretical) questions.

My analysis of the Academy Commission follows the above outline. The evidence presented in Fresnel's memoir did not constitute a sufficient test of Fresnel's theory, and the Commission, rightly, could not decide whether it was correct or not. So they devised a new experiment, one that was sufficient. What made the new experiment sufficient was primarily that it had an adequately high probability of rejecting a mistaken model.

Probabilities, however, are not the only component in a decision-theoretic analysis of the logic of testing. We must also assume the existence of "epistemic" or "scientific" values. I say "values" rather than "utilities" because a satisficing strategy, like maximin, can be applied with as weak a value structure as a mere ordering—a full-fledged utility function is not necessary. This is an additional virtue of satisficing as a general decision strategy. Still, those who question this approach may ask whether there are any such things as scientific values and, if so, whether they can play the role assigned to them by this analysis. Here I can only sketch a reply.

In principle we need appeal to only one scientific value, truth. That is, correctly accepting a true hypothesis or rejecting a false one is valued over the reverse. This seems very difficult to deny, except as part of a radical theory of science in which truth plays little or no role.[20] Otherwise the decision-theoretic analysis requires only that the satisfaction level of expected value be strictly less than the value assigned to accepting truth (or rejecting

falsehood). Because the probability of a mistake is strictly greater than zero, our expected payoff is necessarily less than maximal no matter whether H is true or not. If our satisfaction level were equal to the value of a correct decision, no amount of data or care in experimental design would be good enough for us ever to make either choice. Thus we really do not need to delve deeply into questions about the value of truth, e.g., *how much* is truth valued over error. So long as truth is *more* valued, we can assume an arbitrary scale. The interesting question is what determines the satisfaction level. And given a fixed value scale, this question reduces to asking what determines an acceptable level of risk. So we are back to probabilities.

My view, which I can only affirm here, is that the satisfaction level, or level of acceptable risk, is not a function of individuals but of the *institution* of science. The institution decrees that tolerating some risk of error is better than having no theoretical conclusions at all. Yet something more should be forthcoming. It seems that different fields, or the same field at different stages of maturity, have different tolerances for risk of error. Again, it seems not just that scientists in some fields are more risk adverse. Rather, some *fields* are more or less risk adverse. I think there are objective reasons why this is so and why it is proper, but that would be a digression here. The main point is to recognize this as an important question for a theory of science.[21]

One important consequence of introducing values into an account of scientific inference is that it automatically relativizes the acceptance of a theoretical hypothesis to the scientific context

---

[20] Such a view is developed in Larry Laudan's influential book *Progress and its Problems* (Berkeley: University of California Press, 1977).

[21] In several previous papers I have attempted to distinguish two rough types or stages in scientific inquiry, "exploratory" and "confirmatory," and to argue that the satisfaction level, as reflected in the acceptable risk for a mistaken conclusion, is justifiably higher in confirmatory inquiry. See Empirical Probability, Objective Statistical Methods and Scientific Inquiry, in *Foundations of Probability Theory, Statistical Inference and Statistical Theories of Science*, W. L. Harper and C. A. Hooker, Vol. 2 (Dordrecht, Holland: D Reidel, 1976), pp. 63–101; and Testing vs. Information Models of Statistical Inference, in *Logic, Laws and Life*, ed. R. G. Colodny, (Pittsburgh: University of Pittsburgh Press, 1977), pp. 19–70.

characterized by those values. This relativization eliminates what has often been regarded as a fatal objection to the idea that hypotheses are ever "accepted" as being true. The objection is that it would be irrational to regard any hypothesis as true for all purposes or in any possible context. Thus Laplace may have been convinced of the truth of Fresnel's hypothesis, but it would have been irrational to stake the fortunes of the whole French nation on this conclusion. On our analysis, however, Laplace's commitment to the truth of the hypothesis would be restricted to the scientific context, leaving open the question whether the hypothesis was sufficiently well-tested to presume its truth if other values were at stake. This makes the relationship between "pure" and "applied" science more complicated than is often supposed, but that, I would argue, is an added virtue of this approach.[22]

THE WEIGHT OF EVIDENCE

It is a commonplace that the evidence for a theory may be better or worse, and that evidence may accumulate. In short, evidence seems to come in degrees. Our account, however, leads to hypotheses being either "accepted" or "rejected." Does not this account, therefore, run counter to well-established methodological intuitions? I think not, but some explanation is in order.

In the first place, it is not strictly true that our account leaves no room for degrees of support. A test can be more or less stringent (or severe) depending on the probabilities of mistaken acceptance or rejection. The probability of correctly rejecting a mistaken hypothesis, what statisticians call the "power" of a test, is a particularly good measure of the severity of a test. For example, later tests of wave models tended to be better than the early experiments of Fresnel and Arago because they employed fairly precise *quantitative*, rather

than merely qualitative, predictions. The famous 1850 experiment of Foucault and Fizeau on the relative velocity of light in air and water was a much better test because wave models gave a quite precise value for this ratio based on the known relative indices of refraction. The chances of a badly mistaken model yielding the right value to within the known experimental error had to have been very small indeed.

Second, the idea that a theory is a generalization over regions of a domain provides ample room for the idea of accumulating evidence for a theory. As more and more regions of the domain are brought under a given type of model, the evidence in favor of the generalization increases. This is how I would understand the history of the wave theory between 1820 and 1850. As wave models were refined, more and more optical phenomena were shown to fit: diffraction, polarization, double refraction, and so on. By 1850 it was reasonable to conclude that all optical phenomena could be accounted for by suitably specialized wave models.[23]

APPROXIMATION AND SCIENTIFIC REALISM

Peirce said that every scientific conclusion should be doubly qualified by the phrase "probably and approximately." Thus far we have been primarily concerned with the role of probability in the testing of theoretical hypotheses, and, by implication, the way probability "qualifies" our conclusions. It is time to turn to the second of Peirce's qualifications. The need for some such qualification is once again well-illustrated by the Fresnel episode. At the time of his original memoir on diffraction, Fresnel's wave models employed *longitudinal* rather than transverse waves. It so happens that for diffraction phenomena the two types of models give at least qualitatively similar results. This is not

---

[22] This point is developed is somewhat greater detail in both papers mentioned in n. 21.

[23] The useful notion of a "domain" has been developed in a number of papers by Dudley Shapere. See, for example, Scientific Theories and their Domains, in *The Structure of Scientific Theories*, ed: Fred Suppe, (Urbana: University of Illinois Press. 2nd ed., 1977), pp. 518–555.

true in general, however, and it was the switch to transverse wave models several years later that provided the key to a wave explanation of polarization and other previously difficult cases. But what are we to say of the Commission's conclusion after Arago's experiments with the opaque disk? Were they justified in concluding simply that Fresnel's theory is correct, even though this conclusion had later to be modified? Or should the conclusion have been softened by a qualifying "approximately"?

One reason for softening conclusions is the general realization that (with the possible exception of models of microphysical phenomena) no model is likely to capture the full complexity of the phenomena under investigation. Thus no hypothesis asserting a "perfect fit" between a model and a phenomenon is likely to be exactly true. We can be fairly confident on general grounds that there are likely to be at least minor discrepancies, even if these do not show up in existing experiments. Thus, if one desires a conclusion that one does not know in advance to be strictly false, it seems advisable to say that what one accepts as true is not ever H itself, but the more complicated conclusion that "H is approximately true."

This position is reinforced by our account of the testing of theoretical hypotheses. It is required that the testing process be such that a false hypothesis is very likely to lead to a failed prediction and thus to rejection of the hypothesis. But we could never be in the position of knowing that even a very slight difference between the model and the real system would very probably lead to a failed prediction. The most we could ever reasonably claim about a testing process is that it is very likely to detect a type and degree of deviation from the model. The *type* is given by the category of phenomena being studied. Arago's experiment could not possibly detect mistaken features of the model that would not show up in simple diffraction experiments. Nor could it detect *degrees* of deviation beyond the resolving power of his experimental apparatus. If the spot had been of very low intensity, for example, he would have missed it even though the wave model was basically correct. Thus, if the experiment yields a positive con-

clusion, that conclusion must be correspondingly qualified. What we can say is that the real system exhibits the structure of the model in those respects relevant to the domain in question and to a degree that the experiments performed are capable of detecting. This is an elaboration of the simple phrase "H is approximately true."

It is sometimes supposed that in moving from "H is true" to "H is approximately true," one is trading a probable falsehood for a vacuous truth. That this is not so is well illustrated by the Fresnel example. Models of the type Fresnel used for diffraction simply do not work for polarization experiments. And the reason is clear: longitudinal waves do not polarize. The correct conclusion, as was clear at the time, was that any supposed Fresnel theory of polarization was not even approximately true. Of course much more could and needs to be said about approximation, but the general charge of vacuity can be safely dismissed.

Even doubly qualified, our conclusions are still quite solidly realistic. With all qualifications understood, to accept H as approximately correct is to assert that there is a real structure underlying the phenomena, and that this underlying structure, as far as we can tell, reflects the structure of our model. Bas van Frassen has recently raised general objections that apply even to so qualified a version of scientific realism. Since the view of theoretical models embedded in my account is essentially van Fraassen's, it is important to see how his objections may be avoided.[24]

Reformulated in my terminology, van Fraassen's view is that theoretical hypotheses may *refer* to underlying entities and processes, but that no evidence can *justify* accepting claims about such theoretical goings on. Rather, the most we can ever justifiably claim is that our models are "empirically adequate," i.e., that they "save the phenomena." His main direct argument for so restricting our conclusions is that, for any given

---

[24] See n. 13.

evidence, the conclusion of empirical adequacy is necessarily better supported than any realistic conclusion simply because it is logically weaker. The realistic conclusion implies empirical adequacy, but the reverse implication, of course, fails. Van Fraassen tends to state his argument by saying that the empiricist hypothesis of empirical adequacy is *more probable,* for any given evidence, than a realistic hypothesis. The general point, however, does not depend on invoking (logical or subjective) probabilities of hypotheses.

That the empiricists' hypothesis is always *better* supported does not, however, imply that the realists' hypothesis cannot be *adequately* supported. Reformulating the same point, just because empirical adequacy is a *more acceptable* hypothesis, it does not follow that a realistic hypothesis is not *acceptable.* Van Fraassen assumes that only the more probable empiricists' hypothesis could be acceptable. That this assumption is not necessarily justified is reinforced by the logic of satisficing. If we assign *equal* value to the truth of both empiricist and realist hypotheses, the empiricist hypothesis, being more probable, would have greater expected value. But the realist hypothesis might still have "satisfactory" expected value, making it acceptable to a satisficer. But of course a realist would assign *greater* scientific value to true realistic hypotheses, which could give them greater expected value. So a realistic satisficer need not even be in the position of settling for second best.

These considerations do not, of course, settle the issues between realists and empiricists. My objective has been simply to show that one can adopt van Fraassen's formal account of theoretical models without committing oneself to his anti-realist arguments. Van Fraassen himself insists that this separation be possible, but it is useful to see how to make the separation for a particular realistic alternative.

FINAL CONSIDERATIONS

In conclusion, I would like briefly to mention two issues that would have to be treated in any gener-

ally adequate account of scientific inference but that cannot be examined in any detail here. One involves a technical elaboration; the other is philosophically much broader.

The above account treats only deterministic models. This leaves out stochastic models, which yield only statistical predictions. But the account also fails to be adequate to the actual testing of deterministic models. Experiments testing theoretical hypotheses typically require multiple measurements on complex apparatus that, when pushed to their limits of accuracy, yield a spread of values. Thus even tests of deterministic models typically involve testing statistical hypotheses. Testing theoretical hypotheses is therefore generally a two-stage affair. One begins by testing a statistical hypothesis or estimating a statistical parameter in order to determine whether the theoretical prediction has been fulfilled or not. Only after deciding on the truth or falsity of the prediction can one reach a conclusion on the theoretical hypothesis. It turns out, however, that the above account of testing theoretical hypotheses can be extended in a completely natural way to incorporate the statistical level into the whole testing process. No fundamentally new principles need be involved.[25]

The broader issue concerns *justification* of the type involved in traditional philosophical discussions of "the justification of induction." On the above account, whether a proposed test of a theoretical hypothesis is a satisfactory test is itself an empirical question. The judgment that fulfillment of the prediction would be unlikely if the hypothesis tested is not (even approximately) true is an empirical judgment. This opens the way for a typical Humean regress.

Philosophers of science today are much less concerned with Hume's problem than in the recent past. Foundationist justifications, in particular, have largely gone out of fashion. In their place

---

[25] This point is further developed in the two papers mentioned in n. 21 above.

are discussions of the "rationality" of the scientific process. I regard this development as a "progressive problem shift." The new program, however, requires a sound theory of the scientific process before one can fruitfully inquire after the rationality of that process. We do not yet have such a theory. Indeed, one of the main defects of current theories is that they lack good accounts of the empirical testing of theoretical hypotheses. We may hope this is just a temporary situation, part of the general over-reaction to positivism. In any case, only when we achieve a more balanced picture of the scientific enterprise itself shall we be in a position to develop better ideas about the nature of scientific justification and rationality.[26]

---

[26] My own version of a "nonfoundationist" justification of induction is developed in The Epistemological Roots of Scientific Knowledge, *Minnesota Studies in the Philosophy of Science,* Vol. VI, *Induction, Probability and Confirmation,* G. Maxwell and R. M. Anderson, eds., (Minneapolis: University of Minnesota Press, 1975), pp. 212–261.

THE HISTORICAL DEVELOPMENT OF SCIENTIFIC KNOWLEDGE

4

In the last section we witnessed some of the controversy that has surrounded the issue of the appraisal of claims to scientific knowledge. As we saw, philosophers of science have fundamentally disagreed not only about how such claims are or ought to be appraised but also about the units of scientific knowledge and appraisal themselves—whether they are best construed as individual theories, systems of theories, research programmes, theoretical hypotheses, or the like.

But controversy has also surrounded the *results* of scientific appraisal, especially the pattern of development that those results have taken over time. Two important questions have been debated under this head. The first question concerns the historical development of *scientific fields:* In what way has the knowledge generated in individual scientific fields changed over time? The second question concerns the historical development of *science as a whole:* To what extent has the knowledge generated in the various scientific fields been moving toward the ideal of unified science, a single comprehensive and unified explanatory system of theories? In what follows we shall briefly discuss the main positions that have been taken on these two questions. This preliminary material will be followed by readings representing the main positions. We shall then be in a position to consider, in Section V, our final question regarding the results of scientific enquiry: Is scientific knowledge a literally true account of the way the world is?

THE DEVELOPMENT OF SCIENTIFIC FIELDS: CONSERVATION VERSUS CHANGE

Perusing almost any science text gives one the impression that, by and large, science has developed in a cumulative way. More specifically, the impression is that, after, perhaps, an initial period of groping toward the right questions and the right methods, the history of a scientific field has consisted in a series of individual discoveries and inventions—namely, the ones reported in the field's texts; that, one by one, in a process like the addition of bricks to a building, scientists—working with the same methods, aims, and problems as their modern counterparts, and observing the same world—have added another fact, concept, law, or theory to the modern body of technical knowledge. Consider, for example, elementary physics texts. What you are likely to find described and applied in them are Galileo's laws dealing with the motion of objects (falling stones, pendula, balls on inclined planes) near the surface of the earth, Kepler's laws dealing with the motion of the planets around the sun, Newton's more general laws of motion and law of universal gravitation dealing with the motion and causes of motion of any terrestrial and celestial object whatever, Einstein's still more general theory of relativity dealing with the motion and causes of motion of atomic and nuclear particles as well as all terrestrial and celestial objects, and so on. These laws and theories are represented in such physics texts as permanent additions to scientific knowledge, obtained by using sound scientific procedures. And they are represented as progressively revealing the truth about the world.

This cumulative model of scientific development—that a scientific field typically develops by adding new knowledge to the knowledge already accumulated—implicit in much science textbook writing as well as in much of the older history and justificationist philosophy of science, has been widely criticized during more than two decades of discussion on scientific change. Two alternative views have proved influential in that discussion: the evolutionary model of scientific development, associated with Karl Popper, and the revolutionary model of scientific development, associated with Thomas Kuhn. In addition, a promising new gradualist model of scientific development has recently been proposed by Larry Laudan. We shall sketch each of these models in turn.

The Evolutionary Model of Scientific Development

According to the cumulative model of scientific development, as we have seen, laws like those formulated by Galileo, Kepler, Newton, and Einstein are permanent additions to scientific knowledge, progressively revealing the truth about the world. But only the slightest investigation will demonstrate that this account is inaccurate. After all, Galileo's and Kepler's laws are incompatible with Newtonian mechanics; for example, according to Galileo's laws the acceleration due to gravity of an object near the surface of the earth is constant, whereas according to Newtonian mechanics that acceleration varies with the height of the object from the surface of the earth. And Newtonian mechanics is, likewise, incompatible with Einstein's theory; according to Newtonian mechanics, for example, the mass of an object is a constant property, whereas according to Einsteinian theory the mass of an object varies with its velocity. Newtonian mechanics *corrects* Galileo's and Kepler's laws: They are a good approximation to the more accurate laws deducible from it. Newtonian mechanics does not add to or generalize or explain Galileo's and Kepler's laws. And, similarly, Einstein's theory corrects Newtonian mechanics. How can we capture this prevalent kind of situation in a model of scientific development?

According to the evolutionary model proposed by Karl Popper, science is a means used by human beings to adapt to their environment. Such adaptation starts with the dominant scientific theories of a field (an inherited structure), which are then exposed to an environment of experimental tests. In response to negative results of such tests (challenges from the environment), new tentative theories (variations of the inherited structure) are produced by methods that are at least partly random. The new tentative theories must, of course, lead to at least some results that conflict with those of the original theories—must, therefore, be incompatible with the original theories—or they could not hope to deal with the negative experimental results faced by the original theories. A natural selection from the new tentative theories then follows, allowing only the more well-adapted theories to survive and be transmitted in turn.

Thus, according to the evolutionary model of scientific development, the new theories in a field are *replacements* of, rather than additions to, older theories in the field. In this sense the development of the field is not cumulative. But in another sense, we are told, that development *is* cumulative, for the new theories in a field typically yield results at least as good as those of their predecessors in all those areas in which the predecessors were successful, while yielding different and better results in other areas as well. Thus, the new theories typically preserve the successes of their predecessors while adding to them, allowing a closer adaptation to nature. Indeed, according to the evolutionary model, this preservation of old successes and addition of new successes is the mark of scientific progress, allowing rational assessment of scientific change.

In "The Rationality of Scientific Revolutions," Karl Popper sets out the evolutionary model of scientific development.

The Revolutionary Model of Scientific Development

According to the revolutionary model of scientific development associated with Thomas Kuhn, the kind of cumulative scientific development described in the evolutionary model never really occurs. After all, we are told, the new theories that replace older theories give scientists new ways of thinking about the world, new ways of describing the world, including observable objects and events, even new ways of seeing the world. Indeed, in a sense, the new theories give scientists new worlds to investigate—a Newtonian world in which objects naturally move in straight lines rather than a Galilean world in which they naturally move in circles, or an Einsteinian world in which the shape, size, mass, and other properties of objects vary with one's frame of reference rather than a Newtonian world in which such properties are intrinsic to their objects. Such new theories, moreover, give scientists new methods of investigating these new worlds— for example, rules of inference that allow the postulation of unobservable objects rather than rules of inference that preclude the postulation of such objects. Such new theories also give scientists new goals to pursue when investigating these new worlds, such as the goal of explaining phenomena in terms of entities and processes that are better understood than what is to be explained, or that can be represented by mechanical models, or that are picturable, or the like.

The conclusion, according to the revolutionary model, is that when theories change, the world of scientists, their methods, and their goals, and thus, the successes these allow, change as well. The historical development of a scientific field is thus a succession of scientific revolutions, a succession, that is, of radical shifts of theory and associated fact, methods, and goals, with (unlike the cumulative model) no progress toward one complete set of truths about the world, and (unlike the evolutionary model) no progress toward ever more successful accounts of the world. Progress nonetheless occurs. It occurs between scientific revolutions, as each new theory is developed and extended to new areas of application. And it occurs across scientific revolutions as well. At least the scientific community most intimately involved with a revolutionary change of theory would represent that change as progress, and, we are told, as practitioners of the relevant specialty they are the ones best fitted by training and experience to judge.

In "The Function of Dogma in Scientific Research" and "The Nature and Necessity of Scientific Revolutions," Thomas Kuhn gives his now-classic defense of the revolutionary model of scientific development.

The Gradualist Model of Scientific Development

The gradualist model of scientific development espoused by Larry Laudan presents yet another account of scientific change. According to this account, new theories have given scientists new worlds to investigate, but, as a matter of historical fact, they have not always given scientists new methods of investigating these new worlds or new goals to pursue when investigating them. Indeed, we are told, scientific theories, methods, and goals have tended to function as independent elements in the history of science. Sometimes the theories of a scientific field have changed, sometimes its methods, and sometimes its goals. Occasionally two of these elements have changed simultaneously. But rarely have all three changed at once. To be sure, the great transitions in the history of science—for example, from an Aristotelian to a Newtonian worldview, or from nineteenth-century mechanistic psychology to psychoanalysis—that did involve changes of all three kinds of elements, have appeared to us as abrupt Kuhnian revolutionary changes because our characterizations of these changes have compressed or telescoped a number of gradual changes (one element at a time) into one abrupt change.

The historical development of a scientific field, according to the gradualist model, is thus a succession of separate changes of theory, methods, and goals—that is, a more gradual version of the kind of development described in the revolutionary model. Like the revolutionary model (and unlike the cumulative model) the gradualist model allows no progress toward one complete set of truths about the world, and like the revolutionary model (and unlike the evolutionary model) it allows no progress toward ever more successful accounts of the world. But unlike the revolutionary model it allows progress of another sort. Thus, if a scientific community's methods fail to justify their theories, or if their methods fail to promote their goals, or if their goals prove to be utopian, the scientific community will have compelling reasons for replacing one element or another of their worldview with an element that does the job better. And, once made, that replacement will represent progress. In short, the gradualist model, unlike the revolutionary model, allows the sort of progress that occurs when a change of one component of a scientific field (for example, its methods) occurs, and is rationally justified, given the character of its other components (its theories and goals).

In "Dissecting the Holist Picture of Scientific Change," Larry Laudan argues for the gradualist model of scientific development.

Summary

We have now considered four models of scientific development—the cumulative model, the evolutionary model, the revolutionary model, and the gradualist model. Each has offered us a different account of scientific progress and a correspondingly different account of the typical historical development of scientific fields. Thus, according to the cumulative model, a scientific field progresses when it gains new facts, concepts, laws, or theories by correct applications of scientific method, and the typical historical development of a scientific field is a succession of such additions. According to the evolutionary model, a scientific field progresses when it replaces its current theories with new, more successful theories, and the typical historical development of a scientific field is a succession of such replacements. According to the revolutionary model, a scientific field progresses when it replaces its current theories and associated facts, methods, and goals with new theories and associated facts, methods, and goals, and the typical historical development of a scientific field is a succession of such radical replacements. And finally, according to the gradualist model, a scientific field progresses when it justifiably replaces one or more of its current theories, methods, or goals with new theories, methods, or goals, and the typical historical development of a scientific field is a succession of such limited replacements.

How do you choose among these alternative models of scientific development? Obviously a careful reading of each of the selections that follow will be helpful, particularly if you pay close attention to the reasons given by each author for his position, and the examples offered in support or illustration. You might then consider how closely each model fits selected noncontroversial examples of scientific progress. These might be cases the authors themselves take up, or cases already familiar to you or in which you have an interest. Furthermore, how closely does each model fit other cases in other scientific fields? Bear in mind that a model that fits one scientific field fairly well, at least for some part of its history, may not fit other scientific fields nearly as well (not every scientific field may develop in the same way), so that we may need different models of scientific development for different scientific fields. And bear in mind that some hybrid of the different models, or some model of your own creation, might be better yet.

THE DEVELOPMENT OF SCIENCE AS A WHOLE: UNITY VS. PLURALISM

Could a completely developed psychology explain all the phenomena dealt with by sociology, economics, political science, and the other social sciences, and a completely developed biology explain all the phenomena dealt with by psychology? Could a completely developed chemistry, in turn, explain all the phenomena dealt with by biology, and a completely developed physics explain all the phenomena dealt with by chemistry? In short, could a completely developed physics explain *all* phenomena—are all phenomena, at bottom, physical in nature?

The question of how scientific fields have developed over time leads naturally to the question of how science as a whole has developed over time; that is, through all the additions or replacements of laws and theories, methods, and goals in all the various scientific fields, has science been moving towards a unified result? Is one picture of the world emerging, or are a number of disparate pictures emerging instead?

Many scientists as well as philosophers of science have assumed that, since the world that science is investigating is one, the ultimate result of that investigation should also be one. The unified result these individuals have in mind is a state of science in which the theories of some one discipline, usually thought to be physics, would be able to explain all observational data. To describe this state of science more clearly, let us envision science divided into six levels of theories dealing with the following six levels of objects: (6) social groups; (5) multicellular living things; (4) cells; (3) molecules; (2) atoms; and (1) elementary particles. And let us speak of the ''reduction'' of the theories of one level to the theories of the next lower level when the lower-level theories can explain all the observational data explained by the higher-level theories. In this case the number of theories really needed for explanation of such data would be reduced to those on the lower level. And the objects really needed for explanation of such data would correspondingly be reduced to those on the lower level. Leaving out questions of convenience, we could then simply omit the higher-level theories and objects from science as superfluous for explanatory purposes. In these terms the unity of science would be a state of science in which the theories of each level would be reduced to theories of the next lower level, the theories of the lowest level being those to which all the theories of science would finally be reduced in a cumulative way. These theories of the lowest level would thus be the theories which could explain all observational data, and the objects of the lowest level they dealt with would thus be the only objects needed to explain all observational data. These theories of the lowest level would thus be the final and complete result of the scientific enterprise.

So much for the nature of a unified science. Has science actually been moving toward this kind of unity? Paul Oppenheim and Hilary Putnam, in their classic ''Unity of Science as a Working Hypothesis,'' and Dudley Shapere, in his more recent ''Unity and Method in Contemporary Science,'' argue that science has indeed been moving toward this kind of unity, while Patrick Suppes, in his recent ''The Plurality of Science,'' argues that science has, in fact, been moving in the opposite direction—toward greater pluralism. The evidence Oppenheim and Putnam present in favor of a movement toward unity includes examples of a variety of successful reductions of theories between all successive pairs of the six levels cited above, as well as such indirect evidence as successes at synthesizing things of each level out of things of the next lower level, and evidence to the effect that each level is, in evolution, prior to the one above it. For his own part Shapere surveys developments in the history of the physical and biological sciences to show that, despite numerous setbacks along the way, there has been an overall tendency toward more and more comprehensive unification of the various fields of science.

Suppes, arguing *against* a movement toward unity, points out that we cannot have reduction of the theories of the different sciences to the theories dealing with elementary particles because, despite all the research that has gone into the question, we simply do not know what these theories and their postulated elementary particles are. Nor is there reason to believe that we will one day find them out, given the continual revision of our views regarding them and the continual increase of complexity of high-energy physics and elementary particle theory. Nor is there reason to believe that the theories of one branch of science will one day be able to explain the observational data explained by the theories of other branches of science, given that the experimental languages of the different branches of science— the languages in which such observational data are expressed—have been diverging rather than converging. In the end you will have to decide which side makes the stronger case.

The Rationality of Scientific Revolutions

Karl Popper

The title of this series of Spencer lectures, *Progress and Obstacles to Progress in the Sciences,* was chosen by the organizers of the series. The title seems to me to imply that progress in science is a good thing, and that an obstacle to progress is a bad thing, a position held by almost everybody, until quite recently. Perhaps I should make clear at once that I accept this position, although with some slight and fairly obvious reservations to which I shall briefly allude later. Of course, obstacles which are due to the inherent difficulty of the problems tackled are welcome challenges. (Indeed, many scientists were greatly disappointed when it turned out that the problem of tapping nuclear energy was comparatively trivial, involving no new revolutionary change of theory.) But stagnation in science would be a curse. Still, I agree with Professor Bodmer's suggestion that scientific advance is only a *mixed* blessing.[1] Let us face it: Blessings *are* mixed, with some exceedingly rare exceptions.

My talk will be divided into two parts. The first part (Sections I–VIII) is devoted to progress in science, and the second part (Sections IX–XIV) to some of the social obstacles to progress.

Remembering Herbert Spencer, I shall discuss progress in science largely *from an evolutionary point of view*—more precisely, from the point of view of the theory of natural selection. Only the end of the first part (that is, Section VIII), will be spent in discussing the progress of science *from a logical point of view,* and in proposing *two rational criteria* of progress in science, which will be needed in the second part of my talk.

In the second part I shall discuss a few obstacles to progress in science, more especially ideological obstacles; and I shall end (Sections XI–XIV) by discussing the distinction between, on the one hand, *scientific revolutions,* which are subject to rational criteria of progress, and on the other hand, *ideological revolutions,* which are only rarely rationally defensible. It appeared to me that this distinction was sufficiently interesting to call my lecture "The Rationality of Scientific Revolutions." The emphasis here must be, of course, on the word "scientific."

I

I now turn to progress in science. I will be looking at progress in science from a biological or evolutionary point of view. I am far from suggesting that this is the most important point of view for examining progress in science. But the biological approach offers a convenient way of introducing the two leading ideas of the first half of my talk. They are the ideas of *instruction* and of *selection.*

From a biological or evolutionary point of view, science, or progress in science, may be regarded as a means used by the human species to adapt itself to the environment: to invade new environmental niches, and even to invent new envi-

I wish to thank Troels Eggers Hansen, The Rev. Michael Sharratt, Dr. Herbert Spengler, and Dr. Martin Wenham for critical comments on this lecture.

[1] See, in the present series of Herbert Spencer Lectures, the concluding remark of the contribution by Professor W. F. Bodmer. My own misgivings concerning scientific advance and stagnation arise mainly from the changed spirit of science, and from the unchecked growth of Big Science which endangers great science. (See Section IX of this lecture.) Biology seems to have escaped this danger so far, but not, of course, the closely related dangers of large-scale application.

From *Problems of Scientific Revolution: Progress and Obstacles to Progress in the Sciences,* The Herbert Spencer Lectures 1973, Rom Harré, Ed. (1975), pp. 72–101. Copyright 1975, 1981 by Sir Karl Popper and reprinted by permission of the author.

ronmental niches.[2] This leads to the following problem.

We can distinguish between three levels of adaptation: genetic adaptation; adaptive behavioral learning; and scientific discovery, which is a special case of adaptive behavioral learning. My main problem in this part of my talk will be to enquire into the similarities and dissimilarities between the strategies of progress or adaptation on the *scientific* level and on those two other levels: the *genetic* level and the *behavioral* level. And I will compare the three levels of adaptation by investigating the role played on each level by *instruction* and by *selection*.

II

In order not to lead you blindfolded to the result of this comparison I will anticipate at once my main thesis. It is a thesis asserting the *fundamental similarity of the three levels,* as follows.

On all three levels—genetic adaptation, adaptive behavior, and scientific discovery—the mechanism of adaptation is fundamentally the same.

This can be explained in some detail.

Adaptation starts from an inherited *structure* which is basic for all three levels: *the gene structure of the organism.* To it corresponds, *on* the behavioral level, *the innate repertoire* of the types of behavior which are available to the organism, and on the scientific level, *the dominant scientific conjectures or theories.* These *structures* are always transmitted by *instruction,* on all three levels: by the replication of the coded genetic instruction on the genetic and the behavioral levels, and by social tradition and imitation on the behavioral and the scientific levels. On all three levels, the *instruction* comes from *within the structure.* If mutations or variations or errors occur, then these are new instructions, which also arise *from within the*

structure, rather than *from without,* from the environment.

These inherited structures are exposed to certain pressures, or challenges, or problems: to selection pressures; to environmental challenges; to theoretical problems. In response, variations of the genetically or traditionally inherited *instructions* are produced[3] *by* methods which are at least partly *random.* On the genetic level, these are mutations and recombinations[4] of the coded instruction; on the behavioral level, they are tentative variations and recombinations within the repertoire; on the scientific level, they are new and revolutionary tentative theories. On all three levels we get new tentative trial instructions, or, briefly, tentative trials.

It is important that these tentative trials are changes that originate *within* the individual structure in a more or less random fashion—on all three levels. The view that they are *not* due to instruction from without, from the environment, is supported (if only weakly) by the fact that very similar organisms may sometimes respond in very different ways to the same new environmental challenge.

The next stage is that of *selection* from the available mutations and variations: those of the new tentative trials which are badly adapted are eliminated. *This is the stage of the elimination of error.* Only the more or less well adapted trial instructions survive and are inherited in their turn. Thus we may speak of *adaptation by "the method of trial and error"* or better, by "the method of trial and the elimination of error." The elimination of error, or of badly adapted trial instructions, is also called *natural selection:* it is a kind of "negative feedback." It operates on all three levels.

It is to be noted that in general *no equilibrium state of adaptation* is reached by any one applica-

---

[2] The formation of membrane proteins, of the first viruses, and of cells, may perhaps have been among the earliest inventions of new environmental niches, though it is possible that other environmental niches (perhaps networks of enzymes invented by otherwise naked genes) may have been invented even earlier.

[3] It is an open problem whether one can speak in these terms ("in response") about the genetic level (compare my conjecture about responding mutagens in Section V). Yet if there were no variations, there could not be adaptation or evolution; and so we can say that the occurrence of mutations is either partly controlled by a need for them, or functions as if it was.

[4] When in this lecture I speak, for brevity's sake, of *mutation,* the possibility of recombination is of course always tacitly included.

tion of the method of trial and the elimination of error, or by natural selection. First, because no perfect or optimal trial solutions to the problem are likely to be offered; secondly—and this is more important—because the emergence of new structures, or of new instructions, involves a change in the environmental situation. New elements of the environment may become relevant; and in consequence, new pressures, new challenges, new problems may arise, as a result of the structural changes which have arisen from within the organism.

On the genetic level the change may be a mutation of a gene, with a consequent change of an enzyme. Now the network of enzymes forms the more intimate environment of the gene structure. Accordingly, there will be a change in this intimate environment; and with it, new relationships between the organism and the more remote environment may arise; and further, new selection pressures.

The same happens on the behavioral level, for the adoption of a new kind of behavior can be equated in most cases with the adoption of a new ecological niche. As a consequence, new selection pressures will arise, and new genetic changes.

On the scientific level, the tentative adoption of a new conjecture or theory may solve one or two problems, but it invariably opens up many *new* problems; for a new revolutionary theory functions exactly like a new and powerful sense organ. If the progress is significant then the new problems will differ from the old problems: The new problems will be on a radically different level of depth. This happened, for example, in relativity; it happened in quantum mechanics; and it happens right now, most dramatically, in molecular biology. In each of these cases, new horizons of unexpected problems were opened up by the new theory.

This, I suggest, is the way in which science progresses. And our progress can best be gauged by comparing our old problems with our new ones. If the progress that has been made is great, then the new problems will be of a character undreamt of before. There will be deeper problems, and, besides, there will be more of them. The fur-

ther we progress in knowledge, the more clearly we can discern the vastness of our ignorance.[5]

I will now sum up my thesis.

On all the three levels which I am considering—the genetic, the behavioral, and the scientific levels—we are operating with inherited structures which are passed on by instruction, either through the genetic code or through tradition. On all the three levels, new structures and new instructions arise by trial changes from *within the structure:* by tentative trials which are subject to natural selection or the elimination of error.

III

So far I have stressed the *similarities* in the working of the adaptive mechanism on the three levels. This raises an obvious problem: What about the *differences?*

The main difference between the genetic and the behavioral level is this. Mutations on the genetic level are not only random but completely "blind," in two senses.[6] First, they are in no way goal directed. Secondly, the survival of a mutation cannot influence the further mutations, not even the frequencies or probabilities of their occurrence; though admittedly, the *survival* of a mutation may sometimes determine what kind of mutations may possibly *survive* in future cases. On the behavioral level, trials are also more or less random, but they are no longer completely "blind" in either of the two senses mentioned. First, they are goal directed; and secondly, animals may learn from the outcome of a trial: They may learn to avoid the type of trial behavior which has led to a failure. (They may even avoid it in cases in which it could have succeeded.) Similarly, they may also

---

[5] The realization of our ignorance has become pinpointed as a result, for example, of the astonishing revolution brought about by molecular biology.

[6] For the use of the term *blind* (especially in the second sense) see D. T. Campbell, "Methodological Suggestions from a Comparative Psychology of Knowledge Processes," *Inquiry* **2**, 152–82 (1959); "Blind Variation and Selective Retention in Creative Thought as in Other Knowledge Processes," *Psychol. Rev.* **67**, 380–400 (1960); and "Evolutionary Epistemology," in *The Philosophy of Karl Popper,* The Library of Living Philosophers (ed. P. A. Schilpp), pp. 413–63, The Open Court Publishing Co., La Salle, Illinois (1974).

learn from success; and successful behavior may be repeated, even in cases in which it is not adequate. However, a certain degree of "blindness" is inherent in all trials.[7]

Behavioral adaptation is usually an intensely active process: The animal—especially the young animal at play—and even the plant, are actively investigating the environment.[8]

This activity, which is largely genetically programmed, seems to me to mark an important difference between the genetic level and the behavioral level. I may here refer to the experience which the Gestalt psychologists call "insight;" an experience that accompanies many behavioral discoveries.[9] However, it must not be overlooked

that even a discovery accompanied by "insight" may be *mistaken:* Every trial, even one with "insight," is of the nature of a conjecture or a hypothesis. Köhler's apes, it will be remembered, sometimes hit with "insight" on what turns out to be a mistaken attempt to solve their problem; and even great mathematicians are sometimes misled by intuition. Thus animals and men have to try out their hypotheses; they have to use the method of trial and of error elimination.

On the other hand I agree with Köhler and Thorpe[10] that the trials of problem-solving animals are in general not completely blind. Only in extreme cases, when the problem which confronts the animal does not yield to the making of hypotheses, will the animal resort to more or less blind and random attempts in order to get out of a disconcerting situation. Yet even in these attempts, goal-directedness is usually discernible, in sharp contrast to the blind randomness of genetic mutations and recombinations.

Another difference between genetic change and adaptive behavioral change is that the former *always* establishes a rigid and almost invariable genetic structure. The latter, admittedly, leads *sometimes* also to a fairly rigid behavior pattern which is dogmatically adhered to; radically so in the case of "imprinting" (Konrad Lorenz); but in other cases it leads to a flexible pattern which allows for differentiation or modification—for example, it may lead to exploratory behavior, or to what Pavlov called the "freedom reflex."[11]

On the scientific level, discoveries are revolutionary and creative. Indeed, a certain creativity

---

[7] While the "blindness" of trials is relative to what we have found out in the past, randomness is relative to a set of elements (forming the "sample space"). On the genetic level these "elements" are the four nucleotide bases; on the behavioral level they are the constituents of the organism's repertoire of behavior. These constituents may assume different weights with respect to different needs or goals, and the weights may change through experience (lowering the degree of "blindness").

[8] On the importance of active participation, see R. Held and A. Hein, "Movement-produced Stimulation in the Development of Visually Guided Behavior," *J. Comp. Physiol. Psychol.* **56,** 872–6 (1963); cf. J. C. Eccles *Facing Reality,* pp. 66–7. The activity is, at least partly, one of producing hypotheses: see J. Krechevsky, "'Hypothesis' versus 'Chance' in the Pre-solution Period in Sensory Discrimination-learning," *Univ. Calif. Publ. Psychol.* **6,** 27–44 (1932) (reprinted in *Animal Problem Solving* [ed. A. J. Riopelle], pp. 183–97, Penguin Books, Hardmondsworth [1967].

[9] I may perhaps mention here some of the differences between my views and the views of the Gestalt school. (Of course, I accept the fact of Gestalt perception; I am only dubious about what may be called Gestalt philosophy.)

I conjecture that the unity, or the articulation, of perception is more closely dependent on the motor control systems and the efferent neural systems of the brain than on afferent systems, that it is closely dependent on the behavioral repertoire of the organism. I conjecture that a spider or a mouse will never have insight (as had Köhler's ape) into the possible unity of the two sticks which can be joined together, because handling sticks of that size does not belong to their behavioral repertoire. All this may be interpreted as a kind of generalization of the James-Lange theory of emotions (1884; see William James, *The Principles of Psychology,* Vol. II, pp. 449 ff. [1809] Macmillan and Co., London), extending the theory from our emotions to our perceptions (especially to Gestalt perceptions), which thus would not be "given" to us (as in Gestalt theory) but rather "made" by us, by decoding (comparatively "given") clues. The fact that the clues may mislead (optical illusions in man; dummy illusions in animals, etc.) can be explained by the biological need to impose our behavioral interpretations upon highly simplified clues. The conjecture that our decoding of what the senses tell us depends on our behavioral repertoire may explain part of the gulf that lies between animals and man, for through the evolution of the human language our repertoire has become unlimited.

[10] See W. H. Thorpe, *Learning and Instinct in Animals,* pp. 99 ff. Methuen, London (1956); 1963 edn, pp. 100–47; W. Köhler, *The Mentality of Apes* (1925); Penguin Books edn, (1957), pp. 166 ff.

[11] See I. P. Pavlov, *Conditioned Reflexes,* esp. pp. 11–12, Oxford University Press (1927). In view of what he calls "exploratory behavior" and the closely related "freedom behavior"— both obviously genetically based—and of the significance of these for scientific activity, it seems to me that the behavior of behaviorists who aim to supersede the value of freedom by what they call "positive reinforcement" may be a symptom of an unconscious hostility to science. Incidentally, what B. F. Skinner (cf. his *Beyond Freedom and Dignity* (1972) Cape, London) calls "the literature of freedom" did not arise as a result of negative reinforcement, as he suggests. It arose, rather, with Aeschylus and Pindar, as a result of the victories of Marathon and Salamis.

may be attributed to all levels, even to the genetic level: New trials, leading to new environments and thus to new selection pressures, create new and revolutionary results on all levels, even though there are strong conservative tendencies built into the various mechanisms of instruction.

Genetic adaptation can of course operate only within the time span of a few generations—at the very least, say, one or two generations. In organisms which replicate very quickly this may be a short time span, and there may be simply no room for behavioral adaptation. More slowly reproducing organisms are compelled to invent behavioral adaptation in order to adjust themselves to quick environmental changes. They thus need a behavioral repertoire, with types of behavior of greater or lesser latitude or range. The repertoire, and the latitude of the available types of behavior can be assumed to be genetically programmed; and since, as indicated, a new type of behavior may be said to involve the choice of a new environmental niche, new types of behavior may indeed be genetically creative, for they may in their turn determine new selection pressures and thereby indirectly decide upon the future evolution of the genetic structure.[12]

On the level of scientific discovery two new aspects emerge. The most important one is that scientific theories can be formulated linguistically, and that they can even be published. Thus they become objects outside ourselves: objects open to investigation. As a consequence, they are now open to *criticism*. Thus we can get rid of a badly fitting theory before the adoption of the theory makes us unfit to survive: By criticizing our theories we can let our theories die in our stead. This is of course immensely important.

The other aspect is also connected with language. It is one of the novelties of human language that it encourages story telling, and thus *creative imagination*. Scientific discovery is akin to explanatory story telling, to myth making and to poetic imagination. The growth of imagination enhances of course the need for some control, such as, in science, inter-personal criticism—the friendly hostile cooperation of scientists which is partly based on competition and partly on the common aim to get nearer to the truth. This, and the role played by instruction and tradition, seems to me to exhaust the main sociological elements inherently involved in the progress of science; though more could be said of course about the social obstacles to progress, or the social dangers inherent in progress.

IV

I have suggested that progress in science, or scientific discovery, depends on *instruction* and *selection:* on a conservative or traditional or historical element, and on a revolutionary use of trial and the elimination of error by criticism, which includes severe empirical examinations or tests; that is, attempts to probe into the possible weaknesses of theories, attempts to refute them.

Of course, the individual scientist may wish to establish his theory rather than to refute it. But from the point of view of progress in science, this wish can easily mislead him. Moreover, if he does not himself examine his favorite theory critically, others will do so for him. The only results which will be regarded by them as supporting the theory will be the failures of interesting attempts to refute it; failures to find counter-examples where such counter-examples would be most expected, in the light of the best of the competing theories. Thus it need not create a great obstacle to science if the

---

[12] Thus exploratory behavior and problem-solving create new conditions for the evolution of genetic systems, conditions which deeply affect the natural selection of these systems. One can say that once a certain latitude of behavior has been attained—as it has been attained even by unicellular organisms (see especially the classic work of H. S. Jennings, *The Behavior of the Lower Organisms,* Columbia University Press, New York [1906]—the initiative of the organism in selecting its ecology or habitat takes the lead, and natural selection within the new habitat follows the lead. In this way, Darwinism can simulate Lamarckism, and even Bergson's "creative evolution." This has been recognized by strict Darwinists. For a brilliant presentation and summary of the history, see Sir Alister Hardy, *The Living Stream,* Collins, London (1965), especially Lectures VI, VII, and VIII, where many references to earlier literature will be found, from James Hutton (who died in 1797) onwards (see pp. 178 ff.). See also Ernst Mayr, *Animal Species and Evolution,* The Belknap Press, Cambridge, Mass., and Oxford University Press, London (1963), pp. 604 ff. and 611; Erwin Schrödinger, *Mind and Matter,* Cambridge University Press (1958), Ch. 2; F. W. Braestrup, "The Evolutionary Significance of Learning," in *Vidensk. Meddr dansk naturh. Foren.* **134,** 89–102 (1971) (with a bibliography); and also my first Herbert Spencer Lecture (1961) now in my *Objective Knowledge,* Clarendon Press, Oxford (1972, 1973).

individual scientist is biased in favor of a pet theory. Yet I think that Claude Bernard was very wise when he wrote: "Those who have an excessive faith in their ideas are not well fitted to make discoveries.[13]

All this is part of the critical approach to science, as opposed to the inductivist approach; or of the Darwinian or eliminationist or selectionist approach, as opposed to the Lamarckian approach, which operates with the idea of *instruction from without,* or from the environment, while the critical or selectionist approach only allows *instruction from within*—from within the structure itself.

In fact, I contend that *there is no such thing as instruction from without the structure,* or the passive reception of a flow of information which impresses itself on our sense organs. All observations are theory impregnated: There is no pure, disinterested, theory-free observation. (To see this, we may try, using a little imagination, to compare human observation with that of an ant or a spider.)

Francis Bacon was rightly worried about the fact that our theories may prejudice our observations. This led him to advise scientists that they should avoid prejudice by purifying their minds of all theories. Similar recipes are still given.[14] But to attain objectivity we cannot rely on the empty mind: Objectivity rests on criticism, on critical discussion, and on the critical examination of experiments.[15] And we must recognize, particularly, that our very sense organs incorporate what amount to prejudices. I have stressed before (in Section II) that theories are like sense organs. Now

I wish to stress that our sense organs are like theories. They *incorporate* adaptive theories (as has been shown in the case of rabbits and cats). And these theories are the result of natural selection.

V

However, not even Darwin or Wallace, not to mention Spencer, saw that there is no instruction from without. They did not operate with purely selectionist arguments. In fact, they frequently argued on Lamarckian lines.[16] In this they seem to have been mistaken. Yet it may be worthwhile to speculate about possible limits to Darwinism, for we should always be on the lookout for possible alternatives to any dominant theory.

I think that two points might be made here. The first is that the argument against the genetic inheritance of acquired characteristics (such as mutilations) depends upon the existence of a genetic mechanism in which there is a fairly sharp distinction between the gene structure and the remaining part of the organism, the soma. But this genetic mechanism must itself be a late product of evolution, and it was undoubtedly preceded by various other mechanisms of a less sophisticated kind. Moreover, certain very special kinds of mutilations *are* inherited; more particularly, mutilations of the gene structure by radiation. Thus if we assume that the primeval organism was a naked gene then we can even say that every non-lethal mutilation to this organism would be inherited. What we cannot say is that this fact contributes in any way to an explanation of genetic adaptation, or of genetic learning, except indirectly, via natural selection.

The second point is this. We may consider the very tentative conjecture that, as a somatic response to certain environmental pressures, some chemical mutagen is produced, increasing what is called the spontaneous mutation rate. This would be a kind of semi-Lamarckian effect, even though *adaptation* would still proceed only by the elimi-

---

[13] Quoted by Jacques Hadamard, *The Psychology of Invention in the Mathematical Field,* Princeton University Press (1945), and Dover edition (1954), p. 48.

[14] Behavioral psychologists who study "experimenter bias" have found that some albino rats perform decidedly better than others if the experimenter is led to believe (wrongly) that the former belong to a strain selected for high intelligence: see, "The Effect of Experimenter Bias on the Performance of the Albino Rat," *Behav. Sci.* **8,** 183–9 (1963). The lesson drawn by the authors of this paper is that experiments should be made by "research assistants who do not know what outcome is desired" (p. 188). Like Bacon, these authors pin their hopes on the empty mind, forgetting that the expectations of the director of research may communicate themselves, without explicit disclosure, to his research assistants, just as they seem to have communicated themselves from each research assistant to his rats.

[15] Compare my *Logic of Scientific Discovery,* Section 8, and my *Objective Knowledge.*

[16] It is interesting that Charles Darwin in his later years believed in the occasional inheritance even of mutilations. See his *The Variation of Animals and Plants under Domestication,* 2nd edn, Vol. i, pp. 466–70 (1875).

nation of mutations; that is, by natural selection. Of course, there may not be much in this conjecture, as it seems that the spontaneous mutation rate suffices for adaptive evolution.[17]

These two points are made here merely as a warning against too dogmatic an adherence to Darwinism. Of course, I do conjecture that Darwinism is right, even on the level of scientific discovery; and that it is right even beyond this level, that it is right even on the level of artistic creation. We do not discover new facts or new effects by copying them, or by inferring them inductively from observation; or by any other method of instruction by the environment. We use, rather, the method of trial and the elimination of error. As Ernst Gombrich says, "making comes before matching:"[18] the active production of a new trial structure comes before its exposure to eliminating tests.

VI

I suggest therefore that we conceive the way science progresses somewhat on the lines of Niels Jerne's and Sir Macfarlane Burnet's theories of antibody formation.[19] Earlier theories of antibody formation assumed that the antigen works as a negative template for the formation of the antibody. This would mean that there is *instruction from without*, from the invading antibody. The fundamental idea of Jerne was that the instruction or information which enables the antibody to recognize the antigen is, literally, inborn, that it is part of the gene structure, though possibly subject to a repertoire of mutational variations. It is conveyed by the genetic code, by the chromosomes of the specialized cells which produce the antibodies; and the immune reaction is a result of growth-stimulation given to these cells by the antibody–antigen complex. Thus these cells are *selected* with the help of the invading environment (that is, with the help of the antigen), rather than instructed. (The analogy with the selection—and the modification—of scientific theories is clearly seen by Jerne, who in this connection refers to Kierkegaard, and to Socrates in the *Meno*.)

With this remark I conclude my discussion of the biological aspects of progress in science.

VII

Undismayed by Herbert Spencer's cosmological theories of evolution, I will now try to outline the cosmological significance of the contrast between *instruction from within the structure,* and *selection from without, by the elimination of trials.*

To this end we may note first the presence, in the cell, of the gene structure, the coded instruction, and of various chemical substructures,[20] the latter in random Brownian motion. The process of instruction by which the gene replicates proceeds as follows. The various substructures are carried (by Brownian motion) to the gene, in random fashion, and those which do not fit fail to attach themselves to the DNA structure; while those which fit, *do* attach themselves (with the help of enzymes). By this process of trial and selection,[21] a kind of photographic negative or complement of the genetic instruction is formed. Later, this complement

---

[17] Specific mutagens (acting selectively, perhaps on some particular sequence of codons rather than on others) are not known, I understand. Yet their existence would hardly be surprising in this field of surprises, and they might explain mutational "hot spots." At any rate, there seems to be a real difficulty in concluding from the absence of known specific mutagens that specific mutagens do not exist. Thus it seems to me that the problem suggested in the text (the possibility of a reaction to certain strains by the production of mutagens) is still open.

[18] Cf. Ernst Gombrich, *Art and Illusion* (1960), and later editions. (See the Index under "making and matching.")

[19] See Niels Kai Jerne, "The Natural Selection Theory of Antibody Formation: Ten Years Later," in *Phage and the Origin of Molecular Biology* (ed. J. Cairns et al.), pp. 301–12 (1966); also "The Natural Selection Theory of Antibody Formation," *Proc. Natn. Acad. Sci.* **41,** 849–57 (1955); "Immunological Speculations," *A. Rev. Microbiol* **14,** 341–58 (1960); "The Immune System," *Scient. Am.* **229,** 52–60. See also Sir Macfarlane Burnet, "A Modification of Jerne's Theory of Antibody Production, Using the Concept of Clonal Selection," *Aust. J. Sci.* **20,** 67–9 (1957); *The Clonal Selection Theory of Acquired Immunity,* Cambridge University Press (1959).

[20] What I call *structures* and *substructures* are called *integrons* by Francois Jacob, *The Logic of Living Systems: A History of Heredity,* pp. 299–324. Allen Lane, London (1974).

[21] Something might be said here about the close connection between "the method of trial and of the elimination of error" and "selection": All selection is error elimination; and what remains—after elimination—as "selected" are merely those trials which have not been eliminated *so far.*

separates from the original instruction; and by an analogous process, it forms again its negative. This negative of the negative becomes an identical copy of the original positive instruction.[22]

The selective process underlying replication is a fast-working mechanism. It is essentially the same mechanism that operates in most instances of chemical synthesis, and also, especially, in processes like crystallization. Yet although the underlying mechanism is selective, and operates by random trials and by the elimination of error, it functions as a part of what is clearly a process of instruction rather than of selection. Admittedly, owing to the random character of the motions involved, the matching processes will be brought about each time in a slightly different manner. In spite of this, the results are precise and conservative: The results are essentially determined by the original structure.

If we now look for similar processes on a cosmic scale, a strange picture of the world emerges which opens up many problems. It is a dualistic world: a world of structures in chaotically distributed motion. The small structures (such as the so-called elementary particles) build up larger structures; and this is brought about mainly by chaotic or random motion of the small structures, under special conditions of pressure and temperature.

The larger structures may be atoms, molecules, crystals, organisms, stars, solar systems, galaxies, and galactic clusters. Many of these structures appear to have a seeding effect, like drops of water in a cloud, or crystals in a solution; that is to say, they can grow and multiply by instruction; and they may persist, or disappear by selection. Some of them, such as the aperiodic DNA crystals[23] which constitute the gene structure of organisms and, with it, their building instructions, are almost infinitely rare and, we may perhaps say, very precious.

I find this dualism fascinating: I mean the strange dualistic picture of a physical world consisting of comparatively stable structures—or rather structural processes—on all micro and macro levels; and of substructures on all levels, in apparently chaotically or randomly distributed motion, a random motion that provides part of the mechanism by which these structures and substructures are sustained, and by which they may seed, by way of instruction, and grow and multiply, by way of selection and instruction. This fascinating dualistic picture is compatible with, yet totally different from, the well-known dualistic picture of the world as indeterministic in the small, owing to quantum-mechanical indeterminism, and deterministic in the large, owing to macro-physical determinism. In fact, it looks as if the existence of structures which do the instructing, and which introduce something like stability into the world, depends very largely upon quantum effects.[24] This seems to hold for structures on

---

[22] The main difference from a photographic reproduction process is that the DNA molecule is not two-dimensional but linear: a long string of four kinds of substructures ("bases"). These may be represented by dots colored either red or green, or blue or yellow. The four basic colors are pairwise negatives (or complements) of each other. So the negative or complement of a string would consist of a string in which red is replaced by green, and blue by yellow; and vice versa. Here the colors represent the four letters (bases) which constitute the alphabet of the genetic code. Thus the complement of the original string contains a kind of translation of the original information into another yet closely related code; and the negative of this negative contains in turn the orginal information, stated in terms of the original (the genetic) code.

This situation is utilized in replication, when first one pair of complementary strings separates and when next two pairs are formed as each of the strings selectively attaches to itself a new complement. The result is the replication of the original structure *by way of instruction*. A very similar method is utilized in the second of the two main functions of the gene (DNA): the control, by way of instruction, of the synthesis of proteins. Though the underlying mechanism of this second process is more complicated than that of replication, it is similar in principle.

[23] The term "aperiodic crystal" (sometimes also "aperiodic solid") is Schrödinger's; see his *What Is Life?*, Cambridge University Press (1944); cf. *What Is Life? and Mind and Matter*, Cambridge University Press, pp. 64 and 91 (1967).

[24] That atomic and molecular structures have something to do with quantum theory is almost trivial, considering that the peculiarities of quantum mechanics (such as eigenstates and eigenvalues) were introduced into physics in order to explain the structural stability of atoms.

The idea that the structural "wholeness" of biological systems has also something to do with quantum theory was first discussed, I suppose, in Schrödinger's small but great book *What is Life?* (1944), which, it may be said, anticipated both the rise of molecular biology and of Max Delbrück's influence on its development. In this book Schrödinger adopts a consciously ambivalent attitude toward the problem whether or not biology

the atomic, molecular, crystal, organic, and even on the stellar levels (for the stability of the stars depends upon nuclear reactions), while for the supporting random movements we can appeal to classical Brownian motion and to the classical hypothesis of molecular chaos. Thus in this dualist picture of order supported by disorder, or of structure supported by randomness, the role played by quantum effects and by classical effects appears to be almost the opposite from that in the more traditional pictures.

VIII

So far I have considered progress in science mainly from a biological point of view; however,

it seems to me that the following two logical points are crucial.

First, in order that a new theory should constitute a discovery or a step forward it should conflict with its predecessor; that is to say, it should lead to at least some conflicting results. But this means, from a logical point of view, that it should contradict[25] its predecessor: It should overthrow it.

In this sense, progress in science—or at least striking progress—is always revolutionary.

My second point is that progress in science, although revolutionary rather than merely cumulative,[26] is in a certain sense always conservative: A new theory, however revolutionary, must always be able to explain fully the success of its predecessor. In all those cases in which its predecessor was successful, it must yield results at least as good as those of its predecessor and, if possible, better results. Thus in these cases the predecessor theory must appear as a good approximation to the new theory, while there should be, preferably, other cases where the new theory yields different and better results than the old theory.[27]

---

will turn out to be reducible to physics. In Chapter 7, 'Is Life Based on the Laws of Physics,'' he says (about living matter) first that "we must be prepared to find it working in a manner that cannot be reduced to the ordinary laws of physics" (*What is Life? and Mind and Matter,* p. 81). But a little later he says that "the new principle" (that is to say, "order from order") "is not alien to physics": It is "nothing else than the principle of quantum physics again" (in the form of Nernst's princple) (*What is Life? and Mind and Matter,* p. 88). My attitude is also an ambivalent one: On the one hand, I do not believe in complete reducibility; on the other hand, I think that *reduction must be attempted;* for even though it is likely to be only partially successful, even a very partial success would be a very great success.

Thus my remarks in the text to which this note is appended (and which I have left substantially unchanged) were not meant as a statement of reductionism: All I wanted to say was that quantum theory seems to be involved in the phenomenon of "structure from structure" or "order from order."

However, my remarks were not clear enough; for in the discussion after the lecture Professor Hans Motz challenged what he believed to be my reductionism by referring to one of the papers of Eugene Wigner ("The Probability of the Existence of a Self-reproducing Unit," Ch. 15 of his *Symmetries and Reflections: Scientific Essays,* pp. 200–8, M.I.T. Press [1970]. In this paper Wigner gives a kind of proof of the thesis that the probability is zero for a quantum theoretical system to contain a subsystem which reproduces itself. (Or, more precisely, the probability is zero for a system to change in such a manner that at one time it contains some subsystem and later a second subsystem which is a copy of the first.) I have been puzzled by this argument of Wigner's since its first publication in 1961; and in my reply to Motz I pointed out that Wigner's proof seemed to me refuted by the existence of Xerox machines (or by the growth of crystals), which must be regarded as quantum mechanical rather than "biotonic" systems. (It may be claimed that a Xerox copy of a crystal does not reproduce itself with sufficient precision; yet the most puzzling thing about Wigner's paper is that he does not refer to degrees of precision, and that absolute exactness or "the apparently virtually absolute reliability," as he puts it on p. 208—which is not required—is, it seems, excluded at once by Pauli's principle.) I do not think that either the reducibility of biology to physics or else its irreducibility can be proved; at any rate not at present.

---

[25] Thus Einstein's theory *contradicts* Newton's theory (although it contains Newton's theory as an approximation): In contradistinction to Newton's theory, Einstein's theory shows, for example, that in strong gravitational fields there cannot be a Keplerian elliptic orbit with appreciable eccentricity but without corresponding precession of the perihelion (as observed of Mercury).

[26] Even the collecting of butterflies is *theory*-impregnated (*butterfly* is a *theoretical* term, as is *water:* It involves a set of expectations). The recent accumulation of evidence concerning elementary particles can be interpreted as an accumulation of falsifications of the early electromagnetic theory of matter.

[27] An even more radical demand may be made; for we may demand that if the apparent laws of nature should change, then the new theory, invented to explain the new laws, should be able to explain the state of affairs both before and after the change, and also the change itself, from universal laws and (changing) initial conditions (cf. my *Logic of Scientific Discovery,* Section 79, esp. p. 253).

By stating these logical criteria for progress, I am implicitly rejecting the fashionable (anti-rationalistic) suggestion that two different theories such as Newton's and Einstein's are incommensurable. It may be true that two scientists with a verificationist attitude towards their favored theories (Newtonian and Einsteinian physics, say) may fail to understand each other. But if their attitude is critical (as was Newton's and Einstein's) they will understand both theories and see how they are related. See, for this problem, the excellent discussion of the comparability of Newton's and Einstein's theories by Troels Eggers Hansen in his paper. "Confrontation and Objectivity," *Danish Yb. Phil.* **7,** 13–72 (1972).

The important point about the two logical criteria which I have stated is that they allow us to decide of any new theory, even before it has been tested, whether it will be better than the old one, provided it stands up to tests. But this means that, in the field of science, we have something like a criterion for judging the quality of a theory as compared with its predecessor, and therefore a criterion of progress. And so it means that progress in science can be assessed rationally.[28] This possibility explains why, in science, only progressive theories are regarded as interesting; and it thereby explains why, as a matter of historical fact, the history of science is, by and large, a history of progress. (Science seems to be the only field of human endeavor of which this can be said.)

As I have suggested before, scientific progress is revolutionary. Indeed, its motto could be that of Karl Marx: "Revolution in permanence." However, scientific revolutions are rational in the sense that, in principle, it is rationally decidable whether or not a new theory is better than its predecessor. Of course, this does not mean that we cannot blunder. There are many ways in which we can make mistakes.

An example of a most interesting mistake is reported by Dirac.[29] Schrödinger found, but did not publish, a relativistic equation of the electron, later called the Klein–Gordon equation, before he found and published the famous non-relativistic equation which is now called by his name. He did not publish the relativistic equation because it did not seem to agree with the experimental results as interpreted by the preceding theory. However, the discrepancy was due to a faulty interpretation of empirical results, and not to a fault in the relativistic equation. Had Schrödinger published it, the problem of the equivalence between his wave mechanics and the matrix mechanics of Heisenberg and Born might not have arisen, and the history of modern physics might have been very different.

It should be obvious that the objectivity and the rationality of progress in science is not due to the personal objectivity and rationality of the scientist.[30] Great science and great scientists, like great poets, are often inspired by non-rational intuitions. So are great mathematicians. As Poincaré and Hadamard have pointed out,[31] a mathematical proof may be discovered by unconscious trials, guided by an inspiration of a decidedly aesthetic character, rather than by rational thought. This is true, and important. But obviously, it does not make the result, the mathematical proof, irrational. In any case, a proposed proof must be able to stand up to critical discussion, to its examination by competing mathematicians. And this may well induce the mathematical inventor to check, rationally, the results which he reached unconsciously or intuitively. Similarly, Kepler's beautiful Pythagorean dreams of the harmony of the world system did not invalidate the objectivity, the testability, the rationality of his three laws, nor the rationality of the problem which these laws posed for an explanatory theory.

With this, I conclude my two logical remarks on the progress of science; and I now move on to the second part of my lecture, and with it to remarks which may be described as partly sociological, and which bear on *obstacles* to progress in science.

---

[28] The logical demands discussed here (cf. Ch. 10 of my *Conjectures and refutations* and Ch. 5 of *Objective Knowledge),* although they seem to me of fundamental importance, do not, of course, exhaust what can be said about the rational method of science. For example, in my *Postscript* (which has been in galley proofs since 1957, but which I hope will still be published one day) I have developed a theory of what I call metaphysical research programmes. This theory, it might be mentioned, in no way clashes with the theory of testing and of the revolutionary advance of science which I have outlined here. An example which I gave there of a metaphysical research programme is the use of the propensity theory of probability, which seems to have a wide range of applications.

What I say in the text should not be taken to mean that rationality depends on having a criterion of rationality. Compare my criticism of "criterion philosophies" in "Addendum I, Facts, Standards, and Truth," to Vol. ii of my *Open Society.*

[29] The story is reported by Paul A. M. Dirac, "The Evolution of the Physicist's Picture of Nature," *Scient. Am.* **208,** No. 5, 45–53 (1963); see esp. p. 47.

[30] Cf. my criticism of the so-called "sociology of knowledge" in Ch. 23 of my *Open Society,* and pp. 155 f. of my *Poverty of Historicism.*

[31] Cf. Jacques Hadamard, *The Psychology of Invention in the Mathematical Field* (see note 13 above).

IX

I think that the main obstacles to progress in science are of a social nature and that they may be divided into two groups: economic obstacles and ideological obstacles.

On the economic side poverty may, trivially, be an obstacle (although great theoretical and experimental discoveries have been made in spite of poverty). In recent years, however, it has become fairly clear that affluence may also be an obstacle: Too many dollars may chase too few ideas. Admittedly, even under such adverse circumstances progress *can* be achieved. But the spirit of science is in danger. Big Science may destroy great science, and the publication explosion may kill ideas: Ideas, which are only too rare, may become submerged in the flood. The danger is very real, and it is hardly necessary to enlarge upon it, but I may perhaps quote Eugene Wigner, one of the early heroes of quantum mechanics, who sadly remarks, ''The spirit of science has changed.''[32]

This is indeed a sad chapter. But since it is all too obvious I shall not say more about the economic obstacles to progress in science; instead, I will turn to discuss some of the ideological obstacles.

X

The most widely recognized of the ideological obstacles is ideological or religious intolerance, usually combined with dogmatism and lack of imagination. Historical examples are so well known that I need not dwell upon them. Yet it should be noted that even suppression may lead to progress. The martyrdom of Giordano Bruno and the trial of Galileo may have done more in the end for the progress of science than the Inquisition could do against it.

The strange case of Aristarchus and the original heliocentric theory opens perhaps a different problem. Because of his heliocentric theory Aristarchus was accused of impiety by Cleanthes, a Stoic. But this hardly explains the obliteration of the theory. Nor can it be said that the theory was too bold. We know that Aristarchus's theory was supported, a century after it was first expounded, by at least one highly respected astronomer (Seleucus).[33] And yet, for some obscure reason, only a few brief reports of the theory have survived. Here is a glaring case of the only too frequent failure to keep alternative ideas alive.

Whatever the details of the explanation, the failure was probably due to dogmatism and intolerance. But new ideas should be regarded as precious, and should be carefully nursed, especially if they seem to be a bit wild. I do not suggest that we should be eager to accept new ideas *just* for the sake of their newness. But we should be anxious not to suppress a new idea even if it does not appear to us to be very good.

There are many examples of neglected ideas, such as the idea of evolution before Darwin, or Mendel's theory. A great deal can be learned about obstacles to progress from the history of these neglected ideas. An interesting case is that of the Viennese physicist Arthur Haas who in 1910 partly anticipated Niels Bohr. Haas published a theory of the hydrogen spectrum based on a quantization of J. J. Thomson's atom model: Rutherford's model did not yet exist. Haas appears to have been the first to introduce Planck's quantum of action into atomic theory with a view to deriving the spectral constants. In spite of his use of Thomson's atom model, Haas almost succeeded in his derivation; and as Max Jammer explains in detail, it seems quite possible that the theory of Haas (which was taken seriously by Sommerfeld) indirectly influenced Niels Bohr.[34] In Vienna, however, the theory was rejected out of hand; it was ridiculed and decried as a silly joke by Ernst Lecher (whose early experiments had impressed

---

[32] A conversation with Eugene Wigner, *Science* **181**, 527–33 (1973); see p. 533.

[33] For Aristarchus and Seleucus see Sir Thomas Heath, *Aristarchus of Samos*, Clarendon Press, Oxford (1966).

[34] See Max Jammer, *The Conceptual Development of Quantum Mechanics*, pp. 40–2, McGraw-Hill, New York (1966).

Heinrich Hertz[35]), one of the professors of physics at the University of Vienna, whose somewhat pedestrian and not very inspiring lectures I attended some eight or nine years later.

A far more surprising case, also described by Jammer,[36] is the rejection in 1913 of Einstein's photon theory, first published in 1905, for which he was to receive the Nobel prize in 1921. This rejection of the photon theory formed a passage within a petition recommending Einstein for membership of the Prussian Academy of Science. The document, which was signed by Max Planck, Walther Nernst, and two other famous physicists, was most laudatory and asked that a slip of Einstein's (such as they obviously believed his photon theory to be) should not be held against him. This confident manner of rejecting a theory which, in the same year, passed a severe experimental test undertaken by Millikan, has no doubt a humorous side; yet it should be regarded as a glorious incident in the history of science, showing that even a somewhat dogmatic rejection by the greatest living experts can go hand in hand with a most liberal-minded appreciation: These men did not dream of suppressing what they believed was mistaken. Indeed, the wording of the apology for Einstein's slip is most interesting and enlightening. The relevant passage of the petition says of Einstein: "That he may sometimes have gone too far in his speculations, as for example in his hypothesis of light quanta, should not weigh too heavily against him. For nobody can introduce, even into the most exact of the natural sciences, ideas which are really new, without sometimes taking a risk."[37] This is well said, but it is an understatement. One has always to take the risk of being mistaken and also the less important risk of being misunderstood or misjudged.

However, this example shows, drastically, that even great scientists sometimes fail to reach that self-critical attitude which would prevent them from feeling very sure of themselves while gravely misjudging things.

Yet a limited amount of dogmatism is necessary for progress: Without a serious struggle for survival in which the old theories are tenaciously defended, none of the competing theories can show their mettle, that is, their explanatory power and their truth content. Intolerant dogmatism, however, is one of the main obstacles to science. Indeed, we should not only keep alternative theories alive by discussing them, but we should systematically look for new alternatives; and we should be worried whenever there are no alternatives—whenever a dominant theory becomes too exclusive. The danger to progress in science is much increased if the theory in question obtains something like a monopoly.

XI

But there is even a greater danger: A theory, even a scientific theory, may become an intellectual fashion, a substitute for religion, an entrenched ideology. And with this I come to the main point of this second part of my lecture—the part that deals with obstacles to progress in science, to the distinction between scientific revolutions and ideological revolutions.

For in addition to the always important problem of dogmatism and the closely connected problem of ideological intolerance, there is a different and, I think, a more interesting problem. I mean the problem which arises from certain links between science and ideology, links which do exist but which have led some people to conflate science and ideology and to muddle the distinction between scientific and ideological revolutions.

I think that this is quite a serious problem at a time when intellectuals, including scientists, are prone to fall for ideologies and intellectual fashions. This may well be due to the decline of reli-

---

[35] See Heinrich Hertz, *Electric Waves,* Macmillan and Co., London (1894); Dover edn, New York (1962), pp. 12, 187 f., 273.

[36] See Jammer, op. cit., pp. 43 f., and Théo Kahan, "Un document historique de l'académie des sciences de Berlin sur l'activité scientific d'Albert Einstein" (1913), *Archs. Int. Hist. Sci.* **15,** 337–42 (1962); see esp. p. 340.

[37] Compare Jammer's slightly different translation, loc. cit.

gion, to the unsatisfied and unconscious religious needs of our fatherless society.[38] During my lifetime I have witnessed, quite apart from the various totalitarian movements, a considerable number of intellectually highbrow and avowedly nonreligious movements with aspects whose religious character is unmistakable once your eyes are open to it.[39] The best of these many movements was that which was inspired by the father figure of Einstein. It was the best, because of Einstein's always modest and highly self-critical attitude and his humanity and tolerance. Nevertheless, I shall later have a few words to say about what seem to me the less satisfactory aspects of the Einsteinian ideological revolution.

I am not an essentialist, and I shall not discuss here the essence or nature of "ideologies." I will merely state very generally and vaguely that I am going to use the term "ideology" for *any nonscientific* theory or creed or view of the world which proves attractive, and which interests people, including scientists. (Thus there may be very helpful and also very destructive ideologies from, say, a humanitarian or a rationalist point of view.[40]) I need not say more about ideologies in

order to justify the sharp distinction which I am going to make between science[41] and "ideology," and further, between *scientific revolutions* and *ideological revolutions*. But I will elucidate this distinction with the help of a number of examples.

These examples will show, I hope, that it is important to distinguish between a scientific revolution in the sense of a rational overthrow of an established scientific theory by a new one and all processes of "social entrenchment" or perhaps "social acceptance" of ideologies, including even those ideologies which incorporate some scientific results.

XII

As my first example I choose the Copernican and Darwinian revolutions, because in these two cases a scientific revolution gave rise to an ideological revolution. Even if we neglect here the ideology of "Social Darwinism,"[42] we can distinguish a scientific and an ideological component in both these revolutions.

The Copernican and Darwinian revolutions were *ideological* insofar as they both changed man's view of his place in the Universe. They clearly were *scientific* insofar as each of them overthrew a dominant scientific theory: a domi-

---

[38] Our Western societies do not, by their structure, satisfy the need for a father figure. I discussed the problems that arise from this fact briefly in my (unpublished) William James Lectures in Harvard (1950). My late friend, the psychoanalyst Paul Federn, showed me shortly afterwards an earlier paper of his devoted to this problem.

[39] An obvious example is the role of prophet played, in various movements, by Sigmund Freud, Arnold Schönberg, Karl Kraus, Ludwig Wittgenstein, and Herbert Marcuse.

[40] There are many kinds of "ideologies" in the wide and (deliberately) vague sense of the term I used in the text, and therefore many aspects to the distinction between science and ideology. Two may be mentioned here. One is that scientific theories can be distinguished or "demarcated" (see note 41) from non-scientific theories which, nevertheless, may strongly influence scientists and even inspire their work. (This influence, of course, may be good or bad or mixed.) A very different aspect is that of entrenchment: A scientific theory may function as an ideology if it becomes socially entrenched. This is why, when speaking of the distinction between scientific revolutions and ideological revolutions, I include among ideological revolutions changes in non-scientific ideas which may inspire the work of scientists and also changes in the social entrenchment of what may otherwise be a scientific theory. (I owe the formulation of the points in this note to Jeremy Shearmur who has also contributed to other points dealt with in this lecture.)

---

[41] In order not to repeat myself too often, I did not mention in this lecture my suggestion for a criterion of the empirical character of a theory (falsifiability or refutability as the criterion of demarcation between empirical theories and non-empirical theories). Since in English "science" means "empirical science," and since the matter is sufficiently fully discussed in my books, I have written things like the following (for example, in *Conjectures and Refutations*, p. 39): " . . . in order to be ranked as scientific, [statements] must be capable of conflicting with possible, or conceivable, observations." Some people seized upon this like a shot (as early as 1932, I think.) "What about your own gospel?" is the typical move. (I found this objection again in a book published in 1973.) My answer to the objection, however, was published in 1934 (see my *Logic of Scientific Discovery*, Ch 2, Section 10 and elsewhere). I may restate my answer: My gospel is not "scientific," that is, it does not belong to empirical science, but it is, rather, a (normative) *proposal*. My gospel (and also my answer) is, incidentally, criticizable, though not just by observation, and it has been criticized.

[42] For a criticism of Social Darwinism see my *Open Society*, Ch. 10, note 71.

nant astronomical theory and a dominant biological theory.

It appears that the ideological impact of the Copernican and also of the Darwinian theory was so great because each of them clashed with a religious dogma. This was highly significant for the intellectual history of our civilization, and it had repercussions on the history of science (for example, because it led to a tension between religion and science). And yet, the historical and sociological fact that the theories of both Copernicus and Darwin clashed with religion is completely irrelevant for the rational evaluation of the scientific theories proposed by them. Logically it has nothing whatsoever to do with the *scientific* revolution started by each of the two theories.

It is therefore important to distinguish between scientific and ideological revolutions particularly in those cases in which the ideological revolutions interact with revolutions in science.

The example, more especially, of the Copernican ideological revolution may show that even an ideological revolution might well be described as "rational." However, while we have a logical criterion of progress in science—and thus of rationality—we do not seem to have anything like general criteria of progress or of rationality outside science (although this should not be taken to mean that outside science there are no such things as standards of rationality). Even a highbrow intellectual ideology which bases itself on accepted scientific results may be irrational, as is shown by the many movements of modernism in art (and in science), and also of archaism in art, movements which in my opinion are intellectually insipid since they appeal to values which have nothing to do with art (or science). Indeed, many movements of this kind are just fashions which should not be taken too seriously.[43]

Proceeding with my task of elucidating the distinction between scientific and ideological revolutions, I will now give several examples of major scientific revolutions which did not lead to any ideological revolution.

The revolution of Faraday and Maxwell was, from a scientific point of view, just as great as that of Copernicus, and possibly greater: It dethroned Newton's central dogma—the dogma of central forces. Yet it did *not* lead to an ideological revolution, though it inspired a whole generation of physicists.

J. J. Thomson's discovery (and theory) of the electron was also a major revolution. To overthrow the age-old theory of the indivisibility of the atom constituted a scientific revolution easily comparable to Copernicus's achievement: When Thomson announced it, physicists thought he was pulling their legs. But it did not create an ideological revolution. And yet, it overthrew both of the two rival theories which for 2400 years had been fighting for dominance in the theory of matter—the theory of indivisible atoms, and that of the continuity of matter. To assess the revolutionary significance of this breakthrough it will be sufficient to remind you that it introduced structure as well as electricity into the atom, and thus into the constitution of matter. Also, the quantum mechanics of 1925 and 1926, of Heisenberg and of Born, of de Broglie, of Schrödinger and of Dirac, was essentially a quantization of the theory of the Thomson electron. And yet Thomson's scientific revolution did not lead to a new ideology.

Another striking example is Rutherford's overthrow in 1911 of the model of the atom proposed by J. J. Thomson in 1903. Rutherford had accepted Thomson's theory that the positive charge must be distributed over the whole space occu-

---

[43] Further to my use of the vague term "ideology" (which includes all kinds of theories, beliefs, and attitudes, including some that may influence scientists) it should be clear that I intend to cover by this term not only historicist fashions like "modernism," but also serious, and rationally discussable, metaphysical and ethical ideas. I may perhaps refer to Jim Erikson, a former student of mine in Christchurch, New Zealand, who once said in a discussion: "We do not suggest that science invented intellectual honesty, but we do suggest that intellectual honesty invented science." A very similar idea is to be found in Ch. ix ("The Kingdom and the Darkness") of Jacques Monod's book *Chance and Necessity,* Knopf, New York (1971). See also my *Open Society,* Vol. ii, Ch. 24 ("The Revolt against Reason"). We might say, of course, that an ideology which has learned from the critical approach of the sciences is likely to be more rational than one which clashes with science.

pied by the atom. This may be seen from his reaction to the famous experiment of Geiger and Marsden. They found that when they shot alpha particles at a very thin sheet of gold foil, a few of the alpha particles—about one in twenty thousand—were reflected by the foil rather than merely deflected. Rutherford was incredulous. As he said later, "It was quite the most incredible event that has ever happened to me in my life. It was almost as incredible as if you fired a fifteen-inch shell at a piece of tissue paper and it came back and hit you."[44] This remark of Rutherford's shows the utterly revolutionary character of the discovery. Rutherford realized that the experiment refuted Thomson's model of the atom, and he replaced it by his nuclear model of the atom. This was the beginning of nuclear science. Rutherford's model became widely known, even among non-physicists. But it did not trigger off an ideological revolution.

One of the most fundamental scientific revolutions in the history of the theory of matter has never even been recognized as such. I mean the refutation of the electromagnetic theory of matter which had become dominant after Thomson's discovery of the electron. Quantum mechanics arose as part of this theory, and it was essentially this theory whose "completeness" was defended by Bohr against Einstein in 1935, and again in 1949. Yet in 1934 Yukawa had outlined a new quantum-theoretical approach to nuclear forces which resulted in the overthrow of the electromagnetic theory of matter after forty years of unquestioned dominance.[45]

There are many other major scientific revolutions which failed to trigger off any ideological revolution; for example, Mendel's revolution (which later saved Darwinism from extinction). Others are X-rays, radioactivity, the discovery of isotopes, and the discovery of superconductivity. To all these, there was no corresponding ideological revolution. Nor do I see as yet an ideological revolution resulting from the breakthrough of Crick and Watson.

XIII

Of great interest is the case of the so-called Einsteinian revolution—I mean Einstein's scientific revolution, which among intellectuals had an ideological influence comparable to that of the Copernican or Darwinian revolutions.

Of Einstein's many revolutionary discoveries in physics, there are two which are relevant here.

The first is special relativity, which overthrows Newtonian kinematics, replacing Galileo invariance by Lorentz invariance.[46] Of course, this revo-

---

[44] Lord Rutherford, "The Development of the Theory of Atomic Structure," in J. Needham and W. Pagel (eds), *Background of Modern Science*, pp. 61–74, Cambridge University Press (1938); the quotation is from p. 68.

[45] See my "Quantum Mechanics without 'the Observer'," in *Quantum Theory and Reality* (ed. Mario Bunge), esp. pp. 8–9, Springer-Verlag, New York (1967). (It will form a chapter in my forthcoming volume *Philosophy and Physics*.)

The fundamental idea (that the inertial mass of the electron is in part explicable as the inertia of the moving electromagnetic field) that led to the electromagnetic theory of matter is due to J. J. Thomson, "On the Electric and Magnetic Effects Produced by the Motion of Electrified Bodies," *Phil. Mag.* (5th Ser.) **11**, 229–49 (1881), and to O. Heaviside, "On the Electromagnetic Effects due to the Motion of Electrification through a Dialectric,"

Phil. Mag. (5th Ser.) **27**, 324–39 (1889). It was developed by W. Kaufmann ("Die magnetische und elektrische Ablenkbarkeit der Bequerelstrahlen und die scheinbare Masse der Elektronen," *Gött. Nachr.* 143–55 [1901], "Ueber die elektromagnetische Masse des Elektrons," 291–6 [1902], "Ueber die 'Elektromagnetische Masse' der Elektronen," 90-103 [1903]) and M. Abraham ("Dynamik des Elektrons," *Gött. Nachr.* 20–41 [1902], "Prinzipien der Dynamik des Elektrons," *AnnIn Phys.* [4th Ser.], **10**, 105–79 [1903]) into the thesis that the mass of the electron is a purely electromagnetic effect. (See W. Kaufmann, "Die elektromagnetische Masse des Elektrons," *Phys. Z.* **4**, 54–7 [1902–3] and M. Abraham, "Prinzipien der Dynamik des Elektrons," *Phys. Z.* **4**, pp. 57–63 [1902–3] and M. Abraham, *Theorie der Elektrizität*, Vol. ii, pp. 136–249, Leipzig [1905].) The idea was strongly supported by H. A. Lorentz, "Elektromagnetische verschijnselen in een stelsel dat zich met willekeurige snelheid, kleiner dan die van het licht, beweegt," *Versl. gewone Vergad. wis- en natuurk. Afd. K. Akad. Wet. Amst.* **12**, second part, 986–1009 (1903–4), and by Einstein's special relativity, leading to results deviating from those of Kaufmann and Abraham. The electromagnetic theory of matter had a great ideological influence on scientists because of the fascinating possibility of *explaining matter*. It was shaken and modified by Rutherford's discovery of the nucleus (and the proton) and by Chadwick's discovery of the neutron, which may help to explain why its final overthrow by the theory of nuclear forces was hardly taken notice of.

[46] The revolutionary power of special relativity lies in a new point of view which allows the derivation and interpretation of the Lorentz tranformations from two simple first principles. The

lution satisfies our criteria of rationality: The old theories are explained as approximately valid for velocities which are small compared with the velocity of light.

As to the ideological revolution linked with this scientific revolution, one element of it is due to Minkowski. We may state this element in Minkowski's own words. "The views of space and time I wish to lay before you," Minkowski wrote, " . . . are radical. Henceforth space by itself, and time by itself, are doomed to fade away into mere shadows, and only a kind of union of the two will preserve an independent reality."[47] This is an intellectually thrilling statement. But it is clearly not science; it is ideology. It became part of the ideology of the Einsteinian revolution. But Einstein himself was never quite happy about it. Two years before his death he wrote to Cornelius Lanczos: "One knows so much and comprehends so little. The four-dimensionality with the [Minkowski signature of] $+ + + -$ belongs to the latter category."

A more suspect element of the ideological Einsteinian revolution is the fashion of operationalism or positivism—a fashion which Einstein later rejected, although he himself was responsible for it, owing to what he had written about the operational definition of simultaneity. Although, as Einstein later realized,[48] operationalism is, logically, an untenable doctrine, it has been very influential ever since, in physics, and especially in behaviorist psychology.

With respect to the Lorentz transformations, it does not seem to have become part of the ideology that they limit the validity of the transitivity of simultaneity: The principle of transitivity remains valid within each inertial system while it becomes invalid for the transition from one system to another. Nor has it become part of the ideology that general relativity, or more especially Einstein's cosmology, allows the introduction of a preferred cosmic time and consequently of preferred local spatio-temporal frames.[49]

General relativity was in my opinion one of the greatest scientific revolutions ever, because it clashed with the greatest and best tested theory ever—Newton's theory of gravity and of the solar system. It contains, as it should, Newton's theory as an approximation; yet it contradicts it in several points. It yields different results for elliptic orbits of appreciable eccentricity; and it entails the astonishing result that any physical particle (photons included) which approaches the center of a gravitational field with a velocity exceeding six-tenths of the velocity of light is not accelerated by the gravitational field, as in Newton's theory, but decelerated: that is, not attracted by a heavy body, but repelled.[50]

This most surprising and exciting result has stood up to tests, but it does not seem to have become part of the ideology.

It is this overthrow and correction of Newton's

greatness of this revolution can be best gauged by reading Abraham's book (Vol. ii, referred to in note 45 above). This book, which is slightly earlier than Poincaré's and Einstein's papers on relativity, contains a full discussion of the problem situation, of Lorentz's theory of the Michelson experiment, and even of Lorentz's local time. Abraham comes, for example on pp. 143 f. and 370 f., quite close to Einsteinian ideas. It even seems as if Max Abraham was better informed about the problem situation than was Einstein. Yet there is no realization of the revolutionary potentialities of the problem situation; quite the contrary. For Abraham writes in his Preface, dated March 1905: "The theory of electricity now appears to have entered a state of quieter development." This shows how hopeless it is even for a great scientist like Abraham to foresee the future development of his science.

[47] See H. Minkowski, "Space and Time," in A. Einstein, H. A. Lorentz, H. Weyl, and H. Minkowski, *The Principle of Relativity*, Methuen, London (1923) and Dover edn, New York, p. 75. For the quotation from Einstein's letter to Cornelius Lanczos, later in the same paragraph of my text, see C. Lanczos, "Rationalism and the Physical World," in R. S. Cohen and B. Wartofski (eds), *Boston Studies in the Philosophy of Science*, Vol. 3, pp. 181–98 (1967); see p. 198.

[48] See my *Conjectures and Refutations*, p. 114 (with footnote 30); also my *Open Society*, Vol. ii, p. 20, and the criticism in my *Logic of Scientific Discovery*, p. 440. I pointed out this criticism in 1950 to P. W. Bridgman, who received it most generously.

[49] See A. D. Eddington, *Space Time and Gravitation*, pp. 162 f., Cambridge University Press (1935). It is interesting in this context that Dirac (on p. 46 of the paper referred to in note 29 above) says that he now doubts whether four-dimensional thinking is a fundamental requirement of physics. (It is a fundamental requirement for driving a motor car.)

[50] More precisely, a body falling from infinity with a velocity $v > c/3^{1/2}$ toward the center of a gravitational field will be constantly decelerated in approaching this center.

theory which from a scientific (as opposed to an ideological) point of view is perhaps most significant in Einstein's general theory. This implies, of course, that Einstein's theory can be compared point by point with Newton's[51] and that it preserves Newton's theory as an approximation. Nevertheless, Einstein never believed that his theory was true. He shocked Cornelius Lanczos in 1922 by saying that his theory was merely a passing stage; he called it "ephemeral."[52] And he said to Leopold Infeld[53] that the left-hand side of his field equation[54] (the curvature tensor) was as solid as a rock, while the right-hand side (the momentum—energy tensor) was as weak as straw.

In the case of general relativity, an idea which had considerable ideological influence seems to have been that of a curved four-dimensional space. This idea certainly plays a role in both the scientific and the ideological revolution. But this makes it even more important to distinguish the scientific from the ideological revolution.

However, the ideological elements of the Einsteinian revolution influenced scientists, and thereby the history of science; and this influence was not all to the good.

First of all, the myth that Einstein had reached his result by an essential use of epistemological and especially operationalist methods had in my opinion a devastating effect upon science. (It is irrelevant whether you get your results—especially good results—by dreaming them, or by drinking black coffee, or even from a mistaken

epistemology.)[55] Secondly, it led to the belief that quantum mechanics, the second great revolutionary theory of the century, must outdo the Einsteinian revolution, especially with respect to its epistemological depth. It seems to me that this belief affected some of the great founders of quantum mechanics,[56] and also some of the great founders of molecular biology.[57] It led to the dominance of a subjectivist interpretation of quantum mechanics; an interpretation which I have been combating for almost forty years. I cannot here describe the situation, but while I am aware of the dazzling achievement of quantum mechanics (which must not blind us to the fact that it is seriously incomplete[58]) I suggest that the orthodox interpretation of quantum mechanics is not part of physics, but an ideology. In fact, it is part of a modernistic ideology; and it has become a scientific fashion which is a serious obstacle to the progress of science.

XIV

I hope that I have made clear the distinction between a scientific revolution and the ideological revolution which may sometimes be linked with it. The ideological revolution may serve rationality or it may undermine it. But it is often nothing but an intellectual fashion. Even if it is linked to a scientific revolution it may be of a highly irrational

---

[51] See the reference to Troels Eggers Hansen cited in note 27 above; and Peter Havas, "Four-dimensional Formulations of Newtonian Mechanics and Their Relation to the Special and the General Theory of Relativity," *Revs mod. Phys.* **36,** 938–65 (1964), and "Foundation Problems in General Relativity," in *Delaware Seminar in the Foundations of Physics* (ed. M. Bunge), pp. 124–48 (1967). Of course, the comparison is not trivial: see, for example, pp. 52 f. of E. Wigner's book referred to in note 24 above.

[52] See C. Lanczos, op. cit., p. 196.

[53] See Leopold Infeld, *Quest,* p. 90. Victor Gollancz, London (1941).

[54] See A. Einstein, "Die Feldgleichungen der Gravitation," *Sber. Akad. Wiss. Berlin,* Part 2, 844–7 (1915); "Die Grundlage der allgemeinen Relativitätstheorie," *Annln Phys.,* (4th Ser.) **49,** 769–822 (1916).

[55] I believe that §2 of Einstein's famous paper, "Die Grundlage der allgemeinen Relativitätstheorie" (see Note 54 above; English translation, "The Foundation of the General Theory of Relativity," *The Principle of Relativity,* pp. 111–64; see note 47 above) uses most questionable epistemological arguments *against* Newton's absolute space and *for* a very important theory.

[56] Especially Heisenberg and Bohr.

[57] Apparently it affected Max Delbrück; see *Perspectives in American History,* Vol. 2, Harvard University Press (1968), "Emigré Physicists and the Biological Revolution," by Donald Fleming, pp. 152–89, especially Sections iv and v. (I owe this reference to Professor Mogens Blegvad.)

[58] It is clear that a physical theory which does not explain such constants as the electric elementary quantum (or the fine structure constant) is incomplete, to say nothing of the mass spectra of the elementary particles. See my paper, "Quantum Mechanics without 'the Observer'," referred to in note 45 above.

character, and it may consciously break with tradition.

But a scientific revolution, however radical, cannot really break with tradition, since it must preserve the success of its predecessors. This is why scientific revolutions are rational. By this I do not mean, of course, that the great scientists who make the revolution are, or ought to be, wholly rational beings. On the contrary: Although I have been arguing here for the rationality of scientific revolutions, my guess is that should individual scientists ever become "objective and rational" in the sense of "impartial and deatched," then we should indeed find the revolutionary progress of science barred by an impenetrable obstacle.

The Function of Dogma in Scientific Research[1]

Thomas S. Kuhn

At some point in his or her career every member of this Symposium has, I feel sure, been exposed to the image of the scientist as the uncommitted searcher after truth. He is the explorer of nature— the man who rejects prejudice at the threshold of his laboratory, who collects and examines the bare and objective facts, and whose allegiance is to such facts and to them alone. These are the characteristics which make the testimony of scientists so valuable when advertising proprietary products in the United States. Even for an international audience, they should require no further elaboration. To be scientific is, among other things, to be objective and open-minded.

Probably none of us believes that in practice the real-life scientist quite succeeds in fulfilling this ideal. Personal acquaintance, the novels of Sir Charles Snow, or a cursory reading of the history of science provides too much counter-evidence. Though the scientific enterprise may be open-minded, whatever this application of that phrase may mean, the individual scientist is very often not. Whether his work is predominantly theoretical or experimental, he usually seems to know, before his research project is even well under way, all but the most intimate details of the result which that project will achieve. If the result is quickly forthcoming, well and good. If not, he will struggle with his apparatus and with his equations until, if at all possible, they yield results which conform to the sort of pattern which he has foreseen from the start. Nor is it only through his own research that the scientist displays his firm convictions about the phenomena which nature can yield and about the ways in which these may be fitted to theory. Often the same convictions show even more clearly in his response to the work produced by others. From Galileo's reception of Kepler's research to Nägeli's reception of Mendel's, from Dalton's rejection of Gay Lussac's results to Kelvin's rejection of Maxwell's, unexpected novelties of fact and theory have characteristically been resisted and have often been rejected by many of the most creative members of the professional scientific community. The historian, at least, scarcely needs Planck to remind him that "A new scientific truth is not usually presented in a way that convinces its opponents . . . ; rather they gradually die off, and a rising generation is familiarized with the truth from the start."[2]

---

[1] The ideas developed in this paper have been abstracted, in a drastically condensed form, from the first third of my forthcoming monograph, *The Structure of Scientific Revolutions*, which will be published during 1962 by the University of Chicago Press. Some of them were also partially developed in an earlier essay, "The Essential Tension: Tradition and Innovation in Scientific Research," which appeared in Calvin W. Taylor (ed.), *The Third (1959) University of Utah Research Conference on the Identification of Creative Scientific Talent* (Salt Lake City, 1959). [*Editor's note: The Structure of Scientific Revolutions* was published in 1962; the second edition was published in 1970—both by the University of Chicago Press.]

On this whole subject see also I. B. Cohen, "Orthodoxy and Scientific Progress," *Proceedings of the American Philosophical Society*, XCVI (1952) 505–12, and Bernard Barber, "Resistance by Scientists to Scientific Discovery", *Science, CXXIV* (1961) 596–602. I am indebted to Mr. Barber for an advance copy of that helpful paper. Above all, those concerned with the importance of quasi-dogmatic commitments as a requisite for productive scientif research should see the works of Michael Polanyi, particularly his *Personal Knowledge* (Chicago, 1958) and *The Logic of Liberty* (London, 1951). The discussion which follows this paper will indicate that Mr. Polanyi and I differ somewhat about what scientists are committed to, but that should not disguise the very great extent of our agreement about the issues discussed explicitly below.

[2] *Wissenschaftliche Selbstbiographie* (Leipzig, 1948) 22, my translation.

Familiar facts like these—and they could easily be multiplied—do not seem to bespeak an enterprise whose practitioners are notably open-minded. Can they at all be reconciled with our usual image of productive scientific research? If such a reconciliation has not seemed to present fundamental problems in the past, that is probably because resistance and preconception have usually been viewed as extraneous to science. They are, we have often been told, no more than the product of inevitable *human* limitations; a proper scientific method has no place for them; and that method is powerful enough so that no mere human idiosyncrasy can impede its success for very long. On this view, examples of a scientific *parti pris* are reduced to the status of anecdotes, and it is that evaluation of their significance that this essay aims to challenge. Verisimilitude, alone, suggests that such a challenge is required. Preconception and resistance seem the rule rather than the exception in mature scientific development. Furthermore, under normal circumstances they characterize the very best and most creative research as well as the more routine. Nor can there be much question where they come from. Rather than being characteristics of the aberrant individual, they are community characteristics with deep roots in the procedures through which scientists are trained for work in their profession. Strongly held convictions that are prior to research often seem to be a precondition for success in the sciences.

Obviously I am already ahead of my story, but in getting there I have perhaps indicated its principal theme. Though preconception and resistance to innovation could very easily choke off scientific progress, their omnipresence is nonetheless symptomatic of characteristics upon which the continuing vitality of research depends. Those characteristics I shall collectively call the dogmatism of mature science, and in the pages to come I shall try to make the following points about them. Scientific education inculcates what the scientific community had previously with difficulty gained—a deep commitment to a particular way of viewing the world and of practicing science in it. That commitment can be, and from time to time is, replaced by another, but it cannot be merely given up. And, while it continues to characterize the community of professional practitioners, it proves in two respects fundamental to productive research. By defining for the individual scientist both the problems available for pursuit and the nature of acceptable solutions to them, the commitment is actually constitutive of research. Normally the scientist is a puzzle-solver like the chess player, and the commitment induced by education is what provides him with the rules of the game being played in his time. In its absence he would not be a physicist, chemist, or whatever he has been trained to be.

In addition, commitment has a second and largely incompatible research role. Its very strength and the unanimity with which the professional group subscribes to it provides the individual scientist with an immensely sensitive detector of the trouble spots from which significant innovations of fact and theory are almost inevitably educed. In the sciences most discoveries of unexpected fact and all fundamental innovations of theory are responses to a prior breakdown in the rules of the previously established game. Therefore, though a quasi-dogmatic commitment is, on the one hand, a source of resistance and controversy, it is also instrumental in making the sciences the most consistently revolutionary of all human activities. One need make neither resistance nor dogma a virtue to recognize that no mature science could exist without them. Before examining further the nature and effects of scientific dogma, consider the pattern of education through which it is transmitted from one generation of practitioners to the next. Scientists are not, of course, the only professional community that acquires from education a set of standards, tools, and techniques which they later deploy in their own creative work. Yet even a cursory inspection of scientific pedagogy suggests that it is far more likely to induce professional rigidity than education in other fields, excepting, perhaps, systematic theology. Admittedly the following epitome is biased toward the American pattern, which I know best. The contrasts at which it aims must, however, be visible, if muted, in European and British education as well.

Perhaps the most striking feature of scientific

education is that, to an extent quite unknown in other creative fields, it is conducted through textbooks, works written especially for students. Until he is ready, or very nearly ready, to begin his own dissertation, the student of chemistry, physics, astronomy, geology, or biology is seldom either asked to attempt trial research projects or exposed to the immediate products of research done by others—to, that is, the professional communications that scientists write for their peers. Collections of "source readings" play a negligible role in *scientific* education. Nor is the science student encouraged to read the historical classics of his field—works in which he might encounter other ways of regarding the questions discussed in his text, but in which he would also meet problems, concepts and standards of solution that his future profession had long since discarded and replaced.[3] Whitehead somewhere caught this quite special feature of the sciences when he wrote, "A science that hesitates to forget its founders is lost."

An almost exclusive reliance on textbooks is not all that distinguishes scientific education. Students in other fields are, after all, also exposed to such books, though seldom beyond the second year of college and even in those early years not exclusively. But in the sciences different textbooks display different subject matters rather than, as in the humanities and many social sciences, exemplifying different approaches to a single problem field. Even books that compete for adoption in a single science course differ mainly in level and pedagogic detail, not in substance or conceptual structure. One can scarcely imagine a physicist's or chemist's saying that he had been forced to begin the education of his third-year class almost from first principles because its previous exposure to the field had been through books that consistently violated his conception of the discipline. Remarks of that sort are not by any means unprecedented in several of the social sciences.

Apparently scientists agree about what it is that every student of the field must know. That is why, in the design of a pre-professional curriculum, they can use textbooks instead of eclectic samples of research.

Nor is the characteristic technique of textbook presentation altogether the same in the sciences as elsewhere. Except in the occasional introductions that students seldom read, science texts make little attempt to describe the *sorts* of problems that the professional may be asked to solve or to discuss the *variety* of techniques that experience has made available for their solution. Instead, these books exhibit, from the very start, concrete problem-solutions that the profession has come to accept as paradigms, and they then ask the student, either with a pencil and paper or in the laboratory, to solve for himself problems closely modelled in method and substance upon those through which the text has led him. Only in elementary language instruction or in training a musical instrumentalist is so large or essential a use made of "finger exercises." And those are just the fields in which the object of instruction is to produce with maximum rapidity strong "mental sets" or *Einstellungen*. In the sciences, I suggest, the effect of these techniques is much the same. Though scientific development is particularly productive of consequential novelties, scientific education remains a relatively dogmatic initiation into a pre-established problem-solving tradition that the student is neither invited nor equipped to evaluate.

The pattern of systematic textbook education just described existed in no place and in no science (except perhaps elementary mathematics) until the early nineteenth century. But before that date a number of the more developed sciences clearly displayed the special characteristics indicated above, and in a few cases had done so for a very long time. Where there were no textbooks there had often been universally received paradigms for the practice of individual sciences. These were scientific achievements reported in books that all the practitioners of a given field knew intimately and admired, achievements upon which they modelled their own research and which provided them with a measure of their own

---

[3] The individual sciences display some variation in these respects. Students in the newer and also in the less theoretical sciences—e.g., parts of biology, geology, and medical science—are more likely to encounter both contemporary and historical source materials than those in, say, astronomy, mathematics, or physics.

accomplishment. Aristotle's *Physica,* Ptolemy's *Almagest,* Newton's *Principia* and *Opticks,* Franklin's *Electricity,* Lavoisier's *Chemistry,* and Lyell's *Geology*—these works and many others all served for a time implicitly to define the legitimate problems and methods of a research field for succeeding generations of practitioners. In their day each of these books, together with others modelled closely upon them, did for its field much of what textbooks now do for these same fields and for others besides.

All of the works named above are, of course, classics of science. As such their role may be thought to resemble that of the main classics in other creative fields, for example the works of a Shakespeare, a Rembrandt, or an Adam Smith. But by calling these works, or the achievements which lie behind them, paradigms rather than classics, I mean to suggest that there is something else special about them, something which sets them apart both from some other classics of science and from all the classics of other creative fields.

Part of this "something else" is what I shall call the exclusiveness of paradigms. At any time the practitioners of a given specialty may recognize numerous classics, some of them—like the works of Ptolemy and Copernicus or Newton and Descartes—quite incompatible one with the other. But that same group, if it has a paradigm at all, can have only one. Unlike the community of artists— which can draw simultaneous inspiration from the works of, say, Rembrandt *and* Cézanne and which therefore studies both—the community of astronomers had no alternative to choosing *between* the competing models of scientific activity supplied by Copernicus and Ptolemy. Furthermore, having made their choice, astronomers could thereafter neglect the work which they had rejected. Since the sixteenth century there have been only two full editions of the *Almagest,* both produced in the nineteenth century and directed exclusively to scholars. In the mature sciences there is no apparent function for the equivalent of an art museum or a library of classics. Scientists know when books, and even journals, are out of date. Though they do not then destroy them, they do, as any historian of

science can testify, transfer them from the active departmental library to desuetude in the general university depository. Up-to-date works have taken their place, and they are all that the further progress of science requires.

This characteristic of paradigms is closely related to another, and one that has a particular relevance to my selection of the term. In receiving a paradigm the scientific community commits itself, consciously or not, to the view that the fundamental problems there resolved have, in fact, been solved once and for all. That is what Lagrange meant when he said of Newton: "There is but one universe, and it can happen to but one man in the world's history to be the interpreter of its laws."[4] The example of either Aristotle or Einstein proves Lagrange wrong, but that does not make the fact of his commitment less consequential to scientific development. Believing that what Newton had done need not be done again, Lagrange was not tempted to fundamental reinterpretations of nature. Instead, he could take up where the men who shared his Newtonian paradigm had left off, striving both for neater formulations of that paradigm and for an articulation that would bring it into closer and closer agreement with observations of nature. That sort of work is undertaken only by those who feel that the model they have chosen is entirely secure. There is nothing quite like it in the arts, and the parallels in the social sciences are at best partial. Paradigms determine a developmental pattern for the mature sciences that is unlike the one familiar in other fields.

That difference could be illustrated by comparing the development of a paradigm-based science with that of, say, philosophy or literature. But the same effect can be achieved more economically by contrasting the early developmental pattern of almost any science with the pattern characteristic of the same field in its maturity. I cannot here avoid putting the point too starkly, but

---

[4] Quoted in this form by S. F. Mason, *Main Currents of Scientific Thought* (New York, 1956) 254. The original, which is identical in spirit but not in words, seems to derive from Delambre's contemporary éloge, *Memoires de . . . l'Institut . . . , année 1812,* 2nd part (Paris, 1816) p. xlvi.

what I have in mind is this. Excepting in those fields which, like biochemistry, originated in the combination of existing specialties, paradigms are a relatively late acquisition in the course of scientific development. During its early years a science proceeds without them, or at least without any so unequivocal and so binding as those named illustratively above. Physical optics before Newton or the study of heat before Black and Lavoisier exemplifies the pre-paradigm developmental pattern that I shall immediately examine in the history of electricity. While it continues, until, that is, a first paradigm is reached, the development of a science resembles that of the arts and of most social sciences more closely than it resembles the pattern which astronomy, say, had already acquired in antiquity and which all the natural sciences make familiar today.

To catch the difference between pre- and post-paradigm scientific development, consider a single example. In the early eighteenth century, as in the seventeenth and earlier, there were almost as many views about the nature of electricity as there were important electrical experimenters, men like Hauksbee, Gray, Desaguliers, Du Fay, Nollet, Watson, and Franklin. All their numerous concepts of electricity had something in common—they were partially derived from experiment and observation and partially from one or another version of the mechanico-corpuscular philosophy that guided all scientific research of the day. Yet these common elements gave their work no more than a family resemblance. We are forced to recognize the existence of several competing schools and sub-schools, each deriving strength from its relation to a particular version (Cartesian or Newtonian) of the corpuscular metaphysics, and each emphasizing the particular cluster of electrical phenomena which its own theory could do most to explain. Other observations were dealt with by *ad hoc* elaborations or remained as outstanding problems for further research.[5]

One early group of electricians followed seventeenth-century practice, and thus took attraction and frictional generation as the fundamental electrical phenomena. They tended to treat repulsion as a secondary effect (in the seventeenth century it had been attributed to some sort of mechanical rebounding) and also to postpone for as long as possible both discussion and systematic research on Gray's newly discovered effect, electrical conduction. Another closely related group regarded repulsion as the fundamental effect, while still another took attraction and repulsion together to be equally elementary manifestations of electricity. Each of these groups modified its theory and research accordingly, but they then had as much difficulty as the first in accounting for any but the simplest conduction effects. Those effects provided the starting point for still a third group, one which tended to speak of electricity as a "fluid" that ran through conductors rather than as an "effluvium" that emanated from non-conductors. This group, in its turn, had difficulty reconciling its theory with a number of attractive and repulsive effects.[6]

At various times all these schools made significant contributions to the body of concepts, phenomena, and techniques from which Franklin drew the first paradigm for electrical science. Any definition of the scientist that excludes the members of these schools will exclude their modern successors as well. Yet anyone surveying the de-

---

[5] Much documentation for this account of electrical development can be retrieved from Duane Roller and Duane H. D. Roller, *The Development of the Concept of Electric Charge: Electricity from the Greeks to Coulomb* (Harvard Case Histories in Experimental Science, VIII, Cambridge, Mass., 1954) and from I. B. Cohen, *Franklin and Newton: An Inquiry into Speculative Newtonian Experimental Science and Franklin's Work in Electricity as an Example Thereof* (Philadelphia, 1956). For analytic detail I am, however, very much indebted to a still unpublished paper by my student, John L. Heilbron, who has also assisted in the preparation of the three notes that follow.

[6] This division into schools is still somewhat too simplistic. After 1720 the basic division is between the French school (Du Fay, Nollet, etc.) who base their theories on attraction–repulsion effects and the English school (Desaguliers, Watson, etc.) who concentrate on conduction effects. Each group had immense difficulty in explaining the phenomena that the other took to be basic. (See, for example, Needham's report of Lemonier's investigations, in *Philosophical Transactions*, XLIV, 1746, p. 247). Within each of these groups, and particularly the English, one can trace further subdivision depending upon whether attraction or repulsion is considered the more fundamental electrical effect.

velopment of electricity before Franklin may well conclude that, though the field's practitioners were scientists, the immediate result of their activity was something less than science. Because the body of belief he could take for granted was very small, each electrical experimenter felt forced to begin by building his field anew from its foundations. In doing so his choice of supporting observation and experiment was relatively free, for the set of standard methods and phenomena that every electrician must employ and explain was extraordinarily small. As a result, throughout the first half of the century, electrical investigations tended to circle back over the same ground again and again. New effects were repeatedly discovered, but many of them were rapidly lost again. Among those lost were many effects due to what we should now describe as inductive charging and also Du Fay's famous discovery of the two sorts of electrification. Franklin and Kinnersley were surprised when, some fifteen years later, the latter discovered that a charged ball which was repelled by rubbed glass would be attracted by rubbed sealing-wax or amber.[7] In the absence of a well-articulated and widely received theory (a desideratum which no science possesses from its very beginning and which few if any of the social sciences have achieved today), the situation could hardly have been otherwise. During the first half of the eighteenth century there was no way for electricians to distinguish consistently between electrical and non-electrical effects, between laboratory accidents and essential novelties, or between striking demonstration and experiments which revealed the essential nature of electricity.

This is the state of affairs which Franklin changed.[8] His theory explained so many—though not all—of the electrical effects recognized by the various earlier schools that within a generation all electricians had been converted to some view very like it. Though it did not resolve quite all disagreements, Franklin's theory was electricity's first paradigm, and its existence gives a new tone and flavor to the electrical researches of the last decades of the eighteenth century. The end of inter-school debate ended the constant reiteration of fundamentals; confidence that they were on the right track encouraged electricians to undertake more precise, esoteric, and consuming sorts of work. Freed from concern with any and all electrical phenomena, the newly united group could pursue selected phenomena in far more detail, designing much special equipment for the task and employing it more stubbornly and systematically than electricians had ever done before. In the hands of a Cavendish, a Coulomb, or a Volta the collection of electrical facts and the articulation of electrical theory were, for the first time, highly directed activities. As a result the efficiency and effectiveness of electrical research increased immensely, providing evidence for a societal version of Francis Bacon's acute methodological dictum: "Truth emerges more readily from error than from confusion."

Obviously I exaggerate both the speed and the completeness with which the transition to a paradigm occurs. But that does not make the phenomenon itself less real. The maturation of electricity as a science is not coextensive with the entire de-

---

[7] Du Fay's discovery that there are two sorts of electricity and that these are mutually attractive but self-repulsive is reported and documented in great experimental detail in the fourth of his famous memoirs on electricity: "De l'Attraction & Répulsion des Corps Electriques," Memoires de . . . l'Académie . . . de l'année 1733 (Paris, 1735) 457–76. These memoirs were well known and widely cited, but Desaguliers seems to be the only electrician who, for almost two decades, even mentions that some charged bodies will attract each other (Philosophical Transactions . . . , XLII, 1741–2, pp. 140–3). For Franklin's and Kinnersley's "surprise" see I. B. Cohen (ed.), Benjamin Franklin's Experiments: A New Edition of Franklin's Experiments and Observations on Electricity(Cambridge, Mass., 1941) 250–5. Note also that, though Kinnersley had produced the effect, neither he nor Franklin seems ever to have recognized that two resinously charged bodies would repel each other, a phenomenon directly contrary to Franklin's theory.

[8] The change is not, of course, due to Franklin alone nor did it occur overnight. Other electricians, most notably William Watson, anticipated parts of Franklin's theory. More important, it was only after essential modifications, due principally to Aepinus, that Franklin's theory gained the general currency requisite for a paradigm. And even then there continued to be two formulations of the theory: the Franklin–Aepinus one-fluid form and a two-fluid form due principally to Symmer. Electricians soon reached the conclusion that no electrical test could possibly discriminate between the two theories. Until the discovery of the battery, when the choice between a one-fluid and two-fluid theory began to make an occasional difference in the design and analysis of experiments, the two were equivalent.

velopment of the field. Writers on electricity during the first four decades of the eighteenth century possessed far more information about electrical phenomena than had their sixteenth- and seventeenth-century predecessors. During the half-century after 1745 very few new sorts of electrical phenomena were added to their lists. Nevertheless, in important respects the electrical writings of the last two decades of the century seemed further removed from those of Gray, Du Fay, and even Franklin than are the writings of these early eighteenth-century electricians from those of their predecessors a hundred years before. Some time between 1740 and 1780 electricians, as a group, gained what astronomers had achieved in Antiquity, students of motion in the Middle Ages, of physical optics in the late seventeenth century, and of historical geology in the early nineteenth. They had, that is, achieved a paradigm, possession of which enabled them to take the foundation of their field for granted and to push on to more concrete and recondite problems.[9] Except with the advantage of hindsight, it is hard to find another criterion that so clearly proclaims a field of science.

These remarks should begin to clarify what I take a paradigm to be. It is, in the first place, a fundamental scientific achievement and one which includes both a theory and some exemplary applications to the results of experiment and observation. More important, it is an open-ended achievement, one which leaves all sorts of research still to be done. And, finally, it is an accepted achievement in the sense that it is received by a group whose members no longer try to rival it or to create alternates for it. Instead, they attempt to extend and exploit it in a variety of ways to which I shall shortly turn. That discussion of the work that paradigms leave to be done will make both their role and the reasons for their special

efficacy clearer still. But first there is one rather different point to be made about them. Though the reception of a paradigm seems historically prerequisite to the most effective sorts of scientific research, the paradigms which enhance research effectiveness need not be and usually are not permanent. On the contrary, the developmental pattern of mature science is usually from paradigm to paradigm. It differs from the pattern characteristic of the early or pre-paradigm period not by the total elimination of debate over fundamentals, but by the drastic restriction of such debate to occasional periods of paradigm change.

Ptolemy's *Almagest* was not, for example, any less a paradigm because the research tradition that descended from it had ultimately to be replaced by an incompatible one derived from the work of Copernicus and Kepler. Nor was Newton's *Opticks* less a paradigm for eighteenth-century students of light because it was later replaced by the ether-wave theory of Young and Fresnel, a paradigm which in its turn gave way to the electromagnetic displacement theory that descends from Maxwell. Undoubtedly the research work that any given paradigm permits results in lasting contributions to the body of scientific knowledge and technique, but paradigms themselves are very often swept aside and replaced by others that are quite incompatible with them. We can have no recourse to notions like the "truth" or "validity" of paradigms in our attempt to understand the special efficacy of the research which their reception permits.

On the contrary, the historian can often recognize that in declaring an older paradigm out of date or in rejecting the approach of some one of the pre-paradigm schools a scientific community has rejected the embryo of an important scientific perception to which it would later be forced to return. But it is very far from clear that the profession delayed scientific development by doing so. Would quantum mechanics have been born sooner if nineteenth-century scientists had been more willing to admit that Newton's corpuscular view of light might still have something significant to teach them about nature? I think not, although in the arts, the humanities, and many social sci-

---

[9] Note that this first electrical paradigm was fully effective only until 1800, when the discovery of the battery and the multiplication of electrochemical effects initiated a revolution in electrical theory. Until a new paradigm emerged from that revolution, the literature of electricity, particularly in England, reverted in many respects to the tone characteristic of the first half of the eighteenth century.

ences that less doctrinaire view is very often adopted toward classic achievements of the past. Or would astronomy and dynamics have advanced more rapidly if scientists had recognized that Ptolemy and Copernicus had chosen equally legitimate means to describe the earth's position? That view was, in fact, suggested during the seventeenth century, and it has since been confirmed by relativity theory. But in the interim it was firmly rejected together with Ptolemaic astronomy, emerging again only in the very late nineteenth century when, for the first time, it had concrete relevance to unsolved problems generated by the continuing practice of non-relativistic physics. One could argue, as indeed by implication I shall, that close eighteenth- and nineteenth-century attention either to the work of Ptolemy or to the relativistic views of Descartes, Huygens, and Leibniz would have delayed rather than accelerated the revolution in physics with which the twentieth century began. Advance from paradigm to paradigm rather than through the continuing competition between recognized classics may be a functional as well as a factual characteristic of mature scientific development.

Much that has been said so far is intended to indicate that—except during occasional extraordinary periods to be discussed in the last section of this paper—the practitioners of a mature scientific specialty are deeply committed to some one paradigm-based way of regarding and investigating nature. Their paradigm tells them about the sorts of entities with which the universe is populated and about the way the members of that population behave; in addition, it informs them of the questions that may legitimately be asked about nature and of the techniques that can properly be used in the search for answers to them. In fact, a paradigm tells scientists so much that the questions it leaves for research seldom have great intrinsic interest to those outside the profession. Though educated men as a group may be fascinated to hear about the spectrum of fundamental particles or about the processes of molecular replication, their interest is usually quickly exhausted by an account of the beliefs that already underlie research on these

problems. The outcome of the individual research project is indifferent to them, and their interest is unlikely to awaken again until, as with parity non-conservation, research unexpectedly leads to paradigm-change and to a consequent alteration in the beliefs which guide research. That, no doubt, is why both historians and popularizers have devoted so much of their attention to the revolutionary episodes which result in change of paradigm and have so largely neglected the sort of work that even the greatest scientists necessarily do most of the time.

My point will become clearer if I now ask what it is that the existence of a paradigm leaves for the scientific community to do. The answer—as obvious as the related existence of resistance to innovation and as often brushed under the carpet—is that scientists, given a paradigm, strive with all their might and skill to bring it into closer and closer agreement with nature. Much of their effort, particularly in the early stages of a paradigm's development, is directed to articulating the paradigm, rendering it more precise in areas where the original formulation has inevitably been vague. For example, knowing that electricity was a fluid whose individual particles act upon one another at a distance, electricians after Franklin could attempt to determine the quantitative law of force between particles of electricity. Others could seek the mutual interdependence of spark length, electroscope deflection, quantity of electricity, and conductor-configuration. These were the sorts of problems upon which Coulomb, Cavendish, and Volta worked in the last decades of the eighteenth century, and they have many parallels in the development of every other mature science. Contemporary attempts to determine the quantum mechanical forces governing the interactions of nucleons fall precisely in this same category, paradigm-articulation.

That sort of problem is not the only challenge which a paradigm sets for the community that embraces it. There are always many areas in which a paradigm is assumed to work but to which it has not, in fact, yet been applied. Matching the paradigm to nature in these areas often engages much of the best scientific talent in any generation. The eighteenth-century attempts to develop a Newtonian theory of vibrating strings provide one significant example, and the current work on a quantum mechanical theory of solids provides another. In addition, there is always much fascinating work to be done in improving the match between a paradigm and nature in an area where at least limited agreement has already been demonstrated. Theoretical work on problems like these is illustrated by eighteenth-century research on the perturbations that cause planets to deviate from their Keplerian orbits as well as by the elaborate twentieth-century theory of the spectra of complex atoms and molecules. And accompanying all these problems and still others besides is a recurring series of instrumental hurdles. Special apparatus had to be invented and built to permit Coulomb's determination of the electrical force law. New sorts of telescopes were required for the observations that, when completed, demanded an improved Newtonian perturbation theory. The design and construction of more flexible and more powerful accelerators is a continuing desideratum in the attempt to articulate more powerful theories of nuclear forces. These are the sorts of work on which almost all scientists spend almost all of their time.[10]

Probably this epitome of normal scientific research requires no elaboration in this place, but there are two points that must now be made about it. First, all of the problems mentioned above were paradigm-dependent, often in several ways. Some—for example, the derivation of perturbation terms in Newtonian planetary theory—could not even have been stated in the absence of an appropriate paradigm. With the transition from Newtonian to relativity theory a few of them became different problems and not all of these have yet been solved. Other problems—for example, the attempt to determine a law of electric forces—could be and were at least vaguely stated before the emergence of the paradigm with which they

were ultimately solved. But in that older form they proved intractable. The men who described electrical attractions and repulsions in terms of effluvia attempted to measure the resulting forces by placing a charged disc at a measured distance beneath one pan of a balance. Under those circumstances no consistent or interpretable results were obtained. The prerequisite for success proved to be a paradigm that reduced electrical action to a gravity-like action between point particles at a distance. After Franklin electricians thought of electrical action in those terms; both Coulomb and Cavendish designed their apparatus accordingly. Finally, in both these cases and in all the others as well a commitment to the paradigm was needed simply to provide adequate motivation. Who would design and build elaborate special-purpose apparatus, or who would spend months trying to solve a particular differential equation, without a quite firm guarantee that his effort, if successful, would yield the anticipated fruit?

This reference to the anticipated outcome of a research project points to the second striking characteristic of what I am now calling normal, or paradigm-based, research. The scientist engaged in it does not at all fit the prevalent image of the scientist as explorer or as inventor of brand new theories which permit striking and unexpected predictions. On the contrary, in all the problems discussed above everything but the detail of the outcome was known in advance. No scientist who accepted Franklin's paradigm could doubt that there was a law of attraction between small particles of electricity, and they could reasonably suppose that it would take a simple algebraic form. Some of them had even guessed that it would prove to be an inverse square law. Nor did Newtonian astronomers and physicists doubt that Newton's laws of motion and of gravitation could ultimately be made to yield the observed motions of the moon and planets even though, for over a century, the complexity of the requisite mathematics prevented good agreements being uniformly obtained. In all these problems, as in most others that scientists undertake, the challenge is not to uncover the unknown but to obtain the known. Their fascination lies not in what success may be ex-

---

[10] The discussion in this paragraph and the next is considerably elaborated in my paper, "The Function of Measurement in Modern Physical Science," *Isis*, LII (1961) 161–93.

pected to disclose but in the difficulty of obtaining success at all. Rather than resembling exploration, normal research seems like the effort to assemble a Chinese cube whose finished outline is known from the start.

Those are the characteristics of normal research that I had in mind when, at the start of this essay, I described the man engaged in it as a puzzle-solver, like the chess player. The paradigm he has acquired through prior training provides him with the rules of the game, describes the pieces with which it must be played, and indicates the nature of the required outcome. His task is to manipulate those pieces within the rules in such a way that the required outcome is produced. If he fails, as most scientists do in at least their first attacks upon any given problem, that failure speaks only to his lack of skill. It cannot call into question the rules that his paradigm has supplied, for without those rules there would have been no puzzle with which to wrestle in the first place. No wonder, then, that the problems (or puzzles) which the practitioner of a mature science normally undertakes presuppose a deep commitment to a paradigm. And how fortunate it is that that commitment is not lightly given up. Experience shows that, in almost all cases, the reiterated efforts, either of the individual or of the professional group, do at last succeed in producing within the paradigm a solution to even the most stubborn problems. That is one of the ways in which science advances. Under those circumstances can we be surprised that scientists resist paradigm-change? What they are defending is, after all, neither more nor less than the basis of their professional way of life.

By now one principal advantage of what I began by calling scientific dogmatism should be apparent. As a glance at any Baconian natural history or a survey of the pre-paradigm development of any science will show, nature is vastly too complex to be explored even approximately at random. Something must tell the scientist where to look and what to look for, and that something, though it may not last beyond his generation, is the paradigm with which his education as a scientist has supplied him. Given that paradigm and the

requisite confidence in it, the scientist largely ceases to be an explorer at all, or at least to be an explorer of the unknown. Instead, he struggles to articulate and concretize the known, designing much special-purpose apparatus and many special-purpose adaptations of theory for that task. From those puzzles of design and adaptation he gets his pleasure. Unless he is extraordinarily lucky, it is upon his success with them that his reputation will depend. Inevitably the enterprise which engages him is characterized, at any one time, by drastically restricted vision. But within the region upon which vision is focused the continuing attempt to match paradigms to nature results in a knowledge and understanding of esoteric detail that could not have been achieved in any other way. From Copernicus and the problem of precession to Einstein and the photo-electric effect, the progress of science has again and again depended upon just such esoterica. One great virtue of commitment to paradigms is that it frees scientists to engage themselves with tiny puzzles.

Nevertheless, this image of scientific research as puzzle-solving or paradigm-matching must be, at the very least, thoroughly incomplete. Though the scientist may not be an explorer, scientists do again and again discover new and unexpected sorts of phenomena. Or again, though the scientist does not normally strive to invent new sorts of basic theories, such theories have repeatedly emerged from the continuing practice of research. But neither of these types of innovation would arise if the enterprise I have been calling normal science were always successful. In fact, the man engaged in puzzle-solving very often resists substantive novelty, and he does so for good reason. To him it is a change in the rules of the game and any change of rules is intrinsically subversive. That subversive element is, of course, most apparent in major theoretical innovations like those associated with the names of Copernicus, Lavoisier, or Einstein. But the discovery of an unanticipated phenomenon can have the same destructive effects, although usually on a smaller group and for a far shorter time. Once he had performed his first follow-up experiments, Roentgen's glowing screen demonstrated that previously standard cathode ray equipment was behaving in ways for which no one had made allowance. There was an unanticipated variable to be controlled; earlier researches, already on their way to becoming paradigms, would require re-evaluation; old puzzles would have to be solved again under a somewhat different set of rules. Even so readily assimilable a discovery as that of X rays can violate a paradigm that has previously guided research. It follows that, if the normal puzzle-solving activity were altogether successful, the development of science could lead to no fundamental innovations at all.

But of course normal science is not always successful, and in recognizing that fact we encounter what I take to be the second great advantage of paradigm-based research. Unlike many of the early electricians, the practitioner of a mature science knows with considerable precision what sort of result he should gain from his research. As a consequence he is in a particularly favorable position to recognize when a research problem has gone astray. Perhaps, like Galvani or Roentgen, he encounters an effect that he knows ought not to occur. Or perhaps, like Copernicus, Planck, or Einstein, he concludes that the reiterated failures of his predecessors in matching a paradigm to nature is presumptive evidence of the need to change the rules under which a match is to be sought. Or perhaps, like Franklin or Lavoisier, he decides after repeated attempts that no existing theory can be articulated to account for some newly discovered effect. In all of these ways and in others besides the practice of normal puzzle-solving science can and inevitably does lead to the isolation and recognition of anomaly. That recognition proves, I think, prerequisite for almost all discoveries of new sorts of phenomena and for all fundamental innovations in scientific theory. After a first paradigm has been achieved, a breakdown in the rules of the pre-established game is the usual prelude to significant scientific innovation.

Examine the case of discoveries first. Many of them, like Coulomb's law or a new element to fill an empty spot in the periodic table, present no problem. They were not "new sorts of phenomena" but discoveries anticipated through a paradigm and achieved by expert puzzle-solvers: That sort of discovery is a natural product of what I have been calling normal science. But not all discoveries are of that sort: Many could not have been anticipated by any extrapolation from the known; in a sense they had to be made "by accident." On the other hand the accident through which they emerged could not ordinarily have occurred to a man just looking around. In the mature sciences discovery demands much special equipment, both conceptual and instrumental, and that special equipment has invariably been developed and deployed for the pursuit of the puzzles of normal research. Discovery results when that equipment fails to function as it should. Furthermore, since some sort of at least temporary failure occurs during almost every research project, discovery results only when the failure is particularly stubborn or striking and only when it seems to raise questions about accepted beliefs and procedures. Established paradigms are thus often doubly prerequisite to discoveries. Without them the project that goes astray would not have been undertaken. And even when the project has gone astray, as most do for a while, the paradigm can help to determine whether the failure is worth pursuing. The usual and proper response to a failure in puzzle-solving is to blame one's talents or one's tools and to turn next to another problem. If he is not to waste time, the scientist must be able to discriminate essential anomaly from mere failure.

That pattern—discovery through an anomaly that calls established techniques and beliefs in doubt—has been repeated again and again in the course of scientific development. Newton discovered the composition of white light when he was unable to reconcile measured dispersion with that predicted by Snell's recently discovered law of refraction.[11] The electric battery was discovered when existing detectors of static charges failed to behave as Franklin's paradigm said they should.[12] The planet Neptune was discovered through an effort to account for recognized anomalies in the

---

[11] See my "Newton's Optical Papers" in I. B. Cohen (ed.), *Isaac Newton's Papers & Letters on Natural Philosophy* (Cambridge, Mass., 1958) 27–45.

[12] Luigi Galvani, *Commentary on the Effects of Electricity on Muscular Motion*, trans. by M. G. Foley with notes and an introduction by I. B. Cohen (Norwalk, Conn., 1954) 27–9.

orbit of Uranus.[13] The element chlorine and the compound carbon monoxide emerged during attempts to reconcile Lavoisier's new chemistry with laboratory observations.[14] The so-called noble gases were the products of a long series of investigations initiated by a small but persistent anomaly in the measured density of atmospheric nitrogen.[15] The electron was posited to explain some anomalous properties of electrical conduction through gases, and its spin was suggested to account for other sorts of anomalies observed in atomic spectra.[16] Both the neutron and the neutrino provide other examples, and the list could be extended almost indefinitely.[17] In the mature sciences unexpected novelties are discovered principally after something has gone wrong.

If, however, anomaly is significant in preparing the way for new discoveries, it plays a still larger role in the invention of new theories. Contrary to a prevalent, though by no means universal, belief, new theories are not invented to account for observations that have not previously been ordered by theory at all. Rather, at almost all times in the development of any advanced science, all the facts whose relevance is admitted seem either to fit existing theory well or to be in the process of conforming. Making them conform better provides many of the standard problems of normal science. And almost always committed scientists succeed in solving them. But they do not always succeed, and, when they fail repeatedly

and in increasing numbers, then their sector of the scientific community encounters what I am elsewhere calling "crisis." Recognizing that something is fundamentally wrong with the theory upon which their work is based, scientists will attempt more fundamental articulations of theory than those which were admissible before. (Characteristically, at times of crisis, one encounters numerous different versions of the paradigm theory.[18]) Simultaneously they will often begin more nearly random experimentation within the area of difficulty, hoping to discover some effect that will suggest a way to set the situation right. Only under circumstances like these, I suggest, is a fundamental innovation in scientific theory both invented and accepted.

The state of Ptolemaic astronomy was, for example, a recognized scandal before Copernicus proposed a basic change in astronomical theory, and the preface in which Copernicus described his reasons for innovation provides a classic description of the crisis state.[19] Galileo's contributions to the study of motion took their point of departure from recognized difficulties with medieval theory, and Newton reconciled Galileo's mechanics with Copernicanism.[20] Lavoisier's new chemistry was a product of the anomalies created jointly by the proliferation of new gases and the first systematic

---

[13] Angus Armitage, *A Century of Astronomy* (London, 1950) 111–15.

[14] For chlorine see Ernst von Meyer, *A History of Chemistry from the Earliest Times to the Present Day,* trans. G. M'Gowan (London, 1891) 224–7. For carbon monoxide see Hermann Kopp, *Geschichte der Chemie* (Braunschweig, 1845) III, 294–6.

[15] William Ramsay, *The Gases of the Atmosphere: the History of their Discovery* (London, 1896) Chs. 4 and 5.

[16] J. J. Thomson, *Recollections and Reflections* (New York, 1937) 325–71; T. W. Chalmers, *Historic Researches: Chapters in the History of Physical and Chemical Discovery* (London, 1949) 187–217; and F. K. Richtmeyer, E. H. Kennard and T. Lauritsen, *Introduction to Modern Physics* (5th ed., New York, 1955) 212.

[17] Ibid, pp. 466–470; and Rogers D. Rusk, *Introduction to Atomic and Nuclear Physics* (New York, 1958) 328–30.

---

[18] One classic example, for which see the reference cited below in the next note, is the proliferation of geocentric astronomical systems in the years before Copernicus's heliocentric reform. Another, for which see J. R. Partington and D. McKie, "Historical Studies of the Phlogiston Theory," *Annals of Science,* II (1937) 361–404, III (1938) 1–58, 337–71, and IV (1939) 113–49, is the multiplicity of "phlogiston theories" produced in response to the general recognition that weight is always gained on combustion and to the experimental discovery of many new gases after 1760. The same proliferation of versions of accepted theories occurred in mechanics and electromagnetism in the two decades preceding Einstein's special relativity theory. (E. T. Whittaker, *History of the Theories of Aether and Electricity,* 2nd ed., 2 vols., London 1951–53, I, Ch. 12, and II, Ch. 2. I concur in the widespread judgment that this is a very biased account of the genesis of relativity theory, but it contains just the detail necessary to make the point here at issue.)

[19] T. S. Kuhn, *The Copernican Revolution: Planetary Astronomy in the Development of Western Thought* (Cambridge, Mass., 1957) 133–40.

[20] For Galileo see Alexandre Koyré, *Études Galiléennes* (3 vols., Paris, 1939); for Newton see Kuhn, op. cit. pp. 228–60 and 289–91.

studies of weight relations.[21] The wave theory of light was developed amid growing concern about anomalies in the relation of diffraction and polarization effects to Newton's corpuscular theory.[22] Thermodynamics, which later came to seem a superstructure for existing sciences, was established only at the price of rejecting the previously paradigmatic caloric theory.[23] Quantum mechanics was born from a variety of difficulties surrounding black-body radiation, specific heat, and the photo-electric effect.[24] Again the list could be extended, but the point should already be clear. New theories arise from work conducted under old ones, and they do so only when something is observed to have gone wrong. Their prelude is widely recognized anomaly, and that recognition can come only to a group that knows very well what it would mean to have things go right.

Because limitations of space and time force me to stop at this point, my case for dogmatism must remain schematic. I shall not here even attempt to deal with the fine structure that scientific development exhibits at all times. But there is another more positive qualification of my thesis, and it requires one closing comment. Though successful research demands a deep commitment to the status quo, innovation remains at the heart of the enterprise. Scientists are *trained* to operate as puzzle-solvers from established rules, but they are also *taught* to regard themselves as explorers and inventors who know no rules except those dictated by nature itself. The result is an acquired tension, partly within the individual and partly within the community, between professional skills on the one hand and professional ideology on the other. Almost certainly that tension and the ability to sustain it are important to science's success. Insofar as I have dealt exclusively with the dependence of research upon tradition, my discussion is inevitably one-sided. On this whole subject there is a great deal more to be said.

But to be one-sided is not necessarily to be wrong, and it may be an essential preliminary to a more penetrating examination of the requisites for successful scientific life. Almost no one, perhaps no one at all, needs to be told that the vitality of science depends on the continuation of occasional tradition-shattering innovations. But the apparently contrary dependence of research upon a deep commitment to established tools and beliefs receives the very minimum of attention. I urge that it be given more. Until that is done, some of the most striking characteristics of scientific education and development will remain extraordinarily difficult to understand.

---

[21] For the proliferation of gases see Partington, *A Short History of Chemistry* (2nd ed., London, 1948) Ch. 6; for the role of weight relations see Henry Guerlac, "The Origin of Lavoisier's Work on Combustion," *Archives internationales d'histoire des sciences,* XII (1959) 113–35.

[22] Whittaker, *Aether and Electricity,* II, 94–109; William Whewell, *History of the Inductive Sciences* (revised ed., 3 vols., London, 1847) II, 213–71; and Kuhn, "Function of Measurement," p. 181 n.

[23] For a general account of the beginnings of thermodynamics (including much relevant bibliography) see my "Energy Conservation as an Example of Simultaneous Discovery" in Marshall Clagett (ed.), *Critical Problems in the History of Science* (Madison, Wisc., 1959) 321–56. For the special problems presented to caloric theorists by energy conservation see the Carnot papers, there cited in n. 2, and also S. P. Thompson, *The Life of William Thomson, Baron Kelvin of Largs* (2 vols., London, 1910) Ch. 6.

[24] Richtmeyer et al., *Modern Physics,* pp. 89–94, 124–32, and 409–14; Gerald Holton, *Introduction to Concepts and Theories in Physical Science* (Cambridge, Mass., 1953) 528–45.

The Nature and Necessity of Scientific Revolutions

Thomas Kuhn

. . . . What are scientific revolutions, and what is their function in scientific development? . . . [S]cientific revolutions are here taken to be those non-cumulative developmental episodes in which an older paradigm is replaced in whole or in part by an incompatible new one. There is more to be said, however, and an essential part of it can be introduced by asking one further question. Why should a change of paradigm be called a revolution? In the face of the vast and essential differences between political and scientific development, what parallelism can justify the metaphor that finds revolutions in both?

One aspect of the parallelism must already be apparent. Political revolutions are inaugurated by a growing sense, often restricted to a segment of the political community, that existing institutions have ceased adequately to meet the problems posed by an environment that they have in part created. In much the same way, scientific revolutions are inaugurated by a growing sense, again often restricted to a narrow subdivision of the scientific community, that an existing paradigm has ceased to function adequately in the exploration of an aspect of nature to which that paradigm itself had previously led the way. In both political and scientific development the sense of malfunction that can lead to crisis is prerequisite to revolution. Furthermore, though it admittedly strains the metaphor, that parallelism holds not only for the major paradigm changes, like those attributable to Copernicus and Lavoisier, but also for the far smaller ones associated with the assimilation of a new sort of phenomenon, like oxygen or X rays. Scientific revolutions . . . need seem revolutionary only to those whose paradigms are affected by

them. To outsiders they may, like the Balkan revolutions of the early twentieth century, seem normal parts of the developmental process. Astronomers, for example, could accept X rays as a mere addition to knowledge, for their paradigms were unaffected by the existence of the new radiation. But for men like Kelvin, Crookes, and Roentgen, whose research dealt with radiation theory or with cathode ray tubes, the emergence of X rays necessarily violated one paradigm as it created another. That is why these rays could be discovered only through something's first going wrong with normal research.

This genetic aspect of the parallel between political and scientific development should no longer be open to doubt. The parallel has, however, a second and more profound aspect upon which the significance of the first depends. Political revolutions aim to change political institutions in ways that those institutions themselves prohibit. Their success therefore necessitates the partial relinquishment of one set of institutions in favor of another, and in the interim, society is not fully governed by institutions at all. Initially it is crisis alone that attenuates the role of political institutions as we have already seen it attenuate the role of paradigms. In increasing numbers individuals become increasingly estranged from political life and behave more and more eccentrically within it. Then, as the crisis deepens, many of these individuals commit themselves to some concrete proposal for the reconstruction of society in a new institutional framework. At that point the society is divided into competing camps or parties, one seeking to defend the old institutional constellation, the others seeking to institute some new one.

From Chapter IX of *The Structure of Scientific Revolutions* by Thomas Kuhn, 2nd edition (1970), pp. 92–110. © 1962, 1970 by the University of Chicago Press. Reprinted by permission of the author and University of Chicago Press.

And, once that polarization has occurred, *political recourse fails*. Because they differ about the institutional matrix within which political change is to be achieved and evaluated, because they acknowledge no supra-institutional framework for the adjudication of revolutionary difference, the parties to a revolutionary conflict must finally resort to the techniques of mass persuasion, often including force. Though revolutions have had a vital role in the evolution of political institutions, that role depends upon their being partially extrapolitical or extrainstitutional events.

The remainder of this essay aims to demonstrate that the historical study of paradigm change reveals very similar characteristics in the evolution of the sciences. Like the choice between competing political institutions, that between competing paradigms proves to be a choice between incompatible modes of community life. Because it has that character, the choice is not and cannot be determined merely by the evaluative procedures characteristic of normal science, for these depend in part upon a particular paradigm, and that paradigm is at issue. When paradigms enter, as they must, into a debate about paradigm choice, their role is necessarily circular. Each group uses its own paradigm to argue in that paradigm's defense.

The resulting circularity does not, of course, make the arguments wrong or even ineffectual. The man who premises a paradigm when arguing in its defense can nonetheless provide a clear exhibit of what scientific practice will be like for those who adopt the new view of nature. That exhibit can be immensely persuasive, often compellingly so. Yet, whatever its force, the status of the circular argument is only that of persuasion. It cannot be made logically or even probabilistically compelling for those who refuse to step into the circle. The premises and values shared by the two parties to a debate over paradigms are not sufficiently extensive for that. As in political revolutions, so in paradigm choice—there is no standard higher than the assent of the relevant community. To discover how scientific revolutions are effected, we shall therefore have to examine not only the impact of nature and of logic, but also the techniques of persuasive argumentation effective within the quite special groups that constitute the community of scientists.

To discover why this issue of paradigm choice can never be unequivocally settled by logic and experiment alone, we must shortly examine the nature of the differences that separate the proponents of a traditional paradigm from their revolutionary successors. . . . We have, however, already noted numerous examples of such differences, and no one will doubt that history can supply many others. What is more likely to be doubted than their existence—and what must therefore be considered first—is that such examples provide essential information about the nature of science. Granting that paradigm rejection has been a historic fact, does it illuminate more than human credulity and confusion? Are there intrinsic reasons why the assimilation of either a new sort of phenomenon or a new scientific theory must demand the rejection of an older paradigm?

First notice that if there are such reasons, they do not derive from the logical structure of scientific knowledge. In principle, a new phenomenon might emerge without reflecting destructively upon any part of past scientific practice. Though discovering life on the moon would today be destructive of existing paradigms (these tell us things about the moon that seem incompatible with life's existence there), discovering life in some less well-known part of the galaxy would not. By the same token, a new theory does not have to conflict with any of its predecessors. It might deal exclusively with phenomena not previously known, as the quantum theory deals (but, significantly, not exclusively) with subatomic phenomena unknown before the twentieth century. Or again, the new theory might be simply a higher level theory than those known before, one that linked together a whole group of lower level theories without substantially changing any. Today, the theory of energy conservation provides just such links between dynamics, chemistry, electricity, optics, thermal theory, and so on. Still other compatible relationships between old and new theories can be conceived. Any and all of them might be exemplified by the historical process through which science has developed. If they were, scientific development would be genuinely cumulative. New sorts of phenomena would simply disclose order in an aspect of nature where none had been seen before. In the evolution of science new knowledge would replace ignorance rather than replace knowledge of another and incompatible sort.

Of course, science (or some other enterprise, perhaps less effective) might have developed in that fully cumulative manner. Many people have believed that it did so, and most still seem to suppose that cumulation is at least the ideal that historical development would display if only it had not so often been distorted by human idiosyncrasy. There are important reasons for that belief. . . . Nevertheless, despite the immense plausibility of that ideal image, there is increasing reason to wonder whether it can possibly be an image of *science*. After the pre-paradigm period the assimilation of all new theories and of almost all new sorts of phenomena has in fact demanded the destruction of a prior paradigm and a consequent conflict between competing schools of scientific thought. Cumulative acquisition of unanticipated novelties proves to be an almost non-existent exception to the rule of scientific development. The man who takes historic fact seriously must suspect that science does not tend toward the ideal that our image of its cumulativeness has suggested. Perhaps it is another sort of enterprise.

If, however, resistant facts can carry us that far, then a second look at the ground we have already covered may suggest that cumulative acquisition of novelty is not only rare in fact but improbable in principle. Normal research, which *is* cumulative, owes its success to the ability of scientists regularly to select problems that can be solved with conceptual and instrumental techniques close to those already in existence. (That is why an excessive concern with useful problems, regardless of their relation to existing knowledge and technique, can so easily inhibit scientific development.) The man who is striving to solve a problem defined by existing knowledge and technique is not, however, just looking around. He

knows what he wants to achieve, and he designs his instruments and directs his thoughts accordingly. Unanticipated novelty, the new discovery, can emerge only to the extent that his anticipations about nature and his instruments prove wrong. Often the importance of the resulting discovery will itself be proportional to the extent and stubbornness of the anomaly that foreshadowed it. Obviously, then, there must be a conflict between the paradigm that discloses anomaly and the one that later renders the anomaly lawlike. . . .

The same argument applies even more clearly to the invention of new theories. There are, in principle, only three types of phenomena about which a new theory might be developed. The first consists of phenomena already well explained by existing paradigms, and these seldom provide either motive or point of departure for theory construction. When they do . . . the theories that result are seldom accepted, because nature provides no ground for discrimination. A second class of phenomena consists of those whose nature is indicated by existing paradigms but whose details can be understood only through further theory articulation. These are the phenomena to which scientists direct their research much of the time, but that research aims at the articulation of existing paradigms rather than at the invention of new ones. Only when these attempts at articulation fail do scientists encounter the third type of phenomena, the recognized anomalies whose characteristic feature is their stubborn refusal to be assimilated to existing paradigms. This type alone gives rise to new theories. Paradigms provide all phenomena except anomalies with a theory-determined place in the scientist's field of vision.

But if new theories are called forth to resolve anomalies in the relation of an existing theory to nature, then the successful new theory must somewhere permit predictions that are different from those derived from its predecessor. That difference could not occur if the two were logically compatible. In the process of being assimilated, the second must displace the first. Even a theory like energy conservation, which today seems a logical superstructure that relates to nature only through independently established theories, did not develop historically without paradigm destruction. Instead, it emerged from a crisis in which an essential ingredient was the incompatibility between Newtonian dynamics and some recently formulated consequences of the caloric theory of heat. Only after the caloric theory had been rejected could energy conservation become part of science.[1] And only after it had been part of science for some time could it come to seem a theory of a logically higher type, one not in conflict with its predecessors. It is hard to see how new theories could arise without these destructive changes in beliefs about nature. Though logical inclusiveness remains a permissible view of the relation between successive scientific theories, it is a historical implausibility.

A century ago it would, I think, have been possible to let the case for the necessity of revolutions rest at this point. But today, unfortunately, that cannot be done because the view of the subject developed above cannot be maintained if the most prevalent contemporary interpretation of the nature and function of scientific theory is accepted. That interpretation, closely associated with early logical positivism and not categorically rejected by its successors, would restrict the range and meaning of an accepted theory so that it could not possibly conflict with any later theory that made predictions about some of the same natural phenomena. The best-known and the strongest case for this restricted conception of a scientific theory emerges in discussions of the relation between contemporary Einsteinian dynamics and the older dynamical equations that descend from Newton's *Principia*. From the viewpoint of this essay these two theories are fundamentally incompatible in the sense illustrated by the relation of Copernican to Ptolemaic astronomy: Einstein's theory can be accepted only with the recognition that Newton's was wrong. Today this remains a minority view.[2] We must therefore examine the most prevalent objections to it.

The gist of these objections can be developed as follows. Relativistic dynamics cannot have shown Newtonian dynamics to be wrong, for Newtonian dynamics is still used with great success by most engineers and, in selected applications, by many physicists. Furthermore, the propriety of this use of the older theory can be proved from the very theory that has, in other applications, replaced it. Einstein's theory can be used to show that predictions from Newton's equations will be as good as our measuring instruments in all applications that satisfy a small number of restrictive conditions. For example, if Newtonian theory is to provide a good approximate solution, the relative velocities of the bodies considered must be small compared with the velocity of light. Subject to this condition and a few others, Newtonian theory seems to be derivable from Einsteinian, of which it is therefore a special case.

But, the objection continues, no theory can possibly conflict with one of its special cases. If Einsteinian science seems to make Newtonian dynamics wrong, that is only because some Newtonians were so incautious as to claim that Newtonian theory yielded entirely precise results or that it was valid at very high relative velocities. Since they could not have had any evidence for such claims, they betrayed the standards of science when they made them. In so far as Newtonian theory was ever a truly scientific theory supported by valid evidence, it still is. Only extravagant claims for the theory—claims that were never properly parts of science—can have been shown by Einstein to be wrong. Purged of these merely human extravagances, Newtonian theory has never been challenged and cannot be.

Some variant of this argument is quite sufficient to make any theory ever used by a significant group of competent scientists immune to attack. The much-maligned phlogiston theory, for example, gave order to a large number of physical and chemical phenomena. It explained why bodies burned—they were rich in phlogiston—and why metals had so many more properties in common than did their ores. The metals were all compounded from different elementary earths combined with phlogiston, and the latter, common to

---

[1] Silvanus P. Thompson, *Life of William Thomson Baron Kelvin of Largs* (London, 1910), I, 266–81.

[2] See, for example, the remarks by P. P. Wiener in *Philosophy of Science*, XXV (1958), 298.

all metals, produced common properties. In addition, the phlogiston theory accounted for a number of reactions in which acids were formed by the combustion of substances like carbon and sulphur. Also, it explained the decrease of volume when combustion occurs in a confined volume of air—the phlogiston released by combustion "spoils" the elasticity of the air that absorbed it, just as fire "spoils" the elasticity of a steel spring.[3] If these were the only phenomena that the phlogiston theorists had claimed for their theory, that theory could never have been challenged. A similar argument will suffice for any theory that has ever been successfully applied to any range of phenomena at all.

But to save theories in this way, their range of application must be restricted to those phenomena and to that precision of observation with which the experimental evidence in hand already deals.[4] Carried just a step further (and the step can scarcely be avoided once the first is taken), such a limitation prohibits the scientist from claiming to speak "scientifically" about any phenomenon not already observed. Even in its present form the restriction forbids the scientist to rely upon a theory in his own research whenever that research enters an area or seeks a degree of precision for which past practice with the theory offers no precedent. These prohibitions are logically unexceptionable. But the result of accepting them would be the end of the research through which science may develop further.

By now that point too is virtually a tautology. Without commitment to a paradigm there could be no normal science. Furthermore, that commitment must extend to areas and to degrees of precision for which there is no full precedent. If it did not, the paradigm could provide no puzzles that

had not already been solved. Besides, it is not only normal science that depends upon commitment to a paradigm. If existing theory binds the scientist only with respect to existing applications, then there can be no surprises, anomalies, or crises. But these are just the signposts that point the way to extraordinary science. If positivistic restrictions on the range of a theory's legitimate applicability are taken literally, the mechanism that tells the scientific community what problems may lead to fundamental change must cease to function. And when that occurs, the community will inevitably return to something much like its pre-paradigm state, a condition in which all members practice science but in which their gross product scarcely resembles science at all. Is it really any wonder that the price of significant scientific advance is a commitment that runs the risk of being wrong?

More important, there is a revealing logical lacuna in the positivist's argument, one that will reintroduce us immediately to the nature of revolutionary change. Can Newtonian dynamics really be *derived* from relativistic dynamics? What would such a derivation look like? Imagine a set of statements, $E_1, E_2, \ldots, E_n$, which together embody the laws of relativity theory. These statements contain variables and parameters representing spatial position, time, rest mass, etc. From them, together with the apparatus of logic and mathematics, is deducible a whole set of further statements, including some that can be checked by observation. To prove the adequacy of Newtonian dynamics as a special case, we must add to the E_i's additional statements, like $(v/c)^2 \ll 1$, restricting the range of the parameters and variables. This enlarged set of statements is then manipulated to yield a new set, $N_1, N_2, \ldots, N_m$, which is identical in form with Newton's laws of motion, the law of gravity, and so on. Apparently Newtonian dynamics has been derived from Einsteinian, subject to a few limiting conditions.

Yet the derivation is spurious, at least to this point. Though the N_i's are a special case of the laws of relativistic mechanics, they are not Newton's Laws. Or at least they are not unless those laws are reinterpreted in a way that would have been impossible until after Einstein's work. The

[3] James B. Conant, *Overthrow of the Phlogiston Theory* (Cambridge, 1950), pp. 13–16; and J. R. Partington, *A Short History of Chemistry* (2d ed.; London, 1951), pp. 85–88. The fullest and most sympathetic account of the phlogiston theory's achievements is by H. Metzger, *Newton, Stahl, Boerhaave et la doctrine chimique* (Paris, 1930), Part II.

[4] Compare the conclusions reached through a very different sort of analysis by R. B. Braithwaite, *Scientific Explanation* (Cambridge, 1953), pp. 50–87, esp. p. 76.

variables and parameters that in the Einsteinian E_i's represented spatial position, time, mass, etc., still occur in the N_i's; and they there still represent Einsteinian space, time, and mass. But the physical referents of these Einsteinian concepts are by no means identical with those of the Newtonian concepts that bear the same name. (Newtonian mass is conserved; Einsteinian is convertible with energy. Only at low relative velocities may the two be measured in the same way, and even then they must not be conceived to be the same.) Unless we change the definitions of the variables in the N_i's, the statements we have derived are not Newtonian. If we do change them, we cannot properly be said to have *derived* Newton's Laws, at least not in any sense of "derive" now generally recognized. Our argument has, of course, explained why Newton's Laws ever seemed to work. In doing so it has justified, say, an automobile driver in acting as though he lived in a Newtonian universe. An argument of the same type is used to justify teaching earth-centered astronomy to surveyors. But the argument has still not done what it purported to do. It has not, that is, shown Newton's Laws to be a limiting case of Einstein's. For in the passage to the limit it is not only the forms of the laws that have changed. Simultaneously we have had to alter the fundamental structural elements of which the universe to which they apply is composed.

This need to change the meaning of established and familiar concepts is central to the revolutionary impact of Einstein's theory. Though subtler than the changes from geocentrism to heliocentrism, from phlogiston to oxygen, or from corpuscles to waves, the resulting conceptual transformation is no less decisively destructive of a previously established paradigm. We may even come to see it as a prototype for revolutionary reorientations in the sciences. Just because it did not involve the introduction of additional objects or concepts, the transition from Newtonian to Einsteinian mechanics illustrates with particular clarity the scientific revolution as a displacement of the conceptual network through which scientists view the world.

These remarks should suffice to show what might, in another philosophical climate, have been taken for granted. At least for scientists, most of the apparent differences between a discarded scientific theory and its successor are real. Though an out-of-date theory can always be viewed as a special case of its up-to-date successor, it must be transformed for the purpose. And the transformation is one that can be undertaken only with the advantages of hindsight, the explicit guidance of the more recent theory. Furthermore, even if that transformation were a legitimate device to employ in interpreting the older theory, the result of its application would be a theory so restricted that it could only restate what was already known. Because of its economy, that restatement would have utility, but it could not suffice for the guidance of research.

Let us, therefore, now take it for granted that the differences between successive paradigms are both necessary and irreconcilable. Can we then say more explicitly what sorts of differences these are? The most apparent type has already been illustrated repeatedly. Successive paradigms tell us different things about the population of the universe and about that population's behavior. They differ, that is, about such questions as the existence of subatomic particles, the materiality of light, and the conservation of heat or of energy. These are the substantive differences between successive paradigms, and they require no further illustration. But paradigms differ in more than substance, for they are directed not only to nature but also back upon the science that produced them. They are the source of the methods, problem-field, and standards of solution accepted by any mature scientific community at any given time. As a result, the reception of a new paradigm often necessitates a redefinition of the corresponding science. Some old problems may be relegated to another science or declared entirely "unscientific." Others that were previously non-existent or trivial may, with a new paradigm, become the very archetypes of significant scientific achievement. And as the problems change, so, often, does the standard that distinguishes a real scientific solution from a mere metaphysical speculation, word game, or mathematical play. The normal-scientific tradition that emerges from a scientific revolution is not only incompatible but often actually incommensurable with that which has gone before.

The impact of Newton's work upon the normal seventeenth-century tradition of scientific practice provides a striking example of these subtler effects of paradigm shift. Before Newton was born the "new science" of the century had at last succeeded in rejecting Aristotelian and scholastic explanations expressed in terms of the essences of material bodies. To say that a stone fell because its "nature" drove it toward the center of the universe had been made to look a mere tautological wordplay, something it had not previously been. Henceforth the entire flux of sensory appearances, including color, taste, and even weight, was to be explained in terms of the size, shape, position, and motion of the elementary corpuscles of base matter. The attribution of other qualities to the elementary atoms was a resort to the occult and therefore out of bounds for science. Molière caught the new spirit precisely when he ridiculed the doctor who explained opium's efficacy as a soporific by attributing to it a dormitive potency. During the last half of the seventeenth century many scientists preferred to say that the round shape of the opium particles enabled them to sooth the nerves about which they moved.[5]

In an earlier period explanations in terms of occult qualities had been an integral part of productive scientific work. Nevertheless, the seventeenth century's new commitment to mechanico-corpuscular explanation proved immensely fruitful for a number of sciences, ridding them of problems that had defied generally accepted solution and suggesting others to replace them. In dynamics, for example, Newton's three laws of motion are less a product of novel experiments than of the attempt to reinterpret well-known observations in terms of the motions and interactions of primary neutral corpuscles. Consider just one con-

crete illustration. Since neutral corpuscles could act on each other only by contact, the mechanico-corpuscular view of nature directed scientific attention to a brand-new subject of study, the alteration of particulate motions by collisions. Descartes announced the problem and provided its first putative solution. Huyghens, Wren, and Wallis carried it still further, partly by experimenting with colliding pendulum bobs, but mostly by applying previously well-known characteristics of motion to the new problem. And Newton embedded their results in his laws of motion. The equal "action" and "reaction" of the third law are the changes in quantity of motion experienced by the two parties to a collision. The same change of motion supplies the definition of dynamical force implicit in the second law. In this case, as in many others during the seventeenth century, the corpuscular paradigm bred both a new problem and a large part of that problem's solution.[6]

Yet, though much of Newton's work was directed to problems and embodied standards derived from the mechanico-corpuscular world view, the effect of the paradigm that resulted from his work was a further and partially destructive change in the problems and standards legitimate for science. Gravity, interpreted as an innate attraction between every pair of particles of matter, was an occult quality in the same sense as the scholastics' "tendency to fall" had been. Therefore, while the standards of corpuscularism remained in effect, the search for a mechanical explanation of gravity was one of the most challenging problems for those who accepted the *Principia* as paradigm. Newton devoted much attention to it and so did many of his eighteenth-century successors. The only apparent option was to reject Newton's theory for its failure to explain gravity, and that alternative, too, was widely adopted. Yet neither of these views ultimately triumphed. Unable either to practice science without the *Principia* or to make that work conform to the corpuscular standards of the seventeenth cen-

---

[5] For corpuscularism in general, see Marie Boas, "The Establishment of the Mechanical Philosophy," *Osiris,* X (1952), 412–541. For the effect of particle-shape on taste, see ibid., p. 483.

[6] R. Dugas, *La mécanique au XVIIᵉ siècle* (Neuchatel, 1954), pp. 177–85, 284–98, 345–56.

tury, scientists gradually accepted the view that gravity was indeed innate. By the mid-eighteenth century that interpretation had been almost universally accepted, and the result was a genuine reversion (which is not the same as a retrogression) to a scholastic standard. Innate attractions and repulsions joined size, shape, position, and motion as physically irreducible primary properties of matter.[7]

The resulting change in the standards and problem-field of physical science was once again consequential. By the 1740s, for example, electricians could speak of the attractive "virtue" of the electric fluid without thereby inviting the ridicule that had greeted Molière's doctor a century before. As they did so, electrical phenomena increasingly displayed an order different from the one they had shown when viewed as the effects of a mechanical effluvium that could act only by contact. In particular, when electrical action-at-a-distance became a subject for study in its own right, the phenomenon we now call charging by induction could be recognized as one of its effects. Previously, when seen at all, it had been attributed to the direct action of electrical "atmospheres" or to the leakages inevitable in any electrical laboratory. The new view of inductive effects was, in turn, the key to Franklin's analysis of the Leyden jar and thus to the emergence of a new and Newtonian paradigm for electricity. Nor were dynamics and electricity the only scientific fields affected by the legitimization of the search for forces innate to matter. The large body of eighteenth-century literature on chemical affinities and replacement series also derives from this supramechanical aspect of Newtonianism. Chemists who believed in these differential attractions between the various chemical species set up previously unimagined experiments and searched for new sorts of reactions. Without the data and the chemical concepts developed in that process, the later work of Lavoisier and, more particularly, of Dalton

would be incomprehensible.[8] Changes in the standards governing permissible problems, concepts, and explanations can transform a science. . . .

Other examples of these nonsubstantive differences between successive paradigms can be retrieved from the history of any science in almost any period of its development. For the moment let us be content with just two other and far briefer illustrations. Before the chemical revolution, one of the acknowledged tasks of chemistry was to account for the qualities of chemical substances and for the changes these qualities underwent during chemical reactions. With the aid of a small number of elementary "principles"—of which phlogiston was one—the chemist was to explain why some substances are acidic, others metalline, combustible, and so forth. Some success in this direction had been achieved. We have already noted that phlogiston explained why the metals were so much alike, and we could have developed a similar argument for the acids. Lavoisier's reform, however, ultimately did away with chemical "principles," and thus ended by depriving chemistry of some actual and much potential explanatory power. To compensate for this loss, a change in standards was required. During much of the nineteenth-century failure to explain the qualities of compounds was no indictment of a chemical theory.[9]

Or again, Clerk Maxwell shared with other nineteenth-century proponents of the wave theory of light the conviction that light waves must be propagated through a material ether. Designing a mechanical medium to support such waves was a standard problem for many of his ablest contemporaries. His own theory, however, the electromagnetic theory of light, gave no account at all of a medium able to support light waves, and it clearly made such an account harder to provide than it had seemed before. Initially, Maxwell's theory was widely rejected for those reasons. But, like Newton's theory, Maxwell's proved difficult

[7] I. B. Cohen, *Franklin and Newton: An Inquiry into Speculative Newtonian Experimental Science and Franklin's Work in Electricity as an Example Thereof* (Philadelphia, 1956), Chaps. vi–vii.

[8] For electricity, see ibid, Chaps. viii–ix. For chemistry, see Metzger, op. cit., Part I.

[9] E. Meyerson, *Identity and Reality* (New York, 1930), Chap. x.

to dispense with, and as it achieved the status of a paradigm, the community's attitude toward it changed. In the early decades of the twentieth century Maxwell's insistence upon the existence of a mechanical ether looked more and more like lip service, which it emphatically had not been, and the attempts to design such an ethereal medium were abandoned. Scientists no longer thought it unscientific to speak of an electrical "displacement" without specifying what was being displaced. The result, again, was a new set of problems and standards, one which, in the event, had much to do with the emergence of relativity theory.[10]

These characteristic shifts in the scientific community's conception of its legitimate problems and standards would have less significance to this essay's thesis if one could suppose that they always occurred from some methodologically lower to some higher type. In that case their effects, too, would seem cumulative. No wonder that some historians have argued that the history of science records a continuing increase in the maturity and refinement of man's conception of the nature of science.[11] Yet the case for cumulative development of science's problems and standards is even harder to make than the case of cumulation of theories. The attempt to explain gravity, though fruitfully abandoned by most eighteenth-century scientists, was not directed to an intrinsically illegitimate problem; the objections to innate forces were neither inherently unscientific nor metaphysical in some pejorative sense. There are no external standards to permit a judgment of that sort. What occurred was neither a decline nor a raising of standards, but simply a change demanded by the adoption of a new paradigm. Furthermore, that change has since been reversed and could be again. In the twentieth century Einstein succeeded in explaining gravitational attrac-

tions, and that explanation has returned science to a set of canons and problems that are, in this particular respect, more like those of Newton's predecessors than of his successors. Or again, the development of quantum mechanics has reversed the methodological prohibition that originated in the chemical revolution. Chemists now attempt, and with great success, to explain the color, state of aggregation, and other qualities of the substances used and produced in their laboratories. A similar reversal may even be underway in electromagnetic theory. Space, in contemporary physics, is not the inert and homogenous substratum employed in both Newton's and Maxwell's theories; some of its new properties are not unlike those once attributed to the ether; we may someday come to know what an electric displacement is.

By shifting emphasis from the cognitive to the normative functions of paradigms, the preceding examples enlarge our understanding of the ways in which paradigms give form to the scientific life. Previously, we had principally examined the paradigm's role as a vehicle for scientific theory. In that role it functions by telling the scientist about the entities that nature does and does not contain and about the ways in which those entities behave. That information provides a map whose details are elucidated by mature scientific research. And since nature is too complex and varied to be explored at random, that map is as essential as observation and experiment to science's continuing development. Through the theories they embody, paradigms prove to be constitutive of the research activity. They are also, however, constitutive of science in other respects, and that is now the point. In particular, our most recent examples show that paradigms provide scientists not only with a map but also with some of the directions essential for map-making. In learning a paradigm the scientist acquires theory, methods, and standards together, usually in an inextricable mixture. Therefore, when paradigms change, there are usually significant shifts in the criteria determining the legitimacy both of problems and of proposed solutions.

That observation returns us to the point from which this section began, for it provides our first

---

[10] E. T. Whittaker, *A History of the Theories of Aether and Electricity*, II (London, 1953), 28–30.

[11] For a brilliant and entirely up-to-date attempt to fit scientific development into this Procrustean bed, see C. C. Gillispie, *The Edge of Objectivity: An Essay in the History of Scientific Ideas* (Princeton, 1960).

explicit indication of why the choice between competing paradigms regularly raises questions that cannot be resolved by the criteria of normal science. To the extent, as significant as it is incomplete, that two scientific schools disagree about what is a problem and what a solution, they will inevitably talk through each other when debating the relative merits of their respective paradigms. In the partially circular arguments that regularly result, each paradigm will be shown to satisfy more or less the criteria that it dictates for itself and to fall short of a few of those dictated by its opponent. There are other reasons, too, for the incompleteness of logical contact that consistently characterizes paradigm debates. For example, since no paradigm ever solves all the problems it defines and since no two paradigms leave all the same problems unsolved, paradigm debates always involve the question: Which problems is it more significant to have solved? Like the issue of competing standards, that question of values can be answered only in terms of criteria that lie outside of normal science altogether, and it is that recourse to external criteria that most obviously makes paradigm debates revolutionary . . . .

Dissecting the Holist Picture of Scientific Change

Larry Laudan

It is now more than twenty years since the appearance of Thomas Kuhn's *The Structure of Scientific Revolutions*. For many of us entering the field two decades ago, that book made a powerful difference. Not because we fully understood it; still less because we became converts to it. It mattered, rather, because it posed in a particularly vivid form some direct challenges to the empiricism we were learning from the likes of Hempel, Nagel, Popper, and Carnap.

Philosophers of science of that era had no doubts about whom and what the book was attacking. If Kuhn was right, all the then-reigning methodological orthodoxies were simply wrong. It was a good deal less clear what Kuhn's positive message amounted to, and not entirely because many of Kuhn's philosophical readers were too shocked to read him carefully. Was he saying that theories were really and always incommensurable so that rival scientists invariably misunderstood one another, or did he mean it when he said that the problem-solving abilities of rival theories could be objectively compared? Did he really believe that accepting a new theory was a "conversion experience," subject only to the Gestalt-like exigencies of the religious life? In the first wave of reaction to Kuhn's bombshell, answers to such questions were not easy to find.

Since 1962 most of Kuhn's philosophical writings have been devoted to clearing up some of the ambiguities and confusions generated by the language of the first edition of *The Structure of Scientific Revolutions*. By and large, Kuhn's message has been an ameliorative and conciliatory one, to such an extent that some passages in his later writings make him sound like a closet positivist. More than one commentator has accused the later Kuhn of taking back much of what made his message interesting and provocative in the first place.[1]

But that is not entirely fair, for if many of Kuhn's clarifications have indeed taken the sting out of what we once thought Kuhn's position was, there are several issues about which the later Kuhn is both clear *and* controversial. Significantly, several of those are central to the themes of this essay . . . .

Kuhn, then, will be my immediate target, but I would be less than candid if I did not quickly add that the views I discuss here have spread considerably beyond the Kuhnian corpus. To some degree, almost all of us who wrote about scientific change in the 1970s (present company included) fell prey to some of the confusions I describe. In trying to characterize the mechanisms of theory change, we have tended to lapse into sloppy language for describing change. However, because Kuhn's is the best-known account of scientific change, and because Kuhn most overtly makes several of the mistakes I want to discuss, this chapter focuses chiefly on his views. Similar criticisms can be raised with varying degrees of severity against authors as diverse as Foucault, Lakatos, Toulmin, Holton, and Laudan.

---

[1] Alan Musgrave spoke for many of Kuhn's readers when he noted, apropos of the second edition of *The Structure of Scientific Revolutions*, that in "his recent writings, then, Kuhn disowns most of the challenging ideas ascribed to him by his critics . . . the new, more real Kuhn who emerges . . . [is] but a pale reflection of the old, revolutionary Kuhn" (Musgrave, 1980, p. 51).

From Chapter 4 of *Science and Values* by Larry Laudan (1984), pp. 67–102, 141–144. Reprinted by permission of University of California Press.

KUHN ON THE UNITS OF SCIENTIFIC CHANGE

It is notorious that the key Kuhnian concept of a paradigm is multiply ambiguous. Among its most central meanings are the following three: First and foremost, a paradigm offers a conceptual framework for classifying and explaining natural objects. That is, it specifies in a generic way the sorts of entities that are thought to populate a certain domain of experience and it sketches out how those entities generally interact. In short, every paradigm will make certain claims about what populates the world. Such ontological claims mark that paradigm off from others, since each paradigm is thought to postulate entities and modes of interaction which differentiate it from other paradigms. Second, a paradigm will specify the appropriate methods, techniques, and tools of inquiry for studying the objects in the relevant domain of application. Just as different paradigms have different ontologies, so they involve substantially different methodologies. (Consider, for instance, the very different methods of research and theory evaluation associated with behaviorism and cognitive psychology respectively.) These methodological commitments are persistent ones, and they characterize the paradigm throughout its history. Finally, the proponents of different paradigms will, according to Kuhn, espouse different sets of cognitive goals or ideals. Although the partisans of two paradigms may (and usually do) share some aims in common, Kuhn insists that the goals are not fully overlapping between followers of rival paradigms. Indeed, to accept a paradigm is, for Kuhn, to subscribe to a complex of cognitive values which the proponents of no other paradigm accept fully.

Paradigm change, on this account, clearly represents a break of great magnitude. To trade in one paradigm for another is to involve oneself in changes at each of . . . three levels . . . : We give up one ontology for another, one methodology for another, and one set of cognitive goals for another. Moreover, according to Kuhn, this change is *simultaneous* rather than *sequential.* . . .

. . . Kuhn portrays paradigm changes in ways that make them seem to be abrupt and global ruptures in the life of a scientific community. So great is this supposed transition that several of Kuhn's critics have charged that, despite Kuhn's proclaimed intentions to the contrary, his analysis inevitably turns scientific change into a nonrational or irrational process. In part, but only in part, it is Kuhn's infelicitous terminology that produces this impression. Notoriously, he speaks of the acceptance of a new paradigm as a "conversion experience,"[2] conjuring up a picture of the scientific revolutionary as a born-again Christian, long on zeal and short on argument. At other times he likens paradigm change to an "irreversible Gestalt-shift."[3] Less metaphorically, he claims that there is never a point at which it is "unreasonable" to hold onto an old paradigm rather than to accept a new one.[4] Such language does not encourage one to imagine that paradigm change is exactly the result of a careful and deliberate weighing-up of the respective strengths of rival contenders. But impressions based on some of Kuhn's more lurid language can probably be rectified by cleaning up some of the vocabulary of *The Structure of Scientific Revolutions,* a task on which Kuhn has been embarked more or less since the book first appeared.[5] No changes of terminology, however, will alter the fact that some central features of Kuhn's model of science raise serious roadblocks to a rational analysis of scientific change. The bulk of this chapter is devoted to examining some of those impediments. Before we turn to that examination, however, I want to stress early on that my complaint with Kuhn is not merely that he has failed to give any normatively robust or rational account of theory change, serious as that failing is. As I show below, he has failed even at the descriptive or narrative task of offering an accurate story about the manner in

---

[2] Kuhn, 1962.

[3] Ibid.

[4] Ibid., p. 159.

[5] As Kuhn himself remarks, he has been attempting "to eliminate misunderstandings for which my own past rhetoric is doubtless partially responsible" (1970, pp. 259–260).

which large-scale changes of scientific allegiance occur.

But there is a yet more fundamental respect in which Kuhn's approach presents obstacles to an understanding of the dynamics of theory change. Specifically, by insisting that individual paradigms have an integral and static character—that changes take place only between, rather than within, paradigms—Kuhn has missed the single feature of science which promises to mediate and rationalize the transition from one world view or paradigm to another. Kuhn's various writings on this subject leave the reader in no doubt that he thinks the parts of a paradigm go together as an inseparable package. As he puts it in *The Structure of Scientific Revolutions*, "In learning a paradigm the scientist acquires theory, methods, and standards together, usually in an *inextricable* mix."[6] This theme of the inextricable and inseparable ingredients of a paradigm is a persistent one in Kuhn's work. One key aim of this chapter is to show how drastically we need to alter Kuhn's views about how tightly the pieces of a paradigm's puzzle fit together before we can expect to understand how paradigmlike change occurs.

Loosening Up the Fit

Without too heavy an element of caricature, we can describe world-view models such as Kuhn's along the following lines: One group or faction in the scientific community accepts a particular "big picture." That requires acquiescence in a certain ontology of nature, acceptance of a specific set of rules about how to investigate nature, and adherence to a set of cognitive values about the teleology of natural inquiry (i.e., about the goals that science seeks). On this analysis, large-scale scientific change involves the replacement of one such world view by another, a process that entails the simultaneous repudiation of the key elements of the old picture and the adoption of corresponding (but of course different) elements of the new. In short, scientific change looks something like Figure 1.

WV1 (ontology 1, methodology 1, values 1)

WV2 (ontology 2, methodology 2, values 2)

Figure 1   Kuhn's Picture of Theory Change

When scientific change is construed so globally, it is no small challenge to see how it could be other than a conversion experience. If different scientists not only espouse different theories but also subscribe to different standards of appraisal and ground those standards in different and conflicting systems of cognitive goals, then it is difficult indeed to imagine that scientific change could be other than a whimsical change of style or taste. There could apparently never be compelling grounds for saying that one paradigm is better than another, for one has to ask: Better relative to which standards and whose goals? To make matters worse—much worse—Kuhn often suggested that each paradigm is more or less automatically guaranteed to satisfy its own standards and to fail the standards of rival paradigms, thus producing a kind of self-reinforcing solipsism in science. As he once put it, "To the extent, as significant as it is incomplete, that two scientific schools disagree about what is a problem and what is a solution, they will inevitably talk through each other when debating the merits of their respective paradigms. In the partially circular arguments that regularly result, *each* paradigm will be shown to satisfy more or less the criteria that it dictates for itself and to fall short of those dictated by its opponent."[7] Anyone who writes prose of this sort must think that scientific decision-making is fundamentally capricious. Or at least so many of us thought in the mid- and late 1960s, as philosophers began to digest Kuhn's ideas. In fact, if one looks at several discussions of Kuhn's work dating from that period, one sees this theme repeatedly. Paradigm change, it was said, could not possibly be a reasoned or rational process. Kuhn, we thought, has made science into an irrational "monster."

---

[6] Kuhn, 1962, p. 108; my italics. [p. 274 above]

[7] Ibid., pp. 108–109. [p. 275 above]

Kuhn's text added fuel to the fire by seeming to endorse such a construal of his own work. In a notorious discussion of the shift from the chemistry of Priestley to that of Lavoisier and Dalton, for instance, Kuhn asserted that it was perfectly reasonable for Priestley to hold onto phlogiston theory, just as it was fully rational for most of his contemporaries to be converting to the oxygen theory of Lavoisier. According to Kuhn, Priestley's continued adherence to phlogiston was reasonable because—given Priestley's cognitive aims and the methods he regarded as appropriate—his own theory continued to look good. Priestley lost the battle with Lavoisier, not because Priestley's paradigm was objectively inferior to its rivals, but rather because most of the chemists of the day came to share Lavoisier's and Dalton's views about what was important and how it should be investigated.

The clear implication of such passages in Kuhn's writings is that interparadigmatic debate is necessarily inconclusive and thus can never be brought to rational closure. When closure does occur, it must therefore be imposed on the situation by such external factors as the demise of some of the participants or the manipulation of the levers of power and reward within the institutional structure of the scientific community. Philosophers of science, almost without exception, have found such implications troubling, for they directly confute what philosophers have been at pains for two millennia to establish: to wit, that scientific disputes, and more generally all disagreements about matters of fact, are in principle open to rational clarification and resolution. It is on the strength of passages such as those I have mentioned that Kuhn has been charged with relativism, subjectivism, irrationalism, and a host of other sins high on the philosopher's hit list.

There is some justice in these criticisms of Kuhn's work, for . . . Kuhn has failed over the past twenty years to elaborate any coherent account of consensus formation, that is, of the manner in which scientists could ever agree to support one world view rather than another. But that flaw, serious though it is, can probably be remedied. . . . [W]e solve the problem of consensus once we realize that *the various components of a world view are individually negotiable and individually replaceable in a piecemeal fashion* (that is, in such a manner that replacement of one element need not require wholesale repudiation of all the other components). Kuhn himself grants, of course, that some components of a world view can be revised; that is what "paradigm articulation" is all about. But for Kuhn, as for such other world view theorists as Lakatos and Foucault, the central commitments of a world view, its "hard core" (to use Lakatos's marvelous phrase), are not revisable—short of rejecting the entire world view. The core ontology of a world view or paradigm, along with its methodology and axiology, comes on a take-it-or-leave-it basis. Where these levels of commitment are concerned, Kuhn (along with such critics of his as Lakatos) is an uncompromising holist. Consider, for instance, his remark: "Just because it is a transition between incommensurables, the transition between competing paradigms cannot be made a step at a time . . . like the Gestalt-switch, it must occur all at once or not at all."[8] Kuhn could hardly be less ambiguous on this point.

But paradigms or research programs need not be so rigidly conceived, and typically they are not so conceived by scientists; nor, if we reflect on it a moment, should they be so conceived. . . . [T]here are complex justificatory interconnections among a scientist's ontology, his methodology, and his axiology. If a scientist's methodology fails to justify his ontology; if his methodology fails to promote his cognitive aims; if his cognitive aims prove to be utopian—in all these cases the scientist will have compelling reasons for replacing one component or other of his world view with an element that does the job better. Yet he need not modify everything else.

To be more precise, the choice confronting a scientist whose world view is under strain in this manner need be nothing like as stark as the choice sketched in Figure 1 (where it is a matter of sticking with what he knows best unchanged or throwing that over for something completely different), but rather a choice where the modification of one

---

8 Ibid., p. 149.

core element—while retaining the others—may bring a decided improvement. Schematically, the choice may be one between

$$O^1 \ \& \ M^1 \ \& \ A^1 \qquad (1)$$

and

$$O^2 \ \& \ M^1 \ \& \ A^1 \qquad (2)$$

Or, between (1) and

$$O^1 \ \& \ M^2 \ \& \ A^1 \qquad (3)$$

Or, to exhaust the simple cases, it may be between (1) and

$$O^1 \ \& \ M^1 \ \& \ A^2 \qquad (4)$$

. . . [C]hoices like those between (1) and (2), or between (1) and (3), are subject to strong normative constraints. And . . . choices of the sort represented between (1) and (4) are also, under certain circumstances, equally amenable to rational analysis.

In all these examples there is enough common ground between the rivals to engender hope of finding an "Archimedean standpoint" which can rationally mediate the choice. When such commonality exists, there is no reason to regard the choice as just a matter of taste or whim; nor is there any reason to say of such choices, as Kuhn does (recall his characterization of the Priestley–Lavoisier exchange), that there can be no compelling grounds for one preference over another. Provided theory change occurs one level at a time, there is ample scope for regarding it as a thoroughly reasoned process.

But the crucial question is whether change actually does occur in this manner. If one thinks quickly of the great transitions in the history of science, they *seem* to preclude such a stepwise analysis. The shift from (say) an Aristotelian to a Newtonian world view clearly involved changes on all three levels. So, too, did the emergence of psychoanalysis from nineteenth-century mechanistic psychology. But before we accept this wholesale picture of scientific change too quickly, we should ask whether it might not acquire what plausibility it enjoys only because our characterizations of such historical revolutions make us compress or telescope a number of gradual changes (one level at a time, as it were) into what, at our distance in time, can easily appear as an abrupt and monumental shift.

By way of laying out the core features of a more gradualist (and, I argue, historically more faithful) picture of scientific change, I will sketch a highly idealized version of theory change. Once it is in front of us, I will show in detail how it makes sense of some real cases of scientific change. Eventually, we will want a model that can show how one might move from an initial state of disagreement between rival traditions or paradigms to consensus about which one is better. But, for purposes of exposition, I want to begin with a rather simpler situation, namely, one in which consensus in favor of one world view or tradition gives way eventually to consensus in favor of another, without scientists ever being faced with a choice as stark as that between two well-developed, and totally divergent, rival paradigms. My "tall tale," represented schematically in Figure 2, might go like this: At any given time, there will be at least one set of values, methods, and theories which one can identify as operating in any field or subfield of science. Let us call this collective C_1, and its components T_1, M_1, and A_1. These components typically stand in . . . complex justificatory relationships to one another . . . ; that is, A_1 will justify M_1 and harmonize with T_1; M_1 will justify T_1 and exhibit the realizability of A_1; and T_1 will constrain M_1 and exemplify A_1. Let us suppose that someone then proposes a new theory, T_2, to replace T_1. The rules M_1 will be consulted and they may well indicate grounds for preferring T_2 to T_1. Suppose that they do, and that we thereby replace T_1 with T_2. As time goes by, certain scientists may develop reservations about M_1 and propose a new and arguably superior methodology, M_2. Now a choice must be made between M_1 and M_2. As we have seen, that requires determining whether M_1 or M_2 offers more promise of realizing our aims. Since that determination will typically be an empirical matter, both A_1 and the then-prevailing theory, T_2, will have to be consulted to ascertain whether M_1 or M_2 is optimal for securing A_1. Suppose that, in comparing the relative efficacy of achieving the shared values, A_1, cogent

Changing element   Adjudicating factors

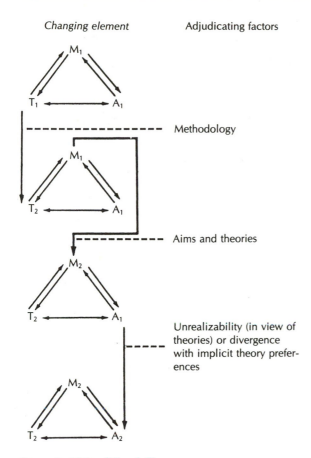

Methodology

Aims and theories

Unrealizability (in view of theories) or divergence with implicit theory preferences

Figure 2 Unitraditional Change

arguments can be made to show that M_2 is superior to M_1. Under the circumstances, assuming scientists behave rationally, M_2 will replace M_1. This means that as new theories, T_3, T_4, . . . , T_n, emerge later, they will be assessed by rules M_2 rather than M_1. Suppose, still further along in this fairy tale, we imagine a challenge to the basic values themselves. Someone may, for instance, point to new evidence suggesting that some element or other of A_1 is unrealizable. Someone else may point out that virtually none of the theories accepted by the scientific community as instances of good science exemplify the values expressed in A_1. (Or, it may be shown that A_1 is an inconsistent set in that its component aspirations are fundamentally at odds with one another.) Under such circumstances, scientists may rationally decide to

abandon A_1 and to take up an alternative, consistent set of values, A_2, should it be available . . .

Now that we have this hypothetical sequence before us, let us imagine a historian called Tom, who decides many years later to study this episode. He will doubtless be struck by the fact that a group of scientists who once accepted values A_1, rules M_1, and theory T_1 came over the course of, say, a decade or two to abandon the whole lot and to accept a new complex, C_2, consisting of A_2, M_2, and T_2. Tom will probably note, and rightly too, that the partisans of C_2 have precious little in common with the devotees of C_1. Surely, Tom may well surmise, here was a scientific revolution if ever there was one, for there was dramatic change at every level. If Tom decides to call the view that scientists eventually came to hold "Paradigm 2," and the view from which they began "Paradigm 1," then he will be able to document the existence of a massive paradigm shift between what (at our remoteness in time) appear to be conceptually distant and virtually incommensurable paradigms.

The point, of course, is that a sequence of belief changes which, described at the microlevel, appears to be a perfectly reasonable and rational sequence of events may appear, when represented in broad brushstrokes that drastically compress the temporal dimension, as a fundamental and unintelligible change of world view. This kind of tunnel vision, in which a sequence of gradual shifts is telescoped into one abrupt and mighty transformation, is a folly which every historian is taught to avoid. Yet knowing that one should avoid it and actually doing so are two different things. Once we recognize this fallacy for what it is, we should probably hesitate to accept too quickly the models of the holists and big-picture builders. For, if our fairy story has anything of the truth about it (that is, if change is, or more weakly even if it could be, more piecemeal than the holistic accounts imply), there may yet be room for incorporating changes of methods and of cognitive values into a rational account of scientific activity. My object in the rest of this chapter is to offer some reasons to believe that the fairy tale is a good deal closer to the mark than its holistic rivals.

But before I present the evidence needed for demythologizing my story, we have to add a new twist to it. As I pointed out above, this story concerns what I call a "unitraditional paradigm shift." It reveals how it might be possible for scientists, originally advocates of one tradition or paradigm, to come around eventually to accept what appears to be a very different view of the world, not to say a very different view of what science is. I call such a change unitraditional because it is not prompted or provoked by the availability of a well-articulated rival world view. If you like, the unitraditional picture explains how one could get paradigm change by developments entirely internal to the dynamic of a particular paradigm. More interesting, and more challenging, is the problem of multitraditional paradigm shifts, that is, basic changes of world view which arise from competition between rival paradigms. To deal with such cases, we need to complicate our fairy story a bit.

Here, we need to imagine two of our complexes already well developed, and radically divergent (i.e., with different ontologies, different methodologies, and different axiologies). If we ask under what circumstances it would be reasonable for the partisans of C_1 to abandon it and accept C_2, some answers come immediately to mind. Suppose, for instance, it can be shown that the central theories of C_1 look worse than the theories of C_2, even by the standards of C_1. . . . Kuhn denies that this is possible, since he says that the theories associated with a particular paradigm will always look better by its standards than will the theories of rival paradigms. . . . But as we have already seen, there is no way of guaranteeing in advance that the methods and standards of C_1 will always give the epistemic nod to theories associated with C_1, since it is always possible (and has sometimes happened) that rival paradigms to C_1 will develop theories that do a better job of satisfying the methodological demands of C_1 than do the theories developed within C_1 itself. Alternatively, suppose someone shows that there is a set of methods M_3 which is more nearly optimal than M_1 for achieving the aims of C_1, and that those methods give the epistemic nod to the theories of C_2 rather than those of C_1. Or, suppose that someone shows that

the goals of C_1 are deeply at odds with the attributes of some of the major theories of science—theories that the partisans of C_1 themselves endorse—and that, by contrast, the cognitive values of C_2 are typified by those same theories. Again, new evidence might emerge that indicates the nonrealizability of some of the central cognitive aims of C_1 and the achievability of the aims of C_2. In all these circumstances (and several obvious ones which I shall not enumerate), the only reasonable thing for a scientist to do would be to give up C_1 and to embrace C_2.

. . . [W]e see that the transition from one paradigm or world view to another can itself be a step-wise process, requiring none of the wholesale shifts in allegiance at every level required by Kuhn's analysis. The advocates of C_1 might, for instance, decide initially to accept many of the substantive theories of C_2, while still retaining for a time the methodology and axiology of C_1. At a later stage they might be led by a different chain of arguments and evidence to accept the methodology of C_2 while retaining C_1's axiology. Finally, they might eventually come to share the values of C_2. As William Whewell showed more than a century ago, precisely some such series of shifts occurred in the gradual capitulation of Cartesian physicists to the natural philosophy of Newton.[9]

In effect, I am claiming the solution of the problem of consensus formation in the multiparadigm situation to be nothing more than a special or degenerate instance of unitraditional change. It follows that, if we can show that the unitraditional fairy tale has something going for it, then we will solve both forms of the consensus-formation problem simultaneously. The core question is whether the gradualist myth, which I have just sketched out, is better supported by the historical record than the holistic picture associated with Kuhn.

One striking way of formulating the contrast

---

[9] See Whewell's remarkably insightful essay of 1851, where he remarks, apropos the transition from one global theory to another: "the change . . . is effected by a transformation, or series of transformations, of the earlier hypothesis, by means of which it is brought nearer and nearer to the second [i.e., later]" (1851, p. 139).

between the piecemeal and the holistic models, and thus designing a test to choose between them, is to ask a fairly straightforward question about the historical record: Is it true that the major historical shifts in the methodological rules of science and in the cognitive values of scientists have invariably been contemporaneous with one another *and* with shifts in substantive theories and ontologies? The holistic account is clearly committed to an affirmative answer to the question. Indeed, it is a straightforward corollary of Kuhn's analysis that changes in rules or values, when they occur, will occur only when a scientific revolution takes place, that is, only when there is a concomitant shift in theories, methods, and values. A change in values without an associated change in basic ontology is not a permissible variation countenanced in the Kuhnian scheme.[10] Nor is a change in methods possible for Kuhn without a paradigm change. Kuhn's analysis flatly denies that the values and norms of a "mature" science can shift in the absence of a revolution. Yet there are plenty of examples one may cite to justify the assertion made here that changes at the three levels do not always go together. I shall mention two such examples.

Consider, first, a well-known shift at the level of methodological rules. From the time of Bacon until the early nineteenth century most scientists subscribed to variants of the rules of inductive inference associated with Bacon, Hume, and Newton. The methods of agreement, difference, and concomitant variations were a standard part of the repertoire of most working scientists for two hundred years. These rules, at least as then understood, foreclosed the postulation of any theoreti-cal or hypothetical entities, since observable bodies were the only sort of objects and properties to which one could apply traditional inductive methods. More generally . . . , thinkers of the Enlightenment believed it important to develop rules of inquiry which would exclude unobservable entities and bring to heel the tendency of scientists to indulge their *l'esprit de système*. Newton's famous third rule of reasoning in philosophy, the notorious "hypotheses non fingo," was but a particularly succinct and influential formulation of this trenchant empiricism.

It is now common knowledge that by the late nineteenth century this methodological orientation had largely vanished from the writings of major scientists and methodologists. Whewell, Peirce, Helmholtz, Mach, Darwin, Hertz, and a host of other luminaries had, by the 1860s and 1870s, come to believe that it was quite legitimate for science to postulate unobservable entities, and that most of the traditional rules of inductive reasoning had been superseded by the logic of hypothetico-deduction. Elsewhere I have described this shift in detail.[11] What is important for our purposes is both that it occurred and when it occurred. That it took place would be denied, I think, by no one who studies the record; determining precisely when it occurred is more problematic, although probably no scholar would quarrel with the claim that it comes in the period from 1800 to 1860. And a dating as fuzzy as that is sufficient to make out my argument.

For here we have a shift in the history of the explicit methodology of the scientific community as significant as one can imagine—from methods of enumerative and eliminative induction to the method of hypothesis—occurring across the spectrum of the theoretical sciences, from celestial mechanics to chemistry and biology. . . . Yet where is the larger and more global scientific revolution of which this methodological shift was the concomitant? There were of course revolutions, and important ones, in this period. Yet this change

---

[10] Some amplification of this point is required. Kuhn evidently believes that there are some values that transcend specific paradigms. He mentions such examples as the demand for accuracy, consistency, and simplicity. The fortunes of these values are not linked to specific paradigms. Thus, if they were to change, such change would presumably be independent of shifts in paradigms. In Kuhn's view, however, these values have persisted unchanged since the seventeenth century. Or, rather, scientists have invoked these values persistently since that time; strictly speaking, on Kuhn's analysis, these values are changing constantly, since each scientist interprets them slightly differently. For a detailed discussion of Kuhn's handling of these quasi-shared values, see the final section of this chapter.

[11] See Laudan, 1981.

in methodology cannot be specifically linked to any of the familiar revolutions of the period. The method of hypothesis did not become the orthodoxy in science of the late nineteenth century because it rode on the coattails of any specific change in ontology or scientific values. So far as I can see, this methodological revolution was independent of any particular program of research in any one of the sciences, which is not to say that it did not reflect some very general tendencies appearing across the board in scientific research. The holist model, which would have us believe that changes in methodological orientation are invariably linked to changes in values and ontology, is patently mistaken here. Nor, if one reflects on the nature of methodological discussion, should we have expected otherwise. . . . [M]ethodological rules can reasonably be criticized and altered if one discovers that they fail optimally to promote our cognitive aims. If our aims shift, as they would in a Kuhnian paradigm shift, we would of course expect a reappraisal of our methods of inquiry in light of their suitability for promoting the new goals. But, even when our goals shift not at all, we sometimes discover arguments and evidence which indicate that the methods we have been using all along are not really suitable for our purposes. Such readjustments of methodological orientation, in the absence of a paradigm shift . . . pose a serious anomaly for Kuhn's analysis.

What about changes in aims, as opposed to rules? Is it not perhaps more plausible to imagine, with Kuhn, that changes of cognitive values are always part of broader shifts of paradigm or world view? Here again, the historical record speaks out convincingly against this account. Consider, very briefly, one example: the abandonment of "infallible knowledge" as an epistemic aim for science. As before, my historical account will have to be "potted" for purposes of brevity; but there is ample serious scholarship to back up the claims I shall be making.[12]

That scholarship has established quite con-vincingly that, during the course of the nineteenth century, the view of science as aiming at certainty gave way among most scientists to a more modest program of producing theories that were plausible, probable, or well tested. As Peirce and Dewey have argued, this shift represents one of the great watersheds in the history of scientific philosophy: the abandonment of the quest for certainty. More or less from the time of Aristotle onward, scientists had sought theories that were demonstrable and apodictically certain. Although empiricists and rationalists disagreed about precisely how to certify knowledge as certain and incorrigible, all agreed that science was aiming exclusively at the production of such knowledge. This same view of science largely prevailed at the beginning of the nineteenth century. But by the end of that century this demonstrative and infallibilist ideal was well and truly dead. Scientists of almost every persuasion were insistent that science could, at most, aspire to the status of highly probable knowledge. Certainty, incorrigibility, and indefeasibility ceased to figure among the central aims of most twentieth-century scientists.

The full story surrounding the replacement of the quest for certainty by a thoroughgoing fallibilism is long and complicated; I have attempted to sketch out parts of that story elsewhere.[13] What matters for our purposes here is not so much the details of this epistemic revolution, but the fact that this profound transformation was not specifically associated with the emergence of any new scientific paradigms or research programs. The question of timing is crucial, for it is important to see that this deep shift in axiological sensibilities was independent of any specific change in scientific world view or paradigm. No new scientific tradition or paradigm in the nineteenth century was associated with a specifically fallibilist axiology. Quite the reverse, fallibilism came to be associated with virtually every major program of scientific research by the mid- to late nineteenth century. Atomists and antiatomists, wave theorists and particle theorists, Darwinians and Lamarck-

---

[12] For an extensive bibliography on this issue, see Laudan, 1968.

[13] See Laudan, 1981.

ians, uniformitarians and catastrophists—all subscribed to the new consensus about the corrigibility and indemonstrability of scientific theories. A similar story could be told about other cognitive values which have gone the way of all flesh. The abandonment of intelligibility, of the requirement of picturable or mechanically constructible models of natural processes, of the insistence on "complete" descriptions of nature—all reveal a similar pattern. The abandonment of each of these cognitive ideals was largely independent of shifts in basic theories about nature.

Once again, the holistic approach leads to expectations that are confounded by the historical record. Changes in values and changes in substantive ontologies or methodologies show no neat isomorphism. Change certainly occurs at all levels, and sometimes changes are concurrent, but there is no striking covariance between the timing of changes at one level and the timing of those at any other. I conclude from such examples that scientific change is substantially more piecemeal than the holistic model would suggest. Value changes do not always accompany, nor are they always accompanied by, changes in scientific paradigm. Shifts in methodological rules may, but need not, be associated with shifts in either values or ontologies. The three levels, although unquestionably interrelated, do not come as an inseparable package on a take-it-or-leave-it basis.

This result is of absolutely decisive importance for understanding the processes of scientific change. Because these changes are not always concomitant, we are often in a position to hold one or two of the three levels fixed while we decide whether to make modifications at the disputed level. The existence of these (temporarily) fixed and thus shared points of perspective provides a crucial form of triangulation. Since theories, methodologies, and axiologies stand together in a kind of justificatory triad, we can use those doctrines about which there is agreement to resolve the remaining areas where we disagree. The uncontested levels will not always resolve the controversy, for underdetermination is an ever present possibility. But the fact that the levels of agreement are sometimes insufficient to terminate

the controversy provides no comfort for Kuhn's subjectivist thesis that those levels of agreement are never sufficient to resolve the debate. As logicians say, we need to be very careful about our quantifiers here. Some writers have not always exercised the care they should. Kuhn, for instance, confusedly slides from (a) the correct claim that the shared values of scientists are, in certain situations, incapable of yielding unambiguously a preference between two rival theories to (b) the surely mistaken claim that the shared values of scientists are never sufficient to warrant a preference between rival paradigms. Manifestly in some instances, the shared rules and standards of methodology are unavailing. But neither Kuhn nor anyone else has established that the rules, evaluative criteria, and values to which scientists subscribe are generally so ambiguous in application that virtually any theory or paradigm can be shown to satisfy them. And we must constantly bear in mind the point that, even when theories are underdetermined by a set of rules or standards, many theories will typically be ruled out by the relevant rules; and if one party to a scientific debate happens to be pushing for a theory that can be shown to violate those rules, then the rules will eliminate that theory from contention.

What has led holistic theorists to misdescribe so badly the relations among these various sorts of changes? As one who was himself once an advocate of such an account, I can explain specifically what led me into thinking that change on the various levels was virtually simultaneous. If one focuses, as most philosophers of science have, on the processes of justification in science, one begins to see systemic linkages among what I earlier called factual, methodological, and axiological ideas. One notices further that beliefs at all three levels shift through time. Under the circumstances it is quite natural to conjecture that these various changes may be interconnected. Specifically, one can imagine that the changes might well be simultaneous, or at least closely dependent on one another. The suggestion is further borne out—at least to a first approximation—by an analysis of some familiar scientific episodes. It is clear, for instance, that the scientific revolution of the seventeenth century brought with it changes in theories, ontologies, rules, and values. Equally, the twentieth-century revolution in relativity theory and quantum mechanics brought in its wake a shift in both methodological and axiological orientations among theoretical physicists. But as I have already suggested, these changes came seriatim, not simultaneously. More to the point, it is my impression that the overwhelming majority of theory transitions in the history of science (including shifts as profound as that from creationist biology to evolution, from energeticist to atomistic views on the nature of matter, from catastrophism to uniformitarianism in geology, from particle to wave theories of light) have not taken place by means of Gestalt-like shifts at all levels concurrently. Often, change occurs on a single level only (e.g., the Darwinian revolution or the triumph of atomism, where it was chiefly theory or ontology that changed); sometimes it occurs on two levels simultaneously; rarely do we find an abrupt and wholesale shift of doctrines at all three levels.

This fact about scientific change has a range of important implications for our understanding of scientific debate and scientific controversy. Leaving aside the atypical case of simultaneous shifts at all three levels . . . , it means that most instances of scientific change—including most of the events we call scientific revolutions—occur amid a significant degree of consensus at a variety of levels among the contending parties. Scientists may, for instance, disagree about specific theories yet agree about the appropriate rules for theory appraisal. They may even disagree about both theories and rules but accept the same cognitive values. Alternatively, they may accept the same theories and rules yet disagree about the cognitive values they espouse. In all these cases there is no reason to speak (with Kuhn) of "incommensurable choices" or "conversion experiences," or (with Foucault) about abrupt "ruptures of thought," for there is in each instance the possibility of bringing the disagreement to rational closure. Of course, it may happen in specific cases that the mechanisms of rational adjudication are of no avail, for the parties may be contending about matters that are underdetermined by the beliefs and standards the contending parties share in common. But, even here, we can still say that there are rational rules governing the game being played, and that the moves being made (i.e., the beliefs being debated and the arguments being arrayed for and against them) are in full compliance with the rules of the game.

Above all, we must bear in mind that it has never been established that such instances of holistic change constitute more than a tiny fraction of scientific disagreements. Because such cases are arguably so atypical, it follows that sociologists and philosophers of science who predicate their theories of scientific change and cognition on the presumed ubiquity of irresolvable standoffs between monolithic world views (of the sort that Kuhn describes in *Structure of Scientific Revolutions*) run the clear risk of failing to recognize the complex ways in which rival theories typically share important background assumptions in common. To put it differently, global claims about the immunity of interparadigmatic disputes to rational adjudication (and such claims are central in the work of both Kuhn and Lakatos) depend for their plausibility on systematically ignoring the piecemeal character of most forms of scientific change and on a gross exaggeration of the impotence of rational considerations to bring such disagreements to closure. Beyond that, I have argued that, even if interparadigmatic clashes had the character Kuhn says they do (namely, of involving little or no overlap at any of the three levels), it still would not follow that there are no rational grounds for a critical and comparative assessment of the rival paradigms. In sum, no adequate support has been provided for the claim that clashes between rival scientific camps can never, or rarely ever, be resolved in an objective fashion. The problem of consensus formation, which I earlier suggested was the great Kuhnian enigma, . . . can be resolved, but only if we realize that science has adjudicatory mechanisms whose existence has gone unnoticed by Kuhn and the other holists.

But it would be misleading to conclude this treatment of Kuhn and the holist theory of theory change on such a triumphal note, for we have yet to confront directly and explicitly another relevant side of Kuhn's work: specifically, his claim, elaborated through a variety of arguments, that methodological rules and shared cognitive values (on which I have laid so much stress as instruments of closure and consensus formation) are impotent to resolve large-scale scientific disagreement. We must now turn to that task directly.

KUHN'S CRITIQUE OF METHODOLOGY

Several writers (e.g., Quine, Hesse, Goodman) have asserted that the rules or principles of scientific appraisal underdetermine theory choice. For reasons I have tried to spell out elsewhere,[14] such a view is badly flawed. Some authors, for instance, tend to confuse the logical underdetermination of theories by data with the underdetermination of theory choice by methodological rules. Others (e.g., Hesse and Bloor) have mistakenly taken the logical underdetermination of theories to be a license for asserting the causal underdetermination of our theoretical beliefs by the sensory evidence to which we are exposed.[15] But there is a weaker, and much more interesting, version of the thesis of underdetermination, which has been developed most fully in Kuhn's recent writings. Indeed, it is one of the strengths of Kuhn's challenge to traditional philosophy of science that he has "localized" and given flesh to the case for underdetermination, in ways that make it prima facie much more telling. In brief, Kuhn's view is this: If we examine situations where scientists are required to make a choice among the handful of paradigms that confront them at any time, we discover that the relevant evidence and appropriate methodological standards fail to pick out one contender as unequivocally superior to its extant rival(s). I call such situations cases of "local" underdetermination, by way of contrasting them with the more global forms of underdetermination (which say, in effect, that the rules are

insufficient to pick out any theory as being uniquely supported by the data). Kuhn offers four distinct arguments for local underdetermination. Each is designed to show that, although methodological rules and standards do constrain and delimit a scientist's choices or options, those rules and standards are never sufficient to compel or unequivocally to warrant the choice of one paradigm over another.

1. The "Ambiguity of Shared Standards" Argument

Kuhn's first argument for methodological underdetermination rests on the purported ambiguity of the methodological rules or standards that are shared by advocates of rival paradigms. The argument first appeared in *The Structure of Scientific Revolutions* (1962) and has been extended considerably in his later *The Essential Tension* (1977). As he put it in the earlier work, "lifelong resistance [to a new theory] . . . is not a violation of scientific standards . . . though the historian can always find men—Priestley, for instance—who were unreasonable to resist for as long as they did, he will not find a point at which resistance becomes illogical or unscientific."[16] Many of Kuhn's readers were perplexed by the juxtaposition of claims in such passages as these. On the one hand, we are told that Priestley's continued refusal to accept the theory of Lavoisier was "unreasonable"; but we are also told that Priestley's refusal was neither "illogical" nor "unscientific." To those inclined to think that being "scientific" (at least in the usual sense of that term) required one to be "reasonable" about shaping one's beliefs, Kuhn seemed to be talking gibberish. On a more sympathetic construal, Kuhn seemed to be saying that a scientist could always interpret the applicable standards of appraisal, whatever they might be, so as to "rationalize" his own paradigmatic preferences, whatever they might be. This amounts to claiming that the methodological rules or standards of science never make a real or deci-

---

[14] See Laudan, forthcoming.

[15] See ibid. for a lengthy treatment of some issues surrounding underdetermination of theories.

[16] Kuhn, 1962, p. 159.

sive difference to the outcome of a process of theory choice; if any set of rules can be used to justify any theory whatever, then methodology would seem to amount to just so much window dressing. But that construal, it turns out, is a far cry from what Kuhn intended. As he has made clear in later writings, he wants to bestow a positive, if (compared with the traditional view) much curtailed, role on methodological standards in scientific choice.

What Kuhn apparently has in mind is that the shared criteria, standards, and rules to which scientists explicitly and publicly refer in justifying their choices of theory and paradigm are typically "ambiguous" and "imprecise," so much so that "individuals [who share the same standards] may legitimately differ about their application to concrete cases.[17] Kuhn holds that, although scientists share certain cognitive values "and must do so if science is to survive, they do not all apply them in the same way. Simplicity, scope, fruitfulness, and even accuracy can be judged differently (which is not to say they may be judged arbitrarily) by different people."[18] Because, then, the shared standards are ambiguous, two scientists may subscribe to "exactly the same standard" (say, the rule of simplicity) and yet endorse opposing viewpoints.

Kuhn draws some quite large inferences from the presumed ambiguity of the shared standards or criteria. Specifically, he concludes that every case of theory choice must involve an admixture of objective and subjective factors, since (in Kuhn's view) the shared, and presumably objective, criteria are too amorphous and ambiguous to warrant a particular preference. He puts the point this way: "I continue to hold that the algorithms of individuals are all ultimately different by virtue of the subjective considerations with which each [scientist] must complete the objective criteria before any computations can be done."[19] As this passage makes clear, Kuhn believes that, because the shared criteria are too imprecise to justify a choice, and because—despite that imprecision—scientists do manage to make choices, those choices *must* be grounded in individual and subjective preferences different from those of his fellow scientists. As he says, "every individual choice between competing theories depends on a mixture of objective and subjective factors, or of shared and individual criteria."[20] And, the shared criteria "are not by themselves sufficient to determine the decisions of individual scientists."[21]

This very ambitious claim, if true, would force us to drastically rethink our views of scientific rationality. Among other things, it would drive us to the conclusion that every scientist has different reasons for his theory preferences from those of his fellow scientists. The view entails, among other things, that it is a category mistake to ask (say) why physicists think Einstein's theories are better than Newton's; for, on Kuhn's analysis, there must be as many different answers as there are physicists. We might note in passing that this is quite an ironic conclusion for Kuhn to reach. Far more than most writers on these subjects, he has tended to stress the importance of community and socialization processes in understanding the scientific enterprise. Yet the logic of his own analysis drives him to the radically individualistic position that every scientist has his own set of reasons for theory preferences and that there is no real consensus whatever with respect to the grounds for theory preference, not even among the advocates of the same paradigm. Seen from this perspective, Kuhn tackles what I earlier called the problem of consensus by a maneuver that trivializes the problem; for if we must give a separate and discrete explanation for the theory preferences of each member of the scientific community—which is what Kuhn's view entails—then we are confronted with a gigantic mystery at the collective level, to wit, why the scientists in a given discipline—each supposedly operating with his own individualistic and

---

[17] Kuhn, 1977, p. 322. [p. 198 above]

[18] Ibid., p. 262.

[19] Ibid., p. 329. [p. 202 above]

[20] Ibid., p. 325; see also p. 324. [p. 200 above]

[21] Ibid., p. 325. [p. 199 above]

idiosyncratic criteria, each giving a different "gloss" to the criteria that are shared—are so often able to agree about which theories to bet on. But we can leave it to Kuhn to sort out how he reconciles his commitment to the social psychology of science with his views about the individual vagaries of theory preference. What must concern us is the question whether Kuhn has made a plausible case for thinking that the shared or collective criteria must be supplemented by individual and subjective criteria.

The first point to stress is that Kuhn's thesis purports to apply to all scientific rules or values that are shared by the partisans of rival paradigms, not just to a selected few, notoriously ambiguous ones. We can grant straightaway that some of the rules, standards, and values used by scientists ("simplicity" would be an obvious candidate) exhibit precisely that high degree of ambiguity which Kuhn ascribes to them. But Kuhn's general argument for the impotence of shared rules to settle disagreements between scientists working in different paradigms cannot be established by citing the occasional example. Kuhn must show us, for he claims as much, that there is something in the very nature of those methodological rules that come to be shared among scientists which makes the application of those rules or standards invariably inconclusive. He has not established this result, and there is a good reason why he has not: It is false. To see that it is, one need only produce a methodological rule widely accepted by scientists which can be applied to concrete cases without substantial imprecision or ambiguity. Consider, for instance, one of Kuhn's own examples of a widely shared scientific standard, namely, the requirement that an acceptable theory must be internally consistent and logically consistent with accepted theories in other fields. (One may or may not favor this methodological rule. I refer to it here only because it is commonly regarded, including by Kuhn, as a methodological rule that frequently plays a role in theory evaluation.)

I submit that we have a very clear notion of what it is for a theory to be internally consistent, just as we understand perfectly well what it means for a theory to be consistent with accepted beliefs.

Moreover, on at least some occasions we can tell whether a particular theory has violated the standard of (internal or external) consistency. Kuhn himself, in a revealing passage, grants as much; for instance, when comparing the relative merits of geocentric and heliocentric astronomy, Kuhn says that "the consistency criterion, by itself, therefore, spoke unequivocally for the geocentric tradition.[22] (What he has in mind is the fact that heliocentric astronomy, when introduced, was inconsistent with the then-reigning terrestrial physics, whereas the assumptions of geocentric astronomy were consistent with that physics.) Note that in this case we have a scientific rule or criterion "speaking unequivocally" in favor of one theory and against its rival. Where are the inevitable imprecision and ambiguity which are supposed by Kuhn to afflict all the shared values of the scientific community? What is ambiguous about the notion of consistency? The point of these rhetorical questions is to drive home the fact that, even by Kuhn's lights, some of the rules or criteria widely accepted in the scientific community do not exhibit that multiplicity of meanings which Kuhn has described as being entirely characteristic of methodological standards.

One could, incidentally, cite several other examples of reasonably clear and unambiguous methodological rules. For instance, the requirements that theories should be deductively closed or that theories should be subjected to controlled experiments have not generated a great deal of confusion or disagreement among scientists about what does and does not constitute closure or a control. Or, consider the rule that theories should lead successfully to the prediction of results unknown to their discoverer; so far as I am aware, scientists have not differed widely in their construal of the meaning of this rule. The significance of the nonambiguity of many methodological concepts and rules is to be found in the fact that such nonambiguity refutes one of Kuhn's central arguments for the incomparability of paradigms and for its corollary, the impotence of methodology as a

---

[22] Ibid., p. 323. [p. 199 above]

guide to scientific rationality. There are at least some rules that are sufficiently determinate that one can show that many theories clearly fail to satisfy them. We need not supplement the shared content of these objective concepts with any private notions of our own in order to decide whether a theory satisfies them.

2. The "Collective Inconsistency of Rules" Argument

As if the ambiguity of standards was not bad enough, Kuhn goes on to argue that the shared rules and standards, when taken as a collective, "repeatedly prove to conflict with one another."[23] For instance, two scientists may each believe that empirical accuracy and generality are desirable traits in a theory. But, when confronted with a pair of rival (and thus incompatible) theories, one of which is more accurate and the other more general, the judgments of those scientists may well differ about which theory to accept. One scientist may opt for the more general theory; the other, for the more accurate. They evidently share the same standards, says Kuhn, but they end up with conflicting appraisals. Kuhn puts it this way: " . . . in many concrete situations, different values, though all constitutive of good reasons, dictate different conclusions, different choices. In such cases of value-conflict (e.g., one theory is simpler but the other is more accurate) the relative weight placed on different values by different individuals can play a decisive role in individual choice.[24]

Because many methodological standards do pull in different directions, Kuhn thinks that the scientist can pretty well go whichever way he likes. Well, not quite any direction he likes, since—even by Kuhn's very liberal rules—it would be unreasonable for a scientist to prefer a theory (or paradigm) which failed to satisfy any of the constraints. In Kuhn's view, we should expect scientific disagreements or dissensus to emerge specifically in those cases where (a) no available

theory satisfied all the constraints and (b) every extant theory satisfied some constraints not satisfied by its rivals. That scientists sometimes find themselves subscribing to contrary standards, I would be the first to grant. . . . But Kuhn is not merely saying that this happens occasionally; he is asserting that such is the nature of any set of rules or standards that any group of reasonable scientists might accept. As before, our verdict has to be that Kuhn's highly ambitious claim is just that; he never shows us why families of methodological rules should always or even usually be internally inconsistent. He apparently expects us to take his word for it that he is just telling it as it is.[25] I see no reason why we should follow Kuhn in his global extrapolations from the tiny handful of cases he describes. On the contrary, there are good grounds for resisting, since there are plenty of sets of consistent methodological standards. Consider, for instance, one of the most influential documents of nineteenth-century scientific methodology, John Stuart Mill's *System of Logic*. Mill offered there a set of rules or canons for assessing the soundness of causal hypotheses. Nowadays those rules are still called "Mill's methods," and much research in the natural and social sciences utilizes them, often referring to them as the methods of agreement, difference, and concomitant variations. To the best of my knowledge, no one has ever shown that Mill's methods exhibit a latent tendency toward contradiction or conflict of the sort that Kuhn regards as typical of systems of methodological rules. To go back further in history, no one has ever shown that Bacon's or Descartes's or Newton's or Herschel's famous canons of reasoning are internally inconsistent. The fact that numerous methodologies of science may be cited which have never been shown to be inconsistent casts serious doubts on Kuhn's claim that any methodological standards apt to be shared by rival scientists will tend to exhibit mutual inconsistencies.

---

[23] Ibid., p. 322. [p. 198 above]

[24] Kuhn, 1970, p. 262.

[25] "What I have said so far is primarily simply descriptive of what goes on in the sciences at times of theory choice" (Kuhn, 1977, p. 325). [p. 200 above]

Kuhn could have strengthened his argument considerably if, instead of focusing on the purported tensions in sets of methodological rules, he had noted, rather, that whenever one has more than one standard in operation, it is conceivable that we will be torn in several directions. And this claim is true, regardless of whether the standards are strictly inconsistent with one another or not (just so long as there is not a complete covariance between their instances). If two scientists agree to judge theories by two standards, then it is trivially true that, depending upon how much weight each gives to the two standards, their judgments about theories may differ. Before we can make sense of how to work with several concurrent standards, we have to ask (as Kuhn never did) about the way in which these standards do (or should) control the selection of a preferred theory. Until we know the answer to that question, we will inevitably find that the standards are of little use in explaining scientific preferences. Kuhn simply assumes that all possible preference structures (i.e., all possible differential weightings of the applicable standards) are equally viable or equally likely to be exemplified in a working scientist's selection procedures. . . .

To sum up the argument to this point: I have shown that Kuhn is wrong in claiming that all methodological rules are inevitably ambiguous and in claiming that scientific methodologies consisting of whole groups of rules always or even usually exhibit a high degree of internal "tension." Since these two claims were the linchpins in Kuhn's argument to the effect that shared criteria "are not by themselves sufficient to determine the decisions of individual scientists,"[26] we are entitled to say that Kuhn's effort to establish a general form of local underdetermination falls flat.

3. The Shifting Standards Argument

Equally important to Kuhn's critique of methodology is a set of arguments having to do with the manner in which standards are supposed to vary

from one scientist to another. In treating Kuhn's views on this matter, I follow Gerald Doppelt's excellent and sympathetic explication of Kuhn's position.[27] In general, Kuhn's model of science envisages two quite distinct ways in which disagreements about standards might render scientific debate indeterminate or inconclusive. In the first place, the advocates of different paradigms may subscribe to different methodological rules or evaluative criteria. Indeed, *may* is too weak a term here, for, as we have seen, Kuhn evidently believes that associated with each paradigm is a set of methodological orientations that are (at least partly) at odds with the methodologies of all rival paradigms. Thus, he insists that whenever a "paradigm shift" occurs, this process produces "changes in the standards governing permissible problems, concepts and explanations."[28] This is quite a strong claim. It implies, among other things, that the advocates of different paradigms invariably have different views about what constitutes a scientific explanation and even about what constitutes the relevant facts to be explained (viz., the "permissible problems") If Kuhn is right about these matters, then debate between the proponents of two rival paradigms will involve appeal to different sets of rules and standards associated respectively with the two paradigms. One party to the dispute may be able to show that his theory is best by his standards, while his opponent may be able to claim superiority by his.

As I have shown in detail earlier in this chapter, Kuhn is right to say that scientists sometimes subscribe to different methodologies (including different standards for explanation and facticity). But he has never shown, and I believe him to be chronically wrong in claiming, that disagreements about matters of standards and rules neatly coincide with disagreements about substantive matters

---

[26] Kuhn, 1977, p. 325. [p. 199 above]

[27] Doppelt, 1978. Whereas Kuhn's own discussion of these questions in *The Structure of Scientific Revolutions* rambles considerably, Doppelt offers a succinct and perspicacious formulation of what is, or at least what should have been, Kuhn's argument. Although I quarrel with Doppelt's analysis at several important points, my own thoughts about these issues owe a great deal to his writings.

[28] Kuhn, 1962, p. 104. [p. 273 above]

of scientific ontology. Rival scientists advocating fundamentally different theories or paradigms often have the same standards of assessment (and interpret them identically); on the other hand, adherents to the same paradigm will frequently espouse different standards. In short, methodological disagreements and factual disagreements about basic theories show no striking covariances of the kind required to sustain Kuhn's argument about the instrinsic irresolvability of interparadigmatic debate. It was the thrust of my earlier account of "piecemeal change" to show why Kuhn's claims about irresolvability will not work.

But, of course, a serious issue raised by Kuhn still remains before us. If different scientists sometimes subscribe to different standards of appraisal (and that much is surely correct), then how is it possible for us to speak of the resolution of such disagreements as anything other than an arbitrary closure? . . . Provided there are mechanisms for rationally resolving disagreements about methodological rules and cognitive values . . . the fact that scientists often disagree about such rules and values need not, indeed should not, be taken to show that there must be anything arbitrary about the resolution of such disagreements.

4. The Problem-Weighting Argument

As I have said earlier, Kuhn has another argument up his sleeve which he and others think is germane to the issue of the rationality of comparative theory assessment. Specifically, he insists that the advocates of rival paradigms assign differential degrees of importance to the solution of different sorts of problems. Because they do, he says that they will often disagree about which theory is better supported, since one side will argue that it is most important to solve a certain problem, while the other will insist on the centrality of solving a different problem. Kuhn poses the difficulty in these terms: "If there were but one set of scientific problems, one world within which to work on them, and one set of standards for their solution, paradigm competition might be settled more or less routinely by some process like counting the number of problems solved by each. But, in fact,

these conditions are never met completely. The proponents of competing paradigms are always at least slightly at cross purposes . . . the proponents will often disagree about the list of problems that any candidate for paradigm must resolve."[29]

In this passage Kuhn runs together two issues which it is well to separate: One concerns the question (just addressed in the preceding section) about whether scientists have different standards of explanation or solution; the other (and the one that concerns us here) is the claim that scientists working in different paradigms want to solve different problems and that, because they do, their appraisals of the merits of theories will typically differ. So we must here deal with the case where scientists have the same standards for what counts as solving a problem but where they disagree about which problems are the most important to solve. As Kuhn puts it, "scientific controversies between the advocates of rival paradigms involve the question: which problems is it more significant to have solved? Like the issue of competing standards, that question of values can be answered only in terms of criteria that lie outside of normal science altogether."[30] Kuhn is surely right to insist that partisans of different global theories or paradigms often disagree about which problems it is most important to solve. But the existence of such disagreement does not establish that interparadigmatic debate about the epistemic support of rival paradigms is inevitably inconclusive or that it must be resolved by factors that lie outside the normal resources of scientific inquiry.

At first glance, Kuhn's argument seems very plausible: The differing weights assigned to the solution of specific problems by the advocates of rival paradigms may apparently lead to a situation in which the advocates of rival paradigms can each assert that their respective paradigms are the best because they solve precisely those problems they respectively believe to be the most important. No form of reasoning, insists Kuhn, could convince either side of the merits of the opposition or

---

[29] Ibid., pp. 147–148.

[30] Ibid., p. 110.

of the weakness of its own approach in such circumstances.

To see where Kuhn's argument goes astray in this particular instance, we need to dissect it at a more basic level. Specifically, we need to distinguish two quite distinct senses in which solving a problem may be said to be important. A problem may be important to a scientist just in the sense that he is particularly curious about it. Equally, it may be important because there is some urgent social or economic reason for solving it. Both sorts of considerations may explain why a scientist regards it as urgent to solve the problem. Such concerns are clearly relevant to explaining the motivation of scientists. But these senses of problem importance have no particular epistemic or probative significance. When we are assessing the evidential support for a theory, when we are asking how well supported or well tested that theory is by the available data, we are not asking whether the theory solves problems that are socially or personally important. Importance, in the sense chiefly relevant to this discussion, is what we might call epistemic or probative importance. One problem is of greater epistemic or probative significance than another if the former constitutes a more telling test of our theories than does the latter.

So, if Kuhn's point is to be of any significance for the epistemology of science (or, what amounts to the same thing, if we are asking how beliefworthy a theory is), then we must imagine a situation in which the advocates of different paradigms assign conflicting degrees of epistemic import to the solution of certain problems. Kuhn's thesis about such situations would be, I presume, that there is no rational machinery for deciding who is right about the assignment of epistemic weight to such problems. But that seems wrongheaded, or at least unargued, for philosophers of science have long and plausibly maintained that the primary function of scientific epistemology is precisely to ascertain the (epistemic) importance of any piece of confirming or disconfirming evidence. It is not open to a scientist simply to say that solving an arbitrarily selected problem (however great its subjective significance) is of high probative value. Indeed, it is often true that the

epistemically most salient problems are ones with little or no prior practical or even heuristic significance. (Consider that Brownian motion was of decisive epistemic significance in discrediting classical thermodynamics, even though such motion had little intrinsic interest prior to Einstein's showing that such motion was anomalous for thermodynamics.) The whole point of the theory of evidence is to desubjectify the assignment of evidential significance by indicating the kinds of reasons that can legitimately be given for attaching a particular degree of epistemic importance to a confirming or refuting instance. Thus, if one maintains that the ability of a theory to solve a certain problem is much more significant epistemically than its ability to solve another, one must be able to give reasons for that epistemic preference. Put differently, one has to show that the probative significance of the one problem for testing theories of a certain sort is indeed greater than that of the other. He might do so by showing that the former outcome was much more surprising than or more general than the latter. One may thus be able to motivate a claim for the greater importance of the first problem over the second by invoking relevant epistemic and methodological criteria. But if none of these options is open to him, if he can answer the question, "Why is solving this problem more important probatively than solving that one?" only by replying, in effect, "because I am interested in solving this rather than that," then he has surrendered any claim to be shaping his beliefs rationally in light of the available evidence.

We can put the point more generally: The rational assignment of any particular degree of probative significance to a problem must rest on one's being able to show that there are viable methodological and epistemic grounds for assigning that degree of importance rather than another. Once we see this, it becomes clear that the degree of empirical support which a solved problem confers on a paradigm is not simply a matter of how keenly the proponents of that paradigm want to solve the problem.

Let me expand on this point by using an example cited extensively by both Kuhn and Doppelt: the Daltonian "revolution" in chemistry. As Doppelt summarizes the Kuhnian position, " . . . the pre-Daltonian chemistry of the phlogiston theory and the theory of elective affinity achieved reasonable answers to a whole set of questions effectively abandoned by Dalton's new chemistry.[31] Because Dalton's chemistry failed to address many of the questions answered by the older chemical paradigm, Kuhn thinks that the acceptance of Dalton's approach deprived "chemistry of some actual and much potential explanatory power.[32] Indeed, Kuhn is right in holding that, during most of the nineteenth century, Daltonian chemists were unable to explain many things that the older chemical traditions could make sense of. On the other hand, as Kuhn stresses, Daltonian chemistry could explain a great deal that had eluded earlier chemical theories. In short, "the two paradigms seek to explain different kinds of observational data, in response to different agendas of problems."[33] This "loss" of solved problems during transitions from one major theory to another is an important insight of Kuhn's . . . . But this loss of problem-solving ability through paradigm change, although real enough, does not entail, as Kuhn claims, that proponents of old and new paradigms will necessarily be unable to make congruent assessments of how well tested or well supported their respective paradigms are.

What leads Kuhn and Doppelt to think otherwise is their assumption that the centrality of a problem on one's explanatory agenda necessarily entails one's assigning a high degree of epistemic or probative weight to that problem when it comes to determining how well supported a certain theory or paradigm is. But that assumption is usually false. In general, the observations to which a reasonable scientist attaches the most probative or epistemic weight are those instances that test a theory especially "severely" (to use Popper's splendid term). The instances of greatest probative weight in the history of science (e.g., the oblate shape of the "spherical" earth, the Arago disk experiment, the bending of light near the sun, the

recession of Mercury's perihelion, the reconstitution of white light from the spectrum) have generally not been instances high on the list of problems that scientists developed their theories to solve. A test instance acquires high probative weight when, for example, it involves testing one of a theory's surprising or counterintuitive predictions, or when it represents a kind of crucial experiment between rival theories. The point is that a problem or instance does not generally acquire great probative strength in testing a theory simply because the advocates of that theory would like to be able to solve the problem. Quite the reverse, many scientists and philosophers would say. After all, it is conventional wisdom that a theory is not very acutely tested if its primary empirical support is drawn from the very sort of situations it was designed to explain. Most theories of experimental design urge—in sharp contrast with Kuhn—that theories should not be given high marks simply because they can solve the problems they were invented to solve. In arguing that the explanatory agenda a scientist sets for himself automatically dictates that scientist's reasoned judgments about well-testedness, Kuhn and Doppelt seem to have profoundly misconstrued the logic of theory appraisal.

Let us return for a moment to Kuhn's Dalton example. If I am right, Dalton might readily have conceded that pre-Daltonian chemistry solved a number of problems that his theory failed to address. Judged as theories about the qualitative properties of chemical reagents, those theories could even be acknowledged as well supported *of their type.* But Dalton's primary interests lie elsewhere, for he presumably regarded those earlier theories as failing to address what he considered to be the central problems of chemistry. But this is not an epistemic judgment; it is a pragmatic one. It amounts to saying: "These older theories are well-tested and reliable theories for explaining certain features of chemical change; but those features happen not to interest me very much." In sum, Kuhn and Doppelt have failed to offer us any grounds for thinking that a scientist's judgment about the degree of evidential support for a paradigm should or does reflect his personal views

[31] Doppelt, 1978, p. 42.

[32] Kuhn, 1962, p. 107. [p. 273 above]

[33] Ibid., p. 43.

about the problems he finds most interesting. That, in turn, means that one need not share an enthusiasm for a certain paradigm's explanatory agenda in order to decide whether the theories that make up that paradigm are well tested or ill tested. It appears to me that what the Kuhn-Doppelt point really amounts to is the truism that scientists tend to invest their efforts exploring paradigms that address problems those scientists find interesting. That is a subjective and pragmatic matter which can, and should, be sharply distinguished from the question whether one paradigm or theory is better tested or better supported than its rivals. Neither Kuhn nor Doppelt has made plausible the claim that, because two scientists have different degrees of interest in solving different sorts of problems, it follows that their epistemic judgments of which theories are well tested and which are not will necessarily differ.

We are thus in a position to conclude that the existence of conflicting views among scientists about which problems are interesting apparently entails nothing about the *incompatibility* or *incommensurability* of the epistemic appraisals those scientists will make. That in turn means that these real differences of problem-solving emphasis between advocates of rival paradigms do nothing to undermine the viability of a methodology of comparative theory assessment, insofar as such a methodology is epistemically rather than pragmatically oriented. It seems likely that Kuhn and Doppelt have fallen into this confusion because of their failure to see that acknowledged differences in the motivational appeal of various problems to various scientists constitutes no rationale for asserting the existence of correlative differences in the probative weights properly assigned to those problems by those same scientists.

The appropriate conclusion to draw from the features of scientific life to which Kuhn and Doppelt properly direct our attention is that the pursuit of (and doubtless the recruitment of scientists into)

rival paradigms is influenced by pragmatic as well as by epistemic considerations. That is an interesting thesis, and probably a sound one, but it does nothing to undermine the core premise of scientific epistemology: that there are principles of empirical or evidential support which are neither paradigm-specific, hopelessly vague, nor individually idiosyncratic. More important, these principles are sometimes sufficient to guide our preferences unambiguously.[34]

REFERENCES

Doppelt, Gerald (1978). "Kuhn's Epistemological Relativism: An Interpretation and Defense," *Inquiry* 21:33–86.

Gutting, Gary, ed. (1980). *Paradigms and Revolutions.* Notre Dame: University of Notre Dame Press.

Kuhn, Thomas (1962). *The Structure of Scientific Revolutions.* Chicago: University of Chicago Press.

———— (1970). "Reflections on My Critics." In I. Lakatos and A. Musgrave, *Criticism and the Growth of Knowledge.* Cambridge: Cambridge University Press.

———— (1977). *The Essential Tension.* Chicago: University of Chicago Press.

Laudan, Larry (1968). "Theories of Scientific Method from Plato to Mach," *History of Science* 7:1–63.

———— (1981). *Science and Hypothesis.* Dordrecht: Reidel.

———— (forthcoming). *Science and Method.*

Musgrave, Alan (1980). "Kuhn's Second Thoughts." In Gutting, 1980.

Whewell, William (1851). "Of the Transformation of Hypotheses in the History of Science," *Transactions of the Cambridge Philosophical Society* 9:139–147.

---

[34] Even on the pragmatic level, however, it is not clear that the Doppeltian version of Kuhn's relativistic picture of scientific change will stand up, for Doppelt is at pains to deny that there can be any short-term resolution between the advocates of rival axiologies. If the arguments of the preceding chapter have any cogency, it seems entirely possible that pragmatic relativism, every bit as much as its epistemic counterpart, is question begging.

Unity of Science as a Working Hypothesis

Paul Oppenheim
Hilary Putnam

INTRODUCTION

The expression "Unity of Science" is often encountered, but its precise content is difficult to specify in a satisfactory manner. It is the aim of this paper to formulate a precise concept of Unity of Science and to examine to what extent that unity can be attained.

A concern with Unity of Science hardly needs justification. We are guided especially by the conviction that Science of Science, i.e., the meta-scientific study of major aspects of science, is the natural means for counterbalancing specialization by promoting the integration of scientific knowledge. The desirability of this goal is widely recognized—for example, many universities have programs with this end in view—but it is often pursued by means different from the one just mentioned, and the conception of the Unity of Science might be especially suited as an organizing principle for an enterprise of this kind.

As a preliminary, we will distinguish, in order of increasing strength, three broad concepts of Unity of Science:

First, Unity of Science in the weakest sense is attained to the extent to which all the terms of science[1] are reduced to the terms of some one

discipline (e.g., physics, or psychology). This concept of *Unity of Language* (12) may be replaced by a number of sub-concepts depending on the manner in which one specifies the notion of "reduction" involved. Certain authors, for example, construe reduction as the *definition* of the terms of science by means of those in the selected basic discipline (reduction by means of biconditionals [47]); and some of these require the definitions in question to be analytic, or "true in virtue of the meanings of the terms involved" (epistemological reduction); others impose no such restriction upon the biconditionals effecting reduction. The notion of reduction we shall employ is a wider one and is designed to include reduction by means of biconditionals as a special case.

Second, Unity of Science in a stronger sense (because it implies Unity of Language, whereas the reverse is not the case) is represented by *Unity of Laws* (12). It is attained to the extent to which the laws of science become reduced to the laws of some one discipline. If the ideal of such an all-comprehensive explanatory system were realized, one could call it *Unitary Science* (18, 19, 20, 80). The exact meaning of "Unity of Laws" depends, again, on the concept of "reduction" employed.

Third, Unity of Science in the strongest sense is realized if the laws of science are not only reduced to the laws of some one discipline, but the laws of that discipline are in some intuitive sense "unified" or "connected." It is difficult to see how this last requirement can be made precise, and it will not be imposed here. Nevertheless, trivial realizations of "Unity of Science" will be excluded, for example, the simple conjunction of several

---

AUTHORS' NOTE: We wish to express our thanks to C. G. Hempel for constructive criticism. The responsibility for any shortcomings is, however, exclusively ours.

[1] Science, in the wider sense, may be understood as including the formal disciplines, mathematics, and logic, as well as the empirical ones. In this paper, we shall be concerned with science only in the sense of empirical disciplines, including the socio-humanistic ones.

From *Concepts, Theories, and the Mind-body Problem,* Herbert Feigl, Michael Scriven, and Grover Maxwell, Eds., *Minnesota Studies in the Philosophy of Science,* Vol. II (1958), pp. 3–36. Reprinted by permission of University of Minnesota Press.

branches of science does not *reduce* the particular branches in the sense we shall specify.

In the present paper, the term "Unity of Science" will be used in two senses to refer, first, to an ideal *state* of science, and, second, to a pervasive *trend* within science, seeking the attainment of that ideal.

In the first sense, "Unity of Science" means the state of unitary science. It involves the two constituents mentioned above: unity of vocabulary, or "Unity of Language," and unity of explanatory principles, or "Unity of Laws." That Unity of Science, in this sense, can be fully realized constitutes an over-arching meta-scientific hypothesis which enables one to see a unity in scientific activities that might otherwise appear disconnected or unrelated, and which encourages the construction of a unified body of knowledge.

In the second sense, Unity of Science exists as a trend within scientific inquiry, whether or not unitary science is ever attained, and notwithstanding the simultaneous existence (and, of course, legitimacy) of other, even *incompatible,* trends.

The expression "Unity of Science" is employed in various other senses, of which two will be briefly mentioned in order to distinguish them from the sense with which we are concerned. In the first place, what is sometimes referred to is something that we may call the *Unity of Method* in science. This might be represented by the thesis that all the empirical sciences employ the same standards of explanation, of significance, of evidence, etc.

In the second place, a radical reductionist thesis (of an alleged "logical," not an empirical kind) is sometimes referred to as the thesis of the Unity of Science. Sometimes the "reduction" asserted is the definability of all the terms of science in terms of *sensationalistic predicates* (10); sometimes the notion of "reduction" is wider (11) and predicates referring to *observable qualities of physical things* are taken as basic (12). These theses are epistemological ones, and ones which today appear doubtful. The epistemological uses of the terms "reduction," "physicalism," "Unity of Science," etc., should be carefully distinguished from the use of these terms in the present paper.

UNITY OF SCIENCE AND MICRO-REDUCTION

In this paper we shall employ a concept of reduction introduced by Kemeny and Oppenheim in their paper on the subject (47), to which the reader is referred for a more detailed exposition. The principal requirements may be summarized as follows: Given two theories T_1 and T_2, T_2 is said to be *reduced* to T_1 if and only if:

1. The vocabulary of T_2 contains terms not in the vocabulary of T_1.

2. Any observational data explainable by T_2 are explainable by T_1.

3. T_1 is at least as well systematized as T_2. (T_1 is normally more complicated than T_2; but this is allowable, because the reducing theory normally explains more than the reduced theory. However, the "ratio" so to speak, of simplicity to explanatory power should be at least as great in the case of the reducing theory as in the case of the reduced theory.)[2]

Kemeny and Oppenheim also define the reduction of a branch of science B_2 by another branch B_1 (e.g., the reduction of chemistry to physics). Their procedure is as follows: Take the accepted theories of B_2 at a given time t as T_2. Then B_2 *is reduced to B_1 at time t* if and only if there is some theory T_1 in B_1 at t such that T_1 reduces T_2 (47). Analogously, if *some* of the theories of B_2 are reduced by some T_1 belonging to branch B_1 at t, we shall speak of a *partial reduction* of B_2 to B_1 at t. This approach presupposes (1) the familiar assumption that some division of the total vocabulary of both branches into theoretical and observational terms is given, and (2) that the two

---

[2] By a *theory* (in the widest sense) we mean any hypothesis, generalization, or law (whether deterministic or statistical), or any conjunction of these; likewise by *phenomena* (in the widest sense) we shall mean either particular occurrences or theoretically formulated general patterns. Throughout this paper, *explanation* (*explainable,* etc.) is used as defined in Hempel and Oppenheim (35) [parts of which are reprinted above, pp. 30–43]. As to *explanatory power,* there is a definite connection with *systematic power.* See Kemeny and Oppenheim (46, 47).

branches have the same observational vocabulary.

The essential feature of a *micro*-reduction is that the branch B_1 deals with the parts of the objects dealt with by B_2. We must suppose that corresponding to each branch we have a specific universe of discourse U_{Bi};[3] and that we have a part–whole relation, Pt (75; 76, especially p. 91). Under the following conditions we shall say that the reduction of B_2 to B_1[4] is a *micro-reduction*: B_2 is reduced to B_1; and the objects in the universe of discourse of B_2 are wholes which possess a decomposition (75; 76, especially p. 91) into proper parts, all of which belong to the universe of discourse of B_1. For example, let us suppose B_2 is a branch of science which has multicellular living things as its universe of discourse. Let B_1 be a branch with cells as its universe of discourse. Then the things in the universe of discourse of B_2 can be decomposed into proper parts belonging to the universe of discourse of B_1. If, in addition, it is the case that B_1 reduces B_2 at the time t, we shall say that *B_1 micro-reduces B_2 at time t*.

We shall also say that a branch B_1 is a *potential micro-reducer* of a branch B_2 if the objects in the universe of discourse of B_2 are wholes which possess a decomposition into proper parts, all of which belong to the universe of discourse of B_1. The definition is the same as the definition of "micro-reduces" except for the omission of the clause "B_2 is reduced to B_1."

Any microreduction constitutes a step in the direction of *Unity of Language* in science. For, if B_1 reduces B_2, it explains everything that B_2 does (and normally, more besides). Then, even if we cannot define in B_1 analogues for some of the theoretical terms of B_2, we can *use B_1 in place of B_2*. Thus any reduction, in the sense explained, permits a "reduction" of the total vocabulary of sci-

ence by making it possible to dispense with some terms.[5] Not every reduction moves in the direction of Unity of Science; for instance reductions *within* a branch lead to a simplification of the vocabulary of science, but they do not necessarily lead in the direction of Unity of Science as we have characterized it (although they may at times fit into that trend). However, *micro*-reductions, and even partial micro-reductions, insofar as they permit us to replace some of the terms of one branch of science by terms of another, *do* move in this direction.

Likewise, the micro-reduction of B_2 to B_1 moves in the direction of *Unity of Laws*; for it "reduces" the total number of scientific laws by making it possible, in principle, to dispense with the laws of B_2 and explain the relevant observations by using B_1.

The relations "micro-reduces" and "potential micro-reducer" have very simple properties: (1) they are transitive (this follows from the transitivity of the relations "reduces" and "Pt"); (2) they are irreflexive (no branch can micro-reduce itself); (3) they are asymmetric (if B_1 micro-reduces B_2, B_2 never micro-reduces B_1). The two latter properties are not purely formal; however, they require for their derivation only the (certainly true) empirical assumption that there does not exist an infinite descending chain of proper parts, i.e., a series of things x_1, x_2, x_3 . . . such that x_2 is a proper part of x_1, x_3 is a proper part of x_2, etc.

The just-mentioned *formal* property of the relation "micro-reduces"—its transitivity—is of great importance for the program of Unity of Science. It means that micro-reductions have a *cumulative* character. That is, if a branch B_3 is micro-reduced to B_2, and B_2 is in turn micro-reduced to B_1, then B_3 is automatically micro-reduced to B_1. This simple fact is sometimes overlooked in objections[6] to the theoretical possibility of attaining unitary science by means of micro-reduction. Thus it has been contended that one manifestly

---

[3] If we are willing to adopt a "Taxonomic System" for classifying all the things dealt with by science, then the various classes and subclasses in such a system could represent the possible "universes of discourse." In this case, the U_{Bi} of any branch would be associated with the extension of a taxonomic term in the sense of Oppenheim (62).

[4] Henceforth, we shall as a rule omit the clause "at time t."

[5] Oppenheim (62, Section 3) has a method for measuring such a reduction.

[6] Of course, in some cases, such "skipping" does occur in the process of micro-reduction, as shall be illustrated later on.

cannot explain human behavior by reference to the laws of atomic physics. It would indeed be fantastic to suppose that the simplest regularity in the field of psychology could be explained directly—i.e., "skipping" intervening branches of science—by employing subatomic theories. But one may believe in the attainability of unitary science without thereby committing oneself to this absurdity. It is not absurd to suppose that psychological laws may eventually be explained in terms of the behavior of individual neurons in the brain; that the behavior of individual cells—including neurons—may eventually be explained in terms of their biochemical constitution; and that the behavior of molecules—including the macro-molecules that make up living cells—may eventually be explained in terms of atomic physics. If this is achieved, then psychological laws will have, *in principle*, been reduced to laws of atomic physics, although it would nevertheless be hopelessly impractical to try to derive the behavior of a single human being directly from his constitution in terms of elementary particles.

Unitary science certainly does not exist today. But will it ever be attained? It is useful to divide this question into two subquestions: (1) If unitary science can be attained at all, *how* can it be attained? (2) *Can* it be attained at all?

First of all, there are various abstractly possible ways in which unitary science might be attained. However, it seems very doubtful, to say the least, that a branch B_2 could be reduced to a branch B_1, if the things in the universe of discourse of B_2 are not themselves in the universe of discourse of B_1 and also do not possess a decomposition into parts in the universe of discourse of B_1. ("They don't speak about the same things.")

It does not follow that B_1 must be a potential *micro*-reducer of B_2, i.e., that all reductions are micro-reductions.

There are many cases in which the reducing theory and the reduced theory belong to the same branch, or to branches with the same universe of discourse. When we come, however, to branches with different universes—say, physics and psychology—it seems clear that the possibility of reduction depends on the existence of a structural

connection between the universes via the "Pt" relation. Thus one cannot plausibly suppose—for the present at least—that the behavior of inorganic matter is explainable by reference to psychological laws; for inorganic materials do not consist of living parts. One supposes that psychology may be reducible to physics, but not that physics may be reducible to psychology!

Thus, the only method of attaining unitary science that appears to be seriously available at present is micro-reduction.

To turn now to our second question, *can* unitary science be attained? We certainly do not wish to maintain that it has been *established* that this is the case. But it does not follow, as some philosophers seem to think, that a tentative acceptance of the hypothesis that unitary science can be attained is therefore a mere "act of faith." We believe that this hypothesis is *credible;*[7] and we shall attempt to support this in the latter part of this paper, by providing empirical, methodological, and pragmatic reasons in its support. We therefore think the assumption that unitary science can be attained through cumulative micro-reduction recommends itself *as a working hypothesis.*[8] That is, we believe that it is in accord with the standards of reasonable scientific judgment to tentatively accept this hypothesis and to work on the assumption that further progress can be made in this direction, without claiming that its truth has been established, or denying that success may finally elude us.

REDUCTIVE LEVELS

As a basis for our further discussion, we wish to consider now the possibility of ordering branches in such a way as to indicate the major potential

---

[7] As to degree of *credibility*, see Kemeny and Oppenheim (45, especially p. 307).

[8] The "acceptance, as an overall fundamental working hypothesis, of the reduction theory, with physical science as most general, to which all others are reducible; with biological science less general; and with social science least general of all" has been emphasized by Hockett (37, especially p. 571).

micro-reductions standing between the present situation and the state of unitary science. The most natural way to do this is by their universes of discourse. We offer, therefore, a system of *reductive levels* so chosen that a branch with the things of a given level as its universe of discourse will always be a potential micro-reducer of any branch with things of the next higher level (if there is one) as its universe of discourse.

Certain conditions of adequacy follow immediately from our aim. Thus:

1. There must be several levels.

2. The number of levels must be finite.

3. There must be a unique lowest level (i.e., a unique "beginner" under the relation "potential micro-reducer"); this means that success at transforming all the *potential* micro-reductions connecting these branches into *actual* micro-reductions must, *ipso facto,* mean reduction to a single branch.

4. Any thing of any level except the lowest must possess a decomposition into things belonging to the next lower level. In this sense each level will be as it were a "common denominator" for the level immediately above it.

5. Nothing on any level should have a part on any higher level.

6. The levels must be selected in a way which is "natural"[9] and justifiable from the standpoint of present-day empirical science. In particular, the step from any one of our reductive levels to the next lower level must correspond to what is, scientifically speaking, a crucial step in the trend toward overall physicalistic reduction.

The accompanying list gives the levels we shall employ;[10] the reader may verify that the six conditions we have listed are all satisfied.

6 . . . . .Social groups
5 . . . .(Multicellular) living things
4 . . . . .Cells
3 . . . . .Molecules
2 . . . . .Atoms
1 . . . . .Elementary particles

Any whole which possesses a decomposition into parts, all of which are on a given level, will be counted as also belonging to that level. Thus each level includes all higher levels. However, the highest level to which a thing belongs will be considered the "proper" level of that thing.

This inclusion relation among our levels reflects the fact that scientific laws which apply to the things of a given level and to all combinations of those things also apply to all things of higher level. Thus a physicist, when he speaks about "all physical objects," is also speaking about living things—but not qua living things.

We maintain that each of our levels is *necessary* in the sense that it would be utopian to suppose that one might reduce all of the major theories or a whole branch concerned with any one of our six levels to a theory concerned with a lower level, *skipping* entirely the *immediately* lower level; and we maintain that our levels are *sufficient* in the sense that it would *not* be utopian to suppose that a major theory on any one of our levels *might* be directly reduced to the next lower level. (Although this is *not* to deny that it may be convenient, in special cases, to introduce intervening steps.)

However, this contention is significant only if we suppose some set of *predicates* to be associated with each of these levels. Otherwise, as has been pointed out,[11] *trivial* micro-reductions would

---

[9] As to *natural,* see Hempel (33, p. 52), and Hempel and Oppenheim (34, pp. 107, 110).

[10] Many well known hierarchical orders of the same kind (including some compatible with ours) can be found in modern writings. It suffices to give the following quotation from an article by L. von Bertalanffy (95, p. 164): "Reality, in the modern conception, appears as a tremendous hierarchical order of organized entities, leading, in a superposition of many levels, from physical and chemical to biological and sociological systems. Unity of Science is granted, not by an utopian reduction of all sciences to physics and chemistry, but by the structural uniformities of the different levels of reality." As to the last sentence, we refer on pp. 298–299 to the problem noted. Von Bertalanffy has done pioneer work in developing a General System Theory that, in spite of some differences of emphasis, is an interesting contribution to our problem.

[11] The following example is a slight modification of the one given in Hempel and Oppenheim (35, p. 148). See also Rescher and Oppenheim (76, pp. 93, 94).

be possible; e.g., we might introduce the property "Tran" (namely, the property of being an atom of a transparent substance) and then "explain the transparency of water in terms of properties on the atomic level," namely, by the hypothesis that all atoms of water have the property Tran. More explicitly, the explanation would consist of the statements

(a) $(x)(x$ is transparent $\equiv (y)(y$ is an atom of $x \supset$ Tran $(y))$

(b) $(x)(x$ is water $\supset (y)(y$ is an atom of $x \supset$ Tran $(y))$

To exclude such trivial "micro-reductions," we shall suppose that with each level there is associated a list of the theoretical predicates normally employed to characterize things on that level at present (e.g., with level 1, there would be associated the predicates used to specify spatio-temporal coordinates, mass-energy, and electric charge). And when we speak of a theory concerning a given level, we will mean not only a theory whose universe of discourse is that level, but one whose predicates belong to the appropriate list. Unless the hypothesis that theories concerning level n + 1 can be reduced by a theory concerning level n is restricted in this way, it lacks any clear empirical significance.

If the "part-whole" ("Pt") relation is understood in the wide sense, that x Pt y holds if x is spatially or temporally contained in y, then everything, continuous or discontinuous, belongs to one or another reductive level; in particular to level 1 (at least), since it is a whole consisting of elementary particles. However, one may wish to understand *whole* in a narrower sense (as "structured organization of elements"[12]). Such a specialization involves two essential steps: (1) the construction of a calculus with such a narrower

notion as its primitive concept, and (2) the definition of a particular "Pt" relation satisfying the axioms of the calculus.

Then the problem will arise that some things do not belong to any level. Hence a theory dealing with such things might not be micro-reduced even if all the micro-reductions indicated by our system of levels were accomplished; and for this reason, unitary science might not be attained.

For a trivial example, "a man in a phone booth" is an aggregate of things on different levels which we would not regard as a whole in such a narrower sense. Thus, such an "object" does not belong to any reductive level; although the "phone booth" belongs to level 3 and the man belongs to level 5.

The problem posed by such aggregates is not serious, however. We may safely make the assumption that the behavior of "man in phone booths" (to be carefully distinguished from "men in phone booths") could be completely explained given (a) a complete physicochemical theory (i.e., a theory of levels up to 3, including "phone booths"), and (b) a complete individual psychology (or more generally, a theory of levels up to 5). With this assumption in force, we are able to say: If we can construct a theory that explains the behavior of all the objects in our system of levels, then it will also handle the aggregates of such objects.

THE CREDIBILITY OF OUR WORKING HYPOTHESIS

John Stuart Mill asserts (55, Book VI, Chapter 7) that since (in our wording) human social groups are wholes whose parts are individual persons, the "laws of the phenomena of society" are "derived from and may be resolved into the laws of the nature of individual man." In our terminology, this is to suggest that it is a logical truth that theories concerning social groups (level 6) can be *micro-reduced* by theories concerning individual living things (level 5); and, *mutatis mutandis*, it would have to be a logical truth that theories con-

---

[12] See Rescher and Oppenheim (76, p. 100), and Rescher (75). Of course, nothing is intrinsically a "true" whole; the characterization of certain things as "wholes" is always a function of the point of view, i.e. of the particular "Pt" relation selected. For instance, if a taxonomic system is given, it is very natural to define "Pt" so that the "wholes" will correspond to the things of the system. Similarly for *aggregate* see Rescher and Oppenheim (76, p. 90, n. 1).

cerning any other level can be micro-reduced by theories concerning the next lower level. As a consequence, what we have called the "working hypothesis" that unitary science can be attained would likewise be a logical truth.

Mill's contention is, however, not so much *wrong* as it is vague. What is one to count as "the nature of individual man"? As pointed out above (p. 300–301) the question whether theories concerning a given reductive level can be reduced by a theory concerning the next lower level has empirical content only if the theoretical vocabularies are specified; that is, only if one associates with each level, as we have supposed to be done, a particular set of theoretical concepts. Given, e.g., a sociological theory T_2, the question whether there exists a true psychological theory T_1 *in a particular vocabulary* which reduces T_2 is an empirical question. Thus our "working hypothesis" is one that can only be justified on empirical grounds.

Among the factors on which the degree of credibility of *any* empirical hypothesis depends are (45, p. 307) the *simplicity* of the hypothesis, the *variety* of the evidence, its *reliability,* and, last but not least, the *factual support* afforded by the evidence. We proceed to discuss each of these factors.

As for the *simplicity*[13] of the hypothesis that unitary science can be attained, it suffices to consider the traditional alternatives mentioned by those who oppose it. "Hypotheses" such as Psychism and Neo-Vitalism assert that the various objects studied by contemporary science have special parts or attributes, unknown to present-day science, in addition to those indicated in our system of reductive levels. For example, men are said to have not only cells as parts; there is also an immaterial "psyche"; living things are animated by "entelechies" or "vital forces"; social groups are moved by "group minds." But, in none of these cases are we provided *at present* with postulates or coordinating definitions which would per-

mit the derivation of testable predictions. Hence, the claims made for the hypothetical entities just mentioned lack any clear scientific meaning; and as a consequence, the question of supporting evidence cannot even be raised.

On the other hand, if the effort at micro-reduction should seem to fail, we cannot preclude the introduction of theories postulating presently unknown relevant parts or presently unknown relevant attributes for some or all of the objects studied by science. Such theories are perfectly admissible, provided they have genuine explanatory value. For example, Dalton's chemical theory of molecules might not be reducible to the best available theory of atoms at a given time if the latter theory ignores the existence of the electrical properties of atoms. Thus the hypothesis of micro-reducibility,[14] as the meaning is specified at a particular time, may be false because of the insufficiency of the theoretical apparatus of the reducing branch.

Of course, a new working hypothesis of micro-reducibility, obtained by enlarging the list of attributes associated with the lowest level, might then be correct. However, if there are presently unknown attributes of a more radical kind (e.g., attributes which are relevant for explaining the behavior of living, but not of non-living things), then no such simple "repair" would seem possible. In this sense, Unity of Science is an alternative to the view that it will eventually be necessary to *bifurcate* the conceptual system of science, by the postulation of new entities or new attributes unrelated to those needed for the study of inanimate phenomena.

The requirement that there be *variety* of evidence assumes a simple form in our present case. If all the past successes referred to a single pair of levels, then this would be poor evidence indeed

---

[13] See Kemeny and Oppenheim (47, n. 6). A suggestive characterization of *simplicity* in terms of the "entropy" of a theory has been put forward by Rothstein (78). Using Rothstein's terms, we may say that any micro-reduction moves in the direction of lower entropy (greater organization).

[14] The statement that B_2 is *micro-reducible* to B_1 means (according to the analysis we adopt here) that some true theory belonging to B_1—i.e., some true theory with the appropriate vocabulary and universe of discourse, whether accepted or not, and whether it is ever even written down or not—micro-reduces every true theory of B_2. This seems to be what people have in mind when they assert that a given B_2 may not be reduced to a given B_1 at a certain time, but may nonetheless be reducible (micro-reducible) to it.

that theories concerning each level can be re-duced by theories concerning a lower level. For example, if all the past successes were on the atomic level, we should hardly regard as justified the inference that laws concerning social groups can be explained by reference to the "individual psychology" of the members of those groups. Thus, the first requirement is that one should be able to provide examples of successful micro-re-ductions between several pairs of levels, prefera-bly between all pairs.

Second, within a given level what is required is, preferably, examples of different kinds, rather than a repetition of essentially the same example many times. In short, one wants good evidence that *all* the phenomena of the given level can be micro-reduced.

We shall present below a survey of the past successes in each level. This survey is, of course, only a sketch; the successful micro-reductions and projected micro-reductions in biochemistry alone would fill a large book. But even from this sketch it will be apparent, we believe, how great the vari-ety of these successful micro-reductions is in both the respects discussed.

Moreover, we shall, of course, present only evidence from authorities regarded as *reliable* in the particular area from which the theory or exper-iment involved is drawn.

The important factor *factual support* is dis-cussed only briefly now, because we shall devote to it many of the following pages and would other-wise interrupt our presentation.

The first question raised in connection with any hypothesis is, of course, what *factual support* it possesses; that is, what confirmatory or discon-firmatory evidence is available. The evidence sup-porting a hypothesis is conveniently subdivided into that providing *direct* and that providing *indi-rect* factual support. By the direct factual support for a hypothesis we mean, roughly,[15] the propor-tion of confirmatory as opposed to disconfirma-tory instances. By the indirect factual support, we

mean the inductive support obtained from other well-confirmed hypotheses that lend credibility to the given hypothesis. While intuitively adequate quantitative measures of direct factual support have been worked out by Kemeny and Op-penheim,[16] no such measures exist for indirect factual support. The present paper will rely only on intuitive judgments of these magnitudes and will not assume that quantitative explicata will be worked out.

As our hypothesis is that theories of each re-ductive level can be micro-reduced by theories of the next lower level, a "confirming instance" is simply any successful micro-reduction between any two of our levels. The *direct* factual support for our hypothesis is thus provided by the *past successes* at reducing laws about the things on each level by means of laws referring to the parts on lower (usually, the next lower) levels. In the sequel, we shall survey the past successes with respect to each pair of levels.

As *indirect* factual support, we shall cite evi-dence supporting the hypothesis that each reduc-tive level is, in evolution and ontogenesis (in a wide sense presently to be specified) prior to the one above it. The hypothesis of *evolution* means here that (for n = 1 . . . 5) there was a time when there were things of level n, but no things of any higher level. This hypothesis is highly speculative on levels 1 and 2; fortunately the micro-reducibil-ity of the molecular to the atomic level and of the atomic level to the elementary particle level is rel-atively well established on other grounds.

Similarly, the hypothesis of ontogenesis is that, in certain cases, for any *particular* object on level n, there was a time when it did not exist, but when some of its parts on the next lower level existed; and that it developed or was causally produced out of these parts.[17]

The reason for our regarding evolution and ontogenesis as providing indirect factual support

---

[15] See Kemeny and Oppenheim (45, p. 307); also for "related concepts," like Carnap's "degree of confirmation" see Carnap (13).

[16] As to degree of credibility see Kemeny and Oppenheim (45, especially p. 307).

[17] Using a term introduced by Kurt Lewin (48), we can also say in such a case: Any particular object on level n is *genidentical* with these parts.

for the Unity of Science hypothesis may be formulated as follows:

Let us, as is customary in science, assume causal determination as a guiding principle, i.e., let us assume that things that appear later in time can be accounted for in terms of things and processes at earlier times. Then, if we find that there was a time when a certain whole did not exist, and that things on a lower level came together to form that whole, it is very natural to suppose that the characteristics of the whole can be causally explained by reference to these earlier events and parts; and that the theory of these characteristics can be micro-reduced by a theory involving only characteristics of the parts.

For the same reason, we may cite as further indirect factual support for the hypothesis of empirical Unity of Science the various successes at *synthesizing* things of each level out of things on the next lower level. Synthesis strongly increases the evidence that the characteristics of the whole in question are causally determined by the characteristics, including spatio-temporal arrangement, of its parts by showing that the object is produced, under controlled laboratory conditions, whenever parts with those characteristics are arranged in that way.

The consideration just outlined seems to us to constitute an argument against the view that, as objects of a given level combine to form wholes belonging to a higher level, there appear certain new phenomena which are "emergent" (35, p. 151; 76, p. 93) in the sense of being forever irreducible to laws governing the phenomena on the level of the parts. What our argument opposes is not, of course, the obviously true statement that there are many phenomena which are not reducible by currently available theories pertaining to lower levels; our working hypothesis rejects merely the claim of absolute irreducibility, unless such a claim is supported by a theory which has a sufficiently high degree of credibility; thus far we are not aware of any such theory. It is not sufficient, for example, simply to advance the claim that certain phenomena considered to be specifically human, such as the use of verbal language, in an abstract and generalized way, can never be

explained on the basis of neurophysiological theories, or to make the claim that this conceptual capacity distinguishes man in principle and not only in degree from nonhuman animals.

Let us mention in passing certain *pragmatic* and *methodological* points of view which speak in favor of our working hypothesis:

1. It is of *practical* value because it provides a good synopsis of scientific activity and of the relations among the several scientific disciplines.

2. It is, as has often been remarked, *fruitful* in the sense of stimulating many different kinds of scientific research. By way of contrast, belief in the *irreducibility* of various phenomena has yet to yield a single accepted scientific theory.

3. It corresponds *methodologically* to what might be called the "Democritean tendency" in science; that is, the pervasive methodological tendency[18] to try, insofar as is possible, to explain apparently dissimilar phenomena in terms of qualitatively identical parts and their spatio-temporal relations.

PAST SUCCESSES AT EACH LEVEL

By comparison with what we shall find on lower levels, the micro-reduction of level 6 to lower ones has not yet advanced very far, especially in regard to human societies. This may have at least two reasons: First of all, the body of well established theoretical knowledge on level 6 is still rather rudimentary, so that there is not much to be micro-reduced. Second, while various precise theories concerning certain special types of phenomena on level 5 have been developed, it seems as if a good deal of further theoretical knowledge concerning other areas on the same level will be

---

[18] Though we cannot accept Sir Arthur Eddington's idealistic implications, we quote from his *Philosophy of Physical Science* (17, p. 125): "I conclude therefore that our engrained form of thought is such that we shall not rest satisfied until we are able to represent all physical phenomena as an interplay of a vast number of structural units intrinsically alike. All the diversity of phenomena will be then seen to correspond to different forms of relatedness of these units or, as we should usually say, different configurations."

needed before reductive success on a larger scale can be expected.[19] However, in the case of certain very primitive groups of organisms, astonishing successes have been achieved. For instance, the differentiation into social castes among certain kinds of insects has been tentatively explained in terms of the secretion of so-called social hormones (3).

Many writers[20] believe that there are some laws common to all forms of animal association, including that of humans. Of greater potential relevance to such laws are experiments dealing with "pecking order" among domestic fowl (29). In particular, experiments showing that the social structure can be influenced by the amount of male hormone in individual birds suggest possible parallels farther up the evolutionary scale.

With respect to the problems of human social organization, as will be seen presently, two things are striking: (1) The most developed body of theory is undoubtedly in the field of *economics,* and this is at present entirely micro-reductionistic in character; (2) The main approaches to *social* theory are *all* likewise of this character. (The technical term *micro-reduction* is not, of course, employed by writers in these fields. However, many writers have discussed "the Principle of Methodological Individualism";[21] and this is nothing more than the special form our working hypothesis takes in application to human social groups.)

In economics, if very weak assumptions are satisfied, it is possible to represent the way in which an individual orders his choices by means of an individual preference function. In terms of these functions, the economist attempts to explain group phenomena, such as the market, to account for collective consumer behavior, to solve the

problems of welfare economics, etc. As theories for which a micro-reductionistic derivation is accepted in economics we could cite all the standard macro-theories, e.g., the theories of the business cycle, theories of currency fluctuation (Gresham's law to the effect that bad money drives out good is a familiar example), the principle of marginal utility, the law of demand, laws connecting change in interest rate with changes in inventory, plans, equipment, etc. The relevant point is while the economist is no longer dependent on the oversimplified assumption of "economic man," the explanation of economic phenomena is still in terms of the preferences, choices, and actions available to *individuals.*

In the realm of *sociology,* one can hardly speak of any major theory as "accepted." But it is of interest to survey some of the major theoretical approaches from the standpoint of micro-reduction.

On the one hand, there is the *economic determinism* represented by Marx and Veblen. In the case of Marx the assumptions of classical economics are openly made: Individuals are supposed—at least on the average, and in the long run—to act in accordance with their material interests. From this assumption, together with a theory of the business cycle which, for all its undoubted originality, Marx based on the classical laws of the market, Marx derives his major laws and predictions. Thus Marxist sociology is micro-reductionistic in the same sense as classical economics and shares the same basic weakness (the assumption of "economic man").

Veblen, although stressing class interests and class divisions as did Marx, introduces some noneconomic factors in his sociology. His account is ultimately in terms of individual psychology; his hypothesis of "conspicuous consumption" is a brilliant—and characteristic—example.

Max Weber produced a sociology strongly antithetical to Marx's. Yet each of his explanations of group phenomena is ultimately in terms of individual psychology, e.g., in his discussion of political parties, he argues that people *enjoy* working under a "charismatic" leader, etc.

Indeed the psychological (and hence micro-

---

[19] M. Scriven has set forth some suggestive considerations on this subject in his essay, "A Possible Distinction between Traditional Scientific Disciplines and the Study of Human Behavior" (79).

[20] See, e.g., Kartman (43), with many quotations, references, and notes, some of them micro-reductionistic.

[21] This term has been introduced by F. A. Hayek (31). See also Watkins (98, especially pp. 729–732) and Watkins (99). We owe valuable information in economics to W. J. Baumol, Princeton University.

reductionistic) character of the major sociologies (including those of Mannheim, Simmel, etc., as well as the ones mentioned above [54, 86, 94, 103] is often recognized. Thus one may safely say that while there is no one accepted sociological theory, all of these theoretical approaches represent attempted micro-reductions.

Since Schleiden and Schwann (1838/9), it is known that all living things consist of cells. Consequently, explaining the laws valid on level 5 by those on the cell level means micro-reducing all phenomena of plants and animals to level 4.

As instances of past successes in connection with level 5 we have chosen to cite, in preference to other types of example, micro-reductions and projected micro-reductions dealing with *central nervous systems* as wholes and nerve cells as parts. Our selection of these examples has not been determined by anthropocentrism. First of all, substantially similar problems arise in the case of multicellular animals, as nearly all of them possess a nervous system; and, second, the question of micro-reducing those aspects of behavior that are controlled by the central nervous system in man and the higher animals is easily the most significative (85, p. 1) one at this level, and therefore most worth discussing.

Very great activity is, in fact, apparent in the direction of micro-reducing the phenomena of the central nervous system. Much of this activity is very recent; and most of it falls under two main headings: *neurology*, and the *logical design of nerve nets*. (Once again, the technical term *microreduction* is not actually employed by workers in these fields. Instead, one finds widespread and lasting discussion concerning the advantages of "molecular" versus "molar"[22] explanations and concerning "reductionism."[23]

Theories constructed by neurologists are the product of highly detailed experimental work in neuroanatomy, neurochemistry, and neurophysiology, including the study of electric activity of the nervous system, e.g., electroencephalography.[24]

As a result of these efforts, it has proved possible to advance more or less hypothetical explanations on the cellular level for such phenomena as association, memory, motivation, emotional disturbance, and some of the phenomena connected with learning, intelligence, and perception. For example, a theory of the brain has been advanced by Hebb (32) which accounts for all of the above-mentioned phenomena. A classical psychological law, the Weber-Fechner law (insofar as it seems to apply), has likewise been micro-reduced, as a result of the work of Hoagland (36).

We turn now to *the logical design* of nerve nets: The logician Turing[25] proposed (and solved) the problem of giving a characterization of *computing machines* in the widest sense—mechanisms for solving problems by effective series of logical operations. This naturally suggests the idea of seeing whether a "Turing machine" could consist of the elements used in neurological theories of the brain; that is, whether it could consist of a network of neurons. Such a nerve network could then serve as a hypothetical model for the brain.

Such a network was first constructed by McCulloch and Pitts.[26] The basic element is the neuron, which, at any instant, is either *firing* or *not firing* (quiescent). On account of the "all or none"

---

[22] This distinction, first made by C. D. Broad (6, p. 616), adopted by E. C. Tolman (90), C. L. Hull (39), and others, is still in use, in spite of objections against this terminology.

[23] This is the form our working hypothesis takes on this level in this field. See in this connection the often quoted paper by K. MacCorquodale and P. E. Meehl, "On a Distinction between Hypothetical Constructs and Intervening Variables" (52), and some of the discussions in the "Symposium on the Probability Approach in Psychology" (73), as well as references therein, to H. Feigl, W. Koehler, D. Krech, and C. C. Pratt.

[24] As to *neuroanatomy*, see, e.g., W. Penfield (69); as to *neurochemistry*, see, e.g., Rosenblueth (77, especially Chapter 26 for acetylcholine and the summaries on pp. 134–135, 274–275; as to *The Electric Activity of the Nervous System*, see the book of this title by Brazier (5). See this last book also for neuroanatomy, neurophysiology, neurochemistry. See Brazier (5, pp. 128, 129, 152) for micro-reduction of *Gestalt phenomena* mentioned below.

[25] Turing (91, 92). For an excellent popular presentation, see Kemeny (44).

[26] See the often quoted paper by McCulloch and Pitts (53), and later publications by these authors, as well as other papers in this field in the same *Bulletin of Mathematical Biophysics*, e.g., by N. Rashevsky. See also Platt (72) for a "complementary approach that might be called amplifier theory." For more up to date details, see Shannon and McCarthy's (82) *Automata Studies*, including von Neumann's model, discussed by him (82, pp. 43–98).

character of the activity of this basic element, the *nerve net* designed by McCulloch and Pitts constitutes, as it were, a digital computer. The various relations of propositional logic can be represented by instituting suitable connections between neurons; and in this way the hypothetical net can be "programmed" to solve any problem that will yield to a predetermined sequence of logical or mathematical operations. McCulloch and Pitts employ approximately 10^4 elements in their net; in this respect they are well below the upper limit set by neurological investigation, since the number of neurons in the brain is estimated to be of the order of magnitude of 10^{10}. In other respects, their model was, however, unrealistic: No allowance is made for time delay, or for random error, both of which are important features of all biological processes.

Nerve nets incorporating both of these features have been designed by von Neumann. Von Neumann's model employs bundles of nerves rather than single nerves to form a network; this permits the simultaneous performance of each operation as many as 20,000 times as a check against error. This technique of constructing a computer is impractical at the level of present-day technology, von Neumann admits, "but quite practical for a perfectly conceivable, more advanced technology, and for the natural relay-organs (neurons). I.e., it merely calls for micro-componentry, which is not at all unnatural as a concept on this level" (97, p. 87). Still further advances in the direction of adapting these models to neurological data are anticipated. In terms of such nerve nets it is possible to give hypothetical micro-reductions for *memory, exact thinking, distinguishing similarity or dissimilarity of stimulus patterns, abstracting* of "essential" components of a stimulus pattern, *recognition of shape* regardless of form *and of chord* regardless of pitch (phenomena of great importance in Gestalt psychology [5, pp. 128, 129, 152]), *purposeful behavior* as controlled by negative feedback, *adaptive behavior,* and *mental disorders.*

It is the task of the neurophysiologist to test these models by investigating the existence of such nets, scanning units, reverberating networks, and pathways of feedback, and to provide physio-logical evidence of their functioning. Promising studies have been made in this respect.

As past successes in connection with level 4 (i.e., as cases in which phenomena involving whole cells[27] have been explained by theories concerning the molecular level) we shall cite micro-reductions dealing with three phenomena that have a fundamental character for all of biological science: the *decoding, duplication,* and *mutation* of the genetic information that is ultimately responsible for the development and maintenance of order in the cell. Our objective will be to show that at least one well-worked-out micro-reducing theory has been advanced for each phenomenon.[28] (The special form taken by our working hypothesis on this level is "methodological mechanism.")

Biologists have long had good evidence indicating that the genetic information in the cell's nucleus—acting as an "inherited message"—exerts its control over cell biochemistry through the production of specific protein catalysts (enzymes) that mediate particular steps (reactions) in the chemical order that is the cell's life. The problem of *"decoding"* the control information in the nucleus thus reduces to how the specific molecules that comprise it serve to specify the construction of specific protein catalysts. The problem of *duplication* (one aspect of the overall problem of inheritance) reduces to how the molecules of genetic material can be copied—like so many "blueprints." And the problem of *mutation* (elementary step in the evolution of new inheritable messages) reduces to how "new" forms of the genetic molecules can arise.

In the last twenty years evidence has accumulated implicating *desoxyribose nucleic acid* (DNA) as the principal "message-carrying" molecule and constituting the genetic material of the chromo-

---

[27] Throughout this paper, *cell* is used in a wide sense, i.e., "unicellular" organism or single cell in a multicellular organism.

[28] For more details and much of the following, see Simpson, Pittendrigh and Tiffany (87), Goldschmidt (28), and Horowitz (38). For valuable suggestions we are indebted to C. S. Pittendrigh, who also coined the terms "message carrying molecule" and "languages of surface" used in our text.

somes. Crick and Watson's[29] brilliant analysis of DNA structure leads to powerful micro-reducing theories that explain the decoding and duplication of DNA. It is known that the giant molecules that make up the nucleic acids have, like proteins (49, 66, 67), the structure of a backbone with side groups attached. But, whereas the proteins are polypeptides, or chains of amino-acid residues (slightly over 20 kinds of amino acids are known), the nucleic acids have a phosphate-sugar backbone, and there are only 4 kinds of side groups, all of which are nitrogen bases (purines and pyrimidines). Crick and Watson's model contains a pair of DNA chains wound around a common axis in the form of two interlocking helices. The two helices are held together (forming a helical "ladder") by hydrogen bonds between pairs of the nitrogen bases, one belonging to each helix. Although 4 bases occur as side groups, only 2 of 16 conceivable pairings are possible, for steric reasons. These 2 pairs of bases recur along the length of the DNA molecule and thus invite a picturesque analogy with the dots and dashes of the Morse code. They can be arranged in any sequence: There is enough DNA in a single cell of the human body to encode in this way 1000 large textbooks. The model can be said to imply that the genetic "language" of the inherited control message is a "language of surfaces": The information in DNA structure is decoded as a sequence of amino acids in the proteins which are synthesized under ultimate DNA control. The surface structure of the DNA helix, dictated by the sequence of base pairs, specifies like a template[30] the sequence of amino acids laid down end to end in the fabrication of polypeptides.

Watson and Crick's model immediately suggests how the DNA might produce an exact copy of itself—for transmission as an inherited message to the succeeding generation of cells. The DNA molecule, as noted above, consists of two inter-woven helices, each of which is the complement of the other. Thus each chain may act as a mold on which a complementary chain can be synthesized. The two chains of a DNA molecule need only unwind and separate. Each begins to build a new complement onto itself, as loose units, floating in the cell, attach themselves to the bases in the single DNA chain. When the process is completed, there are two pairs of chains where before there was only one![31]

Mutation of the genetic information has been explained in a molecular (micro-reduction) theory advanced some years ago by Delbrück.[32] Delbrück's theory was conceived long before the newer knowledge of DNA was available; but it is a very general model in no way vitiated by Crick and Watson's model of the particular molecule constituting the genetic material. Delbrück, like many others, assumed that the gene is a single large "nucleo-protein" molecule. (This term is used for macromolecules, such as viruses and the hypothetical "genes," which consist of protein and nucleic acid. Some recent theories even assume that an entire chromosome is a single such molecule.) According to Delbrück's theory, different quantum levels within the atoms of the molecule correspond to different hereditary characteristics. A mutation is simply a quantum jump of a rare type (i.e., one with a high activation energy). The observed variation of the spontaneous mutation rate with temperature is in good quantitative agreement with the theory.

Such hypotheses and models as those of Crick and Watson, and of Delbrück, are at present far from suffcient for a complete micro-reduction of the major biological generalizations, e.g., evolution and general genetic theory (including the problem of the control of development). But they constitute an encouraging start toward this ulti-

---

[29] See in reference to the following discussion Watson and Crick (100), also (101), and (102), and Crick (15).

[30] Pauling and Delbrück (68). A micro-reducing theory has been proposed for these activities using the "lock-key" model. See Pauling, Campbell and Pressman (65), and Burnet (8).

[31] For a mechanical model, see von Neumann (96) and Jacobson (40).

[32] See Timoféeff-Ressovsky (89, especially pp. 108–138). It should, however, be noted that since Delbrück's theory was put forward, his model has proved inadequate for explaining genetic facts concerning mutation. And it is reproduced here only as a historical case of a micro-reducing theory that, in its day, served valuable functions.

mate goal and, to this extent, an indirect support for our working hypothesis.

Only in the twentieth century has it been possible to micro-reduce to the atomic and in some cases directly to the subatomic level most of the *macro-physical* aspects of matter (e.g., the high fluidity of water, the elasticity of rubber, and the hardness of diamond) as well as the *chemical* phenomena of the elements, i.e., those changes of the peripheral electrons which leave the nucleus unaffected. In particular, electronic theories explain, e.g., the laws governing valence, the various types of bonds, and the "resonance" of molecules between several equivalent electronic structures. A complete explanation of these phenomena and those of the Periodic Table is possible only with the help of Pauli's exclusion principle, which states in one form that no two electrons of the same atom can be alike in all of 4 "quantum numbers." While some molecular laws are not yet micro-reduced, there is every hope that further successes will be obtained in these respects. Thus Pauling (63, 64) writes:

There are still problems to be solved, and some of them are great problems—an example is the problem of the detailed nature of catalytic activity. We can feel sure, however, that this problem will in the course of time be solved in terms of quantum theory as it now exists: There seems little reason to believe that some fundamental new principle remains to be discovered in order that catalysis be explained (64).

Micro-reduction of level 2 to level 1 has been mentioned in the preceding section because many molecular phenomena are at present (skipping the atomic level) explained with reference to laws of elementary particles.[33] Bohr's basic (and now somewhat outdated) model of the atom as a kind of "solar system" of elementary particles is today part of everyone's conceptual apparatus, while the mathematical development of theory in its present form is formidable indeed! Thus we shall not attempt to give any details of this success. But the high rate of progress in this field certainly gives

reason to hope that the unsolved problems, especially as to the forces that hold the nucleus together, will likewise be explained in terms of an elementary particle theory.

EVOLUTION, ONTOGENESIS, AND SYNTHESIS

As pointed out on pp. 303–304, *evolution* provides *indirect* factual support for the working hypothesis that unitary science is attainable. Evolution (in the present sense) is an overall phenomenon involving all levels, from 1 through 6; the mechanisms of chance variation and "selection" operate throughout in ways characteristic for the evolutionary level involved.[34] Time scales have, indeed, been worked out by various scientists showing the times when the first things of each level first appeared.[35] (These times are, of course, the less hypothetical, the higher the level involved.) But even if the hypothesis of evolution should fail to hold in the case of certain levels, it is important to note that whenever it *does* hold—whenever it *can* be shown that things of a given level existed before things of the next higher level came into existence—some degree of indirect support is provided to the particular special case of our working hypothesis that concerns those two levels.

The hypothesis of "evolution" is most speculative insofar as it concerns levels 1 to 3. Various cosmological hypotheses are at present undergoing lively discussion.[36] According to one of these, strongly urged by Gamow (24, 25, 26), the first nuclei did not form out of elementary particles until five to thirty minutes after the start of the universe's expansion; molecules may not have

---

[33] We think that, throughout this paper, our usage of thing language also on this level is admissible in spite of well-known difficulties and refer, e.g., to Born (4) and Johnson (42).

[34] See, e.g., Broad (6, especially p. 93), as to "a general tendency of one order to combine with each other under suitable conditions to form complexes of the next order." See also Blum (1 and 2, especially p. 608); Needham (59, especially pp. 184–185); and Dodd (16).

[35] This wording takes care of *regression,* a reversal of trend, illustrated, e.g., by parasitism.

[36] For a clear survey of cosmological hypotheses see the twelve articles published in the issue of *Scientific American* cited under Gamow (26).

been able to exist until considerably later. Most present-day cosmologists still subscribe to such evolutionary views of the universe, i.e., there was a "zero point" from which the evolution of matter began, with diminishing density through expansion. However, H. Bondi, T. Gold, and F. Hoyle have advanced a conflicting idea, the "steady state" theory, according to which there is no "zero point" from which the evolution of matter began, but matter is continuously created, so that its density remains constant in spite of expansion. There seems to be hope that these rival hypotheses will be submitted to specific empirical tests in the near future. But, fortunately, we do not have to depend on hypotheses that are still so highly controversial: As we have seen, the micro-reducibility of molecular and atomic phenomena is today not open to serious doubt.

Less speculative are theories concerning the origin of life (transition from level 3 to level 4). Calvin (9; Fox, 22) points out that four mechanisms have been discovered which lead to the formation of amino acids and other organic materials in a mixture of gases duplicating the composition of the primitive terrestrial atmosphere.[37] These have, in fact, been tested experimentally with positive results. Many biologists today accept with Oparin (61) the view that the evolution of life as such was not a single chance event but a long process possibly requiring as many as two billion years, until precellular living organisms first appeared.

According to such views, "chemical evolution" gradually leads in an appropriate environment to evolution in the familiar Darwinian sense. In such a process, it hardly has meaning to speak of a point at which "life appeared." To this day controversies exist concerning the "dividing line" between living and non-living things. In particular, viruses are classified by some biologists as *living,* because they exhibit *self-duplication* and *mu-*

tability; but most biologists refuse to apply the term to them, because viruses exhibit these characteristic phenomena of life only due to activities of a living cell with which they are in contact. But, wherever one draws the line,[38] non-living molecules preceded primordial living substance, and the latter evolved gradually into highly organized living units, the unicellular ancestors of all living things. The "first complex molecules endowed with the faculty of reproducing their own kind" must have been synthesized—and with them the beginning of evolution in the Darwinian sense—a few billion years ago, Goldschmidt (27, p. 84) asserts: "All the facts of biology, geology, paleontology, biochemistry, and radiology not only agree with this statement but actually prove it."

Evolution at the next two levels (from level 4 to level 5, and from 5 to 6) is not speculative at all, but forms part of the broad line of Darwinian evolution, so well marked out by the various kinds of evidence referred to in the statement just quoted. The line of development is again a continuous one;[39] and it is to some extent arbitrary (as in the case of "living" versus "non-living") to give a "point" at which true multicellulars first appeared, or at which an animal is "social" rather than "solitary." But in spite of this arbitrariness, it is safe to say that:

a. Multicellulars evolved from what were originally competing single cells; the "selection" by the environment was in this case determined by the superior survival value of the cooperative structure.[40]

b. Social animals evolved from solitary ones for

---

[37] Perhaps the most sensational method is an experiment suggested by H. C. Urey and made by S. L. Miller (56, 57), according to which amino acids are formed when an electric discharge passes through a mixture of methane, hydrogen, ammonia, and water.

[38] "Actually life has many attributes, almost any one of which we can reproduce in a nonliving system. It is only when they all appear to a greater or lesser degree in the same system simultaneously that we call it living" (Calvin, 9, p. 252). Thus the dividing line between "living" and "nonliving" is obtained by transforming an underlying "multidimensional concept of order" (see Hempel and Oppenheim, 34, pp. 65–77), in a more or less arbitrary way, into a dichotomy. See also Stanley (88, especially pp. 15 and 16 of the reprint of this article).

[39] See note 38 above.

[40] For details, see Lindsey (50, especially pp. 136–139, 152–153, 342–344). See also Burkholder (7).

similar reasons; and, indeed, there were millions of years during which there were *only* solitary animals on earth and not yet their organizations into social structures.[41]

To illustrate *ontogenesis,* we must show that particular things of a particular level have arisen out of particular things of the next lower level. For example, it is a consequence of most contemporary cosmological theories—whether of the evolutionary or of the "steady state" type—that each existent atom must have originally been formed by a union of elementary particles. (Of course an atom of an element may subsequently undergo "transmutation.") However, such theories are extremely speculative. On the other hand, the chemical union of atoms to form molecules is commonplace in nature.

Coming to the higher levels of the reductive hierarchy, we have unfortunately a hiatus at the level of cells. Individual cells do *not,* as far as our observations go, ever develop out of individual molecules; on the contrary, "cells come only from cells," as Virchow stated about one hundred years ago. However, a characteristic example of ontogenesis of things of one level out of things of the next lower level is afforded by the development of multicellular organisms through the process of mitosis and cell division. All the hereditary characteristics of the organism are specified in the "genetic information" carried in the chromosomes of each individual cell, and are transmitted to the resultant organism through cell division and mitosis.

A more startling example of ontogenesis at this level is provided by the *slime molds* studied by Bonner (3). These are isolated amoebae; but, at a certain stage, they "clump" together chemotactically and form a simple multicellular organism, a sausage-like "slug"! This "slug" crawls with comparative rapidity and good coordination. It even has senses of a sort, for it is attracted by light.

As to the level of social groups, we have some ontogenetic data, however slight; for children, according to the well-known studies of Piaget (70, 71) (and other authorities on child behavior), acquire the capacity to cooperate with one another, to be concerned with each other's welfare, and to form groups in which they treat one another as peers, only after a number of years (not before seven years of age, in Piaget's studies). Here one has in a rudimentary form what we are looking for: the ontogenetic development of progressively more social behavior (level 6) by what begin as relatively "egocentric" and unsocialized individuals (level 5).

Synthesis affords factual support for micro-reduction much as ontogenesis does; however, the evidence is better because synthesis usually takes place under *controlled* conditions. Thus it enables one to show that one can obtain an object of the kind under investigation *invariably* by instituting the appropriate causal relations among the parts that go to make it up. For this reason, we may say that success in synthesizing is as strong evidence as one can have for the possibility of micro-reduction, short of actually finding the micro-reducing theory.

To begin on the lowest level of the reductive hierarchy, that one can obtain an atom by bringing together the appropriate elementary particles is a basic consequence of elementary nuclear physics. A common example from the operation of atomic piles is the synthesis of deuterium. This proceeds as one bombards protons (in, e.g., hydrogen gas) with neutrons.

The synthesis of a molecule by chemically uniting atoms is an elementary laboratory demonstration. One familiar example is the union of oxygen and hydrogen gas. Under the influence of an electric spark one obtains the appearance of H_2O molecules.

The next level is that of life. "On the borderline" are the viruses. Thus success at synthesizing a virus out of non-living macro-molecules would count as a first step to the synthesis of cells (which

---

[41] See, e.g., the publications (104, 105, 106) by Wheeler. See also Haskins (30, especially pp. 30–36). Since we are considering evolution on level 6 as a whole, we can refrain from discussing the great difference between, on the one hand, chance mutations, natural selection, and "instinctive" choices and, on the other hand, the specific faculty of man of consciously and willfully directing social evolution in time stretches of specifically small orders of magnitude (see Zilsel, 108).

at present seems to be an achievement for the far distant future).

While success at synthesizing a virus out of atoms is not yet in sight, synthesis out of *non-living* highly complex macro-molecules has been accomplished. At the University of California Virus Laboratory (23), protein obtained from viruses has been mixed with nucleic acid to obtain active virus. The protein does not behave like a virus—it is completely non-infectious. However, the reconstituted virus has the same structure as "natural" virus and will produce the tobacco mosaic disease when applied to plants. Also new "artificial" viruses have been produced by combining the nucleic acid from one kind of virus with the protein from a different kind. Impressive results in synthesizing proteins have been accomplished; e.g., R. B. Woodward and C. H. Schramm (107; see also Nogushi and Hayakawa, 60; and Oparin, 61) have synthesized "protein analogues"—giant polymers containing at least 10,000 amino-acid residues.

At the next level, no one has of course synthesized a whole multicellular organism out of individual cells; but here too there is an impressive partial success to report. Recent experiments have provided detailed descriptions of the manner in which cells organize themselves into whole multicellular tissues. These studies show that even isolated whole cells, when brought together in random groups, could effectuate the characteristic construction of such tissues.[42] Similar phenomena are well known in the case of sponges and freshwater polyps.

Lastly, the "synthesis" of a new social group by bringing together previously separated individuals is extremely familiar, e.g., the organization of new clubs, trade unions, professional associations, etc. One has even the deliberate formation of whole new societies, e.g., the formation of the Oneida community of utopians in the nineteenth century, or of the state of Israel by Zionists in the twentieth.

There have been experimental studies in this field; among them, the pioneer work of Kurt Lewin and his school is especially well known.[43]

CONCLUDING REMARKS

The possibility that all science may one day be reduced to micro-physics (in the sense in which chemistry seems today to be reduced to it), and the presence of a unifying trend toward micro-reduction running through much of scientific activity, have often been noticed both by specialists in the various sciences and by meta-scientists. But these opinions have, in general, been expressed in a more or less vague manner and without very deep-going justification. It has been our aim, first, to provide precise definitions for the crucial concepts involved, and, second, to reply to the frequently made accusations that belief in the attainability of unitary science is "a mere act of faith." We hope to have shown that, on the contrary, a tentative acceptance of this belief, an acceptance of it as a working hypothesis, is *justified,* and that the hypothesis is *credible,* partly on methodological grounds (e.g., the simplicity of the hypothesis, as opposed to the bifurcation that rival suppositions create in the conceptual system of science), and partly because there is really a large mass of direct and indirect evidence in its favor.

The idea of reductive levels employed in our discussion suggests what may plausibly be regarded as a *natural order of sciences.* For this purpose, it suffices to take as "fundamental disciplines" the branches corresponding to our levels. It is understandable that many of the well-known orderings of things[44] have a rough similarity to our reductive levels, and that corresponding orderings of sciences are more or less similar to our order of 6 "fundamental disciplines." Again, several successive levels may be grouped together (e.g., physics today conventionally deals at least with

---

[42] See Moscana (58) and his references, especially to work by the same author and by Paul Weiss.

[43] See Lippitt (51). For recent experiments, see Sherif and Sherif (84, Chapters 6 and 9), and Sherif (83).

[44] See note 10 above.

levels 1, 2, and 3; just as biology deals with at least levels 4 and 5). Thus we often encounter a division into simply physics, biology, and social sciences. But these other efforts to solve a problem which goes back to ancient times[45] have apparently been made on more or less intuitive grounds; it does not seem to have been realized that these orderings are "natural" in a deeper sense, of being based on the relation of *potential micro-reducer* obtaining between the branches of science.

It should be emphasized that these six "fundamental disciplines" are, largely, fictitious ones (e.g., there is no actual branch whose universe of discourse is *strictly* molecules and combinations thereof). If one wishes a less idealized approach, one may utilize a concept in semantical information theory which has been defined by one of us (3). This is the semantical functor: "the amount of information the statement S contains about the class C" (or, in symbols: $inf(S, C)$). Then one can characterize any theory S (or any branch, if we are willing to identify a branch with a conjunction of theories) by a sextuple: namely, inf(S, level 1), inf(S, level 2) . . . inf(S, level 6). This sextuple can be regarded as the "locus" of the branch S in a six-dimensional space. The axes are the loci of the imaginary "fundamental disciplines" just referred to; any real branch (e.g., present-day biology) will probably have a position not quite on any axis, but nearer to one than to the others.

Whereas the orderings to which we referred above generally begin with the historically given branches, the procedure just described reverses this tendency. *First* a continuous order is defined in which any imaginable branch can be located; *then* one investigates the relations among the actually existing branches. These positions may be expected to change with time, e.g., as micro-reduction proceeds, "biology" will occupy a position closer to the "level 1" axis, and so will all the other branches. The continuous order may be described as "Darwinian" rather than "Linnean"; it derives its naturalness, not from agreement with intuitive or customary classifications, but from its high systematic import in the light of the hypothesis that Unity of Science is attainable.

REFERENCES

1. Blum, H. F. *Time's Arrow and Evolution*. Princeton: Princeton Univ. Press, 1951.
2. Blum, H. F. "Perspectives in Evolution," *American Scientist,* 43:595–610 (1955).
3. Bonner, J. T. *Morphogenesis*. Princeton: Princeton Univ. Press, 1952.
4. Born, M. "The Interpretation of Quantum Mechanics," *British Journal for the Philosophy of Science,* 3:95–106 (1953).
5. Brazier, M. A. B. *The Electric Activity of the Nervous System.* London: Sir Isaac Pitman & Sons, Ltd., 1951.
6. Broad, C. D. *The Mind and its Place in Nature.* New York: Harcourt, Brace, 1925.
7. Burkholder, P. R. "Cooperation and Conflict among Primitive Organisms," *American Scientist,* 40:601–631 (1952).
8. Burnet, M. "How Antibodies are Made," *Scientific American,* 191:74–78 (November 1954).
9. Calvin, M. "Chemical Evolution and the Origin of Life," *American Scientist,* 44:248–263 (1956).
10. Carnap, R. *Der logische Aufbau der Welt.* Berlin-Schlachtensee: Im Weltkreis-Verlag, 1928. Summary in N. Goodman, *The Structure of Appearances,* pp. 114–146. Cambridge: Harvard Univ. Press, 1951.
11. Carnap, R. "Testability and Meaning," *Philosophy of Science,* 3:419–471 (1936), and 4:2–40 (1937). Reprinted by Graduate Philosophy Club, Yale University, New Haven, 1950.
12. Carnap, R. *Logical Foundations of the Unity of Science, International Encyclopedia of Unified Science.* Vol. I, pp. 42–62. Chicago: Univ. of Chicago Press, 1938.
13. Carnap, R. *Logical Foundations of Probability.* Chicago: Univ. of Chicago Press, 1950.
14. Comte, Auguste. *Cours de Philosophie Positive.* 6 Vols. Paris: Bachelier, 1830–42.
15. Crick, F. H. C. "The Structure of Hereditary Material," *Scientific American,* 191:54–61 (October 1954).
16. Dodd, S. C. "A Mass-Time Triangle," *Philosophy of Science,* 11:233–244 (1944).
17. Eddington, Sir Arthur. *The Philosophy of Physical*

---

[45] For details, see Flint (21), and Vannerus (93), Auguste Comte in his *Cours de Philosophie Positive,* Première et Deuxième at Leĉons (14), has given a hierarchical order of 6 "fundamental disciplines" that, independently from its philosophical background, is amazingly modern in many respects, as several contemporary authors recognize.

Science. Cambridge: Cambridge University Press, 1949.

18. Feigl, H. "Logical Empiricism," in D. D. Runes (ed.), *Twentieth Century Philosophy,* pp. 371–416. New York: Philosophical Library, 1943. Reprinted in H. Feigl and W. Sellars (eds.), *Readings in Philosophical Analysis.* New York: Appleton-Century-Crofts, 1949.

19. Feigl, H. "Unity of Science and Unitary Science," in H. Feigl and M. Brodbeck (eds.), *Readings in the Philosophy of Science,* pp. 382–384. New York: Appleton-Century-Crofts, 1953.

20. Feigl, H. "Functionalism, Psychological Theory and the Uniting Sciences: Some Discussion Remarks," *Psychological Review,* 62:232–235 (1955).

21. Flint, R. *Philosophy as Scientia Scientiarum and the History of the Sciences.* New York: Scribner, 1904.

22. Fox, S. W. "The Evolution of Protein Molecules and Thermal Synthesis of Biochemical Substances," *American Scientist,* 44:347–359 (1956).

23. Fraenkel-Conrat, H. "Rebuilding a Virus," *Scientific American,* 194:42–47 (June 1956).

24. Gamow, G. "The Origin and Evolution of the Universe," *American Scientist,* 39:393–406 (1951).

25. Gamow, G. *The Creation of the Universe.* New York: Viking Press, 1952.

26. Gamow, G. "The Evolutionary Universe," *Scientific American,* 195:136–154 (September 1956).

27. Goldschmidt, R. B. "Evolution, as Viewed by One Geneticist," *American Scientist,* 40:84–98 (1952).

28. Goldschmidt, R. B. *Theoretical Genetics.* Berkeley and Los Angeles: Univ. of California Press, 1955.

29. Guhl, A. M. "The Social Order of Chickens," *Scientific American,* 194:42–46 (February 1956).

30. Haskins, C. P. *Of Societies and Man.* New York: Norton & Co., 1951.

31. Hayek, F. A. *Individualism and the Economic Order.* Chicago: Univ. of Chicago Press, 1948.

32. Hebb, D. O. *The Organization of Behavior.* New York: Wiley, 1949.

33. Hempel, C. G. *Fundamentals of Concept Formation in the Empirical Sciences,* Vol. II, No. 7 of *International Encyclopedia of Unified Science.* Chicago: Univ. of Chicago Press, 1952.

34. Hempel, C. G., and P. Oppenheim. *Der Typusbegriff im Lichte der neuen Logik; wissenschaftstheoretische Untersuchungen zur Konstitutionsforschung und Psychologie.* Leiden: A. W. Sythoff, 1936.

35. Hempel, C. G., and P. Oppenheim. "Studies in the Logic of Explanation," *Philosophy of Science,* 15:135–175 (1948).

36. Hoagland, H. "The Weber-Fechner Law and the All-or-None Theory," *Journal of General Psychology,* 3:351–373 (1930).

37. Hockett, C. H. "Biophysics, Linguistics, and the Unity of Science," *American Scientist,* 36:558–572 (1948).

38. Horowitz, N. H. "The Gene," *Scientific American,* 195:78–90 (October 1956).

39. Hull, C. L. *Principles of Animal Behavior.* New York: D. Appleton-Century, Inc., 1943.

40. Jacobson, H. "Information, Reproduction, and the Origin of Life," *American Scientist,* 43:119–127 (1955).

41. Jeffress, L. A. *Cerebral Mechanisms in Behavior; the Hixon Symposium.* New York: Wiley, 1951.

42. Johnson, M. "The Meaning of Time and Space in Philosophies of Science," *American Scientist,* 39:412–431 (1951).

43. Kartman, L. "Metaphorical Appeals in Biological Thought," *American Scientist,* 44:296–301 (1956).

44. Kemeny, J. G. "Man Viewed as a Machine," *Scientific American,* 192:58–66 (April 1955).

45. Kemeny, J. G., and P. Oppenheim. "Degree of Factual Support," *Philosophy of Science,* 19:307–324 (1952).

46. Kemeny, J. G., and P. Oppenheim. "Systematic Power," *Philosophy of Science,* 22:27–33 (1955).

47. Kemeny, J. G., and P. Oppenheim. "On Reduction," *Philosophical Studies,* 7:6–19 (1956).

48. Lewin, Kurt. *Der Begriff der Genese.* Berlin: Verlag von Julius Springer, 1922.

49. Linderstrom-Lang, K. U. "How is a Protein Made?" *American Scientist,* 41:100–106 (1953).

50. Lindsey, A. W. *Organic Evolution.* St. Louis: C. V. Mosby Company, 1952.

51. Lippitt, R. "Field Theory and Experiment in Social Psychology," *American Journal of Sociology,* 45:26–79 (1939).

52. MacCorquodale, K., and P. E. Meehl. "On a Distinction Between Hypothetical Constructs and Intervening Variables," *Psychological Review,* 55:95–105 (1948).

53. McCulloch, W. S., and W. Pitts. "A Logical Calculus of the Ideas Immanent in Nervous Activity," *Bulletin of Mathematical Biophysics,* 5:115–133 (1943).

54. Mannheim, K. *Ideology and Utopia.* New York: Harcourt, Brace, 1936.

55. Mill, John Stuart. *System of Logic.* New York: Harper, 1848 (1st ed. London, 1843).

56. Miller, S. L. "A Production of Amino Acids Under Possible Primitive Earth Conditions," *Science,* 117:528–529 (1953).

57. Miller, S. L. "Production of Some Organic Compounds Under Possible Primitive Earth Conditions," *Journal of the American Chemical Society,* 77:2351–2361 (1955).

58. Moscana, A. "Development of Heterotypic Combinations of Dissociated Embryonic Chick Cells,"

Proceedings of the Society for Experimental Biology and Medicine, 92:410–416 (1956).

59. Needham, J. *Time.* New York: Macmillan, 1943.

60. Nogushi, J., and T. Hayakawa. Letter to the Editor, *Journal of the American Chemical Society,* 76:2846–2848 (1954).

61. Oparin, A. I. *The Origin of Life.* New York: Macmillan, 1938 (Dover Publications, Inc. edition, 1953).

62. Oppenheim, P. "Dimensions of Knowledge," *Revue Internationale de Philosophie,* Fascicule 40, Section 7 (1957).

63. Pauling, L. "Chemical Achievement and Hope for the Future," *American Scientist,* 36:51–58 (1948).

64. Pauling, L. "Quantum Theory and Chemistry," *Science,* 113:92–94 (1951).

65. Pauling, L., D. H. Campbell, and D. Pressmann. "The Nature of Forces between Antigen and Antibody and of the Precipitation Reaction," *Physical Review,* 63:203–219 (1943).

66. Pauling, L., and R. B. Corey. "Two Hydrogen-Bonded Spiral Configurations of the Polypeptide Chain," *Journal of the American Chemical Society,* 72:5349 (1950).

67. Pauling, L., and R. B. Corey, "Atomic Coordination and Structure Factors for Two Helical Configurations," *Proceedings of the National Academy of Science* (U.S.), 37:235 (1951).

68. Pauling, L., and M. Delbrück. "The Nature of Intermolecular Forces Operative in Biological Processes," *Science,* 92:585–586 (1940).

69. Penfield, W. "The Cerebral Cortex and the Mind of Man," in P. Laslett (ed.), *The Physical Basis of Mind,* pp. 56–64. Oxford: Blackwell, 1950.

70. Piaget, J. *The Moral Judgment of the Child.* London: Kegan Paul, Trench, Trubner and Company, Ltd., 1932.

71. Piaget, J. *The Language and Thought of the Child.* London: Kegan Paul, Trench, Trubner and Company; New York: Harcourt, Brace, 1926.

72. Platt, J. R. "Amplification Aspects of Biological Response and Mental Activity," *American Scientist,* 44:180–197 (1956).

73. Probability Approach in Psychology (Symposium), *Psychological Review,* 62:193–242 (1955).

74. Rashevsky, N. Papers in general of Rashevsky, published in the *Bulletin of Mathematical Biophysics,* 5 (1943).

75. Rescher, N. "Axioms of the Part Relation," *Philosophical Studies,* 6:8–11 (1955).

76. Rescher, N. and P. Oppenheim. "Logical Analysis of Gestalt Concepts," *British Journal for the Philosophy of Science,* 6:89–106 (1955).

77. Rosenblueth, A. *The Transmission of Nerve Impulses at Neuroeffector Junctions and Peripheral Synapses.* New York: Technological Press of MIT and Wiley, 1950.

78. Rothstein, J. *Communication, Organization, and Science.* Indian Hills, Colorado: Falcon's Wing Press, 1957.

79. Scriven, M. "A Possible Distinction between Traditional Scientific Disciplines and the Study of Human Behavior," in H. Feigl and M. Scriven (eds.), Vol. I, *Minnesota Studies in the Philosophy of Science,* pp. 330–339. Minneapolis: Univ. of Minnesota Press, 1956.

80. Sellars, W. "A Semantical Solution of the Mind-Body Problem," *Methodos,* 5:45–84 (1953).

81. Sellars, W. "Empiricism and the Philosophy of Mind," in H. Feigl and M. Scriven (eds.), *Minnesota Studies in the Philosophy of Science,* Vol. I, pp. 253–329. Minneapolis: Univ. of Minnesota Press, 1956.

82. Shannon, C. E., and J. McCarthy (eds.), *Automata Studies.* Princeton: Princeton Univ. Press, 1956.

83. Sherif, M. "Experiments in Group Conflict," *Scientific American,* 195:54–58 (November 1956).

84. Sherif, M., and C. W. Sherif. *An Outline of Social Psychology.* New York: Harper, 1956.

85. Sherrington, Charles. *The Integrative Action of the Nervous System.* New Haven: Yale Univ. Press, 1948.

86. Simmel, G. *Sociologie.* Leipzig: Juncker und Humblot, 1908.

87. Simpson, G. G., C. S. Pittendrigh, and C. H. Tiffany. *Life.* New York: Harcourt, Brace, 1957.

88. Stanley, W. M. "The Structure of Viruses," reprinted from publication No. 14 of the *American Association for the Advancement of Science, The Cell and Protoplasm,* pp. 120–135 (reprint consulted) (1940).

89. Timoféeff-Ressovsky, N. W. *Experimentelle Mutationsforschung in der Vererbungslehre.* Dresden und Leipzig: Verlag von Theoder Steinkopff, 1937.

90. Tolman, E. C. *Purposive Behavior in Animals and Men.* New York: The Century Company, 1932.

91. Turing, A. M. "On Computable Numbers, With an Application to the Entscheidungsproblem," *Proceedings of the London Mathematical Society,* Ser. 2, 42:230–265 (1936).

92. Turing, A. M. "A Correction," *Proceedings of the London Mathematical Society,* Ser. 2, 43:544–546 (1937).

93. Vannerus, A. *Vetenskapssystematik.* Stockholm: Aktiebolaget Ljus, 1907.

94. Veblen, T. *The Theory of the Leisure Class.* London: Macmillan, 1899.

95. Von Bertalanffy, L. "An Outline of General System Theory," *The British Journal for the Philosophy of Science,* 1:134–165 (1950).

96. Von Neumann, John. "The General and Logical Theory of Automata," in L. A. Jeffress (ed.), *Cerebral Mechanisms in Behavior; The Hixon Sympo-*

sium, pp. 20–41. New York: John Wiley and Sons, Inc., 1951.

97. Von Neumann, John. "Probabilistic Logics and the Synthesis of Reliable Organisms from Unreliable Components," in C. E. Shannon and J. McCarthy (eds.), *Automata Studies.* Princeton: Princeton Univ. Press, 1956.

98. Watkins, J. W. N. "Ideal Types and Historical Explanation," in H. Feigl and M. Brodbeck (eds.), *Readings in the Philosophy of Science,* pp. 723–743. New York: Appleton-Century-Crofts, 1953.

99. Watkins, J. W. N. "A Reply," *Philosophy of Science,* 22:58–62 (1955).

100. Watson, J. D., and F. H. C. Crick. "The Structure of DNA," *Cold Spring Harbor Symposium on Quantitative Biology,* 18:123–131 (1953).

101. Watson, J. D., and F. H. C. Crick. "Molecular Structure of Nucleic Acids—A Structure for Desoxyribosenucleic Acid," *Nature,* 171:737–738 (1953).

102. Watson, J. D., and F. H. C. Crick. "Genetical Implications of the Structure of Desoxyribosenucleic Acid," *Nature,* 171:964–967 (1953).

103. Weber, M. *The Theory of Social and Economic Organization,* translated by A. M. Henderson and T. Persons. New York: Oxford Univ. Press, 1947.

104. Wheeler, W. M. *Social Life Among the Insects.* New York: Harcourt, Brace, 1923.

105. Wheeler, W. M. *Emergent Evolution and the Development of Societies.* New York: Norton & Co., 1928.

106. Wheeler, W. M. "Animal Societies," *Scientific Monthly,* 39:289–301 (1934).

107. Woodward, R. B., and C. H. Schramm. Letter to the Editor, *Journal of the American Chemical Society,* 69:1551 (1947).

108. Zilsel, E. "History and Biological Evolution," *Philosophy of Science,* 7:121–128 (1940).

The Plurality of Science

Patrick Suppes

What I have to say falls under four headings: What is unity of science, unity and reductionism, the search for certainty, and the search for completeness.

WHAT IS UNITY OF SCIENCE SUPPOSED TO BE?

To answer this initial question, I turned to the introductory essay by Otto Neurath [5] for Volume 1, Part 1, of the *International Encyclopedia of Unified Science*. He begins this way:

Unified science became historically the subject of this *Encyclopedia* as a result of the efforts of the unity of science movement, which includes scientists and persons interested in science who are conscious of the importance of a universal scientific attitude.

The new version of the idea of unified science is created by the confluence of divergent intellectual currents. Empirical work of scientists was often antagonistic to the logical constructions of a priori rationalism bred by philosophico-religious systems; therefore, "empiricalization" and "logicalization" were considered mostly to be in opposition—the two have now become synthesized for the first time in history ([5], p. 1).

Later he continues:

All-embracing vision and thought is an old desire of humanity. . . . This interest in combining concepts and statements without empirical testing prepared a certain attitude which appeared in the following ages as metaphysical construction. The neglect of testing facts and using observation statements in connection with all systematized ideas is especially found in the different idealistic systems ([5], pp. 5–6).

I am indebted to Georg Kreisel for a number of penetrating criticisms of the first draft of this paper.

Reprinted from *PSA 1978*, Vol. II, P.D. Asquith and I. Hacking, Eds. East Lansing: Philosophy of Science Association, pp. 3–16. Reprinted by permission of the author and the Philosophy of Science Association.

Later he says:

A universal application of logical analysis and construction to science in general was prepared not only by the systematization of empirical procedure and the systematization of logico-empirical analysis of scientific statements, but also by the analysis of language from different points of view ([5], pp. 16–17).

In the same volume of the *Encyclopedia*, the thesis about the unity of the language of science is taken up in considerably more detail in Carnap's analysis of the logical foundations of the unity of science. He states his well-known views about physicalism and, concerning the terms or predicates of the language, concludes:

The result of our analysis is that the class of observable thing-predicates is a sufficient reduction basis for the whole of the language of science, including the cognitive part of the everyday language ([1], p. 60).

Concerning the unity of laws, Carnap reaches a negative but optimistic conclusion—optimistic in the sense that the reducibility of the laws of one science to another has not been shown to be impossible. Here is what he has to say on the reduction of biological to physical laws:

There is a common language to which both the biological and the physical laws belong so that they can be logically compared and connected. We can ask whether or not a certain biological law is compatible with the system of physical laws, and whether or not it is derivable from them. But the answer to these questions cannot be inferred from the reducibility of the terms. At the present state of the development of science, it is certainly not possible to derive the biological laws from the physical ones. Some philosophers believe that such a derivation is forever impossible because of the very nature of the two fields. But the proofs attempted so far for this thesis are certainly insufficient ([1], p. 60).

Later he has the same sort of thing to say about the reduction of psychology or other social sciences to biology.

A different and less linguistic approach is to contrast the unity of scientific subject matter with the unity of scientific method. Many would agree that different sciences have different subject matters; for example, in no real sense is the subject matter of astronomy the same as that of psychopharmacology. But many would affirm that in spite of the radically different subject matters of science there are important ways in which the methods of science are the same in every domain of investigation. The most obvious and simple examples immediately come to mind. There is not one arithmetic for psychological theories of motivation and another for cosmological theories of the universe. More generally, there are not different theories of the differential and integral calculus or of partial differential equations or of probability theory. There is a great mass of mathematical methods and results that are available for use in all domains of science and that are, in fact, quite widely used in very different parts of science. There is a plausible prima facie case for the unity of science in terms of unity of scientific method. This may be one of the most reasonable meanings to be attached to any central thesis about the unity of science. However, I shall be negative even about this thesis in the sequel.

UNITY AND REDUCTIONISM

What I have said earlier about different sciences having obviously different subject matters was said too hastily because there is a historically important sense of unity. One form or another of reductionism has been central to the discussion of unity of science for a very long time. I concentrate on three such forms: reduction of language, reduction of subject matter, and reduction of method.

Reduction of Language

Carnap's views about the reduction of the language of science to commonsense language about physical objects remain appealing. He states his general thesis in such a way that no strong claims about the reduction of psychology to physics, for example, are implied, and I am sure much is correct about what he has had to say. On the other hand, it seems appropriate to emphasize the very clear senses in which there is no reduction of language. The reduction certainly does not take place in practice, and it may be rightly claimed that the reduction in theory remains in a hopelessly vague state.

There are many ways to illustrate the basis for my skepticism about any serious reduction of language. Part of my thesis about the plurality of science is that the languages of the different branches of science are diverging rather than converging as they become increasingly technical. Let me begin with a personal example. My daughter Patricia is taking a Ph.D. in neurophysiology, and she recently gave me a subscription to what is supposed to be an expository journal, entitled *Neurosciences: Research Program Bulletin*. After several efforts at reading this journal, I have reached the conclusion that the exposition is only for those in nearby disciplines. I quote one passage from an issue dealing with neuron-target cell interactions.

The above studies define the anterograde transsynaptic regulation of adrenergic ontogeny. Black and co-workers (1972b) have also demonstrated that postsynaptic neurons regulate presynaptic development through a retrograde process. During the course of maturation, presynaptic ChAc activity increased 30- to 40-fold (Figure 19), and this rise paralleled the formation of ganglionic synapses (Figure 20). If postsynaptic adrenergic neurons in neonatal rats were chemically destroyed with 6-hydroxydopamine (Figure 24) or immunologically destroyed with antiserum to NGF (Figure 25), the normal development of presynaptic ChAc activity was prevented. These data, viewed in conjunction with the anterograde regulation studies, lead to the conclusion that there is a bidirectional flow of regulatory information at the synapse during development ([6], p. 253).

This is by no means the least intelligible passage. It seems to me it illustrates the cognitive facts of life. The sciences are diverging and there is no reason to think that any kind of convergence will ever occur. Moreover, this divergence is not something of recent origin. It has been present for a long time in that oldest of quantitative sciences, astronomy, and it is now increasingly present throughout all branches of science.

There is another point I want to raise in opposition to a claim made by some philosophers and philosophically minded physicists. Some persons have held that in the physical sciences at least, substantial theoretical unification can be expected in the future and, with this unification, a unification of the theoretical language of the physical sciences, thereby simplifying the cognitive problem of understanding various domains. I have skepticism about this thesis that I shall explain later, but at this point I wish to emphasize that it takes care of only a small part of the difficulties. It is the experimental language of the physical sciences as well as of the other sciences that is difficult to understand, much more so for the outsider than the theoretical language. There is, I believe, no comparison in the cognitive difficulty for a philosopher of reading theoretical articles in quantum mechanics and reading current experimental articles in any developed branch of physics. The experimental literature is simply impossible to penetrate without a major learning effort. There are reasons for this impenetrability that I shall not attempt to go into on this occasion but stipulate to let stand as a fact.

Personally I applaud the divergence of language in science and find in it no grounds for skepticism or pessimism about the continued growth of science. The irreducible pluralism of languages of science is as desirable a feature as is the irreducible plurality of political views in a democracy.

Reduction of Subject Matter

At least since the time of Democritus in the 5th century B.C., strong and attractive theses about the reduction of all phenomena to atoms in motion have been set forth. Because of the striking scientific successes of the atomic theory of matter since the beginning of the 19th century, this theory has dominated the views of plain men and philosophers alike. In one sense, it is difficult to deny that everything in the universe is nothing but some particular swarm of particles. Of course, as we move into the latter part of the 20th century, we recognize this fantasy for what it is. We are no longer clear about what we mean by particles or even if the concept as originally stated is anywhere near the mark. The universe is indeed made of something but we are vastly ignorant of what that something is. The more we probe, the more it seems that the kind of simple and orderly view advanced as part of ancient atomism and that seemed so near realization toward the end of the 19th century is even further from being a true description. To reverse the phrase used earlier, it is not swarms of particles that things are made of, but particles that are made of swarms. There are still physicists about who hold that we will one day find the ultimate simples out of which all other things are made, but as such claims have been continually revised and as the complexity of high-energy physics and elementary particle theory has increased, there seems little reason that we shall ever again be able to seriously believe in the strong sense of reduction that Democritus so attractively formulated.

To put the matter in a skeptical fashion, we cannot have a reduction of subject matter to the ultimate physical entities because we do not know what those entities are. I have on another occasion [8] expressed my reasons for holding that Aristotle's theory of matter may be sounder and more sensible than the kind of simpleminded atomistic reductionist views dominating our thinking about the physical world for 200 years.

There is another appealing argument against reduction of subject matter in the physical sense that does not rest on the controversy about the status of mental events but on what has happened in the development of computers. Perhaps for the first time we have become fully and completely aware that the same cognitive structures can be realized in physically radically different ways. I have in mind the fact that we now have computers that are built on quite different physical principles; for example, old computers using vacuum tubes and modern computers using semiconductors can execute exactly the same programs and can perform exactly the same tasks. The differences in physical properties are striking between these two generations of computers. They stand in sharp contrast to different generations of animal species, which have very similar physical constitutions but which may have very different cultural histories. It has often been remarked upon that men of quite similar constitutions can have quite different thoughts. The computer case stands this argument on its head—it is not that the hardware is the same and the software different but rather that the hardware is radically different and the software of thoughts the same. Reduction in this situation, below the level of the concepts of information processing, seems wholly uninteresting and barren. Reduction to physical concepts is not only impractical but also theoretically empty.

The same kinds of arguments against reductionism of subject matter can be found even within physics. A familiar example is the currently accepted view that it is hopeless to try to solve the problems of quantum chemistry by applying the fundamental laws of quantum mechanics. It is hopeless in the same way that it is hopeless to program a computer to play the perfect chess game by always looking ahead to all possible future moves. The combinatorial explosion is so drastic and so overwhelming that theoretical arguments can be given that not only now but also in the future it will be impossible by direct computation to reduce the problems of quantum chemistry to problems of ordinary quantum mechanics. Quantum chemistry, in spite of its proximity to quantum mechanics, is and will remain an essentially autonomous discipline. At the level of computability, reduction is not only practically impossible but theoretically so as well.

An impressive substantive example of reduction is the reduction of large parts of mathematics to set theory. But even here, the reduction to a single subject matter of different parts of mathematics has a kind of barren formality about it. It is not that the fact of the reduction is conceptually uninteresting but rather that it has limited interest and does not say much about many aspects of mathematics. Mathematics, like science, is made up of many different subdisciplines, each going its own way and each primarily sensitive to the nuances of its own subject matter. Moreover, as we have reached for a deeper understanding of the foundations of mathematics we have come to real-

ize that the foundations are not to be built on a bedrock of certainty but that, in many ways, developed parts of mathematics are much better understood than the foundations themselves. As in the case of physics, an effort of reduction is now an effort of reduction to we know not what.

In many ways a more significant mathematical example is the reduction of computational mathematics to computability by Turing machines, but as in the case of set theory, the reduction is irrelevant to most computational problems of theoretical or practical interest.

Reduction of Method

As I remarked earlier, many philosophers and scientists would claim that there is an important sense in which the methods of science are the same in every domain of investigation. Some aspects of this sense of unity, as I also noted, are well recognized and indisputable. The common use of elementary mathematics and the common teaching of elementary mathematical methods for application in all domains of science can scarcely be denied. But it seems to me it is now important to emphasize the plurality of methods and the vast difference in methodology of different parts of science. The use of elementary mathematics—and I emphasize *elementary* because almost all applications of mathematics in science are elementary from a mathematical standpoint—as well as the use of certain elementary statistical methods does not go very far toward characterizing the methodology of any particular branch of science. As I have emphasized earlier, it is especially the experimental methods of different branches of science that have radically different form. It is no exaggeration to say that the handbooks of experimental method for one discipline are generally unreadable by experts in another discipline (the definition of "discipline" can here be quite narrow). Physicists working in solid-state physics cannot intelligibly read the detailed accounts of method in other parts of physics. This is true even of less developed sciences like psychology. Physiological psychologists use a set of experimental methods that are foreign to psychologists specializing, for example, in educational test theory, and correspondingly the intricate details of the methodology of test construction will be unknown to almost any physiological psychologist.

Even within the narrow domain of statistical methods, different disciplines have different statistical approaches to their particular subject matters. The statistical tools of psychologists are in general quite different from those of economists. Moreover, within a single broad discipline like physics, there are in different areas great variations in the use of statistical methods, a fact that has been well documented by Paul Humphreys [2].

The unity of science arose to a fair degree as a rallying cry of philosophers trying to overcome the heavy weight of 19th-century German idealism. A half century later the picture looks very different. The period since the *Encyclopedia of Unified Science* first appeared has been the era of greatest development and expansion of science in the history of thought. The massive enterprise of science no longer needs any philosophical shoring up to protect it from errant philosophical views. The rallying cry of unity followed by three cheers for reductionism should now be replaced by a patient examination of the many ways in which different sciences differ in language, subject matter, and method, as well as by synoptic views of the ways in which they are alike.

Related to unity and reduction are the two long-standing themes of certainty of knowledge and completeness of science. In making my case for the plurality of science, I want to say something about both of these unsupported dogmas.

THE SEARCH FOR CERTAINTY

From Descartes to Russell, a central theme of modern philosophy has been the setting forth of methods by which certainty of knowledge can be achieved. The repeatedly stated intention has been to find a basis that is, on the one hand, certain and, on the other hand, adequate for the remaining superstructure of knowledge, including science. The introduction of the concept of sense data and the history of the use of this concept have dominated the search for certainty in knowledge, especially in the empirical tradition, as an alternative to direct rational knowledge of the universe.

All of us can applaud the criticism of rationalism and the justifiable concern not to accept the possibility of direct knowledge of the world without experience. But it was clearly in a desire to compete with the kind of foundation that rationalism offered that the mistaken additional step was taken of attempting to ground knowledge and experience in a way that guaranteed certainty for the results. The reduction of the analysis of experience to sense data is itself one of the grand and futile themes of reductionism, in this case largely driven by the quest for certainty. Although it is not appropriate to pursue the larger epistemological issues involved, I would like to consider some particular issues of certainty that have been important in the development of modern scientific methods.

Errors of Measurement

With the development of scientific methodology and probability theory in the 18th century, it was recognized that not only did errors in measurement arise but also that a systematic theory of these errors could be given. Fundamental memoirs on the subject were written by Simpson, Lagrange, Laplace, and others. For our purposes, what is important about these memoirs is that there was no examination of the question of the existence or nonexistence of an exact value for the quantity being measured. It was implicit in these 18th-century developments, as it was implicit in Laplace's entire theory of probability, that probabilistic considerations, including errors, arise from ignorance of true causes and that the physical universe is so constituted that in principle we should be able to achieve the exact true value of any measurable physical quantities. Throughout the 19th century it was implicit that it was simply a matter of tedious and time-consuming effort to refine the measured values of any quantity one more significant digit. Nothing fundamental stood in the way of making such a refinement. It is a curious and conceptually interesting fact that, so far as I know, no one in this period enunciated the thesis that this was all a mistake, that there were continual random fluctuations in all continuous real quantities, and that the concept of an exact value had no clear meaning.

The development of quantum mechanics in this century made physicists reluctantly but conclusively recognize that it did not make sense to claim that any physical quantity could be measured with arbitrary precision in conjunction with the simultaneous measurement of other related physical quantities. It was recognized that the inability to make exact measurement is not due to technological inadequacies of measuring equipment but is central to the fundamental theory itself.

Even within the framework of quantum mechanics, however, there has tended to be a large conceptual equivocation on the nature of uncertainty. On the one hand, the claim has been that interference from the measuring apparatus makes uncertainty a necessary consequence. In this context some aspects of uncertainty need to be noted. It is not surprising that if we measure human beings at different times and places we expect to get different measurements of height and weight. But in the case of quantum mechanics what is surprising is that variation is found in particles submitted to "identical" experimental preparations. Once again a thesis of simplicity and unity is at work. Electrons should differ only in numerical identity, not in any of their properties. And if this is not true of electrons, there should be finer particles discoverable that do satisfy such a principle of identity.

The other view, and the sounder one in my judgment, is that random fluctuations are an intrinsic part of the behavior of microscopic phenomena. No process of measurement is needed to generate these fluctuations; they are a part of nature and lead to a natural view of the impossibility of obtaining results of arbitrary precision about microscopic physical quantities.

If we examine the status of theory and experiments in other domains of science, it seems to me that similar claims about the absence of certainty can be made. The thrust for certainty associated with classical physics, British empiricism, and Kantian idealism is now spent.

THE SEARCH FOR COMPLETENESS

Views about the unity of science, coupled with views about the reduction of knowledge to an epistemologically certain basis like that of sense data, are often accompanied by an implicit doctrine of completeness. Such a doctrine is often expressed by assumptions about the uniformity of nature and assumptions about the universe being ultimately totally ordered and consequently fully knowable in character. Unity, certainty, and completeness can easily be put together to produce a delightful philosophical fantasy.

In considering problems of completeness, I begin with logic and mathematics but have as my main focus the subsequent discussion of the empirical sciences.

Logical Completeness

Logic is the one area of experience in which a really satisfactory theory of completeness has been developed. The facts are too familiar to require a detailed review. The fundamental result is Gödel's completeness theorem that in first-order logic a formula is universally valid if and only if it is logically provable. Thus, our apparatus of logical derivation is adequate to the task of deriving any valid logical formula, that is, any logical truth. What we have in first-order logic is a happy match of syntax and semantics.

On the other hand, as Kreisel has emphasized in numerous publications (e.g., [4]), this match of syntax and semantics is not used in the proof of logical theorems. Rather, general set-theoretical and topological methods are continually drawn upon. One reason is that proofs given in the syntax of elementary logic are psychologically opaque and therefore in nontrivial cases easily subject to error. Another is that it is not a natural setting for studying the relation of objects that are the focus of the theory to other related objects; as an example, even the numerical representation theorem for simple orderings cannot be proved in first-order fashion. Completeness of elementary logic is of some conceptual interest, but from a practical mathematical standpoint useless.

Incompleteness of Arithmetic

The most famous incompleteness result occurs at an elementary level, namely, at the level of arithmetic or elementary number theory. In broad conceptual terms, Gödel's result shows that any formal system whose language is rich enough to represent a minimum of arithmetic is incomplete. A much earlier and historically important incompleteness result was the following.

Incompleteness of Geometric Constructions

The three classical construction problems that the ancient Greeks could not solve by elementary means were those of trisecting an angle, doubling a cube, and squaring a circle. It was not until the 19th century that these constructions were shown to be impossible by elementary means, thereby establishing a conceptually important incompleteness result for elementary geometry.

Incompleteness of Set Theory

In the latter part of the 19th century, on the basis of the work of Frege in one direction and Cantor in another, it seemed that the theory of sets or classes was the natural framework within which to construct the rest of mathematics. Research in the 20th century on the foundations of set theory, some of it recent, has shown that there is a disturbing sense of incompleteness in set theory, when formulated as a first-order theory. The continuum hypothesis as well as the axiom of choice is independent of other principles of set theory, and, as in the case of geometry, a variety of set theories can be constructed, at least first-order set theories.

The continuum hypothesis, for example, is decidable in second-order set theory, but we do not yet know in which way, that is, as true or false. Thus there is clearly less freedom for variation in second-order set theory, but also at present much less clarity about its structure. The results of these various investigations show unequivocally that the hope for some simple and complete foundation of mathematics is not likely to be attained.

Theories with Standard Formalization

The modern logical sense of completeness for theories with standard formalization, that is, theories formalized within first-order logic, provides a sharp and definite concept that did not exist in the past. Recall that the characterization of completeness in this context is that a theory is complete if and only if every sentence of the theory is either valid in the theory or inconsistent with the theory—that is, its negation is valid in the theory.

Back of this well-defined logical notion is a long history of discussions in physics that are vaguer and less sharply formulated but that have a similar intuitive content.

Kant's Sense of Completeness

Although there is no time here to examine this history, it is worth mentioning the high point of its expression as found in Kant's *Metaphysical Foundations of Natural Science*. Kant's claim is not for the completeness of physics but for the completeness of the metaphysical foundations of physics. After giving the reason that it is desirable to separate heterogeneous principles in order to locate errors and confusions, he gives as the second reason the argument concerning completeness.

There may serve as a second ground for recommending this procedure the fact that in all that is called metaphysics the absolute completeness of the sciences may be hoped for, which is of such a sort as can be promised in no other kind of cognitions; and therefore just as in the metaphysics of nature in general, so here also the completeness of the metaphysics of corporeal nature may be confidently expected . . . .

The schema for the completeness of a metaphysical system, whether of nature in general or of corporeal nature in particular, is the table of the categories. For there are no more pure concepts of the understanding, which can concern the nature of things. ([3], pp. 10–11).

It need scarcely be said that Kant's argument in terms of the table of the categories scarcely satisfied 18th-century mathematical standards, let alone modern ones. His argument for completeness was not subtle, but his explicit focus on the issue of completeness was important and original.

The Unified Field Theory

After Kant, there was important system building in physics during the 19th century, and there were attempts by Kelvin, Maxwell, and others to reduce all known physical phenomena to mechanical models, but these attempts were not as imperialistic and forthright in spirit as Kant's. A case can be made, I think, for taking Einstein's general theory of relativity, especially the attempt at a unified field theory, as the real successor to Kant in the attempt to obtain completeness. I do not want to make the parallel between Kant and Einstein too close, however, for Einstein does not hold an a priori metaphysical view of the foundations of physics. What they do share is a strong search for completeness of theory. Einstein's goal was to find a unified field theory defining one common structure from which all forces of nature could be derived. In the grand version of the scheme, for given boundary conditions, the differential equations would have a unique solution for the entire universe, and all physical phenomena would be encompassed within the theory. The geometrodynamics of John Wheeler and his collaborators is the most recent version of the Einstein vision. Wheeler, especially, formulates the problem in a way that is reminiscent of Descartes: "Are fields and particles foreign entities immersed *in* geometry, or are they nothing *but* geometry?" ([9], p. 361).

Had the program of Einstein and the later program of Wheeler been carried to completion, my advocacy of skepticism toward the problem of completeness in empirical science would have to retreat from bold assertion of inevitable incompleteness. However, it seems to me that there is, at least in the current scientific temperament, total support for the thesis of incompleteness. Grand building of theories has currently gone out of fashion in fields as far apart as physics and sociology, and there seems to be a deeper appreciation of the problems of ever settling, in any definitive way, the fundamental laws of complex phenomena.

As the examples I have mentioned—and many others that I have not—demonstrate, in most areas of knowledge it is too much to expect theories to have a strong form of completeness. What we have learned to live with in practice is an appropriate form of completeness, but we have not built this working practice explicitly into our philosophy as thoroughly as we might. It is apparent from various examples that weak forms of completeness may be expected for theories about restricted areas of experience. It seems wholly inappropriate, unlikely, and, in many ways, absurd to expect theories that cover large areas of experience, or, in the most grandiose cases, *all* of experience, to have a strong degree of completeness.

The application of working scientific theories to particular areas of experience is almost always schematic and highly approximate in character. Whether we are predicting the behavior of elementary particles, the weather, or international trade—any phenomenon, in fact, that has a reasonable degree of complexity—we can hope only to encompass a restricted part of the phenomenon.

It is sometimes said that it is exactly the role of experimentation to isolate particular fragments of experience that can be dealt with in relatively complete fashion. This is, I think, more a dogma of philosophers who have not engaged in much experimentation than it is of practicing experimental scientists. When involved in experimentation, I have been struck by how much my schematic views of theories also apply to experimental work. First one concrete thing and then another is abstracted and simplified to make the data fit within the limited set of concepts of the theory being tested.[1]

Let me put the matter another way. A common philosophical conception of science is that it is an ever closer approximation to a set of eternal truths that hold always and everywhere. Such a conception of science can be traced from Plato through Aristotle and onward to Descartes, Kant, and more recent philosophers, and this account has no doubt been accepted by many scientists as well. It is my own view that a much better case can be

---

[1] This idea is developed in some detail in Suppes [7].

made for the kind of instrumental conception of science set forth in general terms by Peirce, Dewey, and their successors. In this view, scientific activity is perpetual problem solving. No area of experience is totally and completely settled by providing a set of basic truths; but rather, we are continually confronted with new situations and new problems, and we bring to these problems and situations a potpourri of scientific methods, techniques, and concepts, which in many cases we have learned to use with great facility.

The concept of objective truth does not directly disappear in such a view of science, but what we might call the cosmological or global view of truth is looked at with skepticism just as is a global or cosmological view of completeness. Like our own lives and endeavors, scientific theories are local and are designed to meet a given set of problems. As new problems arise new theories are needed, and in almost all cases the theories used for the old set of problems have not been tested to the fullest extent feasible nor been confirmed as broadly or as deeply as possible, but the time is ripe for something new, and we move on to something else. Again this conception of science does not mean that there cannot be continued correction in a sequence of theories meeting a particular sequence of problems; but it does urge that the sequence does not necessarily converge. In fact, to express the kind of incompleteness I am after, we can even make the strong assumption that in many domains of experience the scientific theory that replaces the best old theory is always an improvement, and therefore we have a kind of monotone increasing sequence. Nonetheless, as in the case of a strictly monotone increasing sequence of integers, there is no convergence to a finite value—the sequence is never completed—and so it is with scientific theories. There is no bounded fixed result toward which we are converging or that we can hope ever to achieve. Sci-

entific knowledge, like the rest of our knowledge, will forever remain pluralistic and highly schematic in character.

REFERENCES

1. Carnap, R. "Logical Foundations of the Unity of Science." In *International Encyclopedia of Unified Science*, Volume 1, Part 1. Edited by O. Neurath, et al. Chicago: University of Chicago Press, 1938. Pages 42–62.

2. Humphreys, P. *Inquiries in the Philosophy of Probability: Randomness and Independence.* Unpublished Ph.D. Dissertation, Stanford University, 1976. Xerox University Microfilms Publication No. 76–18774.

3. Kant, Immanuel. *Die metaphysischen Anfangsgründe der Naturwissenschaft*, 1786 (As reprinted as *Metaphysical Foundations of Natural Science* [trans.] J. Ellington. Indianapolis: Bobbs-Merrill, 1970. Pages 1–134).

4. Kreisel, G. "Informal Rigor and Completeness Proofs." In *Problems in the Philosophy of Mathematics.* Edited by I. Lakatos. Amsterdam: North-Holland, 1967. Pages 138–171.

5. Neurath, O. "Unified Science as Encyclopedic Integration." In *International Encyclopedia of Unified Science*, Volume 1, Part 1. Edited by O. Neurath, et al. Chicago: University of Chicago Press, 1938. Pages 1–27.

6. Smith, B. H., and Kreutzberg, G. W. "Neuron-target Cell Interactions." *Neurosciences Research Program Bulletin* 14(1976): 211–453.

7. Suppes, P. "Models of Data." In *Logic, Methodology and Philosophy of Science: Proceedings of the 1960 International Congress.* Edited by E. Nagel, et al. Stanford, Calif.: Stanford University Press, 1962. Pages 252–261.

8. ———. "Aristotle's Concept of Matter and Its Relation to Modern Concepts of Matter." *Synthese* 28(1974): 27–50.

9. Wheeler, J. A. "Curved Empty Space-time as the Building Material of the Physical World: An Assessment." In *Logic, Methodology and Philosophy of Science: Proceedings of the 1960 International Congress.* Edited by E. Nagel, et al. Stanford, Calif.: Stanford University Press, 1962. Pages 361–374.

Unity and Method in Contemporary Science*

Dudley Shapere

Listen: there's a hell of a good universe next door;
let's go.

—*e.e. cummings*

I

One of the most striking features of the history of science is that, despite numerous setbacks along the way, there has, overall, been a tendency toward the development of more and more comprehensive unification of the various fields of science. Newton fused terrestrial and planetary motions into a unified theory at the end of the seventeenth century. But it was in the second half of the nineteenth century that unification of scientific fields began in earnest. In spite of the differences between electricity and magnetism (and between various types of electricity) which had been noted by investigators beginning with Gilbert, Faraday was able to provide a unified treatment of those types of phenomena. His approach was developed and given a mathematically precise formulation by Maxwell, who was also able to extend it

further by incorporating light into the same theory. The study of heat too was assimilated to other areas, partly to the theory of radiation and partly to the theory of the motion of particles. As if in protest against what Einstein called the "profound formal difference" between the nineteenth century's treatment of electromagnetism and light by a continuous (wave) theory on the one hand, and of matter in terms of a discrete particle theory on the other, the twentieth century provided a unification of those domains in the quantum theory. With that theory came, too, an understanding of the periodic table of chemical elements and of the bonding of those elements into larger complexes, as well as of the spectra of chemical substances.

The years between the development of quantum mechanics in the late 1920s and the Second World War were concerned largely with extension rather than with unification of pre-existing areas; the period saw, among other things, the beginnings of understanding of the electromagnetic force (beginnings of quantum electrodynamics), of radioactive decay, and of the nuclear force (Yukawa exchange-particle theory). Postwar physicists generalized these results in a clear recognition that there are three fundamental types of forces important in elementary particle interactions, the electromagnetic, the weak, and the strong, and in particular developed the theory of the electromagnetic force, quantum electrodynamics, into the most successful scientific theory ever devised. (The fourth recognized force, gravitation, is too weak to play any effective role except where large masses are involved.) But the vast number of particles discovered during the postwar period, and the existence of four apparently independent fundamental forces, again awakened the

---

* [Note added, 1982] Some of the scientific ideas described in this paper—particularly in the portions on elementary particle physics—are by now outdated, the paper having been written in 1976. However, the more general points I made here remain valid, embodying as they do features which have been characteristic of the scientific approach throughout recent times and remain so despite the dramatic advances of the past six years. Since those points, and the features of the scientific cases on which they rest, are important . . . , I have therefore kept the article in its original form. There would have been little point in bringing the scientific discussions up to date, only to find them again superseded in a few years, unless it could be shown that science has altered so drastically in the past six years that those features are no longer found in it. And even then, as always, there might be important lessons to learn even from such ancient science as that of the mid-1970s.

From "Unification and Fractionation in Science: Significance and Prospects," in *The Search for Absolute Values: Harmony Among the Sciences,* Proceedings of the Fifth International Conference of the Unity of the Sciences (Washington, D.C., 1976), pp. 867–880. Reprinted by permission of the International Cultural Foundation Press.

urge toward unification. As regards the multitude of elementary particles, Gell-Mann and Ne'eman showed that the hadrons (particles interacting via the strong force) fall into well-defined families which are representations of the symmetry group SU(3). A further representation of that group, corresponding to no known particles, constituted a family of three; when appropriate quantum numbers were assigned to the members of this family, it was found that the quantum numbers of all hadrons could be obtained as the result of adding the quantum numbers of this family in pairs (mesons) or triplets (baryons). These "quarks" could therefore be considered to be the constituents of hadrons. More recently still, the addition of further quantum numbers ("charm" and "color") and of a fourth quark, in order to account for the stability of the π (or J) particle, has produced the suggestion, at least, of an analogy between hadrons and leptons (particles not participating in the strong interaction): As there are four fundamental leptons (electron, muon, and their respective neutrinos), so also there are now four fundamental hadrons; like the leptons, the quarks appear to be dimensionless points and therefore true candidates for the status of being "fundamental" (i.e., with no further internal structure); and the leptons and quarks have the same spin (1/2). The analogy is far from complete: For example, leptons do not combine to form composite structures, as do quarks; further, leptons are observed in experiments, while quarks, if they exist as free particles, seem somehow to evade all attempts to observe them. (The fact that the charges of quarks are fractions of those of leptons may not be a serious disanalogy, as Han and Nambu have shown.) Nevertheless, the analogy is there, and its existence, coupled with increasing experimental success of the four-quark hypothesis, cannot help but suggest some deeper relationship between those particles which interact via the strong force and those which do not.

As regards the four fundamental forces, after enormous obstacles had been overcome, a unification of the electromagnetic and weak interactions is now available (unified gauge theory of Salam and Weinberg), and there is hope of extending that theory to cover the strong interactions. The unified gauge and colored- and charmed-quark theories are bound together, so that the prospect of a giant step in the direction of a unified theory of elementary particles and three of the four fundamental forces now lies before us. (The possibility that there are further forces—and indications are growing that there are at least two others, a "superweak" and a "semistrong" force—could not detract from the significance of such unification as has, hopefully, been achieved, but would only set a challenge for further unification.)

The application of spectroscopy to analysis of chemical composition made it possible—despite Auguste Comte's pronouncement of the impossibility of our ever knowing the composition of the stars—to ascertain that the stars are made of the same substances as are found on earth. The development of an understanding, in terms of quantum theory, of how spectra are produced, together with the theory of elementary particle interactions, has provided an understanding of the processes of stellar evolution, and has, with the further occasional cooperation of the theory of general relativity, led to an understanding of the synthesis, evolution, and relative abundances of the chemical elements. The alliance of general relativity and elementary particle theory, especially when coupled with recent observations, has even made possible reasonably-based theories of the origin of the universe in a "hot big bang."

Thus far I have surveyed some examples of unification in the physical sciences; but the biological sciences cannot be omitted from this picture. Some examples of unification in those areas are the following. Despite the apparent conflict between Darwinian evolutionary theory and Mendelian genetics at the beginning of the twentieth century, those areas were shown to be consistent by Fisher, Haldane, and Wright; further integration at the hands of Dobzhansky, Rensch, Simpson, Mayr and many others, produced a "Synthetic Theory of Evolution" which was at least consistent with, and to a considerable degree explanatory of, evidence from a number of fields which had hitherto seemed incompatible. Chemical understanding of biological inheritance began to be achieved in detail in the mid-twentieth century and has begun to penetrate the area of organismic development. The work of Oparin and his successors showed that Darwin had been too pessimistic in forecasting that the origin of life could never be an object of scientific investigation, and numerous mechanisms are now known for the production of at least the basic constituents of self-replicating macromolecules. The study of the animal brain, though still rudimentary, has produced associations of various conscious functions with specific regions of the brain, giving reason to expect that improved understanding of, for example, human psychology will ultimately be forthcoming from such investigations. (Except for this remark, I will limit my discussion in this paper to the physical and biological sciences.)

Taken together, the developments I have described provide a broad and coherent picture of the universe and man's place in it. In outline, the picture goes something like this. The universe—at least the one we know—began in (or at least became after a fraction of a second) a hot (of the order of 10^{12}–10^{13} K) dense (around 10^{14} g/cm^3) soup of elementary particles. From this state, after a few minutes (for which period the detailed calculations that can be made are nothing short of mind-boggling), emerged a matter–radiation equilibrium in which the matter consisted of roughly 75 percent hydrogen nuclei (protons) and 25 percent helium nuclei (alpha particles). Further cooling enabled electrons, after a few hundred thousand years, to combine with these nuclei, ending the matter–radiation coupling. At some time a few million years later, inhomogeneities developed in the cloud of matter; these inhomogeneities, or at least those of an appropriate size, collapsed gravitationally to form clusters of galaxies, sub-inhomogeneities (or at least those of an appropriate size) collapsing within the larger inhomogeneities to form galaxies. As the galaxies took shape, stars began to form and evolve within them; under the conditions of high temperature and pressure existing in the interiors of those stars, hydrogen and helium underwent nuclear reactions which produced many of the heavier elements; those stars

which ultimately died in violent explosions (and which, in the process of exploding, created further heavy elements) spewed those heavier elements into the interstellar medium, where they became available for the birth of later-generation, heavy-element-enriched stars. Some proportion of those later-generation stars can be expected to be born with planetary systems; on some of these planets, under favorable circumstances, the production of complex molecules, and ultimately of self-replicating macromolecules, will eventuate in the evolution of higher forms of life. The transmission of hereditary information from generation to generation of these living creatures, as well as the variations in that information which lead to evolutionary changes, and the development and functioning of individual organisms, can be understood in terms of chemical processes and the physical processes which affect and ultimately explain them.

We thus obtain a coherent view of the evolution of the universe and of life in it as a continuous process understandable in terms of the same ultimate laws. Not all of the parts of this picture are equally well-grounded. I am not thinking here of the fact that the "details" of the picture are far from being worked out, or that the picture has yet to be extended to many areas; although the working out of details often produces surprising problems which ultimately upset the grander scheme, the difficulties I am thinking of are known ones which cannot be dismissed as due merely to lack of detailed knowledge. Nor am I thinking of the fact that parts of the picture may ultimately come to be looked on as mere "limiting cases" of some larger theory. Let me explain the sorts of problems I have in mind by beginning with an example of a difficulty that can be considered to be the result of a need to "fill in details." This difficulty concerns the birth of stars from an interstellar medium. Small dark globules and highly localized infrared sources have been observed which are presumably "protostars," stars (or at least stellar "placentas") in the very early stages of birth, fragmenting from a larger cloud of gas and dust and collapsing toward a stage where nuclear reactions will be initiated in their interiors. And certain stars are observed which, there is reason to believe, are only relatively recently born. However, how the protostars uncouple from their environment, and what happens between the observed putative protostar stage and the emergence of the fully-born star is unknown. Though the critical factors can be listed, their precise contributions are uncertain and the problem is highly complex. Nevertheless, there is good reason to believe *that* the general "fragmentation-and-collapse" account of stellar birth is "on the right track," and that it is only the details of *how* this takes place that are not yet understood.

The situation is presumably the same with regard to the transition from laboratory synthesis of relatively small constituents of DNA (or some presumably primitive analogue) to the production of the giant self-replicating macromolecule itself: The gap is enormous and not yet understood. Here, however, there is a hitch that was not present in the case of the "gap" between protostars and stars: In the case of stars, observational evidence indicates that star formation is relatively widespread and therefore has at least a decent probability of occurrence given a proper interstellar medium and proper conditions which are themselves fairly common. But in the case of the evolution of life from inorganic molecules, we have only one planet to look at—one case in which such evolution has actually occurred. And in the absence of an understanding of a mechanism for evolution from relatively small macromolecules to huge self-replicating ones, we do not know what the probabilities of such an occurrence are. In spite of the overwhelming statistics that astronomers like to throw at us about the probable numbers of planets in the universe having conditions favorable to life (once produced), the probability of nature jumping the gap from chemistry to biology may yet be so low that earth's life may be unique or near-unique in the universe, vast as it is. The "filling in of details" in this case thus has ramifications beyond those of the star-formation gap: There, the probability of gap-jumping—the existence of a mechanism, however little understood, which is widespread in the universe—was not in question; here, it is.

Yet a third level of difficulty, this time by no means reducible to a matter of "filling in details," occurs in the case of the birth of galaxy clusters and galaxies. Luckily for theoreticians, observational evidence (such as the apparent black-body character of the 3°K microwave background radiation) indicates that the universe is, in the large, homogeneous and isotropic, and that such conditions held in the early universe, before galaxies and clusters of galaxies fragmented out. Where, then, did the *inhomogeneities* postulated in our picture of the origin of galaxy clusters come from? (The theoretician no longer seems so fortunate.) In a universe in which quantum theory holds, fluctuations would arise spontaneously; these *might* be amplified in the relatively dense conditions of the early universe, and inhomogeneities of the proper size (galaxy-cluster-size and galaxy-size) *might* be selected out as ones which would collapse rather than be washed out. But thus far, no good theory of galaxy (or galaxy cluster) formation along these or any other lines has been forthcoming. However, the situation here is potentially more dangerous than mere lack of a good theory might suggest. Two independent considerations in particular make this so. First: Evidence is now very strong that the nuclei of galaxies are regions from which enormous amounts of matter (and energy) are expelled, presumably periodically. Ambartsumian and others have suggested that the expelled matter is the source of new galaxies. The nuclei of the new galaxies might in turn carry the matter-producing capability. (There is even some hint of evidence that some small galaxies may have been ejected from larger ones.) On this view, the collapse theory of galaxy (or galaxy cluster) formation, already burdened with the problem of the origin of appropriately-sized inhomogeneities, would be rejected in favor of a "little-bang" theory of their origin. The second relevant consideration is this: Why are clusters of galaxies still in existence if, as the cosmological inhomogeneity theory alleges, they were formed several billion years ago? If they are to have the gravitational stability required for such a long life, the clusters would have to have a certain mass to counterbalance their motions. The observed masses, however, fall short of the minimum required in every specific cluster for which mass-estimates are available, and by factors ranging from five to fifty or more. (Needless to say, estimating the total mass of a cluster of galaxies is a risky business; but could the observational uncertainties be of such a magnitude? and all in the same direction, of underestimation?) Is the missing mass present in "invisible" form—black holes, dead stars and galaxies, for example? There are difficulties with such proposals, and one must remember with soberness that once before when there was a "missing mass" problem (the advance of the perihelion of Mercury), the problem was solved not by finding the missing mass but by revolutionizing physics. Taken together with the problem of the origin of inhomogeneities, these two considerations cannot but lessen our confidence in the "collapse of cosmological inhomogeneities" part of our picture; they suggest that Ambartsumian's alternative cannot be dismissed out of hand. Indeed, were it not for the black-body character of the microwave background radiation, the observed helium abundance in the universe, and some other difficulties, one might be tempted to reconsider the Steady-State theory, with matter being continually (or at least sporadically) created in galactic nuclei rather than in intergalactic space. Nevertheless, although the history of science has often witnessed supposedly dead theories rise, phoenix-like, from their ashes, the objections against the Steady-State theory seem at present insurmountable; and Ambartsumian's suggestion is too undeveloped to be called a theory. (And how are we supposed to account for the huge amounts of matter and energy somehow produced out of the galactic nuclei? Would it be genuine creation *ex nihilo?* What would then become of the principle of conservation of energy? An alternative that has been suggested—not easy to swallow—is that matter comes through a "white hole" from another universe.) Hence, despite its difficulties, and in view of the slim observational evidence in its favor (distribution of globular clusters and of older stars), the cosmological theory of the origin of galaxies and galaxy clusters remains the best available. (However, that theory may be in for further trouble

if small-scale anisotropies in the microwave background radiation continue not to be detected. Such anisotropies would be expected, on the cosmological theory of the origin of galaxy clusters, as relics of the original inhomogeneities.)

In this case, the nature of the difficulty may be summarized as follows: (1) contrary to the "lack of details" kind of problem, in this case the initial (or relatively early) conditions (the inhomogeneities or their relics) are not observed; (2) it is difficult, in the light of other considerations, to see how the appropriate conditions could be realized (how the appropriate inhomogeneities could arise); (3) there are other independent considerations which suggest an alternative possible explanation; (4) that alternative, however, is not as palatable as the theory available (in the present case because it has not been developed in detail, and because its development would seem to call for radical revision of other well-grounded ideas, or else for the introduction of radically new ideas for which there is little or no other warrant). This is one type of difficulty that might be classified under the heading of a *fundamental theoretical problem*—as opposed to the star-formation "filling in details" type of difficulty, which appears almost certain to be a *problem of theoretical incompleteness.*

These are far from the only known reasons for hesitancy about the picture I have drawn. One can of course expect a sensible caution about the cosmological portions of the picture, involving as they do such enormous extrapolations; and one can expect a tentative attitude toward the most recent attempts at synthesis. Heisenberg went to his grave opposing the quark theory, and we must remember that quarks are, after all, unobserved; and one would suppose that a scientific theory would have to be very good indeed if it is to maintain that the fundamental postulated entities are unobserv*able.* And as I remarked earlier, the symmetry between quarks and leptons is very incomplete. But there are also difficulties in parts of the picture that are of longer standing. The strong interaction borders on the intractable; the origin of planetary systems is still shrouded in obscurities; the origin of taxa higher than the species level remains something of an embarrassment for evolutionary theory; the problem of development in biology remains complex and very incompletely solved; the later stages of stellar evolution are still unclear, as indeed is the ultimate fate of the universe—whether it will go on expanding forever (as seems to be the slightly favored view at present) or will ultimately collapse again to a singularity, and, if so, whether it will "bounce" to produce yet another in a possibly continuous train of successive universes. These and their like can perhaps be said to be merely open questions, problems of theoretical incompleteness—matters of detail or extension of present knowledge and theory—rather than fundamental theoretical problems, overt threats to present theory (though some may have larger philosophical ramifications than others). But there are more serious difficulties too, which, though in some cases they differ significantly in general character from the problem of galaxy cluster formation, deserve to rank with the latter as fundamental theoretical problems, as dark clouds on the horizon of contemporary science. Whatever happens to our interpretation of quasars, something drastic may well happen to current physics. If quasars are "local"—relatively nearby—then we must account for their very large red shifts in some way other than as indications of great distance—possibly as effects of a large gravitational field (but then why are no other effects of the field observed?), or in terms of some entirely new law (but will that affect our interpretation of other red shifts as indicating an expansion of the universe?). If they are "cosmological"—very far away—we are faced with the problem of explaining energy production that appears to put even nuclear fusion to shame. In particular, if quasars turn out to be related to galactic nuclei (and there are strong indications that they are), then we again face the problem of the origin and nature of galaxies. There are difficulties with either alternative. In every problem in science there is the possibility of the unforeseeable; but in this case, unlike most others, we can as it were see that the unforeseeable is a *significant* possibility. Again, the failure to detect neutrinos from the sun has cast doubt on our theories of stellar evolution, and some have suggested that it indicates some shortcoming in

our grasp of elementary particle interactions. Quantum theory and general relativity remain apart, and years of trying have not produced agreed-on progress toward their synthesis, or even general agreement as to how to try. For all its success in dealing with phenomena in a wide range of domains, the quantum theory has in the past decade or two been subjected to a revival of controversy as to its interpretation. Is a deterministic hidden-variable theory still feasible? Is precise determination of simultaneous position and momentum of a particle really impossible? One interpretation (Everett-Wheeler "relative state" interpretation) of quantum theory, which has the virtue of consistency if not of initial plausibility, has it that the universe splits into two independent universes on the occasion of every measurement, the two universes corresponding to the alternative possible outcomes of the measurement. With that, we have flirted, in this survey, with the possibility of parallel universes, successive universes, and now with possible universes being actualized. The past history of science has time and again produced new ideas that far outstripped prior imagination; speculation about other universes, though still on the borders, has entered the domain of science. We must be prepared for the possibility that there are indeed more things in heaven and earth than are dreamt of in our present picture of the universe. Even other universes.

But while we must keep an open mind about possible radical revisions of the picture of the universe and of life in it which I outlined earlier, we must also recognize that it is, I think it is fair to say, the picture within which the majority of physicists, chemists, and biologists today work. They work within it not in the sense that they accept it dogmatically, but in the sense that they believe it to be, overall, the picture best supported by present evidence, and that they believe the present task of science to be the development of the details of that picture, its further extension, and its testing and confrontation with alternative reasonable possibilities, especially in those parts of the picture which seem weakest. Much of the picture, indeed, seems unlikely to be rejected: What evidence could reasonably be expected that would lead us to deny, after all, that galaxies are stellar systems far beyond the Milky Way? that dinosaurs existed in the past? that DNA is at least implicated in heredity? And so on for a multitude of details which form the basis of much of our present picture. It is possible, of course—as philosophers since Descartes have been fond of reminding us—that these and indeed all facets of the picture may ultimately be rejected. But the logical possibility that we may be wrong, though it may be a reason for open-mindedness, is not itself a reason for skepticism or even for timid and indiscriminate caution. (This is the reason why I have emphasized that the difficulties I have been concerned with are *known* difficulties, which are, after all, the only ones we can hope to do something about.) And even in those regions of our picture for which we do have positive reasons for worry, we must not forget that, in the light of the available evidence, one picture may well be better than any of the available alternatives.

One final point in this all-too-sketchy survey of some aspects of the unity of the current scientific picture of the universe: There will be some who will claim that my account is "reductionistic," and who will claim that—for example—biology is *not* "reduced" to chemistry because all details of biological processes are not deducible from the chemistry of those processes. In this vein, since the details of the helium atom are not in general deducible from basic quantum-theoretical considerations as is the case with the hydrogen atom, one might as well say that physics has not been reduced to physics. If this is meant to imply that, to the extent that we cannot make such deductions, we do not have an *understanding* of the helium atom in terms of quantum theory (or of biology in terms of chemistry), then perhaps the fault lies in the deductive interpretation of understanding (or "explanation") which decrees that only deduction produces understanding. We do, after all, have such understanding despite the lack of precise deduction; and a more adequate account of "understanding" should allow for this. No doubt there is much in biology that is not understood in terms of chemistry; perhaps it can never be. But if this turns out to be the case, it will be because of specific aspects of the world, and

not because of some prior philosophical strictures about what *understanding* (or *explaining*) means.

II

In the preceding discussion I argued that, as a result of the evolution of scientific thought, there has emerged a broad and coherent picture of the universe and of life in it, a view which, while incomplete and in some aspects open to serious question, is at present the best picture available. In the present section I will argue that this process of unification has not been restricted to the integration of beliefs about the world, but that there has also been a progressive tendency toward unification of those beliefs with the methods employed to attain well-grounded beliefs. That is, I will argue, the methods we consider appropriate for arriving at well-grounded beliefs about the world have come more and more to be shaped by those very beliefs, and have evolved with the evolution of knowledge.

Such a view of the intimate relation between knowledge and the methods of gaining knowledge flies in the face of the traditional sharp bifurcation of the two. For it is, and long has been, commonly assumed that there exists a unique method, the "scientific" or "empirical" or "experimental" method, allegedly discovered or at least first systematically applied in the seventeenth century, which can be formulated wholly independently of, and is wholly unaffected by, the knowledge which is arrived at by its means. It is as though scientific method is a set of abstract and immutable rules, like the rules of chess, independent of the strategies of the game but governing what strategies are possible.

Yet the most strenuous efforts of scientists and philosophers have failed to produce agreement as to precisely what that method is. Indeed, general philosophical theories about science according to which there is an eternal scientific method, which, once discovered, needs only to be applied to generate knowledge, but which itself will not alter in the light of that knowledge, have proved to be either empty or false. Consider, for example, the view that science does not (or should not) admit concepts referring to what is "in principle" unobservable. The phrase "in principle" is a slippery one; but on any reasonable interpretation, what is "observable," even "in principle," changes with the development of new techniques, discoveries, and theories (think of the "direct observation" of the core of the sun by observing neutrinos). And on the other hand, perhaps the quark theory, if it is ultimately accepted, will have taught us not only something about nature, but also about what to do in explaining nature: about a role for the unobservable that was not allowed for by the straitjackets of philosophies of science that take observability to be something that is laid down forever. Similarly, what is "verifiable" and "falsifiable" can only be determined by the way things are, and our *beliefs about* what is verifiable and falsifiable can only be determined by our beliefs about the way things are. What for yesterday's science was considered unverifiable (hypotheses about the constitution of the stars, or about the origin of life) may today be a legitimate part of science; what some consider to be beyond the "line of demarcation" of the legitimately scientific (the unobservable, the unverifiable, the unfalsifiable) may at some stage, for good reasons, come to be a legitimate part of science (confined quarks, whose existence is unverifiable—unless, of course, we are willing to stretch the meaning of "verifiable" so that their existence is "verifiable" even though they are "unobservable"; but the philosophy of science has long been acquainted with the bankruptcy of such moves). Observability, verifiability, falsifiability, criteria for being a legitimate scientific problem (as opposed to a "pseudo-problem"), criteria for being a scientific possibility (as opposed to "metaphysics")—all these come, more and more in the development of science, to depend on the substantive content of accepted (well-grounded) scientific belief, and change with changes in that content. A sketch of some important developments in the history of science will indicate some ways in which this has come about.

In the seventeenth century, the boundaries between science, philosophy, theology, and mysticism were not drawn sharply. This fact must not be seen as evidence of some sort of intellectual schizophrenia on the part of the scientists concerned, or as an indication that they sometimes did science "badly." Consider Kepler: He was probably the first thinker to insist that every detail of our experience be accounted for precisely in terms of underlying mathematical laws. All experience was for Kepler interconnected by mathematical (for him, geometrical) relationships, and those interrelationships were clues to still deeper ones. In the light of this belief, Kepler felt compelled to ask not only such questions as, What is the precise relationship between the orbital speed of a planet and its distance from the sun? but also—*and in the same spirit*—What is the relation between the color of a planet and its distance? and, Given two planets forming a given angle at a person's birthplace at the time of his birth, what relationship does this fact have to his later life? and, What is the relationship between the "harmonies" in the motions of the planets and the harmonies in music (and in art and meteorology and . . .)? Angles formed by planets with locations on earth were as much "details of our experience" as, and had as much significance as, the angles swept out by a planetary radius vector in a given time. Within the general framework of his geometrical approach, Kepler knew no constraints on the kinds of questions to ask or the kinds of observable relationships it was appropriate to ask them about. Such constraints would later be introduced in the light of accumulating knowledge. For Newton, the planets were just further material bodies, obeying the law of inertia and exerting and responding to gravitational forces; their relative positions had nothing to do with either man or music. On the other hand, Newton still regarded theological considerations as relevant to his science: Indeed, he saw his science as implying the necessity of periodic miraculous intervention by God in order to preserve the stability of the universe against the continual decrease in "quantity of motion" (momentum) due to collisions, against the disruption of the solar system through mutual planetary perturbations, and against either gravitational collapse in a universe containing a finite amount of matter, or a cancellation of all net gravitational forces in an infinite universe containing an infinite amount of matter (Bentley-Seeliger paradox). Laplace, having seen the resolution of problems about elastic and inelastic collisions and conservation principles that had plagued Newton's era, and himself claiming to have shown that planetary perturbations are self-correcting in the long run—but forgetting about the Bentley paradox—was able to inform Napoleon that science had no need of the hypothesis of God.

In such ways, as science progresses, constraints come to be imposed on the kinds of questions to be asked, and on the kinds of possibilities that can be legitimately envisaged, in science. But the development of such "rules of the game" is not all negative—not always a matter of cutting out questions and possibilities that had hitherto been considered legitimate. For the progress of science also, at various stages, through new discoveries, approaches, techniques, and theories, opens the door to new possibilities—new questions and new alternatives that were before ruled out as illegitimate or perhaps even self-contradictory or inconceivable. The work of Gauss and Riemann opened the way for thinking of a space

with variable characteristics—a possibility which Newton, with good reasons at the time, rejected as self-contradictory in dismissing Descartes' similar suggestion. And no one needs to be reminded that quantum mechanics and relativity opened the floodgates for questions and theoretical concepts which would previously have been rejected out of hand. The idea that quantum theory contains its own theory of measurement, and even refashions the rules of logic in its own image, is completely consistent with the viewpoint I have suggested.

That viewpoint maintains that method not only determines the course of science, but is itself shaped by the knowledge attained in that enterprise. In many ways, scientific method is more like military strategy than it is like the rules of chess: The strategy shapes the course of the campaign, but is itself responsive to the lay of the land, and to the armaments that become available to it; and it adjusts to new situations and new devices. Science has not only tended to move toward unification of its substantive beliefs; it has also tended to move toward unification of belief and method. It has learned how to learn in the very process of learning.

REALISM VERSUS ANTI-REALISM: THE ONTOLOGICAL IMPORT OF SCIENTIFIC KNOWLEDGE

5 Do the theories of science give a literally true account of the way the world is? Do the entities and processes they postulate really exist? Consider one such theory, Copernican astronomy. When it was proposed in the middle of the sixteenth century, a small group of astronomers thought that its central hypothesis—that the earth moves while the sun and stars do not, the actual motions of the earth explaining the merely apparent motions of the sun and stars—was literally true. The hypothesis was, after all, supported by a wide variety of observational evidence, and it did, after all, lead to the discovery of new facts. What's more, Copernican astronomy explained facts that its predecessor, Ptolemaic astronomy, merely postulated (for example, that the five visible planets, but not the sun or moon, show retrograde motion), and it provided determinate values of quantities that Ptolemaic astronomy had not (for example, the distances of the planets). Most astronomers, however, while granting that Copernicus's theory was an improvement over Ptolemy's in regard to both observational accuracy and theoretical adequacy, still emphasized that Copernicus's theory conflicted with other accepted knowledge (for example, Holy Scripture and Aristotelian physics), and was, at any rate, only one of the systems that could be constructed to account for the observational data. They concluded that Copernicus's theory was merely a calculating device, useful for deriving important astronomical information, but not to be taken as literally true. Who was right?

This kind of question seemed settled in Part 3. There we considered six major approaches to theory testing currently in the forefront of discussion: (1) justificationism; (2) falsificationism; (3) conventionalism; (4) the methodology of scientific research programmes; (5) Thomas Kuhn's sociological approach; and (6) the testing paradigm of scientific inference. All six approaches allowed that a scientific theory is tested by deducing from it consequences regarding observable states of affairs that are then compared with the results of observation and experiment. But the approaches differed regarding what might follow from such a comparison. For justificationism, falsificationism, and the testing paradigm of scientific inference, true observational consequences warranted a judgment regarding the *truth* of a theory—either that it is probably true (for justificationism), or that it is possibly true (for falsificationism), or simply that it is true (for the testing paradigm), whereas false observational consequences warranted a judgment that the theory is false. For conventionalism, the methodology of scientific research programmes, and Kuhn's sociological approach, on the other hand, neither true nor false observational consequences warranted *any* judgment regarding the truth or falsity of the theory. Instead, these approaches suggested that a scientific theory is accepted or rejected on the basis of considerations other than its truth (or possible truth or probable truth) or falsity, such as its relative simplicity (for conventionalism) or its progressiveness (for the research programmes of the methodology of scientific research programmes) or its accuracy, consistency, scope, simplicity, and fruitfulness (for Kuhn's sociological approach). And nothing regarding the truth or falsity of the theory was held to follow from such features of it.

In short, by the end of Part 3, if you had accepted the testing paradigm of scientific inference, justificationism, or falsificationism, you would have said that the theories of science do, or probably do, or possibly do, give a literally true account of the way the world is. On the other hand, if you had accepted conventionalism, the methodology of scientific research programmes, or Kuhn's sociological approach, you would have said that the theories of science do not give a literally true account of the way the world is—you would have said this, that is, unless you had an independent argument to the effect that simplicity or progressiveness or the like is a mark of truth.

But then, in Part 4, we investigated the historical development of scientific knowledge. In particular, we considered four models of scientific development—an older cumulative model, and the more current evolutionary, revolutionary, and gradualist models. Each of these models offered us a different account of scientific progress and a correspondingly different account of the typical historical development of scientific fields. Thus, according to the cumulative model, a scientific field progresses when it gains new facts, concepts, laws, or theories by correct applications of scientific method, and the typical historical development of a scientific field is a succession of such additions. According to the evolutionary model, a scientific field progresses when it replaces its current theories with new, more successful theories, and the typical historical development of a scientific field is a succession of such replacements. According to the revolutionary model, a scientific field progresses when it replaces its current theories and associated facts, methods, and goals with new theories and associated facts, methods, and goals, and the typical historical development of a scientific field is a succession of such radical replacements. And finally, according to the gradualist model, a scientific field progresses when it justifiably replaces one or more of its current theories, methods, or goals with new theories, methods, or goals, and the typical historical development of a scientific field is a succession of such limited replacements.

In short, by the end of Part 4, if you had accepted the evolutionary, revolutionary, or gradualist models of scientific development you would have said that scientific theories are regularly replaced—are regularly *falsified*, in the language of justificationism, falsificationism, and the testing paradigm of scientific inference. In other words, you would have said that *all* scientific theories have been falsified, save for the current ones. And you would have said that the current theories will likewise be falsified in the future as well. By the end of Part 4, then, only if you had accepted the much maligned cumulative model of scientific development could you still have said that the theories of science give a literally true account of the way the world is.

What, then, is the answer—realism, the view that the theories of science give a literally true account of the way the world is, or anti-realism, the view that the theories of science are mere calculating devices, useful fictions, convenient methods of representation, or the like, helpful only for predicting and organizing purely observational truths about the world? Without a doubt the majority of scientists and philosophers of science today lean toward realism, and many arguments have been offered in its support. Thus, it has been said that only realism allows the explanation of regularities in observable phenomena; only realism can explain the usefulness of scientific theories, and, in fact, make sense of the distinction between correct and merely useful, but false, scientific theories; only realism can explain the ongoing success of mature scientific fields; and the like. In "Arguments Concerning Scientific Realism," Bas van Fraassen surveys these and other main arguments for scientific realism. He concludes, however, that they are all wanting.

The case for anti-realism has also been judged wanting, however. For example, it has been said that anti-realism is unable to account for scientists' interest in testing remote implications of their theories (if a theory is merely a calculating device or method of representation, after all, then failure of a test will constitute, not a refutation, but only a limitation of the theory's applicability). Again, it has been said that anti-realism is unable to account for cases in which what was once merely theoretical—for example, the circulation of the blood, or viruses, or the mountains on the moon—is now actually observable, and hence, real. In response to these and other purported shortcomings of anti-realism, a number of distinguished philosophers are currently elaborating new versions of anti-realism. According to one such version, the theories of science give, not a literally true account of the way the world is, but, at best, an account true in another sense. In this other sense, this "acceptance" sense, of truth, the truth of an account of the way the world is amounts to the fact that a certain class of subjects would accept the account under a certain set of circumstances—for example, perfectly rational agents would accept the account under circumstances ideally suited to knowledge acquisition, or conscientious and well-intentioned, but not perfectly rational, agents would accept the account under circumstances marking a serious dialogue of the kind that makes for consensus, where consensus is attainable. According to another new version of anti-realism, the one developed by van Fraassen, the theories of science give, not a literally true account of the way the world is, but only an empirically adequate account—that is, an account true only of the observable things and events of the world. In "And Not Anti-Realism Either," Arthur Fine explores these new versions of anti-realism. He concludes, however, that they are just as inadequate as older versions of anti-realism.

If both realism and anti-realism appear inadequate, however, what position ought we to take? Fine argues in favor of a "natural ontological attitude" toward science, an attitude that eschews both realism and anti-realism. Such an attitude, Fine stipulates, allows science to speak for itself—that is, provide its own local interpretations of its own results, rather than be interpreted by either realism or anti-realism in a global way. If we take this attitude, Fine suggests, then the global interpretations of realism and anti-realism will appear as idle overlays to science: not necessary, not warranted, and, in the end, probably not even intelligible.

In "Realism and Instrumentalism in Pre-Newtonian Astronomy" and "Experimentation and Scientific Realism," Michael Gardner and Ian Hacking seem to be doing exactly what Fine suggests: letting science—theoretical science for Gardner and experimental science for Hacking—speak for itself. And in so doing they both conclude that the usual way of conceiving the realism-anti-realism question must be changed. Considering Gardner first, he has pointed out in earlier work that the realism-anti-realism question, as usually conceived, is the question whether scientific theories are correctly interpreted realistically—that is, as literally true—or instrumentalistically—that is, as merely convenient devices for summarizing, systematizing, deducing, and so on, observable facts. This question, Gardner has suggested, requires a single answer applicable to all theories. But a question such as this, about the proper interpretation of scientific theories, should be settled through an examination of particular actual scientific theories rather than in general terms, given the possibility that the question might have different answers for different theories. Indeed, a common pattern in the history of science is that a theory is first put forward or accepted merely as an idealization or calculational device and only later comes to be regarded as literally true. Gardner has thus suggested a successor question to the realism-anti-realism question: Under what conditions is it reasonable to accept a theory on a realistic interpretation (as literally true) rather than on an instrumentalist interpretation (as not literally true but convenient for summarizing, systematizing, deducing, and so on a given body of information)? In "Realism and Instrumentalism in Pre-Newtonian Astronomy," which is part of a program aimed at answering this question, Gardner examines in detail the debate over the status of Copernican astronomy in the sixteenth century. He finds that Copernican astronomy was accepted on a realistic interpretation or on an instrumentalist interpretation depending on whether the theory was thought to satisfy or fail to satisfy conditions like the following: (1) the theory satisfies the laws of physics; (2) the theory is consistent with other putative knowledge (for example, the Scriptures); (3) the theory is consistent with all observational data; (4) the theory contains only determinate quantities; (5) the theory is able to predict novel facts; (6) the theory has a central hypothesis supported by a large variety of evidence; (7) the theory is within the realm of possible human knowledge; (8) the theory explains facts that competing theories merely postulate; and (9) the theory agrees with some of the nonobservational claims of some previous theories purporting to explain the same observations. If, as is plausible, these conditions, which are operative in the case of Copernican astronomy, are also found to be operative in a variety of other cases in which the realism-instrumentalism issue has arisen, we might then accept them as good reasons for adopting a theory on a realistic interpretation. The justification for such an answer to our new version of the realism-anti-realism question would, of course, be that the answer agrees with the judgments of most good scientists of the past and present on most of the relevant occasions.

Hacking's suggested revision of the realism-anti-realism question takes a different form from Gardner's. Focusing on experimental science rather than theoretical science, Hacking suggests, in essence, that we ask: Under what conditions is it reasonable to accept the entities postulated by a theory (and this includes processes, states, fields, and the like) as real existents rather than as mere hypothetical entities? Like Gardner's revised version of the realism-anti-realism question, this version allows us to form different judgments about the entities postulated by different theories and by the same theory at different stages of development. But unlike Gardner's version, this version of the realism-anti-realism question focuses on the reality of the entities postulated by a theory rather than on the truth of the theory. And this is as it should be, according to Hacking, given that a false theory as well as a true one might postulate real entities, and that different, and even incompatible, theories have frequently postulated the same entities (think of all the different theories that have postulated electrons or atoms).

Finally, based on the widespread and, Hacking thinks, reasonable practices of experimental scientists, Hacking offers the following answer to his revised version of the realism-anti-realism question: When scientists' understanding of the causal properties of postulated entities allows them to use such entities as tools to investigate other aspects of nature, then it is reasonable to accept such entities as real existents. Note that accepting such entities as real existents does not commit scientists to accepting as true any particular theory in which the entities are postulated.

Are we now in a position to answer the realism-anti-realism question? We have considered three versions of this question:

1. Do the theories of science give a literally true account of the way the world is? Or are they mere calculating devices, useful fictions, convenient methods of representation, only empirically adequate but not true, or only true in some non-literal sense?

2. Under what conditions is it reasonable to accept a theory on a realistic interpretation (as literally true) rather than on an instrumentalist interpretation (as not literally true, but convenient for summarizing, systematizing, deducing, and so on a given body of information)?

3. Under what conditions is it reasonable to accept the entities postulated by a theory (and this includes processes, states, fields, and the like) as real existents rather than as mere hypothetical entities?

We have also considered some of the factors that motivate particular answers to the realism-anti-realism question in one or another of its versions:

a. The nature of scientific theory testing: Is it correctly described by justificationism, falsificationism, conventionalism, the methodology of scientific research programmes, Thomas Kuhn's sociological approach, or the testing paradigm of scientific inference?

b. The nature of scientific development: Is it correctly described by the cumulative model, the evolutionary model, the revolutionary model, or the gradualist model?

c. The need to explain various features of science (such as the usefulness of its theories or its ongoing success) and the need to explain various features of the world (such as regularities in observable phenomena)

d. The past and present practices of theoretical scientists in cases in which the realism-anti-realism issue has arisen

e. The present (and past?) practices of experimental scientists in cases in which the realism-anti-realism issue arises

The extreme difficulty of the realism-anti-realism question should now be apparent. Indeed, not only is the form of the question controversial, and the factors that need to be considered complex, but also these factors may very well conflict with one another. Thus, for example, your view of theory testing may conflict with the past and present practices of theoretical scientists in cases in which the realism-anti-realism issue has arisen. In our consideration of theory testing, after all, no provision was made for different modes of theory acceptance, such as accepting a theory as literally true vs. accepting it as useful but not literally true. Again, as we have seen, your view of theory testing may conflict with your view of scientific development—justificationism, for example, leading you to say that theories with much positive evidence and no negative evidence in their behalf are probably true, whereas the evolutionary model of scientific development leads you to say that such theories will be shown to be false. Such conflicts must, of course, be resolved before an answer to the realism-anti-realism question can be had, and in resolving them you may need to revise or refine one or more of factors (a)–(e) and even one of questions (1)–(3). But take heart: In making these revisions or refinements you will be putting the final touches on your own unified and comprehensive philosophy of science.

Arguments Concerning Scientific Realism

Bas van Fraassen

The rigor of science requires that we distinguish well the undraped figure of nature itself from the gay-colored vesture with which we clothe it at our pleasure.

> —Heinrich Hertz, quoted by Ludwig Boltzmann, letter to *Nature*, 28 February 1895

In our century, the first dominant philosophy of science was developed as part of logical positivism. Even today, such an expression as "the received view of theories" refers to the views developed by the logical positivists, although their heyday preceded the Second World War.

. . . I shall examine and criticize the main arguments that have been offered for scientific realism. These arguments occurred frequently as part of a critique of logical positivism. But it is surely fair to discuss them in isolation, for even if scientific realism is most easily understood as a reaction against positivism, it should be able to stand alone. The alternative view which I advocate—for lack of a traditional name I shall call it *constructive empiricism*—is equally at odds with positivist doctrine.

SCIENTIFIC REALISM AND CONSTRUCTIVE EMPIRICISM

In philosophy of science, the term "scientific realism" denotes a precise position on the question of how a scientific theory is to be understood, and what scientific activity really is. I shall attempt to define this position, and to canvass its possible alternatives. Then I shall indicate, roughly and briefly, the specific alternative which I shall advocate. . . .

Statement of Scientific Realism

What exactly is scientific realism? A naive statement of the position would be this: The picture which science gives us of the world is a true one, faithful in its details, and the entities postulated in science really exist—the advances of science are discoveries, not inventions. That statement is too naive; it attributes to the scientific realist the belief that today's theories are correct. It would mean that the philosophical position of an earlier scientific realist such as C. S. Peirce had been refuted by empirical findings. I do not suppose that scientific realists wish to be committed, as such, even to the claim that science will arrive in due time at theories true in all respects—for the growth of science might be an endless self-correction; or worse, Armageddon might occur too soon.

But the naive statement has the right flavor. It answers two main questions: It characterizes a scientific theory as a story about what there really is, and scientific activity as an enterprise of discovery, as opposed to invention. The two questions of what a scientific theory is, and what a scientific theory does, must be answered by any philosophy of science. The task we have at this point is to find a statement of scientific realism that shares these features with the naive statement, but does not saddle the realists with unacceptably strong consequences. It is especially important to make the statement as weak as possible if we wish to argue against it, so as not to charge at windmills.

As clues I shall cite some passages, most of which will also be examined below in the contexts of the authors' arguments. A statement of Wilfrid Sellars is this:

to have good reason for holding a theory is *ipso facto* to have good reason for holding that the entities postulated by the theory exist.[1]

This addresses a question of epistemology, but also throws some indirect light on what it is, in Sellars's opinion, to hold a theory. Brian Ellis, who calls himself a scientific entity realist rather than a scientific realist, appears to agree with that statement of Sellars, but gives the following formulation of a stronger view:

I understand scientific realism to be the view that the theoretical statements of science are, or purport to be, true generalized descriptions of reality.[2]

This formulation has two advantages: It focuses on the understanding of the theories without reference to reasons for belief, and it avoids the suggestion that to be a realist you must believe current scientific theories to be true. But it gains the latter advantage by use of the word *purport,* which may generate its own puzzles.

Hilary Putnam, in a passage which I shall cite again [later], gives a formulation which he says he learned from Michael Dummett:

A realist (with respect to a given theory or discourse) holds that (1) the sentences of that theory are true or false; and (2) that what makes them true or false is something external—that is to say, it is not (in general) our sense data, actual or potential, or the structure of our minds, or our language, etc.[3]

He follows this soon afterwards with a further formulation which he credits to Richard Boyd:

That terms in mature scientific theories typically refer (this formulation is due to Richard Boyd), that the theories accepted in a mature science are typically approximately true, that the same term can refer to the same thing even when it occurs in different theories—these statements are viewed by the scientific

realist . . . as part of any adequate scientific description of science and its relations to its objects.[4]

None of these were intended as definitions. But they show I think that truth must play an important role in the formulation of the basic realist position. They also show that the formulation must incorporate an answer to the question what it is to *accept* or *hold* a theory. I shall now propose such a formulation, which seems to me to make sense of the above remarks, and also renders intelligible the reasoning by realists which I shall examine below—without burdening them with more than the minimum required for this.

Science aims to give us, in its theories, a literally true story of what the world is like; and acceptance of a scientific theory involves the belief that it is true. This is the correct statement of scientific realism.

Let me defend this formulation by showing that it is quite minimal, and can be agreed to by anyone who considers himself a scientific realist. The naive statement said that science tells a true story; the correct statement says only that it is the aim of science to do so. The aim of science is of course not to be identified with individual scientists' motives. The aim of the game of chess is to checkmate your opponent; but the motive for playing may be fame, gold, and glory. What the aim is determines what counts as success in the enterprise as such; and this aim may be pursued for any number of reasons. Also, in calling something *the* aim, I do not deny that there are other subsidiary aims which may or may not be means to that end: Everyone will readily agree that simplicity, informativeness, predictive power, explanation are (also) virtues. Perhaps my formulation can even be accepted by any philosopher who considers the most important aim of science to be something which only *requires* the finding of true theories—given that I wish to give the weakest

---

[1] *Science, Perception and Reality* (New York: Humanities Press, 1962); cf. the footnote on p. 97. See also my review of his *Studies in Philosophy and its History,* in *Annals of Science,* January 1977.

[2] Brian Ellis, *Rational Belief Systems* (Oxford: Blackwell, 1979), p. 28.

[3] Hilary Putnam, *Mathematics, Matter and Method* (Cambridge: Cambridge University Press, 1975), Vol. 1, pp. 69f.

---

[4] Putnam, op. cit., p. 73, n. 29. The argument is reportedly developed at greater length in Boyd's forthcoming book *Realism and Scientific Epistemology* (Cambridge University Press).

formulation of the doctrine that is generally acceptable.

I have added "literally" to rule out as realist such positions as imply that science is true if "properly understood" but literally false or meaningless. For that would be consistent with conventionalism, logical positivism, and instrumentalism. I will say more about this below; and also on pp. 356–357, where I shall consider Dummett's views further.

The second part of the statement touches on epistemology. But it only equates acceptance of a theory with belief in its truth.[5] It does not imply that anyone is ever rationally warranted in forming such a belief. We have to make room for the epistemological position, today the subject of considerable debate, that a rational person never assigns personal probability 1 to any proposition except a tautology. It would, I think, be rare for a scientific realist to take this stand in epistemology, but it is certainly possible.[6]

To understand qualified acceptance we must first understand acceptance *tout court*. If acceptance of a theory involves the belief that it is true,

then tentative acceptance involves the tentative adoption of the belief that it is true. If belief comes in degrees, so does acceptance, and we may then speak of a degree of acceptance involving a certain degree of belief that the theory is true. This must of course be distinguished from belief that the theory is approximately true, which seems to mean belief that some member of a class centering on the mentioned theory is (exactly) true. In this way the proposed formulation of realism can be used regardless of one's epistemological persuasion.

Alternatives to Realism

Scientific realism is the position that scientific theory construction aims to give us a literally true story of what the world is like, and that acceptance of a scientific theory involves the belief that it is true. Accordingly, anti-realism is a position according to which the aim of science can well be served without giving such a literally true story, and acceptance of a theory may properly involve something less (or other) than belief that it is true.

What does a scientist do then, according to these different positions? According to the realist, when someone proposes a theory, he is asserting it to be true. But according to the anti-realist, the proposer does not assert the theory; *he displays it,* and claims certain virtues for it. These virtues may fall short of truth: empirical adequacy, perhaps; comprehensiveness, acceptability for various purposes. This will have to be spelled out, for the details here are not determined by the denial of realism. For now we must concentrate on the key notions that allow the generic division.

The idea of a literally true account has two aspects: The language is to be literally construed; and so construed, the account is true. This divides the anti-realists into two sorts. The first sort holds that science is or aims to be true, properly (but not literally) construed. The second holds that the language of science should be literally construed, but its theories need not be true to be good. The anti-realism I shall advocate belongs to the second sort.

[5] Hartry Field has suggested that "acceptance of a scientific theory involves the belief that it is true" be replaced by "any reason to think that any part of a theory is not, or might not be, true, is reason not to accept it." The drawback of this alternative is that it leaves open what epistemic attitude acceptance of a theory does involve. This question must also be answered, and as long as we are talking about full acceptance—as opposed to tentative or partial or otherwise qualified acceptance—I cannot see how a realist could do other than equate that attitude with full belief. (That theories believed to be false are used for practical problems, for example, classical mechanics for orbiting satellites, is of course a commonplace.) For if the aim is truth, and acceptance requires belief that the aim is served . . . I should also mention the statement of realism at the beginning of Richard Boyd, "Realism, Underdetermination, and a Causal Theory of Evidence," *Noûs*, **7** (1973), 1–12. Except for some doubts about his use of the terms *explanation* and *causal relation* I intend my statement of realism to be entirely in accordance with his. Finally, see C. A. Hooker, "Systematic Realism," *Synthese*, **26** (1974), 409–97; esp. pp. 409 and 426.

[6] More typical of realism, it seems to me, is the sort of epistemology found in Clark Glymour's book, *Theory and Evidence* (Princeton: Princeton University Press, 1980), except of course that there it is fully and carefully developed in one specific fashion. (See esp. his chapter "Why I Am Not a Bayesian" for the present issue.) But I see no reason why a realist, as such, could not be a Bayesian of the type of Richard Jeffrey, even if the Bayesian position has in the past been linked with anti-realist and even instrumentalist views in philosophy of science.

It is not so easy to say what is meant by a literal construal. The idea comes perhaps from theology, where fundamentalists construe the Bible literally, and liberals have a variety of allegorical, metaphorical, and analogical interpretations, which "demythologize." The problem of explicating "literal construal" belongs to the philosophy of language. . . . [B]elow, where I briefly examine some of Michael Dummett's views, I shall emphasize that "literal" does not mean "truth-valued." The term "literal" is well enough understood for general philosophical use, but if we try to explicate it we find ourselves in the midst of the problem of giving an adequate account of natural language. It would be bad tactics to link an inquiry into science to a commitment to some solution to that problem. The following remarks, and those on pp. 356–357, should fix the usage of "literal" sufficiently for present purposes.

The decision to rule out all but literal construals of the language of science rules out those forms of anti-realism known as *positivism* and *instrumentalism*. First, on a literal construal, the apparent statements of science really are statements, *capable of* being true or false. Secondly, although a literal construal can elaborate, it cannot change logical relationships. (It is possible to elaborate, for instance, by identifying what the terms designate. The "reduction" of the language of phenomenological thermodynamics to that of statistical mechanics is like that: Bodies of gas are identified as aggregates of molecules, temperature as mean kinetic energy, and so on.) On the positivists' interpretation of science, theoretical terms have meaning only through their connection with the observable. Hence they hold that two theories may in fact *say the same thing* although in form they contradict each other. (Perhaps the one says that all matter consists of atoms, while the other postulates instead a universal continuous medium; they will say the same thing nevertheless if they agree in their observable consequences, according to the positivists.) But two theories which contradict each other in such a way can "really" be saying the same thing only if they are not literally construed. Most specifically, if a theory says that something exists, then a literal construal may

elaborate on what that something is, but will not remove the implication of existence.

There have been many critiques of positivist interpretations of science, and there is no need to repeat them. . . .

Constructive Empiricism

To insist on a literal construal of the language of science is to rule out the construal of a theory as a metaphor or simile, or as intelligible only after it is "demythologized" or subjected to some other sort of "translation" that does not preserve logical form. If the theory's statements include "There are electrons," then the theory says that there are electrons. If in addition they include "Electrons are not planets," then the theory says, in part, that there are entities other than planets.

But this does not settle very much. It is often not at all obvious whether a theoretical term refers to a concrete entity or a mathematical entity. Perhaps one tenable interpretation of classical physics is that there are no concrete entities which are forces—that "there are forces such that . . ." can always be understood as a mathematical statement asserting the existence of certain functions. That is debatable.

Not every philosophical position concerning science which insists on a literal construal of the language of science is a realist position. For this insistence relates not at all to our epistemic attitudes toward theories, nor to the aim we pursue in constructing theories, but only to the correct understanding of *what a theory says*. (The fundamentalist theist, the agnostic, and the atheist presumably agree with each other [though not with liberal theologians] in their understanding of the statement that God, or gods, or angels exist.) After deciding that the language of science must be literally understood, we can still say that there is no need to believe good theories to be true, nor to believe *ipso facto* that the entities they postulate are real.

Science aims to give us theories which are empirically adequate; and acceptance of a theory involves as belief only that it is empirically adequate. This is the statement of the anti-realist position I advocate; I shall call it *constructive empiricism*.

This formulation is subject to the same qualifying remarks as that of scientific realism on pp. 343–345 above. In addition it requires an explication of "empirically adequate." For now, I shall leave that with the preliminary explication that a theory is empirically adequate exactly if what it says about the observable things and events in this world is true—exactly if it "saves the phenomena." A little more precisely: Such a theory has at least one model that all the actual phenomena fit inside. I must emphasize that this refers to *all* the phenomena; these are not exhausted by those actually observed, nor even by those observed at some time, whether past, present, or future. . . .

The distinction I have drawn between realism and anti-realism, insofar as it pertains to acceptance, concerns only how much belief is involved therein. Acceptance of theories (whether full, tentative, to a degree, etc.) is a phenomenon of scientific activity which clearly involves more than belief. One main reason for this is that we are never confronted with a complete theory. So if a scientist accepts a theory, he thereby involves himself in a certain sort of research programme. That programme could well be different from the one acceptance of another theory would have given him, even if those two (very incomplete) theories are equivalent to each other with respect to everything that is observable—insofar as they go.

Thus acceptance involves not only belief but a certain commitment. Even for those of us who are not working scientists, the acceptance involves a commitment to confront any future phenomena by means of the conceptual resources of this theory. It determines the terms in which we shall seek explanations. If the acceptance is at all strong, it is exhibited in the person's assumption of the role of explainer, in his willingness to answer questions *ex cathedra*. Even if you do not accept a theory, you can engage in discourse in a context in which language use is guided by that theory—but acceptance produces such contexts. There are similarities in all of this to ideological commitment. A commitment is of course not true or false: The confidence exhibited is that it will be *vindicated*.

This is a preliminary sketch of the *pragmatic* dimension of theory acceptance. Unlike the epistemic dimension, it does not figure overtly in the disagreement between realist and anti-realist. But because the amount of belief involved in acceptance is typically less according to anti-realists, they will tend to make more of the pragmatic aspects. It is as well to note here the important difference. Belief that a theory is true, or that it is empirically adequate, does not imply, and is not implied by, belief that full acceptance of the theory will be vindicated. To see this, you need only consider here a person who has quite definite beliefs about the future of the human race, or about the scientific community and the influences thereon and practical limitations we have. It might well be, for instance, that a theory which is empirically adequate will not combine easily with some other theories which we have accepted in fact, or that Armageddon will occur before we succeed. Whether belief that a theory is true, or that it is empirically adequate, can be equated with belief that acceptance of it would, under ideal research conditions, be vindicated in the long run, is another question. It seems to me an irrelevant question within philosophy of science, because an affirmative answer would not obliterate the distinction we have already established by the preceding remarks. (The question may also assume that counterfactual statements are objectively true or false, which I would deny.)

Although it seems to me that realists and anti-realists need not disagree about the pragmatic aspects of theory acceptance, I have mentioned it here because I think that typically they do. We shall find ourselves returning time and again, for example, to requests for explanation to which realists typically attach an objective validity which anti-realists cannot grant.

THE THEORY/OBSERVATION "DICHOTOMY"

For good reasons, logical positivism dominated the philosophy of science for thirty years. In 1960, the first volume of *Minnesota Studies in the Philos-*

ophy of Science published Rudolf Carnap's "The Methodological Status of Theoretical Concepts," which is, in many ways, the culmination of the positivist programme. It interprets science by relating it to an observation language (a postulated part of natural language which is devoid of theoretical terms). Two years later this article was followed in the same series by Grover Maxwell's "The Ontological Status of Theoretical Entities," in title and theme a direct counter to Carnap's. This is the *locus classicus* for the new realists' contention that the theory/observation distinction cannot be drawn.

I shall examine some of Maxwell's points directly, but first a general remark about the issue. Such expressions as "theoretical entity" and "observable–theoretical dichotomy" are, on the face of it, examples of category mistakes. Terms or concepts are theoretical (introduced or adapted for the purposes of theory construction); entities are observable or unobservable. This may seem a little point, but it separates the discussion into two issues. Can we divide our language into a theoretical and non-theoretical part? On the other hand, can we classify objects and events into observable and unobservable ones?

Maxwell answers both questions in the negative, while not distinguishing them too carefully. On the first, where he can draw on well-known supportive essays by Wilfrid Sellars and Paul Feyerabend, I am in total agreement. All our language is thoroughly theory-infected. If we could cleanse our language of theory-laden terms, beginning with the recently introduced ones like "VHF receiver," continuing through "mass" and "impulse" to "element" and so on into the prehistory of language formation, we would end up with nothing useful. The way we talk, and scientists talk, is guided by the pictures provided by previously accepted theories. This is true also, as Duhem already emphasized, of experimental reports. Hygienic reconstructions of language such as the positivists envisaged are simply not on. . . .

But does this mean that we must be scientific realists? We surely have more tolerance of ambiguity than that. The fact that we let our language be guided by a given picture, at some point, does not show how much we believe about that picture. When we speak of the sun coming up in the morning and setting at night, we are guided by a picture now explicitly disavowed. When Milton wrote *Paradise Lost* he deliberately let the old geocentric astronomy guide his poem, although various remarks in passing clearly reveal his interest in the new astronomical discoveries and speculations of his time. These are extreme examples, but show that no immediate conclusions can be drawn from the theory-ladenness of our language.

However, Maxwell's main arguments are directed against the observable–unobservable distinction. Let us first be clear on what this distinction was supposed to be. The term "observable" classifies putative entities (entities which may or may not exist). A flying horse is observable—that is why we are so sure that there aren't any—and the number seventeen is not. There is supposed to be a correlate classification of human acts: An unaided act of perception, for instance, is an observation. A calculation of the mass of a particle from the deflection of its trajectory in a known force field, is not an observation of that mass.

It is also important here not to confuse *observing* (an entity, such as a thing, event, or process) and *observing that* (something or other is the case). Suppose one of the Stone Age people recently found in the Philippines is shown a tennis ball or a car crash. From his behavior, we see that he has noticed them; for example, he picks up the ball and throws it. But he has not seen *that* it is a tennis ball, or *that* some event is a car crash, for he does not even have those concepts. He cannot get that information through perception; he would first have to learn a great deal. To say that he does not see the same things and events as we do, however, is just silly; it is a pun which trades on the ambiguity between seeing and seeing that. (The truth-conditions for our statement "x observes *that* A" must be such that what concepts x has, presumably related to the language x speaks if he is human, enter as a variable into the correct truth definition, in some way. To say that x observed the tennis ball, therefore, does not imply at all that x observed that it was a tennis ball; that would require some conceptual awareness of the game of tennis.)

The arguments Maxwell gives about observability are of two sorts: one directed against the possibility of drawing such distinctions, the other against the importance that could attach to distinctions that can be drawn.

The first argument is from the continuum of cases that lie between direct observation and inference:

there is, in principle, a continuous series beginning with looking through a vacuum and containing these as members: looking through a windowpane, looking through glasses, looking through binoculars, looking through a low-power microscope, looking through a high-power microscope, etc., in the order given. The important consequence is that, so far, we are left without criteria which would enable us to draw a non-arbitrary line between "observation" and "theory".[7]

This continuous series of supposed acts of observation does not correspond directly to a continuum in what is supposed observable. For if something can be seen through a window, it can also be seen with the window raised. Similarly, the moons of Jupiter can be seen through a telescope; but they can also be seen without a telescope if you are close enough. That something is observable does not automatically imply that the conditions are right for observing it now. The principle is:

X is observable if there are circumstances which are such that, if X is present to us under those circumstances, then we observe it.

This is not meant as a definition, but only as a rough guide to the avoidance of fallacies.

We may still be able to find a continuum in what is supposed detectable: Perhaps some things can only be detected with the aid of an optical microscope, at least; perhaps some require an

electron microscope, and so on. Maxwell's problem is: Where shall we draw the line between what is observable and what is only detectable in some more roundabout way?

Granted that we cannot answer this question without arbitrariness, what follows? That "observable" is a *vague predicate*. There are many puzzles about vague predicates, and many sophisms designed to show that, in the presence of vagueness, no distinction can be drawn at all. In Sextus Empiricus, we find the argument that incest is not immoral, for touching your mother's big toe with your little finger is not immoral, and all the rest differs only by degree. But predicates in natural language are almost all vague, and there is no problem in their use; only in formulating the logic that governs them.[8] A vague predicate is usable provided it has clear cases and clear counter-cases. Seeing with the unaided eye is a clear case of observation. Is Maxwell then perhaps challenging us to present a clear counter-case? Perhaps so, for he says "I have been trying to support the thesis that any (non-logical) term is a *possible* candidate for an observation term."

A look through a telescope at the moons of Jupiter seems to me a clear case of observation, since astronauts will no doubt be able to see them as well from close up. But the purported observation of micro-particles in a cloud chamber seems to me a clearly different case—if our theory about what happens there is right. The theory says that if a charged particle traverses a chamber filled with saturated vapor, some atoms in the neighborhood of its path are ionized. If this vapor is decompressed, and hence becomes supersaturated, it condenses in droplets on the ions, thus marking the path of the particle. The resulting silver-grey line is similar (physically as well as in appearance) to the vapor trail left in the sky when a jet passes.

[7] G. Maxwell. "The Ontological Status of Theoretical Entities." *Minnesota Studies in Philosophy of Science,* III (1962), p. 7.

[8] There is a great deal of recent work on the logic of vague predicates; especially important, to my mind, is that of Kit Fine ("Vagueness, Truth, and Logic," *Synthese,* **30** (1975), 265–300) and Hans Kamp. The latter is currently working on a new theory of vagueness that does justice to the "vagueness of vagueness" and the context-dependence of standards of applicability for predicates.

Suppose I point to such a trail and say: "Look, there is a jet!"; might you not say: "I see the vapor trail, but where is the jet?" Then I would answer: "Look just a bit ahead of the trail . . . there! Do you see it?" Now, in the case of the cloud chamber this response is not possible. So while the particle is detected by means of the cloud chamber, and the detection is based on observation, it is clearly not a case of the article's being observed.

As second argument, Maxwell directs our attention to the "can" in "what is observable is what can be observed." An object might of course be temporarily unobservable—in a rather different sense: It cannot be observed in the circumstances in which it actually is at the moment, but could be observed if the circumstances were more favorable. In just the same way, I might be temporarily invulnerable or invisible. So we should concentrate on "observable" *tout court,* or on (as he prefers to say) "unobservable in principle." This Maxwell explains as meaning that the relevant scientific theory *entails* that the entities cannot be observed in any circumstances. But this never happens, he says, because the different circumstances could be ones in which we have different sense organs—electron-microscope eyes, for instance.

This strikes me as a trick, a change in the subject of discussion. I have a mortar and pestle made of copper and weighing about a kilo. Should I call it breakable because a giant could break it? Should I call the Empire State Building portable? Is there no distinction between a portable and a console record player? The human organism is, from the point of view of physics, a certain kind of measuring apparatus. As such it has certain inherent limitations—which will be described in detail in the final physics and biology. It is these limitations to which the "able" in "observable" refers—our limitations, *qua* human beings.

As I mentioned, however, Maxwell's article also contains a different sort of argument: Even if there is a feasible observable/unobservable distinction, this distinction has no importance. The point at issue for the realist is, after all, the reality of the entities postulated in science. Suppose that these entities could be classified into observable

and others; what relevance should that have to the question of their existence?

Logically, none. For the term "observable" classifies putative entities and has logically nothing to do with existence. But Maxwell must have more in mind when he says: "I conclude that the drawing of the observational–theoretical line at any given point is an accident and a function of our physiological make-up, . . . and, therefore, that it has no ontological significance whatever."[9] No ontological significance if the question is only whether "observable" and "exists" imply each other—for they do not; but significance for the question of scientific realism?

Recall I defined scientific realism in terms of the aim of science and epistemic attitudes. The question is what aim scientific activity has, and how much we shall believe when we accept a scientific theory. What is the proper form of acceptance: belief that the theory, as a whole, is true; or something else? To this question, what is observable by us seems eminently relevant. Indeed, we may attempt an answer at this point: To accept a theory is (for us) to believe that it is empirically adequate—that what the theory says *about what is observable* (by us) is true.

It will be objected at once that, on this proposal, what the anti-realist decides to believe about the world will depend in part on what he believes to be his, or rather the epistemic community's, accessible range of evidence. At present, we count the human race as the epistemic community to which we belong; but this race may

---

[9] Op. cit., p. 15. . . . At this point . . . I may be suspected of relying on modal distinctions which I criticize elsewhere. After all, I am making a distinction between human limitations and accidental factors. A certain apple was dropped into the sea in a bag of refuse, which sank; relative to that information it is necessary that no one ever observed the apple's core. That information, however, concerns an accident of history, and so it is not human limitations that rule out observation of the apple core. But unless I assert that some facts about humans are essential, or physically necessary, and others accidental, how can I make sense of this distinction? This question raises the difficulty of a philosophical retrenchment for modal language. This I believe to be possible through an ascent to pragmatics. In the present case, the answer would be, to speak very roughly, that the scientific theories we accept are a determining factor for the set of features of the human organism counted among the limitations to which we refer in using the term "observable." . . .

mutate, or that community may be increased by adding other animals (terrestrial or extra-terrestrial) through relevant ideological or moral decisions ("to count them as persons"). Hence the anti-realist would, on my proposal, have to accept conditions of the form

> If the epistemic community changes in fashion *Y*, then my beliefs about the world will change in manner *Z*.

To see this as an objection to anti-realism is to voice the requirement that our epistemic policies should give the same results independent of our beliefs about the range of evidence accessible to us. That requirement seems to me in no way rationally compelling; it could be honored, I should think, only through a thoroughgoing scepticism or through a commitment to wholesale leaps of faith. But we cannot settle the major questions of epistemology *en passant* in philosophy of science; so I shall just conclude that it is, on the face of it, not irrational to commit oneself only to a search for theories that are empirically adequate, ones whose models fit the observable phenomena, while recognizing that what counts as an observable phenomenon is a function of what the epistemic community is (that *observable* is *observable-to-us*).

The notion of empirical adequacy in this answer will have to be spelled out very carefully if it is not to bite the dust among hackneyed objections. . . . But the point stands: Even if observability has nothing to do with existence (is, indeed, too anthropocentric for that), it may still have much to do with the proper epistemic attitude to science.

INFERENCE TO THE BEST EXPLANATION

A view advanced in different ways by Wilfrid Sellars, J.J.C. Smart, and Gilbert Harman is that the canons of rational inference require scientific realism. If we are to follow the same patterns of inference with respect to this issue as we do in science itself, we shall find ourselves irrational unless we assert the truth of the scientific theories we accept. Thus Sellars says: "As I see it, to have good reason for holding a theory is *ipso facto* to have good reason for holding that the entities postulated by the theory exist."[10]

The main rule of inference invoked in arguments of this sort is the rule of *inference to the best explanation*. The idea is perhaps to be credited to C. S. Peirce,[11] but the main recent attempts to explain this rule and its uses have been made by Gilbert Harman.[12] I shall only present a simplified version. Let us suppose that we have evidence *E*, and are considering several hypotheses, say *H* and *H'*. The rule then says that we should infer *H* rather than *H'* exactly if *H* is a better explanation of *E* than *H'* is. (Various qualifications are necessary to avoid inconsistency: We should always try to move to the best overall explanation of all available evidence.)

It is argued that we follow this rule in all "ordinary" cases; and that if we follow it consistently everywhere, we shall be led to scientific realism, in the way Sellars's dictum suggests. And surely there are many telling "ordinary" cases: I hear scratching in the wall, the patter of little feet at midnight, my cheese disappears—and I infer that a mouse has come to live with me. Not merely that these apparent signs of mousely presence will continue, not merely that all the observable phenomena will be as if there is a mouse, but that there really is a mouse.

Will this pattern of inference also lead us to belief in unobservable entities? Is the scientific realist simply someone who consistently follows the rules of inference that we all follow in more mun-

---

[10] See n. 1 above.

[11] Cf. P. Thagard, doctoral dissertation, University of Toronto, 1977, and "The Best Explanation: Criteria for Theory Choice." *Journal of Philosophy*, **75** (1978), 76–92.

[12] "The Inference to the Best Explanation." *Philosophical Review*, **74** (1965), 88–95 and "Knowledge, Inference, and Explanation," *American Philosophical Quarterly*, **5** (1968), 164–73. Harman's views were further developed in subsequent publications (*Noûs*, 1967; *Journal of Philosophy*, 1968; in M. Swain (ed.), *Induction*, 1970; in H.-N. Castañeda (ed.), *Action, Thought, and Reality*, 1975; and in his book *Thought*, Ch. 10). I shall not consider these further developments here.

dane contexts? I have two objections to the idea that this is so.

First of all, what is meant by saying that we all *follow* a certain rule of inference? One meaning might be that we deliberately and consciously "apply" the rule, like a student doing a logic exercise. That meaning is much too literalistic and restrictive; surely all of mankind follows the rules of logic much of the time, while only a fraction can even formulate them. A second meaning is that we act in accordance with the rules in a sense that does not require conscious deliberation. That is not so easy to make precise, since each logical rule is a rule of permission (*modus ponens* allows you to infer *B* from *A* and (if *A then B*), but does not forbid you to infer (*B or A*) instead). However, we might say that a person behaved in accordance with a set of rules in that sense if every conclusion he drew could be reached from his premises via those rules. But this meaning is much too loose; in this sense we always behave in accordance with the rule that any conclusion may be inferred from any premise. So it seems that to be following a rule, I must be willing to believe all conclusions it allows, while definitely unwilling to believe conclusions at variance with the ones it allows—or else, change my willingness to believe the premises in question.

Therefore the statement that we all follow a certain rule in certain cases is a *psychological hypothesis* about what we are willing and unwilling to do. It is an empirical hypothesis, to be confronted with data, and with rival hypotheses. Here is a rival hypothesis: We are always willing to believe that the theory which best explains the evidence is empirically adequate (that all the observable phenomena are as the theory says they are).

In this way I can certainly account for the many instances in which a scientist appears to argue for the acceptance of a theory or hypothesis on the basis of its explanatory success. (A number of such instances are related by Thagard.[13]) For, remember: I equate the acceptance of a scientific theory with the belief that it is empirically adequate. We have therefore two rival hypotheses concerning these instances of scientific inference, and the one is apt in a realist account, the other in an anti-realist account.

Cases like the mouse in the wainscoting cannot provide telling evidence between those rival hypotheses. For the mouse *is* an observable thing; therefore "there is a mouse in the wainscoting" and "All observable phenomena are as if there is a mouse in the wainscoting" are totally equivalent; each implies the other (given what we know about mice).

It will be countered that it is less interesting to know whether people do follow a rule of inference than whether they ought to follow it. Granted; but the premise that we all follow the rule of inference to the best explanation when it comes to mice and other mundane matters—that premise is shown wanting. It is not warranted by the evidence, because that evidence is not telling *for* the premise *as against* the alternative hypothesis I proposed, which is a relevant one in this context.

My second objection is that even if we were to grant the correctness (or worthiness) of the rule of inference to the best explanation, the realist needs some further premise for his argument. For this rule is only one that dictates a choice when given a set of rival hypotheses. In other words, we need to be committed to belief in one of a range of hypotheses before the rule can be applied. Then, under favorable circumstances, it will tell us which of the hypotheses in that range to choose. The realist asks us to choose between different hypotheses that explain the regularities in certain ways; but his opponent always wishes to choose among hypotheses of the form "theory *T* is empirically adequate." So the realist will need his special extra premise that every universal regularity in nature needs an explanation before the rule will make realists of us all. And that is just the premise that distinguishes the realist from his opponents (and which I shall examine in more detail . . . below). . . .

I have kept this discussion quite abstract; but more concrete arguments by Sellars, Smart, and Putnam will be examined below. It should at least

---

[13] See n. 11 above.

be clear that there is no open-and-shut argument from common sense to the unobservable. Merely following the ordinary patterns of inference in science does not obviously and automatically make realists of us all.

LIMITS OF THE DEMAND FOR EXPLANATION

In this section and the next . . . , I shall examine arguments for realism that point to explanatory power as a criterion for theory choice. That this is indeed a criterion I do not deny. But these arguments for realism succeed only if the demand for explanation is supreme—if the task of science is unfinished, *ipso facto,* as long as any pervasive regularity is left unexplained. I shall object to this line of argument, as found in the writings of Smart, Reichenbach, Salmon, and Sellars, by arguing that such an unlimited demand for explanation leads to a demand for hidden variables, which runs contrary to at least one major school of thought in twentieth-century physics. I do not think that even these philosophers themselves wish to saddle realism with logical links to such consequences; but realist yearnings were born among the mistaken ideals of traditional metaphysics.

In his book *Between Science and Philosophy,* Smart gives two main arguments for realism. One is that only realism can respect the important distinction between *correct* and *merely useful* theories. He calls "instrumentalist" any view that locates the importance of theories in their use, which requires only empirical adequacy and not truth. But how can the instrumentalist explain the usefulness of his theories?

Consider a man (in the sixteenth century) who is a realist about the Copernican hypothesis but instrumentalist about the Ptolemaic one. He can explain the instrumental usefulness of the Ptolemaic system of epicycles because he can prove that the Ptolemaic system can produce almost the same predictions about the apparent motions of the planets as does the Copernican hypothesis. Hence the assumption of the realist truth of the Copernican hypothesis explains the instrumental usefulness of the Ptolemaic one. Such an

explanation of the instrumental usefulness of certain theories would not be possible if *all* theories were regarded as merely instrumental.[14]

What exactly is meant by "such an explanation" in the last sentence? If no theory is assumed to be true, then no theory has its usefulness explained as following from the truth of another one—granted. But would we have less of an explanation of the usefulness of the Ptolemaic hypothesis if we began instead with the premise that the Copernican gives implicitly a very accurate description of the motions of the planets as observed from earth? This would not assume the truth of Copernicus's heliocentric hypothesis, but would still entail that Ptolemy's simpler description was also a close approximation of those motions.

However, Smart would no doubt retort that such a response pushes the question only one step back: What explains the accuracy of predictions based on Copernicus's theory? If I say, the empirical adequacy of that theory, I have merely given a verbal explanation. For of course Smart does not mean to limit his question to actual predictions—it really concerns all actual and possible predictions and retrodictions. To put it quite concretely: What explains the fact that all observable planetary phenomena fit Copernicus's theory (if they do)? From the medieval debates, we recall the nominalist response that the basic regularities are merely brute regularities and have no explanation. So here the anti-realist must similarly say: That the observable phenomena exhibit these regularities, because of which they fit the theory, is merely a brute fact, and may or may not have an explanation in terms of unobservable facts "behind the phenomena"—it really does not matter to the goodness of the theory, nor to our understanding of the world.

Smart's main line of argument is addressed to exactly this point. In the same chapter he argues as follows. Suppose that we have a theory *T* which postulates micro-structure directly, and macro-structure indirectly. The statistical and approxi-

---

[14] J.J.C. Smart, *Between Science and Philosophy* (New York: Random House, 1968), p. 151.

mate laws about macroscopic phenomena are only partially spelled out perhaps, and in any case derive from the precise (deterministic or statistical) laws about the basic entities. We now consider theory *T'*, which is part of *T*, and says only what *T* says about the macroscopic phenomena. (How *T'* should be characterized I shall leave open, for that does not affect the argument here.) Then he continues:

I would suggest that the realist could (say) . . . that the success of *T'* is explained by the fact that the original theory *T* is true of the things that it is ostensibly about; in other words by the fact that there really are electrons or whatever is postulated by the theory *T*. If there were no such things, and if *T* were not true in a realist way, would not the success of *T'* be quite inexplicable? One would have to suppose that there were innumerable lucky accidents about the behavior mentioned in the observational vocabulary, so that they behaved miraculously *as if* they were brought about by the nonexistent things ostensibly talked about in the theoretical vocabulary.[15]

In other passages, Smart speaks similarly of "cosmic coincidences." The regularities in the observable phenomena must be explained in terms of deeper structure, for otherwise we are left with a belief in lucky accidents and coincidences on a cosmic scale.

I submit that if the demand for explanation implicit in these passages were precisely formulated, it would at once lead to absurdity. For if the mere fact of postulating regularities, without explanation, makes *T'* a poor theory, *T* will do no better. If, on the other hand, there is some precise limitation on what sorts of regularities can be postulated as basic, the context of the argument provides no reason to think that *T'* must automatically fare worse than *T*.

In any case, it seems to me that it is illegitimate to equate being a lucky accident, or a coincidence, with having no explanation. It was by coincidence that I met my friend in the market—but I can explain why I was there, and he can explain why he came, so together we can explain how this meeting happened. We call it a coincidence, not because the occurrence was inexplicable, but because we did not severally go to the market in order to meet.[16] There cannot be a requirement upon science to provide a theoretical elimination of coincidences, or accidental correlations in general, for that does not even make sense. There is nothing here to motivate the demand for explanation, only a restatement in persuasive terms. . . .

LIMITS TO EXPLANATION: A THOUGHT EXPERIMENT

Wilfrid Sellars was one of the leaders of the return to realism in philosophy of science and has, in his writings of the past three decades, developed a systematic and coherent scientific realism. I have discussed a number of his views and arguments elsewhere; but will here concentrate on some aspects that are closely related to the arguments of Smart, Reichenbach, and Salmon just examined.[17] Let me begin by setting the stage in the way Sellars does.

There is a certain oversimplified picture of science, the "levels picture," which pervades positivist writings and which Sellars successfully demolished.[18] In that picture, singular observable facts ("this crow is black") are scientifically explained by general observable regularities ("all crows are black"), which in turn are explained by highly theoretical hypotheses not restricted in what they say to the observable. The three levels are commonly called those of *fact,* of *empirical law,* and of *theory.* But, as Sellars points out, theories do not explain, or even entail such empirical

[15] Ibid., pp. 150f.

[16] This point is clearly made by Aristotle, *Physics,* II, Chs. 4–6 (see esp. 196ᵃ 1–20; 196ᵇ 20–197ᵃ 12).

[17] See my "Wilfrid Sellars on Scientific Realism," *Dialogue,* **14** (1975), 606–16; W. Sellars, "Is Scientific Realism Tenable?", pp. 307–34 in F. Suppe and P. Asquith (eds.), *PSA 1976* (East Lansing, Mich.: Philosophy of Science Association, 1977), vol. II, 307–34; and my "On the Radical Incompleteness of the Manifest Image," ibid., 335–43; and see n. 1 above.

[18] W. Sellars, "The Language of Theories," in his *Science, Perception, and Reality* (London: Routledge and Kegan Paul, 1963).

laws—they only show why observable things obey these so-called laws to the extent they do.[19] Indeed, perhaps we have no such empirical laws at all: All crows are black—except albinos: water boils at 100°C—provided atmospheric pressure is normal; a falling body accelerates—provided it is not intercepted, or attached to an aeroplane by a static line; and so forth. On the level of the observable we are liable to find only putative laws heavily subject to unwritten *ceteris paribus* qualifications.

This is, so far, only a methodological point. We do not really expect theories to "save" our common everyday generalizations, for we ourselves have no confidence in their strict universality. But a theory which says that the micro-structure of things is subject to *some* exact, universal regularities must imply the same for those things themselves. This, at least, is my reaction to the points so far. Sellars, however, sees an inherent inferiority in the description of the observable alone, an incompleteness which requires (*sub specie* the aims of science) an introduction of an unobservable reality behind the phenomena. This is brought out by an interesting "thought-experiment."

Imagine that at some early stage of chemistry it had been found that different samples of gold dissolve in *aqua regia* at different rates, although "as far as can be observationally determined, the specimens and circumstances are identical."[20] Imagine further that the response of chemistry to this problem was to postulate two distinct microstructures for the different samples of gold. Observationally unpredictable variation in the rate of dissolution is explained by saying that the samples are mixtures (not compounds) of these two (observationally identical) substances, each of which has a fixed rate of dissolution.

In this case we have explanation through laws which have no observational counterparts that can play the same role. Indeed, no explanation seems possible unless we agree to find our physical vari-

ables outside the observable. But science aims to explain, must try to explain, and so must require a belief in this unobservable micro-structure. So Sellars contends.

There are at least three questions before us. Did this postulation of micro-structure really have no new consequences for the observable phenomena? Is there really such a demand upon science that it must explain—even if the means of explanation bring no gain in empirical predictions? And thirdly, could a *different* rationale exist for the use of a micro-structure picture in the development of a scientific theory in a case like this?

First, it seems to me that these hypothetical chemists did postulate new observable regularities as well. Suppose the two substances are A and B, with dissolving rates x and x + y and that every gold sample is a mixture of these substances. Then it follows that every gold sample dissolves at a rate no lower than x and no higher than x + y; *and* that between these two any value may be found—to within the limits of accuracy of gold mixing. None of this is implied by the data that different samples of gold have dissolved at various rates between x and x + y. So Sellars's first contention is false.

We may assume, for the sake of Sellars's example, that there is still no way of predicting dissolving rates any further. Is there then a categorical demand upon science to explain this variation which does not depend on other observable factors? . . . [A] precise version of such a demand (Reichenbach's principle of the common cause) could result automatically in a demand for hidden variables, providing a "classical" underpinning for indeterministic theories. Sellars recognized very well that a demand for hidden variables would run counter to the main opinions current in quantum physics. Accordingly he mentions ". . . the familiar point that the irreducibly and lawfully statistical ensembles of quantum-mechanical theory are mathematically inconsistent with the assumption of hidden variables."[21] Thus, he restricts the demand for explanation, in effect, to just those

[19] Op. cit., p. 121.

[20] Ibid., p. 121.

[21] Ibid., p. 123.

cases where it is *consistent* to add hidden variables to the theory. And consistency is surely a logical stopping point.

This restriction unfortunately does not prevent the disaster. For while there are a number of proofs that hidden variables cannot be supplied so as to turn quantum mechanics into a classical sort of deterministic theory, those proofs are based on requirements much stronger than consistency. To give an example, one such assumption is that two distinct physical variables cannot have the same statistical distributions in measurement on all possible states.[22] Thus it is assumed that, if we cannot point to some possible difference in empirical predictions, then there is no real difference at all. If such requirements were lifted, and consistency alone were the criterion, hidden variables could indeed be introduced. I think we must conclude that science, in contrast to scientific realism, does not place an overriding value on explanation in the absence of any gain for empirical results.

Thirdly, then, let us consider how an anti-realist could make sense of those hypothetical chemists' procedure. After pointing to the new empirical implications which I mentioned two paragraphs ago, he would point to methodological reasons. By imagining a certain sort of microstructure for gold and other metals, say, we might arrive at a theory governing many observationally disparate substances; and this might then have implications for new, wider empirical regularities when such substances interact. This would only be a hope, of course; no hypothesis is guaranteed to be fruitful—but the point is that the true demand on science is not for explanation *as such*, but for imaginative pictures which have a hope of suggesting new statements of observable regularities and of correcting old ones. . . .

. . . THE ULTIMATE ARGUMENT

. . . In . . . "What is Mathematical Truth," Putnam . . . gives what I shall call the *Ultimate*

Argument. He begins with a formulation of realism which he says he learned from Michael Dummett:

A realist (with respect to a given theory or discourse) holds that (1) the sentences of that theory are true or false; and (2) that what makes them true or false is something external—that is to say, it is not (in general) our sense data, actual or potential, or the structure of our minds, or our language, etc.[23]

This formulation is quite different from the one I have given even if we instantiate it to the case in which that theory or discourse is science or scientific discourse. Because the wide discussion of Dummett's views has given some currency to his usage of these terms, and because Putnam begins his discussion in this way, we need to look carefully at this formulation.

In my view, Dummett's usage is quite idiosyncratic. Putnam's statement, though very brief, is essentially accurate. In his "Realism," Dummett begins by describing various sorts of realism in the traditional fashion, as disputes over whether there really exist entities of a particular type. But he says that in some cases he wishes to discuss, such as the reality of the past and intuitionism in mathematics, the central issues seem to him to be about other questions. For this reason he proposes a new usage: He will take such disputes

as relating, not to a class of entities or a class of terms, but to a class of *statements* . . . . Realism I characterize as the belief that statements of the disputed class possess an objective truth-value, independently of our means of knowing it: They are true or false in virtue of a reality existing independently of us. The anti-realist opposes to this the view that statements of the disputed class are to be understood only by reference to the sort of thing which we count as evidence for a statement of that class.[24]

Dummett himself notes at once that nominalists are realists in this sense.[25] If, for example, you say

[22] See my "Semantic Analysis of Quantum Logic," in C. A. Hooker (ed.), *Contemporary Research in the Foundations and Philosophy of Quantum Theory* (Dordrecht: Reidel, 1973), Part III, Sects. 5 and 6.

[23] See n. 3 above.

[24] Michael Dummett, *Truth and Other Enigmas* (Cambridge, Mass.: Harvard University Press, 1978), p. 146 (see also pp. 358–61).

[25] Dummett adds to the cited passage that he realizes that his characterization does not include all the disputes he had mentioned, and specifically excepts nominalism about abstract entities. However, he includes scientific realism as an example (op. cit., pp. 146f.).

that abstract entities do not exist, and sets are abstract entities, hence sets do not exist, then you will certainly accord a truth-value to all statements of set theory. It might be objected that if you take this position then you have a decision procedure for determining the truth-values of these statements (*false* for existentially quantified ones, *true* for universal ones, apply truth tables for the rest). Does that not mean that, on your view, the truth-values are not independent of our knowledge? Not at all; for you clearly believe that if we had not existed, and *a fortiori* had had no knowledge, the state of affairs with respect to abstract entities would be the same.

Has Dummett perhaps only laid down a necessary condition for realism, in his definition, for the sake of generality? I do not think so. In discussions of quantum mechanics we come across the view that the particles of microphysics are real and obey the principles of the theory, but at any time t when "particle x has exact momentum p" is true then "particle x has position q" is neither true nor false. In any traditional sense, this is a realist position with respect to quantum mechanics.

We note also that Dummett has, at least in this passage, taken no care to exclude non-literal construals of the theory, as long as they are truth-valued. The two are not the same; when Strawson construed "The king of France in 1905 is bald" as neither true nor false, he was not giving a non-literal construal of our language. On the other hand, people tend to fall back on non-literal construals typically in order to be able to say, "properly construed, the theory is true."

Perhaps Dummett is right in his assertion that what is really at stake, in realist disputes of various sorts, is questions about language—or, if not really at stake, at least the only serious philosophical problems in those neighborhoods. Certainly the arguments in which he engages are profound, serious, and worthy of our attention. But it seems to me that his terminology ill accords with the traditional one. Certainly I wish to define scientific realism so that it need not imply that all statements in the theoretical language are true or false (only that they are all capable of being true or false, that is, there are conditions for each under which it has

a truth-value); to imply also that the aim·at least is that the theories should be true. And the contrary position of constructive empiricism is not anti-realist in Dummett's sense, since it also assumes scientific statements to have truth-conditions entirely independent of human activity or knowledge. But then, I do not conceive the dispute as being about language at all.

In any case Putnam himself does not stick with this weak formulation of Dummett's. A little later in the paper he directs himself to scientific realism *per se,* and formulates it in terms borrowed, he says, from Richard Boyd. The new formulation comes in the course of a new argument for scientific realism, which I shall call the Ultimate Argument:

the positive argument for realism is that it is the only philosophy that doesn't make the success of science a miracle. That terms in mature scientific theories typically refer (this formulation is due to Richard Boyd), that the theories accepted in a mature science are typically approximately true, that the same term can refer to the same thing even when it occurs in different theories—these statements are viewed by the scientific realist not as necessary truths but as part of the only scientific explanation of the success of science, and hence as part of any adequate scientific description of science and its relations to its objects.[26]

Science, apparently, is required to explain its own success. There is this regularity in the world, that scientific predictions are regularly fulfilled; and this regularity, too, needs an explanation. Once *that* is supplied we may perhaps hope to have reached the *terminus de jure?*

The explanation provided is a very traditional one—*adequatio ad rem,* the "adequacy" of the theory to its objects, a kind of mirroring of the structure of things by the structure of ideas—Aquinas would have felt quite at home with it.

Well, let us accept for now this demand for a scientific explanation of the success of science. Let us also resist construing it as merely a restatement of Smart's "cosmic coincidence" argument, and view it instead as the question why we have

---

26 See n. 4 above.

successful scientific theories at all. Will this realist explanation with the Scholastic look be a scientifically acceptable answer? I would like to point out that science is a biological phenomenon, an activity by one kind of organism which facilitates its interaction with the environment. And this makes me think that a very different kind of scientific explanation is required.

I can best make the point by contrasting two accounts of the mouse who runs from its enemy, the cat. St. Augustine already remarked on this phenomenon, and provided an intensional explanation: The mouse *perceives that* the cat is its enemy, hence the mouse runs. What is postulated here is the "adequacy" of the mouse's thought to the order of nature: The relation of enmity is correctly reflected in his mind. But the Darwinist says: Do not ask why the *mouse* runs from its enemy. Species which did not cope with their natural enemies no longer exist. That is why there are only ones who do.

In just the same way, I claim that the success of current scientific theories is no miracle. It is not even surprising to the scientific (Darwinist) mind. For any scientific theory is born into a life of fierce competition, a jungle red in tooth and claw. Only the successful theories survive—the ones which *in fact* latched on to actual regularities in nature.[27]

---

[27] Of course, we can ask specifically why the *mouse* is one of the surviving species, how *it* survives, and answer this, on the basis of whatever scientific theory we accept, in terms of its brain and environment. The analogous question for theories would be why, say, Balmer's formula for the line spectrum of hydrogen survives as a successful hypothesis. In that case too we explain, on the basis of the physics we accept now, why the spacing of those lines satisfies the formula. Both the question and the answer are very different from the global question of the success of science, and the global answer of realism. The realist may now make the *further* objection that the anti-realist cannot answer the question about the mouse specifically, nor the one about Balmer's formula, in this fashion, since the answer is in part an assertion that the scientific theory, used as basis of the explanation, is true. This is a quite different argument, which I . . . take up in Ch. 4, Sect. 4, and Ch. 5 [of *The Scientific Image*].

In his most recent publications and lectures Hilary Putnam has drawn a distinction between two doctrines, metaphysical realism and internal realism. He denies the former and identifies his preceding scientific realism as the latter. While I have at present no commitment to either side of the metaphysical dispute, I am very much in sympathy with the critique of Platonism in philosophy of mathematics, which forms part of Putnam's arguments. Our disagreement about scientific (internal) realism would remain, of course, whenever we came down to earth after deciding to agree or disagree about metaphysical realism, or even about whether this distinction makes sense at all.

And Not Anti-Realism Either*

Arthur Fine

EPIGRAPHS

1. *Realism:* "Out yonder there was this huge world, which exists independently of us human beings. . . . The mental grasp of this extra-personal world hovered before me as the highest goal . . . ."

Albert Einstein, "Autobiographical Notes"

2. *Anti-Realism:* "to get at something absolute without going out of your own skin!"

William James, letter to Tom Ward, October 9, 1868

INTRODUCTION

As my title suggests, this paper is another episode in a continuing story. In the last episode the body of realism was examined, the causes of its death identified, and then the project of constructing a suitable successor for these post-realist times was begun ([3]). I called that successor the "natural ontological attitude" or NOA, for short, and I shall return to it below. In today's episode, however, the subject of criticism becomes anti-realism, and this is a live and, therefore, a shiftier target. For the death of realism has revived interest in several anti-realist positions and, appropriately enough, recent philosophical work has explored modifications of these anti-realisms to see whether they can be refurbished in order to take over, from realism, as the philosophy-of-science "of choice." My first object here will be to show that just as realism will not do for this choice position, neither will anti-realism. That job accomplished, I shall then sing some more in praise of NOA.

To understand anti-realism we have first to backtrack a bit and re-examine realism. Given the diverse array of philosophical positions that have sought the "realist" label, it is probably not possible to give a sketch of realism that will encompass them all. Indeed, it may be hopeless to try, even, to capture the essential features of realism. Yet that is indeed what I hope to do in identifying the core of realism with the following ideas. First, realism holds that there exists a definite world; that is, a world containing entities with relations and properties that are to a large extent independent of human acts and agents (or the possibilities thereof). Secondly, according to realism, it is possible to obtain a substantial amount of reliable and relatively observer-independent information concerning this world and its features, information not restricted, for example, to just observable features. I shall refer to these components of realism as (1) belief in a definite world-structure and (2) belief in the possibility of substantial epistemic access to that structure. This realism becomes "scientific" when we add to it a third component, namely, (3) the belief that science aims at (and, to some extent, achieves) all the epistemic access to the definite world structure that realism holds to be possible.

This sketch of realism highlights the ontological features that seem to me characteristic of it. But there is a semantic aspect as well. For in order to see science as working toward the achievement of the realist goal of substantial access to features of the definite world-structure, the theories and principles of science must be understood to be *about* that world-structure. Thus the *truth* of scientific assertions gets a specifically realist interpretation; namely, as a *correspondence* with features of the definite world structure.

I can put it very succinctly this way. The realist adopts a standard, model-theoretic, correspon-

* This paper was written during the tenure of a Guggenheim Fellowship. I want to thank the Foundation for their support. Thanks, too, to Micky Forbes for struggling with me through the ideas and their expression.

dence theory of truth, where the model is just the definite world structure posited by realism and where correspondence is understood as a relation that reaches right out to touch the world. (See [4] and [10].)

The "anti-realisms" that I want to examine and reject here all oppose the three tenets of realism understood as above (in spirit, if not always in words). They also reject the characteristically realist picture of truth as external-world correspondence. They divide among themselves over the question of whether or not that realist picture of truth ought to be replaced by some other picture. But they agree (again in spirit, if not in words) that although the realist has the aim of science wrong, in his third tenet above, it is important for us to understand what the correct aim of science is. This agreement is the mark of what I shall call "scientific" anti-realism. And the disagreement over offering truth pictures, then, divides the scientific anti-realists into those who are truthmongers and those who are not.

TRUTHMONGERS

The history of philosophy has witnessed a rather considerable trade in truth; including wholesale accounts like correspondence and coherence theories, or consensus and pragmatic theories, or indexical and relativist theories. There have also been special reductions available including phenomenalisms and idealisms. Among scientific anti-realists the wholesalers, recently, have tried to promote some kind of consensus-cum-pragmatic picture. I will try to give this picture a canonical representation so that we can identify the features that these particular anti-realisms have in common. So represented, it portrays the truth of a statement P as amounting to the fact that a certain class of subjects would accept P under a certain set of circumstances. If we let the subjects be "perfectly rational" agents and the circumstances be "ideal" ones for the purposes of the knowledge trade (perhaps those marking the Peircean limit?), then we get the picture of truth as ideal rational acceptance, and this is the picture that Hilary Put-

nam paints for his "internal realism."[1] If the subjects are not perfectly rational and yet conscientious and well-intentioned about things, and we let the circumstances be those marking a serious dialogue of the kind that makes for consensus, where consensus is attainable, then we get the Wittgensteinean position that Richard Rorty calls "epistemological behaviorism."[2] Finally, if our subjects are immersed in the matrix of some paradigm and the circumstances are those encompassed by the values and rules of the paradigm, then we get the specifically paradigm-relative concept of truth (and of reference) that is characteristic of Thomas Kuhn's anti-realism ([8]). With these three applications in mind, I want to examine the merits—which is to say, to point out the demerits—of this sort of acceptance theory of truth.

Let us first be clear that these acceptance pictures of truth make for an anti-realist attitude towards science. That is a somewhat subtle issue, for the old Machian debates over the reality of molecules and atoms might suggest that realism turns on the putative truth (or not) of certain existence claims, especially claims about the existence of "unobservables." Since acceptance theories of truth, of the sort outlined above, might very well issue in the truth of such existence claims, one might be tempted to suggest, as well, that holders of acceptance theories could be realists. While there is no doubt a distinction to be drawn between those who do and those who do not believe in the existence, let us say, of magnetic monopoles; I think it would be a mistake to take that as distinguishing the realists from the others.[3] For it is not the *form* of a claim held true that marks off realism, it is rather the significance or content of the claim. The realist, say, wants to know

---

[1] Putnam [11] is an extended discussion, usefully supplemented by Putnam [13] and [14]. Originally, rational acceptability was merely offered as a "picture" of truth. But later it emerged as a "characterization," and as providing "the only sense in which we have a vital and working notion of it." ([14]:5)

[2] Rorty [15]. In his symposium talk for the March, 1983 Pacific Division, APA meetings (in Berkeley), Rorty announced a new position that he called "revisionary pragmatism." This new stance pulls back from various of Rorty's earlier commitments, including some of his ideas about truth. I have not been able to figure out, however, just what it rejects or what it retains.

[3] [See p. 361.]

whether there *really* are magnetic monopoles. He understands that in the way explained above, so that a positive answer here would signify a sort of reaching *out* from electrodynamic discourse *to* the very stuff of the world. The fact that scientific practice involves serious monopole talk, including what is described as manipulating monopoles and intervening in their behavior, does not even begin to address the issue of realism. For what realism is after is a very particular interpretation of that practice. This is exactly the interpretation that the picture of truth-as-acceptance turns us away from.

The special sort of correspondence that is built into the realist conception of truth orients us to face "*out* on the world," striving in our science to grab hold of significant chunks of its definite structure. The idea of truth as acceptance, however, turns us right around again to look back at our own collective selves, and at the interpersonal features that constitute the practice of the truth-game. (Compare the two epigraphs.) This turnabout makes for a sort of Ptolemaic counterrevolution. We are invited to focus on the mundane roots of truth-talk, and its various mundane purposes and procedures. Concepts having to do with acceptance provide a rich setting for all these mundane happenings. If we then take truth just to *be* the right sort of acceptance we reap a bonus for, when we bring truth down to earth in this way, we obtain insurance against the inherent, metaphysical aspects of realism.

I can well understand how the sight of realism unveiled might bring on disturbing, metaphysical shudders. And it's understandable, I think, that we should seek the seeming security provided by sheltering for awhile in a nest of interpersonal rela-

tions. But it would be a mistake to think that we will find truth there. For the anti-realism expressed in the idea of truth-as-acceptance is just as metaphysical and idle as the realism expressed by a correspondence theory.

I have not been able to locate a significant line of argument in the recent literature that moves to supply the warrant for an acceptance theory of truth. Rather, as I have noted, these anti-realists seem to have taken shelter in that corner mainly in reaction to realism. For when one sees that the realist conception of truth creates a gap that keeps the epistemic access one wants always just beyond reach, it may be tempting to try to refashion the idea of truth in epistemic terms in order, literally, to make the truth accessible. What allows the truthmongers to think that this is feasible, so far as I can tell, is a common turning toward behaviorism. In one way or another, these anti-realists seem sympathetic to the behaviorist idea that the working practices of conceptual exchange exhaust the meaning of that exchange, giving it its significance and providing it with its content. Thus we come to the idea that if the working practices of the truth exchange are the practices of acceptance, then acceptance is what truth is all about, and nothing but acceptance.

I do not have any new critique to offer concerning the flaws in behaviorism. Just about everyone recognizes that various special applications of behaviorism are wrong; for example, operationalism, or Watson-Skinnerism. So too, just about everyone has a sense of the basic error; namely, that behaviorism makes out everything it touches to be less than it is, fixing limits where none exist. Such, indeed, is the way of these anti-realisms: they fix the concept of truth, pinning it down to acceptance. One certainly has no more warrant for imposing this constraint on the basic concept of truth, however, than the operationalist has for imposing his constraints on more derivative concepts (like length or mass).

In fact, I think the warrant for behaviorism with regard to truth is considerably more suspicious than anything the operationalist ever had in mind. For whatever might possibly warrant the behaviorist conception of truth-as-acceptance

---

[3] Cartwright [1] and Hacking [5] and [6] adopt this way of distinguishing a significant form of realism. See my [3] and [4] for a critique. The only background that seems to me to support the idea that the truth of certain existence claims makes for realism is an account of truth as external-world correspondence. I do not believe that Hacking adopts such a view. I do not know about Cartwright. I might mention here that Putnam's tactic of calling his position a kind of realism (an "internal" kind), while also seeing in it a "transcendental idealism" ([12]: 6), seems founded on nothing more than the amusing idea that whatever is not solipsism is, *ipso facto*, a realism. See ([13]: 162) and ([14]: 13).

should at least make that a conception we can take in and understand. Even if, as some maintain, truth is merely a regulative ideal, it must still be an ideal we can understand, strive for, believe in, glimpse—and so forth. But if, as the behaviorist holds, judgments of truth are judgments of what certain people would accept under certain circumstances, what are the ground rules for arriving at those judgments, and working with them as required? Naively, it looks like what we are called upon to do is to extrapolate from what *is* the case with regard to actual acceptance behavior to what *would be* the case under the right conditions. But how are we ever to establish what *is* the case, in order to get this extrapolation going, when that determination itself calls for a prior, successful round of extrapolation? It appears that acceptance locks us into a repeating pattern that involves an endless regress. Moreover, if we attend to the counterfactuality built into the "would accept" in the truth-as-acceptance formula, then I think we encounter a similar difficulty. To understand this conception of truth we must get a sense of how things would be were they different in certain respects from what they are now. Whatever your line about counterfactuals, this understanding involves at least either the idea of truth in altered circumstances, or the idea of truth in these actual circumstances. But each alternative here folds in upon itself, requiring in turn further truths. I believe there is no grounding for this process unless we turn away from the acceptance picture at some point.

It seems to me that the acceptance idea never *can* get off the ground, and that we cannot actually understand the picture of truth that it purports to offer. If we think otherwise that is probably because we are inclined to read into the truthmongers' project some truths (or ideas of truth) not having to do with acceptance at all—perhaps, even, some truths via correspondence! Thus, with respect to warrant and intelligibility, the acceptance picture emerges as quite on a par with the correspondence picture.[4]

There is, as I have noted, a very close connection between these two conceptions. It is a typical dialectic that binds the metaphysics of realism to the metaphysics of behaviorism. Realism reaches out for *more* than can be had. Behaviorism reacts by pulling back to the "secure" ground of human behavior. In terms of that it tries to impose a limit, short of what realism has been searching for. The limit imposed by behaviorism, however, is simply *less* than what we require. So realism reacts by positing something more, and then reaches out for it again. What we can learn from this cycle is just what makes it run, and how to stop it.

Both the scientific realist and the scientific anti-realist of the acceptance sort share an attitude toward the concept of truth. They think it is appropriate to give a theory, or account, or perhaps just a "picture" of truth. As Hilary Putnam pleads,

> But if all notions of rightness, both epistemic and (metaphysically) realist are eliminated, then what are our statements but noisemakings? What are our thoughts but *mere* subvocalizations? . . . Let us recognize that one of our fundamental self-conceptualizations, in Rorty's phrase, is that we are *thinkers,* and that *as* thinkers we are committed to there being *some* kind of truth, some kind of correctness which is substantial and not merely "disquotational." ([14]: 20–21)

Of course we are all committed to there being some kind of truth. But need we take that to be something like a "natural" kind? This essentialist idea is what makes the cycle run, and we can stop it if we stop conceiving of truth as a substantial something, something for which theories, accounts, or even pictures are appropriate. To be sure, the anti-realist is quite correct in his diagnosis of the disease of realism, and in his therapeutic

---

[4] Other ways of displaying the gap between "truth" and the favored version of acceptance would be to ask whether the

acceptance formula is true, or what "accept as true" comes to under the formula, or what now would guarantee the idempotency of "is true." Pursuing such lines of inquiry, along with the ones in the text, will show that the sense and grammar of truth is not that of acceptance. But, of course, it does not follow that truth is not acceptance (really!). Nor could such lines of inquiry really subvert the program of replacing "truth" by acceptance, if one were determined to carry on with the program. One can always dodge the arguments and, where that fails, bite the argumentative bullets. In philosophy, as in other areas of rational discourse, inquiry must end in judgments. One can try to inform and tutor good judgment, but it cannot be compelled—not even by good-looking reasons.

recommendation to pay attention to how human beings actually operate with the family of truth concepts. Where he goes wrong is in trying to fashion out of these practices a completed concept of truth as a substantial something, one that will then act as a limit for legitimate human aspirations. If we do not join him in this undertaking and if we are also careful not to replace this anti-realist limit on truth by something else that goes beyond practice, then we shall have managed to avoid both realism and these truthmongering anti-realisms as well.

EMPIRICISM

But there are other anti-realisms to contend with. One well-known brand is empiricism, and this has made some notable progress in the sophisticated version that Bas van Fraassen calls "constructive empiricism" ([18]). This account avoids the reductive and foundationalist tendency of earlier empiricisms that sought to ground all truths in a sense-data or phenomenalist base. It also avoids the modification of this idea that ensnared logical-empiricism: the conception of a theory as a deductively closed logical system on the vocabulary of which there is imposed an epistemologically significant distinction between observables and unobservables. Instead, constructive empiricism takes a semantical view of a scientific theory; it views it as a family of models. And it lets science itself dictate what is or is not observable, where the "able" part refers to us and our limitations according to science. As for truth, it does not engage in trade but plumps for a literal construal.[5]

The important concept for this brand of empiricism is the idea of empirical adequacy. This idea applies to theories, conceived of as above. Such a theory is empirically adequate just in case it has some model in which all truths about observables are represented. If truths about observables are called "phenomena," then a theory is empirically adequate just in case it saves the phenomena, *all* the phenomena. The distinctively anti-realist thesis of constructive empiricism is twofold: (1) that science aims only to provide theories that are empirically adequate and (2) that acceptance of a theory involves as belief only that it *is* empirically adequate. The intended contrast is with a realism that posits true theories as the goal of science and that takes acceptance of a theory to be belief in the truth of the theory. Since truth here is to be taken literally, the realist could well be committed to believing in the existence of unobservable entities literally, but never the constructive empiricist.

Indeed this brand of empiricism, along with its ancestors, involves a strong limitation on what it is legitimate for us to believe (in the sense of believe to be true). Where science is taken as the legitimating basis, we are allowed to believe that the scientific story about observables is true, and no more than that. It seems to me that there are two obvious testing points to probe with regard to any stance that seeks to impose limits on our epistemic attitudes. The first is to see whether the boundary can be marked off in a way that does not involve suspicious or obnoxious assumptions. The second is to see what the rationale is for putting the boundary just there, and to what extent that implacement is arbitrary. Let me take these in order.

A difficulty of the first sort begins to show up as soon as we ask why an attitude of belief is appropriate for the scientific judgment that something is observable. After all, that is supposed to be just another bit of science, and so our empiricism says that it is a candidate for affirmative belief (as op-

---

[5] Although van Fraassen ([18]: Esp. 9–11) is quite explicit about taking truth literally, he also seems tempted by the interpretative metaphor of realist-style correspondence. "A statement is true exactly if the actual world accords with the statement." ([18]: 90) "I would still identify the truth of a theory with the condition that there is an exact correspondence between reality and one of its models." ([18]: 197) If van Fraassen is taken literally, in these passages, then for him truth *is*, literally, real-world correspondence. If this were correct, then van Fraassen's empiricism would appear to be a restricted version of realism, a version where the epistemic access is restricted to observables. This makes his "anti-realism" seem considerably less radical than one might have thought. I, at any rate, had thought his idea of literal truth included the notion that "truth" was not to be fur-

ther interpreted. On this understanding I thought that if he were persuaded out of his attachment to observables, then his ideas would fit right in with NOA (see below). But now I think that may be wrong. If we were to make constructive empiricism lose its attachment to observables, we would (it seems) merely have regained realism, full blown.

posed to agnostic reserve) just in case it is itself a judgment entirely within the realm of observables (according to science). What does that mean? Well, one might suppose that since the judgment that something is observable has a simple subject/predicate form, then both the subject of the judgment and the predicate must refer to what science holds to be observable. So, for example, the judgment that carrots are mobile would be a candidate for belief if, as we suppose, science classifies both carrots and mobility as observables. What then of the judgment that carrots are observable? In order for *it* to be a candidate for belief, we must suppose that science classifies both carrots and observability as observables. But now I think we ought to come to a full stop.

For if we accept the moves made so far, then we see that the combination of first, limiting belief to the observable and, second, letting science determine what counts as observable, has a terribly odd consequence. Namely, in order to believe in any scientific judgment concerning what is observable, we must take as a presupposition that the "property" or "characteristic" (or whatever) of "being observable" is itself an observable, *according to science*. Thus when we go down the list of entities supposedly using our science to determine which ones are observable and which not, the property of "being observable" must be classified as well, and indeed it must come out as observable. But this is surely something forced on us *a priori* by this empiricist philosophical stance. If there actually were such a property as "being observable," and science did actually classify it, who is to say how it must come out—or even whether it must come out at all as observable or not. *Science* is supposed to speak here, not philosophy. Thus if we accept the moves in the argument, this empiricism is suspiciously near to an inconsistency: It forces the hand of science exactly where it is supposed to follow it.

What then if we try to reject some move in the argument? What shall we question? Surely the requirement that we respect grammar and ask separately of subject and predicate whether it refers to an observable is not a necessary one. After all, to speak somewhat realistically, who can tell how a judgment confronts the world? Let us then give up the grammatical requirement and think again how to deal with the judgment that something is an observable; that is, how to construe it as a judgment entirely within the realm of observables. If I judge, scientifically, that carrots are observable, then I suppose I would have to identify some properties or features of carrots and show that these would induce the right sort of effects in an interaction, one party to which is a human being, *qua* observing instrument. To back up the counterfactual, here, (what effects would be induced) certainly several laws would enter the argument, very likely connecting entities that may themselves not be observable. Now, according to the empiricism at issue, I do not have to believe this whole theoretical story, only its observational part. *That* I do have to believe if it is to warrant my belief in the observability of carrots. But since the question here was precisely how to identify the observational part of a simple judgment (that carrots are observable) I think I am stuck. I do not know what to believe in my scientific story that issues in the observability of carrots, unless I can pick out its observational parts. And I cannot identify a part of the story as observational unless I can support that identification by means of beliefs based on observational parts of still other covering stories. I really think that we cannot break out of this cycle—or rather break in to get it going—without some external stipulations, or the like, as to what to believe to be observable. Thus an aprioristic resolution of the philosophical squabble over what to take as observable seems required by this empiricism, just as it was by the older ones.

There is, however, a deft maneuver that could get things going again. It is simply not to raise the question of observability where what is at stake is itself a judgment of observability. Thus we could exempt those special judgments from the test of observability and allow ourselves to believe them in just the way that we would if they had actually passed the test. Indeed if we allow this exception for judgments of observability, then no difficulties seem to arise by way of beliefs being sanctioned that are not really warranted. But if we try to avoid obnoxious assumptions concerning what is observable by granting exemptions from the general empiricist rule in certain special cases, then why—we must ask—should that rule be necessary for the others? This brings us to the second testing point for a philosophy that seeks to impose limits on one's epistemic attitudes; namely, to examine the rationale for the limit—especially to see how arbitrary it is.

We can push this question hard if we recognize that there is a loosely graded vocabulary concerning observability. We do, after all, draw a distinction between what is *observable,* which is rather strict, and what is *detectable,* which is somewhat looser. To get a feel for the distinction, we might, for instance, picture the difference here as between what we would "observe," in the right circumstances, with our sense organs as they are and what we would "detect" in those same circumstances were our eyes, for example, replaced by electron microscopes. In this grading system atoms . . . would count as detectable but not (strictly) observable. It seems to me that distinctions of this sort are, in fact, at work in the vocabulary of observation, and van Fraassen certainly recognizes some such ([18]: 16–17). With this in mind . . . I think we can make the question of observability, as a warrant for belief, very acute by asking why restrict the realm of belief to what is observable, as opposed, say, to what is detectable?

I think the question is acute, because I cannot imagine any answer that would be compelling. Are we supposed to refrain from believing in atoms, and various truths about them, because we are concerned over the possibility that what the electron microscope reveals is merely an artifact of the machine? If this is our concern, then we can address it by applying the cautious and thorough procedures and analyses involved in the use and construction of that machine, as well as the cross-checks from other detecting devices, to evaluate the artifactuality (or not) of the atomic phenomena. If we can do this satisfactorily according to tough standards, are we then still not supposed to frame beliefs about atoms, and why not now? Surely the end product of such inquiries, when each one pursues a specific area of uncertainty or

possible error, can only be a very compelling scientific documentation of the grounds for believing that we are, actually, detecting atoms.[6] Faced with such substantial reasons for believing that we are detecting atoms what, except purely *a priori* and arbitrary conventions, could possibly dictate the empiricist conclusion that, nevertheless, we are unwarranted actually to engage in *belief* about atoms? What holds for detectability holds as well for the other information-bearing modalities, ones that may be even more remotely connected with strict observability. The general lesson is that, in the context of science, adopting an attitude of belief has as warrant precisely that which science itself grants, nothing more but certainly nothing less.[7]

The stance of empiricism, like that of the truthmongers, is (in part) a moral stance. They both regard metaphysics, and in particular the metaphysics of realism, as a sin. They both move in the direction of their anti-realism in order to avoid that sin. But the behaviorism to which the truthmongers turn, as we have seen, locks them into a comic dance with realism, a *pas de deux* as wickedly metaphysical as ever there was. The empiricist, I think, carries a comparable taint. For when he sidesteps science and moves into his courtroom, there to pronounce his judgments of where to believe and where to withhold, he avoids metaphysics only by committing, instead, the sin of epistemology. We ought not to follow him in this practice. Indeed, I think courtesy requires, at this point, a discreet withdrawal.

NOA: THE NATURAL ONTOLOGICAL ATTITUDE

The "isms" of this paper each derive from a philosophical program in the context of which they

---

[6] The themes just touched on, especially the insistence on the specificity of scientific doubt and on following the scientific rationale that informs the vocabulary of observation, are forcefully elaborated by Shapere [16]. Part B ("intervening") of Hacking [6] is also required reading here.

[7] See Hellman ([7]: esp. 247–248) for some cosmological "unobservables" in which we might have good scientific grounds for belief. But do not forget more familiar sorts of objects either, like unconscious (or "subliminal") causal factors in our behavior or, even, the nightly activity we call "dreaming"!

seek to place science. The idea seems to be that when science is put in that context its significance, rationality, and purpose, as it were, just click into place. Consequently, the defense of these "isms," when a defense is offered, usually takes the form of arguing that the favorite one is better than its rivals because it makes better sense of science than do its rivals.[8]

What are we to conclude from this business of placing science in a context, supplying it with an aim, attempting to make better sense of it, and so forth? Surely, it is that realism and anti-realism alike view science as susceptible to being set in context, provided with a goal, and being made sense of. And what manner of object, after all, could show such susceptibilities other than something that could not or did not do these very things for itself? What binds realism and anti-realism together is this. They see science as a set of practices in need of an interpretation, and they see themselves as providing just the right interpretation.

But science is not needy in this way. Its history and current practice constitute a rich and meaningful setting. In that setting questions of goals or aims or purposes occur spontaneously and *locally*. For what purpose is a particular instrument being used, or why use a tungsten filament here rather than a copper one? What significant goals would be accomplished by building accelerators capable of generating energy levels in excess of 10^4 GeV? Why can we ignore gravitational effects in the analysis of Compton scattering? Etc. These sorts of questions have a teleological cast and, most likely, could be given appropriate answers in terms of ends, or goals, or the like. But when we are asked what is the aim of science itself, I think we find ourselves in a quandary, just as we do when asked "What is the purpose of life?" or in-

deed the corresponding sort of question for any sufficiently rich and varied practice or institution. As we grow up I think we learn that such questions really do not require an answer, but rather they call for an empathetic analysis to get at the cognitive (and temperamental) sources of the question, and then a program of therapy to help change all that.

Let me try to collect up my thoughts by means of a metaphor (or is it an allegory?). The realisms and anti-realisms seem to treat science as a sort of grand performance, a play, or opera, whose production requires interpretation and direction. They argue among themselves as to whose "reading" is best.[9] I have been trying to suggest that if science is a performance, then it is one where the audience and crew play as well. Directions for interpretation are also part of the act. If there are questions and conjectures about the meaning of this or that, or its purpose, then there is room for those in the production too. The script, moreover, is never finished, and no past dialogue can fix future action. Such a performance is not susceptible to a reading or interpretation in any global sense, and it picks out its own interpretations, locally, as it goes along.

To allow for such an open conception of science, the attitude one adopts must be neither realist nor anti-realist. It is the attitude I want to call your attention to under the name of NOA, the natural ontological attitude. The quickest way to get a feel for NOA is to understand it as undoing the idea of interpretation, and the correlative idea of invariance (or essence).

The attitude that marks NOA is just this: Try to

---

[8] "However, there is also a positive argument for constructive empiricism—it makes better sense of science, and of scientific activity, than realism does and does so without inflationary metaphysics." ([18]: 73) I think van Fraassen speaks here for all the anti-realists. While I cannot recommend this defense of anti-realism, I think van Fraassen's own critique of the explanationist defenses of realism is very incisive, especially if complemented with the attack of Laudan [9]. My [3] contains a meta-theorem showing why such explanationist (or coherentist) defenses of realism are bound to fail.

[9] This way of putting it suggests that the philosophies of realism and anti-realism are much closer to the hermeneutical tradition than (most of) their proponents would find comfortable. Similarly, I think the view of science that has emerged from these "isms" is just as contrived as is the shallow, mainline view of the hermeneuts (science as control and manipulation, involving only dehumanized and purely imaginary models of The World). In opposition to this, I do not suggest that science is hermeneutic-proof, but rather that in science, as elsewhere, hermeneutical understanding has to be gained *from the inside*. It should not be prefabricated to meet external, philosophical specifications. There is, then, no legitimate hermeneutical *account* of science, but only a hermeneutical activity that is a lively part of science itself.

take science on its own terms, and try not to read things into science. If one adopts this attitude, then the global interpretations, the "isms" of scientific philosophies, appear as idle overlays to science: not necessary, not warranted and, in the end, probably not even intelligible. It is fundamental to NOA that science has a history, rooted indeed in everyday thinking. But there need not be any aspects invariant throughout that history, and hence, contrary to the isms, no necessary uniformity in the overall development of science (including projections for the future). NOA is, therefore, basically at odds with the temperament that looks for definite boundaries demarcating science from pseudo-science, or that is inclined to award the title "scientific" like a blue ribbon on a prize goat. Indeed the anti-essentialist aspect of NOA is intended to be very comprehensive, applying to all the concepts used in science, even the concept of truth.

Thus NOA is inclined to reject *all* interpretations, theories, construals, pictures, etc. of truth, just as it rejects the special correspondence theory of realism and the acceptance pictures of the truthmongering anti-realisms. For the concept of truth is the fundamental semantical concept. Its uses, history, logic, and grammar are sufficiently definite to be partially catalogued, at least for a time. But it cannot be "explained" or given an "account of" without circularity. Nor does it require anything of the sort. The concept of truth is open-ended, growing with the growth of science. Particular questions (Is this true? What reason do we have to believe in the truth of that? Can we find out whether it is true? Etc.) are addressed in well-known ways. The significance of the answers to those questions is rooted in the practices and logic of truth-judging (which practices, incidentally, are by no means confined to acceptance, or the like), but that significance branches out beyond current practice along with the growing concept of truth. For, present knowledge not only redistributes truth-values among past judgments, present knowledge also re-evaluates the whole character of past practice. There is no saying, in advance, how this will go. Thus there is no projectible sketch now of what truth signifies, nor of what

areas of science (eg. "fundamental laws") truth is exempt from—nor ever will there be. Some questions, of course, are not settled by the current practices of truth judging. Perhaps some never will be settled.

NOA is fundamentally a heuristic attitude, one that is compatible with quite different assessments of particular scientific investigations; say, investigations concerning whether or not there are magnetic monopoles. At the time of this writing the scientific community is divided on this issue. There is a long history of experimental failure to detect monopoles, and one recent success—maybe. I believe that there are a number of new experiments under way, and considerable theoretical work that might narrow down the detectable properties of monopoles.[10] In this context various ways of putting together the elements that enter into a judgment about monopoles will issue in various attitudes toward them, ranging from complete agnosticism to strong belief. NOA is happy with any of these attitudes. All that NOA insists is that one's ontological attitude towards monopoles, and everything else that might be collected in the scientific zoo (whether observable or not), be governed by the very same standards of evidence and inference that are employed by science itself. This attitude tolerates all the differences of opinion, and all the varieties of doubt and skepticism, that science tolerates. It does not, however, tolerate the prescriptions of empiricism, or of other doctrines that externally limit the commitments of science. Nor does it overlay the judgment say, that monopoles do exist, with the special readings of realism or of the truthmongering anti-realisms. NOA tries to let science speak for itself, and it trusts in our native ability to get the message without having to rely on metaphysical or epistemological hearing aids.

I promised to conclude these reflections by singing in praise of NOA. The refrain I had in mind is an adaptation of a sentiment that Einstein once expressed concerning Mozart. Einstein said that the music of Mozart (read "NOA") seems so natu-

---

[10] See [17] for a review.

ral that, by contrast, the music of other composers (read "realism" or "anti-realism") sounds artificial and contrived.

REFERENCES

[1] N. Cartwright, *How the Laws of Physics Lie* (Oxford: Oxford University Press, 1983).

[2] A. Fine, "The Young Einstein and the Old Einstein," in R. Cohen et al. (eds.), *Essays in Memory of Imre Lakatos* (Dordrecht, Holland: Reidel, 1976): 145–159.

[3] ———, "The Natural Ontological Attitude" in J. Leplin (ed.), *Scientific Realism* (Berkeley, CA: University of California Press, 1984).

[4] ———, "Is Scientific Realism Compatible with Quantum Physics?," *Noûs*, 1984.

[5] I. Hacking, "Experimentation and Scientific Realism" in J. Leplin (eds.), *Scientific Realism* (Berkeley, CA: University of California Press, 1984).

[6] ———, *Representing and Intervening*, (Cambridge, MA: Cambridge University Press, 1983).

[7] G. Hellman, "Realist Principles," *Philosophy of Science* 50(1983): 227–249.

[8] T. S. Kuhn, *The Structure of Scientific Revolutions,* 2nd Edition (Chicago: University of Chicago Press, 1970).

[9] L. Laudan, "A Confutation of Convergent Realism," *Philosophy of Science* 48(1981): 19–49.

[10] ———, "Realism without the Real," *Philosophy of Science,* 1984.

[11] H. Putnam, *Reason, Truth and History* (Cambridge: Cambridge University Press, 1981).

[12] ———, "Quantum Mechanics and the Observer," *Erkenntnis* 16(1981): 193–220.

[13] ———, "Why There Isn't a Ready-Made World," *Synthese* 51(1982): 141–167.

[14] ———, "Why Reason Can't Be Naturalized," *Synthese* 52(1982): 3–23.

[15] R. Rorty, *Philosophy and the Mirror of Nature* (Princeton: Princeton University Press, 1979).

[16] D. Shapere, "The Concept of Observation in Science and Philosophy," *Philosophy of Science* 49(1982): 485–525.

[17] W. P. Trower and B. Cabrera, "Magnetic Monopoles: Evidence since the Dirac Conjecture," *Foundations of Physics* 13(1983): 195–216.

[18] B. van Fraassen, *The Scientific Image* (Oxford: Clarendon Press, 1980).

Realism and Instrumentalism in Pre-Newtonian Astronomy

Michael R. Gardner

INTRODUCTION

There is supposed to be a problem in the philosophy of science called "realism versus instrumentalism." In the version with which I am concerned, this supposed problem is whether scientific theories in general are put forward as true, or whether they are put forward as untrue but nonetheless convenient devices for the prediction (and retrodiction) of observable phenomena.

I have argued elsewhere (1979) that this problem is misconceived. Whether a theory is put forward as true or merely as a device depends on various aspects of the theory's structure and content, and on the nature of the evidence for it. I illustrated this thesis with a discussion of the nineteenth-century debates about the atomic theory. I argued that the atomic theory was initially regarded by most of the scientific community as a set of false statements useful for the deduction and systematization of the various laws regarding chemical combination, thermal phenomena, etc.; and that a gradual transition occurred in which the atomic theory came to be regarded as a literally true picture of matter. I claimed, moreover, that the historical evidence shows that this transition occurred because of increases in the theory's proven predictive power; because of new determinations of hitherto indeterminate magnitudes through the use of measurement results and well-

tested hypotheses; and because of changes in some scientists' beliefs about what concepts may appear in fundamental explanations. I posed it as a problem in that paper whether the same or similar factors might be operative in other cases in the history of science; and I suggested that it might be possible, on the basis of an examination of several cases in which the issue of realistic vs. instrumental acceptance of a theory has been debated, to put forward a (normative) theory of when it is reasonable to accept a theory as literally true and when as only a convenient device.

For simplicity I shall usually speak of the acceptance-status of a theory as a whole. But sometimes it will be helpful to discuss individual hypotheses within a theory, when some are to be taken literally and others as conceptual devices.

In the present paper I would like to discuss a closely analogous case—the transition, during the Copernican revolution, in the prevailing view of the proper purpose and correlative mode of acceptance of a theory of the planetary motions. I shall briefly discuss the evidence—well known to historians—that from approximately the time of Ptolemy until Copernicus, most astronomers held that the purpose of planetary theory is to permit the calculations of the angles at which the planets appear from the earth at given times, and not to describe the planets' true orbits in physical space. For a few decades after Copernicus's death, except among a handful of astronomers, his own theory was accepted (if at all) as only the most recent and most accurate in a long series of untrue prediction-devices. But eventually the Copernican theory came to be accepted as the literal truth, or at least close to it. That this transition occurred is

This material is based upon work supported by the National Science Foundation under Grants No. SOC 77-07691 and SOC 78-26194. I am grateful for comments on an earlier draft by Ian Hacking, Geoffrey Hellman, Roger Rosenkrantz, Robert Rynasiewicz and Ferdinand Schoeman.

From Sections 1, 8, 9, 10, and 11 of "Realism and Instrumentalism in Pre-Newtonian Astronomy" by Michael Gardner, in *Testing Scientific Theories,* John Earman, Ed., *Minnesota Studies in the Philosophy of Science,* Vol. X © 1983 Minneapolis: University of Minnesota, pp. 201–202, 237–265. Used by permission.

well known; why it occurred has not been satisfactorily explained, as I shall try to show. I shall then try to fill in this gap in the historical and philosophical literature. In the concluding section I shall also discuss the relevance of this case to theses, other than the one just defined, which go by the name "realism.". . .

THE INSTRUMENTALIST RECEPTION OF COPERNICANISM

In the half-century or so after the publication of *De Revolutionibus,* Copernicus's theory was widely perceived as an improvement upon Ptolemy's in regard to observational accuracy and theoretical adequacy, and yet was almost universally regarded as untrue or at best highly uncertain (Kuhn 1957, pp. 185–188; Westman 1972a, pp. 234–236). A concise expression of instrumental acceptance occurs in an astronomical textbook of 1594 by Thomas Blundeville: "Copernicus . . . affirmeth that the earth turneth about and that the sun standeth still in the midst of the heavens, by help of which false supposition he hath made truer demonstrations of the motions and revolutions of the celestial spheres, than ever were made before" (quoted in Johnson 1937, p. 207).

Crucial in promoting this point of view, especially in the leading German universities, was a group of astronomers led by Phillipp Melanchthon (1497–1560) of the University of Wittenberg. Generally speaking, their opinion was that Copernicus's theory was credible primarily just in regard to its determinations of observed angles; that it was preferable to Ptolemy's in that it eschewed the abhorrent equant*; but that the new devices needed to be transformed into a geostatic frame of reference, since the earth does not really move (Westman 1975a, pp. 166–167). For example, Melanchthon praised parts of Copernicus's theory in 1549 for being "so beautifully put together"

and used some of his data, but held that the theory must be rejected on a realistic interpretation because it conflicts with Scripture and with the Aristotelian doctrine of motion (Westman 1975a, p. 173). Similarly, Melanchthon's distinguished disciple Erasmus Reinhold was plainly more impressed by the fact that "we are liberated from an equant by the assumption of this [Copernican] theory" (as Rheticus had put it in Rosen 1959, p. 135) than by the theory's revolutionary cosmology. On the title page of his own copy of *De Revolutionibus,* Reinhold wrote out Copernicus's principle of uniform motion in red letters. And in his annotations he consistently singled out for summary and comment Copernicus's accomplishments in eliminating the equant, because of which (he said) "the science of the celestial motions was almost in ruins; the studies and works of this author have restored it." Thus Reinhold saw Copernicus entirely as the reactionary thinker he in some respects was, returning astronomy to its true foundations on uniform circular motions. In contrast, the paucity of Reinhold's annotations on the cosmological arguments of Book I indicates little interest, and in an unpublished commentary on Copernicus's work he maintained a neutral stance on the question of whether the earth really moves. But there was no doubt in his mind that Copernicus's geometric constructions provided a superior basis for computing planetary positions, and the many users of Reinhold's *Prutenic Tables* (1551) found out he was right, whatever their own cosmological views (Westman 1975a, pp. 174–178).

An especially influential advocate of instrumental acceptance in our sense—i.e., with an explicit denial of truth—of the Copernican theory was Caspar Peucer, Melanchthon's successor as rector at Wittenberg. Like his predecessor and mentor, Peucer used Copernican values for various parameters, but denied the theory's truth on Scriptural and Aristotelian physical grounds in his popular textbook of 1553. He also suggested in 1568 that if certain parts of Copernicus's theory were reforrnulated in a geostatic frame, "then I believe that the same [effects] would be achieved without having to change the ancient hypotheses" (quoted in Westman 1975a, pp. 178–181).

---

* [a mathematical device developed to aid in the reconciliation of Ptolemaic astronomy with the results of accurate observation—editor]

We have already seen one reason why the Wittenberg school refused to grant realistic acceptance to the Copernican theory: namely, that on a realistic interpretation the theory conflicts with Aristotelian physics and with Holy Scripture. (. . . [A] parallel argument from Aristotelian physics had often been given against a realistically interpreted Ptolemaic theory.) But let us consider whether something else was involved as well. Westman makes some intriguing suggestions about this:

> . . . what the Wittenberg Interpretation *ignored* was as important as that which it either asserted or denied. In the writings both public and private of nearly every author of the generation which first received the work of Copernicus, the new analysis of the relative *linear* distances of the planets is simply passed over in silence. . . . questions about the Copernican ordering of the planets were not seen as important topics of investigation. In annotated copies of *De Revolutionibus* which are datable from the period *circa* 1543–1570, passages in Book I extolling the newly discovered harmony of the planets and the eulogy to the sun, with its Hermetic* implications, were usually passed over in silence (Westman 1975a, pp. 167, 181). . . .

Although Westman deserves our thanks for pointing this out, he makes no effort to explain why a lack of interest in Copernicus's planetary harmony and distances was associated with a witholding of realistic acceptance. Can we get any deeper? Consider first the question of distances, deferring that of harmony. In another paper (1979) I argued that a principle P operative in the nineteenth-century debates about the reality of atoms was that *it is an objection to the acceptance of a theory on a realistic interpretation that it contains or implies the existence of indeterminate quantities.* . . . [T]his principle played at least some role in astronomy: Ptolemy's theory had indeterminate planetary distances and tended to be refused realistic acceptance. One might well wonder, however, how this principle could explain refusal to accept the literal truth of Copernicus's theory, since he did make the planetary distances determinate. The answer appeals to a variant of P

called P': *Persons who either reject or ignore a theory's determinations of magnitudes from measurements via its hypotheses will tend to refuse it realistic acceptance.* P', though not precisely a corollary of P, is plausible given P: Someone who rejects a theory's magnitude-determinations is likely to do so because he regards the hypotheses used as not well tested and hence regards the magnitudes as indeterminate; and someone who ignores the determinations is unaware of some of the support for realistic acceptance. Principle P' certainly fits the behavior as described by Westman of the first-generation response to Copernicus, especially among the Wittenberg group.

It also fits Johannes Praetorius (1537–1616), who studied astronomy at Wittenberg and later taught there and elsewhere. He expressed his instrumental acceptance of the Copernican theory as follows in a manuscript begun in 1592:

> Now, just as everyone approves the calculations of Copernicus (which are available to all through Erasmus Reinhold under the title *Prutenic Tables*), so everyone clearly abhors his hypotheses on account of the multiple motion of the earth. . . . we follow Ptolemy, in part, and Copernicus, in part. That is, if one retains the suppositions of Ptolemy, one achieves the same goal that Copernicus attained with his new constructions (Westman 1975b, p. 293).

Like others associated with Wittenberg, Praetorius was most impressed by the improvements in observational accuracy over Ptolemy and even over Copernicus himself, that were achieved by Reinhold on Copernican assumptions, and by Copernicus's elimination of the "absurd" equant. But unlike the first generation at his school, he paid careful attention to Copernicus's determinations of the planetary distances and to his evocations of the planetary system's "harmony" or "symmetry" (i.e., unified overall structure) that the new theory makes evident. Thus in lectures written in 1594 he listed Copernicus's values for the planetary distances and remarked about them: "this symmetry of all the orbs appears to fit together with the greatest consonance so that nothing can be inserted between them and no space remains to be filled. Thus, the distance from the convex orb of Venus to the concave orb of Mars takes up 730 earth

---

* [magical—editor]

semidiameters, in which space the great orb contains the moon and earth and moving epicycles*" (quotations etc. in Westman 1975b, pp. 298–299).

Another point emerges from this quotation: Praetorius evidently followed the tradition of thinking of the planets as moving on solid spheres. This assumption created difficulties for him when he attempted to transform Copernicus's system into a geostatic one. For he found that using Copernicus's distances, "there would occur a great confusion of orbs (especially with Mars). . . . because it would then occupy not only the Sun's orb but also the great part of Venus'. . . ." Since intersections of the spheres are impossible, he argued, Copernicus's distances "simply cannot be allowed." He therefore roughly doubled the distance to Saturn, on the ground that there will still be plenty of distance to the stars, and claimed that with that done, "nothing prohibits us . . . from making Mars' orb greater so that it will not invade the territory of the Sun." (Westman 1975b, p. 298) Plainly, on Praetorius's version of the Copernican theory, the planetary distances are indeterminate: they are set through entirely theoretical considerations regarding the relative sizes of the spheres, instead of being computed from observational data via well-tested hypotheses. Because he rejected Copernicus's determinations of the distances, it is in accord with principle *P′* that he rejected Copernicus's theory on a realistic interpretation. And since the distances are indeterminate (even though specified) on his own theory, it is in accordance with our principle *P* that he granted instrumental acceptance to his own astronomical theory, since he refused realistic acceptance to any:

. . . the astronomer is free to devise or imagine circles, epicycles and similar devices although they might not exist in nature. . . . The astronomer who endeavors to discuss the truth of the positions of these or those bodies acts as a Physicist and not as an astronomer—and, in my opinion, he arrives at nothing with certainty (Westman 1975b, p. 303).

---

* [one of the mathematical devices used to explain the motion of the planets—editor]

This quotation reveals that Praetorius was influenced by two additional factors . . . counting against realistic acceptance of an astronomical theory. One is that *the theory is independent of physics:* that it is either outside the domain of physics, or if literally interpreted is inconsistent with the true principles of physics. (. . . Ptolemy, who seems sometimes to have been thinking of parts of his theory as mere devices, held to the first kind of independence; and . . . Proclus used the second as an argument against realistic acceptance of a Ptolemaic theory.) The second factor influencing Praetorius was the argument, also found in Proclus and others, that no realistically interpreted astronomical theory can be known to be true.

Another argument . . . found in the pre-Copernican period (e.g., in Proclus) against realistic acceptance of any planetary theory was that alternative systems of orbits may be compatible with the appearances; and that no particular system, therefore, can be asserted as literally true. A strengthened version of principle *P*—no theory *T* containing indeterminate quantities should receive realistic acceptance—is closely related to Proclus's principle, since various settings of the indeterminate parameters in *T* would in some cases produce various alternative theories equally compatible with the data. But although the notion that indeterminate quantities count against realistic acceptance continued to play a role in post-Copernican astronomy, Proclus's principle came under attack and seems not to have played much (if any) role in the thinking of instrumentally Copernican astronomers. For example, the influential Jesuit astronomer Christopher Clavius wrote in 1581 that it is not enough merely to speculate that there *may* be some other method than ours of accounting for the celestial appearances. For the argument to have any force, our opponents must actually produce the alternative. And if it turns out to be a "more convenient way [specifically, of dealing with the appearances] . . . we shall be content and will give them very hearty thanks." But failing such a showing, we are justified in believing that the best theory we actually have (Ptolemy's, he thought) is "highly probable"; for the use of Proclus's principle would destroy not just realistically interpreted astronomy, but all of natural philosophy: "If they cannot show us some better way, they certainly ought to accept this way, inferred as it is from so wide a variety of phenomena; unless in fact they wish to destroy . . . Natural Philosophy. . . . For as often as anyone inferred a certain cause from its observable effects, I might say to him precisely what they say to us—that forsooth it may be possible to explain those effects by some cause as yet unknown to us" (Blake 1960, pp. 31–37). Although this gets us ahead of and even beyond our story, eventually a principle very much like Clavius's appeared as Newton's fourth rule of reasoning in philosophy:

In experimental philosophy we are to look upon propositions inferred by general induction from phenomena as accurately or very nearly true, notwithstanding any contrary hypotheses that may be imagined, till such time as other phenomena occur by which they may either be made more accurate, or liable to exceptions.

This rule we must follow, that the argument of induction may not be evaded by hypotheses (Newton 1934, p. 400).

Newton's rule is a stronger critical tool than Clavius's, since even if the alternative "hypothesis" is actually produced (but, by definition of "hypothesis," not by deduction from phenomena), Newton refused it consideration, whereas Clavius might even have preferred it if it proved to be more convenient, or better in accord with physics and Scripture.

Clavius thought that although Copernicus's theory was approximately as accurate as Ptolemy's, it was false because it conflicted with physics and Scripture. So he accorded the Copernican theory instrumental acceptance, and the Ptolemaic theory realistic acceptance as an approximation. In addition to consistency with physics and Scripture, he used one other consideration in favor of realistic acceptance which, I have argued elsewhere (1979), was also operative in the nineteenth-century atomic debates. It is progressiveness—i.e., the power of a theory to inform us of "novel" facts, of facts the theory's inventor did not know at the time of the invention. (See my 1982 paper on this definition of "novel.") Thus Clavius

argued in favor of a realistic acceptance of Ptolemy's theory:

But by the assumption of Eccentric* and Epicyclic spheres not only are all the appearances already known accounted for, but also future phenomena are predicted, the time of which is altogether unknown: thus, if I am in doubt whether, for example, the full moon will be eclipsed in September, 1583, I shall be assured by calculation from the motions of the Eccentric and Epicyclic spheres, that the eclipse will occur, so that I shall doubt no further. . . . it is incredible that we force the heavens (but we seem to force them, if the Eccentrics and Epicycles are figments, as our adversaries will have it) to obey the figments of our minds and to move as we will or in accordance with our principles (Blake 1960, p. 34).

Here we have as clear an example as could be desired of an explicit distinction being made between realistic and instrumental acceptance, and of progressiveness being used to decide between them.

The instrumentally Copernican astronomers discussed so far—i.e., astronomers who preferred Copernican angle-determinations but thought the theory needed a geostatic transformation—either ignored or rejected Copernicus's determinations of the planets' distances. But this is not true of the most famous of their group, Tycho Brahe. Like the members of the Wittenberg circle, with whom he had extensive contact, Tycho wrote in 1574 that although Copernicus "considered the course of the heavenly bodies more accurately than anyone else before him" and deserved further credit for eliminating the "absurd" equant, still "he holds certain [theses] contrary to physical principles, for example, . . . that the earth . . . move(s) around the Sun. . . ." He therefore invented his own system, which was essentially Copernicus's subjected to a transformation that left the earth stationary, the sun in orbit around it, and the other planets on moving orbits centered at the sun. Having become convinced that there are no solid spheres carrying the planets, since the comets he had observed would have to penetrate them, he

---

* [one of the mathematical devices used to explain the motion of the planets—editor]

did not share Praetorius's motivation of altering the Copernican distances, and therefore retained them (Westman 1975b, pp. 305–313, 329; see Kuhn 1957, pp. 201–204).

Now the case of Tycho may seem to be anomalous from the standpoint of principles P and P': For Tycho accorded Copernicus's theory only instrumental acceptance, and yet neither ignored nor rejected Copernicus's determinations of the planetary distances. He would have conceded that these quantities were determinate, since he knew they could be computed from observations and certain of Copernicus's hypotheses on the *relative* positions of the planets, hypotheses that Tycho accepted and regarded as well tested. But this objection to P ignores its implicit ceteris paribus clause: P requires only that the determinateness of a theory's quantities should count in favor of realistic acceptance, and that indeterminateness should count against; there may nonetheless be countervailing considerations. Tycho's reasoning is entirely in accord with this notion. In one of his own copies of *De Revolutionibus,* Tycho underlined the passage . . . in which Copernicus stated that his theory links together the planetary distances, and commented on the passage: "The reason for the revival and establishment of the Earth's motion." And next to the passage . . . in which Copernicus spoke of the "symmetry of the universe" made evident by explaining so many varied phenomena in terms of the earth's motion, Tycho wrote: "The testimonies of the planets, in particular, agree precisely with the Earth's motion and thereupon the hypotheses assumed by Copernicus are strengthened" (Westman 1975b, p. 317). Despite these favorable remarks, Tycho rejected the Copernican theory on the sorts of grounds with which we are now familiar: that it conflicts with Scripture, physical theory, and certain observational data—specifically, Tycho's failure to detect the annual stellar parallax* entailed by the earth's motion, and the relatively large ap-

parent sizes of the stars given the great distances entailed by the undetectability of parallax (Dreyer 1953, pp. 360–361). Although these considerations prevailed in his mind, it is still plain from the marginal notes just quoted that in accordance with principle P he counted it in favor of realistic acceptance of the hypothesis of the earth's motion that it made the planetary distances determinate and also (a point not yet discussed in this context) that *it satisfies Copernicus's principle of variety of evidence.* . . .

That variety of evidence (metaphorically, "symmetry" or "harmony") counted in favor of realistic acceptance is also indicated by Westman's remark that in the period of instrumental acceptance of Copernicus's theory his remarks on harmony tended to be ignored.

We can sum up our discussion of the instrumental acceptance of the Copernican theory by listing the factors that, in the immediately post-Copernican period, were counted in favor of, or whose absence was counted against, acceptance on a realistic interpretation:

On such an interpretation, the theory

1. satisfies the laws of physics,

2. is consistent with other putative knowledge (e.g., the Scriptures),

3. is consistent with all observational data,

4. contains only determinate quantities,

5. is able to predict novel facts,

6. has a central hypothesis supported by a large variety of evidence,

7. is within the realm of possible human knowledge.

Failing any of (1)–(3), a theory (if we assume it is still a convenient prediction-device in a certain domain) will tend to be accorded instrumental acceptance (with denial of truth). Supposed failure of (4)–(7) leads only to scepticism regarding truth.

We can now turn to those who accepted the Copernican theory on a realistic interpretation. If the foregoing is correct and complete, we should not find anything new.

---

* [apparent motion of the stars over the course of a year—editor]

REALISTIC ACCEPTANCE OF COPERNICANISM

. . . [T]he first person to accept the Copernican theory as literally true was Copernicus himself. . . . [H]e argued explicitly that his theory satisfies the laws of physics, makes the planetary distances determinate, and has a central hypothesis supported by a wide variety of evidence. He also mentioned no observational data inconsistent with his theory, and implied in his prefatory letter to the Pope that Scripture conflicts with his theory only if "wrongly twisted." Since these considerations were all "in the air" in Copernicus's period as counting in favor of realistic acceptance, I think it is plausible to regard them as his reasons, although he did not make this more obvious by citing them in the context of an explicit distinction between realistic vs. instrumental acceptance.

The second astronomer to give realistic acceptance to Copernicanism was undoubtedly Georg Joachim Rheticus. He left Wittenberg to live and study with Copernicus (from 1539 to 1541), during which time he became familiar with the still unpublished Copernican theory. In 1540 he published *Narratio Prima,* the first printed account of the new theory of "my teacher," as he called Copernicus. In this work he nowhere indicated that he thought the theory to be just a convenient device. Moreover, he claimed (falsely) for unspecified reasons that at least some aspects of the Copernican theory could not be subjected to the sort of geostatic transformation (permitting instrumental acceptance) favored by others associated with Wittenberg: "I do not see how the explanation of precession* is to be transferred to the sphere of stars" (Rosen 1959, pp. 4–5, 10, 164). Finally, in two copies of *De Revolutionibus* he crossed out Osiander's preface with red pencil or crayon (Gingerich 1973c, p. 514). So it is obvious enough that his acceptance was realistic.

---

* [precession of the equinoxes, that is, the occurrence of the equinoxes (times when the sun crosses the equator) earlier in each successive year—editor]

But why? First, he thought the theory is consistent with the most important relevant law of physics—uniform circularity of celestial motion—and all observational data:

. . . you see that here in the case of the moon we are liberated from an equant by the assumption of this theory, which, moreover, corresponds to experience and all the observations. My teacher dispenses with equants for the other planets as well . . . (Rosen 1959, p. 135).

. . . my teacher decided that he must assume such hypotheses as would contain causes capable of confirming the truth of the observations of previous centuries, and such as would themselves cause, we may hope, all future astronomical predictions of the phenomena to be found true (Rosen 1959, pp. 142–143).

It is somewhat puzzling that Copernicus's repudiation of the equant was a basis for both realistic and instrumental acceptance. The explanation is perhaps that his principle of uniformity can be thought of as an aesthetic virtue of a calculation-device—it is "pleasing to the mind" (Copernicus, in Rosen 1959, p. 57)—or as a physical principle (Copernicus 1976, Book I, chapter 4).

In the last quotation from Rheticus, he invoked the criterion of progressiveness (5), since he implied that the predictions were not known to be correct on some other ground (such as simple induction). He also contrasted the Copernican and Ptolemaic hypotheses in regard to the determinateness of planetary distances:

. . . what dispute, what strife there has been until now over the position of the spheres of Venus and Mercury, and their relation to the sun. . . . Is there anyone who does not see that it is very difficult and even impossible ever to settle this question while the common hypotheses are accepted? For what would prevent anyone from locating even Saturn below the sun, provided that at the same time he preserved the mutual proportions of the spheres and epicycle, since in these same hypotheses there has not yet been established the common measure of the spheres of the planets. . . .

However, in the hypotheses of my teacher, . . . (t)heir common measure is the great circle which carries the earth . . . (Rosen 1959, pp. 146–147).

It will be noted that Rheticus ignored the nesting-shell hypothesis* and took the Ptolemaic distances as entirely unspecified. Finally, Rheticus argued that Copernicus's central hypothesis that the earth moves was supported by a wide variety of evidence—specifically, the apparent motions of the five visible planets. "For all these phenomena appear to be linked most nobly together, as by golden chain; and each of the planets, by its position and order and every inequality of its motion, bears witness that the earth moves . . ." (Rosen 1959, p. 165). God arranged the universe thus "lest any of the motions attributed to the earth should seem to be supported by insufficient evidence" (Rosen 1959, p. 161). Rheticus, then, appealed to criteria (1), (3), (4), (5), and (6) for realistic acceptance—criteria, I have argued, that were widely accepted in his period.

Westman is dissatisfied with "rational" explanations (such as the above) of Rheticus's behavior—i.e., explanations in terms of generally applicable and generally applied criteria regarding the theory and the evidence for it: "If today we might defend the rationality of this argument [from unity or harmony] on grounds of its empirical adequacy, its simplicity, and hence its considerable promise for future success, Rheticus went much further: He took it as evidence of the *absolute* truth of the entire theory of Copernicus" (Westman 1975a, pp. 184–186). Rheticus's "excessive zeal," then, requires not a rational but a "psychodynamic" explanation. We should note that Westman appears at this point to be following the psychohistorical analog of the "arationality assumption" widely accepted by sociologists of knowledge: *The sociology of knowledge may step in to explain beliefs if and only if those beliefs cannot be explained in terms of their rational merits*" (this formulation of the assumption and references to writers espousing it are in Laudan 1977, p. 202).

Westman finds himself at a disadvantage by comparison with professional psychoanalysts in that he cannot put Rheticus on the couch and get him to free-associate. Still, the psychohistorian has considerable information with which to work, including the fact that when Rheticus was fourteen his father was convicted of sorcery and beheaded. Westman thinks that part of the reason why Rheticus was attracted to Copernicus and thus to his theory was that "in Copernicus, Rheticus had found a kind and strong father with a streak of youthful rebellion in him: a man who was different, as Rheticus' father had been. . . ." But just as important was the fact that the Copernican system had the sort of unity that Rheticus's father so notably lacked after he had been beheaded. Rheticus had made "determined efforts—in the search for wholeness, strength, and harmony—to unconsciously repair the damage earlier wrought on his father." And Copernicus was a substitute father "who, like the system he created, had a head and a heart which were connected to the same body" (Westman 1975a, pp. 187–189).

Despite my considerable reliance upon and admiration for Professor Westman's brilliant contributions to our understanding of the Copernican revolution, I cannot follow him here. Leaving aside the question of the scientific merit of the general psychological theory on which his explanation of Rheticus's behavior is premised, the main problem with the explanation is that it simply is not needed. Rheticus argued explicitly that Copernicus's theory met certain criteria, and these were criteria used by many writers of his time (and other times) for realistic acceptance. Rheticus himself said that the importance of the "golden chain" unifying the planetary appearances was that it assures that there is sufficient evidence for the earth's motion. There is simply no need (and certainly no direct evidence) for an appeal to symbolic posthumous surgery on his father.

To make this criticism of Westman is not to accept the arationality assumption. In fact, I consider it absurd to deny that there can be both scientific reasons and psychosocial causes for a given cognitive attitude of a scientist. Still, when a psychosocial explanation lacks support for its initial conditions (here, the symbolic import of "unity"),

---

* [the hypothesis, to the effect that there is no space, no emptiness, between planetary spheres (shells), that Ptolemy used to determine the distances of the planets from the earth—editor]

so that the most that can be said for it is that we cannot think of any other explanation of the explanandum, then the existence of a documented rational account undermines the psychosocial one.

Laudan points out that a difficulty in using the arationality assumption is that one cannot apply it correctly unless one has an adequate theory of the rational merits of scientific theories; and, he says, use of an overly simple theory of rationality has been the cause of much confusion in the sociology (and presumably, the psychohistory) of ideas (1977, pp. 205; 242, n. 1). This, I believe, is what has gone wrong in Westman's discussion of Rheticus. "Empirical adequacy . . . simplicity . . . and . . . promise" is just not an adequate description of the scientific merits of Copernicus's arguments. Moreover, it is beside the point that today we think Copernicus's theory has only approximate and not "absolute" truth. Since we have much more astronomical evidence and know much more physics than Rheticus did, the rationality of his beliefs (in the light of his knowledge) cannot be assessed by reference to our knowledge.

Perhaps Westman would concede in response to my criticism that although the unity of the Copernican theory may have provided Rheticus with *reason* to believe it, still we need a psychodynamic explanation of why Rheticus was impressed by this unity in a way others of his generation generally were not. To this I would reply that a perfectly straightforward and plausible explanation of Rheticus's attitude is that he learned the theory from Copernicus's own lips; and since Copernicus obviously thought the "harmony" of his system was one of its main virtues, he no doubt forcefully called it to Rheticus's attention. This explanation is at any rate considerably less speculative than Westman's.

We find realistic acceptance and reasoning similar to that of Copernicus and Rheticus in another early Copernican, Michael Mästlin (1550–1631), whose support was crucial because of the pro-Copernican influence Mästlin exerted on his student Kepler. In his annotations of a copy of *De Revolutionibus,* which are consistently approving

of Copernicus, he complained that Osiander's preface had made the mistake of "shattering [astronomy's] foundations" and suffered from "much weakness in his meaning and reasoning." This indicates that his acceptance was realistic. Commenting on Copernicus's attempts in Book I of *De Revolutionibus* to answer Ptolemy's physical arguments against the earth's motion, he wrote: "He resolves the objections which Ptolemy raises in the Almagest, Book I, chapter 7." So he evidently thought the Copernican theory satisfied the laws of physics. Finally, referring to Copernicus's arguments from determinateness of distances and variety of evidence, he wrote: "Certainly this is the great argument, viz. that all the phenomena as well as the order and magnitude of the orbs are bound together in the motion of the earth. . . . moved by this argument I approve of the opinions and hypotheses of Copernicus" (Quoted in Westman 1975b, pp. 329–334). Mästlin's realistic acceptance, then, was based at least on criteria (1), (4), and (6).

KEPLER

The trend toward realistic acceptance of a heliostatic theory culminated in the work of Kepler. As Duhem wrote, "the most resolute and illustrious representative [of the realistic tradition of Copernicus and Rheticus] is, unquestionably, Kepler" (1960, p. 100). Kepler was quite explicit in making the distinction between realistic and instrumental acceptance of astronomical theories in general and of Copernicus's in particular, and explicit in saying where he stood on these issues. Not only Osiander, but Professor Petrus Ramus of the University of Paris, had asserted that Copernicus's theory used hypotheses that were false. Ramus wrote: "The fiction of hypotheses is absurd . . . would that Copernicus had rather put his mind to the establishing of an astronomy without hypotheses." And he offered his chair at Paris "as the prize for an astronomy constructed without hypotheses." Kepler wrote in his *Astronomia Nova* of 1609 that had Ramus not died in the meantime, "I would of good right claim [his chair] myself, or for Copernicus." He also indignantly revealed that Osiander was the author of the anonymous preface to *De Revolutionibus* and asserted: "I confess it a most absurd play to explain the processes of nature by false causes, but there is no such play in Copernicus, who indeed himself did believe his hypotheses true . . . nor did he only believe, but also proved them true" (Blake 1960, p. 43). Kepler intended to proceed in the same realistic spirit: "I began this work declaring that I would found astronomy not upon fictive hypotheses, but upon physical causes" (Quoted in Westman 1971, p. 128). Astronomy "can easily do without the useless furniture of fictitious circles and spheres" (Kepler 1952, p. 964). In taking such a view Kepler was consciously aware of contributing to a revolution not only in the prevailing theories in astronomy but also in the prevailing view of the field's purposes. He described his work as involving "the unexpected transfer of the whole of astronomy from fictitious circles to natural causes, which were the most profound to investigate, difficult to explain, and difficult to calculate, since mine was the first attempt" (quoted in Gingerich 1973d, p. 304).

According to Kuhn, disagreement over the problems, aims, and methods of a field is one of the things that makes competing schools "incommensurable"—i.e., makes arguments for either of them circular, the choice a matter of "faith" or a "conversion experience" based, sometimes, on "personal and inarticulate aesthetic considerations" rather than on "rational" argument (1970, pp. 41, 94, 151, 158). But in fact Kepler did present rational (if not always decisive) arguments for the shift in astronomical aims that he advocated, grounds for asserting that these aims could and should be achieved. Most of these grounds were neither inarticulate nor merely personal, but were explicitly stated attempts to show that a heliostatic theory could meet the widely used criteria for realistic acceptance.

We saw [p. 373] that one such criterion, in this historical period and others, is progressiveness—prediction of novel facts. Thus we are not surprised to find Kepler arguing as follows in his *Mysterium Cosmographicum* (1596) for an essen-

tially Copernican theory—i.e., one that has the planets somehow orbiting a stationary sun:

My confidence was upheld in the first place by the admirable agreement between his conceptions and all [the objects] which are visible in the sky; an agreement which not only enabled him to establish earlier motions going back to remote antiquity, but also to predict future [phenomena], certainly not with absolute accuracy, but in any case much more exactly than Ptolemy, Alfonso, and other astronomers (quoted in Koyré, 1973, p. 129).

Kepler (*ibid*, p. 133) also echoed Copernicus's and Rheticus's appeals to criterion (6), well-testedness: "Nature likes simplicity and unity. Nothing trifling or superfluous has ever existed: and very often, one single cause is destined by itself to [produce] several effects. Now, with the traditional hypotheses there is no end to the invention [of circles]; with Copernicus, on the other hand, a large number of motions is derived from a small number of circles" (1973, p. 133). As Koyré pointed out, this claim about numbers of circles is an overstatement which had become traditional among Copernicus and his followers. But we can accept the part of this argument alluding to the variety of evidence for the earth's motion.

We also saw [pp. 370–377] that realistic acceptance tended to be associated with belief and interest in the determinate values of the planetary distances that Copernicus's theory and data provided. There can be no doubt that Kepler had both belief and the most intense interest. In 1578 Kepler's teacher Michael Mästlin had published a theory of the motion of the comet of 1577 that asserted that it moved within the heliocentric shell of Venus, a theory that presupposed the Copernican arrangement of the inferior planets and his values for their distances: "I noticed that the phenomena could be saved in no other way than if . . . [the comet's radii] were assumed to be 8420 parts when . . . the semidiameter of the [earth's orbit] is 10,000; and likewise, when the semidiameter of Venus' eccentric is 7193." Kepler wrote in 1596 that Mästlin's theory that the comet "completed its orbit in the same orb as the Copernican Venus" provided "the most important argument for the arrangement of the Copernican orbs" (quotations in Westman, 1972b, pp. 8,22). A second argument for Kepler's acceptance of (at least as approximations) and interest in Copernican determinations of the distances is that the main purpose of his *Mysterium Cosmographicum* was to explain the distances (as well as the number) of the planets on the basis of the assumptions that their spheres are inscribed within a nest formed by the five regular solids. This work was published with an appendix by Mästlin containing improved Copernican calculations of the distances based upon the Prutenic Tables (Westman 1972b, pp. 9–10; Koyré, 1973, pp. 146–147). The third way in which approximately Copernican values for the sun-to-planet distances were important for Kepler was that he held that a planet's orbital period is proportional to its mean distance raised to the 3/2 power, and that its linear speed is inversely proportional to its distance from the sun. And from either premise he deduced his crucial conclusion that the planets are made to revolve in their orbits neither by their supposed souls (Plato) nor their intrinsic nature (Copernicus), but by a physical force originating in the sun (Kepler 1952, p. 895).

A corollary of our principle (4) governing realistic acceptance [p. 371] is that a theory's failure to provide any means at all—let alone well-tested hypotheses—to determine some of its parameters counts against realistic acceptance. Kepler appealed to this corollary when he tried to show that Ptolemy believed his theory was more than a prediction-device: "to predict the motions of the planets Ptolemy did not have to consider the order of the planetary spheres, and yet he did so diligently.[1] (Kepler, forthcoming) Since the hypothesis from which Ptolemy obtained the order (that it corresponds to increasing orbital period) was entirely untested, I do not say that the order was determinate, but only specified.

We have seen earlier that such writers as Proclus and Praetorius argued against realistic acceptance of any astronomical theory on the grounds that knowledge of the full truth of such a theory exceeds merely human capacities and is attainable only by God. Aware of this traditional instrumentalist argument, Kepler felt obligated to argue on theological grounds that there is no *hubris* in claiming to know the true geometry of the cosmos:

Those laws [governing the whole material creation] are within the grasp of the human mind; God wanted us to recognize them by creating us after his own image so that we could share in his own thoughts. For what is there in the human mind besides figures and magnitudes? It is only these which we can apprehend in the right way, and . . . our understanding is in this respect of the same kind as the divine . . . (Letter of 1599, in Baumgardt 1951, p. 50).

To supplement his theological arguments, Kepler also attempted to undermine such support as astronomical scepticism received from the unobservability of the planets' orbits in physical space: "But Osiander . . . (i)f [you say that] this art knows absolutely nothing of the causes of the heavenly motions, because you believe only what you see, what is to become of medicine, in which no doctor ever perceived the inwardly hidden cause of a disease, except by inference from the external bodily signs and symptoms which impinge on the senses, just as from the visible positions of the stars the astronomer infers the form of their motion" (Kepler, forthcoming).

Another epistemological argument we saw was popular among astronomical instrumentalists asserts that since there are, or may be, alternative systems of orbits equally compatible with all observational data, no one system can be asserted as physically correct. About twenty years after the Ptolemaic astronomer Clavius attacked the argument from observational equivalence, Kepler mounted his own attack from a Copernican viewpoint. First, he argued, sets of hypotheses—some true, some false—which have exactly the same observational consequences are found (if ever) far less frequently than those who use the argument from equivalence suppose:

In astronomy, it can scarcely ever happen, and no example occurs to me, that starting out from a posited false hypothesis there should follow what is altogether sound and fitting to the motions of the heavens, or such as one wants demonstrated. For the same result

---

[1] I am grateful to Nicholas Jardine for allowing me to see and quote his unpublished draft translation. His final, published version may be different.

is not always in fact obtained from different hypotheses, whenever someone relatively inexperienced thinks it is (Kepler, forthcoming).

For example, Kepler argued, Magini attempted (1589) to produce a Ptolemaic theory agreeing with the *Prutenic Tables,* but failed to obtain Copernicus's prediction that Mars has a greater parallax than the sun. Kepler believed that whenever two conflicting hypotheses give the same results for a given range of phenomena, at least one of them can be refuted by deriving observational predictions from it in conjunction with new auxiliary hypotheses:

"And just as in the proverb liars are cautioned to remember what they have said, so here false hypotheses which together produce the truth by chance, do not, in the course of a demonstration in which they have been applied to many different matters, retain this habit of yielding the truth, but betray themselves" (Kepler, forthcoming).

Thus a false hypothesis may occasionally yield a true prediction, but only when it chances to be combined with an auxiliary hypothesis containing a compensatory error, as when Copernicus proposed a lunar latitude and a stellar latitude, both too small by the same amount, and thus obtained a correct prediction for an occultation of the star by the moon (Kepler, forthcoming). Conjoined with different auxiliary hypotheses, this one on the moon would certainly "betray itself." Kepler was arguing—exactly in accordance with (6) . . .— that we have good reason to accept a hypothesis realistically when it is supported by a variety of phenomena, where this means "in conjunction with many sets of auxiliary hypotheses." Moreover, he appealed to the rationale for this idea . . . —namely, that it reduces the chance of compensatory errors.

Kepler also considered a somewhat different way of stating the instrumentalist argument from observational equivalence. The Copernican and Ptolemaic hypotheses are concededly both compatible with, and both imply, e.g., the daily motion of the whole heaven. Ptolemy apparently inferred, partly because of this property of his theory, that it is true. But, the objection runs, the Copernicans think Ptolemy was thus led into error.

"So, by the same token, it could be said to Copernicus that although he accounts excellently for the appearances, nevertheless he is in error in his hypotheses" (trans. Jardine 1979, p. 157).

Kepler's rejoinder to this objection is as follows:

For it can happen that the same [conclusion] results from two suppositions which differ in species, because the two are in the same genus and it is in virtue of the genus primarily that the result in question is produced. Thus Ptolemy did not demonstrate the risings and settings of the stars from this as a proximate and commensurate middle term: 'The earth is at rest in the centre'. Nor did Copernicus demonstrate the same things from this as a middle term: 'The earth revolves at a distance from the centre'. It sufficed for each of them to say (as indeed each did say) that these things happen as they do because there occurs a certain separation of motions between the earth and the heaven, and because the distance of the earth from the centre is not perceptible amongst the fixed stars (i.e., there is no detectable parallactic effect]. So Ptolemy did not demonstrate the phenomena from a false or accidental middle term. He merely sinned against the law of essential truth (*kath'auto*), because he thought that these things occur as they do because of the species when they occur because of the genus. Whence it is clear that from the fact that Ptolemy demonstrated from a false disposition of the universe things that are nonetheless true and consonant with the heavens and with our observations—from this fact I repeat—we get no reason for suspecting something similar of the Copernican hypotheses (trans. Jardine 1979, p. 158).

Kepler's point is this: Let H = "The heaven moves (in a certain way) about a stationary earth," E = "The earth moves (in a certain way) within a stationary heaven," R = "The earth and heavens have a (certain) relative motion," and O = "The stars rise and set (in certain ways)." Since H implies O, it may appear that the verification of O supports H. But Aristotle required that in a premise of a "demonstration," or "syllogism productive of scientific knowledge," the predicate must belong to the subject "commensurately and universally," which he took to entail both that it belongs "essentially" and also that the subject is the "primary subject of this attribute." Aristotle's example of a violation of this latter requirement is the statement that any isosceles triangle has angles equal to 180° (*Post. Anal.* I, 2,4; in McKeon 1941). Evidently, then, it would be a "sin" against this requirement to use a specific predicate when a more general one would yield the conclusion. (Thus far I follow Jardine 1979, p. 172.) Kepler's application of this idea to Ptolemy is as follows: The syllogism that leads validly from H to O is not a proper demonstration, since the weaker premise R would suffice; hence the verification of O gives HD*-support only to R, and the falsity of H casts no doubt on HD reasoning.

The supposedly erroneous reasoning that Kepler here attributed to Ptolemy is the same as what occurs in the "tacking paradox," an objection to the HD account of scientific reasoning discussed by Glymour (1980, chapter 2). The paradox is that if hypothesis h entails and is hence HD-supported by evidence e, then the same holds for "$h \& g$," where g is an arbitrary, "tacked on" sentence. Ptolemy obtained support for R (i.e., "H or E"), but then tacked on $\sim E$ and claimed he had support for the conjunction and hence for H.

The difficulty with Kepler's argument (and with the HD account generally) is that it is quite unclear when tacking on is allowed and when it is not. We do not want to say, as Kepler's argument suggests, that no premise is ever HD-confirmed when a weaker one would have sufficed for the deduction. This would entail that whenever one applies, say, Newton's law of gravitation to objects within a certain region, one obtains no support for the law, but only for the hypothesis that the law holds within that region. On the contrary, we can tack on the law's restriction to the region's complement. But why? Thus Kepler's reply to the objection to HD reasoning answers it by revealing another, more damaging one.

When two hypotheses seem to be observationally indistinguishable, one way Kepler thought they could be distinguished is by relating them to what he called "physical considerations": "And though some disparate astronomical hypotheses may yield exactly the same results in astronomy, as Rothmann insisted . . . of his own mutation [geostatic transform] of the Copernican system,

nevertheless a difference arises because of some physical consideration" (Kepler, forthcoming). Physics, in this context, includes dynamics and cosmology—theories of the causes of motion and of the large-scale structure of the universe. His example here is cosmological: Copernicus's system and its geostatic transform differ in that the latter can "avoid postulating the immensity of the fixed stars" required by the former to explain the absence of detectable stellar parallax. Since Kepler had no way to show (without appeal to Copernicus's theory) that more sensitive instruments would detect stellar parallax due to the earth's revolution, this consideration provided no reason to prefer Copernicus's theory to a geostatic transform of it such as Tycho's. But this neutrality was appropriate in a piece titled "A Defense of Tycho Against Ursus."

In other works, however, Kepler used physical considerations—specifically, about the causes of planetary motions—to argue in favor of his own theory, which was Copernican in using a moving earth, non-Copernican in using elliptical orbits. In ancient and medieval astronomy the problem of why the planets move had either not arisen, or had been solved in a very simple way. To the extent that hypothesized motions were viewed as mere computation-devices, the problem of explaining them dynamically did not arise. Motions that were considered physically real, such as those of the spheres carrying the stars or planets, were usually explained as due to the spheres' "nature" or to spiritual intelligences attached to them. But Kepler, in part because he thought that God created nothing haphazardly but followed a rational plan knowable by man, sought to understand why the planets move as they do (Koyré 1973, pp. 120–122).

In accordance with principle (1)—consistency with the laws of physics counts in favor of realistic acceptance—the ideas of physical explanation and realistic interpretation of planetary orbits were intimately connected in Kepler's mind:

Consider whether I have made a step toward establishing a physical astronomy without hypotheses, or rather, fictions, ... The force is fixed in the sun, and the ascent and descent of the planets are likewise

---

* [Hypothetico-Deductive—editor]

fixed according to the greater or lesser apparent emanation from the Sun. These, therefore, are not hypotheses or (as Ramus calls them) figments, but the very truth, as the stars themselves; indeed, I assume nothing but this (quoted in Gingerich 1975, p. 271).

. . . Astronomers should not be granted excessive license to conceive anything they please without reason: on the contrary, it is also necessary for you to establish the probable cause of your Hypotheses which you recommend as the true causes of Appearances. Hence, you must first establish the principles of your astronomy in a higher science, namely Physics or Metaphysics . . . (quoted in Westman, 1972a, p. 261).

In addition to the foregoing arguments based on criteria (1) and (4)–(7) . . . for realistic acceptance—criteria that had been used by earlier writers—Kepler formulated two criteria of his own. One of these might be called "explanatory depth": it counts in favor of realistic acceptance of a theory that

(8) it explains facts that competing theories merely postulate.

After asserting the superior accuracy of Copernicus's retrodictions and predictions, Kepler remarked: "Furthermore, and this is much more important, things which arouse our astonishment in the case of other(s) [astronomers] are given a reasonable explanation by Copernicus. . . ." In particular, Ptolemy merely postulated that the deferent motions of the sun, Mercury, and Venus have the same period (one year). Copernicus, in contrast, could explain this equality on the basis of his theory that the planets revolve around the sun. Transformed into an earth-centered system, this theory yields components of the sun's and each planet's motions that are, as Kepler put it, "projections of the earth's proper motion on to the firmament" (quoted in Koyré 1973, pp. 129, 136–137).

Second, Kepler argued that readers of Ptolemy should be astonished that the five planets, but not the sun and moon, show retrograde motion*,

whereas Copernicus can explain these facts, specifically by saying the five planets have epicycles of such speeds and sizes as to produce retrograde motion but the sun and moon do not. Kepler presumably meant that Copernicus's theory, when transformed geostatically, yields these statements about epicycles. Using Copernicus's figures for the radii and periods of all the planets' heliostatic orbits, one can show that their geostatic transforms will contain combinations of circles producing retrogression. In contrast, the moon, since it shares the earth's heliocentric motion, does not have a component of its geostatic motion that mirrors the earth's orbit and thereby yields retrogression, as does the epicycle of a superior planet. Finally, Kepler argued, since the earth's heliostatic orbit is circular with constant speed, it follows that the sun's geostatic orbit shows no retrogression (Koyré 1973, pp. 136–137).

Kepler's third and fourth points are similar to ones made by Copernicus himself. The third is that Ptolemy postulates but cannot explain the relative sizes of the planets' epicycles, whereas their ratios can be obtained by transforming Copernicus's system into a geostatic one. The fourth is that Ptolemy postulates that, but does not explain why, the superior planets are at the closest point on their epicycles (and hence brightest) when at opposition with the sun, whereas this fact too results from a geostatic transformation of Copernicus's system.

Kepler sometimes said these four arguments are designed to show Copernicus' theory is preferable to Ptolemy's (Koyré 1973, p. 136), and sometimes to unnamed "other" astronomers' (p. 129). It is worth noting, however, that arguments from explanatory depth do not establish the superiority of Copernicus's system to Tycho's. Either of these can explain anything (regarding relative motions within the solar system) asserted by the other, by means of the appropriate transformation. (This symmetric relation does not hold between Copernicus's theory and Ptolemy's, since a heliostatic transformation of the latter would yield few if any features of the former. For example, the transform would have the planets orbiting a moving earth.) Of all Kepler's arguments, it is only the dynamical ones considered above—that there is a

---

* [brief intervals of westward motion that occasionally interrupt the normal eastward motion of the planets—editor]

plausible physical explanation why the planets should move around the sun, but not why the sun should move around the earth carrying the other planets' orbits with it—that favor Copernicus's theory over Tycho's.

The last argument by Kepler that I shall consider has a remarkably contemporary ring. One of Ursus's arguments against Tycho had been an induction on the falsity of all previous astronomical theories (Jardine 1979, p. 168). Kepler's reply was that despite the continuing imperfection of astronomical theories, cumulative progress had nonetheless been made at least since Ptolemy. Erroneous in other respects, Ptolemy's theory at least taught us that "the sphere of the fixed stars is furthest away, Saturn, Jupiter, Mars, follow in order, the Sun is nearer than them, and the Moon nearest of all. These things are certainly true. . . ." Tycho taught us at least that "the Sun is the centre of motion of the five planets," Copernicus that the earth-moon distance varies less than Ptolemy said, and unspecified astronomers established the "ratios of the diameters of the Earth, Sun and Moon. . . . Given that so many things have already been established in the realm of physical knowledge with the help of astronomy, things which deserve our trust from now on and which are truly so, Ursus' despair is groundless" (Kepler, forthcoming). Similarly, Kepler argued in favor of Copernicus that he "denied none of the things in the [ancient] hypotheses which give the cause of the appearances and which agree with observations, but rather includes and explains all of them" (quoted in Jardine 1979, pp. 157–158). This last statement is part of Kepler's reply to the objection that Copernicus's theory might be false even though it saves the phenomena.

Clearly, then, Kepler was appealing to a principle we have not previously come across: It counts in favor of realistic acceptance of a theory that

(9) it agrees with some of the nonobservable claims of some previous theories purporting to explain the same observations.

I say "nonobservational" because the agreed-upon claims Kepler mentioned here were not ob-servable phenomena such as brightness and angular positions, but unobservables such as the planets' orbits. The tacit assumption behind (9) seems to be that if the astronomical theories produced through history were merely a series of devices for predicting observations, there would be relatively little reason to expect them to contain any common non-observational parts: whereas this is what we would expect if the sequence of principal theories contains a growing set of true descriptions of astronomical reality.

CONTEMPORARY REALISMS

I said this argument sounds contemporary because it is echoed with little change in an argument Hilary Putnam has recently discussed, attributing it to R. Boyd[2] (forthcoming). According to this argument, a new and better theory in a given field of science usually implies "the *approximate truth of the theoretical laws of the earlier theories in certain circumstances.*" Further, scientists usually require this feature of new theories in part because they believe that (a) the "laws of a theory belonging to a mature science are typically approximately *true*"; and meeting this requirement is fruitful in part because this belief is true (Putnam 1978, pp. 20–21). Like Kepler, then, Boyd thinks that there is a degree of agreement in the nonobservational hypotheses of successive theories in a given field, and that this tends to show that these hypotheses are (partially or approximately) true and are not just prediction-devices. And like Kepler, Putnam (1978, p. 25) thinks that this consideration helps rescue contemporary science from the charge, based on induction from past theories, that it is probably false (1978, p. 25).

Boyd labels as "realism" the conjunction of (a) above with (b): "terms in a mature science typically *refer*" (Putnam 1978, p. 20). This essay is mainly about a quite different thesis also called

---

[2] I shall assume for the sake of argument that Putnam gives an accurate account of Boyd's thinking, or at least of some stage thereof.

"realism"—the thesis that *scientific theories in general are put forward as true, and accepted because they are believed to be true.* But we have just seen that our astronomical case study has at least some connection with Boyd's kind of realism as well. I should like to conclude with some remarks about the more general question of the relevance of this case-study to various versions of realism.

Let us call the version of realism I have mainly been discussing "purpose-realism," since it is based on a thesis about the purpose of any scientific theory, and identifies acceptance with belief that that purpose is fulfilled. This is the kind of realism stated (and criticized) by van Fraassen: "*Science aims to give us, in its theories, a literally true story of what the world is like; and acceptance of a scientific theory involves the belief that it is true*" (1980, p. 8). Van Fraassen's own opposing position, which he calls "constructive empiricism," is: "*Science aims to give us theories which are empirically adequate* [true regarding observables]; *and acceptance of a theory involves as belief only that it is empirically adequate.*" Now I claim to have shown above and in my 1979 paper that purpose-realism and constructive empiricism are both over-generalizations, and that each holds for some theories but not others. Neither of the theses stated by van Fraassen can accommodate the extensive historical evidence that scientists sometimes believe that a theory is true and sometimes only that it is empirically adequate, and that there are different sets of grounds for these two beliefs.

Consider now the question whether this case study has any further relevance for Boyd's thesis, which we might call "approximation-realism" because it appeals to the concept of approximate truth. We should note first that approximation-realism is very different from purpose-realism. It is one thing to talk about the purpose of scientific theories and what those who accept them therefore believe, and quite another to say when this aim has to some degree actually been accomplished. That this distinction is nonetheless insufficiently appreciated is clear from the fact that Boyd (1976) puts approximation-realism forward as a

rival to an earlier version of van Fraassen's (1976) thesis, which refers to purpose. Another difference between the two theses is that although purpose-realism is sufficiently clear to be refuted, the obscurity of approximation-realism makes its assessment difficult and perhaps impossible. I leave aside the question of what might be meant by a "mature science," and say nothing of the vagueness of "typically." The more difficult question is whether it makes any sense to speak of a law or theory (Boyd 1976) as "approximately true." It certainly makes sense, although the statement is somewhat vague, to say that a particular *value* for a given magnitude is approximately correct—e.g., that "$\theta = 3.28$" is approximately true, because in fact $\theta = 3.29$. But speaking of a *law* or *theory* as "approximately true" raises serious problems. Usually a law or theory refers to several different magnitudes—their values and relations at various times and places. Given two theories, one may be more accurate with respect to some magnitudes, and the other theory more accurate with respect to some others. If this happens, it is quite unclear what it would mean to say that one theory is *on the whole* more accurate than another. Some weights would have to be assigned to the various quantities, and no general way to do this springs readily to mind. It might seem that this problem could be obviated at least in the special case in which, for theories, T_1 and T_2 and *every* common magnitude, T_1's predicted value is never further from (and is sometimes closer to) the true value than T_2's. But Miller (1975) has shown that uniformly greater accuracy in this sense is impossible—at least where the two predictions never lie on different sides of the true value.

To be fair, we should note that Boyd himself concedes that (approximation-) realists still have considerable work to do in developing a concept of approximate truth suitable for stating their thesis. Boyd does not mention that some work relevant to this task has been done by Popper and various of his critics (see Popper 1976, for references). This body of work provides little help to Boyd, however. For Popper's critics have found fatal weaknesses in a number of his explications of "verisimilitude." Worse, Popper's original intuitive concept of verisimilitude was a confusing amalgamation of two quite distinct desiderata of theories—namely, *accuracy* and *strength*. As he put it, "we combine here the ideas of truth and content into . . . the idea of *verisimilitude*" (Popper 1968, pp. 232–233). Thus he supposed it to be evidence for greater verisimilitude that one theory has passed tests that another has failed (greater accuracy), and also that it explains more facts than the other does (greater strength). But combining these two properties into one has at least three disadvantages: (1) it makes the term "verisimilitude" (whose etymology suggests only accuracy) highly misleading; (2) it obscures the question of the relative importance of accuracy vis-à-vis strength as desiderata of theories; and (3) it makes verisimilitude irrelevant to Boyd's problem of explicating the concept of overall accuracy of a theory. If we had a theory which was perfectly accurate (over its domain), we would not say its *accuracy* could be increased by adding to it an arbitrary additional true statement.

I conclude, then, that approximation-realism is too obscure to be assessed and is likely to remain so. (This stricture does not apply to Kepler's somewhat similar view, since he says only that there is a cumulatively growing set of truths upon which the principal astronomers up to any given time have agreed—and this does not presuppose a concept of approximate truth.)

I shall end this essay by considering two final "realistic" theses. Boyd remarks, "What realists really should maintain is that *evidence for a scientific theory* is evidence that both its theoretical claims and its empirical claims are . . . approximately true with respect to certain issues"[3] (Boyd 1976, pp. 633–634). Similarly, Glymour (1976) defines "realism" as "the thesis that to have good reason to believe that a theory is empirically adequate is to have good reason to believe that the entities it postulates are real and, furthermore, that we can and do have such good reasons for some

of our theories." (Glymour has in mind van Fraassen's (1976) concept of empirical adequacy: roughly, that all measurement-reports satisfy the theory.) To avoid the difficulties just discussed, I shall ignore Boyd's use of "approximately" and define "empirical realism" as the thesis that *evidence for a theory's empirical adequacy is evidence for its truth*. This claim is logically independent of claims as to which theories are in fact approximately true, or as to what the purpose of science is, although it might have affinities to such claims. . . . I . . . claim to have shown above and in my 1979 paper that a given body of data may be regarded as good evidence for the empirical adequacy but not for the truth of a theory—as when the theory conflicts with physics, contains indeterminate quantities, lacks proven predictive capability, etc.

Perhaps Boyd would not be much bothered by this argument and would say that the main concern of a "realistically"-minded philosopher is to assert the less specific thesis, which I will call "evidential realism," that *we sometimes have evidence that a theory is true (and not just empirically adequate)*. I claim to have shown that evidential realism is correct, and moreover to have spelled out at least some of the reasons—criteria (1)–(9) above, and acceptability of explanatory basis (in my 1979 paper)—that scientists have counted in favor of a theory's truth over very long historical periods. If someone wants to say that what scientists have considered to be reasons are not really reasons, or are not good enough, I can only reply that such a claim clashes with what I take to be one of the purposes of the philosophy of science—to state explicitly, clearly, and systematically the principles of reasoning that have been and are used in actual scientific practice.

REFERENCES

Armitage, Angus. 1962. *Copernicus, The Founder of Modern Astronomy*. New York: A. S. Barnes.

Baumgardt, Carola. 1951. *Johannes Kepler: Life and Letters*. New York: Philosophical Library.

Bernardus de Virduno. 1961. *Tractatus super total Astrologiam*. Werl/Westf: Dietrich-Coelde-Verlag.

---

[3] From the context, and to avoid triviality, the phrase I have italicized has to be interpreted to mean "instances of (i.e., evidence for) a scientific theory's empirical adequacy."

Blake, Ralph M. 1960. Theory of Hypothesis among Renaissance Astronomers in R. Blake (ed.), *Theories of Scientific Method.* Seattle: University of Washington Press, pp. 22–49.

Bluck, R. S. 1955. *Plato's Phaedo.* London: Routledge & Kegan Paul.

Boyd, Richard. 1976. Approximate Truth and Natural Necessity. *Journal of Philosophy.* 73:633–635.

Boyd, Richard. Forthcoming. *Realism and Scientific Epistemology.* Cambridge: Cambridge University Press.

Carnap, Rudolf. 1956. The Methodological Character of Theoretical Concepts. *The Foundations of Science and the Concepts of Psychology and Psychoanalysis,* in Herbert Feigl and Michael Scriven (eds.), *Minnesota Studies in the Philosophy of Science,* vol. I. Minneapolis: University of Minnesota Press, pp. 33–76.

Copernicus, Nicolaus. 1976. *On the Revolutions of the Heavenly Spheres.* Trans. Alistair M. Duncan. New York: Barnes & Noble. Orig. ed. 1543.

Cornford, Francis M. 1957. *Plato's Cosmology.* Indianapolis: Bobbs-Merrill.

Dreyer, J. L. E. 1953. *A History of Astronomy from Thales to Kepler.* New York: Dover.

Duhem, Pierre. 1969. *To Save the Phenomena.* Trans. Stanley L. Jaki. Chicago: University of Chicago Press. Orig. ed. 1908.

Gardner, Michael R. 1979. Realism and Instrumentalism in 19th-Century Atomism. *Philosophy of Science* 46:1–34.

Gardner, Michael R. 1982. Predicting Novel Facts. *British Journal for the Philosophy of Science.* 33:1–15.

Gingerich, Owen. 1973a. Copernicus and Tycho. *Scientific American* 229:87–101.

Gingerich, Owen. 1973b. A Fresh Look at Copernicus. In *The Great Ideas Today* 1973. Chicago: Encyclopaedia Brittanica, pp. 154–178.

Gingerich, Owen. 1973c. From Copernicus to Kepler: Heliocentrism as Model and as Reality. *Proceedings of the American Philosophical Society* 117:513–522.

Gingerich, Owen. 1973d. Kepler. In *Dictionary of Scientific Biography,* ed. C. C. Gillespie, vol. 7. New York: Scribners, pp. 289–312.

Gingerich, Owen. 1975. Kepler's Place in Astronomy. In *Vistas in Astronomy,* ed. A. & P. Beer, vol. 18. Oxford: Pergamon, pp. 261–278.

Glymour, Clark. 1976. To Save the Noumena. *Journal of Philosophy* 73:635–637.

Glymour, Clark. 1980. *Theory and Evidence.* Princeton: Princeton University Press.

Goldstein, Bernard. 1967. The Arabic Version of Ptolemy's *Planetary Hypotheses. Transactions of the American Philosophical Society,* n.s. vol. 57, part 4:3–12.

Hamilton, Edith and Cairns, Huntington. 1963. *The Collected Dialogues of Plato.* New York: Bollinger Foundation.

Hanson, Norwood R. 1973. *Constellations and Conjectures.* Dordrecht: Reidel.

Hutchins, Robert M. 1952. *Great Books of the Western World,* vol. 16. Chicago: Encyclopaedia Britannica.

Jardine, Nicholas. 1979. The Forging of Modern Realism: Clavius and Kepler against the Sceptics. *Studies in History and Philosophy of Science* 10:141–173.

Johnson, Francis R. 1937. *Astronomical Thought in Renaissance England.* Baltimore: Johns Hopkins Press.

Kepler, Johannes. 1952. *Epitome of Copernican Astronomy.* Trans. C. G. Wallis. Orig. ed. 1618–1621. In Hutchins, 1952, pp. 841–1004.

Kepler, Johannes. Forthcoming. *A Defense of Tycho against Ursus.* Trans. Nicholas Jardine. Written about 1601.

Koyré, Alexander. 1973. *The Astronomical Revolution.* Trans. R. E. W. Maddison. Ithaca: Cornell University Press. Orig. ed. 1961.

Kuhn, Thomas S. 1957. *The Copernican Revolution.* Cambridge, Mass: Harvard University Press.

Kuhn, Thomas S. 1970. *The Structure of Scientific Revolutions.* Chicago: University of Chicago Press.

Lakatos, Imre. 1970. Falsification and the Methodology of Scientific Research Programmes. In *Criticism and the Growth of Knowledge,* ed. Imre Lakatos and Alan Musgrave, pp. 91–195. London: Cambridge University Press.

Lakatos, Imre and Zahar, Elie. 1975. *Why Did Copernicus' Research Program Supersede Ptolemy's?* In Westman (1975c), pp. 354–383.

Laudan, Larry. 1977. *Progress and its Problems.* Berkeley: University of California Press.

Lloyd, G. E. R. 1978. Saving the Appearances. *Classical Quarterly* 28:202–222.

McKeon, Richard. 1941. *The Basic Works of Aristotle.* New York: Random House.

Miller, David. 1975. The Accuracy of Predictions. *Synthèse* 30:159–191.

Nagel, Ernest. 1961. *The Structure of Science.* New York: Harcourt, Brace and World.

Neugebauer, Otto. 1952. *The Exact Sciences in Antiquity.* Princeton: Princeton University Press.

Newton, Isaac. 1934. *Mathematical Principles of Natural Philosophy.* Trans. Andrew Motte and Florian Cajori. Berkeley: University of California Press. Orig. ed. 1687.

Pedersen, Olaf. 1974. *A Survey of the Almagest.* Odense: Odense University Press.

Popper, Karl. 1968. *Conjectures and Refutations.* New York: Harper.

Popper, Karl. 1976. A Note on Verisimilitude. *British Journal for the Philosophy of Science* 27:147–164.

Proclus. 1903. *In Platonis Timaeum Commentaria.* Ed. E. Diehl. Leipzig.

Proclus. 1909. *Hypotyposis Astronomicarum Positionum.* Ed. C. Manitius. Leipzig.

Ptolemy, Claudius. 1952. *The Almagest.* Trans. R. C. Taliaferro. In Hutchins 1952, pp. 1–478.

Ptolemy, Claudius. 1907. *Planetary Hypotheses,* In *Claudii Ptolemae: opera quae extant omnia, volumen II, opera astronomica minora,* ed. J. L. Heiberg, pp. 69–145. Leipzig: B. G. Teubneri.

Putnam, Hilary. 1978. *Meaning and the Moral Sciences.* London: Routledge & Kegan Paul.

Rosen, Edward, trans. 1959. *Three Copernican Treatises.* New York: Dover.

Rosenkrantz, Roger. 1976. Simplicity. In *Foundations of Probability Theory, Statistical Inference, and Statistical Theories of Science,* ed. William A. Harper and C. Hooker, vol. I, pp. 167–203. Dordrecht: Reidel.

Rosenkrantz, Roger. 1977. *Inference, Method, and Decision,* Dordrecht: Reidel.

Sambursky, Samuel. 1962. *The Physical World of Late Antiquity.* London: Routledge & Kegan Paul.

Shapere, Dudley. 1969. Notes Towards a Post-Positivistic Interpretation of Science. In *The Legacy of Logical Positivism,* ed. Stephen Barker and Peter Achinstein, pp. 115–160. Baltimore: Johns Hopkins Press.

van Fraassen, Bas. 1976. To Save the Phenomena. *Journal of Philosophy* 73:623–632.

van Fraassen, Bas. 1980. *The Scientific Image.* Oxford: Clarendon.

Vlastos, Gregory. 1975. *Plato's Universe.* Seattle: University of Washington Press.

Westman, Robert. 1971. *Johannes Kepler's Adoption of the Copernican Hypothesis.* Unpublished doctoral dissertation. Ann Arbor: University of Michigan.

Westman, Robert. 1972a. Kepler's Theory of Hypothesis and the 'Realist Dilemma'. *Studies in History and Philosophy of Science* 3:233–264.

Westman, Robert, 1972b. The Comet and the Cosmos: Kepler, Mästlin and the Copernican Hypothesis. In *The Reception of Copernicus' Heliocentric Theory,* ed. J. Dobrzycki, pp. 7–30. Dordrecht: Reidel.

Westman, Robert. 1975a. The Melanchthon Circle, Rheticus, and the Wittenberg Interpretation of the Copernican Theory, *Isis* 66:165–193.

Westman, Robert. 1975b. *Three Responses to the Copernican Theory: Johannes Praetorius, Tycho Brahe, and Michael Maestlin.* In Westman (1975c), pp. 285–345.

Westman, Robert. 1975c. *The Copernican Achievement.* Berkeley: University of California Press.

Zahar, Elie. 1973. Why Did Einstein's Research Programme Supersede Lorentz's? *British Journal for the Philosophy of Science* 24:95–123, 223–262.

Experimentation and Scientific Realism

Ian Hacking

Experimental physics provides the strongest evidence for scientific realism. Entities that in principle cannot be observed are regularly manipulated to produce new phenomena and to investigate other aspects of nature. They are tools, instruments not for thinking but for doing.

The philosopher's standard "theoretical entity" is the electron. I will illustrate how electrons have become experimental entities, or experimenter's entities. In the early stages of our discovery of an entity, we may test hypotheses about it. Then it is merely a hypothetical entity. Much later, if we come to understand some of its causal powers and use it to build devices that achieve well-understood effects in other parts of nature, then it assumes quite a different status.

Discussions about scientific realism or anti-realism usually talk about theories, explanation, and prediction. Debates at that level are necessarily inconclusive. Only at the level of experimental practice is scientific realism unavoidable—but this realism is not about theories and truth. The experimentalist need only be a realist about the entities used as tools.

A PLEA FOR EXPERIMENTS

No field in the philosophy of science is more systematically neglected than experiment. Our grade school teachers may have told us that scientific method is experimental method, but histories of science have become histories of theory. Experiments, the philosophers say, are of value only when they test theory. Experimental work, they imply, has no life of its own. So we lack even a terminology to describe the many varied roles of experiment. Nor has this one-sidedness done theory any good, for radically different types of theory are used to think about the same physical phenomenon (e.g., the magneto-optical effect). The philosophers of theory have not noticed this and so misreport even theoretical enquiry.

Different sciences at different times exhibit different relationships between "theory" and "experiment." One chief role of experiment is the creation of phenomena. Experimenters bring into being phenomena that do not naturally exist in a pure state. These phenomena are the touchstones of physics, the keys to nature, and the source of much modern technology. Many are what physicists after the 1870s began to call "effects": the photoelectric effect, the Compton effect, and so forth.[1] A recent high-energy extension of the creation of phenomena is the creation of "events," to use the jargon of the trade. Most of the phenomena, effects, and events created by the experimenter are like plutonium: They do not exist in nature except possibly on vanishingly rare occasions.[2]

In this paper I leave aside questions of methodology, history, taxonomy, and the purpose of experiment in natural science. I turn to the purely philosophical issue of scientific realism. Simply

---

[1] C.W.F. Everitt suggests that the first time the word "effect" is used this way in English is in connection with the Peltier effect, in James Clerk Maxwell's 1873 *Electricity and Magnetism,* par. 249, p. 301. My interest in experiment was kindled by conversation with Everitt some years ago, and I have learned much in working with him on our joint (unpublished) paper, "Theory or Experiment, Which Comes First?"

[2] Ian Hacking, "Spekulation, Berechnung und die Erschaffung der Phänomenen," in *Versuchungen: Aufsätze zur Philosophie, Paul Feyerabends,* no. 2, ed. P. Duerr (Frankfort, 1981), 126–158.

From *Philosophical Topics,* Vol. 13, No. 1, 1983, pp. 71–87. Reprinted by permission.

call it "realism" for short. There are two basic kinds: realism about entities and realism about theories. There is no agreement on the precise definition of either. Realism about theories says that we try to form true theories about the world, about the inner constitution of matter and about the outer reaches of space. This realism gets its bite from optimism: We think we can do well in this project and have already had partial success. Realism about entities—and I include processes, states, waves, currents, interactions, fields, black holes, and the like among entities—asserts the existence of at least some of the entities that are the stock in trade of physics.[3]

The two realisms may seem identical. If you believe a theory, do you not believe in the existence of the entities it speaks about? If you believe in some entities, must you not describe them in some theoretical way that you accept? This seeming identity is illusory. *The vast majority of experimental physicists are realists about entities but not about theories.* Some are, no doubt, realists about theories too, but that is less central to their concerns.

Experimenters are often realists about the entities that they investigate, but they do not have to be so. R. A. Millikan probably had few qualms about the reality of electrons when he set out to measure their charge. But he could have been skeptical about what he would find until he found it. He could even have remained skeptical. Perhaps there is a least unit of electric charge, but there is no particle or object with exactly that unit of charge. Experimenting on an entity does not commit you to believing that it exists. Only manipulating an entity, in order to experiment on something else, need do that.

Moreover, it is not even that you use electrons to experiment on something else that makes it impossible to doubt electrons. Understanding some causal properties of electrons, you guess how to build a very ingenious, complex device that enables you to line up the electrons the way you want, in order to see what will happen to something else. Once you have the right experimental idea, you know in advance roughly how to try to build the device, because you know that this is the way to get the electrons to behave in such and such a way. Electrons are no longer ways of organizing our thoughts or saving the phenomena that have been observed. They are now ways of creating phenomena in some other domain of nature. Electrons are tools.

There is an important experimental contrast between realism about entities and realism about theories. Suppose we say that the latter is belief that science aims at true theories. Few experimenters will deny that. Only philosophers doubt it. Aiming at the truth is, however, something about the indefinite future. Aiming a beam of electrons is using present electrons. Aiming a finely tuned laser at a particular atom in order to knock off a certain electron to produce an ion is aiming at present electrons. There is, in contrast, no present set of theories that one has to believe in. If realism about theories is a doctrine about the aims of science, it is a doctrine laden with certain kinds of values. If realism about entities is a matter of aiming electrons next week or aiming at other electrons the week after, it is a doctrine much more neutral between values. The way in which experimenters are scientific realists about entities is entirely different from ways in which they might be realists about theories.

This shows up when we turn from ideal theories to present ones. Various properties are confidently ascribed to electrons, but most of the confident properties are expressed in numerous different theories or models about which an experimenter can be rather agnostic. Even people in a team, who work on different parts of the same large experiment, may hold different and mutually

---

[3] Nancy Cartwright makes a similar distinction in her book, *How the Laws of Physics Lie* (Oxford: Oxford University Press, 1983). She approaches realism from the top, distinguishing theoretical laws (which do not state the facts) from phenomenological laws (which do). She believes in some "theoretical" entities and rejects much theory on the basis of a subtle analysis of modeling in physics. I proceed in the opposite direction, from experimental practice. Both approaches share an interest in real life physics as opposed to philosophical fantasy science. My own approach owes an enormous amount to Cartwright's parallel developments, which have often preceded my own. My use of the two kinds of realism is a case in point.

incompatible accounts of electrons. That is because different parts of the experiment will make different uses of electrons. Models good for calculations on one aspect of electrons will be poor for others. Occasionally, a team actually has to select a member with a quite different theoretical perspective simply to get someone who can solve those experimental problems. You may choose someone with a foreign training, and whose talk is well-nigh incommensurable with yours, just to get people who can produce the effects you want.

But might there not be a common core of theory, the intersection of everybody in the group, which is the theory of the electron to which all the experimenters are realistically committed? I would say common lore, *not* common core. There are a lot of theories, models, approximations, pictures, formalisms, methods, and so forth involving electrons, but there is no reason to suppose that the intersection of these is a theory at all. Nor is there any reason to think that there is such a thing as "the most powerful nontrivial *theory* contained in the intersection of all the theories in which this or that member of a team has been trained to believe." Even if there are a lot of shared beliefs, there is no reason to suppose they form anything worth calling a theory. Naturally, teams tend to be formed from like-minded people at the same institute, so there is usually some real shared theoretical basis to their work. That is a sociological fact, not a foundation for scientific realism.

I recognize that many a scientific realism concerning theories is a doctrine not about the present but about what we might achieve, or possibly an ideal at which we aim. So to say that there is no present theory does not count against the optimistic aim. The point is that such scientific realism about theories has to adopt the Peircean principles of faith, hope, and charity. Scientific realism about entities needs no such virtues. It arises from what we can do at present. To understand this, we must look in some detail at what it is like to build a device that makes the electrons sit up and behave.

OUR DEBT TO HILARY PUTNAM

It was once the accepted wisdom that a word such as "electron" gets its meaning from its place in a network of sentences that state theoretical laws. Hence arose the infamous problems of incommensurability and theory change. For if a theory is modified, how could a word such as "electron" go on meaning the same? How could different theories about electrons be compared, since the very word "electron" would differ in meaning from theory to theory?

Putnam saved us from such questions by inventing a referential model of meaning. He says that meaning is a vector, refreshingly like a dictionary entry. First comes the syntactic marker (part of speech); next the semantic marker (general category of thing signified by the word); then the stereotype (clichés about the natural kind, standard examples of its use, and present-day associations. The stereotype is subject to change as opinions about the kind are modified). Finally, there is the actual referent of the word, the very stuff, or thing, it denotes if it denotes anything. (Evidently dictionaries cannot include this in their entry, but pictorial dictionaries do their best by inserting illustrations whenever possible.)[4]

Putnam thought we can often guess at entities that we do not literally point to. Our initial guesses may be jejune or inept, and not every naming of an invisible thing or stuff pans out. But when it does, and we frame better and better ideas, then Putnam says that, although the stereotype changes, we refer to the same kind of thing or stuff all along. We and Dalton alike spoke about the same stuff when we spoke of (inorganic) acids. J. J. Thomson, H. A. Lorentz, Bohr, and Millikan were, with their different theories and observations, speculating about the same kind of thing, the electron.

There is plenty of unimportant vagueness about when an entity has been successfully "dubbed," as Putnam puts it. "Electron" is the name suggested by G. Johnstone Stoney in 1891 as the name for a natural unit of electricity. He had drawn attention to this unit in 1874. The name

---

[4] Hilary Putnam, "How Not to Talk About Meaning," "The Meaning of 'Meaning,' " and other papers in *Mind, Language and Reality*, Philosophical Papers, Vol. 2 (Cambridge: Cambridge University Press, 1975).

was then applied to the subatomic particles of negative charge, which J. J. Thomson, in 1897, showed cathode rays consist of. Was Johnstone Stoney referring to the electron? Putnam's account does not require an unequivocal answer. Standard physics books say that Thomson discovered the electron. For once I might back theory and say that Lorentz beat him to it. Thomson called his electrons "corpuscles," the subatomic particles of electric charge. Evidently, the name does not matter much. Thomson's most notable achievement was to measure the mass of the electron. He did this by a rough (though quite good) guess at e, and by making an excellent determination of e/m, showing that m is about 1/1800 the mass of the hydrogen atom. Hence it is natural to say that Lorentz merely postulated the existence of a particle of negative charge, while Thomson, determining its mass, showed that there is some such real stuff beaming off a hot cathode.

The stereotype of the electron has regularly changed, and we have at least two largely incompatible stereotypes, the electron as cloud and the electron as particle. One fundamental enrichment of the idea came in the 1920s. Electrons, it was found, have angular momentum, or "spin." Experimental work by O. Stern and W. Gerlach first indicated this, and then S. Goudsmit and G. E. Uhlenbeck provided the theoretical understanding of it in 1925. Whatever we think, Johnstone Stoney, Lorentz, Bohr, Thomson, and Goudsmit were all finding out more about the same kind of thing, the electron.

We need not accept the fine points of Putnam's account of reference in order to thank him for giving us a new way to talk about meaning. Serious discussion of inferred entities need no longer lock us into pseudo-problems of incommensurability and theory change. Twenty-five years ago the experimenter who believed that electrons exist, without giving much credence to any set of laws about electrons, would have been dismissed as philosophically incoherent. Now we realize it was the philosophy that was wrong, not the experimenter. My own relationship to Putnam's account of meaning is like the experimenter's relationship to a theory. I do not literally believe Putnam, but I am happy to employ his

account as an alternative to the unpalatable account in fashion some time ago.

Putnam's philosophy is always in flux. His account of reference was intended to bolster scientific realism. But now, at the time of this writing (July 1981), he rejects any "metaphysical realism" but allows "internal realism."[5] The internal realist acts, in practical affairs, as if the entities occurring in his working theories did in fact exist. However, the direction of Putnam's metaphysical anti-realism is no longer scientific. It is not peculiarly about natural science. It is about chairs and livers too. He thinks that the world does not naturally break up into our classifications. He calls himself a transcendental idealist. I call him a transcendental nominalist. I use the word "nominalist" in the old-fashioned way, not meaning opposition to "abstract entities" like sets, but meaning the doctrine that there is no nonmental classification in nature that exists over and above our own human system of naming.

There might be two kinds of internal realist, the instrumentalist about science and the scientific realist. The former is, in practical affairs where he uses his present scheme of concepts, a realist about livers and chairs but thinks that electrons are only mental constructs. The latter thinks that livers, chairs, and electrons are probably all in the same boat, that is, real at least within the present system of classification. I take Putnam to be an internal scientific realist rather than an internal instrumentalist. The fact that either doctrine is compatible with transcendental nominalism and internal realism shows that our question of scientific realism is almost entirely independent of Putnam's internal realism.

INTERFERING

Francis Bacon, the first and almost last philosopher of experiments, knew it well: The experimenter sets out "to twist the lion's tail." Experi-

---

[5] These terms occur in, e.g., Hilary Putnam, *Meaning and the Moral Sciences* (London: Routledge and Kegan Paul, 1978), 123–130.

mentation is interference in the course of nature; "nature under constraint and vexed; that is to say, when by art and the hand of man she is forced out of her natural state, and squeezed and molded."[6] The experimenter is convinced of the reality of entities, some of whose causal properties are sufficiently well understood that they can be used to interfere *elsewhere* in nature. One is impressed by entities that one can use to test conjectures about other, more hypothetical entities. In my example, one is sure of the electrons that are used to investigate weak neutral currents and neutral bosons. This should not be news, for why else are we (nonskeptics) sure of the reality of even macroscopic objects, but because of what we do with them, what we do to them, and what they do to us?

Interference and interaction are the stuff of reality. This is true, for example, at the borderline of observability. Too often philosophers imagine that microscopes carry conviction because they help us see better. But that is only part of the story. On the contrary, what counts is what we can do to a specimen under a microscope, and what we can see ourselves doing. We stain the specimen, slice it, inject it, irradiate it, fix it. We examine it using different kinds of microscopes that employ optical systems that rely on almost totally unrelated facts about light. Microscopes carry conviction because of the great array of interactions and interferences that are possible. When we see something that turns out to be unstable under such play, we call it an artifact and say it is not real.[7]

Likewise, as we move down in scale to the truly unseeable, it is our power to use unobservable entities that makes us believe they are there. Yet, I blush over these words "see" and "observe." Philosophers and physicists often use these words in different ways. Philosophers tend to treat opacity to visible light as the touchstone of reality, so that anything that cannot be touched or seen with the naked eye is called a theoretical or inferred entity. Physicists, in contrast, cheerfully talk of observing the very entities that philosophers say are not observable. For example, the fermions are those fundamental constituents of matter such as electron neutrinos and deuterons and, perhaps, the notorious quarks. All are standard philosophers' "unobservable" entities. C. Y. Prescott, the initiator of the experiment described below, said in a recent lecture, that "of these fermions, only the t quark is yet unseen. The failure to observe $t\bar{t}$ states in e^+e^- annihilation at PETRA remains a puzzle."[8] Thus, the physicist distinguishes among the philosophers' "unobservable" entities, noting which have been observed and which not. Dudley Shapere has just published a valuable study of this fact.[9] In his example, neutrinos are used to see the interior of a star. He has ample quotations such as "neutrinos present the only way of directly observing" the very hot core of a star.

John Dewey would have said that fascination with seeing-with-the-naked-eye is part of the spectator theory of knowledge that has bedeviled philosophy from earliest times. But I do not think Plato or Locke or anyone before the nineteenth century was as obsessed with the sheer opacity of objects as we have been since. My own obsession with a technology that manipulates objects is, of course, a twentieth-century counterpart to positivism and phenomenology. Its proper rebuttal is not a restriction to a narrower domain of reality, namely, to what can be positivistically seen with the eye, but an extension to other modes by which people can extend their consciousness.

MAKING

Even if experimenters are realists about entities, it does not follow that they are right. Perhaps it is a

---

[6] Francis Bacon, *The Great Instauration*, in *The Philosophical Works of Francis Bacon*, trans. Ellis and Spedding, ed. J. M. Robertson (London, 1905), 252.

[7] Ian Hacking, "Do We See Through a Microscope?" *Pacific Philosophical Quarterly* 62 (1981): 305–322.

[8] C. Y. Prescott, "Prospects for Polarized Electrons at High Energies," SLAC-PUB-2630, Stanford Linear Accelerator, October 1980, p. 5.

[9] "The Concept of Observation in Science and Philosophy," *Philosophy of Science* 49 (1982): 485–526. See also K. S. Shrader-Frechette, "Quark Quantum Numbers and the Problem of Microphysical Observation," *Synthèse* 50 (1982): 125–146, and ensuing discussion in that issue of the journal.

matter of psychology: Maybe the very skills that make for a great experimenter go with a certain cast of mind which objectifies whatever it thinks about. Yet this will not do. The experimenter cheerfully regards neutral bosons as merely hypothetical entities, while electrons are real. What is the difference?

There are an enormous number of ways in which to make instruments that rely on the causal properties of electrons in order to produce desired effects of unsurpassed precision. I shall illustrate this. The argument—it could be called the "experimental argument for realism"—is not that we infer the reality of electrons from our success. We do not make the instruments and then infer the reality of the electrons, as when we test a hypothesis, and then believe it because it passed the test. That gets the time order wrong. By now we design apparatus relying on a modest number of home truths about electrons, in order to produce some other phenomenon that we wish to investigate.

That may sound as if we believe in the electrons because we predict how our apparatus will behave. That too is misleading. We have a number of general ideas about how to prepare polarized electrons, say. We spend a lot of time building prototypes that do not work. We get rid of innumerable bugs. Often we have to give up and try another approach. Debugging is not a matter of theoretically explaining or predicting what is going wrong. It is partly a matter of getting rid of "noise" in the apparatus. "Noise" often means all the events that are not understood by any theory. The instrument must be able to isolate, physically, the properties of the entities that we wish to use, and damp down all the other effects that might get in our way. *We are completely convinced of the reality of electrons when we regularly set to build—and often enough succeed in building— new kinds of device that use various well understood causal properties of electrons to interfere in other more hypothetical parts of nature.*

It is not possible to grasp this without an example. Familiar historical examples have usually become encrusted by false theory-oriented philosophy or history, so I will take something new. This is a polarizing electron gun whose acronym is

PEGGY II. In 1978, it was used in a fundamental experiment that attracted attention even in *The New York Times*. In the next section I describe the point of making PEGGY II. To do that, I have to tell some new physics. You may omit reading this and read only the engineering section that follows. Yet it must be of interest to know the rather easy-to-understand significance of the main experimental results, namely, that parity is not conserved in scattering of polarized electrons from deuterium, and that, more generally, parity is violated in weak neutral-current interactions.[10]

PARITY AND WEAK NEUTRAL CURRENTS

There are four fundamental forces in nature, not necessarily distinct. Gravity and electromagnetism are familiar. Then there are the strong and weak forces (the fulfillment of Newton's program, in the *Optics,* which taught that all nature would be understood by the interaction of particles with various forces that were effective in attraction or repulsion over various different distances, i.e., with different rates of extinction).

Strong forces are 100 times stronger than electromagnetism but act only over a minuscule distance, at most the diameter of a proton. Strong forces act on "hadrons," which include protons, neutrons, and more recent particles, but not electrons or any other members of the class of particles called "leptons."

The weak forces are only 1/10,000 times as strong as electromagnetism, and act over a distance 100 times greater than strong forces. But they act on both hadrons and leptons, including electrons. The most familiar example of a weak force may be radioactivity.

---

[10] I thank Melissa Franklin, of the Stanford Linear Accelerator, for introducing me to PEGGY II and telling me how it works. She also arranged discussion with members of the PEGGY II group, some of whom are mentioned below. The report of experiment E-122 described here is "Parity Non-conservation in Inelastic Electron Scattering," C. Y. Prescott et al., in *Physics Letters.* I have relied heavily on the in-house journal, the *SLAC Beam Line,* report no. 8, October 1978, "Parity Violation in Polarized Electron Scattering." This was prepared by the in-house science writer Bill Kirk.

The theory that motivates such speculation is quantum electrodynamics. It is incredibly successful, yielding many predictions better than one part in a million, truly a miracle in experimental physics. It applies over distances ranging from diameters of the earth to 1/100 the diameter of the proton. This theory supposes that all the forces are "carried" by some sort of particle: Photons do the job in electromagnetism. We hypothesize "gravitons" for gravity.

In the case of interactions involving weak forces, there are charged currents. We postulate that particles called "bosons" carry these weak forces.[11] For charged currents, the bosons may be either positive or negative. In the 1970s, there arose the possibility that there could be weak "neutral" currents in which no charge is carried or exchanged. By sheer analogy with the vindicated parts of quantum electrodynamics, neutral bosons were postulated as the carriers in weak neutral interactions.

The most famous discovery of recent high-energy physics is the failure of the conservation of parity. Contrary to the expectations of many physicists and philosophers, including Kant,[12] nature makes an absolute distinction between right-handedness and left-handedness. Apparently, this happens only in weak interactions.

What we mean by right- or left-handed in nature has an element of convention. I remarked that electrons have spin. Imagine your right hand wrapped around a spinning particle with the fingers pointing in the direction of spin. Then your thumb is said to point in the direction of the spin vector. If such particles are traveling in a beam, consider the relation between the spin vector and the beam. If all the particles have their spin vector in the same direction as the beam, they have right-handed (linear) polarization, while if the spin vector is opposite to the beam direction, they have left-handed (linear) polarization.

The original discovery of parity violation showed that one kind of product of a particle decay, a so-called muon neutrino, exists only in left-handed polarization and never in right-handed polarization.

Parity violations have been found for weak *charged* interactions. What about weak *neutral* currents? The remarkable Weinberg-Salam model for the four kinds of force was proposed independently by Stephen Weinberg in 1967 and A. Salam in 1968. It implies a minute violation of parity in weak neutral interactions. Given that the model is sheer speculation, its success has been amazing, even awe-inspiring. So it seemed worthwhile to try out the predicted failure of parity for weak neutral interactions. That would teach us more about those weak forces that act over so minute a distance.

The prediction is: Slightly more left-handed polarized electrons hitting certain targets will scatter than right-handed electrons. Slightly more! The difference in relative frequency of the two kinds of scattering is 1 part in 10,000, comparable to a difference in probability between 0.50005 and 0.49995. Suppose one used the standard equipment available at the Stanford Linear Accelerator Center in the early 1970s, generating 120 pulses per second, each pulse providing one electron event. Then you would have to run the entire SLAC beam for twenty-seven years in order to detect so small a difference in relative frequency. Considering that one uses the same beam for lots of experiments simultaneously, by letting different experiments use different pulses, and considering that no equipment remains stable for even a month, let alone twenty-seven years, such an experiment is impossible. You need enormously more electrons coming off in each pulse—between 1000 and 10,000 more electrons per pulse than was once possible. The first attempt used an instrument now called PEGGY I. It had, in essence, a high-class version of J. J. Thomson's hot cathode. Some lithium was heated and electrons were boiled off. PEGGY II uses quite different principles.

---

[11] The odd-sounding bosons are named after the Indian physicist. S. N. Bose (1894–1974), also remembered in the name "Bose-Einstein statistics" (which bosons satisfy).

[12] But excluding Leibniz, who "knew" there had to be some real, natural difference between right- and left-handedness.

PEGGY II

The basic idea began when C. Y. Prescott noticed (by chance!) an article in an optics magazine about a crystalline substance called gallium arsenide. GaAs has a curious property; when it is struck by circularly polarized light of the right frequencies, it emits lots of linearly polarized electrons. There is a good, rough and ready quantum understanding of why this happens, and why half the emitted electrons will be polarized, three-fourths of these polarized in one direction and one-fourth polarized in the other.

PEGGY II uses this fact, plus the fact that GaAs emits lots of electrons owing to features of its crystal structure. Then comes some engineering—it takes work to liberate an electron from a surface. We know that painting a surface with the right stuff helps. In this case, a thin layer of cesium and oxygen is applied to the crystal. Moreover, the less air pressure around the crystal, the more electrons will escape for a given amount of work. So the bombardment takes place in a good vacuum at the temperature of liquid nitrogen.

We need the right source of light. A laser with bursts of red light (7100 Ångstroms) is trained on the crystal. The light first goes through an ordinary polarizer, a very old-fashioned prism of calcite, or Iceland spar[13]—this gives linearly polarized light. We want circularly polarized light to hit the crystal, so the polarized laser beam now goes through a cunning device called a Pockel's cell, which electrically turns linearly polarized photons into circularly polarized ones. Being electric, it acts as a very fast switch. The direction of circular polarization depends on the direction of current in the cell. Hence, the direction of polarization can be varied randomly. This is important, for we are trying to detect a minute asymmetry between right- and left-handed polarization. Randomizing helps us guard against any systematic "drift" in the equipment.[14] The randomization is generated by a radioactive decay device, and a computer records the direction of polarization for each pulse.

A circularly polarized pulse hits the GaAs crystal, resulting in a pulse of linearly polarized electrons. A beam of such pulses is maneuvered by magnets into the accelerator for the next bit of the experiment. It passes through a device that checks on a proportion of polarization along the way. The remainder of the experiment requires other devices and detectors of comparable ingenuity, but let us stop at PEGGY II.

BUGS

Short descriptions make it all sound too easy; therefore, let us pause to reflect on debugging. Many of the bugs are never understood. They are eliminated by trial and error. Let me illustrate three different kinds of bugs: (1) the essential technical limitations that, in the end, have to be factored into the analysis of error; (2) simpler mechanical defects you never think of until they are forced on you; and (3) hunches about what might go wrong.

Here are three examples of bugs:

(1) Laser beams are not as constant as science fiction teaches, and there is always an irremediable amount of "jitter" in the beam over any stretch of time.

(2) At a more humdrum level, the electrons from the GaAs crystal are back-scattered and go back along the same channel as the laser beam used to hit the crystal. Most of them are then deflected magnetically. But some get reflected

---

[13] Iceland spar is an elegant example of how experimental phenomena persist even while theories about them undergo revolutions. Mariners brought calcite from Iceland to Scandinavia. Erasmus Bartholinus experimented with it and wrote it up in 1609. When you look through these beautiful crystals you see double, thanks to the so-called ordinary and extraordinary rays. Calcite is a natural polarizer. It was our entry to polarized light, which for three hundred years was the chief route to improved theoretical and experimental understanding of light and then electromagnetism. The use of calcite in PEGGY II is a happy reminder of a great tradition.

[14] It also turns GaAs, a 3/4 to 1/4 left-hand/right-hand polarizer, into a 50-50 polarizer.

from the laser apparatus and get back into the system. So you have to eliminate these new ambient electrons. This is done by crude mechanical means, making them focus just off the crystal and, thus, wander away.

(3) Good experimenters guard against the absurd. Suppose that dust particles on an experimental surface lie down flat when a polarized pulse hits it, and then stand on their heads when hit by a pulse polarized in the opposite direction. Might that have a systematic effect, given that we are detecting a minute asymmetry? One of the team thought of this in the middle of the night and came down next morning frantically using antidust spray. They kept that up for a month, just in case.[15]

RESULTS

Some 10^{11} events were needed to obtain a result that could be recognized above systematic and statistical error. Although the idea of systematic error presents interesting conceptual problems, it seems to be unknown to philosophers. There were systematic uncertainties in the detection of right- and left-handed polarization, there was some jitter, and there were other problems about the parameters of the two kinds of beam. These errors were analyzed and linearly added to the statistical error. To a student of statistical inference, this is real seat-of-the-pants analysis with no rationale whatsoever. Be that as it may, thanks to PEGGY II the number of events was big enough to give a result that convinced the entire physics community.[16] Left-handed polarized electrons were scattered from deuterium slightly more frequently than right-handed electrons. This was the first convincing example of parity-violation in a weak neutral current interaction.

---

[15] I owe these examples to conversation with Roger Miller of SLAC.

[16] The concept of a "convincing experiment" is fundamental. Peter Gallison has done important work on this idea, studying European and American experiments on weak neutral currents conducted during the 1970s.

COMMENT

The making of PEGGY II was fairly nontheoretical. Nobody worked out in advance the polarizing properties of GaAs—that was found by a chance encounter with an unrelated experimental investigation. Although elementary quantum theory of crystals explains the polarization effect, it does not explain the properties of the actual crystal used. No one has got a real crystal to polarize more than 37 percent of the electrons, although in principle 50 percent should be polarized.

Likewise, although we have a general picture of why layers of cesium and oxygen will "produce negative electron affinity," that is, make it easier for electrons to escape, we have no quantitative understanding of why this increases efficiency to a score of 37 percent.

Nor was there any guarantee that the bits and pieces would fit together. To give an even more current illustration, future experimental work, briefly described later in this paper, makes us want even more electrons per pulse than PEGGY II can give. When the aforementioned parity experiment was reported in *The New York Times,* a group at Bell Laboratories read the newspaper and saw what was going on. They had been constructing a crystal lattice for totally unrelated purposes. It uses layers of GaAs and a related aluminum compound. The structure of this lattice leads one to expect that virtually all the electrons emitted would be polarized. As a consequence, we might be able to double the efficiency of PEGGY II. But, at present, that nice idea has problems. The new lattice should also be coated in work-reducing paint. The cesium-oxygen compound is applied at high temperature. Hence the aluminum tends to ooze into the neighboring layer of GaAs, and the pretty artificial lattice becomes a bit uneven, limiting its fine polarized-electron-emitting properties.[17] So perhaps this will never work. Prescott is simultaneously reviving a souped-up new thermionic cathode to try to get more electrons. Theory would not have told us that PEGGY II would beat

---

[17] I owe this information to Charles Sinclair of SLAC.

out thermionic PEGGY I. Nor can it tell if some thermionic PEGGY III will beat out PEGGY II.

Note also that the Bell people did not need to know a lot of weak neutral current theory to send along their sample lattice. They just read *The New York Times*.

MORAL

Once upon a time, it made good sense to doubt that there were electrons. Even after Thomson had measured the mass of his corpuscles, and Millikan their charge, doubt could have made sense. We needed to be sure that Millikan was measuring the same entity as Thomson. Thus, more theoretical elaboration was needed, and the idea had to be fed into many other phenomena. Solid state physics, the atom, and superconductivity all had to play their part.

Once upon a time, the best reason for thinking that there are electrons might have been success in explanation. Lorentz explained the Faraday effect with his electron theory. But the ability to explain carries little warrant of truth. Even from the time of J. J. Thomson, it was the measurements that weighed in, more than the explanations. Explanations, however, did help. Some people might have had to believe in electrons because the postulation of their existence could explain a wide variety of phenomena. Luckily, we no longer have to pretend to infer from explanatory success (i.e., from what makes our minds feel good). Prescott and the team from the SLAC do not explain phenomena with electrons. They know how to use them. Nobody in his right mind thinks that electrons "really" are just little spinning orbs about which you could, with a small enough hand, wrap your fingers and find the direction of spin along your thumb. There is, instead, a family of causal properties in terms of which gifted experimenters describe and deploy electrons in order to investigate something else, for example, weak neutral currents and neutral bosons. We know an enormous amount about the behavior of electrons. It is equally important to know what does *not* matter to electrons. Thus, we know that bending a polar-

ized electron beam in magnetic coils does not affect polarization in any significant way. We have hunches, too strong to ignore although too trivial to test independently: For example, dust might dance under changes of directions of polarization. Those hunches are based on a hard-won sense of the kinds of things electrons are. (It does not matter at all to this hunch whether electrons are clouds or waves or particles.)

WHEN HYPOTHETICAL ENTITIES BECOME REAL

Note the complete contrast between electrons and neutral bosons. Nobody can yet manipulate a bunch of neutral bosons, if there are any. Even weak neutral currents are only just emerging from the mists of hypothesis. By 1980, a sufficient range of convincing experiments had made them the object of investigation. When might they lose their hypothetical status and become commonplace reality like electrons?—when we use them to investigate something else.

I mentioned the desire to make a better electron gun than PEGGY II. Why? Because we now "know" that parity is violated in weak neutral interactions. Perhaps by an even more grotesque statistical analysis than that involved in the parity experiment, we can isolate just the weak interactions. For example, we have a lot of interactions, including electromagnetic ones, which we can censor in various ways. If we could also statistically pick out a class of weak interactions, as precisely those where parity is not conserved, then we would possibly be on the road to quite deep investigations of matter and antimatter. To do the statistics, however, one needs even more electrons per pulse than PEGGY II could hope to generate. If such a project were to succeed, we should then be beginning to use weak neutral currents as a manipulable tool for looking at something else. The next step toward a realism about such currents would have been made.

The message is general and could be extracted from almost any branch of physics. I mentioned earlier how Dudley Shapere has recently used "observation" of the sun's hot core to illustrate how physicists employ the concept of observation. They collect neutrinos from the sun in an enormous disused underground mine that has been filled with old cleaning fluid (i.e., carbon tetrachloride). We would know a lot about the inside of the sun if we knew how many solar neutrinos arrive on the earth. So these are captured in the cleaning fluid. A few neutrinos will form a new radioactive nucleus (the number that do this can be counted). Although, in this study, the extent of neutrino manipulation is much less than electron manipulation in the PEGGY II experiment, we are nevertheless plainly using neutrinos to investigate something else. Yet not many years ago, neutrinos were about as hypothetical as an entity could get. After 1946 it was realized that when mesons disintegrate giving off, among other things, highly energized electrons, one needed an extra nonionizing particle to conserve momentum and energy. At that time this postulated "neutrino" was thoroughly hypothetical, but now it is routinely used to examine other things.

CHANGING TIMES

Although realisms and anti-realisms are part of the philosophy of science well back into Greek prehistory, our present versions mostly descend from debates at the end of the nineteenth century about atomism. Anti-realism about atoms was partly a matter of physics; the energeticists thought energy was at the bottom of everything, not tiny bits of matter. It also was connected with the positivism of Comte, Mach, K. Pearson, and even J. S. Mill. Mill's young associate Alexander Bain states the point in a characteristic way, apt for 1870:

Some hypotheses consist of assumptions as to the minute structure and operation of bodies. From the nature of the case these assumptions can never be proved by direct means. Their merit is their suitability to express phenomena. They are Representative Fictions.[18]

---

[18] Alexander Bain, *Logic, Deductive and Inductive* (London and New York, 1870), 362.

"All assertions as to the ultimate structure of the particles of matter," continues Bain, "are and ever must be hypothetical. . . . The kinetic theory of heat serves an important intellectual function." But we cannot hold it to be a true description of the world. It is a representative fiction.

Bain was surely right a century ago, when assumptions about the minute structure of matter could not be proved. The only proof could be indirect, namely, that hypotheses seemed to provide some explanation and helped make good predictions. Such inferences, however, need never produce conviction in the philosopher inclined to instrumentalism or some other brand of idealism.

Indeed, the situation is quite similar to seventeenth-century epistemology. At that time, knowledge was thought of as correct representation. But then one could never get outside the representations to be sure that they corresponded to the world. Every test of a representation is just another representation. "Nothing is so much like an idea as an idea," said Bishop Berkeley. To attempt to argue to scientific realism at the level of theory, testing, explanation, predictive success, convergence of theories, and so forth is to be locked into a world of representations. No wonder that scientific anti-realism is so permanently in the race. It is a variant on "the spectator theory of knowledge."

Scientists, as opposed to philosophers, did, in general, become realists about atoms by 1910. Despite the changing climate, some anti-realist variety of instrumentalism or fictionalism remained a strong philosophical alternative in 1910 and in 1930. That is what the history of philosophy teaches us. The lesson is: Think about practice, not theory. Anti-realism about atoms was very sensible when Bain wrote a century ago. Anti-realism about *any* submicroscopic entities was a sound doctrine in those days. Things are different now. The "direct" proof of electrons and the like is our ability to manipulate them using well-understood low-level causal properties. Of course, I do not claim that reality is constituted by human manipulability. Millikan's ability to determine the charge of the electron did something of great importance for the idea of electrons—more,

I think, than the Lorentz theory of the electron. Determining the charge of something makes one believe in it far more than postulating it to explain something else. Millikan got the charge on the electron; but better still, Uhlenbeck and Goudsmit in 1925 assigned angular momentum to electrons, brilliantly solving a lot of problems. Electrons have spin, ever after. The clincher is when we can put a spin on the electrons, and thereby get them to scatter in slightly different proportions.

Surely, there are innumerable entities and processes that humans will never know about. Perhaps there are many in principle we can never know about, since reality is bigger than us. The best kinds of evidence for the reality of a postulated or inferred entity is that we can begin to measure it or otherwise understand its causal powers. The best evidence, in turn, that we have this kind of understanding is that we can set out, from scratch, to build machines that will work fairly reliably, taking advantage of this or that causal nexus. Hence, engineering, not theorizing, is the best proof of scientific realism about entities. My attack on scientific anti-realism is analogous to Marx's onslaught on the idealism of his day. Both say that the point is not to understand the world but to change it. Perhaps there are some entities which in theory we can know about only through theory (black holes). Then our evidence is like that furnished by Lorentz. Perhaps there are entities which we shall only measure and never use. The experimental argument for realism does not say that only experimenter's objects exist.

I must now confess a certain skepticism, about, say, black holes. I suspect there might be another representation of the universe, equally consistent with phenomena, in which black holes are precluded. I inherit from Leibniz a certain distaste for occult powers. Recall how he inveighed against Newtonian gravity as occult. It took two centuries to show he was right. Newton's ether was also excellently occult—it taught us lots: Maxwell did his electromagnetic waves in ether, H. Hertz confirmed the ether by demonstrating the existence of radio waves. Albert A. Michelson figured out a way to interact with the ether. He thought his experiment confirmed G. G. Stoke's ether drag theory, but, in the end, it was one of the many things that made ether give up the ghost. A skeptic such as myself has a slender induction: Long-lived theoretical entities which do not end up being manipulated commonly turn out to have been wonderful mistakes.